JOHN WILLIS'

THEATRE WORLD

1977–1978 SEASON

VOLUME 34

CROWN PUBLISHERS, INC.
ONE PARK AVENUE
NEW YORK, N.Y. 10016

"Gentlemen Prefer Blondes"
(1949)

with Steve Reeves (L), David Atkinson (R)
in "The Vamp" (1955)

"Wonderful Town"
(1954)

"Show Girl"
(1961)

"Hello, Dolly!"
(1964)

with Sid Caesar
in "4 on a Garden" (1971)

"Lorelei"
(1973)

"The Bed Before Yesterday"
(1976)

with George Burns
(1976)

"Hello, Dolly!"
(1978)

2

1948   1954   1964   1970   1978

TO
CAROL CHANNING

one of the brightest and most delightfully unique stars in contemporary musical history—a truly dedicated actress whose professional attitude and record for performances is unmatched. Since "Lend an Ear," she has never failed to captivate and endear herself to audiences. The theatre has been gratefully enriched because of her talents. For those who are privileged to know her, sincerity, warmth and generosity make her a treasured friend.

Brian Murray, Barnard Hughes in "Da"

Martha Swope Ph...

Winner of New York Drama Critics Circle, "Tony," Drama Desk and Outer Critics Circle
awards for "Best Play." Mr. Hughes received a "Tony" for Best Actor.

CONTENTS

EDITOR: JOHN WILLIS

Staff: Alberto Cabrera, Maltier Hagan, Don Nute, Ron Reagan, Stanley
Reeves, William Schelble

Staff Photographers: Joseph Abeles, Bert Andrews, Ron Reagan, Van Williams

THE SEASON IN REVIEW
June 1, 1977–May 31, 1978

This season's record-breaking boxoffice receipts might give the impression that it was a season of great quality as well. That is not the view from this aisle seat. According to *Variety*, the trade weekly, attendance decreased 2% from the record set last season. The inflationary spiral is responsible for this season's record receipts. A healthy observation was that the grosses for touring shows exceeded total grosses for Broadway. The 18 productions held over from past seasons produced a "booking jam" and reduced the number of new productions to less than the 1976–77 record. It was good to have theatres fully booked, but unfortunate that the quality of the presentations was generally mediocre. The emergence of several promising new playwrights was an encouraging note for the season, as was the seeming diversification in the taste of the audiences who were more willing to buy tickets for productions that received less than rave reviews—another healthy trend for the theatre.

The most honored play of the season was the Irish import "Da" that received the American Theatre Wing Antoinette Perry ("Tony"), New York Drama Critics Circle, Drama Desk, and Outer Critics Circle awards as "Best Play." Its director, Melvin Bernhardt, received a "Tony," as did Barnard Hughes and Lester Rawlins for "Outstanding Actor" and "Featured Actor," respectively. Jessica Tandy and Hume Cronyn were the stars of the two-character play "The Gin Game" that won the Pulitzer Prize. Miss Tandy received a "Tony" for "Oustanding Actress in a Play." Other notable new plays were the ubiquitous Neil Simon's "Chapter Two" that brought a "Featured Actress" "Tony" to Ann Wedgeworth, "Deathtrap," "Cold Storage" with Martin Balsam and Len Cariou in excellent characterizations, "Miss Margarida's Way" with Estelle Parsons giving a bravura performance, "The Water Engine," James Earl Jones as a memorable "Paul Robeson," and "An Almost Perfect Person" with Colleen Dewhurst again proving her great versatility and talent. Revivals included "A Touch of the Poet" with Jason Robards and Geraldine Fitzgerald, "Tartuffe" with John Wood, and "Dracula" with a skillful performance by Frank Langella. This production received a "Tony" for "Outstanding Revival."

Other impressive performances were given by Bibi Andersson, Anne Bancroft, Victor Borge, Patricia Elliott, Morgan Freeman, Victor Garber, Anita Gillette, Cliff Gorman, Tammy Grimes, Dorian Harewood, Judd Hirsch, Monte Markham, Mary Martin, Brian Murray, Betsy Palmer, Anthony Quayle, Richard Seer, Colin Stinton, Max von Sydow, James Whitmore, and Marian Winters.

Many of the new musicals (a misnomer for most) seemed to challenge the aural endurance of the audience. Sound amplification became almost unbearable for some of the productions. There was also a departure from the traditional musical format with a book or storyline, and a veering toward the old formula for revues. This was true of "Ain't Misbehavin'" that received a "Tony" for "Best Musical," as well as citations from the New York Drama Critics Circle, Drama Desk, and Outer Critics Circle. Nell Carter of the cast won a "Tony" for "Outstanding Featured Actress in a Musical," and the other four cast members (Andre DeShields, Armelia McQueen, Ken Page, Charlaine Woodard) also gave performances that deserved awards. The "Tony" for "Outstanding Actress in a Musical" went to Liza Minnelli in "The Act"—again, not a musical, but a glorified nightclub act. Winners of the "Tony" for "Outstanding Actor" and "Featured Actor in a Musical" were John Cullum and Kevin Kline, respectively, in "On the 20th Century," one of the season's few "book musicals." Other new musical productions of note were "Dancin'," "The Best Little Whorehouse in Texas," "Runaways," and the revivals of "Hello, Dolly!" and "Man of La Mancha" with Carol Channing and Richard Kiley in their original title roles. Additional noteworthy performances in musicals were given by Yul Brynner, Wayne Cilento, Carlin Glynn, Joel Higgins, Judy Kaye, Swoosie Kurtz, Florence Lacey, Patti LuPone, Roger Minami, Melba Moore, Gilbert Price, Lee Roy Reams, Ann Reinking, and Don Scardino.

Off-Broadway had fewer openings this season than last, but the number of Off-Off-Broadway openings increased tremendously. On April 28, 1978 Actors Equity Association (AEA) rejected and delayed action on new codes that virtually would have eliminated the 200 or more OOB theatres. An alternate plan and decision must be reached by Oct. 30, 1978. AEA signed new contracts with the League of New York Theatres and Producers that brought increases in minimum pay for its members. An exemplary project that culminated in "42nd Street Theatre Row" was dedicated on May 13, 1978 with the support and presence of Vice President and Mrs. Walter Mondale. The OOB organization has converted former "porno parlors" into performing space for eight companies, reclaiming a portion of that historical street and neighborhood. The increasing professionalism, influence and importance of OB, OOB, and regional theatres became even more apparent this season when ten of their productions were ultimately moved to Broadway, including the "Tony" and Pulitzer Prize winners. On June 9, 1977, Joseph Papp announced the removal of his New York Shakespeare Festival organization from Lincoln Center's beautiful Beaumont and Newhouse theatres because of their tremendous financial burden. After the closing of his production of "The Cherry Orchard" (with a brilliant performance by Irene Worth), both houses unfortunately remained empty for the remainder of the season. Instead of the customary Shakespeare, Mr. Papp reopened in Central Park his Lincoln Center productions of "The Threepenny Opera" and "Agamemnon." The initially well-received Brooklyn Academy of Music Theatre Company formed an alliance with the Center Theatre Group at the Ahmanson Theatre in Los Angeles to co-produce and exchange plays each year. This season's offering was "The Devil's Disciple." Other outstanding productions away from "The Main Stem" were "Family Business," "Uncommon Women and Others," "K," "Mandrake," "Moliere in Spite of Himself," "P.S. Your Cat Is Dead," "A Life in the Theatre," "Molly," "Native Son," "The Promise," "A Bistro Car on the CNR," "Life of Galileo," "Patio/Porch," "The Biko Inquest," "The Second Greatest Entertainer . . .," "Catsplay," "The Play's the Thing," "The Elusive Angel," "The 5th of July," "The Offering," "One Crack Out," "A Prayer for My Daughter," "Othello," and "The Show-Off."

Those worthy of mention for their Off-Broadway performances include Maureen Anderman, Vasili Bogazianos, Jeffrey DeMunn, George Dzundza, Ronnie Claire Edwards, Peter Evans, Fanny Flagg, Al Freeman, Jr., Jeff Goldblum, Christopher Goutman, Margaret Hilton, William Hurt, Earle Hyman, Laurence Luckinbill, Marcia McClain, Bill Moor, Ellis Rabb, Gordana Rashovich, Charles Repole, Patrick Rose, Bo Rucker, Dick Shawn, Norman Snow, Henrietta Valor and Fritz Weaver.

From this season's calendar, other notes for the record include the loss of two theatres: the Harkness to demolition, and the prestigious Henry Miller to discotheque. . . . The Lyceum and Radio City Music Hall were declared historical landmarks, the latter for at least a year. . . . Because of a power failure on Wednesday night, July 13, 1977, theatres and New York City experienced another blackout but for only 25 hours. A few productions completed performances, but most closed and all resumed on Thursday. . . . To honor Alfred Lunt, one of our greatest actors who died Aug. 3, 1977, marquee lights were dimmed for the second time in Broadway history. . . . Walter Kerr, the *New York Times* Sunday Drama Critic, received the Pulitzer Prize for criticism—the first time a theatre writer has been so honored for his criticism. . . . Critic Clive Barnes moved from the *NY Times* to the *NY Post* and was succeeded by Richard Eder. Martin Gottfried resigned as drama critic of the *NY Post*. Each season the English theatre ordinarily supplies Broadway with several productions. This year there was only one, "The Merchant," that ran for a week. . . . A happy end to the season was the beginning of a new system for taxis: queuing for fares in the theatre district after final curtains. However, the demand seemed to be greater than the supply.

Jessica Tandy, Hume Cronyn in "The Gin Game"

Left: Tony Martinez, Richard Kiley in "Man of La Mancha"

BROADWAY CALENDAR
June 1, 1976 through May 31, 1977

Estelle Parsons In "Miss Margarida's Way"

Left: Yul Brynner, Constance Towers in "The King and I"

Carol Channing in "Hello, Dolly!"

Frank Langella in "Dracula"

7

CIRCLE IN THE SQUARE THEATRE
Opened Thursday, June 16, 1977.*
Circle in the Square (Theodore Mann, Artistic Director; Paul Libin, Managing Director) presents:

THE IMPORTANCE OF BEING EARNEST

By Oscar Wilde; Director, Stephen Porter; Scenery, Zack Brown; Costumes, Ann Roth; Lighting, John McLain; Wigs and Hair Styles, Paul Huntley; Production Associates, Atsumi Kolba; Jolly Nelson; Wardrobe Supervisor, Virginia Merkel; Production Assistants, Gordon Bendall, William Callum, Mona Finston, Michael Rosen, Paul Schneeberger, Leslie McCullough, M. M. O'Flaherty, Christine Pittel, Sharyn Kolberg, Nicole Thomas

CAST

Algernon Moncrieff	John Glover
Lane, Manservant	Munson Hicks
John Worthing	James Valentine
Lady Bracknell	Elizabeth Wilson
Hon. Gwendolen Fairfax	Patricia Conolly
Cecily Cardew	Kathleen Widdoes
Miss Prism, Governess	Mary Louise Wilson
Rev. Canon Chasuble	G Wood
Merriman, Butler	Thomas Ruisinger

STANDBYS AND UNDERSTUDIES: Dorothy Blackburn (Bracknell/Prism), Munson Hicks (Algernon), John Rose (Worthing/Lane/Merriman), Barbara Berge (Gwendolen/Cecily), Thomas Ruisinger (Chausible)

A comedy in three acts. The action takes place in Algernon Moncrieff's flat in Half-Moon Street, and the Manor House in Woolton.

Company Manager: William Conn
Press: Merle Debuskey, David Roggensack
Stage Managers: Randall Brooks, James Bernardi

* Closed Aug. 28, 1977 after 85 performances and 23 previews.

Martha Swope Photos

Kathleen Widdoes, John Glover, Patricia Conolly, James Valentine, Elizabeth Wilson, G Wood, Mary Louise Wilson Top Left: Kathleen Widdoes, John Glover

WINTER GARDEN
 Opened June 1, 1977.*
 David Krebs and Steven Leber present:

BEATLEMANIA

Songs written by John Lennon, Paul McCartney, George Harrison; Editorial Content, Robert Rabinowitz, Bob Gill, Lynda Obst; Visuals Director, Charles E. Hoefler; Multi-Media Images, Robert Rabinowitz, Bob Gill, Shep Kerman, Kathleen Rabinowitz; Original Concept, Steven Leber, David Krebs, Jules Fisher; All songs, except where indicated, licensed by ATV Music Group; Scenery, Robert D. Mitchell; Lighting, Jules Fisher; Sound, Abe Jacob; Musical Supervision, Sandy Yaguda; Hair Stylist, Phyllis Della; Special Consultant, Murray the K; Production Supervision, Jules Fisher

CAST

Joe Pecorino
Mitch Weissman
Leslie Fradkin
Justin McNeill

ALTERNATES: Randy Clark (Joe Pecorino), Reed Kailing (Mitch Weissman), P. M. Howard (Leslie Fradkin), Bobby Taylor (Justin McNeill)

SONGS: "Let's Twist Again," "Roll Over Beethoven," "Bye Bye Love," "Hound Dog," "I Want to Hold Your Hand," "She Loves You," "Help!," "If I Fell," "Can't Buy Me Love," "Day Tripper," "Yesterday," "Eleanor Rigby," "We Can Work It Out," "Nowhere Man," "A Day in the Life," "Strawberry Fields Forever," "Penny Lane," "Magical Mystery Tour," "Lucy in the Sky with Diamonds," "Lady Madonna," "The Fool on the Hill," "Got to Get You into My Life," "Michelle," "Get Back," "Come Together," "With a Little Help from My Friends," "All You Need Is Love," "Revolution," "Helter Skelter," "Hey Jude," "I Am the Walrus," "The Long and Winding Road," "Let It Be."

A musical entertainment, in two acts and nine scenes, celebrating the 1960's.

General Management: Marvin A. Krauss Associates
Company Manager: David Lawlor
Press: Elizabeth A. Rodman, Sharon Mear
Stage Managers: Rovert V. Straus, John Actman, Gary Schnell

* Still playing May 31, 1978.

Mitch Weissman

Emily Yancy

PALACE THEATRE
Opened Thursday, September 15, 1977.*
Eugene V. Wolsk presents:

MAN OF LA MANCHA

Book, Dale Wasserman; Music, Mitch Leigh; Lyrics, Joe Darion; Production and Musical Staging, Albert Marre; Setting and Lighting, Howard Bay; Costumes, Howard Bay, Patton Campbell; Music Arrangements, Music Makers; Assistant to the Director, Greg Hirsch; Musical Director, Robert Brandzel; Wardrobe, Robert Mooney; Hairdresser, Charles LoPresto; Music Coordinator, Earl Shendell; Production Assistant, Adam Marre

CAST

Don Quixote/Cervantes	Richard Kiley
Sancho	Tony Martinez
The Horse	Ben Vargas
The Mule	Hector Mercado
The Innkeeper	Bob Wright
Maria, the Innkeeper's Wife	Marceline Decker
Pedro, Head Muleteer	Chev Rodgers
Anselmo, a Muleteer	Ted Forlow
Juan, a Muleteer	Mark Holliday
Tenorio, a Muleteer	Ben Vargas
Paco, a Muleteer	Anthony DeVecchi
Jose, a Muleteer	Hector Mercado
Aldonza	Emily Yancy
Fermina, a Slavey	Joan Susswein
Guitarist	Robin Polseno
Jorge, a Muleteer	Edmond Varrato
Fernando, a Muleteer	David Wasson
Antonia	Harriett Conrad
The Housekeeper	Margret Coleman
The Padre	Taylor Reed
Dr. Carrasco	Ian Sullivan
The Barber	Ted Forlow
Moorish Dancer	Joan Susswein
The Captain	Renato Cibelli
Guards	Michael St. Paul, David Wasson

STANDBYS AND UNDERSTUDIES: Joan Susswein (Aldonza-/Antonia), Edmond Varrato (Sancho/Barber), Mark Holliday (Anselmo/Padre), Renato Cibelli (Innkeeper), David Wasson (Padre/Carrasco), Marceline Decker (Housekeeper), Kay Vance (Maria/Fermina/Moorish Dancer), Anthony DeVecchi (Pedro/-The Horse/The Mule), Michael St. Paul (Captain)

MUSICAL NUMBERS: "Man of La Mancha," "It's All the Same," "Dulcinea," "I'm Only Thinking of Him," "I Really Like Him," "What Does He Want of Me," "Little Bird, Little Bird," "Barber's Song," "Golden Helmet of Mambrino," "To Each His Dulcinea," "The Quest," "The Combat," "The Abduction," "The Dubbing," "Moorish Dance," "Aldonza," "The Knight of the Mirrors," "A Little Gossip," "The Psalm"

A musical performed without intermission. The action takes place in a dungeon in Seville at the end of the Sixteenth Century, and in various other places in the imagination of Miguel de Cervantes.

Production Manager: Patrick Horrigan
Company Manager: Chuck Eisler
Press: John A. Prescott
Stage Managers: Patrick Corrigan, Greg Hirsch, Kay Vance

* Closed Dec. 31, 1977 after 124 performances and 3 previews. Original production opened at ANTA Washington Square Theatre Nov. 22, 1965 and played 2350 performances. Revived at Vivian Beaumont Theater June 22, 1972 for 140 performances. See THEATRE WORLD Volumes 22 and 29.

**Top Left and Below: Tony Martinez
and Richard Kiley**

CIRCLE IN THE SQUARE THEATRE

Opened Sunday, September 25, 1977.*

Circle in the Square (Theodore Mann, Artistic Director; Paul Libin, Managing Director) presents:

TARTUFFE

By Moliere; English verse translation by Richard Wilbur; Director, Stephen Porter, Scenery and Costumes, Zack Brown; Lighting, John McLain; Wigs and Hairstyles, Paul Huntley; Wardrobe, Virginia Merkel; Associate Manager, Alan C. Wasser; Music Supervisor, Earl Shendell

CAST

Flipote, Mme. Pernelle's maid .... Ruth Livingston
Dorine, Mariane's lady's-maid .... Patricia Elliott
Mme. Pernelle, Orgon's mother .... Mildred Dunnock
Elmire, Orgon's wife .... Tammy Grimes
Mariane, Orgon's daughter .... Swoosie Kurtz
Damis, Orgon's son .... Ray Wise
Cleante, Orgon's brother-in-law .... Peter Coffield
Orgon, Elmire's husband .... Stefan Gierasch
Valere, in love with Mariane .... Victor Garber
Tartuffe, a hypocrite .... John Wood
M. Loyal .... Roy Brocksmith
Police Officer .... Jim Broaddus
Deputies .... Timothy Landfield, Steven Gilborn

UNDERSTUDIES: Roy Brocksmith (Tartuffe), Jim Broaddus (Cleante), Ruth Livingston (Mme. Pernelle/Dorine), Johanna Leister (Elmire/Mariane/Flipote), Timothy Landfield (Valere/Damis), Steven Gilborn (Orgon/Loyal/Officer)

A comedy presented in two acts. The action takes place in Orgon's home in 17th Century Paris.

Company Manager: William Conn
Press: Merle Debuskey, David Roggensack
Stage Managers: Randall Brooks, James Bernardi

* Closed Nov. 20, 1977 after 65 performances and 26 previews.

Martha Swope Photos

Stefan Gierasch, Swoosie Kurtz, Peter Coffield, Tammy Grimes, Patricia Elliott Top: John Wood

11

MAJESTIC THEATRE
Opened Tuesday, September 20, 1977.*
United Euram presents the 1977 Music and Dance Festival
from the Soviet Union:

ESTRADA

Artistic Director, Nikolai Laktionov; Administrative Director,
Nadezhda Kazantzeva; Choreographer, Tamara Golovanova; Pro-
duction Supervisor, M. William Lettich; Production Manager,
Savely Onishchenko

CAST

Nani Bregvadze
Grigori Davidenko
Vladimir Kononovich
Natalia Kiriushkin
Oleg Kiriushkin
Larisa Kudeyarova

Yefim Levinson
Galina Korzina
Orera
Pesnyary
Vladimir Serov
Souvenir Ensemble

PROGRAM

PART I: "Moscow Nights," "Korobeiniki," "Four Contemporary
Byelorussian Folk Songs," "Dva Kuma," "Northern Festive
Dance," "A Friendship That Never Came to Be," "Puppet
Sketches," "Barynya"
PART II: "Sabre Dance," "Give My Regards to Broadway," "Bicy-
cle on the Wire," "Serdtse," "Svetlyachok," "Tbiliso," "Dorogoy
Dlinoyu," "Acrobatic Sketch with a Hoop," "Gypsy Fantasy,"
"Acrobatic Sketch," "Specialty," "Potekha," Finale

Company Managers: Nahman Levinson, John Scott
Press: Dan Langan, Patt Dale, Melissa Burdick, Steven J. Caffery

* Closed Sept. 24, 1977 after 7 performances.

The Rasshivkins

AMBASSADOR THEATRE
Opened Tuesday, September 26, 1977.*
Joseph Papp presents the New York Shakespeare Festival Pro-
duction of:

MISS MARGARIDA'S WAY

Written and Directed by Roberto Athayde; Setting and Costumes,
Santo Loquasto; Lighting, Martin Tudor; Associate Producer, Bernard Gersten; Production Supervisor, Jason Steven Cohen; Production Manager, Andrew Mihok; Technical Director, Mervyn Haines,
Jr.

CAST

Miss Margarida .... Estelle Parsons
One of her students .... Colin Garrey
The rest of her students .... The Audience

Presented in two acts. The action takes place at the present time
in Miss Margarida's classroom.

General Manager: Robert Kamlot
Company Manager: Bob MacDonald
Press: Merle Debuskey, Sol Jacobson, Richard Kornberg
Stage Managers: Penny Gebhard, Colin Garrey

* Closed Jan. 1, 1978 after 98 performances and 7 previews. It was
moved from the Public/Newman Theater where it played 42 performances.

Dan Asher Photos

Estelle Parsons
(also Right Center)

IMPERIAL THEATRE
Opened Monday, October 3, 1977.*
The Edgewood Organization (Lewis Friedman, John W. Ballard, Executive Directors) presents:

VICTOR BORGE
in
"Comedy with Music"
with
Marylyn Mulvey

Designed by Neil Peter Jampolis; Miss Mulvey's gown by Donald Brooks; Associate Producers, Dean Lenz, Allison McLeod; Art Director, Kenneth Hanson; Associate Lighting Designer, Jane Reisman

A musical entertainment by Victor Borge in two parts.

General Managers: McCann & Nugent
Company Manager: Richard Grayson
Press: James Murtha, Bernard Gurtman, Constance Shuman
Stage Manager: Don Judge

* Closed Nov. 16, 1977 after 64 performances and 3 previews.

**Right: Victor Borge, and below
with Marylyn Mulvey**

Cleo Laine

MINSKOFF THEATRE
Opened Wednesday, October 5, 1977.*
Ron Delsener presents:

CLEO ON BROADWAY

Lighting Supervised by Andrea Wilson; Musical Direction and Arrangements, John Dankworth; Tour Management, Elliott Ames; Personal Management, Laurie Mansfield; Management Associate, David Wyler; Management Assistant, Eric Angelson; Production Technician, Mitch Miller; Associate to Mr. Delsener, Stan Feig; Production Assistant, Kathi Gorringe

CAST

Cleo Laine
Bill Conti
John Dankworth Orchestra

A musical program presented without intermission.

General Management: Marvin A. Krauss Associates
Press: Elizabeth Rodman, Harriett Trachtenberg, Harold Lubin
Stage Manager: Elliott Ames

* Closed Oct. 9, 1977 after limited engagement of 6 performances.

13

Loretta Devine, Trudy Perkins, Charlaine Woodard

BILTMORE THEATRE
Opened Wednesday, October 5, 1977.*
Michael Butler in association with K. H. Nezhad presents:

HAIR

Book and Lyrics, Gerome Ragni, James Rado; Music, Galt MacDermot; Director, Tom O'Horgan; Choreography, Julie Arenal; Associate Producer, George Milman; Scenic Design, Robin Wagner; Lighting, Jules Fisher; Costumes, Nancy Potts; Sound, Abe Jacob; Musical Direction, Denzil A. Miller, Jr.; Vocal Direction, Patrick Flynn; Assistant Choreographer, Wesley Fata; Wardrobe Supervisor, Warren Morrill;

CAST

Claude	Randall Easterbrook
Berger	Michael Hoit
Woof	Scott Thornton
Hud	Cleavant Derricks
Sheila	Ellen Foley
Jeanie	Iris Rosenkrantz
Dionee	Alaina Reed
Crissy	Kristen Vigard
Shopping Cart Lady	Michael Leslie
Mothers	Annie Golden, Louis Mattioli, Perry Arthur
Fathers	James Rich, Eva Charney, Martha Wingate
Principals	Carl Woerner, Michael Leslie, Linda Myers
Tourist Couple	Perry Arthur, Carl Woerner
General Grant	Carl Woerner
Abraham Lincoln	Linda Myers
Sergeant	Byron Utley
Parents	Lori Wagner, James Rich

TRIBE: Perry Arthur, Emily Bindiger, Paul Binotto, Eva Charney, Loretta Devine, Doug Katsaros, Michael Leslie, Louis Mattioli, Linda Myers, Raymond Patterson, James Rich, James Sbano, Deborah Van Valkenburgh, Lori Wagner, Doug Wall, Martha Wingate, Carl Woerner, Charlaine Woodard

UNDERSTUDIES: Scott Thornton (Claude), Doug Katsaros (Berger), Deborah Van Valkenburgh (Sheila), Byron Utley (Hud), Iris Rosenkrantz (Jeannie), Charlaine Woodard (Dionne), James Rich (Woof), Soni Moreno (Crissy)

MUSICAL NUMBERS: "Aquarius," "Donna," "Hashish," "Sodomy," "Colored Spade," "Manchester," "Ain't Got No," "Dead End," "I Believe in Love," "Air," "Initials," "I Got Life," "Going Down," "Hair," "My Conviction," "Easy to Be Hard," "Don't Put It Down," "Frank Mills," "Be-In," "Where Do I Go," "Electric Blues," "White Boys," "Walking in Space," "Abie Baby," "Three-Five-Zero-Zero," "What a Piece of Work Is Man," "Good Morning Starshine," "The Bed," "Flesh Failures"

"The American Tribal Love Rock Musical" in two acts. The action takes place in the East Village in New York City during the 1960's.

General Manager: Eugene V. Wolsk
Company Manager: Steven Suskin
Press: Gifford/Wallace, Eileen McMahon
Stage Managers: Seth M. M. Sternberg, Eva Charney

* Closed Nov. 6, 1977 after 43 performances and 79 previews. Original production opened Oct. 17, 1967 and played 1742 performances. See THEATRE WORLD Vol. 24.

Curt Kaufman Photos

**Top Left: Soni Moreno, Annie Golden,
Loretta Devine
Below: Perry Arthur, James Rich, Louis
Mattioli, Doug Wall holding Cleavant Derricks,
Doug Katsouros**

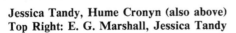

Jessica Tandy, Hume Cronyn (also above)
Top Right: E. G. Marshall, Jessica Tandy

JOHN GOLDEN THEATRE
Opened Thursday, October 6, 1977.*
The Shubert Organization (Gerald Schoenfeld, Chairman; Bernard B. Jacobs, President) presents:

THE GIN GAME

By D. L. Coburn; Director, Mike Nichols; Produced by Hume Cronyn and Mike Nichols; Setting, David Mitchell; Costumes, Bill Walker; Lighting, Ronald Wallace; Production Supervisor, Nina Seely; Wardrobe Supervisor, Lillias Norel

CAST

Fonsia Dorsey .... Jessica Tandy†1
Weller Martin .... Hume Cronyn†2

A comedy in two acts and four scenes. The action takes place at the present time in a home for the elderly.

General Managers: McCann & Nugent
Company Manager: James Mennen
Press: David Powers, Barbara Carroll
Stage Manager: William Chance

* Still playing May 31, 1978. Winner of 1978 Pulitzer Prize. Miss Tandy received a 1978 "Tony" for Outstanding Performance by an Actress.
† Succeeded by: 1. Maureen Stapleton, 2. E. G. Marshall

Martha Swope Photos

E. G. Marshall, Maureen Stapleton

HELEN HAYES THEATRE
Opened Thursday, October 13, 1977.*
Burry Fredrik, Irwin Meyer, Stephen R. Friedman in association with William Donnell present:

THE NIGHT OF THE TRIBADES

By Per Olov Enquist; Translated by Ross Shideler; Director, Michael Kahn; Scenery, Lawrence King; Costumes, Jane Greenwood; Lighting, John McLain; Associate Producers, Sally Sears, Marilyn Strauss; Production Supervisor, Frank C. Prince; Wardrobe Supervisor, Luha Decker; Production Assistant, De Paskos; Hairstylist, Hector Garcia

CAST

Siri von-Essen-Strindberg	Bibi Andersson
August Strindberg	Max von Sydow
Viggo Schiwe	Werner Klemperer
Marie Caroline David	Eileen Atkins
Photographer	Bill Moor

UNDERSTUDIES: Katherine McGrath (Siri/Marie), Bill Moor (Strindberg/Schiwe), Richard Humphrey (Photographer)

A drama in two acts. The action takes place on the stage of the Dagmar Theatre in Copenhagen, March 1889.

General Managers: David Lawlor, Helen Nickerson
Company Manager: David Lawlor
Press: Shirley Herz, Louise Weiner Ment
Stage Managers: Suzanne Egan, Richard Humphrey

* Closed Oct. 22, 1977 after 12 performances and 7 previews.

Cliff Moore Photos

**Right: Eileen Atkins, Max von Sydow,
Bibi Andersson (also top)**

Eileen Atkins, Bibi Andersson

Max von Sydow, Werner Klemperer

16

MARTIN BECK THEATRE
Opened Thursday, October 20, 1977.*
Jujamcyn Theaters, Elizabeth Ireland McCann, John Wulp,
Victor Lurie, Nelle Nugent, Max Weitzenhoffer present:

DRACULA

By Hamilton Deane and John L. Balderston; From Bram Stoker's
novel "Dracula"; Director, Dennis Rosa; Scenery and Costumes
Designed by Edward Gorey; Scenery Supervision, Lynn Pecktal;
Costume Supervision, John David Ridge; Lighting, Roger Morgan;
Wardrobe Supervisor, Rosalie Lahm; Special Effects, Chic Silber

CAST

Lucy Seward	Ann Sachs
Miss Wells	Gretchen Oehler
Jonathan Harker	Alan Coates
Dr. Seward	Dillon Evans
Abraham Van Helsing	Jerome Dempsey
R. M. Renfield	Richard Kavanaugh
Butterworth	Baxter Harris
Count Dracula	Frank Langella

STANDBYS AND UNDERSTUDIES: Lloyd Battista (Dracula),
Stephen Scott (Van Helsing), Baxter Harris (Dracula), Louis
Beachner (Seward/Renfield/Butterworth), Malcolm Stewart (Harker/Butterworth), Charles Kindl (Van Helsing/Seward/Renfield)

A melodrama in three acts and four scenes. The action takes place
in the 1920's in the library of Dr. Seward's sanatorium in Purley,
England, in Lucy's boudoir, and in a vault.

Company Manager: Susan Gustafson
Press: Solters & Roskin, Joshua Ellis, Milly Schoenbaum
Stage Managers: Marnel Sumner, Charles Kindl, Malcolm
Stewart

* Still playing May 31, 1978. Received 1978 "Tonys" for Most
Innovative Production of a Revival, and Best Costume Design

Martha Swope Photos

**Right: Gretchen Oehler, Frank Langella;
Richard Kavanaugh, Jerome Dempsey Top:
Ann Sachs, Alan Coates, Frank Langella**

**Dillon Evans, Jerome Dempsey, Alan
Coates, Ann Sachs**

Frank Langella, Ann Sachs

17

LONGACRE THEATRE
Opened Tuesday, October 25, 1977.*
Arthur Whitelaw, Jack Schlissel and Leonard Soloway present:

SOME OF MY BEST FRIENDS

By Stanley Hart; Director, Harold Prince; Designed by Eugene Lee; Lighting, Ken Billington; Costumes, Franne Lee; Associate Producers, Donald Tick, Martin Markinson; Wardrobe Supervisor, Joseph Busheme

CAST

Andrew Mumford	Ted Knight
Albert	Gavin Reed
Irving Buxbaum	Lee Wallace
Lawrence Mumford	Bob Balaban
Dorothy Mumford	Alice Drummond
Sari	Trish Hawkins
Baby	Ralph Williams
Delivery Boy/Urchins	Joseph Scalzo

STANDBYS AND UNDERSTUDIES: Lee Goodman (Andrew/Irving), Lynne Stuart (Dorothy), Rudolph Willrich (Albert/Lawrence), Laure Mattos (Sari), Joseph Scalzo (Baby)

A comedy in two acts and four scenes. The action takes place at the present time in the living room studio of Andrew Mumford in Manhattan.

Manager: Jay Kingwill
Press: Max Eisen, Judy Jacksina, Barbara Glenn
Stage Manager: Ben Strobach, Joseph Scalzo

* Closed Oct. 29, 1977 after 7 performances and 8 previews.

Left: Ted Knight, Alice Drummond
Top: Ted Knight, Trish Hawkins, Bob Balaban

Gavin Reed, Ted Knight

Gavin Reed, Lee Wallace

George Hearn, Colleen Dewhurst, Rex Robbins
Right: Rex Robbins, Colleen Dewhurst

BELASCO THEATRE
Opened Thursday, October 27, 1977.*
Burry Fredrik and Joel Key Rice present:

AN ALMOST PERFECT PERSON

By Judith Ross; Director, Zoe Caldwell; Set and Lighting, Ben Edwards; Costumes, Jane Greenwood; Associate Producers, Sally Sears, Nadine Koval, William Livingston; Production Supervisor, Frank C. Prince; Wardrobe Supervisor, Harriet Wallerstein; Production Assistants, Nadine Koval, De Paskos

CAST

Irene Porter .... Colleen Dewhurst
Dan Michael Connally .... George Hearn
Jerry Leeds .... Rex Robbins
Announcer's Voice .... Gary Alexander Azerier
Understudy: Jess Osuna

A comedy in two acts and three scenes. The action takes place in Irene Porter's apartment on New York City's Upper West Side at the present time.

General Manager: David Lawlor
Company Manager: Milton Moss
Press: Shirley Herz, Louise Weiner Ment
Stage Managers: Peter Lawrence, Robert Bruyr

* Closed Jan. 28, 1978 after 108 performances and 5 previews.

Cliff Moore Photos

Colleen Dewhurst, George Hearn

MAJESTIC THEATRE
Opened Saturday, October 29, 1977.*
The Shubert Organization presents the Cy Feuer and Ernest H. Martin Production of:

THE ACT

Book, George Furth; Music, John Kander; Lyrics, Fred Ebb; Director, Martin Scorsese; Choreography, Ron Lewis; Scenery, Tony Walton; Lighting, Tharon Musser; Costumes, Halston; Sound, Abe Jacob; Musical Direction, Stanley Lebowsky; Orchestrations, Ralph Burns; Dance Music Arrangements, Ronald Melrose; Vocal and Choral Arrangements, Earl Brown; Hairstylists, Sydney Guilaroff, Carol Shurley; Production Assistants, William Taradash, Linda Brumfield

CAST

Lenny Kanter	Christopher Barrett
Michelle Craig	Liza Minnelli
Dan Connors	Barry Nelson†1
Arthur	Roger Minami
Charley Price	Mark Goddard
Molly Connors	Gayle Crofoot†2
The Girls	Carol Estey, Laurie Dawn Skinner†3
The Boys	Wayne Cilento†4, Michael Leeds, Roger Minami, Albert Stephenson
Dance Alternates	Claudia Asbury†5, Brad Witsger†6

STANDBYS AND UNDERSTUDIES: Mace Barrett (Connors), Christopher Barrett (Connors/Schreiber/Price), Laurie Dawn Skinner (Molly), Claudia Asbury (Dance Standby for Miss Minnelli)

MUSICAL NUMBERS: "Shine It On," "It's the Strangest Thing," "Bobo's," "Turning," "Little Do They Know," "Arthur in the Afternoon," "Hollywood, California," "The Money Tree," "City Lights," "There When I Need Him," "Hot Enough for You?," "My Own Space"

A musical in two acts. The action takes place at the Hotel Las Vegas at the present time and concerns Michelle Craig's nightclub act and her memories.

General Managers: Joseph Harris, Ira Bernstein
Press: Merle Debuskey, Leo Stern, William Shelble
Stage Managers: Robert Corpora, Mark Gero, Richard Lombard

* Closed July 1, 1978 after 233 performances and 6 previews. Miss Minnelli received "Tony" for Outstanding Actress in a Musical.
† Succeeded by: 1. Gower Champion, 2. Laurie Dawn Skinner, 3. Claudia Asbury, 4. Danny Buraczeski, 5. Karen DiBianco, 6. Steve Anthony

Martha Swope Photos

Top: Barry Nelson, Liza Minnelli Right: Arnold Soboloff, Minnelli, Mark Goddard

Roger Minami, Gayle Crofoot, Albert Stephenson, Liza Minnelli, Carol Estey, Wayne Cilento, Laurie Dawn Skinner, Michael Leeds

MOROSCO THEATRE
Opened Monday, November 14, 1977.*
The Theatre Guild presents:

GOLDA

By William Gibson; Director, Arthur Penn; Producers, Philip Langner, Armina Marshall, Marilyn Langner; Scenery and Costumes, Santo Loquasto; Lighting and Projections, Jules Fisher; Visuals, Lucie D. Grosvenor; Hairstylists, J. Roy Helland, Marlies Termine-Vallant; Production Assistant, Linda Laundra; Production Associates, Jack Hogan, Mary Jane Vineburgh, Andrew Behar; Wardrobe Supervisor, James Roberts

CAST

Allon/Menachem/D.P.	James Tolkan
Lior/Father/American/D.P./Cabinet Member	Richard Kuss
Moshe Dayan/D.P.	Ben Hammer
Elazar/D.P.	Nicholas La Padula
Galili/D.P.	Harry Davis
Cabinet Member/TV Interviewer/British Commandant/ Bearded Man	Sam Schacht
Golda Meir	Anne Bancroft
Lou/D.P.	Vivian Nathan
Dinitz (Simcha)/D.P./Cabinet Member	Zack Matalon
Mother/Sarile/D.P.	Frances Chaney
Golda as a child/Sarile as a child/Ruthie	Justine Litchman
Sister/Arab Woman/Adolescent Grandchild/American Girl/ D.P.	Alice Golembo
Body Guard/Arab/Adolescent Grandson/TV Crew/Cabinet Member	Eric Booth
Morris/D.P.	Gerald Hiken
Arab Escort/Bar-Lev/D.P.	Ernest Graves
Arab/Adolescent Grandson/TV Crew/Army Messenger/ D.P.	Phillip Cates
Arab Woman/Clara as a young girl/D.P.	Corinne Neuchateau
King Abdullah/Ben-Gurion/Religious Minister/D.P.	Sam Gray
Gideon/Modke	Josh Freund
Grandson/D.P.	Michael Brown
Menachem as a boy/Nahum	Glenn Scarpelli
Clara/D.P.	Rebecca Schull
D.P./Israeli Citizens	David C. Jones, Robert Levine
D.P.	Judy Unger

STANDBYS AND UNDERSTUDIES: Tresa Hughes (Golda), Gene Gross (Allon/Lior/Ben-Gurion/Elazar/Bar-Lev/Dinitz), David C. Jones (Arab Escort/King Abdullah/Cabinet Member), Rebecca Schull (Lou/Sarile/Mother), Robert Levine (Morris/-Menachem/American/Bearded Man), Corinne Neuchateau (Adolescent Grandchild/American Girl), Michael Brown (Young Menachem/Nahum/Modke/Gideon), Judy Unger (Young Golda/-Ruthie/Sarile as a child)

A "partial portrait" of Golda Meir in 2 acts and 22 scenes.

General Manager: Victor Samrock
Press: Joe Wolhandler, Peter Wolhandler, Silvia Perchuk
Stage Managers: Wayne Carson, Peter Dowling

* Closed Feb. 16, 1978 because of Miss Bancroft's illness. It had played 93 performances and 16 previews.

Top Right: Sam Schacht, Vivian Nathan, Anne Bancroft, Eric Booth, Phillip Cates Below: (seated) Frances Chaney, Anne Bancroft, (standing) Glenn Scarpelli, James Tolkan, Eric Booth, Alice Golembo, Phillip Cates

Anne Bancroft

PLYMOUTH THEATRE
Opened Wednesday, November 16, 1977.*
The Shubert Organization, John F. Kennedy Center for the
Performing Arts, Roger Berlind, Eddie Kulukundis in associa-
tion with SRO Productions Limited present:

THE MERCHANT

By Arnold Wesker; Director, John Dexter; Scenery and Costumes, Jocelyn Herbert; Lighting, Andy Phillips; Lighting Supervision, Andrea Wilson; Management Associate, David Wyler;
Management Assistant, Eric Angelson; Wardrobe Supervisor, Eric
Harrison; Hairstylists, Howard Rodney, Karol Coeyman; Production Assistant, Patrick Chmel; Wigs, Paul Huntley

CAST

Shylock Kolner (A Jew of Venice)	Joseph Leon
Antonio Querini (A Merchant)	John Clements
Portia Contarini (An Heiress)	Roberta Maxwell
Nerissa (Portia's maid)	Gloria Gifford
Jessica Kolner (Shylock's daughter)	Julie Garfield
Rivka Kolner (Shylock's sister)	Marian Seldes
Abtalion da Modena (Shylock's tutor)	Boris Tumarin
Tubal di Ponti (Shylock's partner)	John Seitz
Solomon Usque (Playwright)	Jeffrey Horowitz
Rebecca da Mendes (Daughter of Portuguese banker)	Angela Wood
Bassanio Visconti (Antonio's godson)	Nicolas Surovy
Graziano Sanudo (Antonio's assistant)	Riggs O'Hara
Lorenzo Pisani (Bassanio's friend)	Everett McGill
Moses of Castelazzo (Painter)	Leib Lensky
Girolamo Priuli (Doge of Venice)	William Roerick
Servant	Rebecca Malka
Venetians	Russ Banham, Mark Blum, Philip Carroll, James David Cromer, Brian Meister, John Tyrrell

UNDERSTUDIES: John Seitz (Shylock), Rebecca Malka (Jessica/-
Portia/Nerissa/Rebecca), William Roerick (Antonio), Angela
Wood (Rivka/Nerissa), Leib Lensky (Abtalion), Philip Carroll (Us-
que/Moses/Girolamo/Tubal), James David Cromar (Bassanio),
John Tyrrell (Graziano), Russ Banham (Lorenzo), Pat DeRousie
(Jessica/Rebecca), Brian Meister (Abtalion), Mark Blum (Moses-
/Usque)

A play in two acts. The action takes place during 1563 in Venice
and Belmont.

General Manager: Marvin A. Krauss
Company Manager: G. Warren McClane
Press: Merle Debuskey, Susan L. Schulman
Stage Managers: Brent Peek, Pat DeRousie, Brian Meister, Mark Blum

* Closed Nov. 20, 1977 after 6 performances and 8 previews.

Martha Swope Photos

**Right: Everett McGill, Julie Garfield;
Riggs O'Hara, Everett McGill, Nicolas Surovy**

Joseph Leon, Marian Seldes

James Whitmore

FORTY-SIXTH STREET THEATRE
Opened Tuesday, November 1, 1977.*
Don Saxon and Kevin Brown in association with Kathy Raitt
present the George Spota/Four Star International Production
of:

BULLY

By Jerome Alden; Director, Peter H. Hunt; Setting and Costumes,
John Conklin; Lighting, Peter H. Hunt; Associate Producer, Dan
Lieberman; Production Supervisor, Mitch Miller

CAST

Theodore Roosevelt .... James Whitmore

A one-character play in two acts, relating the adventures of Theodore Roosevelt.

Company Manager: Jo Rosner
Press: Faith Geer
Stage Managers: Martha Knight, Leanna Lenhart

* Closed Nov. 6, 1977 after 8 performances and 8 previews.

Ken Howard Photo

LONGACRE THEATRE
Opened Wednesday, November 23, 1977.*
Hal Zeiger presents:

JESUS CHRIST SUPERSTAR

Music, Andrew Lloyd Webber; Lyrics, Tim Rice; Director, William Daniel Grey; Choreography and Movement, Kelly Carrol; Musical Direction, Peter Phillips; Wardrobe Supervisor, Joan Lucas

CAST

Judas Iscariot	Patrick Jude
Jesus of Nazareth	Willian Daniel Grey
Mary Magdalene	Barbara Niles
First Priest/Apostle	Doug Lucas
Second Priest/Apostle	Richard Tolin
Caiaphas	Christopher Cable
Annas	Steve Schochet
Simon Zealotes	Bobby London
Peter	Randy Martin
Pontius Pilate	Randy Wilson
Soldier/Tormentor	D. Bradley Jones
Soldier/Tormentor	George Bernhard
Soul Girls	Freida Ann Williams, Pauletta Pearson, Claudette Washington
Maid by the Fire	Celeste Hogan
Apostles	David Cahn, Ken Samuels, Lennie Del Duca
King Herod	Mark Syers

UNDERSTUDIES: Randy Wilson (Jesus), Steve Schochet (Judas), Freida Ann Williams (Magdalene), Steve Schochet (Pilate), Doug Lucas (Caiaphas), Alan Blair, Kelly Carrol (Chorus)

MUSICAL NUMBERS: "Heaven on Their Minds," "What's the Buza," "Strange Thing Mystifying," "Everything's All Right," "This Jesus Must Die," "Hosanna," "Simon Zealotes," "Poor Jerusalem," "Pilate's Dream," "The Temple," "I Don't Know How to Love Him," "Damned for All Time," "The Last Supper," "Gethsemane," "The Arrest," "Peter's Denial," "Pilate and Christ," "King Herod's Song," "Could We Start Again, Please," "Judas' Death," "Trial before Pilate," "Superstar," "John 19:41"

A musical in two acts.

Company Manager: Manuel L. Levine
Stage Managers: Chuck Linker, Rick Ralston, Alan Blair

* Closed Feb. 12, 1978 after 96 performances. Original production opened at the Mark Hellinger Theatre Oct. 12, 1971 and closed July 1, 1973 after 711 performances. See THEATRE WORLD, Vol. 28.
(No photos available)

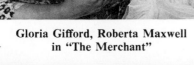

**Gloria Gifford, Roberta Maxwell
in "The Merchant"**

MARK HELLINGER THEATRE
Opened Wednesday, November 23, 1977.*
Larry Tarnofsky presents:

LOU RAWLS ON BROADWAY
with
The MFSB Orchestra

Production Design, Salvatore Tagliarino; Lighting Supervision, Fred Allison; Special Musical Arrangements, Joe Mehe, Larry Farrow; Sound, Gary Ross Sound; Sound Supervision, C. C. Cope; Musical Director, Denny Gore; Associate Producer, Glenn Lipnick; Management Associate, David Wyler; Management Assistant, Eric Angelson; Lighting and Multi-Media Design, Stig Edgren

An evening of song in two acts with Lou Rawls and vocalists Althea Rogers, Debbie Morris, Cindy Jordan.

General Manager: Marvin A. Krauss
Press: Elizabeth A. Rodman, Harriett Trachtenberg, Sharon Mear, Ron Harris

* Closed Dec. 4, 1977 after limited engagement of 15 performances.

Harry Langdon Photo
Top: Lou Rawls

IMPERIAL THEATRE
  Opened Sunday, December 4, 1977.*
  Emanuel Azenberg presents:

CHAPTER TWO

By Neil Simon; Director, Herbert Ross; Scenery, William Ritman; Costumes, Noel Taylor; Lighting, Tharon Musser; Wardrobe Supervisor, Harry Edwards; Hairstylist, Frances LoDrini; Production Assistants, Jane Robison, Matt Schoengood

CAST

George Schneider	Judd Hirsch†
Leo Schneider	Cliff Gorman
Jennie Malone	Anita Gillette
Faye Medwick	Ann Wedgeworth

STANDBYS: Dick Latessa (George/Leo), Andrea Adler (Jennie), Jean DeBaer (Faye)

A comedy in two acts. The action takes place in Jennifer Malone's upper East Side apartment and George Schneider's lower Central Park West apartment in Manhattan, from late February to mid-spring of the present time.

Manager: Jose Vega
Company Manager: Susan Bell
Press: Bill Evans, Mark Hunter
Stage Managers: Charles Blackwell, Lani Sundsten

* Still playing May 31, 1978. Miss Wedgeworth received a 1978 "Tony" for Outstanding Featured Actress in a Play.
† Succeeded by David Groh

Jay Thompson Photos

Left: Anita Gillette, Ann Wedgeworth, Cliff Gorman, Judd Hirsch

Cliff Gorman, Ann Wedgeworth

Judd Hirsch, Anita Gillette

CIRCLE IN THE SQUARE THEATRE
Opened Thursday, December 15, 1977 *
Circle in the Square (Theodore Mann, Artistic Director; Paul Libin, Managing Director) presents:

SAINT JOAN

By George Bernard Shaw; Director, John Clark; Scenery, David Jenkins; Costumes, Zack Brown; Lighting, John McLain; Wigs and Hairstyles, Paul Huntley; Wardrobe Supervisor, Virginia Merkel

CAST

Robert de Baudricourt/English Soldier	Roy Cooper
Steward/Warwick's Page	Armin Shimerman
Joan	Lynn Redgrave
Bertrand de Poulengey/Stranger	Peter Van Norden
Court Page	Pendleton Brown
Archbishop of Rheims	Tom Aldredge
Monseigneur de la Tremouille	Tom Klunis
Gilles de Rais	Kenneth Gray
Captain La Hire	Ed Setrakian
Dauphin, later Charles VII	Robert LuPone
Duchess de la Tremouille	Gwendolyn Brown
Dunois, Bastard of Orleans	Joseph Bova
Dunois' Page	Stephen Lang
Richard de Beauchamp, Earl of Warwick	Philip Bosco
Chaplain de Stogumber	Robert Gerringer
Peter Cauchon, Bishop of Beauvais	Paul Shyre
The Inquisitor	Paul Sparer
Canon John D'Estivet	John Rose
Canon de Courcelles	Stephen Lang
Brother Martin Ladvenu	Nicholas Hormann
Executioner	Jim Broaddus

Court Ladies, Courtiers,
Soldiers, Monks .... Jim Broaddus, Pendleton Brown, Kenneth Gray, Sarah-Jane Gwillim, Nicholas Hormann, Stephen Lang, John Rose, Armin Shimerman, Peter Van Norden

UNDERSTUDIES: Sarah-Jane Gwillim (Joan), Jim Broaddus (Poulengey/Stranger/La Hire/Tremouille), Robert Gerringer (Baudricourt), Kenneth Gray (D'Estivet), Tom Klunis Beauchamp/Cauchon), Stephen Lang (Dauphin/Steward), John Rose (Archbishop/Stogumber/Inquisitor), Ed Setrakian (Dunois), Armin Shimerman (de Courcelles/English Soldier), Peter Van Norden (Executioner), Pendleton Brown (Ladvenu)

A drama performed in two acts and six scenes with an epilogue.

Company Manager: William Conn
Press: Merle Debuskey, David Roggensack
Stage Managers: Randall Brooks, James Bernardi

* Closed Feb. 19, 1978 after 77 performances and 23 previews.

Martha Swope Photos

Top: Nicholas Hormann, Lynn Redgrave Right: Robert Gerringer, Philip Bosco, Paul Shyre, Armin Shimerman

Lynn Redgrave, and above with Joseph Bova, Robert LuPone, Paul Sparer 25

HELEN HAYES THEATRE
Opened Wednesday, December 28, 1977.*
Elliot Martin presents:

A TOUCH OF THE POET

By Eugene O'Neill; Director, Jose Quintero; Setting and Lighting,
Ben Edwards; Costumes, Jane Greenwood; Wardrobe Supervisor,
William Campbell; Hairstylist, Joe Blitz; Assistant to the Producer,
Norma Eckroate

CAST

Mickey Maloy	Barry Snider
Jamie Cregan	Milo O'Shea
Sara Melody	Kathryn Walker
Nora Melody	Geraldine Fitzgerald
Cornelius Melody	Jason Robards
Dan Roche	Walter Flanagan
Paddy O'Dowd	Dermot McNamara
Patch Riley	Richard Hamilton
Deborah (Mrs. Henry Harford)	Betty Miller
Nicholas Gadsby	George Ede

STANDBYS: Milo O'Shea (Cornelius), Louisa Horton (Nora/-
Deborah), Walter Flanagan (Jamie), Linda Martin (Sara), Wally
Peterson (Gadsby/Patch/Dan), Dermot McNamara (Mickey), John
Handy (Paddy)

A drama in two acts. The action takes place in the dining room
of Melody's Tavern in a village a few miles from Boston on July 27,
1828.

General Manager: Leonard A. Mulhern
Company Manager: Malcolm Allen
Press: Seymour Krawitz, Louise Weiner Ment, Patricia MacLean
Krawitz
Stage Managers: Mitch Erickson, John Handy

* Closed Apr. 30, 1978 after 141 performances and 8 previews.
Original production with Eric Portman, Helen Hayes, Kim Stanley and Betty Field opened at the Helen Hayes Theatre Oct. 2,
1958 and played 292 performances. See THEATRE WORLD
Vol. 15.

Martha Swope Photos

**Right: Geraldine Fitzgerald, Kathryn Walker, Jason
Robards, George Ede, Dermot McNamara Top: Jason
Robards, Milo O'Shea**

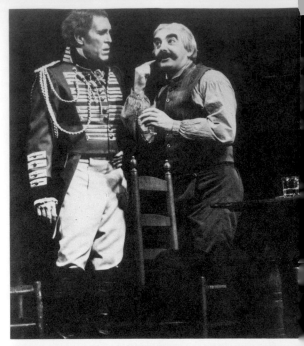

Betty Miller, Jason Robards

Kathryn Walker, Geraldine Fitzgerald

LYCEUM THEATRE
Opened Thursday, December 29, 1977.*
Claire Nichtern and Ashton Springer in association with Irene
Miller present:

COLD STORAGE

By Ronald Ribman; Director, Frank Corsaro; Set and Costume
Design, Karl Eigsti; Lighting, William Mintzer; Wardrobe Mistress,
Betsy Jackson; Production Assistant, Mary-Evelyn Card

CAST

Richard Landau	Len Cariou†
Miss Madurga	Ruth Rivera
Joseph Parmigian	Martin Balsam

STANDBYS AND UNDERSTUDIES: George Guidall (Landau),
Ginny Greedman (Miss Madurga)

A comedy in two acts. The action takes place at the present time
on a hospital roof garden in New York City.

General Management: Theatre Management Associates
Company Manager: Charles Willard
Press: Max Eisen, Judy Jacksina, Barbara Glenn
Stage Managers: Clint Jakeman, Ginny Freedman

* Closed June 4, 1978 after 180 performances and 8 previews Produced originally at American Place Theatre Apr. 6, 1977 and
closed May 8, 1977 after 47 performances.
† Succeeded by George Guidall

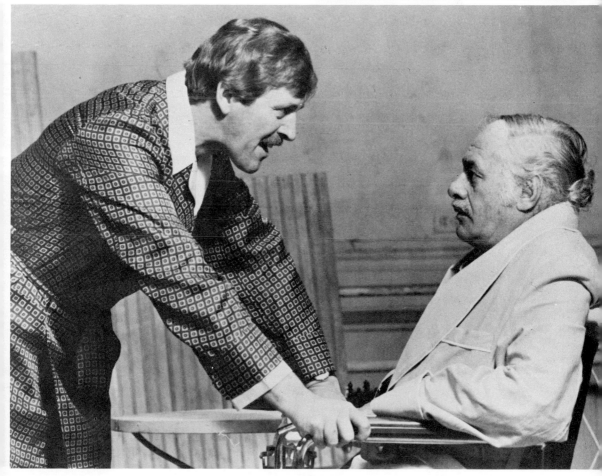

Len Cariou, Martin Balsam

FORTY-SIXTH STREET THEATRE
Opened Monday, January 9, 1978.*
The Kennedy Center in association with Cheryl Crawford presents:

DO YOU TURN SOMERSAULTS?

By Aleksei Arbuzov; Translated by Ariadne Nicolaeff; Director, Edwin Sherin; Scenery, Oliver Smith; Costumes, Ann Roth; Lighting, Ken Billington; Incidental Music, Charles Gross; Presented by arrangement with the Royal Shakespeare Theatre, Stratford-on-Avon, England; Wardrobe Supervisor, Agnes Farrell; Circus Song Lyrics, Ian Kellam

CAST

Lidya Vasilyevna .... Mary Martin
Rodion Nikolayevich .... Anthony Quayle

A play in two acts and nine scenes. The action takes place in August 1968 on the Riga coast.

General Manager: Ralph Roseman
Company Manager: James Awe
Press: Michael Alpert, Marilynn LeVine, Fred H. Nathan, Randi Cone
Stage Managers: Paul A. Foley, Stephen Nasuta, Marc Schlackman

* Closed Jan. 21, 1978 after 16 performances and 3 previews.

Left: Mary Martin, Anthony Quayle

Mary Martin, Anthony Quayle

BILLY ROSE THEATRE
Opened Saturday, January 14, 1978.*
Shelly Bechok and Jim D'Spain present:

THE NOVEMBER PEOPLE

By Gus Weill; Director, Arthur Sherman; Set, Kert Lundell; Lighting, Thomas Skelton; Costumes, Joseph G. Aulisi; Management Associate, Thelma Cooper; Production Assistant, Shauna Vey; Wardrobe Supervisor, Virginia Sylvain;

CAST

Mitch	Cameron Mitchell
Mary	Jan Sterling
Donny, their younger son	John Uecker
Brian, their older son	James Sutorius
Kathleen, Brian's wife	Pamela Reed

STANDBYS AND UNDERSTUDIES: Ben Kapen (Mitch), Justin Deas (Donny/Brian), Lisabeth Shean (Kathleen)

A drama in two acts. The action takes place at the present time.

General Management: Dorothy Olim Associates
Company Manager: Gail Bell
Press: Shirley Herz, William Schelble
Stage Managers: Alan Hall, Richard Elkow

* Closed Jan. 14, 1978 after one performance and 19 previews.

Bert Andrews Photos

Top: James Sutorius, Pamela Reed, John Uecker, Cameron Mitchell, Jan Sterling

Pamela Reed, James Sutorius, Cameron Mitchell, Jan Sterling

BILTMORE THEATRE

Opened Sunday, January 15, 1978.*

Ken Marsolais, Philip M. Getter and Leonard Soloway present:

CHEATERS

By Michael Jacobs; Director, Robert Drivas; Scenery, Lawrence King; Costumes, Jane Greenwood; Lighting, Ian Calderon; Production Supervisor, Larry Forde; Associate Producers, Donald Tick, Martin Markinson; Wardrobe Supervisor, Joseph Busheme; Hairstylist, Karol Coeyman; Production Assistant, Jeff Goodman

CAST

Monica	Rosemary Murphy
Howard	Lou Jacobi
Sam	Jack Weston
Grace	Doris Roberts
Michelle	Roxanne Hart
Allen	Jim Staskel

STANDBYS: Doris Belack (Monica/Grace), Kurt Knudson (Howard/Sam), Arlene Grayson (Michelle), Steve Scott (Allen)

A comedy in two acts. The action takes place at the present time in rooms in New York City and Union, N.J., and in homes in Larchmont, N.Y., and Englewood, N.J.

Company Manager: Robert H. Wallner
Press: Betty Lee Hunt, Maria Cristina Pucci
Stage Managers: Larry Forde, Arlene Grayson, Steve Scott

* Closed Feb. 11, 1978 after 33 performances and 11 previews.

Ken Howard, Joseph Abeles Photos

**Top: Jim Staskel, Rosemary Murphy,
Jack Weston**

30

**Roxanne Hart, Jim Staskel Above: Doris Roberts,
Jack Weston Top: Lou Jacobi, Rosemary Murphy**

LUNT-FONTANNE THEATRE
Opened Thursday, January 19, 1978.*
Don Gregory presents:

PAUL ROBESON

By Phillip Hayes Dean; Director, Lloyd Richards; Original Staging, Charles Nelson Reilly; Scenery, H. R. Poindexter; Lighting, Ian Calderon; Costumes, Noel Taylor; An International Cinegraph/-Creative Image Production by arrangement with Carmen F. Zollo; Production Coordinator, Ed Gazich; Assistant to Producer, Alana Scott; Production Assistant, Patricia Bowman; Choreographic Consultant, Jaime Rogers

CAST

Paul Robeson .... James Earl Jones
Lawrence Brown .... Burt Wallace

A play about the life of the singer, actor and political activist, Paul Robeson, presented in two parts.

General Manager: Leonard A. Mulhern
Company Manager: L. Liberatore
Press: Seymour Krawitz, Patricia McLean Krawitz, Louise Weiner Ment
Stage Managers: Phil Stein, Louis Mascolo

* Closed Feb. 26, 1978 and re-opened at the Booth Theatre Thursday, March 9, 1978 in repertory with "For Colored Girls Who Have Considered Suicide . . . " Closed Apr. 30, 1978 after a total of 77 performances and 3 previews.

Bert Andrews Photos

Right: James Earl Jones, Burt Williams
Top: James Earl Jones

Rick Saucedo

PALACE THEATRE
Opened Tuesday, January 31, 1978.*
DL Theatrical Productions, Inc. presents:

ELVIS: THE LEGEND LIVES!

Production Concept, John Finocchio, Larry Marshak, David Zann; Directed by Jim Sotos, Henry Scarpelli; Musical Director, Peter Dino; Special Consultant, Paul Lichter; Title Music, Doc Pomus, Bruce Foster; Lighting, Barry Arnold; Sound, Joe Golden; Visual Concepts and Design, Productions Two; General Management, Theatre Now (William Court Cohen, Edward H. Davis, Norman E. Rothstein); Hairstylist, James P. Foley

CAST

Rick Saucedo	The Jordanaires
Will Jordan	D. J. Fontana

Kharisma: Bernice Frazier, Judith O'Dell, April Epps

A musical entertainment in two acts and five scenes, reviewing the life and music of Elvis Presley.

General Managers: Theatre Now, Inc.
Press: Les Schecter, Barbara Schwei, Evelyn Barron
Stage Managers: Robert Bernard, Elise Warner

* Closed Apr. 30, 1978 after 101 performances.

ST. JAMES THEATRE
Opened Sunday, February 19, 1978.*
The Producers Circle 2, Inc. (Robert Fryer, Mary Lea Johnson, James Cresson, Martin Richards) in association with Joseph Harris and Ira Bernstein presents:

ON THE TWENTIETH CENTURY

Book and Lyrics, Betty Comden, Adolph Green; Based on plays by Ben Hecht, Charles MacArthur, Bruce Millholland; Music, Cy Coleman; Director, Harold Prince; Musical Numbers Staged by Larry Fuller; Scenery, Robin Wagner; Costumes, Florence Klotz; Lighting, Ken Billington; Musical Director, Paul Gemignani; Orchestrations, Hershy Kay; Assistant to Mr. Prince, Ruth Mitchell; Furs, Ben Kahn; Associate Producers, Sam Crothers, Andre Pastoria; Production Associates, Nina Goodman, Edward Merkow, Rick Mandel; Business Manager, Frank Scardino; Wardrobe Supervisor, Helen McMahon; Hairstylist and Make-up, Richard Allen; Assistant Conductor, Nick Cerrato

CAST

Priest	Ken Hilliard
Bishop	Charles Rule
Stage Manager	Ray Gill
Joan	Maris Clement
Wardrobe Mistress	Carol Lurie
Actor	Hal Norman
Owen O'Malley	George Coe
Oliver Webb	Dean Dittman
Porters	Keith Davis, Quitman Fludd III, Ray Stephens, Joseph Wise
Congressman Lockwood	Rufus Smith
Conductor Flanagan	Tom Batten
Train Secretary Rogers	Stanley Simmonds
Letitia Primrose	Imogene Coca
Redcap	Mel Johnson, Jr.
Anita	Carol Lugenbeal
Oscar Jaffee	John Cullum
Max Jacobs	George Lee Andrews
Imelda	Willi Burke
Maxwell Finch	David Horwitz
Mildred Plotka/Lily Garland	Madeline Kahn†1
Otto Von Bismark	Sal Mistretta
Bruce Granit	Kevin Kline
Agnes	Judy Kaye†2
Hospital Attendants	Sal Mistretta, Carol Lurie
Dr. Johnson	Willi Burke
Fanny	Peggy Cooper

SINGERS: Susan Cella, Maris Clement, Peggy Cooper, Karen Gibson, Carol Lugenbeal, Carol Lurie, Melanie Vaughan, Linda Poser (Swing), Ray Gill, Ken Hilliard, David Horwitz, Craig Lucas, Sal Mistretta, Hal Norman, Charles Rule, David Vogel, Gerald Teijelo (Swing)

STANDBYS AND UNDERSTUDIES: Judy Kaye (Lily), Peggy Cooper (Letitia), Karen Gibson (Imelda), Ray Gill (Bruce), Craig Lucas (Max), Hal Norman (Webb/Lockwood), Stanley Simmonds (Conductor), David Vogel (O'Malley), Karen Gibson (Dr. Johnson), Melanie Vaughan (Agnes), George Lee Andrews (Oscar)

MUSICAL NUMBERS: "Stranded Again," "On the 20th Century," "I Rise Again," "Indian Maiden's Lament," "Veronique," "I Have Written a Play," "Together," "Never," "Our Private World," "Repent," "Mine," "I've Got It All," "Entr'Acte," "Five Zeros," "Sextet," "She's a Nut," "Max Jacobs," "Babbette," "The Legacy," "Lily, Oscar"

A musical in two acts. The action takes place in the early 1930's, mainly on the 20th Century Limited from Chicago to New York.

General Managers: Joseph Harris, Ira Bernstein
Press: Bill Evans, Mary Bryant, Mark Hunter, Philip Rinaldi
Stage Managers: George Martin, E. Bronson Platt, Gerald Teijelo, Andrew Cadiff

* Still playing May 31, 1978. Received 1978 "Tonys" for Outstanding Actor in a Musical (John Cullum), Outstanding Featured Actor in a Musical (Kevin Kline), Best Book of a Musical, Best Score, Best Lyrics, and Best Set Design.
† Succeeded by: 1. Judy Kaye, 2. Melanie Vaughan

Martha Swope Photos

John Cullum, Madeline Kahn

Top Left: Madeline Kahn, Kevin Kline, Imogene Coca

THE MUSIC BOX
Opened Sunday, February 26, 1978.*
Alfred de Liagre, Jr. and Roger L. Stevens present:

DEATHTRAP

By Ira Levin; Director, Robert Moore; Set, William Ritman; Costumes, Ruth Morley; Lighting, Marc B. Weiss; Wardrobe Supervisor, Mariana Torres; Assistant to Director, George Rondo

CAST

Sidney Bruhl	John Wood
Myra Bruhl	Marian Seldes
Clifford Anderson	Victor Garber
Helga ten Dorp	Marian Winters
Porter Milgrim	Richard Woods

STANDBYS: Jan Farrand (Helga/Myra), Ernie Townsend (Clifford)

A "thriller" in two acts and six scenes. The action takes place at the present time in Sidney Bruhl's study in the Bruhl home in Westport, Connecticut.

General Manager: Oscar E. Olesen
Company Manager: David Hedges
Press: Jeffrey Richards, Bruce Lynn
Stage Managers: Philip Cusack, Lani Sundsten

* Still playing May 31, 1978.

Sy Friedman Photos

**Left: John Wood, Marian Seldes, Marian Winters
Top: John Wood, Marian Seldes, Victor Garber**

Marian Winters, Richard Woods

**John Wood Above: Victor
Garber, Marian Winters**

MARK HELLINGER THEATRE
Opened Wednesday, March 1, 1978.*
Luther Davis presents:

TIMBUKTU!

Book, Luther Davis; Based on musical "Kismet" by Charles Lederer and Luther Davis; From the play by Edward Knoblock; Music and Lyrics, Robert Wright, George Forrest from the themes of Alexander Borodin and African Folk Music; Directed, Choreographed and Costumed by Geoffrey Holder; Scenery, Tony Straiges; Lighting, Ian Calderon; Sound, Abe Jacob; Musical Director/Incidental Music, Charles H. Coleman; Additional Orchestrations, Bill Brohn; Produced in association with Sarnoff International Enterprises, William D. Cunningham, John F. Kennedy Center for the Performing Arts; Associate Producer, Alan Eichler; Assistant to Director, Donald Christy; Hairstylist, Michael Smith; Assistant Musical Director, John Cartwright; Technical Director, Arthur Siccardi; Wardrobe Supervisors, Frank Green, Pixie Esmonde; Production Assistant, David Blackwell; Wigs and Make-up, Stanley James; Assistant Choreographer/Dance Captain, Miguel Godreau; Music Coordinator, Earl Shendell.

CAST

The Chakaba (Stiltwalker)	Obba Babatunde
Beggars	Harold Pierson, Shezwae Powell
Hadji	Ira Hawkins
Marsinah, his daughter	Melba Moore†
Witchdoctor	Harold Pierson
Child	Deborah Waller
M'Ballah of the River	Daniel Barton
Najua, Servant to Sahleem-La-Lume	Eleanor McCoy
The Wazir	George Bell
Chief Policeman	Bruce A. Hubbard
Sahleem-La-Lume	Eartha Kitt
Princesses of Baguezane	Deborah K. Brown, Sharon Cuff, Patricia Lumpkin
Munshi, servant to the Mansa	Miguel Godreau
The Mansa of Mali	Gilbert Price
Orange Merchant	Obba Babatunde
Birds in Paradise	Miguel Godreau, Eleanor McCoy
Antelopes	Obba Babatunde, Luther Fontaine
Woman in the garden	Shezwae Powell
Zubbediya	Vanessa Shaw

CITIZENS OF TIMBUKTU: Obba Babatunde, Gregg Baker, Daniel Barton, Joella Breedlove, Deborah K. Brown, Tony Carroll, Sharon Cuff, Cheryl Cummings, Luther Fontaine, Michael F. Harrison, Dyane Harvey, Marzetta Jones, Jimmy Justice, Eugene Little, Patricia Lumpkin, Joe Lynn, Tony Ndogo, Harold Pierson, Ray Pollard, Shezwae Powell, Ronald Richardson, Vanessa Shaw, Louis Tucker, Deborah Waller, Renee Warren.

UNDERSTUDIES: Gregg Baker (Hadji), Shezwae Powell (Sahleem-La-Lume), Vanessa Shaw (Marsinah), Bruce A. Hubbard (Mansa), Louis Tucker (Wazir), Eugene Little (Munshi), Ronald Richardson (Chief of Police), Dyane Harvey (Najua), Jimmy Justice (M'Ballah), Joella Breedlove (Princesses), Tony Ndogo (Antelopes), Rodney Green, Jan Hazell (Swing Dancers)

MUSICAL NUMBERS: "Rhymes Have I," "Fate," "In the Beginning, Woman," "Baubles, Bangles and Beads," "Stranger in Paradise," "Gesticulate," "Night of My Nights," "My Magic Lamp," "Rahadlakum," "And This Is My Beloved," "Golden Land, Golden Life," "Zubbediya," "Sands of Time"

A musical in 2 acts and 12 scenes. The action takes place in Timbuktu, in the Ancient Empire of Mali, West Africa, in the year 1361, from dawn to dusk to dawn.

General Management: Gatchell & Neufeld, Ltd.
Company Manager: Drew Murphy
Press: Solters & Roskin, Joshua Ellis, Milly Schoenbaum, Sophronia McBride-Pope, Mark Goldstaub
Stage Managers: Donald Christy, Jeanna Belkin, Pat Trott

* Still playing May 31, 1978.
† Succeeded by Vanessa Shaw

Martha Swope Photos

Top Right: Melba Moore, Gilbert Price, Eartha Kitt, Ira Hawkins Below: Melba Moore

**Gilbert Price, Melba Moore, Ira Hawkins
Above: Eartha Kitt, Eleanor McCoy, Ira Hawkins**

LUNT-FONTANNE THEATRE
Opened Sunday, March 5, 1978.*
James M. Nederlander and the Houston Grand Opera present:

HELLO, DOLLY!

Book, Michael Stewart; Based on play "The Matchmaker" by Thornton Wilder; Music and Lyrics, Jerry Herman; Director, Lucia Victor; Choreography, Jack Craig; Conductor, Jack Everly; Associate Producer, Robert A. Buckley; Original production directed and choreographed by Gower Champion; Dance and Incidental Music Arrangements, Peter Howard; Settings, Oliver Smith; Costumes, Freddy Wittop; Lighting, Martin Aronstein; Musical Direction, John L. DeMain; Production Supervision, Jerry Herman; Associate Conductor, Patrick Holland; Wardrobe, Gene Wilson, Kathleen Foster; Hairstyles and Wigs, Paul Huntley

CAST

Mrs. Dolly Gallagher Levi	Carol Channing
Ernestina	P. J. Nelson
Ambrose Kemper	Michael C. Booker
Horse	Carole Banninger, Debra Pigliavento
Horace Vandergelder	Eddie Bracken
Ermengarde	K. T. Baumann
Cornelius Hackl	Lee Roy Reams
Barnaby Tucker	Robert Lydiard
Minnie Fay	Alexandra Korey
Irene Molloy	Florence Lacey
Mrs. Rose	Marilyn Hudgins
Rudolph	John Anania
Judge	Bill Bateman
Court Clerk	Randolph Riscol

TOWNSPEOPLE, WAITERS, ETC.: Diane Abrams, Carole Banninger, JoEla Flood, Marilyn Hudgins, Deborah Moldow, Janyce Nyman, Jacqueline Payne, Debra Pigliavento, Theresa Rakov, Barbara Ann Thompson, Richard Ammon, Bill Bateman, Kyle Cittadin, Ron Crofoot, Don Edward Detrick, Richard Dodd, Rob Draper, David Evans, Tom Garrett, Charlie Goeddertz, James Homan, Alex MacKay, Richard Maxon, Randy Morgan, Randolph Riscol, Mark Waldrop, Swing Dancers: Coby Grossbart, Bubba Rambo

UNDERSTUDIES: Michael C. Booker (Cornelius), Deborah Moldow (Irene), K. T. Baumann (Minnie Fay), John Anania (Vandergelder), Kyle Cittadin (Barnaby), Randy Morgan (Rudolph), Jacqueline Payne (Ermengarde), Theresa Rakov (Ernestina), Rob Draper (Ambrose), Barbara Ann Thompson (Mrs. Rose)

MUSICAL NUMBERS: "I Put My Hand In," "It Takes a Woman," "Put on Your Sunday Clothes," "Ribbons down My Back," "Motherhood," "Dancing," "Before the Parade Passes By," "Elegance," "The Waiters' Gallop," "Hello, Dolly!," "Polka Contest," "It Only Takes a Moment," "So Long, Dearie," Finale.

A musical comedy in 2 acts and 13 scenes. The action takes place in Yonkers and Manhattan in the past.

General Management: Jack Schlissel, Jay Kingwill, Robert Buckley
Company Manager: Morry Efron
Press: Solters & Roskin, Milly Schoenbaum, Fred Nathan, Mark Goldstaub
Stage Managers: Pat Tolson, T. L. Boston, Judith Binus

* Closed July 9, 1978 after 147 performances and 5 previews. Original production with Carol Channing opened at the St. James Theatre Jan. 16, 1964 and played 2844 performances, closing Dec. 27, 1970. See THEATRE WORLD, Vol. 20.

**Top Right: Carol Channing
Below: John Anania, Eddie Bracken,
Carol Channing**

Entire Cast at curtain call

PLYMOUTH THEATRE
Opened Monday, March 6, 1978.*
Joseph Papp presents the New York Shakespeare Festival Production of:

THE WATER ENGINE
and
MR. HAPPINESS

By David Mamet; Director, Steven Schacter; Scenery, John Lee Beatty; Costumes, Laura Crow; Lighting, Dennis Parichy; Music, Alaric Jans; Associate Producer, Bernard Gersten; Wigs, J. Roy Helland; Wardrobe Mistress, Reet Pell; Technical Director, Mervyn Haines, Jr.; Production Supervisor, Jason Steven Cohen; Production Manager, Andrew Mihok

CAST

"Mr. Happiness"
Mr. Happiness .... Charles Kimbrough

"The Water Engine"
Charles Lang (Inventor) .... Dwight Schultz
Rita (His sister) .... Patti LuPone
Morton Gross (A lawyer) .... David Sabin
Lawrence Oberman (A lawyer) .... Bill Moor
Mrs. Varec (Woman from upstairs) .... Barbara Tarbuck
Mr. Wallace (Proprietor of candy store) .... Dominic Chinaese
Bernie (His son) .... Michael J. Miller
Dave Murray (Reporter for the Daily News) ..... Colin Stinton
Sound Effects Man .... Eric Loeb
Announcer .... Paul Milikin
Musician .... Alaric Jans
Lily La Pon .... Patti LuPone

UNDERSTUDIES: Eric Loeb (Lang/Murray), Paul Milikin (Wallace/Oberman/Gross), Dominic Chianese, Jr. (Bernie), JoAnne Belanger (Rita/Mrs. Varec)

A comedy performed without intermission. The action takes place in the studios of SCMJ Radio Station, New York City, during 1934, the second year of "The Century of Progress Exposition."

General Manager: Robert Kamlot
Company Manager: Bob MacDonald
Press: Merle Debuskey, William Schelble
Stage Managers: Jason LaPadura, Harold Apter, Roger Gindi

* Closed March 19, 1978 after 16 performances and 8 previews. Moved to Broadway from the Public/Cabaret Theater where it played 45 performances and 18 previews. Patti LuPone succeeded Annie Hat and Penelope Allen.

Martha Swope Photos

**Left: Dwight Schultz, Patti LuPone, Colin Stinton
Top: David Sabin, Eric Loeb, Dwight Schultz, Bill Moor, Patti LuPone, Barbara Tarbuck, Colin Stinton**

Michael J. Miller

Charles Kimbrough

**Carol Kane Top Right: Carol Kane,
Lori Shelle, Shelley Winters**

BILTMORE THEATRE
Opened Tuesday, March 14, 1978.*
Courtney Burr and Nancy Rosenthal present:

THE EFFECT OF GAMMA RAYS ON
MAN-IN-THE-MOON MARIGOLDS

By Paul Zindel; Director, A. J. Antoon; Setting and Costumes, Peter Harvey; Lighting, Ian Calderon; Original Music, Richard Peaslee; Associate Producers, William King, Charles Blum; Production Associate, Blossom Horowitz; Wardrobe Mistress, Jane Doe

CAST

Tillie .... Carol Kane
Beatrice .... Shelley Winters
Ruth .... Lori Shelle
Nanny .... Isabella Hoopes
Janice Vickery .... Lolly Boroff

UNDERSTUDIES: Lolly Boroff.(Tillie/Ruth), Jill Karyn (Janice)

A Drama in two acts. The action takes place at the present time in the home of Beatrice.

General Manager: Jerry Arrow
Press: Max Eisen, Barbara Glenn
Stage Manager: Murray Gitlin

* Closed March 26, 1978 after 16 performances and 5 previews. Original production opened Off-Broadway April 7, 1970 at the Mercer O'Casey Theatre and closed at the New Theatre May 14, 1972 after 819 performances. See THEATRE WORLD Vol. 26.

Lolly Boroff, Shelley Winters

CIRCLE IN THE SQUARE

Opened Thursday, March 16, 1978.*

Circle in the Square (Theodore Mann, Artistic Director; Paul Libin, Managing Director) presents:

13 RUE DE L'AMOUR

By Georges Feydeau; "Monsieur Chasse" adapted and translated by Mawby Green and Ed Feilbert; Director, Basil Langton; Scenery and Costumes, Zack Brown; Lighting, John McLain; Wigs and Hairstyles, Paul Huntley; Wardrobe Supervisor, Virginia Merkel; Production Assistant, Ted Williams.

CAST

Marie	Jill P. Rose
Tailor	Jim Broaddus
Duchotel	Bernard Fox
Moricet	Louis Jourdan
Leontine	Patricia Elliott
Jean-Pierre	Richard Pilcher
Birabeau	Laurie Main
Madame Spritzer	Kathleen Freeman
Inspector of Police	Ian Trigger
First Policeman	Jim Broaddus
Second Policeman	John Shuman

UNDERSTUDIES: Jill P. Rose (Leontine/Mme. Spritzer), Jim Broaddus (Duchotel/Moricet/Birabeau), John Shuman (Tailor/-Jean-Pierre/Inspector/Policeman)

A farce in three acts. The action takes place during the autumn of 1890 in Paris in the morning room of Monsieur and Madame Duchotel, and in Moricet's bachelor apartment.

Company Manager: William Conn
Press: Merle Debuskey, David Roggensack
Stage Managers: James Bernardi, John Shuman

* Closed May 21, 1978 after 77 performances and 21 previews.

Martha Swope Photos

Top Right: Louis Jourdan

Patricia Elliott, Bernard Fox, Louis Jourdan

Patricia Elliott, Louis Jourdan

BELASCO THEATRE
Opened Sunday, March 19, 1978.*
Edgar Bronfman and Stuart Ostrow present:

STAGES

Written and Produced by Stuart Ostrow; Director, Richard Foreman; Scenery, Douglas W. Schmidt; Costumes, Patricia Zipprodt; Lighting, Pat Collins; Music, Stanley Silverman; Hairstylist, Patrik D. Moreton; Sound, Roger Jay; Wardrobe Supervisor, Clarence Sims; Production Assistants, Jane Rottenbach, Victoria Merrill

CAST

Jack Warden	Diana Davila
Tom Aldredge	Ralph Drischell
Philip Bosco	William Duell
Roy Brocksmith	Caroline Kava
Howland Chamberlin	Manuel Martinez
Gretel Cummings	Lois Smith
Brenda Currin	Max Wright

A play in two acts and five stages: Denial, Anger, Bargaining, Depression, Acceptance

General Managers: Joseph Harris, Ira Bernstein
Company Manager: Nancy Simmons
Press: Betty Lee Hunt, Maria Cristina Pucci, Fred Hoot
Stage Managers: D. W. Koehler, Frank DiFilia

* Closed March 19, 1978 after one performance and 13 previews.

No production photographs
Top Right: Jack Warden

 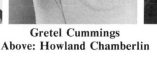 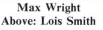 

Roy Brocksmith	**Gretel Cummings**	**Max Wright**	**Diana Davila**
Above: Caroline Kava	**Above: Howland Chamberlin**	**Above: Lois Smith**	**Above: William Duell**

BROADHURST THEATRE
Opened Monday, March 27, 1978.*
Jules Fisher, The Shubert Organization (Gerald Schoenfeld, Chairman; Bernard B. Jacobs, President), Columbia Pictures present:

DANCIN'

Conceived, Directed and Choreographed by Bob Fosse; Scenery, Peter Larkin; Costumes, Willa Kim; Lighting, Jules Fisher; Music and Lyrics, Johann Sebastian Bach, Ralph Burns, George M. Cohan, Neil Diamond, Bob Haggart, Ray Bauduc, Gil Rodin & Bob Crosby, Jerry Leiber & Mike Stoller, Johnny Mercer & Harry Warren, Louis Prima, John Philip Sousa, Carole Bayer Sager & Melissa Manchester, Barry Mann & Cynthia Weil, Felix Powell & George Asaf, Sigmund Romberg & Oscar Hammerstein II, Cat Stevens, Edgard Varese, Jerry Jeff Walker; Producer, Jules Fisher; Associate Producer, Patty Grubman; Music Arranged and Conducted by Gordon Lowry Harrell; Orchestrations, Ralph Burns; Hairstylist, Romaine Greene; Sound, Abe Jacob; Wardrobe Supervisor, Joseph Busheme; Production Assistant, Vicki Stein; Assistants to Mr. Fosse, Kathryn Doby, Christopher Chadman

CAST

Gail Benedict	Vicki Frederick†2
Sandahl Bergman	Linda Haberman
Karen G. Burke	Richard Korthaze
Rene Ceballos	Edward Love
Christopher Chadman	John Mineo
Wayne Cilento	Ann Reinking
Jill Cook	Blane Savage†3
Gregory B. Drotar†1	Charles Ward

Alternates: Christine Colby, William Whitener, Valerie Miller

MUSICAL NUMBERS: "Prologue (Hot August Night)," "Crunchy Granola Suite," "Mr. Bojangles," "Chaconne," "Percussion," "Ionisation," "I Wanna Be a Dancin' Man," "Big Noise from Winettka," "If It Feels Good, Let It Ride," "Easy," "I've Got Them Feelin' Too Good Today Blues," "Was Dog a Doughnut," "Sing, Sing, Sing," "Here You Come Again," "Yankee Doodle Dandy," "Gary Owen," "Stout Hearted Men," "Under the Double Eagle," "Dixie," "When Johnny Comes Marching Home," "Rally Round the Flag," "Pack Up Your Troubles in Your Old Kit Bag," "The Stars and Stripes Forever," "Yankee Doodle Disco," "Dancin'"

"A Musical Entertainment" in 3 acts and 13 scenes.

General Manager: Marvin A. Krauss
Company Manager: G. Warren McClane
Press: Merle Debuskey, Susan L. Schulman, William Schelble
Stage Managers: Phil Friedman, Perry Cline, Richard Korthaze

* Still playing May 31, 1978. Received 1978 "Tonys" for Best Choreography, and Best Lighting.
† Succeeded by: 1. Ross Miles, and Mr. Drotar became an Alternate, 2. Christine Colby, 3. David Gibson

Martha Swope Photos

Top: Blane Savage, Ann Reinking, Charles Ward, Sandahl Bergman Right: Ann Reinking

"Dancin' Man" Above: Opening

ANTA THEATRE
Opened Thursday, March 30, 1978.*
Judith Gordon and Richard S. Bright present:

A HISTORY OF THE AMERICAN FILM

By Christopher Durang; Music, Mel Marvin; Director, David Chambers; Musical Staging, Graciela Daniele; Set, Tony Straiges; Costumes, Marjorie Slaiman; Lighting, William Mintzer; Sound, Lou Shapiro; Musical Direction, Clay Fullum; Orchestrations, Robert M. Freedman; Associate Producers, Marc Howard & Sheila Barbara-Dinah Productions; Hairstylist, Charles Lo Presto

CAST

Maureen Anderman .... Contract Player #8, Blessed Virgin Mother, Speakeasy Patron, Nurse, voice of Anna Karenina, Ma Joad, Cucumber Girl, voice of Sonja Henie
Gary Bayer .... Jimmy
Walter Bobbie ...... Contract Player #1, Michael, Salad Chef
Jeff Brooks .... Contract Player #5, Ticket Man, Newsboy, Young Speakeasy Patron, Young Reporter, Grandma Joad, Mickey
Bryan Clark .... Contract #7, Cop, Bartender, Judge, Edward Mortimer, Von Leffing, Navy Officer, Victor Henreid, Theatre Manager, and voices of Vronsky, John, Academy Award Announcer, F8I Narrator, God
David Cromwell .... Contract Player #4, Jesus, Ferruchi, Ernie the Reporter, Abdhul, Pa Joad, Make-up Man, Harkness, Uncle Sam, Marine Officer, Robot
Ben Halley, Jr. .... Contract Player #3, Piano Man, Viola, Indian, Ito, Sailor, Stuart
Swoosie Kurtz .... Bette
Kate McGregor-Stewart ...... Contract Player #6, Orphanage Lady, Ma O'Reilly, Allison Martimer, Prison Warden, Lettuce Girl, Gold Star Mother, WAC
Joan Pape .... Eve
April Shawhan .... Loretta
Brent Spiner .... Hank
Eric Weitz .... Contract Player #9, God, Little Hit Man, Eric, Santa, Snare, voice of Robot
Mary Catherine Wright .... Contract Player #2, Silent Mother, Bartender's Girl, Clara Mortimer, Carrot Girl
Robert Fisher .... Pianist

UNDERSTUDIES: Stephen James (Hank/Contract Player #1), Carolyn Mignini (Loretta/Contract Players #2 and #8), Robert Polenz (Contract Players #5, #9, #10).

MUSICAL NUMBERS: "The Silent Years," "Minstrel Song," "Shanty Town Romance," "They Can't Prohibit Love," "We're in a Salad," "Euphemism," "Ostende Nobis Tosca," "The Red, the White and the Blue," "Pretty Pin-Up," "Apple Blossom Victory," "Isn't It Fun to Be in the Movies," "Search for Wisdom"

A play with music in two acts.

General Mangement: Dorothy Olim Associates
Company Manager: Gail Bell
Press: David Powers, Barbara Carroll
Stage Managers: Ron Abbott, Gully Stanford, John Beven

* Closed Apr. 16, 1978 after 21 performances and 19 previews.

Martha Swope Photos

Top Right: April Shawhan, Joan Pape, Swoosie Kurtz, David Garrison, Mary Catherine Wright Below: Ben Halley, Jr., Gary Bayer, April Shawhan, Bryan Clark Second from Bottom: Entire Cast

Swoosie Kurtz, Gary Bayer, April Shawhan, David Cromwell, Kate McGregor-Stewart

EUGENE O'NEILL THEATRE
Opened Wednesday, April 12, 1978.*
Roger Berlind, Franklin R. Levy and Mike Wise present:

VINCENT PRICE
(as Oscar Wilde)
in
DIVERSIONS AND DELIGHTS

By John Gay; Director, Joseph Hardy; Setting and Lighting, H. R. Poindexter; Costume, Noel Taylor; Lighting Executed by Barry Arnold; Assistant to director, Grace Johnston; Assistant to producers, Chad Hoffman; Wigs, Renata

An evening spent with "Sebastian Melmouth" on November 28, 1899 in a concert hall on the Rue de la Pepinier, Paris, France. Presented in two acts.

General Management: Theatre Now, Inc.
Assistant General Manager: Charlotte Wilcox
Company Manager: Norman E. Rothstein
Press: Seymour Krawitz, Patricia McLean Krawitz
Stage Managers: David Clive, Janyce Ann Wagner

* Closed Apr. 22, 1978 after 13 performances and 2 previews.

Martha Swope Photos

Left: Vincent Price as Oscar Wilde

Vincent Price as Oscar Wilde

From Top: Morgan Freeman, Howard E. Rollins, Jr., Mansoor Najee-Ullah, Starletta DuPois, Richard Gant, Frank Adu, Dorian Harewood, Brent Jennings
Right: Mansoor Najee-Ullah, Dorian Harewood, Richard Gant, Brent Jennings

AMBASSADOR THEATRE

Opened Sunday, April 16, 1978.*
James Lipton Productions with the Shubert Organization and Ron Dante presents:

THE MIGHTY GENTS

By Richard Wesley; Director, Harold Scott; Scenery, Santo Loquasto; Costumes, Judy Dearing; Lighting, Gilbert V. Hemsley, Jr.; Wardrobe Supervisor, Karen Eifert; Special Movements Consultant, John Parks

CAST

Rita	Starletta DuPois
Frankie	Dorian Harewood
Tiny	Brent Jennings
Lucky	Mansoor Najee-Ullah
Eldridge	Richard Gant
Zeke	Morgan Freeman
Braxton	Howard E. Rollins, Jr.
Father	Frank Adu

STANDBYS AND UNDERSTUDIES: Charles Brown (Frankie/-Father/Braxton), Loretta Greene (Rita), J. Herbert Kerr, Jr. (Lucky/Tiny/Eldridge), Frank Adu (Zeke)

A drama presented without intermission. The action takes place at the present time on the streets of Newark, N.J., and in the apartment of Frankie and Rita.

General Managers: Emanuel Azenberg, Jose Vega
Company Manager: Maurice Schaded
Press: Howard Atlee, Becky Flora, Scott Mauro
Stage Managers: David Taylor, Joseph DePauw

* Closed Apr. 23, 1978 after 9 performances and 7 previews.

Martha Swope Photos

Dorian Harewood, Starletta DuPois
(also top)

43

MOROSCO THEATRE

Opened Monday, May 1, 1978.*

Lester Osterman, Marilyn Strauss, Marc Howard present the Hudson Guild Theatre Production (Craig Anderson, Producer) of:

DA

By Hugh Leonard; Director, Melvin Bernhardt; Set, Marjorie Kellogg; Costumes, Jennifer von Mayrhauser; Lighting, Arden Fingerhut; Technical Adviser, Mitch Miller; Wardrobe Mistress, Toni Baer

CAST

Charlie Now	Brian Murray
Oliver	Ralph Williams
Da	Barnard Hughes
Mother	Sylvia O'Brien
Young Charlie	Richard Seer
Drumm	Lester Rawlins
Mary Tate	Mia Dillon
Mrs. Prynne	Lois de Banzie

STANDBYS AND UNDERSTUDIES: Ruby Holbrook (Mother/Mrs. Prynne), Faith Catlin (Mary Tate), David Naughton (Young Charlie)

A comedy in two acts. The action takes place in a kitchen and places remembered in May 1968 and in times remembered.

General Manager: Richard Horner
Company Manager: Bruce Laffey
Press: Howard Atlee, Becky Flora
Stage Managers: Edward R. Fitzgerald, David Naughton

* Still playing May 31, 1978. Originally produced at the Hudson Guild Theatre for 24 performances (Mar. 10, 1978 – Apr. 2, 1978). Winner of 1978 "Tonys" for Best Play, Outstanding Actor in a Play (Barnard Hughes), Outstanding Featured Actor in a Play (Lester Rawlins), Best Director of a Play. Voted Best Play by NY Drama Critics Circle, Drama Desk, and Outer Critics Circle.

Martha Swope Photos

Standing: Lois De Banzie, Lester Rawlins, Barnard Hughes, Sylvia O'Brien, Ralph Williams, Mia Dillon, Seated: Richard Seer, Brian Murray

Right: Brian Murray, Barnard Hughes, Richard Seer, Mia Dillon

Brian Murray, Richard Seer, Barnard Hughes, Sylvia O'Brien

Lois De Banzie, Barnard Hughes, Richard Seer

44

LONGACRE THEATRE
Opened Tuesday, May 9, 1978.*
Emanuel Azenberg, Dasha Epstein, The Shubert Organization,
Jane Gaynor and Ron Dante present:

AIN'T MISBEHAVIN'

Conceived and Directed by Richard Maltby, Jr.; Based on an idea by Murray Horwitz and Richard Maltby, Jr.; Musical Numbers Staged by Arthur Faria; Music Supervision, Luther Henderson; Associate Director, Murray Horwitz; Orchestrations and Arrangements, Luther Henderson; Vocal Arrangements, William Elliott, Jeffrey Gutcheon; Sets, John Lee Beatty; Costumes, Randy Barcelo; Lighting, Pat Collins; Sound, Otts Munderloh; Hairstylist, Paul Lopez; Wardrobe Supervisor, Warren S. Morrill; Technical Coordinator, Arthur Siccardi; Assistant to Producers, Leslie Butler; Production Assistants, Jane Robison, Lisa Denton, Claudia McAllister, Evan Ross; Originally Produced by The Manhattan Theatre Club (Lynne Meadow, Artistic Director; Barry Grove, Managing Director; Stephen Pascal, Associate Artistic Director; Thomas Bullard, Associate Director)

CAST

Nell Carter	Ken Page
Andre De Shields	Charlaine Woodard
Armelia McQueen	Luther Henderson, Pianist

STANDBYS: Judy Gibson for Nell Carter and Armelia McQueen, Yolanda Graves for Charlaine Woodard, Irving Lee for Andre De Shields and Ken Page

MUSICAL NUMBERS: "Ain't Misbehavin'," "Lookin' Good but Feelin' Bad," "'Taint Nobody's Bizness If I Do," "Honeysuckle Rose," "Squeeze Me," "Handful of Keys," "I've Got a Feeling I'm Falling," "How Ya Baby," "The Jitterbug Waltz," "The Ladies Who Sing with the Band," "Yacht Club Swing," "When the Nylons Bloom Again," "Cash for Your Trash," "Off-Time," "The Joint is Jumpin'," "Spreadin' Rhythm Around," "Lounging at the Waldorf," "The Viper's Drag," "Mean to Me," "Your Feet's Too Big," "That Ain't Right," "Keepin' Out of Mischief Now," "Find Out What They Like," "Fat and Greasy," "Black and Blue," "I'm Gonna Sit Right Down and Write Myself a Letter," "Two Sleepy People," "I've Got My Fingers Crossed," "I Can't Give You Anything But Love," "It's a Sin to Tell a Lie."

A Musical Show based on the music of Thomas "Fats" Waller performed in two acts.

Manager: Jose Vega
Company Manager: Maurice Schaded
Press: Bill Evans, Mark Hunter
Stage Managers: Richard Evans, D. W. Koehler

* Still playing May 31, 1978. Received 1978 "Tonys" for Best Musical, Outstanding Featured Actress in a Musical (Nell Carter), and Best Director of a Musical. Voted Best Musical by NY Drama Critics, Drama Desk, and Outer Critics Circle.

Martha Swope Photos

Top Right: Andre DeShields, Armelia McQueen, Nell Carter, Charlaine Woodard, Ken Page, Luther Henderson

Charlaine Woodard, Ken Page, Armelia McQueen, Andre DeShields, Nell Carter

Armelia McQueen, Nell Carter, Charlaine Woodard

MINSKOFF THEATRE
Opened Wednesday, May 10, 1978.*
Philip Rose and Ellen Madison present:

ANGEL

Book, Ketti Frings, Peter Udell; From Ketti Frings' play "Look Homeward, Angel" based on the novel of the same name by Thomas Wolfe; Music, Gary Geld; Lyrics, Peter Udell; Director, Philip Rose; Choreography, Robert Tucker; Scenery, Ming Cho Lee; Lighting, John Gleason; Costumes, Pearl Somner; Orchestrations, Don Walker; Musical Direction and Dance Arrangements, William Cox; Hair Designs, Patrik D. Moreton; Associate Producers, Karen Wald, Norman Main; Technical Adviser, Mitch Miller; Wardrobe Master, Elonzo Dann

CAST

Helen Gant	Donna Davis
Ben Gant	Joel Higgins
Mrs. Fatty Pert	Patti Allison
Mrs. Snowden	Grace Carney
Eugene Gant	Don Scardino
Eliza Gant	Frances Sternhagen
Will Pentland	Elek Hartman
Florry Mangle	Rebecca Seay
Mrs. Clatt	Justine Johnstone
Jake Clatt	Gene Masoner
Mr. Farrell	Billy Beckham
Miss Brown	Jayne Barnett
Laura James	Leslie Ann Ray
W. O. Grant	Fred Gwynne
Dr. Maguire	Daniel Keyes
Joe Tarkington	Rex David Hays
Reed McKinney	Carl Nicholas
Tim Laughran	Norman Stotz
Madame Victoria	Patricia Englund

STANDBYS AND UNDERSTUDIES: Ann Gardner (Mme. Victoria), Dennis Cooley (Eugene, Farrell), Paul Myrvold (Ben, Jake), Leoni Norton (Laura, Helen, Florry), Laura Waterbury (Mrs. Fatty Pert, Miss Brown)

MUSICAL NUMBERS: "Angel Theme," "All the Comforts of Home," "Like the Eagles Fly," "Make a Little Sunshine," "Fingers and Toes," "Fatty," "Astoria Gloria," "Railbird," "If I Ever Loved Him," "A Dime Ain't Worth a Nickel," "I Got a Dream to Sleep On," "Drifting," "I Can't Believe It's You," "Feelin' Loved," "Medley," "Tomorrow I'm Gonna Be Old," "How Do You Say Goodbye," "Gant's Waltz"

A musical in two acts and four scenes. The action takes place in Altamount, North Carolina during the autumn of 1916 in the Dixieland Boarding House, and in Gant's marble yard and shop.

General Manager: Helen Richards
Company Manager: Charles Willard
Press: Merle Debuskey, Leo Stern
Stage Managers: Steve Zweigbaum, Arturo E. Porazzi, Paul Myrvold

* Closed May 13, 1978 after 5 performances and 6 previews.

Gerry Goodstein Photos

46 **Top: Joel Higgins, Don Scardino, Frances Sternhagen, Fred Gwynne**

Don Scardino, Leslie Ann Ray Above: Fred Gwynne Top: Joel Higgins, Patti Allison

PLYMOUTH THEATRE
Opened Saturday, May 13, 1978.*
Joseph Papp presents the New York Shakespeare Festival Production of:

RUNAWAYS

Written, Composed and Directed by Elizabeth Swados; Setting, Douglas W. Schmidt, Woods Mackintosh; Costumes, Hilary Rosenfeld; Sound, Bill Dreisbach; Lighting, Jennifer Tipton; Associate Producer, Bernard Gersten; Production Supervisor, Jason Steven Cohen; Wardrobe Master, James Roberts; Original Cast Album by Columbia Records

CAST

Hubbell	Bruce Hlibok
Interpreter for Hubbell	Lorie Robinson
A. J.	Carlo Imperato
Jackie	Rachael Kelly
Louis	Ray Contreras
Nikki Kay Kane	Nan-Lynn Nelson
Lidia	Jossie De Guzman
Manny	Randy Ruiz
Eddie	Jon Matthews
Sundar	Bernie Allison
Roby	Venustra K. Robinson
Lazar	David Schechter
Eric	Evan H. Miranda
Iggy	Jonathan Feig
Jane	Kate Schellenbach
Ez	Leonard Brown
Mex-Mongo	Mark Anthony Butler
Melinda	Trini Alvarado
Deidre	Karen Evans
Mocha	Sheila Gibbs

CHORUS: Paula Anderson, Kenya Brome, Jerome Dekie, Karin Dekie, Lisa Dekie, John Gallogly, Timmy Michaels, Toby Parker

MUSICIANS: Judith Fleisher (Piano), John Schimmel (String Bass), Leopoldo F. Fleming (Congas, Timbales, Bongo, Bells), David Sawyer (Trap Set, Triangle), Patience Higgins (Saxophones, Flutes), Elizabeth Swados (Guitar)

UNDERSTUDIES: Carey Bond, Michele Dagavarian, Jerome Dekie, Katherine Diamond, Sheila Gibbs, C. S. Hayward, Michael Laylor, Timmy Michaels, Toby Parker

SONGS AND SPEECHES: "You Don't Understand," "I Had to Go," "Parent/Kid Dance," "Appendectomy," "Where Do People Go," "Footstep," "Once Upon a Time," "Current Events," "Every Now and Then," "Out on the Street," "Minnesota Strip," "Song of a Child Prostitute," "Christmas Puppies," "Lazar's Heroes," "Find Me a Hero," "Scrynatchkielooaw," "The Undiscovered Son," "I Went Back Home," "This Is What I Do When I'm Angry," "The Basketball Song," "Spoons," "Lullaby for Luis," "We Are Not Strangers," "In the Sleeping Line," "Lullaby from Baby to Baby," "Tra Gog Vo In Dein Whole," "I Will Not Tell a Soul," "Revenge Song," "Enterprise," "Sometimes," "Clothes," "Mr. Graffiti," "The Untrue Pigeon," "Senoras de la Noche," "We Have to Die?," "Where Are Those People Who Did 'Hair'?," "Appendectomy II," "Let Me Be a Kid," "To the Dead of Family Wars," "Problem after Problem," "Lonesome of the Road"

A "musical theatre piece" in two acts. The action takes place at the present time on a playground.

General Manager: Robert Kamlot
Company Managers: Bob MacDonald, Roger Gindi
Press: Merle Debuskey, Richard Kornberg
Stage Managers: Gregory Meeh, Peter Glazer, Patricia Morinelli

* Still playing May 31, 1978. Originally produced at Public/Cabaret Theater for 76 performances (Mar. 9, 1978–Apr. 29, 1978).

Martha Swope Photos

Top Right: Elizabeth Swados, Patience Higgins, Leopoldo F. Fleming, Judith Fleisher, David Sawyer, John Schimmel Below: Bruce Hlibok, Diane Lane, Karen Evans

**Nan-Lynn Nelson, Karen Evans, Mark Anthony Butler
Above: Anthony Imperato**

FORTY-SIXTH STREET THEATRE
Opened Sunday, May 14, 1978.*
Stephen R. Friedman and Irwin Meyer in association with Joseph Harris present:

WORKING

From the book by Studs Terkel; Adapted and Directed by Stephen Schwartz; Songs by Craig Carnelia, Micki Grant, Mary Rodgers and Susan Birkenhead, Stephen Schwartz, James Taylor; Dances and Musical Staging, Onna White; Settings, David Mitchell; Costumes, Marjorie Slaiman; Lighting, Ken Billington; Musical Direction and Vocal Arrangements, Stephen Reinhardt; Orchestrations, Kirk Nurock; Dance and Incidental Music, Michele Brourman; Associate to Ms. White, Martin Allen; Associate Director, Nina Faso; Hairstylist, Hector Garcia; Technical Coordinator, Arthur Siccardi; Sound, Jack Mann; Wardrobe Supervisor, Midge Marmo; Assistant Conductor, Kenneth Bichel; Production Assistant, Shauna Vey; Associate Lighting Designer, Shirley Prendergast.

CAST

Steelworker	Brad Sullivan
Parking Lot Attendant/Bus Driver	David Langston Smyrl
Editor/Call Girl	Patti LuPone
Advertising Copy Chief/Hockey Player	Steven Boockvor
Secretary/Telephone Operator/Cleaning Woman/ Bus Driver's Wife	Lynne Thigpen
Corporate Executive/Seaman	Rex Everhart
Stone Mason/Retired Shipping Clerk	Arny Freeman
Newsboy	Matthew McGrath
Teacher/Millworker/Hotel Switchboard Operator/ Seaman's Wife	Bobo Lewis
Supermarket Checker/Stewardess/Waitress	Lenora Nemetz
Boxboy/Bar Pianist/Copy Boy	David Patrick Kelly
Migrant Worker/Interstate Trucker	Joe Mantegna
Gas Meter Reader/Fireman/Salesman/ Tie Salesman	Matt Landers
Housewife	Susan Bigelow
Agency Vice President/Receptionist/ Hospital Aide	Robin Lamont
Model/Salesman's Wife	Terri Treas
Football Coach/Interstate Trucker	Bob Gunton

STANDBYS: Hank Brunjes, James Congdon, Marilyn Cooper

MUSICAL NUMBERS: "All the Livelong Day," "Lovin' Al," "The Mason," "Neat to Be a Newsboy," "Nobody Tells Me How," "Treasure Island Trio," "Un Mejor Dia Vendra," "Just a Housewife," "Millwork," "Nightskate," "Joe," "If I Could've Been," "It's an Art," "Brother Trucker," "Husbands and Wives," "Fathers and Sons," "Cleanin' Women," "Something to Point To"

A musical in two acts. The action takes place at the present time in numerous places of employment.

General Management: Gatchell & Neufeld
Company Manager: Douglas C. Baker
Press: Betty Lee Hunt, Maria Cristina Pucci, Fred Hoot
Stage Managers: Alan Hall, Ruth E. Rinklin, Richard Elkow

* Closed June 4, 1978 after 25 performances and 11 previews.

Roger Greenawalt Photos

Top Right: Lenora Nemetz
Right: Bobo Lewis

Entire Company

Matt Landers, Bob Gunton, Joe Mantegna, Terri Treas

BROADWAY PRODUCTIONS FROM OTHER SEASONS
THAT PLAYED THROUGH THIS SEASON

ALVIN THEATRE
Opened Thursday, April 21, 1977.*
Mike Nichols presents:

ANNIE

Book, Thomas Meehan; Based on "Little Orphan Annie" comic
strip; Music, Charles Strouse; Lyrics, Martin Charnin; Musical
Numbers Choreographed by Peter Gennaro; Director, Martin Charnin; Produced by Irwin Meyer, Stephen R. Friedman, Lewis Allen;
Settings, David Mitchell; Costumes, Theoni V. Aldredge; Lighting,
Judy Rasmuson; Musical Direction and Dance Music Arrangements, Peter Howard; Orchestrations, Philip J. Lang; Produced by
Alvin Nederlander Associates-Icarus Productions; Produced in association with Peter Crane; Assistant Conductor, Robert Billig;
Technical Coordinator, Arthur Siccardi; Wardrobe Supervisor, Ad-
elaide Laurino; Production Assistants, Janice Steele, Stephen Gra-
ham; Hairstylists, Ted Azar, Charles LaFrance; Original Cast
Recording by Columbia Records.

CAST

Molly	Danielle Brisebois
Pepper	Robyn Finn
Duffy	Donna Graham
July	Janine Ruane†1
Tessie	Diana Barrows
Kate	Shelley Bruce†2
Annie	Andrea McArdle†3
Miss Hannigan	Dorothy Loudon
Bundles McCloskey/Sound Effects Man/Ickes	James Hosbein
Dog Catcher/Jimmy Johnson/Honor Guard	Steven Boockvor†4
Dog Catcher/Bert Healy/Hull	Donald Craig
Sandy	Himself
Lt. Ward/Morganthau	Richard Ensslen
Harry/FDR	Raymond Thorne
Sophie/Cecille/A Star to Be/Bonnie Boylan/Perkins	Laurie Beechman
Grace Farrell	Sandy Faison
Drake	Edwin Bordo
Mrs. Pugh/Connie Boylan	Edie Cowan
Annette/Ronnie Boylan	Penny Worth†5
Oliver Warbucks	Reid Shelton†6
Rooster Hannigan	Robert Fitch
Lily	Barbara Erwin
Fred McCracken/Howe	Bob Freschi
NBC Page	Mari McMinn

HOOVERVILLE-ITES, POLICEMEN, SERVANTS, NEW
YORKERS: Laurie Beechman, Steven Boockvor, Edwin Bordo,
Edie Cowan, Donald Craig, Richard Ensslen, Barbara Erwin, Bob
Freschi, James Hosbein, Mari McMinn, Penny Worth

STANDBYS AND UNDERSTUDIES: Kristen Vigard, Shelley
Bruce, Diana Barrows (Annie), Raymond Thorne (Warbucks),
Penny Worth (Hannigan), Mari McMinn (Grace), Steven Boockvor
(Rooster), Kim Fedena (Orphans), Shelley Bruce
(Molly), Donna Graham (July), Donald Craig (FDR/Harry), Edie
Cowan (Lily), Bob Freschi (Drake/Bert), Arf (Sandy), Don Bonnell
(Ensemble Alternate)

MUSICAL NUMBERS: "Maybe," "It's the Hard-Knock Life,"
"Tomorrow," "We'd Like to Thank You," "Little Girls," "I Think
I'm Gonna Like It Here," "N.Y.C.," "Easy Street," "You Won't Be
an Orphan for Long," "You're Never Fully Dressed without a
Smile," "Something Was Missing," "I Don't Need Anything but
You," "Annie," "A New Deal for Christmas."

A musical in 2 acts and 13 scenes. The action takes place December 11–25, 1933 in New York City.

General Management: Gatchell & Neufeld Ltd.
Company Manager: Drew Murphy, Dennis Durcell
Press: David Powers, Barbara Carroll
Stage Managers: Janet Beroza, Jack Timmers, Patrick O'Leary,
Roy Meachum

* Still playing May 31, 1978. Received 1977 NY Drama Critics
Circle and "Tony" Awards for Best Musical. One of its six other
"Tonys" went to Dorothy Loudon for Best Actress in a Musical.
† Succeeded by: 1. Kathy-Jo Kelly, Sarah Jessica Parker, 2. Kim
Fedena, 3. Shelley Bruce, 4. Gary Gendell, 5. Ann Ungar, 6.
Keene Curtis during Mr. Reid's vacation.

Martha Swope Photos
**Top Right: Dorothy Loudon Below: Sandy Faison,
Shelley Bruce, Reid Shelton**

**Laurie Beechman, Shelley Bruce, Reid Shelton,
Sandy Faison Above: Barbara Erwin, Robert
Fitch, Dorothy Loudon**

SHUBERT THEATRE
Opened Sunday, October 19, 1975.*
Joseph Papp presents a New York Shakespeare Festival Production in association with Plum Productions:

A CHORUS LINE

Conceived, Choreographed and Directed by Michael Bennett; Book, James Kirkwood, Nicholas Dante; Music, Marvin Hamlisch; Lyrics, Edward Kleban; Co-Choreographer, Bob Avian; Musical Direction and Vocal Arrangements, Don Pippin; Associate Producer, Bernard Gersten; Setting, Robin Wagner; Costumes, Theoni V. Aldredge; Lighting, Tharon Musser; Sound, Abe Jacob; Music Coordinator, Robert Thomas; Orchestrations, Bill Byers, Hershy Kay, Jonathan Tunick; Assistant to Choreographers and Dance Captain; Baayork Lee; Wardrobe Mistress, Alyce Gilbert; Production Manager, Andrew Mihok; Production Supervisor, Jason Steven Cohen; Original Cast Album by Columbia Records

CAST

Roy	Danny Ruvolo
Kristine	Deborah Geffner
Sheila	Kathrynann Wright
Val	Mitzi Hamilton
Mike	Jim Litten
Butch	Larry G. Bailey†1
Larry	Adam Grammis†2
Maggie	Donna Drake
Richie	Edward Love †3
Tricia	Cynthia Carrillo Onrubia
Tom	Cameron Mason†4
Zach	Kurt Johnson
Mark	Paul Charles†5
Cassie	Vicki Frederick†6
Judy	Sandahl Bergman†7
Lois	Patti D'Beck†8
Don	David Thomé
Bebe	Gillian Scalici†9
Connie	Janet Wong
Diana	Loida Iglesias
Al	Ben Lokey†10
Frank	Tim Cassidy
Greg	Justin Ross
Bobby	Christopher Chadman †11
Paul	Danny Ruvolo†12
Vicki	Crissy Wilzak†13
Barbara	Patti D'Beck
Ed	Mark Fotopoulos
Sam	Steve Riley
Jenny	Candace Tovar

UNDERSTUDIES: Tim Cassidy (Don/Greg/Bobby), Murphy Cross (Val), Patti D'Beck (Cassie), Mark Fotopoulos (Mark/Larry), Troy Garza (Mike), Anthony Inneo (Zach), Carol Marik (Judy/Sheila), Cynthia Carrillo Onrubia (Maggie/Connie/Diana/Bebe), Julie Pars (Val/Kristine/Judy), Steve Riley (Al), Ken Rogers (Richie), Danny Ruvolo (Greg/Larry/Mike/Paul/Al), Candace Tovar (Cassie/Sheila)

MUSICAL NUMBERS: "I Hope I Get It," "I Can Do That," "And....," "At the Ballet," "Sing!," "Hello Twelve, Hello Thirteen, Hello Love," "Nothing," "Dance: Ten, Looks: Three," "The Music and the Mirror," "One," "The Tap Combination," "What I Did for Love," Finale

A musical performed without intermission. The action takes place at an audition at the present time in this theatre.

General Manager: Robert Kamlot
Company Manager: Harris Goldman
Press: Merle Debuskey, Bob Ullman, Richard Kornberg
Stage Managers: Peter Von Mayrhauser, Wendy Mansfield, Danny Ruvolo

* Still playing May 31, 1978. Cited as Best Musical by NY Drama Critics Circle, winner of Pulitzer Prize, 1976 "Tony" Awards for Best Musical, Best Book, Best Score, Best Director, Best Lighting, Best Choreography. A Special Theatre World Award was presented to every member of the creative staff and original cast.
† Succeeded by: 1. Ken Rogers, 2. Paul Charles, 3. A. William Perkins, 4. Anthony Inneo, 5. R. J. Peters, 6. Pamela Sousa, 7. Murphy Cross, 8. Julie Pars, 9. Karen Meister, 10. Don Percassi, 11. Ron Kurowski, 12. Rene Clemente, 13. Carol Marik

Martha Swope Photos

Top Right: Entire Cast
Below: Pamela Sousa

Entire Cast

BOOTH THEATRE
Opened Wednesday, September 15, 1976.*
Joseph Papp and Woodie King, Jr. present.

FOR COLORED GIRLS WHO HAVE CONSIDERED SUICIDE WHEN THE RAINBOW IS ENUF

By Ntozake Shange; Director, Oz Scott; Scenery, Ming Cho Lee; Lighting, Jennifer Tipton; Costumes, Judy Dearing; Choreography, Paula Moss; Associate Producer, Bernard Gersten; A New York Shakespeare Festival Production in association with the Henry Street Settlement's New Federal Theatre; Wardrobe Supervisor, Margaret Faison; Production Supervisor, Jason Steven Cohen

CAST

Lady in Brown	Roxanne Reese
Lady in Yellow	Aku Kadogo†1
Lady in Red	Robbie McCauley†2
Lady in Green	Jonette O'Kelley†3
Lady in Purple	Rise Collins
Lady in Blue	Laurie Carlos
Lady in Orange	Sharita Hunt

UNDERSTUDIES: Robbie McCauley, Andrea Frierson, Anna Horsford

A program of poetry by Ntozake Shange presented without intermission.

Company Manager: Robert Frissell, Sally Campbell
Press: Merle Debuskey, Leo Stern, William Schelble
Stage Managers: John Beven, Fai Walker-Davis, Kellie Williams, Frank Difilia

* Closed July 16, 1978 after 742 performances and 5 previews. Before moving to Broadway, it played 120 performances at the Public/Anspacher Theater. See THEATRE WORLD Vol. 33.
† Succeeded by: 1. Leona Johnson, 2. Saundra McClain, 3. Saundra McPherson

Martha Swope Photos

Top: Roxanne Reese, Sharita Hunt, Laurie Carlos, Robbie McCauley, Rise Collins, Jonette O'Kelley

Jonette O'Kelley, Laurie Carlos, Robbie McCauley

THE LITTLE THEATRE
Opened Saturday, May 21, 1977.*
Jerry Arrow and Jay Broad representing Circle Repertory Company and PAF Playhouse present:

GEMINI

By Albert Innaurato; Director, Peter Mark Schifter; Supervised by Marshall W. Mason; Setting, Christopher Nowak; Costumes, Ernest Allen Smith; Lighting, Larry Crimmins; Sound, Leslie A. DeWeerdt, Jr.; Production Assistants, James Arnemann, Michael Zande, Terry Gusmorino; Wardrobe Supervisor, Kathy Powers, Gordon Needham; Hairstylist, Jose Anselmi; Production Supervisor, Fred Reinglas

CAST

Francis Geminiani	Robert Picardo†1
Bunny Weinbarger	Jessica James
Randy Hastings	Reed Birney
Judith Hastings	Carol Potter†2
Herschel Weinberger	Jonathan Hadary†3
Fran Geminiani	Danny Aiello
Lucille Pompi	Anne DeSalvo†4

UNDERSTUDIES: Dick Boccelli (Fran), Barbara Coggin (Bunny/Lucille), Stephanie Musnick (Judith), Phil Cates (Randy/Francis), Warren Pincus (Herschel)

A comedy in 2 acts and 4 scenes. The action takes place June 1 & 2, 1973 in the Geminiani-Weinberger backyard in South Philadelphia, Pa.

General Managers: Jerry Arrow, R. Robert Lussier
Press: Rima Corben, Glenna Clay
Stage Managers: Fred Reinglas, Dennis Purcell, James Arnemann, Phil Cates

* Still playing May 31, 1978.
† Succeeded by: 1. Dennis Bailey, and during vacations: 2. Stephanie Musnick, 3. Warren Pincus, 4. Stephanie Gordon

Ken Howard Photos

Danny Aiello, Anne DeSalvo, Carol Potter, Reed Birney, Jonathan Hadary, Dennis Bailey
Top Left: Jonathan Hadary, Danny Aiello, Jessica James, Anne DeSalvo, Carol Potter

EDEN THEATRE

Opened Monday, February 14, 1972.* Moved June 7, 1972 to
Broadhurst Theatre, November 21, 1972 to Royale Theatre
Kenneth Waissman and Maxine Fox in association with Anthony D'Amato present:

GREASE

Book, Music and Lyrics, Jim Jacobs, Warren Casey; Director,
Tom Moore; Musical Numbers and Dances Staged by Patricia
Birch; Orchestrations, Michael Leonard; Musical Supervision, Vocal and Dance Arrangements, Louis St. Louis; Scenery, Douglas W.
Schmidt; Costumes, Carrie F. Robbins; Lighting, Karl Eigsti; Musical Direction, Jeremy Stone; Sound, Jack Shearing; Hairstylist, John
Delaat; Production Supervisor, T. Schuyler Smith; Assistant to Producers, Edye Lou Hock; Assistant to Director, Nancy Robbins;
General Management, Theatre Now, Inc.; Wardrobe Supervisor,
Doris Boyhan; Original Cast Album by MGM Records.

CAST

Miss Lynch	Dorothy Leon†1
Patty Simcox	Ilene Kristen†2
Eugene Florczyk	Tom Harris†3
Jan	Garn Stephens†4
Marty	Katie Hanley†5
Betty Rizzo	Adrienne Barbeau†6
Doody	James Canning†7
Roger	Walter Bobbie†8
Kenickie	Timothy Meyers†9
Sonny LaTierri	Jim Borelli†10
Frenchy	Marya Small†11
Sandy Dumbrowski	Carole Demas†12
Danny Zuko	Barry Bostwick†13
Vince Fontaine	Don Billett†14
Johnny Casino/Teen Angel	Alan Paul†15
Cha-Cha DiGregorio	Kathi Moss†16

UNDERSTUDIES: Frank Piegaro (Danny), Lori Ada Jaroslow,
Lesley Berry for female roles, Greg Zadikov, Barry J. Tarallo for
male roles

MUSICAL NUMBERS: "Alma Mater," "Summer Night," "Those
Magic Changes," "Freddy, My Love," "Greased Lightning,"
"Mooning," "Look at Me, I'm Sandra Dee," "We Go Together,"
"Shakin' at the High School Hop," "Born to Hand-Jive," "Beauty
School Drop-Out," "Alone at a Drive-in Movie," "Rock 'n' Roll
Party Queen," "There Were Worse Things I Could Do," "All
Choked Up," Finale

A rock musical in 2 acts and 12 scenes. The action takes place in
the late 1950's.

General Manager: Edward H. Davis
Company Manager: Camille Ranson
Press: Betty Lee Hunt, Maria Cristina Pucci
Stage Managers: Lynne Guerra, Steve Beckler, John Fennessy,
Greg Zadikov

* Still playing May 31, 1978. For original production, see THEATRE WORLD Vol. 28.
† Succeeded by: 1. Sudie Bond, Ruth Russell, 2. Joy Rinaldi, Carol
Culver, Katherine Meloche, Forbesy Russell, 3. Barrey Smith,
Stephen Van Benschoten, Lloyd Alann, Randy Powell, 4. Jamie
Donnelly, Randee Heller, Rebecca Gilchrist, Mimi Kennedy,
Cynthia Darlow, Pippa Pearthree, 5. Meg Bennett, Denise Nettleton, Marilyn Henner, Char Fontane, Diane Stilwell, Sandra Zeeman, 6. Elaine Petricoff, Randee Heller, Livia Genise, Judy Kaye,
Lorelle Brina, 7. Barry J. Tarallo, Bill Vitelli, 8. Richard Quarry,
John Driver, Michael Tucci, Ray DeMattis, Dan Woodard, 9.
John Fennessy, Jerry Zaks, Michael Tucci, Danny Jacobson, 10.
Matt Landers, Albert Insinnia, David Paymer, 11. Ellen March,
Joy Rinaldi, Jill P. Rose, Forbesy Russell, Peggy Lee Brennan, 12.
Ilene Graff, Candice Earley, Robin Lamont, Shannon Fanning,
13. Jeff Conaway, John Lansing, Lloyd Alann, Treat Williams,
Peter Gallagher, 14. Jim Weston, John Holly, Walter Charles,
Stephen M. Groff, 15. Bob Garrett, Philip Casnoff, Joe Rifici,
Philip Casnoff, Frank Piegaro, 16. Robin Vogel.

ETHEL BARRYMORE THEATRE

Opened Sunday, April 17, 1977.*
By arrangement with Joseph Kipness, Terry Allen Kramer and
Harry Rigby present:

I LOVE MY WIFE

Book and Lyrics, Michael Stewart; From a play by Luis Rego;
Music composed and arranged by Cy Coleman; Director, Gene Saks;
Scenery, David Mitchell; Lighting, Gilbert V. Hemsley, Jr.; Cos-
tumes, Ron Talsky; Musical Numbers Staged by Onna White; Musi-
cal Direction, John Miller; Sound, Lou Gonzalez; Associate
Producer, Frank Montalvo; Technical Supervisor, Mitch Miller;
Production Assistant, Jon Puleo; Wardrobe Supervisor, Clarence
Sims, Eric Harrison; Original Cast Album by Atlantic Records

CAST

Cleo	Ilene Graff
Monica	Joanna Gleason†1
Wally	James Naughton†2
Stanley	Michael Mark
Quentin	Joe Saulter
Harvey	John Miller
Norman	Ken Bichel†3
Alvin	Lenny Baker†4

UNDERSTUDIES: Warren Benbow (Quentin), Michael Mark
(Harvey), Joel Mofsenson (Norman), Michael Sergio (Stanley),
Lisby Larson (Cleo/Monica), James Seymour (Alvin), Christine
Ebersole

MUSICAL NUMBERS: "We're Still Friends," "Monica," "By
Threes," "A Mover's Life," "Love Revolution," "Someone Wonderful I Missed," "Sexually Free," "Hey There, Good Times," "Lovers
on Christmas Eve," "Scream," "Everybody Today Is Turning On,"
"Married Couple Seeks Married Couple," "I Love My Wife"

A musical in two acts. The action takes place at the present time
in Trenton, N.J.

General Management: Jack Schlissel, Jay Kingwill
Press: Henry Luhrman, Anne Obert Weinberg, Terry M. Lilly
Stage Managers: Bob Vandergriff, Tony Manzi

* Still playing May 31, 1978.
† Succeeded by: 1. Virginia Sandifur, 2. James Seymour, Brad Blais-
dell, Tom Wopat, Tom Smothers, 3. Mark Franklin, 4. James
Brennan, Lawrence John Moss, Dick Smothers

Laura Pettibone Photos

**Right: Michael Mark, Joseph Saulter, John
Miller, Ken Bichel Above: Virginia Sandifur,
Lenny Baker**

**Ilene Graff, Lenny Baker, James
Naughton, Virginia Sandifur**

**Lenny Baker, Virginia Sandifur
Ilene Graff, James Naughton**

URIS THEATRE
Opened Monday, May 2, 1977.*
Lee Guber and Shelly Gross present:

THE KING AND I

Book and Lyrics, Oscar Hammerstein 2nd; Based on novel "Anna and the King of Siam" by Margaret Landon; Music, Richard Rodgers; Entire Production Directed by Yuriko; Original Choreography, Jerome Robbins; Settings, Peter Wolf; Costumes, Stanley Simmons; Based on original costumes by Irene Sharaff; Lighting, Thomas Skelton; Musical Supervisor and Director, Milton Rosenstock; Sound, Richard Fitzgerald; Associate Producer, Fred Walker; Hairstylist, Werner Sherer; Technical Supervisor, Mitch Miller; Wardrobe Supervisor, Jennifer Bryan; Assistant to Director, Susan Kikuchi; Assistant Conductor, Fred Manzella

CAST

Captain Orton	Larry Swansen
Louis Leonowens	Alan Amick†1
Anna Leonowens	Constance Towers†2
The Interpreter	Jae Woo Lee†3
The Kralahome	Michael Kermoyean†4
The King	Yul Brynner†5
Tuptim	June Angela
Lady Thiang	Hye-Young Choi
Prince Chulalongkorn	Gene Profanato
Princess Ying Yaowalak	Julie Woo
Lun Tha	Martin Vidnovic
Sir Edward Ramsay	John Michael King†6

ROYAL DANCERS AND WIVES: Su Applegate, Jessica Chao, Lei-Lynn Doo, Dale Harimoto, Pamela Kalt, Susan Kikuchi, Faye Fujisaki Mar, Sumiko Murashima, Libby Rhodes, Cecile Santos, Hope Sogawa, Mary Ann Teng, Patricia K. Thomas, Gusti Bogok, Freda Foh Shen, Diane Lam, Mary Ann Teng, Patricia Weber

PRINCESSES AND PRINCES: Ivan Ho, Clark Huang, Annie Lam, Connie Lam, Jennifer Lam, Paul Siu, Tim Waldrip, Kevan Weber, Kym Weber, Julie Woo, Mary Woo, Diana Chan, Susana Chan, Jonathan Chin, Jodrell Dimaculangan, Julian Hsiang, Xavier Rodrigo

NURSES AND AMAZONS: Sidney Smith, Marienne Tatum, Patricia K. Thomas, Rebecca West, Pamela Kalt, VV Matsuoka, Libby Rhodes

PRIESTS AND SLAVES: Kaipo Daniels, Barrett Hong, Jae Woo Lee, Ric Ornellas, Simeon Den, Chandra Tanna, Robert Vega, Henry Yu

STANDBYS AND UNDERSTUDIES: Michael Kermoyan (King), Jo Ann Cunningham (Anna), William Kiehl (King), Pamela Kalt (Anna), Sumiko Murashima (Thiang), Robert Vega (Lun Tha), Freda Foh Shen (Tuptim), Xavier Rodrigo (Prince), Thor Fields (Louis), Kaipo Daniels (Interpreter), Diane Lam (Eliza), Chandra Tanna (Simon), Faye Fujisaki Mar (Angel), Hope Sogawa (Uncle Thomas), Libby Rhodes (Topsy), Dale Harimoto (Little Eva), Ching Gonzalez, Alis-Elaine Anderson (Swing Dancers)

MUSICAL NUMBERS: "I Whistle a Happy Tune," "My Lord and Master," "Hello, Young Lovers," "March of the Siamese Children," "A Puzzlement," "The Royal Bangkok Academy," "Getting to Know You," "We Kiss in a Shadow," "Shall I Tell You What I Think of You?," "Something Wonderful," "Western People Funny," "I Have Dreamed," "The Small House of Uncle Thomas," "Song of the King," "Shall We Dance?," Finale

A musical in two acts. The action takes place in and around the King's palace in Bangkok, Siam, during the 1860's.

General Manager: Theatre Now, Inc.
Company Manager: Robb Lady
Press: Solters & Roskin, Joshua Ellis, Milly Schoenbaum, Fred Nathan, Sophie McBride
Stage Managers: Ed Preston, Conwell Worthington, Thomas J. Rees

* Still playing May 31, 1978.* Original production with Gertrude Lawrence and Yul Brynner opened March 29, 1951 at the St. James Theatre and played 1246 performances.
† Succeeded by: 1. Jason Scott, 2. Angela Lansbury (Apr. 11-30, 1978), 3. Robert Vega (Apr. 11-30, 1978), 4. Jae Woo Lee (Apr. 11-30, 1978), 5. Michael Kermoyan (Apr. 11-30, 1978). 6. Randolph Walker

Michael Baumann/Fuji Photos

Top Right: Yul Brynner, Gene Profanato
Angela Lansbury, Michael Kermoyean

Yul Brynner, Constance Towers
(also above)   55

CORT THEATRE
Opened Tuesday, May 28, 1974.*
Edgar Lansbury, Joseph Beruh, Ivan Reitman present:

THE MAGIC SHOW

Book, Bob Randall; Songs, Stephen Schwartz; Magic, Doug Henning; Direction and Dances, Grover Dale; Setting, David Chapman; Costumes, Randy Barcelo; Lighting, Richard Nelson; Musical Director, Stephen Reinhardt; Dance Arrangements, David Spangler; Assistant to Director, Jay Fox; Associate Producer, Nan Pearlman; Audio, Phil Ramone; Management Associates, Al Isaac, Bob Skerry, Gary Gunas; Wardrobe Supervisor, Teena Maria Charlotta; Music Coordinator, Earl Shendell; Production Assistants, Sam Cristensen, Darrell Jones, Walter Wood, Lee Minter

CAST

Manny	Robert LuPone†1
Feldman	David Ogden Stiers†2
Donna	Annie McGreevey†3
Dina	Cheryl Barnes†4
Cal	Dale Soules†5
Doug	Doug Henning†6
Mike	Ronald Stafford†7
Steve	Loyd Sannes†8
Charmin	Anita Morris†9
Goldfarb	Sam Schact†10

STANDBYS AND UNDERSTUDIES: Steven Peterman (Joe), Nancy Sheehy (Cal/Donna), Rita Rudner (Charmin/Dina), Kevin Marcum (Feldman/Goldfarb), Christopher Lucas (Mike/Steve), Jay Fox (Manny), Timothy Wahrer (Manny)

MUSICAL NUMBERS: "Up to His Old Tricks," "Solid Silver Platform Shoes," "Lion Tamer," "Style," "Charmin's Lament," "Two's Company," "Goldfarb Variations," "Doug's Act," "A Bit of Villainy," "West End Avenue," "Sweet, Sweet, Sweet," "Before Your Very Eyes"

A magic show with music performed without intermission.

General Management: Marvin A. Krauss Associates
Press: Gifford/Wallace, Harvey Kirk
Stage Managers: Herb Vogler, Jay Fox, John Actman, Brennan Roberts

* Still playing May 31, 1978. For original production, see THEATRE WORLD Vol. 30.
† Succeeded by: 1. Clifford Lipson, 2. Timothy Jerome, Kenneth Kimmins, Tom Mardirosian, 3. Lisa Raggio, Cindy Cobitt, 4. Lynne Thigpen, Valerie Williams, 5. Gwendolyn Coleman, 6. Jeffrey Mylett, Joseph Abaldo, 7. Robert Brubett, 8. T. Michael Reed, Christopher Lucas, Timothy Wahrer, 9. Loni Ackerman, Louisa Flaningam, Natalie Mosco, 10. Frederick Wessler

Top Left: Joseph Albaldo, Dale Soules, Robert Brubach, Timothy Wahrer

Cliff Lipson, Natalie Mosco

Lisa Raggio, Ken Kimmins, Valerie Williams

BIJOU THEATRE
Opened Wednesday, March 30, 1977.*
Arthur Shafman International, Ltd. presents:

MUMMENSCHANZ

Production Supervisor, Christopher Dunlop; Production Adviser, Richard G. Miller; Production Associates, Evelyn Gross, Susan Balsam; Created by Andres Bossard, Floriana Frassetto, Bernie Schurch

CAST

Andres Bossard†
Floriana Frassetto
Bernie Schurch

A program of mime in two parts with the use of masks, flexible body wrappings, props and costumes.

Company Managers: John Scott, Don Joslyn
Press: Jeffrey Richards, Bruce Lynn
Stage Managers: Patrick Lecoq, Nancy Finn

* Still playing May 31, 1978.
† Original cast was succeeded by Louis Gilbert, James Greiner, Dominique Weibel

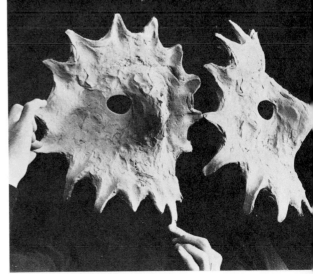

EDISON THEATRE
Opened Friday, September 24, 1976.*
Hillard Elkins, Norman Kean, Robert S. Fishko present:

OH! CALCUTTA!

Devised by Kenneth Tynan; Contributors, Jules Feiffer, Dan Greenburg, Lenore Kandel, John Lennon, Jacques Levy, Leonard Melfi, David Newman, Robert Benton, Sam Shepard, Clovis Trouille, Kenneth Tynan, Sherman Yellen; Music and Lyrics, Robert Dennis, Peter Schickele, Stanley Walden; Additional Music and Lyrics, Stanley Walden, Jacques Levy; Choreography, Margo Sappington; Musical Director, Stanley Walden; Scenery, James Tilton; Lighting, Harry Silverglat; Costumes, Kenneth M. Yount, supervised by James Tilton; Musical Conductors, Michael Tschudin, Norman Bergen; Assistant to Director, Nancy Tribush; Projection Design, Gardner Compton; Production Manager, Sam Stickler; Entire Production Conceived and Directed by Jacques Levy; Technical Supervisor, Jim Bryne; Wardrobe Master, Bruce Horowitz

CAST

Haru Aki†	John Hammil
Jean Andalman	William Knight
Bill Bass	Cy Moore
Dorothy Chansky	Coline Morse
Cress Darwin	Pamela Pilkenton

ACT I: "Taking Off the Robe," "Will Answer All Sincere Replies," "Rock Garden," "Delicious Indignities," "The Paintings of Clovis Trouille," "Suite for Five Letters," "One on One"

ACT II: "Jack and Jill," "Spread Your Love Around," "Was It Good for You Too?," "Coming Together, Going Together"

An erotic musical in two acts.

General Manager: Norman Kean
Company Manager: James Fiore
Press: Les Schecter Associates
Stage Managers: David Rubinstein, Maria DiDia

* Still playing May 31, 1978. Original production opened at the Eden Theatre June 17, 1969 and played 1316 performances before moving to the Belasco Theatre for 606 additional performances.
† During the season, original cast members were succeeded by Cheryl Hartley, Billy Padgett, Katherine Liepe, Scott Baker, Jacqueline Carol, Robert Beau Golden, Mary Hendrickson, September Thorp

Top Right: Cheryl Hartley, Robert Beau Golden

Pamela Pilkenton, John Hammill

**Jacqueline Carol, Robert Beau Golden,
September Thorp**

MAJESTIC THEATRE
Opened Sunday, January 5, 1975.* (Moved May 25, 1977 to
Broadway Theatre)
Ken Harper presents:

THE WIZ

Book, William F. Brown; Based on L. Frank Baum's "The Won-
derful Wizard of Oz"; Music and Lyrics, Charlie Smalls; Director,
Geoffrey Holder; Choreography and Musical Numbers Staged by
George Faison; Musical Direction, Tom Pierson; Settings, Tom H.
John; Costumes, Geoffrey Holder; Lighting, Tharon Musser; Or-
chestrations, Harold Wheeler; Vocal Arrangements, Charles H.
Coleman; Dance Arrangements, Timothy Graphenreed; Manager,
Jose Vega; Sound, Richard J. C. Miller; Wardrobe Supervisors, Jo-
seph Potter, Frank Green, James Hodson; Associate Conductor,
Jack Jeffers; Special Effects, Ronald Vitelli; Wigs and Makeup, Stan-
ley James; Original Cast Album by Atlantic Records

CAST

Aunt Em	Tasha Thomas†1
Toto	Nancy†2
Dorothy	Stephanie Mills
Uncle Henry/Lord High Underling	Ralph Wilcox†3
Tornado	Evelyn Thomas†4
Addaperle	Clarice Taylor†5
Yellow Brick Road	Alvin Davis, Robert Pittman, Aaron Leavy, Stanley Dalton
Scarecrow	Hinton Battle†6
Crows	Renee Rose, Eartha Robinson, Claudia Lewis
Tinman	Tiger Haynes
Lion	Ted Ross†7
Gatekeeper	Danny Beard†8
The Wiz	Andre DeShields†9
Evillene	Mabel King†10
Soldier Messenger	Carl Weaver†11
Winged Monkey	Andy Torres†12
Glinda	Dee Dee Bridgewater†13

MUNCHKINS, KALIDAHS, EMERALD CITY CITIZENS:
Deborah Lynn Bridges, Leslie Butler, Howard Porter, Lois Hayes,
Charles Lavont Williams, Claudia Lewis, Anthony Lawrence, Gayle
Turner, Allison Williams, Dwight Leon, Siri Sat Nam Singh, Renee
Rose, Debbie Fitts, Alvin Davis, Stanley Dalton, Robert Pittman,
Eartha Robinson, Kevin Jeff, Aaron Leavy

PIT SINGERS: Jozella Reed, DeMarest Grey, Sylvester Rickey
Powell, Esther Marrow, Janyse M. Singleton

UNDERSTUDIES: Gayle Turner (Dorothy), Siri Sat Nam Singh,
Howard Porter, Anthony Lawrence (Tin Man), Michael Leslie
(Lion), Charles Lavont Williams, Stanley Dalton (Scarecrow),
Jozella Reed, Ruth Brisbane (Addaperle), Ruth Brisbane (Evillene),
Anthony Lawrence, Sylvester Rickey Powell (Wiz), Janyse M. Sin-
gleton (Glinda), Deborah Burrell (Aunt Em) Carl Hardy, Neisha
Folkes (Swing Dancers)

MUSICAL NUMBERS: "The Feeling We Once Had," "Tornado
Ballet," "He's the Wizard," "Soon as I Get Home," "I Was Born
on the Day before Yesterday," "Ease on Down the Road," "Slide
Some Oil to Me," "Mean Ole Lion," "Kalidah Battle," "Be a Lion,"
"Lion's Dream," "Emerald City Ballet," "So You Want to Meet the
Wizard," "What Would I Do if I Could Feel," "No Bad News,"
"Funky Monkeys," "Everybody Rejoice," "Who Do You Think
You Are," "If You Believe," "Y'All Got It!," "A Rested Body Is
a Rested Mind," "Home"

A musical in 2 acts and 16 scenes with a prologue.

General Managers: Emanuel Azenberg, Eugene V. Wolsk
Company Manager: Susan Bell
Press: Merlin Group, Patt Dale
Stage Managers: Christopher Kelly, Robert Burland, Steven
Shaw, Donald Christy, Clint Jakeman, Robert D. Currie, Lee
Murray, Michael William Schaefer

* Still playing May 31, 1978. For original production, see THE-
ATRE WORLD Vol. 32.
† Succeeded by: 1. Esther Marrow, 2. Westy, Toto, 3. Al Fann,
Toney Watkins, Michael Leslie, 4. Wendy Edmead, Allison Wil-
liams, 5. Jozella Reed during absence, 6. Gregg Burge, Charles
Lavont Williams during Mr. Burge's illness, 7. James Wigfall,
Ken Page, L. Michael Gray, 8. Toney Watkins, Howard Porter,
9. Alan Weeks, Carl Hall, 10. Edye Byrde, Theresa Merritt, Ella
Mitchell, 11. Charles Lavont Williams, 12. Keith Harris, Kevin
Jeff, 13. Deborah Burrell

Martha Swope Photos

**Top Right: Gregg Burge, L. Michael Gray,
Stephanie Mills, Tiger Haynes**

Carl Hall, Stephanie Mills

59

BROOKS ATKINSON THEATRE
Opened Thursday, March 13, 1975.* (Moved May 16, 1978 to Ambassador Theatre)
Morton Gottlieb, Dasha Epstein, Edward L. Schuman, Palladium Productions present:

SAME TIME, NEXT YEAR

By Bernard Slade; Director, Gene Saks; Scenery, William Ritman; Costumes, Jane Greenwood; Lighting, Tharon Musser; Associate Producers, Ben Rosenberg, Warren Crane; Wardrobe Supervisors, Penny Davis, Thelma B. Davis; Hairstylists, Angela Gari, Steve Atha

CAST

Doris .... Ellen Burstyn†1
George .... Charles Grodin†2

STANDBYS: Rochelle Oliver, Peter DeMaio

A comedy in 2 acts and 6 scenes. The action takes place in a guest cottage of a country inn in Northern California from 1951 to 1975.

General Manager: Ben Rosenberg
Company Managers: Martin Cohen, Sam Pagliaro
Press: Solters & Roskin, Milly Schoenbaum, Sophie McBride
Stage Managers: Warren Crane, Kate Pollock, J. S. McKie, Jr., Peter DeMaio

* Still playing May 31, 1978. For original production, see THEATRE WORLD Vol. 31.
† Succeeded by: 1. Joyce Van Patten, Loretta Swit, Sandy Dennis, Hope Lange, Betsy Palmer, 2. Conrad Janis, Ted Bessell, Don Murray, Monte Markham, Charles Kimbrough

Charles Kimbrough, Betsy Palmer
Top: Monte Markham, Betsy Palmer

Betsy Palmer, Don Murray

BROADWAY PRODUCTIONS FROM PAST SEASONS THAT CLOSED THIS SEASON

Title	Opened	Closed	Performances
Pippin	10/23/72	6/12/77	1944
Equus	10/24/74	10/2/77	1209
Shenandoah	1/7/75	8/7/77	1050
Chicago	6/3/75	8/27/77	947
Godspell	6/22/76	9/4/77	527
Sly Fox	12/14/76	2/19/78	505
California Suite	6/10/76	7/2/77	449
Side by Side by Sondheim	4/18/77	3/19/78	390
Otherwise Engaged	2/2/77	10/30/77	311
American Buffalo	1/26/76	6/11/77	135
Anna Christie	4/14/77	7/30/77	127
Basic Training of Pavlo Hummel	4/15/77	9/3/77	121
Lily Tomlin in Appearing Nightly	3/24/77	6/12/77	96
Happy End	5/7/77	7/10/77	75
Toller Cranston's Ice Show	5/19/77	7/10/77	62

PROMENADE THEATRE
  Opened Thursday, June 2, 1977.*
  Kenneth D. Laub presents:

THE 2nd GREATEST ENTERTAINER IN THE WHOLE WIDE WORLD

Written by Dick Shawn; Setting, Akira Yoshimura; Lighting, Marilyn Rennagel; Sound, Ellen Katz

The Entertainer .... Dick Shawn
The Stage Manager .... Stephen Schulefand

An evening of comedy presented in two parts.

General Manager: Al Isaac
Press: Gifford/Wallace
Stage Manager: Christopher Adler

* Closed Aug. 7, 1977 after 78 performances and 19 previews.

Right and Below: Dick Shawn

Adolph Caesar

THEATRE DE LYS
  Opened Tuesday, June 14, 1977.*
  The Negro Ensemble Company presents:

THE SQUARE ROOT OF SOUL

Conceived by Adolph Caesar; Staged by Perry Schwartz; Music, Jothan Callins; Visuals, Makutta Wusaha; Sound, Bruce Strickland
with
Adolph Caesar

A program of poetry presented in two parts.

Press: Howard Atlee, Clarence Allsopp, Becky Flora
Stage Manager: Michael Nunley

* Closed July 10, 1977 after 32 performances. Presented by Adolph Caesar Productions for 16 additional performances through July 24, 1977.

ASTOR PLACE THEATRE
Opened WEdnesday, June 15, 1977.*
Robert E. Richardson presents:

LOVE! LOVE! LOVE!

Written and Composed by Johnny Brandon; Directed and Choreographed by Buck Heller; Musical and Vocal Arrangements and Musical Direction, Clark McClellan; Scenery and Costumes, Don Jensen; Lighting, Jeff Davis

CAST

Michael Calkins   Mel Johnson, Jr.
Pat Lundy   Neva Rae Powers
                    Glory Van Scott

MUSICAL NUMBERS: "The Great-All-American-Power-Driven-Engine," "Searching for Love," "The Battle of Chicago," "Where Did the Dream Go," "I Am You," "Consenting Adults," "Come On In," "Preacher Man," "Age Is a State of Mind," "Searching for Yesterdays," "Somewhere Along the Road," "Reach Out," "Love! Love! Love!," "Empty Spaces," "Look All Around You," "Find Someone to Love," "The Streets of Bed-Stuy," "What Is There to Say?," "Mother's Day," "Lovin'," "What Did We Do Wrong?," "Law and Order," "Middle-Class-Liberal-Blues"

An "All-American Musical 'Bout Love and Other Things" in two acts. The action takes place in the U.S.A. at the present time.

General Manager: Don Joslyn
Press: Saul Richman
Stage Manager: Robert I. Cohen

* Closed July 3, 1977 after 25 performances.

Glory Van Scott   **Neva Rae Powers**

Mel Johnson, Jr.

CHELSEA WESTSIDE CABARET THEATRE
Opened Wednesday, August 17, 1977.*
John A. Vaccaro and James J. Wisner in association with R. Anthony Zeiger present:

CHILDREN OF ADAM

Words and Music, Stan Satlin; Conceived and Directed by John Driver; Musical Direction and Vocal Arrangements, Jimmy Wisner; Choreography, Ruella Frank; Set, Ernest Allen Smith; Lighting, Robert F. Strohmeier; Costumes, Polly P. Smith; Assistant Producer, Bert Stratford; Masque Sound

CAST

Gene Bua   Robert Polenz
Elizabeth Lathram   Roger Rathburn
Karen Philipp   Carole Schweid

MUSICAL NUMBERS: "Dreams," "Mr. & Mrs. Myth," "What's Your Name?," "Move Along," "Sex Is Animal," "It's Really You," "Walkin'," "You've Got to Die to Be Born Again," "Rise in Love," "The Wedding," "The Flowers and the Rainbow," "Life," "It Ain't Easy/Equilib," "Sleep My Child," "I Must Go Now," "Like a Park on Sunday," "Part of the Plan," "I Can Feel," "Sleepin' Around," "The Wooden People," "Cacophony," "Maybe You Can See Yourself," "Just a Feeling," "No More Games," "I Can Make It," "The Sweetest Songs Remain to Be Sung," "Children of Adam"

General Manager: Donald Joslyn
Press: Jeffrey Richards, Penny Vine, Bruce Lynn
Stage Managers: Sari E. Weisman, Robert I. Cohen

* Closed Oct. 9, 1977 after 62 performances and 9 previews.

**Elizabeth Lathrom, Karen Philipp, Gene Bua, Robert Polenz, Roger Rathburn, Carole Schweid
Above: Rathburn, Schweid**

VIVIAN BEAUMONT THEATER
Opened Tuesday, June 28, 1977.*
Joseph Papp presents the New York Shakespeare Festival Production of:

THE CHERRY ORCHARD

By Anton Chekhov; New English version by Jean-Claude van Itallie; Director, Andrei Serban; Scenery and Costumes, Santo Loquasto; Lighting, Jennifer Tipton; Incidental Music, Elizabeth Swados; Dance arranged by Kathryn Posin; Associate Producer, Bernard Gersten; Production Manager, Andrew Mihok; Technical Director, Mervyn Haines, Jr.; Production Supervisor, Jason Steven Cohen; Assistant Director, Richard Jakiel

CAST

Lopakhin, Yermolay Alexeyevich	Raul Julia
Dunyasha, the maid	Christine Estabrook
Yepikhodov, Semyon Panteleyevich, clerk	Max Wright
Anya, Mme. Ranevskaya's daughter	Marybeth Hurt
Ranevskaya, Lyubov Andreyevna	Irene Worth
Varya, her adopted daughter	Priscilla Smith
Gayev, Leonid Andreyevich	George Voskovec
Charlotta Ivanovna, governess	Elizabeth Franz
Simeonov-Pishchik, landowner	C. K. Alexander
Yasha, a valet	Ben Masters
Firs, a valet	Dwight Marfield
Trofimov, Pyotr Sergeyevich, student	David Clennon
A Vagrant	Jon De Vries
Stationmaster	William Duff-Griffin

GUESTS, PEASANTS, SERVANTS: John Ahlburg, Suzanne Collins, Jerry Cunliffe, Jon DeVries, C. S. Hayward, Diane Lane, Jim Siering

UNDERSTUDIES AND STANDBYS: Jacqueline Brookes (Ranevskaya), Gerry Bamman (Lopakhin/Yepikhodov), Suzanne Collins (Varya), Jon De Vries (Trofimov), William Duff-Griffin (Pishchik)

A comedy in four acts, performed with two intermissions. The action takes place on Madame Ranevskaya's estate from May through October.

General Manager: Robert Kamlot
Press: Merle Debuskey, Faith Geer
Stage Managers: Julia Gillett, Don Koehler

* Closed Aug. 7, 1977 after 48 performances.

Sy Friedman Photos

Right: Irene Worth, Raul Julia

Irene Worth, Raul Julia

Dwight Marfield, C. K. Alexander, Priscilla Smith, Irene Worth, George Vosckovec

JONES BEACH THEATRE
Opened Monday, July 4, 1977.*
Guy Lombardo and the Jones Beach State Parkway Authority
present:

FINIAN'S RAINBOW

Book, E. Y. Harburg, Fred Saidy; Music, Burton Lane; Lyrics, E. Y. Harburg; Director, John Fearnley; Choreography, Robert Pagent; Scenery, John W. Keck; Costumes, Winn Morton; Lighting, Richard Nelson; Musical Director, Jay Blackton; Wardrobe Mistress, Agnes Farrell

CAST

Sunny	Raymond Townsend
Buzz Collins	Alan North
Sheriff	John Dorrin
Susan Mahoney, the Silent	Gail Benedict
Henry	Winston Roye
Finian McLonergan	Christopher Hewett
Sharon McLonergan	Beth Fowler
Woody Mahoney	Stanley Grover
Og, a leprechaun	Charles Repole
Howard	Clyde Williams
Senator Bilboard Rawkins	Ronn Carroll
Maude	Phyllis A. Bash
Geologists	Ted Goodridge, Dale Muchmore
Diane	Robbi Smith
John, the preacher	Eugene Edwards
Mr. Robust	Ralph Vucci
Mr. Shears	Lee Cass
Pilgrim Gospeleers	Donald H. Coleman, Eugene Edwards, David Weatherspoon

SHARECROPPERS AND VILLAGERS: Roslyn Burrough, Mary-Pat Carey, Danielle Susan Carter, Helen Castillo, Susan Cella, Heidi Coe, Lynda Farmer, Linda Griffin, Karen W. Hubbard, Lynn Kearney, Elena Malfitano, Gilda Mullette, Laurie Scandurra, Dixie Stewart, Mickey Gunnersen (Swing), Donald H. Coleman, Eugene Edwards, John E. Flynt, Ted Goodridge, Randal Harris, Dale Muchmore, Charles Neal, Michael Page, Rick Schneider, Raymond Townsend, Ralph Vucci, David Weatherspoon, Clyde Williams, Reuben Williams, John Wohl, Arthur Whitfield (Swing)

UNDERSTUDIES: John Dorrin (Finian), Susan Cella (Sharon), John E. Flynt (Woody), John Wohl (Og), Lee Cass (Rawkins), Dale Muchmore (Buzz), Gilda Mullette (Susan), Danielle Susan Carter (Diane), Randal Harris (Robust), Rueben Williams (Henry), David Weatherspoon (Howard)

MUSICAL NUMBERS: Overture, "This Time of the Year," "How Are Things in Glocca Morra?," "Look to the Rainbow," "Old Devil Moon," "Something Sort of Grandish," "Necessity," "When the Idle Poor Become the Idle Rich," "Dance of the Golden Crock," "The Begat," "When I'm Not Near the Girl I Love," Finale

A musical in two acts. The action takes place in Rainbow Valley, and the colonial estate of Senator Rawkins in Missitucky, U.S.A.

Company Manager: Sam Pagliaro
Press: Saul Richman
Stage Managers: Mortimer Halpern, Bernard Pollock, Ralph Vucci

* Closed Sept. 4, 1977 after 58 performances. For original production, see THEATRE WORLD Vol. 3

Liz Lombardo Photos

Christopher Hewett, Charles Repole
Above: Beth Fowler, Charles Repole

Top: Gail Benedict, Charles Repole, Alan North
Left: Beth Fowler, Christopher Hewett, Stanley Grover

BEACON THEATRE

Opened Wednesday, August 31, 1977.*
Kazuko Hillyer with the assistance of the Japan Foundation
presents:

THE GRAND KABUKI

The National Theatre of Japan; Stage Director, Takeshiba Norio; Head of Troupe, Kato Shigeru; General Supervisor, Nagayama Takeomi; General Managers, Imai Masahiko, Suzuki Masako; Simultaneous Translation, Faubion Bowers; Production, Shochiku Co.

CAST

Starring Ennosuke Ichikawa III, with Danshiro Ichikawa IV, Monnosuke Ichikawa VII, Yonekichi Nakamura IV, Dan-en Ichikawa, Juy-en Ichikawa, Tokicho Nakamura, Hidejyu Katacka, Takajiro Ichikawa, Akira Kusanagi, Hirokazu Kihara, Hirotsugu Oishi

PROGRAM: "Kurozuka," "Yoshitsune Senbon Zakura"

Company Manager: David Shapiro
Press: Gurtman & Murtha, Meg Gordean
Stage Manager: Toshi Ogawa

* Closed Sept. 4, 1977 after 7 performances, and returned Sept. 13–18, 1977 for 9 additional performances.

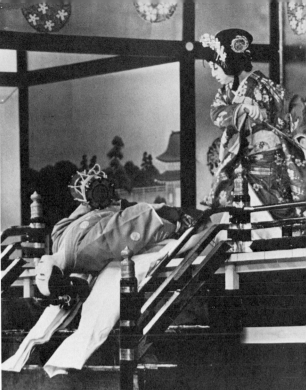

Ennosuke III in "The Fox"

PARK ROYAL CABARET THEATRE

Opened Tuesday, October 4, 1977.*
Roger Ailes and John Fishback with The Comedy Club Company present:

THE PRESENT TENSE

Written by The Cast, Stephen Rosenfield, Haila Strauss, Ralph Buckley, Jeff Sweet (Head Writer); Music and Lyrics, Allen Cohen, Bob Joseph, Alan Menken, Muriel Robinson, Don Siegal, Jeff Sweet, Lee S. Wilkof; Director, Stephen Rosenfield; Musical Director, Skip Kennon; Scenery and Costumes, Paul DePass; Lighting, John Fishback; Assistant Director, Haila Strauss; Associate Producer, Norma Ferrer

CAST

Barbara Brummel	Lianne Kressin
Chris Carroll	Michael Nobel
Jim Cyrus	Lee S. Wilkof

MUSICAL NUMBERS: "Cautiously Optimistic," "Yankee Man," "Margaret," "Come to Cuba," "Song for a Crowded Cabaret," "The Carter Song," "Love Me or Leave Me," "Man on a Subway," "Possum Pie," "Sklip, Dat, Doobee"

A topical satirical revue

Press: Jeffrey Richards, Bruce Lynn
Stage Manager: Haila Strauss

* Closed Oct. 23, 1977 after 23 performances.

Jim Cyrus, Lianne Kressin
Above: Lianne Kressin, Lee S. Wilkof

CHERRY LANE THEATRE
Opened Wednesday, September 27, 1977.*
The Dracula Theatrical Company presents:

THE PASSION OF DRACULA

By Bob Hall and David Richmond; Based on novel by Bram Stoker; Director, Peter Bennett; Sets, Bob Hall, Allen Cornell; Costumes, Jane Tschetter; Lighting and Special Effects, Allen Cornell; Executive Producer, Eric Krebs; Assistant to Producers, David Cleaver; Wardrobe Supervisor, Larry Ensign; Vampire Consultant, Dr. Steven Kaplan

CAST

Jameson	Brian Bell†1
Dr. Cedric Seward	K. Lype O'Dell†2
Prof. Van Helsing	Michael Burg†3
Dr. Helga Van Zandt	Alice White†4
Lord Gordon Godalming	K. C. Wilson
Mr. Renfield	Elliott Vileen†5
Wilhelmina Murray	Giulia Pagano†6
Jonathan Harker	Samuel Maupin†7
Count Dracula	Christopher Bernau†8

Understsy for Ms. Pagano: Sarah Hernstadt

"A Gothic Entertainment" in three acts. The action takes place in England during the autumn of 1911 in the study of Dr. Seward's home.

General Management: Dracula Theatrical Co.
Company Manager: Margay Whitlock
Press: Jeffrey Richards, Bruce Lynn
Stage Managers: Andrea Naier, Sarah Herrnstadt

* Still playing May 31, 1978.
† Succeeded by: 1. Martin LaPlatney, 2. Victor Raider-Wexler, Steve Meyer, Paul Meacham, 3. Stefan Schnabel during his absence, 4. Karen Savage, 5. Robert Schenkkan, 6. Anne Twomey during her absence, 7. Neal Mandell, 8. William Lyman

Left: Christopher Bernau, Giulia Pagano

Christopher Bernau, Giulia Pagano

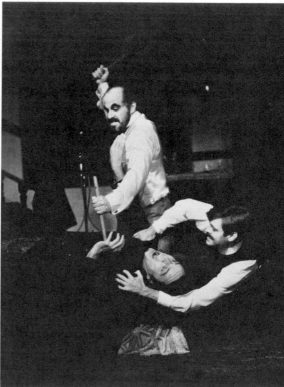

Christopher Bernau, Michael Burg,
Sam Maupin

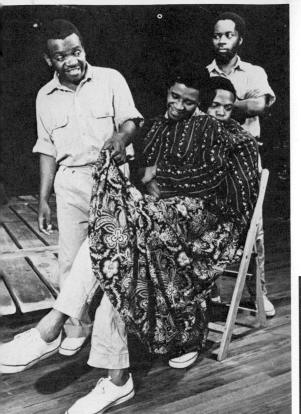

Selaelo Dan Maredi, Themba Ntinga, Fana David Kekana, Seth Sibanda **Right:** Seth Sibanda, Selaelo Dan Maredi, Fana David Kekana, Themba Ntinga

ASTOR PLACE THEATRE

Opened Sunday, October 9, 1977.*

Clyde Kuemmerle in association with the Negro Ensemble Company presents:

SURVIVAL

Written by the cast; Directed and Co-Authored by Mshengu; Additional Staging, Dean Irby; Designed by Clyde Kuemmerle; Music, Selaelo Dan Maredi; Management Associate, Thelma Cooper; Vocal and Acting Coach, Catherine Slade; Wardrobe, Charles Schoonmacker

CAST

Fana David Kekana	Selaelo Dan Maredi
Themba Ntinga	Seth Sibanda

A South African play with music in two acts.

General Management: Dorothy Olim Associates
Company Manager: Gail Bell
Press: Seymour Krawitz, Lewis Harmon
Stage Managers: Harrison Avery, Fana David Kekana

* Closed Nov. 20, 1977 after 47 performances.

Peter Smallman Photo

PLAYHOUSE THEATRE

Opened Friday, October 21, 1977.*

The Labor Theatre in cooperation with the Sanctuary Theatre presents:

NIGHT SHIFT

By Martin Goldsmith; Director, C. R. Portz; Scenery and Lighting, Joe Riley; Technical Director, Larry May; Costumes, Alicia Rogue; Sound, Edward May; Props, David Ticotin; Executive Producer, Bette Craig; Production Assistants, Sandra DeCarolis, Sid Schwartz

CAST

Al Murphy	Rip Torn
Fusco	John D. Swain
Florence Murphy	Barbara Spiegel
Fireman	Owen Hollander
Barber	Shelly Desai
Window Washer	Samm Art Williams
Policeman	David Brooks
Policeman #2	Philip Levy
Model	Amy Wright
Bartender	Paul Ladenheim
Mrs. Darmstetter	Jean Barker
Priest	M. Patrick Hughes

Understudy: William G. Schilling

A drama in two acts.

Press: Chris Kraus
Stage Managers: M. E. Randolph, Paul Ladenheim

* Closed Nov. 6, 1977 after 23 performances.

Rip Torn, John D. Swain

THEATRE DeLYS
Opened Thursday, October 20, 1977.*
Jane Harmon presents:

A LIFE IN THE THEATRE

By David Mamet; Director, Gerald Gutierrez; Incidental Music,
Robert Waldman; Scenery, John Lee Beatty; Lighting, Pat Collins;
Costumes, John David Ridge; Assistant Director, Eileen Wilson;
Wardrobe Master, William Gammon; Production Assistants, Alfred
Grossman, Susan O'Connell; Wigs and Hairstyles, Paul Huntley

CAST

John	Peter Evans†1
Robert	Ellis Rabb†2
Stage Manager	Benjamin Hendrickson†3

UNDERSTUDIES: John Clarkson (Robert), Benjamin Hendrickson (John), James McDonnell (John), Michael Adkins (Stage Manager), Chip Mitchell (John/Stage Manager)

A comedy in two parts. The action takes place at the present time
in various spots around a theatre

General Manager: Albert Poland
Press: Betty Lee Hunt, Maria Cristina Pucci, Fred Hoot
Stage Managers: Frank Hartenstein, Susie Cordon, James
McDonnell, Michael Adkins

* Still playing May 31, 1978.
† Succeeded by: 1. James McDonnell, 2. Jose Ferrer, 3. Michael
Adkins

Roger Greenawalt Photos

**Right: Peter Evans, Ellis Rabb
(also top)**

Ellis Rabb, Peter Evans

Jose Ferrer, James McDonnell

GERSHWIN THEATRE/BROOKLYN COLLEGE
Opened Saturday, October 22, 1977.*
(Moved November 5, 1977 to Norman Thomas Theatre)
Lively and Yiddish Productions in association with David
Carey presents:

ONCE UPON A TIME

Dramatized and Directed by Ben Bonus and Mina Bern; Musical
Director, Renee Solomon; Scenery, Jerry Rothman; Choreography,
Tony Masullo; Lighting, Mallary Perry; Costumes, Sylvia Fried-
lander; Narration, David Carey; Press, Max Eisen

CAST

Ben Bonus	Mina Bern
David Carey	Diane Cypkin
Shmulik Goldstein	Elias Patron
Reizl Bozyk	Chip Garfinkle

Dancers: Tony Masullo, Robert Raimondo, Shirley Stephens,
Lois Silk

ACT I: "The Coachman" in three scenes.

ACT II: "The Family Album," "Honorable Profession," "Chassidic
Chants," "A Letter to Mamma," "The Fair"

* Closed Dec. 18, 1977 after 28 performances.

**Right: David Carey, Mina Bern, Ben Bonus,
Reizl Bozyk Top: Ben Bonus, Mina Bern**

Barry Humphries as Dame Edna Everage

THEATRE FOUR
Opened Wednesday, October 29, 1977.*
Michael White and Arthur Cantor present:

HOUSEWIFE! SUPERSTAR!!

Written by Barry Humphries; Executive Mise en Scene, Ian Da-
vidson; Decor, Brian Thomason; Costumes, Kenneth Everage;
Lighting, Andrea Wilson; Production Assistants, Thomas Madigan,
Marcia Mediate

CAST

Barry Humphries (Dame Edna Everage)
Iris Mason (Pianist)

Program presented without intermission.

General Managers: Robert S. Fishko, Robert Fox
Press: Arthur Cantor, C. George Willard, Bill Miller
Stage Manager: Larry Bussard

* Closed Nov. 20, 1977 after 34 performances and 2 previews.

Craig Russell as Carol Channing
Right: as Bette Midler

Opened Monday, October 31, 1977.*
Jonathan Scharer in association with Stephen Novick presents:

A MAN AND HIS WOMEN

Material by Craig Russell; Music Director, Stephen Stucker; Gowns, Tony Marando; Sound, Bob Casey; Lighting, Consolidated Edification; Wardrobe Master, Russell Elliot; Production Associate, Gaile Burnell

CAST

Craig Russell
and his impressions

A program of Mr. Russell's impressions of famous women presented in two parts.

General Manager: Paul Berkowsky
Press: Elizabeth Rodman, Harold Lubin, Sharon Mear, Harriett Trachtenberg
Stage Manager: Nicholas Plain

* Closed Dec. 31, 1977 after 72 performances.

Jerry Rockwood as Edgar Allan Poe

BIJOU THEATRE
Opened Monday, November 7, 1977.*
Arthur Shafman International, Ltd. presents:

A CONDITION OF SHADOW

Compiled and Written by Jerry Rockwood; Selected material from the works of Edgar Allan Poe; Music Composed and Performed by Thomas Wilt

CAST

Jerry Rockwood

A one-man characterization of the life and works of Edgar Allan Poe.

Press: Jeffrey Richards, Bruce Lynn

* Presented on three consecutive Mondays, closing Nov. 21, 1977.

VILLAGE GATE DOWNSTAIRS

November 17–
Irwin Steiner presents:

NIGHTSONG

Words and Music, Ron Eliroan; Director, Dan Early; Set, Harry Silverglat; Lighting, Jo Mayer; Costumes, Ron Whitehead and Margot Miller; Sound, Alan Stieb; Musical Direction, Jaroslav (Yaron) Jakubovic; General Manager, Churck Aresona; Stage Manager, Karen Winer; Press, Max Eisen, Bruce Cohen

CAST

Ron Eliran
Holly T. Lipton
Dian Sorel
Joy Kohner

MUSICAL NUMBERS: "Looking at Us," "My Land," "Dusty Roads," "Butterfly Child," "I Hear a Song," "Come with Me," "Who Am I?," "Nightsong," "Lady Vagabond," "Music in the City," "Come, Elijah, Come," "Grain of Sand," "All in the Name of Love," "Sweet Fantasy," "Have a Little Fun," "Moments by the Sea," "Young Days," "It Was Worth It," "I Believe."

A musical entertainment in two parts.

Right: Holly T. Lipton, Ron Eliran
**Top: Joy Kohner, Ron Eliran, Holly T.
Lipton, Dian Sorel**

Carol Mayo Jenkins, Emily Frankel

COLONNADES THEATRE LAB

Opened Friday, November 18, 1977.*
Colonnades Theatre Lab presents:

ZINNIA

By Emily Frankel; Director, John Cullum; Choreography, Emily Frankel; Music, Mahler's "Tenth Symphony"; Sets and Costumes, John Falabella; Sound, Michael Jay; Lighting, Randy Becker; Assistant to Director, Kim Jurrius

CAST

Janet McFinney . . . . Carol Mayo Jenkins
Princess Zinnia . . . . Emily Frankel

A play in six scenes, performed without intermission. The action takes place in the present and past.

Press: Eric M. Hamburger & Associates
Stage Manager: Arthur Schwartz

* Closed Apr. 2, 1978 after 41 performances.

THE CUBICULO

November 18–December 5, 1977 (12 performances)
The Cubiculo presents:

THE CUBICULO

Elaine Sulka, Managing Director
Philip Meister, Artistic Director
Deborah Teller, General Manager
Dinah Carlson, Program Coordinator Tenth Season

THE LABORATORY

By June Daniels; Director, Ron Daley; Set and Lighting Design, Preston Yarber; Costumes, Margo LaZaro; Production Manager, Jody Dowdall

CAST

Jane Anderson (Rina), Kermit Brown (Dr. Muncie), Margaret Donohue (Marcie Jones), Lee Kheel (Myrtle Perkins), Stephan Novelli (Randolph Perkins), Andy Murphy (Horace Perkins)

A comedy in 2 acts and 7 scenes. The action takes place during May and July of 1971 in the Perkins' home and in Dr. Muncie's laboratory in Westchester.

Jane Anderson   **Kermit Brown**

Cast of "Streets of Gold"

NEILL GALLERY

Opened Friday, November 25, 1977.*
The Fantasy Factory presents:

THE GATES OF PARADISE

Book, Ed Kuczewski; Music and Lyrics, Bill Vitale; Sets and Projections, W. J. Giampa; Costumes, Milly Russell; Lighting and Sound, Dan Abrahamsen; Orchestrations, Musical Direction, Vocal Arrangements, Richard Fiocca; Dances and Musical Staging, Jay Fox; Director, Bill Vitale

CAST

Raul Aranas, Donna Lee Betz, Marc Castle, Lorraine Davidson, George Harris, Mba Idika, Sharon D. Johnson, Ed Kuczewski, Joan Neuman, Alkis Papoutsis, Raton the Rabbit, Barbara Sandek, Martha Sanders, Rouviere Santana, Jorge Vergne-Fontanez, Louis Zippin

MUSICAL NUMBERS: "Falling Star," "Dying Is," "Canticle Charon," "Montevideo," "The Treeless Leaflets of Times Square," "The Poodle & Canary, also Tom & Jerry Menage a Culinary Croak," "Bad Trip," "The Seamy Side of Heaven," "The Seventh Sacrament," "The Main Event," "Accompaniment," "It's Easy—Let Go," "Passing Through Exotic Places"

A musical play performed without intermission. The action takes place in the Paradise Automat, now or a few years ago.

Stage Manager: Roger Thomas Chaffiotte

* Closed Dec. 18, 1977 after limited engagement of 12 performances.

MANHATTAN CENTER BALLROOM THEATRE
Opened Friday, November 25, 1977.*
Ballet Concepts and The Workmen's Circle present:

THE STREETS OF GOLD

Book and Lyrics, Marvin Gordon; Music, Ted Simons; Director, Scott Redman; Musical Numbers Staged by Tony Masullo; Musical Director, Harrison Fisher; Set Design, Michael Molly; Lighting, Clarke Thornton; Costumes, Christina Giannini; Production Assistants, Grant Brown, David Nathans; Technical Director, Mark Eldrenkamp

CAST

Annie Abbott	Shifee Lovitt
Dorothy Chansky	Donald Mark
Paul Corman	Jared Matesky
Nancy Diaz	Ken Meseroll
Susan Jacks	Gregory Salata
Tom Lantzy	Stuart Silver

MUSICAL NUMBERS: "Streets of Gold," "Hester Street," "Sabbath Blessing," "Greenhorn," "Buy My Passamentaries," "Tammany," "Another Cold Day, Another Sad Penny," "Hottest Knishe," "The Old Ways," "Look Around You," "Kravitz to Snyder to Smith," "Troubles of My Own," "Pogrom Ballet," "Why Can't I?," "Dreidel," "Coney Island," "This Time"

A musical in 2 acts and 24 scenes. The action takes place on the Lower East Side of New York City in 1911.

Stage Manager: Doug Laidlaw

* Closed Dec. 11, 1977 after 12 performances.

Joan Neuman

PROMENADE THEATRE

Opened Tuesday, November 29, 1977.*
Saul Novick and Jomeldin Productions present:

ESTHER

By Carol K. Mack; Director, Joel Zwick; Set, Franco Cola-
vecchia; Costumes, David James; Lighting, Edward M. Greenberg;
Music, Bruce Coughlin; Production Assistants, Paul Baretsky,
Linda Miller

CAST

Ahasuerus	Charles Turner
Haman	John Milligan
Dotus the Scribe	Bruce Kornbluth
Esther/Hadassah	Dianne Wiest
Heghe	Joel Kramer
Mordecai	Stephen Keep

A drama in two acts. The action takes place in Susa, Persia, during
the Fifth Century, B.C.

Company Manager: Don Joslyn
Press: Betty Lee Hunt Associates
Stage Manager: Barrett Nolan

* Closed Dec. 4, 1977 after 8 performances and 8 previews.
(No photos available)

Joel Kramer   **Stephen Keep**

EMANU-EL MIDTOWN YM-YWHA

Opened Thursday, December 1, 1977.*
The Jewish Repertory Theatre in association with the Emanu-
El Midtown YM-YWHA presents:

DANCING IN NEW YORK CITY

By Julius Landau; Director, Ran Avni; Set and Lighting Design,
Howard Kessler; Technical Director, Sol Rosenzweig; Producer,
Ran Avni; Graphics, Christos Peterson; Production Manager, Betsy
Imershein

CAST

Aaron Altman	John McComb
Frank Biancamano	Bernie Rachelle
Rod Bladel	Marilyn Robbins
Herb Duncan	Carol Rosenfeld
Tommy Jenkins	Sel Skolnick

A play performed without intermission. The action takes place at
the present time in New York City.

Stage Managers: Betsy Imershein, Anita Stark, Sol Rosenzweig

* Closed Dec. 25, 1977 after limited engagement of 12 performances.

CHELSEA THEATER CENTER

Opened Thursday, December 8, 1977.*
Podium Management Associates presents:

VOICES FROM THE PAST

Words and Music by Julian Arendt, Bertolt Brecht, Hanns Eisler,
Werner Finck, Robert Gilbert, Friedrich Hollaender, Kurt Tu-
cholsky, Kurt Weill, Frank Wedekind, Carl Zuchmayer, Walter
Mehring, Wolfgang Roth and unknowns; Musical Arranger, Mi-
chael S. Roth; Pianist, Alexandra Ivanoff; Accordionist, William
Schimmel; Drummer, Michael Zuckerman

CAST

Wolfgang Roth

A program of Berlin Theatre and Kabarett Songs from the Golden
'Twenties performed by Wolfgang Roth, and assisting artists.

Press: Susan Bloch, Sally Christiansen, Francis X. Tobin
Stage Manager: David Rosenberg

* Closed Dec. 18, 1977 after 8 performances.

Susan Cook Photo

Wolfgang Roth

ASTOR PLACE THEATRE
Opened Sunday, December 11, 1977.*
Lily Turner presents:

JOE MASIELL NOT AT THE PALACE

Director, James Coco; Choreography, Tod Jackson; Arranged and Conducted by Christopher Bankey; Lighting, James Nesbit Clark; Sets and Costumes, C. Tod Jackson; Assistant to Director, Jack Betts; Sound, George Jacobs; Hairstylist, Bruce Steier; Associate Choreographer, Dennis Michaelson

CAST

Joe Masiell
Debra Dickinson
Anita Ehrler
Gena Ramsel
Nancy Salis

MUSICAL NUMBERS: "When I'm Playin' the Palace," "Everything," "Two for the Road," "You and I," "The Lady Is a Tramp," "Io E' Te," "I Don't Want to Know," "In My Life," "We Were Young," "If You Like the Music," "Here's That Rainy Day," "Money, Money, Money," "This Funny World," "But the World Goes Round," "What Now My Love," "Who," "It will Be My Day," "Madeleine," "Crazy Melody," "Hey Poppa"

A musical program in two parts.

Press: Saul Richman
Stage Manager: James Nesbit Clark

* Closed Jan. 8, 1978 after a limited engagement of 24 performances.

Liz Lombardo Photos

Top Right: Nancy Salis, Joe Masiell, Debra Dickinson, Anita Ehrler, Gena Ramsel (also below)

Cavada Humphrey

VAN DAM THEATRE
December 11, 1977 - January 6, 1978 (12 performances)

HENRY'S DAUGHTER

A one-woman play about the first Queen Elizabeth of England, conceived and performed by: Cavada Humphrey

BARBARANN THEATRE RESTAURANT
Opened Wednesday, December 14, 1977.*
Barbara Beck and John Montgomery present:

IDENTITY
- and other crises -

Music and Lyrics, Ed Dixon; Director, John Montgomery; Music Director, Steven Blier; Costumes, Barbara Beck; Lighting, Michael Spellman; Assistant to Director, Jill Cook

CAST
Ed Dixon
Sigrid Heath

A musical revue.

* Closed Dec. 18, 1977 after a limited engagement of 6 performances.

Ed Dixon, Sigrid Heath
(Barbara Beck Photo)

LIBRARY & MUSEUM OF PERFORMING ARTS
Opened Monday, December 19, 1977.*
Stage Directors & Choreographers Workshop Foundation presents:

JUDY
A Garland of Songs

Created and Staged by Jeffery K. Neill; Musical Adaptation and Direction, Wendell Kindberg; Costumes and Props, Charles W. Roeder; Lighting, Denise Yaney; Producer, Lila Goodman; Piano, Wendell Kindberg; Percussions, James Erwin; Production Assistant, John Vought

CAST
Barbara Coggin
Lou Corato
Peter Marinos
Mary Lynne Metternich
Jacqueline Reilly
Standbys: Jane Portela, J. Douglas James

A "musical entertainment" performed in two parts.
Stage Managers: Denise Yaney, Lucille Miner

* Closed Dec. 21, 1977 after limited engagement of three performances.

Clifford Adams Photo

Wendell Kindberg, Lou Corato, Barbara Coggin, Jacqueline Reilly, Mary Lynne Metternich, Peter Marinos

CORNER LOFT THEATRE
Opened Tuesday, December 27, 1977.*
Ronnie Zolondek and Ora Fishman in association with Rob Anderson, Mary Ann Dreier, Debbie Oltchick, Susan Steele present:

A FINE SUMMER NIGHT

By Michael Shurtleff; Director, Mr. Shurtleff; Title Song by Hugo Napier; Production Consultant, Lee Pucklis; Production Coordinator, Nort Bramesco

CAST
Nicky .... Hugo Napier
Justine .... Anne Gerety
Clarinda .... Suzannah Knight
Charles .... James Congdon

A play in two acts and three scenes. The action takes place at the present time in Justine's duplex apartment, and on the deck of Justine's island home.
Press: Alan Eichler
Stage Managers: Tim Young, Mary Ann Dreier, Debbie Oltchick

* Closed Jan. 8, 1978 after limited engagement of 12 performances.

Hugo Napier, Anne Gerety, James Congdon, Suzannah Knight

COLONNADES THEATRE LAB

December 20, 1977–February 5, 1978 (32 performances)
(Moved January 10, 1978 to Chelsea Theater Center, and January 25, 1978 to Chelsea Westside Theater)
Chelsea Theater Center and the Colonnades Theatre Lab (Michael Lessac, Artistic Director) present:

OLD MAN JOSEPH AND HIS FAMILY

By Romulus Linney; Director, Robert Kalfin; Scenery and Costumes, Carrie F. Robbins; Lighting, Mark DiQuinzio; Music Composed by Ken Guilmartin; Production Manager, Sherman Warner; Technical Director, Thom Shovestull; Assistant to Director, Vic Stornant; Wardrobe Mistress, Rebecca Kreinen; Stage Managers, Arthur J. Schwartz, Katherine Parks; Press, Susan Bloch, Lester Gruner, Sally Christiansen, Francis X. Tobin

CAST

Nesbitt Blaisdell (Chamberlain/Clothdyer/Father of Groom), Jacqueline Cassel (Mary), Louis Giambalvo (Boy/Sheetspreader/-Zeno), Lou Gilbert (Joseph), Donna Haley (Midwife/Mother of Bride/Mother 2), Marcia Hyde (Bride/Mother 1/Old Woman), Peter Kingsley (High Priest/Beggar/Zeno's Father), Berit Lagerwall (Sad Lady/Zeno's Mother/Mother of Groom), Peter Scolari (Herald/Boy/Milo/Groom/Jesus), Charlie Stavola (Boy/Schoolmaster/Father of Bride)

A drama in two acts and ten scenes.

Martha Swope Photos

Left: Lou Gilbert

Jacqueline Cassel, Peter Scolari

Peter Scolari

ASTOR PLACE THEATRE
Opened Wednesday, January 18, 1978.*
Arthur Cantor presents:

MY ASTONISHING SELF

Devised by Michael Voysey from the writings of George Bernard
Shaw; Production Assistants, Thomas Madigan, Mary Beth Mann;
Wardrobe, Dubtex of Dublin

CAST

Donal Donnelly
as
George Bernard Shaw

An "entertainment" in two parts.

Company Manager: Laurel Ann Wilson
Press: C. George Willard, Bill Miller
Stage Manager: Larry Bussard

* Closed March 5, 1978 after 48 performances and 2 previews.

Donal Donnelly as George Bernard Shaw

CONVENT OF THE SACRED HEART
Saturday, February 11, 1978.*
Chesterfield Productions presents:

THE WAY OF THE WORLD

By William Congreve; Director, Cleveland Morris; Choreography, de Lappe/Miller; Costumes, Kenneth M. Yount; Lighting, Barry Andrew Kearsley; Hairstylist, Peg Schierholz; Musicians, The Apple Trio

CAST

Edward Mirabell	Peter DeLaurier
Fainall	Steven Ryan
Waitwell/Sir Rowland	Avrom Berel
Anthony Witwoud	David Boelke
Chauffeur	Dennis Thread
Petulant	William Wright
Mrs. Arabella Fainall	Beverly Shatto
Miss Marwood	Ceal Phelan
Miss Millamant	le Clanché du Rand
Mincing	Anne-Sojourner Wendell
Foible	Carolyn Olga Kruse
Lady Wishfort	Virginia Stevens
Sir Wilfull Witwoud	Peter Boyden

A comedy in five acts performed with one intermission. The action takes place in 1913.

Stage Managers: David Balsom, Peg Schierholz

* Presented for one performance only. No photos available.

Carolyn Olga Kruse   **William Wright**

Avrom Berel   **Beverly Shatto**
Below: Virginia Stevens   **Below: Peter Boyden**

le Clanche du Rand   **David Boelke**

Bruce Sherman, Laurie Lipson, Tony Michael Pann

PARK ROYAL CABARET THEATER
Opened Thursday, February 16, 1978.*
Park Royal Hotel Cabaret Theater presents:

JACQUES BREL IS ALIVE & WELL & LIVING IN PARIS

Production Conception, English Lyrics, Additional Material by Eric Blau, Mort Shuman; Music, Jacques Brel; Based on Brel's Lyrics and Commentary; Musical Director, Richard A. Schacher; Lighting, Sal Sclafani, Chuck Robbins; Production Assistant, Lorna Lable; Creative Consultant, Robert Duva

CAST

Annette Hanington	Bruce Sherman
Laurie Lipson	Tony Michael Pann

A musical revue in two acts.

Stage Manager: Jeane Bee Baretich

* Closed Feb. 18, 1978 after limited engagement of 4 performances.

THE THREE MUSES THEATER

Opened Thursday, February 16, 1978.*
K-H Productions presents:

THE CHANGELING

By Thomas Middleton and William Rowley; Director, Roberto Monticello; Assistant Director-Set Design, Lynn Osborne; Lighting, Scott Robbe; Costumes, Bob Harvey; Costume Master, Antonette Giammarinaro; Sound, Rob Holland

CAST

Warrington Winters (Vermandero), Frank J. Ragazzo (Tomazo de Piracquo), John Rowe (Alonzo de Piracquo/Jasperino), George Holmes (Alsemero), Robert Boyle (Alibius), Charles Fontana (Lollio), Kevin Simons (Pedro), David Silber (Antonio), Steve Prevosto (Franciscus), Antonino Pandolfo (De Flores), Tina Kay (Beatrice-Joanna), Sue Katz (Diaphanta), Georgia Harrell (Isabella), Madwomen: Kathy Helmer, Clare Marshall

A Jacobean revenge tragedy performed in two parts. The action takes place in Alicant in 1622.

Stage Manager: Shari Teitelbaum

* Closed March 5, 1978 after limited engagement of 12 performances.

Top Right: Charles Fontana, Georgia Harrell

DOUBLE IMAGE THEATRE

Opened Friday, February 17, 1978.*
Double Image Theatre presents:

INSUFFICIENT EVIDENCE

By Eleazar Lipsky; Director, Wayne Maxwell; Producer, Helen Waren Mayer; Scenery and Lighting, P. Charles Livermore; Costumes, Betty Sample; Wardrobe Mistress, Debbie McIntyre

CAST

Alston Campbell (Tom Fitch), Michael Arkin (Benjamin Kadinsky), Gene Ruffini (Louis D'Angelo), Richard Southern (Dan Mulvaney), Martha Nazzaro (Alice Kent), Sebastian Stuart (Vincent Ricca), V. Michael Rogers (Harry Purcell), Jack Betts (William Mahler), Kethy Hurley (Doris Flynn), Stan Pearlman (Sheldon Levine), Mark Corum (Joe Wilson), Gessy Lewis (Marie Verlaine), David Ellis (Frank Albany), Manquo (Max Sandoval), M. David Samples (Judge Cook)

A drama in 3 acts and 4 scenes performed with one intermission. The action takes place during 1950 in New York County Homocide Bureau, and the Supreme Court of New York.

Press: David Lipsky
Stage Manager: Dimas Caro

* Closed Feb. 26, 1978 after limited engagement of 9 performances.

Right Center: Martha Nazzaro, M. David Samples, Jack Betts

ACTOR'S PLAYHOUSE

Opened Saturday, March 4, 1978.*
Roy Doliner and Mort Kaplan present:

ZWI KANAR

in a program of mime in two parts. Associate Producer, Ellen N. Brown; Lighting and Sound, Gary Freiberger.

* Closed April 19, 1978 after 15 performances.

Zwi Kanar

THE PRIORY
Opened Wednesday, March 8, 1978.*
Dramacity presents:

PUTTING THEM TO PASTURE

By Vito Gentile, Jr.; Director, RB Naar; Scenery, Pat Plotkin; Costumes, Judity Couzens; Lighting, Larry Naar; Production Manager, Judity Couzens; Assistant Director, Jeff Rubien; Production Assistant, Connie Paragallo; Wardrobe Supervisor, Rena Mintern; Make-up, W. P. Dremack

CAST

ACT I: "Edith Hunt": Lacy J. Thomas (Edith), John Patrick Hart (Ronald), Caesar Carrillo (Tempo), Jon Evans (Butch), Stephen Kelsey (Bobby)

ACT II: "Adelle": Lawrence Cioppa (Tommy), Roy Thomas (Borsalino), Caesar Carrillo (Eddie), Lacy J. Thomas (Adelle), Harry Packwood (Hob Bowling)

ACT III: "Miss Margaret Slope": Lacy J. Thomas (Margaret), John Patrick Hart (J. J. Harwick), Harry Packwood (Frank), Lawrence Cioppa (John Spinner), Paul Espel (John Pratt)

Press: Faith Geer
Stage Manager: Rick Ellis

* Closed March 25, 1978 after limited engagement of 12 performances.

John Patrick Hart, Paul Espel, John Byron, Harry Packwood, Lacy J. Thomas (seated)

PROMENADE THEATRE
Opened Wednesday, March 22, 1978.*
(Moved May 26, 1978 to Circle in the Square/Downtown)
Haskell/Spiegel Productions present:

P. S. YOUR CAT IS DEAD!

By James Kirkwood; Director, Robert Nigrop; Set, Judie Juracek; Lighting, Michael Orris Watson; Costume Coordinator, Wendy Jane Witt; Wardrobe Supervisor, Carol Horne; Hairstylist, Antonio Vangi; Music Coordinator, Alan Eichler; Production Assistant, Mark H. Newman

CAST

Vito	Vasili Bogazianos
Kate	Joan Welles†1
Jimmy	Peter Simon†2
Fred	John Shearin†3

STANDBYS: John Shearin (Jimmy), Stephen Burleigh (Vito/Fred), Ruth Nerken (Kate)

A comedy in two acts and three scenes. The action takes place at the present time in Jimmy Zoole's loft apartment in New York City on New Year's Eve.

Company Manager: Terence Erkkila
Press: Henry Luhrman, Anne Obert Weinberg, Terry M. Lilly
Stage Managers: H. Todd Iveson, Stephen Burleigh

* Still playing May 31, 1978.
† Succeeded by: 1. Claire Malis, Erika Petersen, 2. Warren Burton, 3. David Deardorff

James Kirkwood (author), Claire Malis, John Shearin, Peter Simon, Vasili Bogazianos Above: Simon, Bogazianos

Center Right: John Shearin, Peter Simon, Claire Malis, Vasili Bogazianos

PLAYHOUSE THEATRE
Opened Thursday, March 23, 1978.*
Jeff Britton and Bob Bisaccia present:

A BISTRO CAR ON THE CNR

Music, Patrick Rose; Lyrics, Merv Campone, Richard Ouzounian; Dialogue, D. R. Andersen; Director, Richard Ouzounian; Choreography, Lynne Gannaway; Scenery and Costumes, John Falabella; Lighting, Ned Hallick; Musical Direction, John Clifton; Associate Producer, Jimmy Merrill; Production Assistants, Gary Britton, Michael Crouch; Assistant Musical Director, Robert Grusecki

CAST

Kathy	Marcia McClain
Ted	Patrick Rose
Jessica	Henrietta Valor
Dan	Tom Wopat

MUSICAL NUMBERS: "C.N.R.," "25 Miles," "Guitarist," "Passing By," "Madame La Chanson," "Oh God I'm 30," "Ready or Not," "Sudden Death Overtime," "Bring Back Swing," "Yesterday's Lover," "Four Part Invention," "Nocturne," "La Belle Province," "Ensemble," "Dewey and Sal," "Here I Am Again," "Street Music," "Other People's Houses," "Genuine Grade A Canadian Superstar," "I Don't Live Anywhere Anymore," "The Lady Who Loved to Sing," "Somebody Write Me a Love Song," Finale

A "musical journey" in two acts. The action takes place in a Bistro Car (converted baggage car) on the "Rapido" on its final trip from Toronto to Montreal, Canada.

General Manager: Jeff Britton
Press: Gifford/Wallace, Inc.
Stage Manager: Craig Saeger

* Closed May 14, 1978 after 82 performances.

Laura Pettibone Photos

Right: Tom Wopat, Marcia McClain
Top: Patrick Rose

Pierre Epstein   **Estelle Omens**

VAN DAM THEATRE
Opened Monday, April 3, 1978.*
The Shelter West Company, Inc. presents:

THE BRIGHT AND GOLDEN LAND

By Harry Granick; Director, Len Gochman; Set, James Conway, Michael Holm; Lighting, Lee Amon; Original Music Composed and Performed by David Freedman; Production Coordinator, Marita Lindholm-Gochman; Assistant Director, Ed Rubin; Choreographer, Janis Roswick; Costumes, Susan Segal

CAST

Harry	Chip Zien
Pop	Pierre Epstein
Mom	Estelle Omens
Grandfather/Principal/Joe	Reuben Schafer
Bernie/Rivera	Stephen Mark Weyte
Clara	Darlene Wasko

A comedy-drama in two acts. The action takes place in "the attic of the author's mind."

Press: Max Eisen
Stage Managers: Nancy Ulrich, Susan K. Sternkopf

* Closed Apr. 16, 1978 after 13 performances.

HAVEMEYER LAB/COLUMBIA UNIVERSITY

Opened Wednesday, April 5, 1978.*
Columbia University School of the Arts and The New York Actors' Theater (Laurence Luckinbill, Robin Strasser, Rudy Caringi, Artistic Directors) in association with Penney and Ron Dante, Ilse and Henry Wolf present:

THE LIFE OF GALILEO

By Bertolt Brecht; Translated by Ralph Mannheim and Wolfgang Sauerlander; Director, Rudy Caringi; Sets and Lights, James Tilton; Costumes, Ursula Belden, Elizabeth P. Palmer; Music Composed and Performed by Howard Harris; Technical Director, Robert G. Adams; Producers, Robin Strasser, Andrew Harris; Production Coordinator, John P. Fleming; Assistant to Director, Aaltje Zeilstra; Production Supervisor, Michele Rudnick; Wardrobe Mistress, Ariela Heilman

CAST

Laurence Luckinbill (Galileo Galilei), Jack Magee (Andrea Sarti), Mary Carver (Mrs. Sarti), Michael O'Hare (Ludovico Marsili), Joseph Davidson (Priuli/Old Cardinal), Richard Zavaglia (Sagredo/-Father Clavius/Vanni/Filippo Mucius), Frances James (Virginia), Laurence Attile (Senator/Mathematician/Soldier/Monk/Secretary), Alexander Wells (Senator/Secretary/Peasant), Henry Grossman (Doge/Lord Chamberlain/Gaffone/Ballad Singer), Joel Charap (Grand Duke Cosmo de Medici/Lackey/Monk/Child), Robert Mont (Federzoni), Bernie McInerney (Philosopher/Cardinal Bellarmine/Official/Guard), Samantha Laine (Nun/Balad Singer's Wife), Lillian Jenkins (Woman/Child), Rudy Caringi (Little Monk), Gil Rogers (Cardinal Inquisitor/Clerk), Peter White (Cardinal Barberini, later Pope Urban VIII), Bob Gale (Chalktalker)

A drama in two acts.

Press: Bob Ullman
Stage Manager: Fredric H. Orner

* Closed Apr. 23, 1978 after limited engagement of 20 performances and 7 previews.

Henry Gorssman Photos

Right: Laurence Luckinbill
Top: Jack Magee, Laurence Luckinbill

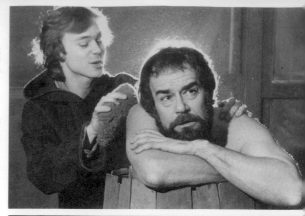

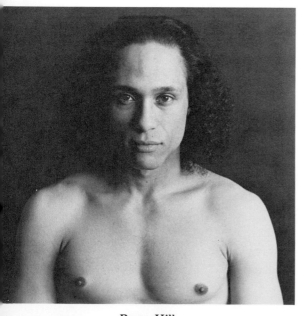

Roger Hill

EVERYMAN THEATRE

Opened Thursday, April 6, 1978.*
The Everyman Company (Geraldine Fitzgerald, Jonathan Ringkamp, Artistic Directors) presents:

HAMLET

By William Shakespeare; Adapted by Geraldine Fitzgerald; Director, Charles Maryan; Choreographer, Chuck Davis; Composer-Music Director, Ron Love; Set, Bil Mikulewicz; Costumes, Badu Onyamache; Lighting, Larry Von Werssowetz; Combat Choreography, A. C. Weary; Sound, Tony Hawkins; Special Adviser, Alan Eichler; Special Consultant, Gabriel Akomolafe; Executive Director, Dolores F. Cregan; Program Coordinator, Ruth Keating; Producers, Hazel Bryant, Peggy Cooper, Dolores F. Cregan, Geraldine Fitzgerald, Jonathan Ringkamp, Mical Whitaker

CAST

Ellis "Skeeter" Williams (Bernardo), Wayne Anthony (Francisco), Ken Threet (Marcellus), Skipper Driscoll (Horatio), Maurice Woods (Ghost/Claudius), Jay Fernandez (Laertes), Bob Lawrence (Polonius), Roger Hill (Hamlet), Yolande Bavan (Gertrude), Jodi Long (Ophelia), Wayne Anthony (Osric), Bill Ferguson (Rosencrantz), Kenneth L. Johnson (Guildenstern), Tazewell Thompson (Player King), Sharon Mackenzie (Player Queen), Kendell Lide (Lucianus), Michele Bonaparte (Lady Player), Gene Harvey (Undertaker), Rogelio Baptiste (Priest), Gisele Richardson (Stranger)

The action takes place at the present time in Elsinor, a small kingdom in West Africa.

Press: Alan Eichler
Stage Managers: Kathleen Phelan, Cheryl Green, Robin Cletis Holder

* Closed Apr. 16, 1978 after limited engagement of 12 performances.

Ron Lieberman Photo

PUERTO RICAN TRAVELING THEATRE
April 11–29, 1978 (18 performances)
The Puerto Rican Traveling Theatre presents the World Premiere of:

THE FM SAFE

By Jaime Carrero; Director, Alba Oms; Set, Robert F. Strohmeier; Lighting, Larry Johnson; Costumes, Maria Ferreira; Administrator, Gary S. Levine; Producer, Miriam Colon; Technical Director, Tim Galvin; Props and Costume Mistress, Wendy Dean; Sound, Phillip Campanella; Stage Manager, Ron Cappa; Press, Alan Eichler

CAST

Vidal . . . . Luis Avalos
Marcelina . . . . Miriam Colon
Professor . . . . Norberto Kerner
Radio II . . . . Jaime Tirelli
Fernando . . . . Freddy Valle
Radio I . . . . Chino Vega

A drama in two acts. Presented in bi-lingual performances.

Miriam Colon, Luis Avalos, Norberto Kerner
Below: Freddy Valle, Chino Vega, Ray Muniz,
Miriam Colon

ASTOR PLACE THEATRE
Opened Wednesday, April 12, 1978.*
Honey Waldman presents:

FAMILY BUSINESS

By Dick Goldberg; Director, John Stix; Scenery, Don Jensen; Lighting, Todd Elmer; Hairstylist, Michael Holland; Production Assistant, Marybeth Mann

CAST

Isaiah Stein . . . . Harold Gary
Jerry Stein . . . . Joel Polis
Norman Stein . . . . David Garfield†
Bobby Stein . . . . Richard Greene
Phil Stein . . . . David Rosenbaum
Young Man . . . . Richard Levine

A drama in three acts. The action takes place in late autumn of 1974 in the main room of Isaiah Stein's home in Beverly, Massachusetts.

General Manager: Lily Turner
Press: Saul Richman, Betty Lee Hunt, Maria Pucci
Stage Manager: Richard Delahanty

* Still playing May 31, 1978.
† Succeeded by David Kagen

Harold Gary, Joel Polis, David Garfield
Above: Richard Greene, Joel Polis

CENTURY THEATRE

Opened Thursday, April 13, 1978.*
Milton Justice in association with Ken Cohen presents:

PATIO/PORCH

By Jack Heifner; Director, Garland Wright; Scenery, John Arnone; Costumes, David James; Lighting, Marc B. Weiss

CAST

Jewel/Lucille .... Ronnie Claire Edwards
Pearl/Dot .... Fannie Flagg
Standby: Tanny McDonald

Two one-act plays ("Patio," "Porch") that take place in a small Texas town.

General Manager: Albert Poland
Press: Merlin Group, Patt Dale, Beatrice Da Silva, Glen Gary
Stage Managers: Lani Ball, Clint Spencer

* Closed Apr. 30, 1978 after 21 performances.

Jack Mitchell Photo

Right: Fannie Flagg, Ronnie Claire Edwards

Divine

HURRAH THEATRE

Opened Sunday, April 16, 1978.*
Bruce Mailman and Ina Meibach Minkin present:

THE NEON WOMAN

By Tom Eyen; Director, Ron Link; Set and Graphics, Herbert Nagle; Lighting, Jack Ranson; Costumes and Make-up, Van Smith; Production Assistant, Jay Bennett

CAST

Maria Duval (Joni), Sweet William Edgar (Kitty LaRue), George Patterson (Speed Gonzalez), William Duff-Griffin (Willy/Senator), Debra Greenfield (Rita), Helen Hanft (Connie), Brenda Bergman (Kim), Lee Corbet (D.A.), Divine (Flash Storm), Hope Stansbury (Laura), Understudies: Jeffrey Herman, Suzanne Smith

"A burlesque" performed without intermission. The action takes place from Jan. 1, 1960 through Nov. 21, 1963 in the Club Neon Woman in Baltimore, Md.

Company Manager: Robert H. Wallner
Press: Alan Eichler, Henry Schissler
Stage Managers: Jack Kalman, Paul Schneeberger

* Closed July 16, 1978 after 92 performances.

Roxanne Lowit Photos

Above: Hope Stansbury, Helen Hanft, George Patterson

ENTERMEDIA THEATRE
Opened Monday, April 17, 1978.*
Universal Pictures presents:

THE BEST LITTLE WHOREHOUSE IN TEXAS

Book, Larry L. King, Peter Masterson; Music and Lyrics, Carol Hall; Directed by Peter Masterson and Tommy Tune; Musical Numbers Staged by Tommy Tune; Costumes, Ann Roth; Sets, Marjorie Kellogg; Lighting, Dennis Parichy; Musical Direction and Vocal Arrangements, Robert Billig; Hairstylist, Michael Gottfried; Sound, John Venable; Associate Choreographer, Thommie Walsh; Musicians, Rio Grande Band; Technical Supervisor, Ronald B. Lindholm; Assistant to Director, Janie Rosenthal; Wardrobe Supervisor, Barbara Steely

CAST

Clint Allmon (Farmer/Melvin P. Thorpe), Pamela Blair (Amber), Lisa Brown (Girl/Dawn/Angelette Imogene Charlene), Cameron Burke† (Slick Dude/Soundman/Ukranian Placekicker/Aggie 1), Gerry Burkhardt (Shy Kid/Dogette/Aggie 7), Jay Bursky (Cowboy/Choirmember/Dogette/Aggie 11/Photographer/Governor's Aide), Tom Cashin (Stage Manager/Camerman/Aggie 12/Specialty Dance), Carol Chambers (Girl/Taddy Jo/Townsperson/Angelette), Don Crabtree (Cokeman/Edsel Mackey), Joan Ellis (Shy), Henderson Forsythe (Sheriff Ed Earl Dodd), Jay Garner (Traveling Salesman/Scruggs/TV Colorman/Governor), Becky Gelke (Choirmember/Jewel), Bradley Clayton King (Cowboy/Leroy Sliney/Melvin Thorpe Singer/Townsperson/Aggie 77), Donna King (Girl/Linda Lou/Angelette), Larry L. King (TV Announcer), J. Frank Lucas (Mayor Rufus Poindexter/Senator Wingwoah), Susan Mansur (Girl/Melvin Thorpe Singer/Doatsey Mae/Reporter 1), Jan Merchant (Choirmember/Beatrice/Melvin Thorpe Singer/Angelette), Edna Milton (Miss Wulla Jean/Townsperson), Louise Quick-Bowen (Girl/Ginger), James Rich (Choirmember/Melvin Thorpe Singer/Townsperson/Photographer/Aggie 17), Marta Sanders (Choirmember/Eloise/Melvin Thorpe Singer/Townsperson), Michael Scott (Cowboy/Dogette/Aggie 71/Photographer/Reporter 3), Paul Ukena, Jr. (Cowboy/Photographer/Dogette/Aggie 21/Reporter 2), Debra Zalkind (Girl/Durla/Angelette), Rio Grande Band: Craig Chambers, Pete Blue, Ben Brogdon, Lynn Frazier, Chris Laird, Ernie Reed

MUSICAL NUMBERS: Prologue, "20 Fans," "A Lil' Ole Bitty Pissant Country Place," "Girl You're a Woman," "Watch Dog Theme," "Texas Has a Whorehouse in It," "24 Hours of Lovin'," "Doatsey Mae," "Angelette March," "The Aggie Song," "Bus from Amarillo," "The Sidestep," "No Lies," "Good Old Girl," "Hard Candy Christmas," Finale

A musical comedy in two acts. The action takes place in the State of Texas

General Management: Jack Schlissel/Jay Kingwill
Company Manager: Steven Suskin
Press: Jeffrey Richards, Maurice Turet, Bruce Lynn, Jeanna Gallo
Stage Managers: Paul J. Phillips, Jay Schlossberg-Cohen

* Closed June 11, 1978 after 85 performances to move to Broadway.
† Succeeded by K. C. Kelly

Ilene Jones Photos

Top Right: Joan Ellis, Debra Zalkind, Jan Merchant, Carlin Glynn, Pamela Blair, Louise Quick Below: Jay Garner, Clint Allmon, J. Frank Lucas Center Right: Delores Hall, Henderson Forsythe, Carlin Glynn

DOWNSTAIRS AT CITY CENTER
Opened Friday, April 28, 1978.*
Jerry B. Livengood presents:

THE CLASS

Conceived, Directed and Choreographed by Jack Johnson; Original Music, Andrew Asch; Settings, Lighting, Multi-Media Effects, John Hawkins; Assistant to Choreographer, Gloria Szymkowicz; Photo Sequences, David Bruce Cratsley; Costumes, Gloria Szymkowicz; Assistant to Producer, Roper R. Christopher

CAST

Rico Costa (Mark)	Robert Raimondo (Bob)
Gisele Ferrari (Bobbie)	Charles C. Sheek (Joe)
Debra Lynn Jones (Heather)	Gloria Szymkowicz (Leslie)
Donna McEntee (Sally)	Whitney Wiemer (Ann)

MUSICAL NUMBERS: "Warm-Up Ballet," "Ann's Fantasy," "Joe's Fantasy," "Heather's Fantasy," "Leslie's Fantasy of Men's Combination," "Supported Adagio," "Leslie's Fantasy of Women's Combination," "Love Duet," "Bob's Fantasy," "Mark's Fantasy," "Leslie's Dance," Finale

A ballet musical in two acts.

Press: Susan Bloch, Francis X. Tobin, Sally Christiansen
Stage Managers: William Schill, Richard Vos

* Closed Apr. 30, 1978 after 4 performances.

Laura Pettibone Photo

Left: Robert Raimondo, Debra Lynn Jones, Donna McEntee, Gisele Ferrari, Rico Costa, Whitney Wiemer

ACTORS PLAYHOUSE
Opened Wednesday, May 3, 1978.*
The Proposition Workshop, Inc. presents:

THE PROPOSITION

Conceived and Directed by Allan Albert; Musical Direction, Robert Hirschhorn, John Lewis, Donald Sosin; Lighting, Dick Williams; Managing Director, Carol Lawhon

CAST

Raymond Baker	Anne Cohen
Timothy Hall	Deborah Reagan
Standby: Shelley Barre	

An improvisational music revue.

General Manager: Richard Seader
Press: Howard Rogut, Helene Greece, Marshall Ballou
Stage Manager: Matthew Cohen

* Closed May 21, 1978 after 24 performances. No photos available.

AMERICAN PLACE THEATRE
Opened Thursday, May 4, 1978.*
Larry Berle by arrangement with SRO Productions presents:

MICHAEL HENNESSY
with
Dan Blegen
Eric Sayer

in an evening of mine and music presented in two parts; Lighting, Michael Pettee; General Management, Robert Brannigan, Charles Eisler; Management Associate, Robert Lorelli

Company Manager: Robert Brannigan
Press: Judy Jacksina, Glenna Freedman
Stage Manager: Michael Pettee

* Closed May 7, 1978 after 6 performances and 2 previews.

Michael Hennessy(C) with Blegen and Sayer

WESTBETH THEATRE CENTER
May 4–21, 1978 (12 performances)
Michael Shepley presents:

FUNERAL MARCH FOR A ONE-MAN BAND

By Ron Whyte; Conceived in collaboration with H. Thomas Moore; Director, Leonard Peters; Music, Mel Marvin; Lyrics, Robert Satuloff; Set, Salvatore Tagliarino; Costumes, Carol Oditz; Lights, Paul Gallo; Musical Director, John McKinney: General Manager; Coral Hawthorne; Technical Director, Samuel Gonzalez; Stage Managers, Laurence Rothenberg, Harold Apter; Press, Ellen Levene, Tom Trenkle.

CAST

Michael	Dwight Schultz
Mr. Chrisolde/Dad	Thomas Toner
Headnurse/Mom	June Squibb
Tiny/Jamie	Rob Derosa
Mike	Dennis Boutsikaris
Joanna	Ellen Barber

A play in two acts. The action takes place at the present time in a hospital room in New York City.

Top Right: Dwight Schultz, Ellen Barber

ST. CLEMENT'S THEATRE
May 10–21, 1978 (12 performances)

ROSA

Book and Lyrics, William Archibald, Based on play by Brenda Forbes; Music, Baldwin Bergersen; Director, Patricia Carmichael; Set, Daniel Thomas Field; Lighting, Curt Ostermann, Costumes, Danny Morgan; Choreography, Roger Preston-Smith; Musical Director, Robert Colston; Music Arranged by Robert Goldstone; Producer, Wendell Minnick; Associate Producer, Phillip Moser; Assistant to Producer, Nora A. Larke; Stage Managers, April Adams, Bill McComb; Production Assistants, Bernard Ferstenberg, Mariann Lewandowski, Penny Morgan; Press, Warren Knowlton

CAST

John Deyle (Dad/Fishmonger/His Grace), Jill Harwood (Maid/Mrs. Guernsey), Ted Houck (Footman/Chef/Bert), Nancy Lipner (Elsie), Everett McGill (Riverton), Donald C. Moore (Edward Prince of Wales), Marnie Mosiman (Maid/Understudy), Kathleen Swan (Maid), Elizabeth Torgersen (Housekeeper/Maid), Steve Vinovich (Henry), Betty Wragge (Mrs. Fricker), Victoria Wyndham (Rosa)

MUSICAL NUMBERS: "Rosa," "Be Kind to the Young," "Time Goes Faster," "The Herb Song," "I Am Royal," "A Place of My Own," "Fame," "Perfection," "Where's My Love A'Wonderin'," "Let Us Charm Each Other," "Fish Soup Song," "Peace Celebration," "From the Bottom of the Sea," "Oh, How We Love You, Mrs. Cornwall," "Dear Friend," "Before It's Too Late."

Ken Howard Photos

Everett McGill, Victoria Wyndham
Right Center: Victoria Wyndham, Donald C. Moore

THEATRE FOUR
Opened Wednesday, May 17, 1978.*
Arthur Cantor by arrangement with Paddington Press Ltd.,
Norman Fenton and Jon Blair presents;

THE BIKO INQUEST

Written and Directed by Norman Fenton and Jon Blair; Prologue,
Donald and Wendy Woods; Sets, Eric Head; Costumes, Patricia
McGourty; Lighting, Clyde Kuemmerle; Production Manager,
Christopher Kelly; Wardrobe Supervisor, Sandra Lee Cottone; Pro-
duction Assistants, Vivien Lind, Thomas C. Madigan, Bruce Peyton

CAST

Mr. Sidney Kentridge	Fritz Weaver
Mr. Martinus Prins	David Gale
Mr. Jan van Rensburg	Bill Moor
Colonel Pieter Goosen	Philip Bosco
Major Harold Snyman	Jess Osuna
Lieutenant Eric Wilken	John Vennema
Prof. Johann David Loubser	James Cook
Prof. Proctor	William Myers
Dr. Ivor Lang	Martin Shakar
Dr. Benjamin Tucker	Carl Low
Dr. Colin Hersch	Jonathan Moore

UNDERSTUDIES: David Gale (Kentridge/Goosen), William Myers (Prins/Tucker), Martin Shakar (Van Rensburg/Snyman),
Charles Helsley (Loubser/Proctor/Hersch), James Cook (Lang)

A drama in two acts. The action takes place in the Old Synagogue
in Pretoria, South Africa, now used as a court room where the
inquest into the death of Stephen Bantu Biko was held from November 14 to December 2, 1977.

Company Manager: Arthur Cantor
Press: C. George Willard
Stage Managers: Christopher Kelly, Charles Helsley

* Closed June 11, 1978 after 31 performances and 6 previews.

Elaine Kirsh Photos

Top Right: Bill Moor, Fritz Weaver, David Gale
Right: Fritz Weaver, Philip Bosco

Fritz Weaver, Jonathan Moore, William Myers, James Cook, David Gale, Martin
Shakar, Carl Low, Jess Osuna, Philip Bosco, John Vennema

Front: Lou Corato, Brian Watson, Eleanor
Reissa Back: David Schall, Beverly Wideman,
Howard Hagan, Geraldine Hanning

INTAR THEATRE
May 19–June 25, 1978 (24 performances)
Intar Hispanic Theatre presents:

CARMENCITA

By Manuel Martin, Jr.; Music, Georges Bizet; Arranged by Cole-
ridge T. Perkinson; Original Score, Tania Leon; Director, Manuel
Martin, Jr.; Choreography, Martial Roumain; Scenery, Sally Locke;
Lighting, Jenny Ball; Costumes, Manuel Yesckas; Musical Director,
Tania Leon; Vocal Director, Angela Bofill; Assistant Director, Mar-
tial Roumain; Assistant Choreographer, Marshall Blake; Production
Manager, John Monge; Artistic Director, Max Ferra; Executive
Director, Lourdes Casal; Production Manager, John Monge; Press,
Howard Atlee, Santiago Pollarsky

CAST

Marshall Blake, Giovanni Cotto, Brenda Feliciano, Carole Garcia,
Felipe Gorostiza, Joey Infante, Adriane Maura, Rosane Michele,
Lorena Palacios, Carmen Rosario, Liz Rosner, Miguel Sierra, Ray-
mond Taylor, Walter Valentino

Carol Lynn Rosegg Photo

Diane Tarleton, Harvey Fierstein

THE CUBICULO
May 12–28, 1978 (12 performances)
Sally E. Parry presents:

REUNION

Book and Lyrics, Melvin H. Freedman, Robert Kornfeld; Music,
Ron Roullier; Additional Songs, Carly Simon, Lucy Simon; Direction and Choreography, Jeffery K. Neill; Sets, Dale Engle; Costumes, Chas W. Roeder; Lighting, Christopher Peabody; Stage
Managers, John Vought, Peter Paulino; Press, Susan L. Schulman

CAST

Wendell Kindberg (Piano), Peter Rivera (Drummer), Lou Corato
(John Donnelly), Eleanor Reissa (Sue Wolczek), Beverly Wideman
(Roseann Campbell), David Schall (David Lerman), Geraldine Han-
ning (Cynthia Parker), Howard Hagan (Kevin Donnelly), Brian
Watson (Avery McGraw)

MUSICAL NUMBERS: "Today," "I'm All It Takes to Make You
Happy," "Young Dreams," "A World I'll Make for Me," "Child-
hood," "Golden Days," "Got to Sing Me a Song," "Reunion," "I'm
Gonna Make It," "That Moment Is Now," "Give Me Love," "All
My Yesterdays," "The Great Wind"

A play with music in two acts. The action takes place in the spring
of 1978 in the Student/Faculty Lounge off the main hallway to the
auditorium on the third day of rehearsal for the reunion show.

Brenda Feliciano, Felipe Gorostiza,
Walter Valentine

PLAYERS THEATRE
Opened Monday, May 22, 1978.*
Players Theatre presents:

INTERNATIONAL STUD

By Harvey Fierstein; Director, Eric Concklin; Costumes, Mardi
Philips; Lighting, Joanna Schielke; Musical Direction and Arrangements, Ned Levy; Sound, George Jacobs

CAST

Piano Man	Ned Levy
Lady Blues	Diane Tarleton
Arnold	Harvey Fierstein
Ed	Richard Dow†

A play in five scenes, performed without intermission. The action
takes place at the present time in a night-club dressing room, the
Stud Bar, Arnold and Ed's apartment.

Press: Jeffrey Richards, Bruce Lynn, Maurice Turet, Jeanna
Gallo
Stage Managers: Lee Evans, Ned Levy

* Still playing May 31, 1978.
† Succeeded by Paul Falzone

PROMENADE THEATRE
Opened Tuesday May 30, 1978.*

Eugene V. Wolsk and Frank Milton present the Manhattan Theatre Club/New York Shakespeare Festival production of:

CATSPLAY

By Istvan Orkeny; Translated by Clara Gyorgyey; Director, Lynne Meadow; Setting, John Lee Beatty; Costumes, Jennifer von Mayrhauser; Lighting, Dennis Parichy; Music, Robert Dennis; Sound, Chuck London; Dramaturge, Andy Wolk; Wardrobe Supervisor, Pat Saphier; Production Assistants, Rosemary Gant, Cheryl Raab, Richard Goodwin, P'nenah Goldstein

CAST

Mrs. Bela Orban	Helen Burns
Giza	Katherine Squire
Paula Krausz	Jane Cronin
Yanos	Charles Mayer
Mrs. Mihaly Almasi	Bette Henritze
Ilona	Susan Sharkey†1
Yoshka	Peter Phillips†2
Victor Vivelli	Robert Gerringer†3
Madame Adelaida Vivelli	Eleanor Phelps†4

A comedy in two acts. The action takes place in the mid-1960's between correspondents Mrs. Bela Orban in Budapest, Hungary, and her sister Giza in Bavaria, Germany.

Manager; Manny Kladitis
Press; Susan L. Schulman
Stage Managers: David S. Rosenak, J. E. Andrews

* Still playing May 31, 1978.
† Succeeded by: 1. Sherry Steiner, 2. Paul Schierhorn, Brad O'Hare, 3. I. M. Hobson, Owen S. Rachleff, 4. Virginia Stevens

Gerry Goodstein Photos

Right: Bette Henritze, Helen Burns
Top: Helen Burns, Jane Cronin

Esther Marrow, Chuck Patterson

HENRY STREET PLAYHOUSE
Opened Wednesday, May 31, 1978.*

Carousel Group, Inc. and Lucy Productions Corp. present:

MAHALIA

Book and Lyrics, Don Evans; Based on "Just Mahalia Baby" by Laurraine Goreau; Original Music, John Lewis; Musical Director, Luther Henderson; Director, Oz Scott; Choreography, Mabel Robinson; Vocal and Choral Arrangements, Brenda Fountain Saunders; Settings, Richard Williams; Costumes, Beverly Parks; Lighting, Victor En Yu Tan; Assistant Choreographer, Ted Williams

CAST

Nat Adderly (Red Beans), Bardell Conner (Choir), Lee Cooper (Choir/Mabel Green), Loretta Devine (Choir), Frances Foster (Aunt Duke/Potion Lady), Andrew Frierson, Fred Gripper (Choir), Edna Goode (Nightclub Inhabitant), William Hardy, Jr. (Brother Maxwell), Lola Holman (Young Mahalia), Esther Marrow (Mahalia), Gayle McKinney (Congregation), Roscoe Orman (Ike Hockinhull), Chuck Patterson (Minters Galloway), Al Perryman (Choir), Otis Sallid (Chafalaya), Rosemary Thompson (Choir), Jimmy Weaver (Nightclub Inhabitant)

MUSICAL NUMBERS: "Great Gettin Up Morning," "When I've Done the Best I Can," "Home Folks," "That's Enough," "Didn't It Rain," "Chi Town Strut," "Gimme a Pigfoot an a Bottle of Beer," "Leaning on the Everlasting Arms," "Chafalaya's Ballet," "Amazin Grace," "Didn't He Ramble," "Higher Ground," "Time to Think of Myself," "Mardi Gras in Chicago," "Take My Hand, Precious Lord," "Move On Up a Little Higher," "Peace," "Blues for Minnis," "His Eye Is on the Sparrow," "Minnis in Eros," Finale

A musical in two acts based on the life of Mahalia Jackson.

General Managers: Liz McCann, Nel Nugent
Press: Howard Atlee, Brent Jennings
Stage Managers: Sharon Brown Levy, Lynn Pannell

* Closed June 11, 1978 after 14 performances.

THE ACTORS STUDIO

Lee Strasberg, Artistic Director
Ellen Chenowith, Studio Coordinator

ACTORS STUDIO
Thursday, June 2–14, 1977 (12 performances)
The Actors Studio presents:

RICHARD THE THIRD

By William Shakespeare; Director, Arthur Sherman; Scenic Design, John Jackson; Costumes, Jane Trapnell; Lighting, Greg Marriner; Music, George Quincy; Executive Producer, Carl Schaeffer; Producer, Deedee Wehle; Associate Director, Carmine Pontilena; Technical Director, John Richmond; Production Assistant, Lauren Barnes; Stage Managers, Michael Wright, J. Michael LaCourse, Paul Lambert

CAST

Ron Leibman, (Duke of Glouster, later Richard), John Sillings (Clarence), Howard Meadow (Brakenbury), Martin Shaker (Hastings), Irma Sandrey (Lady Anne), Janet Ward (Queen Elizabeth), David Tabor (Rivers), Paul Lambert (Dorset), Michael Wager (Buckingham), Anthony Cannon (Stanley), Joan Copeland (Queen Margaret), David Gideon (Catesby), Philip Oxnam (Murderer), Geoffrey Horne (Edward IV), Gary Godiford (Ratcliffe), Elaine Aiken (Duchess of York), Sam Coppola (Bishop), Dylan Harris (Duke of York), Gavin Harris (Prince of Wales), Dan Davin (Lord Mayor), David Westfall (Duke of Norfolk), John Uecker (Tyrell), Philip Oxnam (Richmond), Linda Hamilton (Young Elizabeth), David Hirson (Young George Stanley), Guards: Tom Badal, Tom Ferriter, Charles Prior, Joseph Rinaldo, Tom Wright

A tragedy performed in two parts.

Ron Leibman as Richard III

ACTORS STUDIO
Thursday, October 20–November 6, 1977 (12 performances)
The Actors Studio presents:

THE BEST LITTLE WHOREHOUSE IN TEXAS

Book, Larry L. King, Peter Masterson; Music and Lyrics, Carol Hall; Director, Peter Masterson; Choreographer-Assistant Director, Christopher "Spider" Duncan; Musical Director, George Schneider; Costumes, Jane Trapnell; Lighting, Jay Cohen; Scenery, Kurt Lundell; Executive Producer, Carl Schaeffer; Producer, Jay Cohen; Assistant Producers, Teri Owen, Janie Rosenthal; Stage Managers, Michael Wright, Patricia Saphier, Suzanne Adams. Sarah Jane Smith, Jo Ann Friedman

CAST

Clint Allmon, Barbara Burge, Jan Buttram, Eric Cowley, Christopher Duncan, Joan Ellis, Henderson Forsythe, Tex Gibbons, Gayle Green, Jane Ives, Mallory Jones, John Kegley, K. C. Kelly, Liz Kemp, Brad King, Larry L. King, Thom Kuhl, Susan Mansur, Carlin Glynn, Jay McCormack, Marcie Mullar, J. J. Quinn, Pamela Reed, Elaine Rinehart, Gil Rogers, Marta Sanders, Ed Setrakian, Elliott Swift

For musical numbers see page 85.

Susan Spelman Photo

Seated: Carlin Glynn, Elizabeth Kemp,
Standing: Elaine Rinehart, Mallory Jones, Pamela Reed

ACTORS STUDIO
Monday, January 23–February 12, 1978 (12 performances)
The Actors Studio presents:

ALFRED THE GREAT

Part One of "The Wakefield Trilogy" by Israel Horovitz; Director, Ben Levit; Scenery, Paul Eads; Costumes, Jennifer von Mayrhauser; Lighting, Ann Wrightson; Executive Producer, Carl Schaeffer; Producers, Jay Cohen, Janie Rosenthal; Technical Director, Thomas D. Warren; Production Associates, Arthur Karp, Peter Hackett; Assistant Producer, Diane Peepas; Assistant to Director, Maria Wynn; Stage Managers, Michael Wright, Tess McKeown, Denise Lute

CAST

Alfred	Michael Moriarty
Margaret	Jill O'Hara
Will	Paul Gleason
Emily	Lois Markle

A play in three acts. The action takes place at the present time in the living room of Will and Margaret's home in Wakefield, Massachusetts, at the start of fall.

Sunday, January 29–February 12, 1978 (12 performances)

Susan Spelman Photo

Right: Michael Moriarty, Paul Gleason, Jill O'Hara

OUR FATHER'S FAILING

Part Two of "The Wakefield Trilogy" by Israel Horovitz; Director, Ben Levit

CAST

Sam	Dominic Chianese
Pa	Sully Boyar
Alfred	Michael Moriarty
Emily	Lois Markle

A play in three acts. The action takes place at the end of fall in the back yard of an old folks asylum in Wakefield, Massachusetts, and in the living room of Alfred's home.

Sunday, February 19, 1978. (2 performances)

ALFRED DIES

Part Three of "The Wakefield Trilogy" by Israel Horovitz; Director, Ben Levit

CAST

Alfred	Michael Moriarty
Lynch	Dominic Chianese
Emily	Joanna Miles
Roxy	Madeleine Thornton-Sherwood

A drama in three acts. The action takes place at the end of June and beginning of July in a storage room under the bandstand at the Commons in Wakefield, Mass.

Susan Spelman Photo

Dominic Chianese, Sully Boyar

AMERICAN PLACE THEATRE

Wynn Handman, Director
Julia Miles, Associate Director
Fourteenth Season

AMERICAN PLACE THEATRE
October 16–30, 1977 (27 performances)

COCKFIGHT

By Elaine Jackson; Director, Woodie King, Jr.; Set, C. Richard Mills; Costumes, Ruth Morley; Lighting, Edward M. Greenberg; Administrative Assistants, Gayle Austin, Ellen Ephron; Technical Director, Craig Evans; Costume Mistress, Tommy Rowland; Stage Managers, Nancy Harrington, Jeffrey Richards, Bruce Lynn

CAST

Mary Alice (Reba), Morgan Freeman (Sampson), Charles Brown (Carl), Gylan Kain (Jesse), Cynthia McPherson (Claudia), George Lee Miles (Understudy)

A play in two acts and four scenes. The action takes place in the mid-1970's on a converted farm in the Bay Area near San Francisco, California

Martha Holmes Photos

Right: Mary Alice, Gylan Kain

Mary Alice, Morgan Freeman

AMERICAN PLACE THEATRE
November 20–December 11, 1977 (26 performances)

PASSING GAME

By Steve Tesich; Director, Peter Yates; Set, Kert Lundell; Costumes, Ruth Morley; Lighting, Neil Peter Jampolis; Basketball Sequences Choreographed by Richard D. Morse; Technical Director, Craig Evans; Stage Managers, Nancy Harrington, Jeffrey Rowland; Press, Jeffrey Richards, Bruce Lynn

CAST

Susan MacDonald (Debbie), Paul C. O'Keefe (Randy), William Atherton (Richard), Margaret Ladd (Julie), Pat McNamara (Andrew), Howard E. Rollins, Jr. (Henry), Novella Nelson (Rachel) Standbys: Jacklyn Lee Bartone (Debbie/Julie), Dean Irby (Henry), Barry Jenner (Richard/Andrew), Cynthia McPherson (Rachel)

A drama in two acts. The action takes place at the present time in Upstate New York

Martha Holmes Photos

Right: Howard Rollins, Jr., Novella Nelson

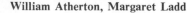

William Atherton, Margaret Ladd   **Howard Rollins, Jr., William Atherton**

AMERICAN PLACE THEATRE
January 13–February 12, 1978 (43 performances)

FEFU AND HER FRIENDS

By Maria Irene Fornes; Directed by Ms. Fornes; Settings, Kert Lundell, Nancy Tobias; Costumes, Theo Barnes; Lighting, Edward M. Greenberg; Wardrobe Mistress, Karen Kain; Stage Managers, Nancy Harrington, Jeffrey Rowland; Press, Jeffrey Richards, Bruce Lynn

CAST

Rebecca Schull (Fefu), Dorothy Lyman (Cindy), Elizabeth Perry (Christina), Margaret Harrington (Julia), Gordana Rashovich (Emma), Connie LoCurto (Paula), Arleigh Richards (Sue), Judith Roberts (Cecilia), Understudy: Kathleen Chalfant

A play in three parts, performed without intermission. The action takes place in New England in the spring of 1935.

Martha Holmes Photos

Right: Dorothy Lyman, Elizabeth Perry

Gordana Rashovich, Rebecca Schull

AMERICAN PLACE THEATRE
March 19–April 2, 1978 (27 performances)

CONJURING AN EVENT

By Richard Nelson; Director, Douglas C. Wager; Set, David Lloyd Gropman; Costumes, William Ivey Long; Lighting, Paul Gallo; Sound, Carol Waaser; Stage Managers, Peggy Peterson, Jeffrey Rowland; Technical Director, Craig Evans; Press, Jeffrey Richards, Bruce Lynn

CAST

Michael Cristofer (Charlie), Sigourney Weaver (Annabella), John Jellison (Waiter), MacIntyre Dixon (Man), Dan Hedaya (Smitty), Frank Hamilton (Sleeves), Standby: John Jellison

A drama in two acts. The action takes place at the present time in the Pen and Pencil Club and in Charlie's apartment.

Martha Holmes Photos

Right: Michael Cristofer, Sigourney Weaver

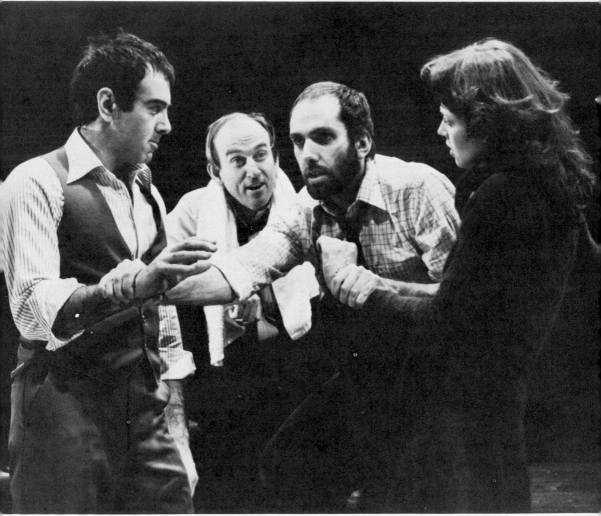

Dan Hedaya, MacIntyre Dixon, Michael Cristofer, Sigourney Weaver

AMERICAN THEATER EXPERIMENT

Dick Gaffield, Artistic Director
Paul McCarren, Managing Director

PERRY STREET THEATRE
March 21–April 16, 1978 (16 performances in repertory)

NATIVE SON

By Paul Green and Richard Wright; Director, Dick Gaffield; Set, Scott Moore; Lighting, William Plachy; Costumes, Walker Hicklin, Gayle Everhart; Musical Director, Greg Gilford; Stage Manager, John David Young

CAST

Bo Rucker (Bigger Thomas), Erma Campbell (Hanna Thomas), Ceal Coleman (Vera Thomas), Terrance Wendell Harris (Buddy Thomas), Sharon O'Donnell (Miss Emmett/Journalist/Stenographer), Kermit Frazier (Jack), Kaydette L. Grant (Clara), Gordon Keys (Gus), Stephen D. Agins (Gus/Rev. Hammond), Harvey Pierce (Dalton), B. Constance Barry (Mrs. Dalton), Danica Galich (Peggy), Kathleen McKiernan (Mary Dalton), Shawn McAllister (Britten), Dimitri Alexander (Jan), Jamie Stolz (Journalist), Robert Johansen (Journalist/Judge/Guard), William Schilling (Max), Francis McDonald (Buckley)

March 28–April 16, 1978 (12 performances in repertory)

A VIEW FROM THE BRIDGE

By Arthur Miller; Director, Paul McCarren; Set, Scott Moore; Lighting, William Plachy; Stage Manager, Peter Shuman

CAST

Del Willard (Alfieri), Alan Wynroth (Eddie), Joseph Patrick Copersito (Louis), Jean Reynolds (Catherine), Margo McKee (Beatrice), at McCord (Marco), Charles Iorio (Tony/Officer), Ron D'Agnessa (Rodolpho)

Al Sussman Photos

Bo Rucker, Erma Campbell, Ceal Coleman, Terrence Harris in "Native Son"

**Alan Wynroth, Ron Dignessa, Jean Reynolds, Patrick McCord, Margo McKee
in "A View from the Bridge"**

**Patricia Hodges, Frances Conroy
in "Mother Courage"**

THE ACTING COMPANY
John Houseman, Producing Artistic Director
Michael Kahn, Alan Schneider, Artistic Directors
Sixth Season

AMERICAN PLACE THEATRE
April 5–19, 1978 (10 performances in repertory)

MOTHER COURAGE AND HER CHILDREN

By Bertolt Brecht; Translated by Ralph Manheim; Director, Alan Schneider; Music and Lyrics, Paul Dessau; Musical Direction, Albert Hague; Settings, Ming Cho Lee; Costumes, Jeanne Button; Lighting, David F. Segal; Wardrobe Supervisor, Carol J. Clow; Technical Director, Peter Carlin; Production Coordinator, Sam Clester; Stage Managers, Daniel Morris, David Bradford, Caroline Yeager; General Manager, Howard Crampton-Smith; Press, The Merlin Group

CAST

Mary Lou Rosato (Mother Courage), Frances Conroy (Kattrin), Kevin Conroy (Eilif), Jeffrey Hayenga (Swiss Cheese), Tom Donaldson (Recruiting Officer/Yvette's Colonel/Soldier), Tom Robbins (Protestant Sgt./Catholic Sgt./Soldier), David Schramm (Cook), James Harper (Swedish General), Anderson Matthews (Chaplain), John Greenleaf (Ordnance Officer/Peasant), Patricia Hodges (Yvette), Henry Stram (Soldier/Stretcher Bearer), Brooks Baldwin (One Eye/Soldier/Lt.), Daniel Corcoran (Stretcher Bearer/Soldier/Young Man), Dennis Bacigalupi (Regimental Clerk/Servant/Young Peasant), Ron Jacobson (Young Soldier), Gregg Almquist (Old Soldier/Peasant), Leslie Geraci (Peasant Woman), Harriet Harris (Old Woman/Peasant)

April 6–22, 1978 (9 performances in repertory)

KING LEAR

By William Shakespeare; Director, John Houseman; Music, Marc Blitzstein; Settings, Ming Cho Lee; Costumes, Nancy Potts; Lighting, David F. Segal; Fights staged by B. H. Barry; Choreography, Elizabeth Keen; Wigs, Jody Thomas; Conductor, Stephen Colvin

CAST

James Harper (Earl of Kent), Gregg Almquist (Earl of Gloucester), Tom Donaldson (Edmund), David Schramm (Lear), Mary Lou Rosato (Goneril), Frances Conroy (Cordelia), Patricia Hodges (Regan), Ron Jacobson (Duke of Burgundy), Daniel Corcoran (King of France/Lear's Knight), Anderson Matthews (Duke of Albany), Tom Robbins (Duke of Cornwall/Herald), Kevin Conroy (Edgar), Brooks Baldwin (Oswald/Soldier/Knight), Dennis Bacigalupi (Fool), Jeffrey Hayenga (Servant/Captain/Soldier), Henry Stram (Servant/Doctor/Soldier/Knight), Ron Jacobson (Gentleman)

April 16 & 23, 1978 (3 performances in repertory)

THE DUCK VARIATIONS

By David Mamet; Director, Gerald Gutierrez; Setting, John Lee Beatty; Costumes, John David Ridge; Lighting, David F. Segal

CAST

Emil Varec .... Richard Ooms
George S. Aronovitz .... David Schramm

April 22 & 23, 1978 (3 performances in repertory)

THE OTHER HALF

A Work in Progress by Elinor Jones; Director, Amy Saltz; Musical Direction, Penna Rose; Musical Staging, Elizabeth Keen; Lighting, Skip Rapoport

CAST

Frances Conroy (Amy Lowell/Sappho/Mary Shelley/Nelly Dean/Dorothea Brooke), Leslie Geraci (Joan Didion/Mrs. Montague/Harriet Smith/Emily Bronte/Catherine Earnshaw), Harriet Harris (Colette/Margaret Cavendish/Fanny Burney/Evelina), Patricia Hodges (Edna St. Vincent Millay/Mrs. Thrale/Christina Rossetti/Charlotte Bronte/Mrs Cadwallader), Diane Kamp (Emma Woodhouse/Anne Bronte/Celia Brooke), Mary Lou Rosato (Virginia Woolf/Aphra Behn/George Eliot) *Martha Swope Photos*

**Top Left: Frances Conroy, Mary Lou Rosato
Below: David Schramm, Mary Lou Rosato
in "Mother Courage"**

Richard Ooms, David Schramm in "The Duck Variations" Top: (L) Frances Conroy, David Schramm, James Harper (R) Anderson Mathews, Mary Lou Rosato, Tom Robbins, Pat Hodge in "King Lear"

BROOKLYN ACADEMY OF MUSIC

Harvy Lichtenstein, President
Judith E. Daykin, Executive Vice President/General Manager

BAM/LEPERCQ SPACE

October 12–20, 1977 (7 Performances)
"i" by Theatre Laboratoire Vicinal of Belgium; Text, Frederic Baal; Acted and Directed by Anne West; Sculpture-Properties, Olivier Strebelle; Producer, Jack Temchin; Press, Jeffrey Richards, Bruce Lynn

Right: Anne West in "i"

BAM/OPERA HOUSE

December 13, 1977–January 1, 1978 (24 performances)

JOSEPH AND THE AMAZING TECHNICOLOR DREAMCOAT

By Tim Rice and Andrew Lloyd Webber; Directed and Choreographed by Graciela Daniele; Originally directed by Frank Dunlop; Production Supervisor, Frank Bayer; Original Design, Nadine Baylis; Set Supervisor, John Pitts; Costume Supervisor, Dona Granata; Lighting, F. Mitchell Dana; Sound, Abe Jacob; Musical Direction, Glen Roven; Assistant to Director, Adam Grammis; General Manager, Berenice Weiler; Stage Managers, Frank Bayer, Robert Beard, Paul Diaz; Press, Louis Sica, John Howlett

CAST

Alan Weeks (Narrator), David-James Carroll (Joseph), Ben Agresti (Reuben), Denny Martin Flinn (Simeon), Michael Hoit (Gad/Butler), Paul Kreppel (Levi), Leonard Piggee (Isaachar), Robert Rhys (Judah), Craig Schaefer (Zebulon), Don Swanson (Napthali), Eric Weitz (Benjamin), Kurt Yahjian (Dan/Baker), Jo Ann Ogawa (Mother), Jill Streisant (Mother), Marybeth Kurdock (Mother/Mrs. Potiphar), Tony Hoty (Jacob), Terry Eno (Potiphar), David Garrison (Egyptian/Ishmaelite), William Parry (Pharaoh), The Brooklyn Boys Chorus

Frederic Ohringer Photos

Alan Weeks, David-James Carroll
(also above)

Alan Weeks, David-James Carroll

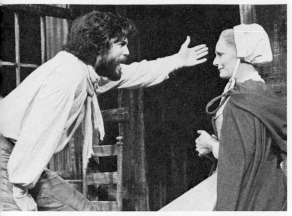

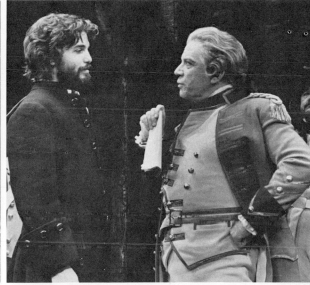

George Rose, Chris Sarandon (also right)
Top: Chris Sarandon, Carole Shelley
Top Right: Barnard Hughes, Margaret Hamilton

BAM/OPERA HOUSE
February 8–March 19, 1978 (19 performances)
The BAM Theatre Company (Frank Dunlop, Director; Berenice Weiler, Administrative Director) in association with the Center Theatre Group/Ahmanson Theatre presents:

THE DEVIL'S DISCIPLE

By George Bernard Shaw; Director, Frank Dunlop; Sets and Costumes, Carl Toms; Lighting, F. Mitchell Dana; Stage Managers, Barbara-Mae Phillips, Norman Abrams, Paul Diaz; Hairstylist, Karol Coeyman

CAST

Margaret Hamilton (Mrs. Dudgeon), Barnard Hughes (Rev. Anderson), George Rose (Gen. Burgoyne), Chris Sarandon (Dick Dudgeon), Carole Shelley (Judith Anderson), Earl Boen (Maj. Swindon), Robert Cornthwaite (Uncle Titus), Luise Heath (Essie), Ken Letner (Chaplain), Allan Lurie (Uncle William), John Orchard (Sergeant), Randy Pelish (Christy), Betty Ramey (Uncle William's wife), Peggy Rea (Uncle Titus' wife), Fred Stuthman (Lawyer Hawkins), Townspeople and Soldiers: Norman Abrams, Timothy Askew, Jason Buzas, Paul Diaz, George McDaniel, Ron Perkins, Rudolf Rainer, Robert Rhys, Rex Stallings, Holly Villaire

Frederic Ohringer Photos

Carole Shelley, Chris Sarandon

BAM/HELEN CAREY PLAYHOUSE
February 22–March 19, 1978 (28 performances)
The BAM Theatre Company presents:

THE PLAY'S THE THING

By Ferenc Molnar; Adapted by P. G. Wodehouse; Director,
Frank Dunlop; Setting, Santo Loquasto; Costumes, Nancy Potts;
Lighting, F. Mitchell Dana; Stage Managers, Frank Bayer, Norman
Abrams, Paul Diaz, Press, Louis Sica, John Howlett

CAST

Rene Auberjonois (Sandor Turai), Stephen Collins (Mell), Kurt
Kasznar (Mansky), Austin Pendleton (Albert Adam), Rex Robbins
(Johann Dwornitschek), George Rose (Almady), Carole Shelley
(Ilona Szabo), Norman Abrams (Lackey), Paul Diaz (Lackey)

Frederic Ohringer Photos

Right: Carole Shelley, George Rose
Right Center: Rene Auberjonois, Kurt
Kasznar, Austin Pendleton

Carole Shelley, Rene Auberjonois

Rex Robbins, Rene Auberjonois

BAM/LEPERCQ SPACE
March 29–April 23, 1978 (31 performances)
The BAM Theatre Company presents:

JULIUS CAESAR

By William Shakespeare; Director, Frank Dunlop; Costumes,
Dona Granata; Lighting, F. Mitchell Dana; Scenic Disposition,
Carole Lee Carroll; Music, Frank Bennett; Speech Consultant, Edith
Skinner; Stage Managers, Barbara-Mae Phillips, Norman Abrams,
Paul Diaz; Press, Louis Sica, John Howlett

CAST

Norman Abrams (Soldier), Terry Alexander (Cinna/Soldier), Rene
Auberjonois (Marcus Brutus), Stephen Davies (Trebonius/
Lucilius), Justin Deas (Decius Brutus/Pindarus), Paul Diaz (Ser-
vant/Soldier), Richard Dreyfus (Cassius), Sheldon Epps (Lepidus/-
Soothsayer), Michael Gennaro (Lucius), Thomas Hulce (Octavius
Caesar), Philip Kraus (Cimber/Strato), Ken Letner (Cicero/-
Titinius), George McDaniel (Popilius Lena/Marullus/Messala),
Austin Pendleton (Marcus Antonius), Paul Perri (Flavius/Ar-
temidorus/Cinna/Volumnius), Rex Robbins (Casca), George Rose
(Julius Caesar), Sloane Shelton (Calpurnia), Rex Stallings (Young
Cato/Servant), Holly Villaire (Portia), People of Rome: Scott Bar-
ton, Robert Bedford, Ronald Jay Berliner, William Campbell,
Jacqueline Cantey, Shawn Charles, Jeffrey Cohen, Lorrie Cook,
John Doerner, Drew Farber, Tyrone Jones, Shiva Kumar, Randi
Lieberman, Lisa Pollack, Evan Turk, Douglas Urbanski, Robert
Wyatt

Richard Dreyfuss, Ken Letner, George McDaniel, Rene Auberjonois, Thomas Hulce, Austin Pendleton
Top Right: Justin Deas, Sloane Shelton, George Rose *(Jack Mitchell Photos)*   **103**

BAM/LEPERCQ SPACE
May 25–June 18, 1978 (30 performances)
The BAM Theatre Company with the cooperation of Goethe House, New York, presents Samuel Beckett's production of:

WAITING FOR GODOT

By Samuel Beckett; Director, Walter D. Asmus; Scenery Supervision, Carole Lee Carroll; Costume Supervision, Dona Granata; Lighting Supervision, Shirley Prendergast; Stage Managers, Frank Bayer, Barbara-Mae Phillips; Production Assistant, William Campbell; Press, Louis Sica, John Howlett

CAST

Michael Egan (Pozzo), Milo O'Shea (Lucky), Austin Pendleton (Estragon), Sam Waterston (Vladimir), R. J. Murray, Jr. (Boy)

Thomas Victor Photos

Left: Austin Pendleton, Sam Waterston

Austin Pendleton, Sam Waterston, Milo O'Shea, Michael Egan

CHELSEA THEATER CENTER

Robert Kalfin, Artistic Director
Michael David, Executive Director
Thirteenth Season

CHELSEA THEATER CENTER/BROOKLYN ACADEMY OF MUSIC
October 18–November 20, 1977 (41 performances)
(Moved November 2, 1977 to Chelsea Westside Theater)
Chelsea Theater Center by arrangement with Oscar Lewenstein presents:

RUM AN COCA COLA

By Mustapha Matura; Director, Donald Howarth; Design, Wolfgang Roth; Costumes, Debra J. Stein; Lighting, William Mintzer; Production Manager, Sherman Warner; Assistant to Director, Richard Hamburger; Stage Managers, Bob Jaffe, Jan Rugh; Press, Susan Bloch, Lester Gruner, Sally Christiansen, Francis X. Tobin

CAST

Creator .... Leon Morenzie
Bird .... Lou Ferguson
Steel Band ...... Kurt Nurse, Brian Griffith, Winston Phillips
Standby: Sullivan Walker

A "serious comedy" performed without intermission. The action takes place on a beach dune in Trinidad.

Martha Swope Photo

Right: Lou Ferguson, Leon Morenzie

Christine Ebersole, Stephen James, Richard Ryder, Stephanie Cotsirilos *(Martha Swope Photo)*

CHELSEA THEATER CENTER/BAM
November 22–December 18, 1977 (32 performances)
(Moved December 7, 1977 to Chelsea Westside Theater)
Chelsea Theater center presents:

GREEN POND

Words, Robert Montgomery; Music, Mel Marvin; Director, David Chambers; Vocal Arrangements and Orchestrations, Mel Marvin; Scenery and Costumes, Marjorie Kellogg; Lighting, Arden Fingerhut; Stage Manager, Dorothy J. Maffeim, Amelia R. Haywood; Assistant to Director, John Lyons; Press, Susan Bloch, Lester Gruner, Sally Christiansen, Francis X. Tobin

CAST

Liz .... Stephanie Cotsirilos
Dana .... Christine Ebersole
Sam .... Stephen James
Frank .... Richard Ryder

MUSICAL NUMBERS: "Green Pond," "Pleasant Company," "Daughter," "I Live Alone," "The Eyes of Egypt," "How We Get Down," "Alligator Meat," "Priceless Relics," "Woman to Woman," "Brother to Brother," "Hurricane," "Hard to Love," "On the Ground at Last"

A musical in two acts. The action takes place somewhere in the American South during the summer of 1976.

CHELSEA THEATER CENTER/BROOKLYN ACADEMY
Opened Wednesday, January 25, 1978.*
Chelsea Theater Center presents the Bread and Puppet Theater with the Word of Mouth Chorus in:

AVE MARIS STELLA

By Josquin Despres; Director, Puppet Designer, Writer, Peter Schumann.

* Closed Jan. 29, 1978 after limited engagement of 6 performances.

"Ave Maris Stella"

CIRCLE REPERTORY COMPANY

Marshall W. Mason, Artistic Director
Jerry Arrow, Executive Director
Ninth Season

CIRCLE REPERTORY COMPANY THEATRE
June 23–September 4, 1977 (78 performances)
Circle Repertory Company presents:

UNSUNG COLE

Conceived and Directed by Norman L. Berman; Songs by Cole Porter; Music and Vocal Arrangements, Norman L. Berman; Music Direction, Leon Odenz; Choreography, Dennis Grimaldi; Setting, Peter Harvey; Costumes, Carol Oditz; Lighting, Arden Fingerhut; Assistant to Director, Brian Ross; Technical Supervisor, Earl Hughes; Company Manager, Dennis Purcell; Stage Managers, Amy Schecter, Carol Patella; Press, Rima Corben

CAST

Gene Lindsey
Mary Louise
Maureen Moore
Anita Morris†
John Sloman

A "musical entertainment" in two acts using the songs of Cole Porter.
†Succeeded by Margery Cohen

Ken Howard Photos

Right: Gene Lindsey, Anita Morris, Maureen Moore, John Sloman, Mary Louise

Gene Lindsey, Mary Louise, Maureen Moore, Anita Morris, John Sloman

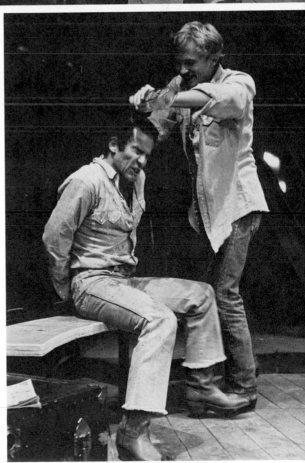

CIRCLE REPERTORY COMPANY THEATRE
October 8–November 27, 1977 (55 performances)
Circle Repertory Company presents:

FEEDLOT

By Patrick Meyers; Director, Terry Schreiber; Setting, Hal Tine;
Lighting, Dennis Parichy; Costumes, Laura Crow; Sound, Charles
London; Stage Managers, Amy Schecter, Michael Herzfeld; Press,
Rima Corben

CAST

Gene Harris	Mark J. Soper
Wesley	Jeff Daniels
Billy Fred	Joseph Ragno
John	James Ray Weeks
Kelly	Edward Seamon

A drama in 2 acts and 3 scenes. The action takes place at the
present time in the control tower of a feedlot in Texas.

Ken Howard Photos

**Top: Mark J. Soper, James Ray Weeks, Edward
Seamon, Joseph Ragno Center: Jeff Daniels,
Joseph Ragno, Mark J. Soper**

Joseph Ragno, Mark J. Soper

CIRCLE REPERTORY COMPANY THEATRE
October 20–November 25, 1977 (23 performances)
(Returned with "Cabin 12" for 26 additional performances
from March 4–April 9, 1978)
Circle Repertory Company Late Show presents:

BRONTOSAURUS

By Lanford Wilson; Director, Daniel Irvine; Setting, Nina Friedman; Costumes, Laura Crow; Lighting, Gary Seltzer; Stage Manager, Amy Schecter; Press, Rima Corben

CAST

The Antique Dealer	Tanya Berezin
The Assistant	Sharon Madden
The Nephew	Jeff Daniels

A play in one act, set at the present time in New York City. The scenes alternate between the shop of the antique dealer and her apartment.

Ken Howard Photo

Right: Sharon Madden, Tanya Berezin

CIRCLE REPERTORY COMPANY THEATRE
December 3, 1977–January 22, 1978 (52 performances)
Circle Repertory Company presents:

ULYSSES IN TRACTION

By Albert Innaurato; Director, Marshall W. Mason; Setting, John Lee Beatty; Costumes, Laura Crow; Lighting, Dennis Parichy; Sound, Charles S. London, George Hansen; Stage Manager, Fred Reinglas; Press, Rima Corben

CAST

Michael Ayr (Bruce Garrick), Jack Davidson (Dr. Stuart Humphreys), Jake Dengel (Leonard Kaufman), Joanna Featherstone (Mae), Trish Hawkins (Emma Konichowski), William Hurt (John Morrisey), Sharon Madden (Doris Reinlos), Ken Kliban (Dr. Steven Klipstader)

A drama in two acts. The action takes place during the spring of 1970 in the rehearsal hall in the Arts Complex of Chapel University, Detroit, Michigan.

Ken Howard Photos

**Front: Jake Dengel, Michael Ayr, Jack Davidson
Back: Sharon Madden, Ken Kliban, William Hurt**

Left Center: Trish Hawkins, William Hurt   Right Center: Jack Davidson, Michael Ayr, William Hurt

CIRCLE REPERTORY COMPANY THEATRE

January 3–20, 1978 (13 performances)
(Returned with "Brontosaurus" for 26 additional performances
from March 4–April 9, 1978)
Circle Repertory Company Late Show presents:

CABIN 12

By John Bishop; Director, Marshall Oglesby; Setting, Gary S. Seltzer; Lighting, Ruth Roberts; Costumes, Irene Nolan; Stage Manager, Joanne Seltzer

CAST

Bob McCullough	Jonathan Hogan
Harold McCullough	Edward Seamon
The Girl	Nancy Snyder
The Man	Michael Ayr

A one-act drama that takes place in a motel cabin in western Virginia at the present time.

Ken Howard Photo

Top Right: Edward Seamon, Jonathan Hogan

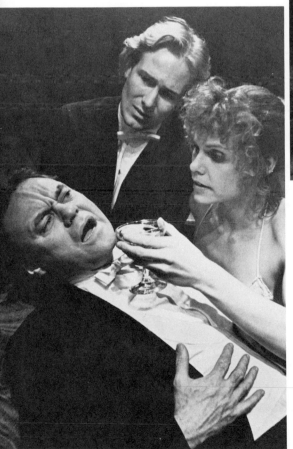

CIRCLE REPERTORY COMPANY THEATRE

February 4–28, 1978 (25 performances)
Circle Repertory Company presents:

LULU

By Frank Wedekind; Director, Rob Thirkield; Setting, John Lee Beatty; Costumes, David Murin; Lighting, Ruth Roberts; Original Music, Norman L. Berman; Sound, Charles S. London; Assistant to Director, David Van Blema; Stage Manager, Amy Schecter; Wardrobe, Irene Nolan; Press, Rima Corben, Glenna Clay

CAST

Michael Ayr (August/Escherich/Ferdinand/Inspector), Robert E. Barnes, Jr. (Kungu Poti), Jacqueline Bertrand (Countess Geschwitz), Jeff Daniels (Schwarz/Hunidei), Jack Davidson (Dr. Schon), Trish Hawkins (Lulu), William Hurt (Alwa Schon), Ken Kliban (Animal Tamer/Roderigo), Sharon Madden (Magelone), Burke Pearson (Prince Escerny/Heilmann/Dr. Hilti), Joyce Reehling (Ludmilla Steinherz), Mariellen Rokosny (Kadidja), William Robertson (Schigolch), Gerard Russak (Dr. Goll/Puntchu), Nancy Snyder (Bianetta Gazil), Mark Soper (Marquis), Danton Stone (Alfred Hugenberg/Groom)

A drama in 3 acts and 7 scenes. The action takes place in Pre-World War I in Germany, Paris and London.

Ken Howard Photos

Jack Davidson, William Hurt, Trish Hawkins
Right Center: William Robertson, Trish Hawkins

CIRCLE REPERTORY COMPANY THEATRE
April 18–September 3, 1978 (140 performances)
Circle Repertory Company presents:

THE 5TH OF JULY

By Lansford Wilson; Director, Marshall W. Mason; Setting, John Lee Beatty; Costumes, Laura Crow; Lighting, Marc B. Weiss; Original Song, Jonathan Hogan; Sound, Chuck London; Assistant to Director, Tony Tenuta; Production Assistant, Terry Lorden; Wardrobe Mistress, Ellen Irving; Stage Managers, Fred Reinglas, Mariellen Rokosny, Andrew Mishkind; Press, Rima Corben, Glenna Clay

CAST

Jeff Daniels (Jed), Jonathan Hogan (John), William Hurt (Kenneth Talley, Jr.), Joyce Reehling (June Talley), Nancy Snyder (Gwen), Helen Stenborg (Aunt Sally), Danton Stone (Weston Hurley), Amy Wright (Shirley)

A comedy-drama in two acts. The action takes place at the Talley Place, a farm near Lebanon, Missouri, on Independence Day 1977 and the following morning.

Ken Howard Photos

Right: Standing: Nancy Snyder, Jonathan Hogan, Amy Wright, Joyce Reehling, (in swing) Helen Stenborg, William Hurt, Seated: Danton Stone, Jeff Daniels

Helen Stenborg, Joyce Reehling, William Hurt, Danton Stone

**William Hurt, Nancy Snyder
Left Center: Nancy Snyder, Jonathan Hogan**

THE CLASSIC THEATRE

Maurice Edwards, Artistic Director

LORETTO THEATRE
September 15–October 2, 1977 (12 performances)

CHARLES THE SECOND

By John Howard Payne and Washington Irving; Director, Warren Kliewer; Song by Sir Henry Rowley Bishop; Producer, Nicholas John Stathis; Technical Director, Michael A. Fink; Costumes, Julia C. Murray, Linda Roots; Set, Thomas Betz; Lighting, Michael A. Fink, Annie Rech; Stage Manager, Deborah Openden

CAST

Don Atkinson (Earl of Rochester), Jonathan Chappell (Capt. Copp), Patricia Cray (Lady Clara), Alan Gilbert (Charles II), Michele LaRue (Mary Copp), John Wyeth (Edward)

LORETTO THEATRE
November 4–20, 1977 (12 performances)

THE MALCONTENT

By John Marston; Directors, Richard Bruno, Maurice Edwards; Producer, Nicholas John Stathis; Costumes, Michele Harris; Lighting, Robert Maloney; Music and Environment, Sal Rasa, Anthony Rasa, Edward Radonic, Gene Ambutter; Technical Director, Michael A. Fink; Production Associates, Anna Sierra, Marie-Louis Silva; Stage Manager, Karen Arrajj

CAST

Maurice Edwards (Giovanni Altofronto), Robert Baines (Pietro Iacomo), John Michalski (Mendoza), Alan Woolf (Celso), Alex Reed (Bilioso), Dan Durning (Passarello), Chris Ceraso (Ferneze), Peter Ruskin (Equato), Steve Pastor (Ferrardo), Patrick Boyington (Page/Mercury), Stephen Zufa (Captain of the Guard), Susannah Halston (Aurelia), Denise Assante (Maria), Carla Ceraso (Emilia), Jacklyn Maddux (Bianca), Madlyn Cates (Maquerelle)

LORETTO PLAYHOUSE
January 27–February 19, 1978 (16 performances)

BREMEN COFFEE

By Rainer Werner Fassbinder; Translated by Anthony Vivis; Director, Manfred Bormann; Producer, Nicholas John Stathis; Design, David Craven; Music, David Hollister; Costumes, Ruth Thomason; Lighting, Richard Kerry; Stage Managers, Robert G. Adams, Alp Deniztekin

CAST

Cynthia Exline (Geesche Gottfried), Thomas Bahring (Miltenberger), Edward Stevlingson (Timm), Helen Kelly (Mother), Eric R. Cowley (Gottfried), Bill Roulet (Father Markus), Ronald Wendschuh (Zimmerman), Al Nazario (Rumpf), Christopher Cooke (Johann), Alp Deniztekin (Bohm), Angelynne Bruno (Luisa Mauer)

LORETTO PLAYHOUSE
March 30–April 16, 1978 (12 performances)

THE COUNTRY GENTLEMAN

By George Villiers and Sir Robert Howard; Director, Maurice Edwards; Producer, Nicholas John Stathis; Set, Ronald Daley; Costumes, Ruth Thomason; Scenic Artist, David Craven; Music, David Frost, Choreography, Vic Stornant; Stage Manager, Malcolm D. Ewen

CAST

John Blazo, Jr. (Lovetruth), Bruce Bouchard (Jack Vapor), Deidre Bryant (Kate), Marisa Cullen (Maid), Dan Durning (Roger Trim), Sarah Fairfax (Philadelphia), Robert Helsel (Worthy), Lucy McMichael (Lucy), Mary Mims (Mistress Finical Fart), Lee Owens (Sir Gravity Empty), Jeff Schoener (Ned/John), Stuart Schoener (Will-/Jacob), Chris Weatherhead (Isabella), Richard Zobel (Tom Slander)

Tom Bahring, Cynthia Exline in "Bremen Coffee"
(Jessie Pavis Photo) **Below: Richard Zobel**
Bruce Bouchard in "Country Gentleman"

LORETTO PLAYHOUSE
May 19–21, 1978 (4 performances)
The Prism Theatre production of:

SATURDAY ADOPTION

By Ron Cowen; Director, Tom Aberger; Design, Paul Everett; Producer, Nicholas John Stathis; Associate Producer, Kathleen A. Moore; Production Coordinator, Rogert G. Adams; Lighting, Jane Rottenbach; Stage Manager, Ana Pacheco

CAST

Jeanne Horn (Mrs. Meridan), Randall Robbins (Meridan), Joseph Adams (Rich), Michael Wiles (Macy), Sundra Jean Williams (Mrs. Stander), Anthony Griffin (Paul)

The action takes place in an American city in 1968.
(No photos available)

Top Right: Maurice Edwards, Madlyn Cates, Denise Assante in "The Malcontent" *(Marbeth Photo)*

111

COUNTERPOINT THEATRE

Howard Green, Artistic Director
Paulene Reynolds, Managing Director
Fred Berry, Company Manager
Fourth Season

COUNTERPOINT THEATRE

November 25–December 12, 1977 (12 performances)
THE HAPPY JOURNEY TO TRENTON AND CAMDEN by
Thornton Wilder; Director, Terry Walker; Set, Milad Ishak; Lights,
Jesse Ira Berger; Costumes, Teri Vasquez; Stage Manager, Bryan
Bradley; Technical Director, Gary Marks; Production Assistant,
Neal Stone. CAST: Elek Hartman (Stage Manager), Carol Grant
(Ma), Michael Mantel (Arthur), Lynn Polan (Caroline), Harold
Oringer (Pa), Mary Anisi (Beulah), and THE LONG CHRISTMAS
DINNER with Carol Grant (Lucia), Hope Cameron (Mother/Er-
mengarde), Harold Oringer (Roderick), Elek Hartman (Brandon),
Don Marlette (Charles), Mary Anisi (Genevieve), Lynn Polan (Nur-
se/Lucia II), Tanny McDonald (Leonora), Neal Stone (Sam), Mi-
chael Mantel (Roderick II)

January 13–30, 1978 (12 performances)
EXIT THE KING by Eugene Ionesco; Director, Howard Green;
Set, Milad Ishak; Lights, Jesse Ira Berger; Costumes, Petrea Macdonald; Music, Lou Rodgers; Stage Manager, Gary Marks; Technical Director, Howard P. Beals, Jr. CAST: Clement Fowler (Berenger
the First), Alice Emerick (Queen Marguerite), Ellen Bry (Queen
Marie), Charles Durand (Doctor/Executioner), Lynn Polan (Juliet-
te/Maid/Nurse), Sanford Morris (Guard)

March 3–30, 1978 (12 performances)
ARTHUR by Ferenc Molnar; *New York Premiere;* Director, How-
ard Green; Set, Tony Giovanetti; Costumes, Deborah Shaw; Techni-
cal Director, W. Scott Allison; Assistant to Director, Mary Ann
Chance. CAST: Kathy Flanagan (Edith), Richard Council (Robert),
Thomas Barbour (Fred), Fred Berry (Captain), Trudi Mathes (Ju-
lie), Neal Stone (Waiter/Andre), Morris Alpern (Hotel Manager/-
Hollingsworth), Howard Green (Renard), Marshall Borden
(Bishop), Charles Durand (Ribaud), Jo Ann Schmidler (Mlle. Bon-
ard), Ed Crowley (Pendix)

April 28–May 15, 1978 (12 performances)
ARMS AND THE MAN by George Bernard Shaw; Director, Isaac
Schambelon; Set, Randi Frank; Costumes, Dennis O'Connor; Stage
Manager, Cindy Russell. CAST: Stephanie Satie (Raina), Carol
Grant (Catherine), Lynn Polan (Louka), Howard Green (Capt.
Bluntschli), Ron Orbach (Russian Officer/Nicola), Jay Bonnell
(Maj. Petkoff), Stephen Stout (Man/Saranoff).

**Right: Sanford Morris, Lynn Polan, Clem Fowler
in "Exit the King" Top: "The Long
Christmas Dinner"**

Thomas Barbour in "Arthur"

**Howard Green, Stephanie Satie
in "Arms and the Man"**

CSC REPERTORY

(Classic Stage Company)
Christopher Martin, Artistic Director
Dennis Turner, Executive Director
Albert Tore, Business Manager
Eleventh Season

ABBEY THEATRE
November 10, 1977–April 2, 1978

COMPANY

Barbara Blackledge, Ted Britton, Ray Dooley, Frank Dwyer, Patrick Egan, Christopher Martin, Christiane McKenna, Brian Rose, Claude Albert Saucier, Harlan Schneider, Noble Shropshire, Karen Sunde, Alberto Tore, Andrew Traines. and Richard Kite, Thomas Lenz, Brian Muehl, Frank Pita, Diana Stagner, Susan Varon, Robert Todd

PRODUCTIONS
(in rotating repertory)

"A MIDSUMMER NIGHT'S DREAM" by William Shakespeare; Direction, Christopher Martin; Design, Clarke Dunham; Costumes, Marianne Powell-Parker; Masks, Joseph Bigelow
"ROSMERSHOLM" by Henrik Ibsen; *World Premiere* of new English translation by Christopher Martin; Directed by Mr. Martin; Design, Clarke Dunham; Costumes, Marianne Powell-Parker
"SERJEANT MUSGRAVE'S DANCE" by John Arden; Director, John Shannon; Design, Phillip Graneto; Costumes, Joseph Bigelow
"THE MAIDS" by Jean Genet, after the translation by Bernard Frechtman; Direction and Production Design by Christopher Martin
World Premiere of "THE RUNNING OF THE DEER" by Karen Sunde; Direction and Design, Christopher Martin; Costumes, Rachel Kurland
"THE MADWOMAN OF CHAILLOT" by Jean Giraudoux, translated by Maurice Valency; Direction and Design, Christopher Martin; Costumes, Rachel Kurland

Gerry Goodstein Photos

Right: Noble Shropshire, Patrick Egan in "The Maids" Top: Noble Shropshire, Christiane McKenna in "Sjt. Musgrave's Dance"

Karen Sunde, Claude Albert Saucier
in "Madwoman of Chaillot"

"The Running of the Deer"

EQUITY LIBRARY THEATRE
INFORMALS

George Wojtasik, Managing Director
Lynn Montgomery, Production Director
Ann B. Grassilli, Producer

LINCOLN CENTER MUSEUM & LIBRARY
Equity Library Theatre Informals Series presents:
September 12, 13, 14, 1977 (3 performances)
JAZZ BABIES: Written, Directed and choreographed by Marc Jordan Gass; Musical Director, Steven Rosenthal; Production Stage Manager, Valerie Laura Imbarrato; Lighting Design, April M. Adams CAST: Adrienne Doucette (Molly), Joel Eagon (Reuben), Susan Edwards (Rosie), Gary Holcombe (Whitey), Charles Leipart (Henry)

October 17, 18, 19, 1977 (3 performances)
BLACK TUESDAY: Episode II/Tony's Story: by Ted Weiant and Joan Stein; Director, Ted Weiant; Lighting Design, Fran Miksits; Sound, Joseph Giardinia, Susan Lewis; Stage Manager, Elizabeth Grayson-Grossman; Producer, Joan Stein. CAST: Roger Brown, Valerie Mahaffey, Judith McIntyre, Cheryl Meguire, John Michalski, Anna Minot, Ken Shuey, Joseph Warren

November 21, 22, 23, 1977 (3 performances)
CELEBRATE MY LOVE by Linda Nerine; Music and Lyrics, Shellen Lubin; Director, Eric Uhler; Set, Carl A. Baldasso; Lighting, Fran Miksits; Costumes, Diane DeBaun; Stage Managers, Bill LaRosa, Newelle McDonald; Technical Director, John Patterson Reed. CAST: Joyce Cohen (Cynthia), Peggy Schoditsch (Barbara), Paul Ukena, Jr. (Gillie)

December 12, 13, 14, 1977 (3 performances)
THE RABINOWITZ GAMBIT by Rose Leiman Goldemberg; Director, June Plager; Designer, Christopher Cleary; Program Editor, Ellen S. Geaney; Stage Manager, Martha R. Jacobs. CAST: Judith Reagan (Niele Teague), Marc Cohen (Jerry), Mitchell Jason (Irving Rabinowitz), Ed Brodow (Blitz), Gregory Macosko (The Etcetera)

January 23, 24, 25, 1978 (3 performances)
"2": Concept, Music and Lyrics by Julie Mandel; Director, Clinton Atkinson; Musical Direction and Vocal Arrangements, Donald Oliver; Choreography, Bick Goss; Puppets, Pady Mark Blackwood; Technical Director, John Patterson Reed; Stage Manager, Mark Keller; Running Crew, David Lobel, Judith A. Snyder. CAST: Ann Hodapp, Hal Watters

February 6, 7, 8, 1978 (3 performances)
HOW FAR IS IT TO BABYLON? by Caryl Young; Stage Manager, Marsha Katzakian. CAST: Gwyda DonHowe (Jeri), Reno Roop (Charlie), Henderson Forsythe (George), Mary Cooper (Edith), Donald Barton (Clive)

March 20, 21, 22, 1978 (3 performances)
THE DIVIDED BED by James V. Hatch and Victoria Sullivan; Director, Warren Kliewer; Set and Lighting Design, Tom Targownik; Stage Manager, Peter Pullman; Technical Director, John Patterson Reed; Program Editor, Bridget Ragan. CAST: John Corey (Bill), John Genke (William), Beth Holland (Eleanor), Elizabeth Ann Reavey (Ellie)

April 17, 18, 19, 1978 (3 performances)
THE ADOPTED MOON by Jack Black; Director, Gregory Macosko; Music, David Friedman; Lighting, M. L. Maretto; Set, John Patterson Reed; Choreography, Michael Lichtefeld; Sound, Showtime Sound Design, Hal Schuler; Stage Manager, Susan Sampliner. CAST: Katherine Bruce (Doreen), Frances Pole (Edna), Michael Lichtefeld (Arlin), Douglas Easley (Mark), Lee Winston (Frank), Arva Holt (Carole), Peter Gatto (Rudy)

May 15, 16, 17, 1978 (3 performances)
A TRIBUTE TO WOMEN conceived and written by Stuart Michaels; Music, Lou Rodgers; Originally Directed by Stuart Michaels assisted by Lou Rodgers; Assistant Director, Audrey Highton; Stage Manager, Joanne Maiello; Music Director, John Klingberg; Costumes, Rene Gladstein. CAST: Linda Fields, Patricia Roark, Elizabeth King, Michael Schilke, Christina Czukor, Keith Lockhart, THE SPECIALIST by Stuart Michaels; Music, Lou Rodgers. CAST: Linda Mulrean (Annabelle), Marcy Jellison (Nora), Brian Stuart (Edward), Ralph Braun (Andre)

Top Right: Ann Hodapp, Reno Roop
Below: Donald Barton, Gwyda DonHowe

EQUITY LIBRARY THEATRE

George Wojtasik, Managing Director
Lynn Montgomery, Production Director
Thirty-fifth Season

EQUITY LIBRARY THEATRE
October 13–23, 1977 (22 performances)

GLAD TIDINGS

By Edward H. Mabley; Director, Bill Herndon; Set, Charles McCarry; Costumes, Madeline Cohen; Lighting, Ann Wrightson; Stage Manager, Nancy Finn; Press, Lewis Harmon, Sol Jacobson

CAST

Kevin Bacon (Terry), Kermit Brown (Gus), Jennifer Dawson (Mrs. MacDonald), Sands Hall (Claire), Diane Linden (Agnes), Etain O'Malley (Maud), Lucy Martin (Ethel), Wayne Miller (Henry), Randall Robbins (Steve)

**Lucy Martin, Randall Robins, Diane Linden
in "Glad Tidings"**

EQUITY LIBRARY THEATRE
November 3–20, 1977 (22 performances

CARNIVAL

Music and Lyrics, Bob Merrill; Book, Michael Stewart; Based on material by Helen Deutsch; Director, Susan Schulman; Choreography, Steven Gelfer; Musical Director, James Fradrich; Scenery, D. J. Markley; Costumes, Patricia Eiben; Lighting, Ruth Roberts; Puppets, Larry Engler; Stage Manager, Victor A. Gelb; Press, Lewis Harmon, Sol Jacobson

CAST

Charles Bari (Roustabout), Jill Cook (Princess Olga), Joel Craig (Marco), Joel Czarlinsky (Roustabout), Kaylyn Dillehay (Magic Girl), Carl Don (Schlegel), J. Oliver Freed (Roustabout), Jeannette Gardner (Gloria Zuwicki), Steven Gelfer (Dr. Glass) Sueanne Gershenson (Lili), Jack Hoffman (Jacquot), Elmore James (Fire Eater), Nancy Kammer (Clown/Juggler/Aerialist), Laura Kenyon (Rosalie), Karen Magee (Gladys), Ted Marriott (Acrobat), Michael Murray (Grobert), Ann Neville (Card Girl), Ross Petty (Paul), Wende Pollock (Greta), Steven Rivellino (Roustabout)

Top Right: Sue Anne Gershenson in "Carnival"

EQUITY LIBRARY THEATRE
December 8–18, 1977 (14 performances)

THE CRUCIBLE

By Arthur Miller; Director, David William Kitchen; Set, Judie Juracek; Lighting, Candice Dunn; Costumes, Donna Meyer; Original Music, Andy Bloor; Stage Manager, Fredric H. Orner; Technical Director, Peter I. Elencovf; Sound, Hal Schuler; Press, Lewis Harmon, Sol Jacobson

CAST

Roger Baron (Willard), Sue Renee Bernstein (Mercy), Michael Burke (Thomas Putnam), Victor Caroli (John Proctor), Thelma Louise Carter (Tituba), Mia Dillon (Mary Warren), Eileen Duerkop (Rachel), Wally Duquet (Francis Nurse), Ann Freeman (Ann Putnam), Pamela Harris (Dinah), Will Hussung (Danforth), Tara Loewenstern (Abigail), Elisa London (Susanna), Basia McCoy (Rebecca Nurse), Paul Meacham (Hathorne), William Pardue (Parris), William Paulson (Hopkins), Arleigh Richards (Mehetabel), William Robertson (Corey), Beatrice Roth (Sarah Good), Lois Ann Saunders (Elizabeth), Nick Savian (Cheever), Joan Shangold (Betty), Ronald Wendschuh (Hale), Toni Wooster (Martha Corey)

Victor Caroli, Lois Ann Saunders in "The Crucible"

EQUITY LIBRARY THEATRE
January 12–29, 1978 (22 performances)

ALLEGRO

Music, Richard Rodgers; Book and Music, Oscar Hammerstein II; Directed and Choreographed by William Koch; Musical Director, Mark Goodman; Scenery, Carl A. Baldasso; Costumes, A. Christina Giannini; Lighting, Jennifer Herrick; Assistant Choreographer, Wende Pollock; Stage Managers, Evan Canary, Martha R. Jacobs, Susan Sampliner; Press, Sol Jacobson, Lewis Harmon

CAST

Sonja Anderson (Marjorie), David Baumunk (Bertram), Judith DeRosa (Grandma Taylor), Adrienne Doucette (Mrs. Lansdale), Florie Freshman (Choir), Teri Gill (Hazel), Daniel Kruger (Joe), Sandy Laufer (Molly), Mary Kay Laughlin (Millie), Craig Mason (Choir), Maida Meyers (Beulah), Linda Motashami (Choir), James Newell (Ned), Howard Pinhasik (Bigby Denby), Barbara Porteus (Emily), Richard Rossomme (Taylor), Myles G. Savage (Cheerleader), Charlie Serrano (Choir), Sheldon Silver (Buckley), Gordon Stanley (Charlie), James Van Treuren (Lansdale), M. Lynne Wieneke (Jennie)

Terri Gill, Sandy Laufer, Gordon Stanley, Adrienne Doucette, Mary Kay Laughlin

COUNT DRACULA

By Ted Tiller; Based on Bram Stoker's novel "Dracula"; Director, Robert Lanchester; Scenery, Randi Frank; Lighting, Robby Monk; Costumes, Polly Smith; Original Music, Andy Bloor; Stage Managers, Ed Oster, David M. Flasck, Grant Brown, Mark Keller; Technical Directors, Peter I. Elencovf, John Patterson Reed; Press, Lewis Harmon, Sol Jacobson

CAST

Robert Blumenfeld (Van Helsing), Ken Bonafons (Hennessey), John Q. Bruce (Jonathan), Rick Meyer (Wesley), Frances Peter (Sybil), John Pielmeier (Renfield), William Shust (Dracula), Ian Stuart (Dr. Seward), Susan Vare (Mina)

**Top Left: Susan Vare, William Shust
in "Count Dracula"**

GAY DIVORCE

Music and Lyrics, Cole Porter; Original Book, Dwight Taylor, Kenneth Webb, Samuel Hoffenstein; Adapted by Robert Brittan; Director, Robert Brink; Musical Direction and Arrangements, Donald Jones; Choreography, Helen Butleroff; Scenery, Phillip Louis Rodzen; Lighting, Jeffrey Schissler; Costumes, Patricia Adshead; Assistant Musical Director, Eric David Stern; Stage Managers, Nancy Harrington, W. Scott Allison, Marsha Hahn, Nancy Kolbeck; Assistant to Production Director, Joan Stein; Pianists, Donald Jones, Eric Stern; Press, Lewis Harmon, Sol Jacobson

CAST

Paul Ames (Teddy), Sydney Anderson (Iris), Bob Ari (Robert), Joseph Billone (Tonetti), Mike Brennan (Porter), Leonard Drum (Waiter), Byron Grant (Pratt), Barbara Hanks (Gladys), Sarilee Kahn (Mimi), Jeri Kansas (Doris), Lynn Marlowe (Pat), Cynthia Meryl (Hortense), Patricia Moline (Barbara), Richard Sabellico (Guy), Dorothy Stanley (Edith), Sonja Stuart (Vivian)

**Right Center: Joseph Billone
in "Gay Divorce"**

THE TAMING OF THE SHREW

By William Shakespeare; Director, John Henry Davis; Composer-Arranger, William Lester; Movement Adviser, Robert DeFrank; Assistant Director, Jack Shannon; Set, David Potts; Costumes, Kenneth M. Yount; Lighting, Todd Lichtenstein; Stage Managers, James Pentecost, David Caine, Arthur Alan Barsamian; Jewelry, Bernard A. Santora; Press, Lewis Harmon, Sol Jacobsen

CAST

Eric Booth (Petruchio), Byron Conner (Musician), Stephanie Cotsirilos (Katherina), William Daprato (Christopher Sly), Robert DeFrank (Tranio), Jessica DuBord (Hostess/Widow), Jeffrey Griglak (Musician), Stephen Guntli (Lord/Pedant), Robert McFarland (Gremio), Robert Paolucci (Vincentio), Irwin Pearl (Biondello/Others), Polly Pen (Musician), Ernie Sabella (Grumio), Robert Schenkkah (Lucentio), Judith Townsend (Bianca), Peter Van Norden (Hortensio), Ed VanNuys (Baptista)

**Peter Van Norden, Robert Schenkkan, Eric Booth, Ed
VanNuys in "The Taming of the Shrew"**

EQUITY LIBRARY THEATRE
May 4–28, 1978 (30 performances)

COMPANY

Music and Lyrics, Stephen Sondheim; Book, George Furth; Director, Robert Nigro; Choreography, Randy Hugill; Musical Director, Eric Stern; Scenery, Richard B. Williams; Lighting, Victor En Yu Tan; Costumes, Mimi Maxmen; Stage Managers, Andrea Naier, Neal Brilliant, Michael Brunner, Mark Keller, Mark Mellender; Press, Sol Jacobson, Lewis Harmon

CAST

Valerie Beaman (April), Joy Bond (Susan), Albert Harris (Robert), Michael Hirsch (Paul), Richard Kevlin-Bell (Harry), Janet MacKenzie (Sarah), Becky McSpadden (Jenny), Bob Morrisey (Peter), Paige O'Hara (Marta), Edward Penn (Larry), Renee Roy (Joanne), Gillian Scalici (Kathy), Lauren White (Amy), Lenny Wolpe (David), Vocal Minority: Alexa Grant, Maureen McNamara, Linda Nenno, Christine Ranck, Patricia Roark, Lynda Karen Smith

Paige O'Hara, Gillian Scalici, Valerie Beaman
in "Company"
Left Center: James Burge, Howard Renensland,
Reily Hendrickson in "The Happy Hunter"

FESTIVAL THEATRE FOUNDATION
Producers: Louise Edmonson, Robert O'Rourke

ST. GEORGE'S CHAPEL
February 22–March 5, 1978 (12 performances)

THE HAPPY HUNTER

By Georges Feydeau; English Adaptation, Barnett Shaw; Director, Robert O'Rourke; Set, Jeffery Pavelka; Costumes, Shephard Goldman; Lighting, John Hastings; Assistant to Producers, Brian Stashick; Stage Managers, Jody Crane, Ralph Cottiers; Press, Edward Hajj

CAST

James C. Burge (Roussel), Reily Hendrickson (Yvonne Chandel), Howard Renensland (Chandel), Linda Christian-Jones (Babette), Alexander Berkeley (Pierre), Ronald Sopyla (Castillo), Sheila Coonan (Mme. De Latour), James Galvin (Inspector), Gary Smith (Policeman), Bill Nabel (Policeman)

ST. GEORGE'S CHAPEL
April 26–May 7, 1978 (12 performances)

LET'S GET A DIVORCE

By Victorien Sardou; English Adaptation, Angela and Robert Goldsby; Director, Robert O'Rourke; Set, Jeffery Pavelka; Costumes, Cheryl Blalock; Lighting, John Hastings; Stage Managers, Bruce M. Kaiden, Nancy Carol Juliber, David Kearse; Press, Reily Hendrickson

CAST

Mary Adams (Cyprienne), Colman de Kay (Bastien), Jonathan Kestly (Ademar), Edith Larkin (Mme. de Valfontaine), John Little (Caretaker/Waiter), Katie Ortlieb (Josepha), Sally Parrish (Mlle. de Lusignan), Howard Renensland (Des Prunelles), Gary Smith (Joseph), Richard Spore (Police Inspector), Jim Swanson (Clavignac), Nina Weiss (Mme. de Brionne)

Gary Smith, Mary Adams, John Little, Howard
Renensland in "Let's Get a Divorce"

GENE FRANKEL THEATRE
Gene Frankel, Executive Director-Producer
Clevedon Kingston, Assistant Producer
Susan Feldman, Assistant Producer

GENE FRANKEL THEATRE
October 7–30, 1977 (12 performances)
KINGDOM by Ali Wadud; Director, Regge Life; Sets, Adalberto Ortiz; Costumes, Leslie Day; Lights, Edward Currelley; Choreography, Dyane M. Harvey; Stage Manager, Merlen Langley; Company Manager, Walter Voza Rivers; Production Coordinator, Clevedon Kingston. CAST: Louise Mike, Joy Moss, Victor Anthony Thomas, Dan Bocharo, Milton Grier
THE CEREMONY by Ali Wadud; CAST: Diane Bivens, Joy Moss, Louise Mike, Bette Howard, Milton Grier, Victor Anthony Thomas
December 19, 1977–January 15, 1978 (25 performances)
THE CONTESSA OF MULBERRY STREET by N. D. Bellitto; Director, Gene Frankel; Assistant Producer, Clevedon Kingston; Set, Wilton Duckworth; Lighting, Candice Dunn; Costumes, Shelley Friedman; Stage Manager, Gina Willens; Press, Max Eisen. CAST: Willi Kirkham (Lia), Lou Criscuolo (Joseph), Keren Liswood (Angela), James Sappho (Johnny), Philip Kraft (Bob), George Igoe (Antonio/Older Hood), Murray Shactman (George/Younger Hood)
February 10–27, 1978 (12 performances)
ZOYA'S APARTMENT by Mikhail Bulzakov; Director, Earl Ostroff; Choreography, Hava Kohav; Musical Composition, Elliot Sokolov; Sets, Sam Gonzalez; Costumes, Judith Fauvell; Lighting, Dan Koetling; Associate Producer, Edward Callaghan; Production Manager, James Fauvell; General Manager, Helene Davis. CAST: Hugh Byrnes, Robert Davis, Linda Gilman, Gail Leinwall, Nancy LeBrun, Raf Michaels, Joseph Capone, Barry Einstein, Pauline Kelly, Dena Malon, Mark Margolis, John Neiman, Mark Cohen, James Fauvell, Hava Kohav, Mary Ann Johnson, Newelle McDonald, Kathleen Roland, Catherine Santaniello
May 5–12, 1978 (12 performances)
THE VERANDAH by Clifford Mason; Production Supervisor, Gene Frankel; Production Coordinator, Susan Feldman; Director, Clifford Mason; Set, Tony Castrigo; Stage Manager, Harrison Avery; Costumes, Pamela Lincoln. CAST: Lee Richardson, Juanita Mahone, Herb Downer, Rosanna Carter, Arnold Wilkerson, Judy Tate, Stephen Harris, Leila Danette, Jodi Long, Lloyd Davis, Harsh Nayyar
June 8–19, 1978 (10 performances)
FRESHWATER by Virginia Woolf; Director, Jon Fraser; Costumes, Joe Bigelow; Lights, William Megalos; Stage Manager, Marylin Daljour. CAST: Connie Rock, J. Nisbet Clark, George Hall, Katherine Rau, Denise Bissette, Paul Merrill, Dianne Trulock, Brendan James, Thomas Sminkey, Mary Francine Golden, Warrington Winters, Peter Pileski, David Hinchman
AN EVENING IN BLOOMSBURY by Victoria Sullivan; Connie Rock, J. Nisbet Clark, George Hall, Katherine Rau, Denise Bissette, Paul Merrill, Dianne Trulock, Brendan James, Thomas Sminkey, Mary Francine Golden, Warrington Winters, Peter Pileski, David Hinchman

"Freshwater" (*Michael Zettler Photo*)
Above: "The Verandah"

Top: Willi Kirkham, James Sappho
Left: Willi Kirkham in "Contessa of Mulberry St."

HUDSON GUILD THEATRE

Craig Anderson, Producing Director
Dennis Luzak, Production Manager

HUDSON GUILD THEATRE
October 9–30, 1977 (24 performances)

TREATS

By Christopher Hampton; Director, Michael Montel; Sets and Lighting, Peter Wexler; Costumes, Donald Brooks, Grief & Co.; Associate Designer, Tom Schwinn; Technical Director, Bill Montgomery; Wardrobe, David Samuel Mankes; Assistant to Director, Billy Serow; Production Assistant, Nell Stifel; Stage Managers, Edward R. Fitzgerald, Amelia Haywood, Christine Banas; Business Manager, Judson Barteaux; Press, Howard Atlee, Clarence Allsopp, Becky Flora

CAST

Ann .... Suzanne Lederer
Patrick .... John Glover
Dave .... Kenneth Welsh

A comedy in two acts. The action takes place at the present time in the main room of Ann's flat in London.

Marinaro Photos

Right: John Glover, Suzanne Lederer, Kenneth Welsh

Suzanne Lederer, Kenneth Welsh

HUDSON GUILD THEATRE

November 23–December 18, 1977 (24 performances)

THE DODGE BOYS

By George Sibbald; Director, Craig Anderson; Setting, Douglas Schmidt; Lighting, John Gleason; Costumes, Sandra Nye; Stage Managers, Edward R. Fitzgerald, Mary Jane de Froscia, Alan Dropkin; Assistant Director, William Serow; Associate Producer, Dennis Luzak; Press, Howard Atlee, Clarence Allsopp, Becky Flora

CAST

Vicky .... Jane Lowry
Bill .... William LeMassena
Harvey .... David Gale
Jimmy .... Ben Slack
Bob .... David Bowman

A drama in three acts. The action takes place at the present time in the automobile showroom of B & B Auto in a large "small town" in the midwest.

Marinaro Photos

Right: Ben Slack, William LeMassena, Jane Lowry
Right Center: David Gale, Ben Slack, Jane Lowry

Josh Clark, Tammy Grimes

HUDSON GUILD THEATRE

January 13–February 12, 1978 (30 performances)

MOLLY

By Simon Gray; Director, Stephen Hollis; Costumes, Patricia Adshead; Setting, Phillip Jung; Lighting, John H. Paull; Original Music, Andy Bloor; Stage Managers, Edward R. Fitzgerald, Mary Jane de Froscia; Assistant Director, Thomas Gardner; Press, Howard Atlee, Clarence Allsopp, Becky Flora

CAST

Molly .... Tammy Grimes
Teddie .... Michael Higgins
Eve .... Margaret Hilton
Oliver .... Josh Clark
Greaves .... Kenneth T. Scott
P.C. .... William A. Serow

A drama in 2 acts and 7 scenes. The action takes place in 1936 in the living room of a house in a small country village in England.

David L. Goodman Photos

Left Center: Michael Higgins, Tammy Grimes

March 10–April 2, 1978 (24 performances)

DA

By Hugh Leonard; Director, Melvin Bernhardt; Set, Marjorie Kellogg; Costumes, Jennifer von Mayrhauser; Lighting, Arden Fingerhut; Technical Director, Scott Glenn; Assistant to Director, Christine Banas; Stage Manager, Edward R. Fitzgerald; Production Assistants, Crystal Williamson, Kathy Gotis; Press, Howard Atlee, Clarence Allsopp, Becky Flora; Production Manager, William Montgomery; Literary Manager/Casting Director, David Kerry Heefner

CAST

Brian Murray (Charlie Now), Paul Rudd (Oliver), Barnard Hughes (Da), Sylvia O'Brien (Mother), Richard Seer (Young Charlie), Lester Rawlins (Drumm), Mia Dillon (Mary Tate), Lois de Banzie (Mrs. Prynne)

A comedy in two acts. The action takes place in a kitchen in May 1968 and later, and places and times remembered.

Marinaro Photos

**Sylvia O'Brien, Richard Seer, Barnard Hughes
Top: Paul Rudd, Brian Murray**

April 26–May 21, 1978 (24 performances)

MY MOTHER WAS A FORTUNE TELLER

Director, Arthur Laurents; Production Supervisor, Craig Anderson; Musical Direction, Herbert Kaplan; Musical Continuity, John Clifton; Musical Staging, Elizabeth Keen; Set, Philipp Jung; Costumes, Bill Kellard; Lighting, Toni Goldin; Multi-Media, Fran Albin; Stage Managers, James Pentecost, Arthur Barsamian; Production Assistant, Jacob Weisbarth; Technical Director, Tim Galvin; Press, Howard Atlee, Becky Flora

with
Phyllis Newman

A one-woman show with 16 musical numbers presented in two parts.

Phyllis Newman

121

IMPOSSIBLE RAGTIME THEATRE (IRT)

Artistic Director, Ted Story
Associate Director, George Ferencz
Co-Producers, Cynthia Crane, Pam Mitchell

IMPOSSIBLE RAGTIME THEATRE

October 22–November 14, 1977 (18 performances)
PLAY STRINDBERG by Friedrich Durrenmatt; Based on Strindberg's "The Dance of Death"; Translation, James Kirkup; Director, Ted Story; Lighting, Gary Porto; Set, Larry Fulton; Costumes, Margo La Zaro; Musical Director, Michael S. Roth; Choreographer, Marcia Milgrom; Assistant Director, Margaret A. Flanagan; Production Manager, Fred Chalfy; Stage Managers, Brian Bonnar, Sharon Bills. CAST: Tom Bade (Kurt), Anita Keal (Alice), Neil McKenzie (Edgar)

December 10, 1977–January 9, 1978 (18 performances)
WOMEN I HAVE KNOWN written and performed by M. Tulis Sessions; Director, Michael T. Gregoric; Set, Larry Fulton; Lighting, Jo Mayer; Production Manager, Mary Vivona

February 3–26, 1978 (18 performances)
SPIDER'S WEB by Agatha Christie; Director, Penelope Hirsch; Set, Trueman Kelley; Costumes, Margo La Zaro; Lighting, Gary Seltzer; Production Manager, Steve Shereff; Assistants to Director, Andy Setticase, George Sumakis; Stage Manager, Ellen Pollack, Musical Consultant, Ricardo Gautreau; Press, Cynthia Crane. CAST: Edwin S. German (Elgin), Donald R. Klecak (Oliver), Johanna Leister (Clarissa), John Lemley (Henry), Harold G. Meyer (Roly), Colin O'Leary (Doctor), Nicholas Saunders (Hugo), Joan Shangold (Pippa), Rudolph Shaw (Constable), E. Frantz Turner (Inspector), William Van Hunter (Jeremy), Nan Wilson (Miss Peake)

March 17–April 15, 1978 (18 performances)
CLASH BY NIGHT by Clifford Odets; Director, Stephan Zuckerman; Sets, Edelmiro Olavarria; Costumes, Margo La Zaro; Lighting, Seltzer; Fighting Choreography, Spencer Cohen; Production Manager, Steve Shereff; Assistant Director, Nancy Zuckerman; Stage Manager, Renata Barile-Sigillo; Technical Director, Arthur Resler. CAST: Marie Cheatham (Mae), Jay Devlin (Jerry), Tim Flanagan (Potter), Erik Fredricksen (Earl), Annette Kurek (Peggy), Don Perkins (Kress), William R. Riker (Father), Michael Zuckerman (Joe)

May 5–26, 1978 (18 performances)
RUSTY AND RICO AND LENA AND LOUIE by Leonard Melfi; Director, John Shearin; Set, Tom Warren; Costumes, Margo La Zaro; Lighting, Curt Ostermann; Sound, Paul E. Garrity; Assistant Director, Gail Starkey; Stage Manager, Lisa Grossman. CAST: Maggie Burke (Rusty/Lena), Justin Deas (Rico/Louie)

Michael Zettler Photos

Top Right: Neil McKenzie, Tom Bade, Anita Keal in "Play Strindberg"

Maggie Burke, Justin Deas in "Rusty & Rico ..."

Marie Cheatham in "Clash by Night" Above: Johanna Leister, Harold G. Meyer in "The Spider's Web"

INTERART THEATRE

Margot Lewitin, Artistic Director

WOMEN'S INTERART CENTER

January 16–February 12, 1978 (19 performances)
WHERE MEMORIES ARE MAGIC AND DREAMS INVENTED by Susan Nanus; Director, Susan Einhorn; Set, Ursula Belden; Lighting, Pat Stern; Costumes, Jean Steinlein; Technical Director, Grant Clifford Logan; Production Assistants, Florence L. Rutherford, Maggie Raywood, Cheryl Moore; Press, Ellen Levene, Sharon Bragin; Stage Manager, Carolyn Greer. CAST: Sylvia Gassell (Rachel), Kay Medford (Rose), Lenore Loveman (Faye), and Michael Kaufman (Harry), Allen Swift (Albert), Laura Copland (Clara)

A play in 3 acts and 9 scenes. The action takes place in 1974, 1950 and 1927, in Manhattan and Brooklyn.

March 30–April 1, 1978 (5 performances)
WHO'S A LADY? an original adaptation by Annette Miller of a wide range of contemporary works dealing with modern woman's quest for identity; Director, Helaine Witkind; Press, Ellen Levene. CAST: Annette Miller, Naomi Thornton, accompanied by Michael Edelstein

May 5–June 4, 1978 (15 performances)
SISTER/SISTER by Clare Coss, Sondra Segal, Roberta Sklar; Directed by Sondra Segal, Roberta Sklar; Lighting, Annie Wrightson; Costumes, Florence Rutherford; Stage Managers, Peggy Imbrie, Pamelia Perkins; Press, Ellen Levene. CAST: Barbara George, Mary Lum, Mary Lyon, Debbie Nitzberg, Sondra Segal

May 5–June 3, 1978 (16 performances)
HEY, RUBE by Janet McReynolds; Director, Vickie Rue; Set and Lighting, Barbara Ling; Costumes, Nanzi Adzima; Sound, Pril Smiley; Associate Director, Alley Mills, Associate Designer, Todd Ruff; Stage Managers, P. J. Hassler, Sally Reid; Press, Ellen Levene. CAST: Michael Margotta (Policeman), Ed Setrakian (Attorney), Avra Petrides (Lois), Rosemary Moore (Anna), Laura Dean (Barbara), Carol Laverne (Darlene), Jack Davidson (Barker), Molly McCarthy (Mabel), Joan Shangold (Ruth), Kathleen Roland (Mrs. Edwards), Rebecca Darke (Psychiatrist), Jan Praver (Snake Woman), Sharon Barr (Lillian)

June 7–26, 1978 (16 performances)
MAGIC AND LIONS conceived and directed by Glenda Dickerson; Prose-Poetry, Ernestine Walker; Music, Janyse Singleton; Additional Music, E. L. James, Bruce Strickland; Set, Tyrone Mitchell; Lighting, Vantile E. Whitfield, Katie Fallon; Costumes, Ellen Lee; Stage Manager, Kenneth L. Johnson; Assistant to Director, Jennifer Nelson; Musical Director, Jimmy Foster; Choreographic Consultants, Carol Pennyfeather, Lee Dobson; Artistic Director, Margot Lewitin; Production Manager, Grant Clifford Logan; Managing Director, Kirsten Beck; Press, Ellen Levene. ENSEMBLE: Lee Dobson, E. L. James, Jacqueline Jones, David LeBron, Carol Pennyfeather, Freda Scott, Bruce Strickland

Laura Pettibone Photos

**Right Center: Trini Alvarado in "Becca", Annette Miller, Naomi Thornton in "Who's a Lady?"
Top: Rosemary Moore, Avra Petrides in "Hey, Rube"**

"Magic and Lions"

Kay Medford, Sylvia Gassell in "Where Memories Are Magic . . ."

JOSEPH JEFFERSON THEATRE COMPANY

Cathy Roskam, Executive Director
John Henry Davis, Associate Director
Marshall Purdy, General Manager

LITTLE CHURCH AROUND THE CORNER
February 23–March 12, 1978 (12 performances)
BED AND BREAKFAST by Marion Fredi Towbin; Director, John Desmond; Set, Richard Williams; Lights, Frances Aronson; Sound, Sam Agar; Costumes, Harry Curtis; Technical Director, Gerald Weinstein; Stage Managers, Mary Burns, Mark Rubinsky, Randy Kaplan; Press, Shirley Herz. CAST: Beatrice Ballance (Linda Kramer), Donald Gantry (Ed Brackman)
October 26–November 12, 1977 (12 performances)
INHERIT THE WIND by Jerome Lawrence and Robert E. Lee; Director, John Henry Davis; Assistant Director, Pamela Caren Billig; Set, Raymond C. Recht; Costumes, Patricia Wiegleb; Lighting, Todd Lichtenstein; Sound, Sam Agar; Musical Director, Bill Lester; Technical Director, John Edward Funke; Stage Manager, Sharon Rosenblum. CAST: Barbara Mathews (Melinda), Lionel Chute (Howard), Sherry Rooney (Rachel), William J. Daprato (Meeker), Sam Blackwell (Bertram), Arthur Berwick (Sillers), Dolores Kenan (Mrs. Krebs), Peter Van Norden (Rev. Brown), Bill Tatum (Corkin), Craig Sechler (Bannister), Winnie Boone (Mrs. Loomis), Ara Watson (Mrs. Blair), Wayne Wofford (Elijah), Richmond Hoxie (Hornbeck), William J. Daprato (Hurdy Gurdy Man), Marvin Einhorn (Mayor), Betty Lee Carlton (Mayor's Wife), Humbert Allen Astredo (Brady), Joen Arliss (Mrs. Brady), William Mahone (Davenport), Ian Martin (Drummond), Ed VanNuys (Judge), Larry C. Lott (Dunlap), Christye John, Bebe Sacks Landis (Townspeople)
November 30–December 17, 1977 (12 performances)

LYRICAL AND SATIRICAL: THE MUSIC OF HAROLD ROME conceived and directed by Julianne Boyd; Musical Director, Vicki H. Carter; Choreographer, Jeff Veazey; Costumes, Rachel Kurland; Sets, Lee Mayman; Lighting, Boyd Masten; Stage Managers, Abigail Harper, Anna Werner; Technical Director, Robert G. Adams. CAST: Cris Groenendaal, Sophie Schwab, Gordon Stanley, Susan Waldman
April 26–May 13, 1978 (12 performances)
MOON CRIES by Midge Maroni; Director, Cathy Roskam; Assistant Director, Ted Kubiak; Set, Vittorio Capecce; Costumes, Polly Lee; Lighting, Norman Coates; Stage Managers, Laura Lawler Tolle, Iris Malsberg, Martin Smith. CAST: Cynthia Exline (Ellen), Nada Rowland (Kate), Gwendolyn Brown (Maggie), David MacEnulty (Mike)
May 31–June 17, 1978 (12 performances)

ALGONQUIN SAMPLER a literary review conceived by Charles Maryan and Fred Voelpel; Director, Charles Maryan; Design, Fred Voelpel; Lighting, John Gleason; Incidental Music, John Clifton; Stage Manager, Malcolm D. Ewen; Technical Director, Larry van Werssowetz; Stage Managers, Malcolm D. Ewen, Carrick Glenn, Samuel Kerr Lockhart, Laura Lawler Toole. CAST: Carrick Glenn, George Hall, Don Hastings, Kathryn Hays, Sam Lockhart, Roy London, William Mahone, Jenny Maybrook, Arlene Nadel, Henrietta Valor

Michael Uffer Photos

Right: Nada Rowand, David MacEnulty in "Moon Cries" Above: "Algonquin Sampler"

**Humbert Allen Astredo in "Inherit the Wind"
Top Right: Beatrice Ballance, Donald Gantry in "Bed & Breakfast"**

Gordon Stanley, Sophie Schwab, Susan Waldman, Chris Groenendaal in "Lyrical and Satirical"

THE LIGHT OPERA OF MANHATTAN

William Mount-Burke, Producer-Director-Conductor
Associate Director, Raymond Allen
Ninth Season

EASTSIDE PLAYHOUSE

June 29, 1977–May 28, 1978

General Manager, Mary Beth Carroll; Assistant General Manager, Todd Pearthree; Stage Manager/Choreographer, Jerry Gotham; Set Design, Louise Krozek; Costumes, James Nadeaux; Costumier, Delores Gamba; Lighting, Peggy Clark; Assistant Musical Director, Brian Molloy; Assistant Conductor, J. Michael Bart; Press, Jean Dalrymple, Todd Pearthree

COMPANY

Raymond Allen, Julio Rosario, Lawrence Raiken, Vashek Pazdera, Gary Ridley, Steven Polcek, Nancy Hoffman, Joan Lader, Diane Armistead, Mark Wolff, Jan Downing, Rosemarie Wright, Peggy DuFour, Michael Harrison, Kenneth Sieger, James Nadeaux, Dennis Curran, Elizabeth Devine, Joanne Jamison, Constance Little, Mary Miller, Kristin Paulus, Jo Shelnutt, Ed Harrison, Bob Main, Calvin Selfridge, Joseph Smith, Jeanne Beauvais, Dennis English, Paul Huck, Georgia McEver, Edward Hustwit, Sheleigah Grube, Karen Kruger, Linda Plona, Michael Barnett, John Palmore, Gary Pitts, Gail Elizabeth Evans, Maeve Gyenes, Marilyn Kaeshian, Francine Katz, Miki Newmark, Hanice Papdos, Linda Plona, Kathy Rogers, Steve Brown, Andrew Callahan, James Lawer, Tom Olmstead, Walter Richardson, Richard Weston, Mary Lee Rubens, Valerie Mondini, Alida Augen, Paul Bufano, Sandy Burnard, Randa Ball, Nancy Breece, William Walsh, Robert Bauckham, Nancy Papale, Katherine Cuba, Danny Bernstein, Robert Berlott, Tom Boyd, Bronwen Brown, Diane Simmons, Lloyd Harris, Sara Taubman, G. Michael Harvey, Ethel Mae Mason, Elizabeth Harr, Katherine Neville, Brian Bonnar, Lindsay Dyett, Cynthia Kolk, Mary Ann Olig, Donna Shanklin, Marilyn Robbins

PRODUCTIONS

"H.M.S. Pinafore," "The Pirates of Penzance," "The Merry Widow," "Naughty Marietta," "The Vagabond King," "Ruddigore," "The Mikado," "The Sorcerer," "Trial by Jury," "Iolanthe," "Mlle. Modiste," "The Grand Duchess of Gerolstein," "Patience," "The Gondoliers"

**Right: Georgia McEver, Gary Ridley
in "Mlle. Modiste" Above: Jeanne Beauvais
(also top), Michael Harrison in
"The Merry Widow"**

**Raymond Allen, Eleanor Wold
in "The Mikado"**

**Georgia McEver
in "Mlle. Modiste"**

LION THEATRE COMPANY
Gene Nye, Producing Director
Garland Wright, Company Director
Ellie Meglio, Managing Director

WESTSIDE AIRLINES TERMINAL
November 25, 1977–February 5, 1978 (54 performances)
K: IMPRESSIONS OF FRANZ KAFKA'S "THE TRIAL" devised by the Lion Theatre Company; Director, Garland Wright; Setting and Lighting, John Arnone, Garland Wright; Costumes, David James; Technical Director, Peter Mainguy; Stage Managers, Steve Shlansky, Gerald Kindfather; Press, Susan Bloch, Francis X. Tobin. CAST: Kim Ameen, Mary E. Baird, Tony Campisi, Janice Fuller, David Gallagher, Gibson Glass, Greg Grove, John Guerrasio, Jim McLure, Gene Nye
May 11–June 4, 1978 (22 performances)
THE DEATH AND LIFE OF JESSE JAMES by Len Jenkin; Director, Gene Nye; Scenery, Henry Millman; Costumes, Bob Wojewodski; Lighting, Frances Aronson; Music, John McKinney; Choreography, Kathy Kramer; Stage Managers, Steve Shlansky, Kathy Arlt; Press, Ellen Levene, Tom Trenkle. CAST: Allan Carlsen (Jesse James), William Brenner (Frank James), James McLure (Bob Ford), John Ingle (Cole Younger), Peter Noel-Duhamel (Huey Dalton), Jerry Lazarus (Louie Dalton), M. Patrick Hughes (Dewey), Maria Cellario (Mrs. James), Tamara Daniel (Mom), Rebecka Malka (Rosita), Janice Fulleer (Conchita), Collette Connor (Pepita), Deirdre Keogh (Child), Don Auspitz (Capt. Sheets/Speedy Gonzalez), John Genke (Reverend/President/-Sheriff), Russell Duffy (Immigrant), Rob Anderson (Commissioner/Interviewer)

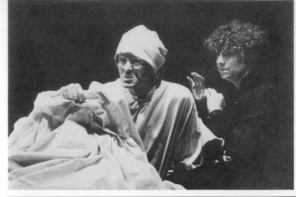

Right: "K" *(Greg Grove Photo)*
Top: Gene Nye, Mary E. Baird in "K"

Peter Noel-Duhamel, John Ingle, Chip Brenner, Allan Carlsen, James McLure, Jerry Lazarus, M. Patrick Hughes in "The Death and Life of Jesse James" *(Laura Pettibone Photo)*

MANHATTAN THEATRE CLUB

Lynne Meadow, Artistic Director
Barry Grove, Managing Director

Associate Artistic Director, Stephan Pascal; Associate Director, Thomas Bullard; Technical Director, Robert Buckler; Business Manager, Connie L. Alexis; Audience Development, Ruby Lerner; Administrative Assistant, Diane de Mailly; Casting-Literary Assistant, Andy Wolk; Technical Assistant, Betsy Tanner; Press, Robert Pontarelli, Caryn Katkin

MANHATTAN THEATRE CLUB

October 26–November 27, 1977 (35 performances)
CHEZ NOUS by Peter Nichols; Director, Lynne Meadow; Associate Director, Richard Maltby, Jr.; Set, John Conklin; Costumes, Nanzi Adzima; Lights, Dennis Parichy; Sound, George Hansen; Stage Manager, Maureen Lynett. CAST: Linda Atkinson, Barbara Caruso, Jim Jansen, Charles Mayer, Christina Pickles, John Tillinger, Sam Waterston

November 2–27, 1977 (20 performances)
THE WAYSIDE MOTOR INN by A. R. Gurey, Jr.; Director, Tony Giordano; Set, David Potts; Costumes, Kenneth M. Yount; Lighting, Spencer Moss; Sound, George Hansen; Stage Manager, Johnna Murray. CAST: Jill Andre, Thomas Barbour, Margaret Barker, John Braden, Gary Cookson, Jill O'Hara, Richard Sale, Catherine Schreiber, Drew Snyder, Wayne Tippit

December 14, 1977–January 15, 1978 (35 performances)
PLAY AND OTHER PLAYS by Samuel Beckett; Director, Alan Schneider; Set and Costumes, Zack Brown; Lights, William Mintzer; Stage Manager, Jody Boese. CAST: Suzanne Costallos, Donald Davis, Sloane Shelton

December 28, 1977–January 22, 1978
DORY PREVIN: LADY WITH A BRAID—a salute to the words and music of Dory Previn; Director, Caymichael Patten; Musical Director, John Lewis; Choreographer, Dalienne Majors; Costumes, Ginna Taulane; Stage Manager, Gene Borio; Associate Artistic Director, Stephan Pascal; Associate Director, Thomas Bullard. CAST: Bob Gunton, Lynne Lipton, Jill O'Hara

December 28, 1977–January 22, 1978
FRANKIE AND ANNIE by Diane Simkin; Director, Paul Schneider; Set, David Potts; Costumes, Anne Wolfe; Lighting, Jeff Davis; Stage Manager, Linda Spohn. CAST: James Albanese, John Andrews, Robin Bartlett, Shelby Brammer, Sarah Chodoff, Gary Cookson, Jim De Marse, Mary Pat Gleason, Mario Carlo Mariani, Wendie Beth Marks, Les Roberts, Lea Scott, Sherry Steiner, Daniel Stern

February 1–March 5, 1978
STATEMENTS AFTER AN ARREST UNDER THE IMMORALITY ACT by Atholt Fugard and SCENES FROM SOWETO by Stephen Wilmer; Director, Thomas Bullard; Sets, David Potts; Costumes, Judy Dearing; Lights, Dennis Parichy; Dialect Coach, Gordon Jacoby; Stage Manager, Jody Boese. CAST: Robert Christian, Veronica Castang, John C. Vennema

Top Right: Sam Waterston, Christina Pickles in "Chez Nous" Below: Margaret Barker, Thomas Barbour in "Wayside Motor Inn"

Suzanne Costallos in "Plays and Other Plays"

John C. Vennema, Robert Christian in "Scenes from Soweto"

(Gerry Goodstein Photos)

MANHATTAN THEATRE CLUB

February 8–March 5, 1978
AIN'T MISBEHAVIN' directed by Richard Maltby, Jr.; Music Supervisor, Luther Henderson; Choreography, Arthur Faria; Vocal Arrangements-Musical Consultant, Jeffrey Gutcheon; Assistant Musical Director, Amina Claudine Myers; Costumes, Pegi Goodman; Associate Director, Murray Horwitz. CAST: Irene Cara, Nell Carter, Andre De Shields, Armelia McQueen, Ken Page

March 1–26, 1978
RED FOX/SECOND HANGING by Don Baker and Dudley Cocke; Director, Michael Posnick; Set, David Potts; Lighting, Curt Ostermann; Associate Director, Dudley Cocke; Stage Manager, Elliott Woodruff. CAST: Don Baker, Gary Slemp, Frankie Taylor

March 8–April 2, 1978
HAS ANYBODY HERE FOUND LOVE directed by Miriam Fond; Lyrics and Book, Lois Wyse; Music, Carol Frankel; Musical Director, Bobby Blume; Stage Manager, Pamela Singer. CAST: Marilyn Caskey, Rosalind Harris, Judith Roberts

April 5–May 7, 1978
CATSPLAY by Istvan Orkeny; Translated by Clara Gyorgyey; Director, Lynne Meadow; Set, John Lee Beatty; Costumes, Jennifer von Mayrhauser; Lighting, Dennis Parichy; Music, Robert Dennis; Sound, Charles London; Dramaturge, Andy Wolk; Stage Manager, David S. Rosenak. CAST: Helen Burns (Bela), Katherine Squire (Giza), Jane Cronin (Paula), Charles Meyer (Yanos), Bette Henritze (Mihaly), Susan Sharkey (Ilona), Peter Phillips (Yoshka), Robert Gerringer (Victor), Eleanor Phelps (Mme. Vivelli). Re-opened Tuesday, May 30, 1978 at Promenade Theatre

April 5–30, 1978
JIM WANN'S COUNTRY CABARET directed by John Haber; Musical Director, Guy Strobel; Stage Manager, Barbara Abel. CAST: Cass Morgan, Kathi Moss, Guy Strobel, Jim Wann

April 5–30, 1978
SAFE HOUSE by Nick Kazan; Director, Jonathan Alper; Set, David Potts; Costumes, Flo Rutherford; Lighting, Bennet Averyt; Stage Manager, Jon Andrews. CAST: John V. Shea (Carl), Paul Schierhorn (Shake), Kaiulani Lee (Hillary), Deborah Hedwall (Tink), Lisabeth Sean (Ruth)

May 3–28, 1978
HAPPY WITH THE BLUES: The Music of Harold Arlen; Director, Julianne Boyd; Musical Director, Vicki Helms Carter; Choreographer, Otis A. Sallid; Stage Manager, David Rosenberg. CAST: Jean Andalman, Barbara Andres, Stephen James, Sarilee Kahn, Orrin Reiley

Right: Orrin Reilley, Barbara Andres in "Happy with the Blues" Above: Gary Slemp, Frankie Taylor, Don Baker in "Red Fox/Second Hanging" Top: Ken Page, Andre DeShields in "Ain't Misbehavin' "

Kaiulani Lee, John Shea
in "Safe House"

Donna Marshall, Maureen Moore, Gary Beach,
Gail Nelson in "By Strouse"

128

MANHATTAN THEATRE CLUB

May 17–June 11, 1978
RIB CAGE by Larry Ketron; Director, Andy Wolk; Set, David Potts; Costumes, Linda Fisher; Lights, Dennis Parichy; Stage Manager, Elliott Woodruff. CAST: Kristin Griffith (Vernie), Grayson Hall (Sheryl), I. M. Hobson (Posten), Lynn Milgrim (Carolyn), David Selby (Hodge), J. T. Walsh (Richard)

November 9–December 4, 1977
BY STROUSE with songs by Charles Strouse; Director, Charles Strouse; Musical Director, David Krane; Staged by Mary Kyte; Stage Manager, Donna Lieberman. CAST: Kim Fedena, Judy Gibson, Laurence Guittard, Maureen Moore. Re-opened February 1, 1978 at Soho Ballroom, and closed April 30, 1978 after 156 performances. Cast changes included Gary Beach, Donna Marshall and Gail Nelson.

May 24–June 18, 1978
STRAWBERRY FIELDS by Stephen Poliakoff; Director, Stephen Pascal; Set, Robert Yodice; Costumes, Judy Dearing; Lighting, Dennis Parichy; Sound, Gary Harris; Stage Manager, Paul Fitzmaurice. CAST: Brad O'Hare, Ralph Seymour, Geraldine Sherman, Susan Sharkey, Nicholas Woodeson

March 15–April 2, 1978 (14 performances)
THE PROMISE by Aleksei Arbuzov; Director, Philip Baloun; Sets, Tom Warren; Lights and Sound, Stephen J. Cramer; Costumes, Margo La Zaro; Projections, Fran Albin; Stage Manager, James Storrow. CAST: John Heard (Marat), Mary Jane Negro (Lika), Christopher Curry (Leonidik)

Right: John Heard, Christopher Curry, Mary-Joan Negro in "The Promise" *(Alissa Margulies Photo)* **Top: Susan Sharkey, Nicholas Woodeson, Brad O'Hare in "Strawberry Fields"** *(Gerry Goodstein Photo)*

NATIONAL BLACK THEATRE

Barbara Ann Teer, Executive Producer
Zuri McKie, Associate Producer

Executive Director, Frederica Teer, Associate Director, Keibu Faison; Stage Managers, Gwen McIver, Otito Smith; Wardrobe, Janice Montague; Press, LaReine LaMar, Phillip Hawkins, Asantewaa Westbrook

NATIONAL BLACK THEATRE

October 22–December 11, 1977
THE RITUAL created and developed by Barbara Ann Teer, based on poem "What If" by Kwame Azular; Original Dialogue and Music developed by Barbara Ann Teer and performing company; Director, Zuri McKie; Musical Director, Nabii Faison; Choreographer, Aseiduwa Collier; Dialogue Adaptation, Sola Roberts. CAST: Adeife Harris, Adetunde Samuel, Amy C. Boyd, Asantewaa Dawn Westbrook, Chiquita Suares, Clair Tait Mason, Dianne Ford, Doris Fontaine, Edward L. Keeler, Jr., Falabu Vivian Grice, Gwendolyn McIver, Jonathan Beale, Lucille Perfit, Marcella Hunter, Oba Watson, Olaitan Valerie Callender, Otito Frank Smith, Sola Gibson Roberts, Tina Hunter, Thomas Mason, Walter Regi Remsey, Wendy Cofield, Yinka Jeppe
SOLJOURNEY INTO TRUTH conceived and created by Barbara Ann Teer; Production Managers, Zuri McKie, Nabii Faison; Stage Manager, Adetunde Samuel; Music Coordinator, Nabii Faison. CAST: Adetunde Samuel, Adeyemi Lythcott, Asieduwa Collier, Ayodele Moore, Donna Stokes, Fela Scott, Keibu Faison, Nabii Faison, Nike Newsam, Otito Smith, Shirley Faison, Sola Roberts, Taraja Samuel, Yinka Jeppe, Zuri McKie

May 5–June 4, 1978
SEVEN COMES UP, SEVEN COMES DOWN by Lonne Elder III with WINE IN THE WILDERNESS by Alice Childress; Director, Adeyemi Lythcott; Co-Producers, Nabii Faison, Zuri McKie; Production Manager, Adetunde Samuel; Set, Paul Davis; Costumes, Pat Vaughn; Stage Manager, Olu Akomolafe; Sound Effects, Adeyemi Lythcott; Lighting, Shirley Prendergrast; Make-up, Desiree Gordon; Production Assistants, Hal Lawson, Wilson Williams, George McKie, Yvonne Stuckey, Julia Berry, Jon Beale, Adeife Harris, Tina Hunter, Dorian King, Naimah Hasam. CAST: Keibu Faison, Dwight Collins, James Pelton, Ayodele Moore, Koya-Doris Fontaine, Valerie Olaitan Callender

Adeyemi Lythcott Photos

wight Collins, Ayodele Moore in "Wine in the Wilderness" Above: ames Pelta, David Pierce, Keibu Faison in "Seven Comes Up ..."

NEGRO ENSEMBLE COMPANY

Douglas Turner Ward, Artistic Director
Tenth Season

Executive Director, Robert Hooks; Administrative Director, Frederick Garrett; General Manager, Coral Hawthorne; Executive Assistant, Deborah McGee; Administrative Assistant, Skip Waters; Press, Howard Atlee, Clarence Allsopp, Becky Flora

ST. MARK'S PLAYHOUSE
November 26, 1977–February 28, 1978 (59 performances)

THE OFFERING

By Gus Edwards; Director, Douglas Turner Ward; Scenery, Raymond C. Recht; Lighting, Paul Gallo; Costumes, Arthur McGee, Technical Director, Samuel Gonzalez; Production Assistant, James Reed; Stage Managers, Horacena J. Taylor, Ron Nguvu

CAST

Bob Tyrone	Douglas Turner Ward
Princess	Olivia Williams
Martin	Charles Weldon
Ginny	Katherine Knowles

A play in two acts. The action takes place at the present time in a basement apartment in West Side Manhattan.

Bert Andrews Photo

Top Right: Katherine Knowles, Charles Welden, Olivia Williams, Douglas Turner Ward

January 19–March 5, 1978 (40 performances)

BLACK BODY BLUES

By Gus Edwards; Director, Douglas Turner Ward; Scenery, Raymond C. Recht; Lighting, Paul Gallo; Costumes, Arthur McGee; Stage Managers, Horacena J. Taylor, Ron Nguvu

CAST

Arthur	Samm-Art Williams
Andy	Norman Bush
Joyce	Catherine E. Slade
Louis	Frankie R. Faison
Fletcher	Douglas Turner Ward

A play in two acts. The action takes place in August at the present time in an apartment in the Broadway-Times Square area of New York City.

Bert Andrews Photo

Right Center: Frankie R. Faison, Samm-Art Williams, Catherine E. Slade

ST. MARK'S PLAYHOUSE
April 14–May 14, 1978 (27 performances)

TWILIGHT DINNER

By Lennox Brown; Director, Douglas Turner Ward; Setting, Samuel Gonzalez; Lighting, James Fauvell

CAST

Jimmy	Leon Morenzie
Elissa	Karen Bernhard
Ray	Reuben Green

Bert Andrews Photo

Karen Bernhard, Leon Morenzie, Reuben Green

THE NEW DRAMATISTS, INC.

June 16, 1977–May 31, 1978

PRODUCTIONS
(Works-in-progress)

WINDCHIMES by Anna Marie Barlow with Mia Heidi, Lois Battle, Augusta Dabney, Bob Shrewsbury, Dan Ziskie, Elsa Raven. TWO MARYS by Warren Kliewer with Ruth Baker, Ed Crowley, Michele LaRue, John Wyeth, Kathleen Phelan. BURNING BRIGHT by Lyle Kessler with Dick Lynch, Gene Davis, Rudy Bond, Sully Boyar, Demo Dimartile, Peter Weller, Pamela Reed, Liz Kemp, Jack Gilpin, Bob Seidenberg. FILIGREE PEOPLE by Peter Dee with Henry Tunney, Linda Russell, Mike Kimberley, Linda Chase, Pat Podell, Glenn Zeitler, Elizabeth Higginbotham. AMAZING GRACE by Peter Maloney with Bill Wiley, Fred Morsell, Cortez Nance, Ellen Sandler, J. T. Walsh, Jean Barker, Graham Beckel, Joan Grant. LOSERS by Donald Wollner with Barnes Miller, Mitchell McGuire, Peter Boyden, Alan North, J. Kevin Scannell, Joan Grant. THE UNDRESSING OF A NUDE by William Andrews with J. J. Lewis, Ingrid Sonnichsen, Joel Simon, Eric Conger, Dan Desmond. CASANOVA by John Wolfson and Ralph Affoumado with Irwin Pearl, Ruth Jaroslow, Michael Enserro, Edmund Lyndeck, Faith Catlin, Spring Condoyan, Ken Shuey, Richard Dahlia, William Starrett, Dottie Dee, Alan Brooks. CARNIVAL DREAMS by Conn Fleming with Elizabeth Ashley, Austin Pendleton, John Cullum, Robert Earl Jones, Allan Benjamin. VOODOO TRILOGY by Frank Gagliano with Barbara Montgomery, Dominic Chianese, Stephanie Cotsirillos, William Rhys, Rosemary DeAngelis, Peter Saputo. WRITERS CAMP by Peter Dee and Albert Lunch with Don Howard, Kathleen Turner, Mary Testa, Dorothy Calo, David Kerry Heefner, Philip LeStrange, Thomas Ryan, Steven Ryan, Kelly Fitzpatrick, Jim Hillgartner, Henson Keys, Elizabeth Higginbotham. MOTHER RYAN by Maurice Noel with Polly Adams, Matthew Cowles, Molly Adams, Parker McCormick, Leora Dana, Robert McFarland, Elise Hunt. DANCIN' TO CALLIOPE by Jack Gilhooley with Graham Beckel, Rosemary DeAngelis, Martina Degnan, Thomas D. Warren. BEIRCE TAKES ON THE RAILROADS! by Phil Bosakowski with Humbert Allen Astredo, Tom Bade, Manuel De Blas, Miles Chapin, Maria Hasen, Dolores Kenan, Terry O'Quinn, Jon Polito, Steve Pudenz, Bruce Robinson, Elizabeth Ruscio, Charles Welch, Susanna Styron. TORNADO by Pat Kolt Staten with Sue Lawless, Shelly Batt, Edmund Williams, Suzanne Ford, Steven Gilborn, Gisela Caldwell, Susan McVeigh, James Scott Bell, Jane Cronin, Dale Carman. THE BEACH CHILDREN by John von Hartz with Bill Randolph, Susan Porretto, Jackie Blue, Mark Margolis, Larry Ross. JUST OFF PARK by Stuart Vaughan with Katherine Manning, Henderson Forsythe, Earl Trussell, Anne Murray. THE BOOTH BROTHERS by Warren Kliewer with Michael Levin, David Aaron, Holly Cameron, Robert Chamberlain, Jonathan Chappell, Hal Davis, Jack Deisler, Jack Gilpin, Michele LaRue, Terry Layman, Charles McKenna, Barnes Miller, Charles Morey, William Newman, Jon Stolzberg, Elsa Raven, David Taylor, James Warden, John Wyeth. THE AMERICAN OASIS by Steven Somkin with Stephen Ahern, Donna Charron, Jack McClure, Fern Howell, Jess Adkins, Charles Mayer, Jerry Rockwood, Marc Burd, Ken Rubenfeld, Adam Lefevre, Janice Wayne, Susan Mell. THE MAN WHO DREW CIRCLES by Barry Berg with Richard Fancy, Richard DeFabees, Robert Chamberlain, Anita Keal, Ruth Klinger. A DISTURBANCE OF MIRRORS by Pat Kolt Staten with Carol Quinn, Shelly Batt, Laure Mattos, Scott Sparks, David Rasche, Eleanor Reissa. THE VERANDAH by Clifford Mason with Herb Downer, Loretta Devine, Thomas Anderson, Estelle Evans, Richard Ward, Judy Tate, Robert Earl Jones, Leila Danette, Jodi Long, Lee K. Richardson, Harsh Nayyar. MOTHERS AND DAUGHTERS by John von Hartz with Ilene Kristen, Lynn Milgrim, Anna Minot, Alan Silver. A SMALL WINTER CRISIS by Warren Kliewer with Mervyn Haines, Jr., Ellen Novack, Deborah Openden, Jonathan Chappell, Martin Shakar, Michele LaRue. THE SUGAR BOWL by Stan Taikeff with Maurice Copeland, John Bruce, Gerald Richards, Clement Fowler, Lynn Cohen, Steve Ryan, Nicholas Kepros, Peter DeLaurier, Clarence Felder, Jerry Zaks, Paul Lambert. THREE MILLION ROSEBUDS by Peter Cookson with David Rasche, Carolyn Lagerfelt, Laure Mattos, John Horton. AVENUE B by Jack Gilhooley with Carlos Cestero, Alma Cuervo, Jim DeMarse, Ilene Kristen. MARVELOUS BROWN by Diane Kagan with Diane Kagan, Doug Higgins, Doug Jones, Edward Seamon, Rudy Hornisch, Roger Morden, Mark Hofmaier. THE PRIVATE EYE OF HIRAM BODONI by Frank Gagliano with Roger Morden, Edward Seamon, Judith Reagan. NAPKIN NOTES by Philip A. Bosakowski with Dann Florek, Debra Mooney, Elizabeth Rusvio, Michael Rockne. FREDERICK JORDAN'S DREAM by Peter Dee with John Bottoms, Deborah Combs, Deborah Rush. IN THE MODERN STYLE by Stanley Taikeff with Richard Patrick-Warner, Lynn Cohen, Dolores Kenan, Bill Nunnery, Jim Carruthers, David Victor Truro,

Robert Earl Jones in "The Verandah" *(Stephan Harty Photo)*

Top: Josephine Nichols, Robin Howard in "Filigree People" *(Joseph Millet Photo)*

Samm-Art Williams, Catherine E. Slade, Norman Bush in "Black Body Blues" *(Bert Andrews Photo)*

Donna Sorbello, Regina David, Leslie-Sarah David. TORNADO by Pat Kolt Staten with Margaret Hamilton, Wendy Goodman, Bill Wiley, Lisabeth Shean, Pat McNamara, Ann Spettell, Jack McClure, Alice Drummond, Steve Vinovich, Laure Mattos. A NEW UNTITLED PLAY by Conn Fleming with John Mintum, William Andrews, Polly Holliday, Suzanne Marley, Chandra Oppenheim.

131

THE PHOENIX THEATRE

T. Edward Hambleton, Managing Director
Marilyn S. Miller, Executive Director
Daniel Freudenberger, Artistic Director

Twenty-fifth Season

MARYMOUNT MANHATTAN THEATRE
October 6–23, 1977 (28 performances)

HOT GROG

Book by Jim Wann; Music and Lyrics, Bland Simpson, Jim Wann; Director, Edward Berkeley; Scenery And Lighting, James Tilton; Costumes, Hilary Rosenfeld; Sound, R. S. D. Weeden; Musical Direction, Jeff Waxman; Musical Staging, Patricia Birch; Associate Choreographer, Mimi Wallace; Fight Choreography, B. H. Barry; Technical Director, Paul H. Everett; Assistant General Manager, Louise M. Bayer; Assistant Manager, Barbara Carrellas; Administrative Assistant, Kathryn Gaffney; Production Manager, Tom Aberger; Wardrobe, Pat Whipple; Stage Managers, James Harker, Barbara Abel; Press, Gifford/Wallace, Inc.

CAST

Mimi Kennedy (Anne Bonney), Patrick Hines (Gov. Eden), Terry O'Quinn (Calico Jack Rackham), Louis Zorich (Blackbeard/Edward Teach), John McCurry (Caesar), Timothy Meyers (Israel Hands), Mary Bracken Phillips (Mr. Read), Rebecca Gilchrist (Savannah), Kathi Moss (Jamaica), Roger Howell (Lt. Rhett).

MUSICAL NUMBERS: "Seizure to Roam," "Got a Notion," "Come on down to the Sea," "Hot Grog," "The Pirates' Life," "The Difference Is Me," "Change in Direction," "Heaven Must Have Been Smiling," "Hack 'Em," "Treasure to Bury/One of Us," "Sea Breeze," "The Chase," "Skye Boat Song," "Marooned," "The Swordfight," "The Head Song," "Drinking Fool," "Bound Away."

A musical in two acts. The action takes place in Coastal Carolina in 1718.

Roger Greenawalt Photo

Mimi Kennedy, Terry O'Quinn, Mary Bracken Phillips

Right: "Uncommon Women and Others"

Below: Alma Cuervo, Ann McDonough, Ellen Parker, Cynthia Herman, Glenn Close, Swoosie Kurtz, Jill Eikenberry, Josephine Nichols in "Uncommon Women"

MARYMOUNT MANHATTAN THEATRE

November 17–December 4, 1977 (28 performances)

UNCOMMON WOMEN AND OTHERS

By Wendy Wasserstein; Director, Steven Robman; Scenery and Lighting, James Tilton; Costumes, Jennifer von Mayrhauser; Technical Director, Paul H. Everett; Production Assistants, Barbara Abel, Pamela Singer; Wardrobe Mistress, Patti Whipple; Stage Managers, Tom Aberger, Madeline Mingino; Press, Gifford/Wallace, Inc.

CAST

Jill Eikenberry (Kate Quin), Ann McDonough (Samantha Stewart), Alma Cuervo (Holly Kaplan), Ellen Parker (Muffet DeNicola), Swoosie Kurtz (Rita Altabel), Josephine Nichols (Mrs. Plumm), Cynthia Herman (Susie Friend), Anna Levine (Carter), Glenn Close (Leilah)

A play in two acts. The action takes place in a restaurant at the present time, and six years earlier at a college for women.

Maureen Anderman, Brad Davis

MARYMOUNT MANHATTAN THEATRE

December 23, 1977–January 8, 1978 (27 performances)

THE ELUSIVE ANGEL

By Jack Gilhooley; Director, Steven Robman; Scenery and Lighting, James Tilton; Costumes, Jennifer von Mayrhauser; Songs, Arthur Miller and Jack Gilhooley; Press, Gifford/Wallace

CAST

Brad Davis (Carlton Pine), Maureen Anderman (Mary Pine), Graham Beckel ("Slick" Jessup), Martha Gaylord ("Bo Peep" Braxton), William Knight (Ken Harrison), Alexa Kenin (Lucy)

A drama in two acts. The action takes place at the present time in the living room of a modest apartment house in a major northern city.

Roger Greenawalt Photos

Graham Beckel, Maureen Anderman

MARYMOUNT MANHATTAN THEATRE

January 12–29, 1978 (28 performances)

ONE CRACK OUT

By David French; Director, Daniel Freudenberger; Scenery, James Tilton; Costumes, Julie Weiss; Lighting, Paul H. Everett; Billiard Consultant, Steve Mizerak; Stage Managers, Tom Aberger, Madeline Mingino; Press, Gifford/Wallace, Inc.

CAST

John Aquino (McKee), Christine Baranski (Wanda), Ed Cambridge (Earl), Al Freeman, Jr. (Bulldog), Teri Garr (Helen), James Greene (Suitcase Sam), Norman Snow (Jack the Hat), Kenneth Welsh (Charlie Evans), Jerry Zaks (Al)

A drama in two acts and eight scenes. The action takes place at the present time in a pool hall, and in Charlie's apartment in Toronto, Canada.

Roger Greenawalt Photos

Left: Al Freeman, Jr.

Christine Baranski, Norman Snow

Kenneth Welsh, Teri Garr

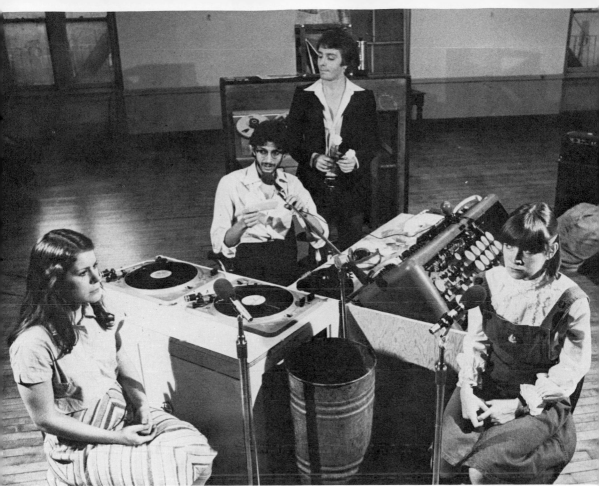

**Christine Estabrook, Jeff Goldblum,
Mark Lamos, Ann McDonough**

MARYMOUNT MANHATTAN THEATRE

June 1–18, 1978 (22 performances)

CITY SUGAR

By Stephen Poliakoff; Director, Daniel Freudenberger; Scenery and Lighting, James Tilton; Costumes and Mannequins, Julie Weiss; Sound and Audio, David Rapkin; Dialect Consultant, Elizabeth Smith; Consulting Disc Jockey, Vin Scelsa; Stage Managers, Tom Aberger, Brian Kremen; Technical Director, Thomas A. Shilhanek; Production Assistant, Kathy Bird; Press, Susan Bloch, Sally Christiansen; Production Coordinator, David Cash

CAST

Christine Estabrook (Nicola Davies), Jeff Goldblum (Leonard Brazil), Russell Horton (John), Mark Lamos (Rex), Anna Levine (Susan), Ann McDonough (Jane)

A "black comedy" in two acts. The action takes place at the present time in a sound studio of a local commercial radio station in Leicester, England; near the frozen foods counter of Liptons supermarket in Leicester; and in Nicola's bedroom in Leicester.

Martha Swope Photos

Jeff Goldblum

135

THE PAPER BAG PLAYERS

September 1977–June 1978

Written, Directed and Designed by Judith Martin; Music Composed by Donald Ashwander; Administrator, Judith Liss; Stage Manager, Peter Jablonski

CAST

Donald Ashwander
Irving Burton
Judith Martin
Jeanne Michels
Cort Miller

PRODUCTIONS: "I Won't Take a Bath," "Everybody, Everybody," "Hot Feet"

Martha Swope Photo

Judith Martin, Irving Burton, Courtney Miller, Jeanne Michels in "Everybody, Everybody"

PLAYWRIGHTS HORIZONS, INC.

Robert Moss, Artistic Director
Andre Bishop, Associate Artistic Director
Jane Moss, Managing Director

Associate Artistic Director/Queens Festival Theater, Philip Himberg; Production Manager, Zoya Wyeth; Press, Joan Egan, Lucy Stille; Audience Development, Roger T. Danforth; Business Manager, Ira Schlosser; Technical Directors, Charles Tyndall, Mary Calhoun, James Fainberg; Assistant Technical Director, Toby Scott

PLAYWRIGHTS HORIZONS
QUEENS FESTIVAL THEATER
June 11–26, 1977 (12 performances)
THE GINGERBREAD LADY by Neil Simon; Director, Rae Allen; Sets, Christina Weppner; Lights, John Giscondi; Costumes, Marcie Begleiter; Stage Manager, Zoya Wyeth. CAST: Thomas Dillon, Helen Gallagher, Dorrie Kavanaugh, Dick LaTessa, Valcour Lavizzo, Kathleen Tolan
June 16–30, 1977 (12 performances)
CRACKS by Martin Sherman; Director, Larry Carpenter; Sets, Ruth A. Wells; Lights, Frances Aronson; Costumes, Jean Steinlein; Stage Manager, Judy Mauer. CAST: Holly Barron, Robert Brian Berger, Joel Brooks, James Cook, Jane Cronin, Julia MacKenzie, Elizabeth Ruscio, William Russ, William Sadler
July 16–31, 1977 (12 performances)
THE PLAYBOY OF THE WESTERN WORLD by John Millington Synge; Director, Michael Montel; Sets, Bob Phillips; Lights, Pat Stern; Costumes, James Edmund Brady; Stage Manager, Belle Baxter. CAST: Jon Peter Benson, Sarah Chodoff, Tom Crawley, Bernard Frawley, Catherine Jacobsen, Kaiulani Lee, Pat McNamara, Marianne Muellerleile, Chris Romilly, David Selby, Jeremiah Supple, Ellen Tovatt
October 15–November 6, 1977 (20 performances)
ANYTHING GOES with Book by Guy Bolton, P. G. Wodehouse, Howard Lindsay, Russell Crouse; Music and Lyrics, Cole Porter; Director, Larry Carpenter; Dances and Musical Numbers Staged by Joey Patton; Musical Direction, Evans Haile; Sets, Christopher Thomas; Lights, Frances Aronson; Costumes, Kenneth M. Yount; Stage Manager, Dorothy Maffei. CAST: Margaret Benczak, Charlie Bernuth, Terry Byrne, Catherine Cappiello, Edmond Dante, Diana Drew, Mark Estes, Ed Evanko, Cookie Harlin, Michael Hayward-Jones, Buck Hobbs, Justine Johnston, Mark Manley, Joe Palmieri, Rick Porter, Bubba Rambo, Sally Ann Swarm, Henrietta Valor
October 20–November 5, 1977 (12 performances) In association with the Second Company of the Williamstown Theater Festival:
GOGOL by Len Jenkins; Director, David Schweizer; Sets, Charles Stone; Lights, Marty Kapell; Costumes, Khorshid Panthaky; Stage Manager, Bonnie Panson. CAST: Michael Arabian, Beverly Barbieri, Sharon Barr, Donna Yvette Brown, Gregory T. Daniel, Kathy Danzer, Lori DeVito, Peter Harris, Brian Kirwin, Randle Mell, Charles Shaw-Robinson, Lisa Sloan, Jeffrey Ware

Nathaniel Tileston Photos

Henrietta Valor, Michael Hayward-Jones in "Anything Goes" Above: Kaiulani Lee, David Selby in "Playboy of the Western World"

Left Top: Helen Gallagher in "The Gingerbread Lady"

PLAYWRIGHTS HORIZONS

October 21–November 19 (15 performances) In Association with the Second Company of the Williamstown Theater Festival:

ANGEL CITY by Sam Shepard; Director Marty Kapell; Sets, Charles Stone; Lights, Marty Kapell; Costumes, Khorshid Panthaky; Stage Manager, Bonnie Panson; CAST: Gregory T. Daniel, Peter Harris, Randle Mell, Charles Shaw-Robinson, Lisa Sloan, Jeffrey Ware.

October 22–November 19, 1977 (13 performances) In Association with The Second Company of the Williamstown Theater Festival:

BACK COUNTY CRIMES by Lanie Robertson; Director, Harold DeFelice; Sets, Marty Kapell; Lights, Marty Kapell; Costumes, Khorshid Panthaky; Stage Manager, Bonnie Panson; CAST: Beverly Barbieri, Sharon Barr, Gregory T. Daniel, Kathy Danzer, Lori DeVito, Deborah Mayo, Randle Mell, Anthony Pasqualini, Charles Shaw-Robinson, Lisa Sloan, Jeffrey Ware

November 3–4, 1977 (2 performances)

S.W.A.K. by Sally Ordway; Director Elinor Renfield; CAST: Alix Elias, Quincy Long, Lane Sanford, Virginia Stephens, D. Victor Truro, Barbara Spiegel.

November 18–19, 1977 (2 performances)

LIBBY AND THE GIANTS by Stephen Hanan; Director, David Boorstin; CAST: Michael Cooke, Miller Lide, Virginia Morris.

November 26–December 18, 1977 (23 performances)

A CHRISTMAS CAROL by Charles Dickens; Adapted by Christopher Cox; Director Christopher Cox; Sets, Richard Williams; Lights, Pat Stern; Costumes, A. Christina Giannini; Sound, Philip Campanella; Stage Manager, Victoria Bradshaw; CAST: Michael Arabian, Sara Birtman-Fox, John Blazo, Jr., Gretel Cummings, Joanne Green, C. S. Hayward, Kathleen Heaney, Christopher Hewett, Prudence Wright Holmes, Stephanie Jose, Court Miller, Timmy Wallace.

December 1–17, 1977 (12 performances)

TWO SMALL BODIES by Neal Bell; Director, Thomas Babe; Sets, Richard Kerry; Lights, James Chaleff; Costumes, William Ivey Long; Stage Manager, Jan Crean; CAST: Catherine Burns, Larry Bryggman

December 8–9, 1977 (2 performances)

DECEMBER TO MAY by Jane Staab; Director, Anthony Hancock; CAST: Malcolm Groome, Bump Heeter, Jessica Hull, Gina Sisk, Jane Staab, Penny White.

January 7–29, 1978 (17 performances)

THE MEMBER OF THE WEDDING by Carson McCullers; Director, Philip Himberg; Sets and Projections, Christopher Thomas; Lights, William D. Anderson; Costumes, Mimi Maxmen, Sound, Walter Mantani; Stage Manager, Amy Chase; CAST: Frank Adu, Beverly Barbieri, Reathel Bean, Cynthia Frost, Michael Gallagher, Mark Hattan, Nancy Mette, Deborah Offner, Tim Rail, Kim Sullivan, Kathy Wells, Beatrice Winde.

January 12–February 12, 1978 (20 performances)

THREE SONS by Richard Lortz; Director, Robert O'Rourke; Sets, Jimmy Cuomo; Lights, Marilyn Rennagel; Costumes, Susan Denison; Stage Manager, Robert Tomlin; CAST: Richard Cox, Joseph Giardina, David Little, Rita Lloyd, Jerry Matz.

February 18–March 12, 1978 (20 performances)

DIAL M FOR MURDER by Frederick Knott; Director, Robert Moss; Sets, Harry Lines; Lights, Todd Lichtenstein; Costumes, Ticia Blackburn; Stage Manager, William Paster; CAST: Robert Baines, Maria Cellario, Drew Keil, William Perley, William Sadler.

February 23–March 26, 1978 (20 performances)

SHAY by Anne Commire; Director, Elinor Renfield; Sets, Jane Thurn; Lights, Pat Stern; Costumes, Michael J Cesario; Sound, Philip Campanella; Stage Manager, Bonnie Panson; CAST: Marvin Chatinover, Avril Gentles, Jack Gilpin, Dallas Greer, Pat Lysinger, Conrad McLaren, Marge Redmond, Shirley Richards.

April 18–30, 1978 (20 performances)

A MIDSUMMER NIGHT'S DREAM by William Shakespeare; Director, Robert Moss, Sets, Richard Kerry; Lights, Toni Goldin; Costumes, Ronald A. Castleman; Sound, Philip Campanella; Choreographer, William A. Dunas; Stage Manager, Ellen Zalk; CAST: Peter Bartlett, Robin Bartlett, Victoria Boothby, Catherine Burns, William Carden, Gilbert Cole, Dan Diggles, Dallas Greer, Mark Hattan, Timothy Hogan, Olgalyn Jolly, Joel Kramer, David Licht, Jeffrey Lorber, David Malamut.

April 18—(30 performances, still running as of May 31, 1978)

HOOTERS by Ted Tally; Director, Gary Pearle; Sets, Charles McCarry; Lights, Frances Aronson; Costumes, Elizabeth Palmer; Stage Manager, Lisa Baker; CAST: Victor Bevine, Michael Kaufman, Christine Lahti, Erika Petersen

May 13–June 4, 1978 (19 performances)

AWAKE AND SING! by Clifford Odets; Director, Alfred Gingold; Sets, Carl A. Baldasso; Lights, Marilyn Rennagel; Costumes, Mary Brownlow; Sound, Philip Campanella; Stage Manager, Victoria Bradshaw; CAST: Jack Aaron, Kim Ameen, Herman O. Arbeit, John Broglio, David Little, Nancy Marchand, Reuben Schafer, Paul Sparer, Fredric Stone.

Nathaniel Tileston Photos

Deborah Offner, Beatrice Winde, Tim Rail in "The Member of the Wedding" Top: Larry Bryggman, Catherine Burns in "Two Small Bodies"

Nancy Marchand, Reuben Schafer in "Awake and Sing" Above: Michael Kaufman, Erika Petersen, Christine Lahti, Victor Bevine in "Hooters"

NEW YORK SHAKESPEARE FESTIVAL PUBLIC THEATER

Joseph Papp, Producer
Bernard Gersten, Associate Producer

General Manager, Robert Kamlot; Production Supervisor, Jason Steven Cohen; Press, Merle Debuskey, Bob Ullman, Richard Kornberg; Production Manager, Andrew Mihok; Costume Shopmaster, Milo Morrow; Director of Play Development, Gail Merrifield; Executive Assistant, Louise Edmonson; Cabaret Director, Craig Zadan; Technical Director, Mervyn Haines, Jr.; Prop Master, Bob Phillips; Audio, Roger Jay; Assistant to General Manager, Linda Cohen; Company Manager, Bob MacDonald

PUBLIC/NEWMAN THEATER
July 31–September 4, 1977.*

MISS MARGARIDA'S WAY

* 42 performances. Re-opened Sept. 26, 1977 at the Ambassador Theatre. See Broadway Calendar page 12.

Estelle Parsons

Virginia Vestoff, John McMartin, Joshua Mostel
(Sy Friedman Photo)

PUBLIC/NEWMAN THEATER
October 12–November 20, 1977 (64 performances)

LANDSCAPE OF THE BODY

By John Guare; Director, John Pasquin; Music and Lyrics, John Guare; Setting and Costumes, Santo Loquasto; Lighting, Jennifer Tipton; Musical Arrangements and Incidental Music, Wally Harper; Pianist, Rod Derefinko; Assistant to Director, Margaret Ownes; Production Assistant, Marge Pfleiderer; Stage Managers, Stephen McCorkle, Trey Altemose

CAST

F. Murray Abraham (Capt. Marvin Holahan), Raymond J. Barry (Masked Man/Dope King of Providence/Bank Teller), Richard Bauer (Raulito), Bonnie Deroski (Margie), Alexa Kenin (Joanne), Shirley Knight (Betty), Anthony Marciona (Donny), Paul McCrane (Bert), Peg Murray (Rosalie), Remak Ramsay (Durwood Peach)

A play in two acts. The action takes place at the present time on a ferry to Nantucket, and in Greenwich Village.

Martha Swope Photo

PUBLIC/ANSPACHER THEATER
October 4–November 27, 1977 (62 performances)

THE MISANTHROPE

By Moliere; Translation, Richard Wilbur; Music and Songs, Jobriath Boone; Additional Songs, Margaret Pine, Arthur Bienstock; Director, Bill Gile; Musical Director, Allen Shawn; Setting, Bill Stabile; Costumes, Carrie F. Robbins; Lighting, Arden Fingerhut; Dance Sequences, Rachel Lampert; Orchestrations, Robert Rodgers, Bill Brohn; Assistant Director, Charles Repole; Assistant to Director, Janet McCall; Wardrobe Melissa Adzima; Stage Managers, D. W. Koehler, Jason LaPadura

CAST

Seth Allen (Acaste), John Bottoms (Philinte), Helen Gallagher (Arsinoe), Paul Hecht (Oronte), John McMartin (Alceste), Joshua Mostel (Dubois), William Parry (Guard), Deborah Rush (Eliante), Virginia Vestoff (Celimene), Ed Zang (Clitandre)

MUSICAL NUMBERS: "Symphonie," "Be Witness to My Madness," "Where in the World?," "The Art of Pleasing Me," "Sonnet," "Paris," "Double," "He Loves to Make a Fuss," "Lovers Manage," "Waltz," "Madam," "The Other Day I Went to an Affair," "We Women," "Substitute," "Second Best," "I Love You More," "Things Are Most Mysterious," "Altogether Too Outrageous," "How Dare You?," "I Confess," Finale.

A comedy with music in five acts with one intermission. The action takes place in Celimene's house in Paris.

Shirley Knight, Paul McCrane, Remak Ramsay

PUBLIC/THEATER CABARET
November 18–December 3, 1977 (19 performances)

TALES OF THE HASIDIM

Conceived, Adapted and Directed by Paul Sills; Music, Fred Kaz; Lighting, Victor En Yu Tan; From Martin Buber's "Tales of the Hasidim"

CAST

Joshua Broder
Severn Darden
Anthony Holland

Mina Kolb
Paul Sand
Eugene Troobnick

Presented in two parts

Anthony Holland, Paul Sand, Mina Kolb
(Martha Swope Photo)

James Lally, John Ferraro

PUBLIC/THE OTHER STAGE
December 6, 1977–April 30, 1978 (174 performances)

THE MANDRAKE

By Niccolo Machiavelli; Translated by Wallace Shawn; Director, Wilford Leach; Music, Richard Weinstock; Set, Wilford Leach; Costumes, Patricia McGourty; Lighting, Victor En Yu Tan; Painting and Set Design Associate, Bob Shaw; Wardrobe Mistress, Melissa Adzima; Stage Managers, Bill McComb, Paca Thomas

CAST

Larry Pine (Brother Timothy) succeeded by John Bottoms, Tom Costello (Professor Nicia), John Ferraro (Ligurio), Corinne Fischer (Lucrezia), James Lally (Callimaco), Thelma Nevitt (Singer), Angela Pietropinto (Madonna Sostrata/Woman at the Church), Wallace Shawn (Prologue/Siro), Paca Thomas (Waiter)

A comedy with music performed without intermission. The action takes place in and around the Piazza della Signoria, at the Trattoria Primavera, at the house of Callimaco and Professor Nicia, and at Il Duomo.

Sy Friedman Photos

**Larry Pine, Corinne Fischer, Angela Pietropinto
Above: James Lally, John Ferraro, Paca Thomas**

PUBLIC/THEATER CABARET

December 11, 1977–February 5, 1978 (17 performances, Sundays only)

WHERE THE MISSISSIPPI MEETS THE AMAZON

Written and Performed by Jessica Hagedorn, Thulani (Davis) Nkabinde, Ntozake Shange; Director, Oz Scott; Costumes, Beverly Parks; Lighting, Victor En Yu Tan; Musical Director, David Murray; Band, Teddy and His Sizzling Romancers; Stage Manager, Peter Glazer

A "poetry event" with dance and jazz.

PUBLIC/NEWMAN THEATER

December 16, 1977–January 29, 1978 (62 performances)

THE DYBBUK
(Between Two Worlds)

By S. Ansky; Translated by Mira Rafalowicz; Director, Joseph Chaikin; New Version developed by Nira Rafalowicz and Joseph Chaikin; Setting, Woods Mackintosh; Costumes, Mary Brecht; Lighting, Beverly Emmons; Assistant to Director, Steve Gomer; Wardrobe, Rita Barbera, Eugene Thomas; Stage Managers, Louis Rackoff, Frank DiFilia

CAST

Richard Bauer (Rabbi Azriel), Robert Blumenfeld (Osher), Shami Chaikin (Chana-Esther/Mother the Groom), Alice Eve Cohen (Woman in Town/Musician), Joseph Davidson (Wedding Guest/ Judge), Bernard Duffy (Henoch/Beggar), Corey Fischer (Maggid), Jenn Hamburg (Pregnant Woman/Beggar), Marcia Jean Kurtz (Leah), Hal Lehrman, Jr. (Student/Beggar), Ellen Maddow (Woman in Town/Basia), Bruce Myers (Chanon), Mark Nelson (Student/ Bridegroom), Marcell Rosenblatt (Woman in Town/Rich Woman), Margo Lee Sherman (Rabbi's Wife/Beggar), Arthur Strimling (Michol/Musician), Jamil Zakkai (Sender),Paul Zimet (Shimson/Musician), Sonia Zomina (Freyda)

Performed without intermission.

PUBLIC/LuESTHER HALL

December 16, 1977–January 22, 1978 (60 performances)

A PHOTOGRAPH:
A Study of Cruelty

By Ntozake Shange; Director, Oz Scott; Scenery, David Mitchell; Costumes, Beverly Parks; Lighting, Victor En Yu Tan; Music, David Murray; Choreography, Marsha Blanc; Visuals, Collis Davis, David Mitchell; Wardrobe, Alvin Perry; Stage Managers, Richard S. Viola, Leanna Lenhart

CAST

Avery Brooks (Sean David), Petronia Paley (Nevada), Michele Shay (Michael), Count Stovall (Earl), Hattie Winston (Claire)

A "poemplay" in two acts

PUBLIC/THEATER CABARET

December 20, 1977–February 11, 1978 (61 performances)*

THE WATER ENGINE

An "American Fable" performed without intermission.

* Re-opened on Broadway Monday, March 6, 1978 at the Plymouth Theatre. See Broadway Calendar page 36.

Martha Swope Photos

Jessica Hagedorn, Thulani (Davis) Nkabinde, Ntozake Shange *(Martha Swope Photo)*

Marcia Jean Kurtz, Richard Bauer
(Inge Morath Photo)

Michael Miller, Colin Stinton   Annie Hat
in "The Water Engine"

PUBLIC/ANSPACHER THEATER
January 16–April 16, 1978 (127 performances)

A PRAYER FOR MY DAUGHTER

By Thomas Babe; Director, Robert Allan Ackerman; Setting, Bil Mikulewicz; Costumes, Bob Wojewodski; Lighting, Arden Fingerhut; Assistant to Director, Nan Harris; Wardrobe, Eugene Thomas; Stage Managers, Kitzi Becker, Andy Lopata

CAST

Jeffrey De Munn (Jack), George Dzundza (Kelly), Laurence Luckinbill (Simon), Alan Rosenberg (Jimmy)

A drama in two acts. The action takes place at the present time in a police precinct station house.

Gerry Goodstein Photo

PUBLIC/LuESTHER HALL
February 26–April 2, 1978 (62 performances)

MUSEUM

By Tina Howe; Director, Max Stafford-Clark; Scenery, Robert Yodice; Costumes, Patricia McGourty; Lighting, Jennifer Tipton; Assistant to Director, Debra Tanklow; Sound, Greg Brennan; Stage Managers, Alan Fox, Robert J. Mooney

CAST

Gerry Bamman (Mr. Hollingsford/First Man/Giorgio), Joel Brooks (Will Willard/Steve Williams), Larry Bryggman (The Guard), Steven Gilborn (Mr. Salt/1st Guard/Elderly Man), Robyn Goodman (Liz/Mira Zadal/Kate Siv), Kathryn Grody (Carol/Gilda Norris), Jane Hallaren (Mrs. Salt/Zoe), Dan Hedaya (Peter Ziff/2nd Guard), Calvin Jung (Fred Izumi), Kaiulani Lee (Annette Froebel/Chloe Trapp), Karen Ludwig (Barbara Zimmer/May/Elderly Woman), Bruce McGill (Michael Wall), Frederikke Meister (Francoise/Ada Bilditsky/Lillian), Lynn Milgrim (Maggie Snow/Barbara Castle/Harriet), Jeffrey David Pomerantz (Bob Lamb/Bill Plaid), Jean-Pierre Stewart (Jean-Claude/Mr. Gregory/2nd Man in Passing), Kathleen Tolan (Balkey/Julie Jenkins), Dianne Wiest (Elizabeth Sorrow/Tink Solheim)

A play performed without intermission. The action takes place in a museum at the present time.

Joseph Abeles Photo

PUBLIC/NEWMAN THEATER
March 2–April 9, 1978 (62 performances)

CURSE OF THE STARVING CLASS

By Sam Shepard; Director, Robert Woodruff; Scenery and Costumes, Santo Loquasto; Lighting, Martin Tudor; Music, Bob Feldman; Assistant to Director, Chris Silva; Stage Managers, Zane Weiner, Patricia M. Morinelli

CAST

John Aquino (Malcolm), Raymond J. Barry (Slater), Olympia Dukakis (Ella), James Gammon (Weston), Eddie Jones (Ellis), Michael J. Pollard (Emerson), Pamela Reed (Emma), Ebbe Roe Smith (Wesley), Kenneth Welsh (Taylor)

A drama in three acts. The action takes place at the present time in a farm house somewhere in the West.

Frederic Ohringer Photo

PUBLIC/THEATER CABARET
March 9–April 29, 1978 (76 performances)*

RUNAWAYS

* Re-opened on Broadway at the Plymouth Theatre on May 13, 1978. See Broadway Calendar page 47.

Jeffrey DeMunn, Laurence Luckinbill, George Dzundza, Alan Rosenberg

Lynn Milgrim, Karen Ludwig, Jeffrey David Pomerantz, Joel Brooks

James Gammon, Ebbe Roe Smith

QUAIGH THEATRE

William H. Lieberson, Artistic Director

Executive Director, Douglas Popper; Managing Director, Ted Mornel; Artistic Consultant, Albert Brower; Production Coordinator, Richard Young; Sound, George Jacobs; Administrative Consultant, Susanne Braham; General Manager, William Douglas; Associate Producer-Company Manager, Sherwood Arthur; Associate Producer, Bob Lefcourt; Press, Max Eisen, Judy Jacsina, Irene Gandy

QUAIGH THEATRE

July 26–October 16, 1977 (58 performances)
COUNSELLOR AT LAW by Elmer Rice; Director, Will Lieberson; Set and Costumes, Christina Giannini; Lighting, Bill McComb; Company Manager, Sherwood Arthur; Stage Managers, Ted Mornel, Glen McLaskey. CAST: Kent Wilson (Bessie), Raymond Faber (Henry), Madeline Shaw (Sarah), Ian Ehrlich (Moreti/Bootblack/Hirschberg), Maxine Taylor-Morris (Zedorah), Ann Saxman (Goldie), John Neary (Charles), Leonard DiSesa (Tedesco), Claudine Catania (Regina), Robert Nersesian (Weinberg), Jay Diamond (Sandler), Kristen Christopher (Lilian), Hart Faber (Messenger), Douglas Popper (Darwin), George Guidall (George Simon), Ralph DeLia (Crayfield), Carolyn Lenz (Cora), Joan Turetzky (Lena), Mel Jurdem (Malone), Richard Spore (Breitstein), Glenn Alterman (David), Dennis Lieberson (Harry), Mike Shari (Richard Dwight, Jr.), Valentina Fratti (Dorothy), Glen McClaskey

November 14–22, 1977 (8 performances)
DRY SHERRY by John Sherry; Director, Martin Oltarsh; Set, John Macgregor; Lights, Bartlett Bigelow; Stage Managers, Greg Brennan, Chris Duffy. CAST: Helen Breed (Julia), Linda Spector (Nurse), Dorothy Farrell (Sarah), Ron Foster (Middie), Jack Betts (Black Jack), Frank P. Ryan (1st Drunk), Bob Clarke (2nd Drunk), Bill Cudlipp (3rd Drunk), Nancy Berg (Cassandra), Rudy Hornish (Simon)

January 5–15, 1978 (13 performances)
THE BEARD by Michael McClure; Director, Philip Minor; Set, John Jobe; Lights, Michael Smith; Stage Manager, Beth Phillips. CAST: Ruth Brandeis (Jean Harlow), Morris Lafon (Billy the Kid)

January 18–27, 1978 (12 performances)
THE THIRD DAUGHTER by Mario Fratti; *American premiere;* Director, Harry F. Thompson; Choreography, Goodloe Lewis; The Austin College Theatre Commpany Production. CAST: Kim Powers (Riccardo), Robert Olson (Roberto), Jeanette Rodriguez (Gina), David Fessenden (Franco), Vicki Goldstein (Lea), Kent Johnson (Bruno), Cynthia Hestand (Dolores), Jennie Greene (Virginia), Selmore Haines (Nerone), Cindy McNabb (Alda), Harry Thompson (Ilario), Laura Vargas (Yvette/Mother)

March 7–19, 1978 (12 performances)
THREE SMALL PLAYS BY THREE BIG PLAYWRIGHTS: AT LIBERTY by Tennesse Williams; Directed by Ted Mornel with Ann Saxman (Mrs. Green), Cam Kornman (Gloria); EPISODE ON AN AUTUMN EVENING by Frederick Durrenmatt; Directed by Bill Lentsch with Warren Ball (Maximilian), Christopher Cooke (Hofer), Joseph Simeon (Secretary), Susan Hoffman (Daisy), Cam Kornman (Vanessa), Glenn Alterman (Manager); THE SWEET-SHOPPE MYRIAM by Ivan Klima; Directed by Ted Mornel with Ruby Payne, Charles Prior, Mel Jurdem, Warren Hall, Janet Croll, Robert Nersesian, McDermott Murphy, Ann Saxman, Glenn Alterman, John Neary, Joseph Simeon, Stephan Hart, Christopher Cooke

March 31–April 9, 1978 (9 performances)
THE EXORCISM OF VIOLENCE by Sidney Morris; Directed by Mr. Morris with Matty Selman (Virgo Boy), Amy Whitman (Clean Lady), Frank Nastasi (Tailor), Kay Williams (Bargain Hunter), Lawrence James (Cool Cat), Ira Lee Collings (Gay Boy), Mona Sands (Chocolate Lady), David Vigliano (Stage Manager)

April 25–May 14, 1978 (18 performances)
DEAD END by Sidney Kingsley; Director, Will Lieberson; Set, Sarah Pryor Oliphant; Lights, Daniel Charles Abrahamsen; Costumes, Don Warshaw; Production Coordinator, Ted Mornel; Stage Managers, George Zagoren, Michael Streich. CAST: Craig Alfano (Dippy), Tony Barbera (G-Man), Stephen Berenson (Milty), Harry Boda (Doorman), Anthony Cardi (Boy), Karin Clauson (Governess), Dorian John Dana (Boy), Peter Jeffries-Ferrara (Spit), Joanne Garahan (Francey), Charles Gemmill (Hilton), Fred Ivory (Angel), Mel Jurdem (Griswald), Hillary Knepper (Rich girl), Joyce Renee Korbin (Mrs. Martin), Christopher Lentsh (Boy), Carolyn Lenz (Kay), Larry Lowy (Boy), John McComb (Milligan), Meridith McComb (Girl), Priscilla Manning (Drina), Mario Mariani (Intern), Roxanne Mellita (Woman), Hal Muchnick (Tommy), John Neary (Baby Face Martin), Tony Page (Hunk), Ruby Payne (Lady with dog), Gerald Oliver (Phillip), Lucy Re (Super), Carol Schaye (Rich Lady), Jeffrey Spolan (Gimpy), Michael Streich (Policeman), Michael Stumm (T. B.), Earl Vedder, Jr. (Jones), Paul Wiley (G-Man)

Peter Jeffries-Ferrara, Stephen Verenson, Michael Stumm, Craig Alfano, Fred Ivory in "Dead End" (*J. F. Peters Photo*)

Left Center: "Tatami" Top: Claudine Catania, George Guidall in "Counsellor-at-Law"

RICHARD MORSE MIME THEATRE

Richard Morse, Artistic Director
September 8, 1977–April 2, 1978

ST. JOHN'S EPISCOPAL CHURCH

COMPANY

Rasa Allen, Gabriel Barre, Mahala Buckingham, Lee Copenhaver, Marty Feldman, Ed Griffith, Peggy Imrie, Gjertine Johansen, Barbara Knight, Digna Landrove, Nancy Lividow, Marisa Lyon, Richard Morse, Charles Penn, Kristin Sakaie, Byam Stevens, Joanne Seltzer (Stage Manager)

PRODUCTIONS

"The Arts and Leisure Section of the New York Times," "Pranks," "Gifts," "Tintinnabula"

Ian Anderson Photos

Left: Rasa Allen, Richard Morse, Gabriel Barre in "Tintinnabula" Below: "The Arts & Leisure Section of the NY Times"

THE RIDICULOUS THEATRICAL COMPANY

Charles Ludlam, Artistic Director

ONE SHERIDAN SQUARE
Opened Tuesday, May 23, 1978*
The Ridiculous Theatrical Company presents in repertory:

CAMILLE freely adapted from "La Dame aux Camilias" by Charles Ludlam; Directed by Mr. Ludlam; Costumes, Mary Brecht; Lighting, Richard Currie; Stage Manager, Robert Fuhrman; Press, Alan Eichler. CAST: John D. Brockmeyer (Baron), Adam McAdam (Nanine), Charles Ludlam (Marguerite), Everett Quinton (Nichette), Richard Currie (Butler), Black-Eyed Susan (Olympe), Lola Pashalinski (Prudence), Bill Vehr (Armand), Richard Currie (Duval, Sr.)
STAGE BLOOD by Charles Ludlam; Directed by Mr. Ludlam. CAST: Adam McAdam (Carleton/Gilbert), Charles Ludlam (Carleton, Jr.), Lola Pashalinski (Helga), John D. Brockmeyer (Jenkins), Bill Vehr (Edmund), Black-Eyed Susan (Elfie)
THE VENTRILOQUIST'S WIFE conceived and executed by Charles Ludlam; Lighting, Robert Fuhrman; Technical Assistant, Jay Sarno; Stage Manager, Everett Quinton; Press, Alan Eichler. CAST: Black-Eyed Susan, Charles Ludlam, Walter Ego

* Still playing May 31, 1978

Right Center: Black-Eyed Susan, Walter Ego, Charles Ludlam in "The Ventriloquist's Wife"
(Gideon Lewin Photo)

Black-Eyed Susan, Bill Vehr, Charles Ludlam, Lola Pashalinski in "Camille" *(John Stern Photo)* **143**

ROUNDABOUT THEATRE

Gene Feist, Michael Fried, Producing Directors
Twelfth Year

ROUNDABOUT STAGE ONE
October 4–30, 1977 (36 performances)

YOU NEVER CAN TELL

By George Bernard Shaw; Director, Tony Tanner; Set, Timothy Galvin; Costumes, V. Jane Suttell; Lighting, Richard Butler; Original Score, Musical Director, Philip Campanella; Hairstylist, Paul Huntley; Assistant to Director, Jeff Passero; Costume Supervisor, Nancy L. Johnson; Technical Coordinator, Gregory A. Roach; Assistant to Producing Directors, Arthur Pearson; Executive Associate, Sharon Legmann; Stage Managers, Tom Gould, Paul Moser; Press, Mark Arnold

CAST

Norman Barrs (Waiter), Ralph Clanton (Crampton), Curt Dawson (Valentine), Rachel Gurney (Mrs. Clandon), Sarah-Jane Gwillim (Gloria), Richard Neilson (M'Comas), Richard Niles (Philip), David Sabin (Bohun), Kristie Thatcher (Dolly)

Ken Howard Photos

Right Top: Entire Cast Below: Kristie Thatcher, Curt Dawson

ROUNDABOUT STAGE TWO
September 6–December 31, 1977 (129 performances)

NAKED

By Luigi Pirandello; Translated by William Murray; Director, Gene Feist; Set, Ron Antone; Lighting, Robert Strohmeier; Costumes, Nancy L. Johnson; Sound Sequences, Philip Campanella; Manager, Geoffrey Hitch; Assistant to Director, Jerry Levine; Stage Manager, Paul Moser; Technical Assistants, Wick O'Brien, Marylou Gillis, Jim Grant, Lewis Mead; Press, Mark Arnold

CAST

Ersilia Drei	Marie Puma
Ludovico Nota	Larkin Ford
Signora Onoria	Nina Dova
Alfredo Cantavalle	Philip Campanella
Franco Laspiga	Lucien Zabielski
Grotto	Richard Sterne

Nina Dova, Lucien Zabielski
144 **Above: Gordon Gould, Fran Brill**

ROUNDABOUT STAGE ONE
January 26–April 9, 1978 (76 performances)

OTHELLO

By William Shakespeare; Director, Gene Feist; Set, Jeff Fiala; Lighting, John McKernon; Costumes, Christina Giannini; Original Score, Philip Campanella; Technical Director, James Dirlam; Movement Consultant, Moni Yakim; Fencing Master, Michael Arabian

CAST

Earle Hyman (Othello), Nicholas Kepros (Iago), Mary Carney (Desdemona), Carmen De Lavallade (Emilia), Edmund Davys (Cassio), Powers Boothe (Roderigo), Wyman Pendleton (Brabantio/Gratiano), Elizabeth Owens (Bianca), John Straub (Duke/Lodovico), Craig Dudley (Montano/Senator), Kale Brown (Officer), Wesley Stevens (Gentleman/Officer), Thomas Brooks (Senator/Officer), Attendants: Michael Arabian, James Scott Bell, Jane Milne, Mary Grace Pizzullo, Thomas M. Ries, Michael S. Strows

Geoffrey Fried Photos

Right: Earle Hyman, Mary Carney
Top: Craig Dudley, Nicholas Kepros, Earle Hyman,
Carmen DeLavallade, Edmund Davys,
Powers Boothe

Craig Dudley, Nicholas Kepros, Earle Hyman,
Edmund Davys Left: Hyman, Kepros

ROUNDABOUT STAGE TWO
January 21–April 9, 1978 (91 performances)

THE PROMISE

By Aleksei Arbuzov; Translated by Ariadne Nicolaeff; Director, Michael Fried; Set, Ron Antone; Costumes, Nancy L. Johnson; Lighting, Robert Strohmeier; Sound Sequences, Philip Campanella; Stage Manager, Paul Moser; Press, Mark Arnold

CAST

Marat	Christopher Goutman
Lika	Marilyn McIntyre
Leonidik	Davis Hall

A drama in 3 acts and 13 scenes. The action takes place in Leningrad between 1942 and 1959.

Geoffrey Fried Photo

Davis Hall, Marilyn McIntyre,
Christopher Goutman

145

ROUNDABOUT STAGE TWO
May 18–July 16, 1978 (104 performances)

THE SHOW-OFF

By George Kelly; Director, John Ulmer; Set, Ron Antone; Costumes, Nancy L. Johnson; Lighting, Robert Strohmeier; Sound Sequences, Philip Campanella; Manager, Michael K. Lippert; Stage Manager, Paul Moser; Hairstylist, Roy Helland; Press, Mark Arnold

CAST

Clara Hyland	Ellen Tovatt
Mrs. Fisher	Polly Rowles
Amy Fisher	Kit LeFever
Frank Hyland	Joseph Costa
Mr. Fisher	Harry Ellerbe
Joe Fisher	Terence Marinan
Aubrey Piper	Paul Rudd
Mr. Gill	Joseph Warren
Mr. Rogers	Ken Costigan

A comedy in 3 acts and 4 scenes. The action takes place in 1924 in the Fisher living room in North Philadelphia, Pa.

Ken Howard Photo

Polly Rowles, Ellen Tovatt, Paul Rudd, Terence Marinan

SPANISH THEATRE REPERTORY COMPANY

Gilberto Zaldivar, Producer
Rene Buch, Artistic Director
June 1, 1977–May 31, 1978

Associate Producer and Resident Designer, Robert Federico; Technical Director, Seth A. Price; Administrative Assistant, Marina Neufeld; Public Relations, Noris Arevalo; Press, Marian Graham; Musical Director, Juan Viccini

GRAMERCY ARTS THEATRE

COMPANY

Ofelia Gonzalez, Virginia Rambal, Teresa Yenque, Nereida Mercado, Vivian DeAngelo, Mirtha Cartaya, Braulio Villar, Parry Roman, Alfonso Manosalvas, Mateo Gomez, Nelson Landrieu, Frank Robles, Raul Davila, Graciela Mas, Rene Sanchez, Juan Billarreal, Elizabeth Pena, Myrna Colon, Nino Roger, Miguel Camarero, Maria Norman, Graciela Lecube, David Crommett, Aida Linares, Alicia Carmona, Yolanda Arenas, Sarita Valle, Carlos Linares

PRODUCTIONS

"La Celestina" by Fernando de Rojas, "La Difunta" by Miguel de Unamuno, "Las Aceitunas" by Lope de Rueda, "Los Habladores" by Miguel de Cervantes, "Los Soles Truncos" by Rene Marquez, "Jardin de Otono" by Diana Raznovich, "La Fiaca" by Ricardo Talesnik, "El Censo" by Emilio Carballido, "Cien Veces No Debo" by Ricardo Talesnik, "Te Juro Juana Que Tengo Ganas" by Emilio Carballido, "La Dama Duende" by Calderon de la Barca, "Bodas de Sangre" by Federico Garcia Lorca, "Los Japoneses No Esperan" by Ricardo Talesnik

Raul Davila, Ofelia Gonzalez in "La Fiaca" *(Gerry Goodstein Photo)*

Left Center: Mirtha Cartaya, Nelson Landrieu in "Blood Wedding" *(Winston Vargas Photo)*

WPA THEATRE

Artistic Directors, Howard Ashman, R. Stuart White
Tenth Season

Managing Director, Kyle Renick; Producing Director, Stephan G. Wells; Technical Director, Edward T. Gianfrancesco; General Manager, Nancy Parent; Press, Alan Eichler

October 13–November 6, 1977 (16 performances)

THE BALLAD OF THE SAD CAFE

By Carson McCullers; Adapted by Edward Albee; Director, R. Stuart White; Original Music, William Flanagan; Set, Edward T. Gianfrancesco; Lighting, Craig Evans; Costumes, Marcia Cox, Margo Russell; Sound, Kathy Giebler; Stage Managers, Beth Prevor, Cheryl Meguire

CAST

John E. Allen (Cousin Lymon), Jill Harwood (Lucy), J. R. Horne (Stumpy), Walter Klavun (Merlie), Kaiulani Lee (Miss Amelia Evans), Parker McCormick (Mrs. Peterson), Alan Mixon (Narrator/Henry Macy), Richard Alexander Milholland (Marvin), Anton Spaeth (Horace), Barbara Stanton (Emma), Don Welch (Rainey 1), Ron Welch (Rainey 2)

December 8–24, 1977 (12 performances)

GOREY STORIES

From the works of Edward Gorey; Adapted by Stephen Currens; Director, Tony Tanner; Music, David Aldrich; Set, Edward Gianfrancesco; Lights, Craig Evans, Costumes, Clifford Capone; Stage Manager, Beth Prevor; Press, Alan Eichler

CAST

Gemze de Lappe (Maid), Tobias Haller (Child), Susan Marchand (Singer), Dennis McGovern (Opera Freak), John Michalski (Hamish), Leon Shaw (Earbrass), Liz Sheridan (Lady Celia), June Squibb (Spinster), Sel Vitella (Butler)

January 27 February 5, 1978 (7 performances)

IF YOU CAN'T SING, THEY'LL MAKE YOU DANCE

By Phillip Hayes Dean; Directed by Mr. Dean; Set, Judie Juracek; Lights, Craig Evans, Lyn Ellis; Costumes, Judy Dearing; Stage Manager, B. J. Boguski

CAST

Marge Eliot (Gloria), Patricia O'Toole (Dee Dee), Frank Adu (Yuseff)

March 2–19, 1978 (12 performances)

APRIL 2, 1979: THE DAY THE BLANCHARDVILLE, N.C. POLITICAL ACTION AND POKER CLUB GOT THE BOMB

By Nicholas Kazan; Director, Douglas Johnson; Set, Vincent Ashbahian; Lighting, Kathy Giebler; Costumes, David Menkes; Production Assistant, Bob Herman; Stage Manager, Paul Holmes; Press, Alan Eichler

CAST

Dann Florek (T. R.), Bill Nunnery (Bob), Harry Orzello (Richard), Don Reeves (Dack), David Swatling (Eddie II), J. T. Walsh (Goose), Ilene Kristen (Tina), Rebecca Gilchrist (Beth)

April 13–May 6, 1978 (16 performances)

EARLY DARK

By Reynolds Price; Director, R. Stuart White; Set, Edward T. Gianfrancesco; Music, H. Ross Levy; Costumes, Marcia Cox; Stage Managers, Beth Prevor, Frances Smith; Press, Alan Eichler

CAST

Corabel Alexander (Sissie), Alexander Berkeley (Milo), Gregory Cassel (Macey), Judy Detar (Marise), Estelle Evans (Mary), Clifford Fetters (Rato), Wendy Fulton (Rosacoke), Anne Gerety (Emma), Eddie Hatch (Sammy), Johanna Hickey (Baby Sister), J. R. Horne (Mason), Rod Houts (Isaac), Philip Henry Kerzner (Heywood), Ms. Lorenzo (Mrs. Ransom), Kathy McKenna (Willie), James Remar (Wesley)

**John E. Allen, Kaiulani Lee
in "Ballad of the Sad Cafe"**
(Edward Gianfrancesco Photo)

**James Remar, Wendy Fulton in "Early Dark"
Above: Gemze de Lappe, Sel Vitella in "Gorey Stories"**
(Ian Anderson Photos)

SULLIVAN STREET PLAYHOUSE
Opened Tuesday, May 3, 1960.*
Lore Noto presents:

THE FANTASTICKS

Book and Lyrics, Tom Jones; Suggested by Edmond Rostand's "Les Romanesques"; Music, Harvey Schmidt; Director, Word Baker; Original Musical Direction and Arrangements, Julian Stein; Designed by Ed Wittstein; Associate Producers, Sheldon Baron, Dorothy Olim, Robert Alan Gold; Assistant Producer, Thad Noto; Production Assistant, John Krug; Original Cast Album by M-G-M Records

CAST

The Narrator	Joseph Gagliano†1
The Girl	Betsy Joslyn†2
The Boy	Bruce Cryer†3
The Boy's Father	Lore Noto
The Girl's Father	David Vogel†4
The Actor	Donald Babcock†5
The Man Who Dies	Liam O'Begley†6
The Mute	John Thomas Waite†7
At the Piano	William F. McDaniel†8
At the Harp	Pattee Cohen†9

MUSICAL NUMBERS: "Overture," "Try to Remember," "Much More," "Metaphor," "Never Say No," "It Depends on What You Pay," "Soon It's Gonna Rain," "Rape Ballet," "Happy Ending," "This Plum Is Too Ripe," "I Can See It," "Plant a Radish," "Round and Round," "They Were You."

A musical in two acts.

General Manager: Toby L. Beckwith
Press: David Powers
Stage Manager: Frank Bouley

* Still playing May 31, 1978. For original production, see THEATRE WORLD, Vol. 16.
† Succeeded by: 1. David Brummel, Michael Tartel, Chapman Roberts, Roger Brown, Douglas Clark, 2. Sarah Rice, Carol Demas, Virginia Gregory, Cheryl Horne, Anne S. Kaye, 3. Ralph Bruneau, Jeff Knight, 4. John High, John J. Martin, Arthur Anderson, Sy Travers, 5. Seamus O'Brien, George Riddle, Russell F. Leib, Elliott Levine, 6. James Cook, Robert Oliver, 7. Tom Flagg, Robert Crest, 8. Penna Rose, 9. Barbara Weiger.

Van Williams Photos

Betsy Joslyn

**Joseph Gagliano, Betsy Joslyn, Jeff Knight
Above: Jeff Knight, Lore Noto**

CIRCLE IN THE SQUARE DOWNTOWN
Opened Thursday, October 14, 1976.*
Circle in the Square (Theodore Mann, Artistic Director; Paul Libin, Managing Director) presents:

THE CLUB

By Eve Merriam; Director, Tommy Tune; Musical Direction and Arrangements, Alexandra Ivanoff; Costumes and Set, Kate Carmel; Lighting, Cheryl Thacker

CAST

Johnny	Marlene Dell
Bertie	Gloria Hodes
Algy	Joanne Beretta
Freddie	Carole Monferdini
Bobby	Julia J. Hafner
Maestro	Memrie Innerarity
Henry	Terri White

UNDERSTUDIES: Frolic Taylor, Gerta Grunen, Patti Harris, Joanne Swanson, Gaelle Spence, Maggie Task, Katherine Benfer, Cookie Harlin, Norma J. Curley, Irene Steiner

A "musical diversion" performed without intermission. All the songs are from the period 1894–1905.

Company Managers: Paul Berkowsky, Jeffrey R. Chernoff
Press: Merle Debuskey, David Roggensack
Stage Managers: Gene Traylor, Kenneth Cox, Clint Spencer, Tom Kelly, Steven Holmes

* Closed May 21, 1978 after 674 performances.

Martha Swope Photo

Julie J. Hafner, Gloria Hodes, Carole Monferdini, Joanne Beretta

CHELSEA WESTSIDE THEATER
Opened Monday, March 22, 1976.*

The Chelsea Theater Center presents the Lion Theatre Company/Playwrights Horizons production of:

VANITIES

By Jack Heifner; Director, Garland Wright; Scenery, John Arnone; Lighting, Patrika Brown; Costumes, David James; Wardrobe Mistress, Gertrude Sloan, Barrie Moss

CAST

Kathy	Jane Galloway†1
Mary	Susan Merson†2
Joanne	Kathy Bates†3

STANDBY: Pat Richardson

A comedy in three acts. The action takes place in 1963 in a gymnasium, in 1968 in a sorority house, and 1974 in the garden of an apartment.

Press: Betty Lee Hunt, Maria Pucci, Fred Hoot
Stage Manager: Dan Early

* Still playing May 31, 1978.
† Succeeded by: 1. Cordis Heard, 2. Monica Merryman, Patricia Miller, 3. Sally Sockwell

Roger Greenawalt Photo

Sally Sockwell, Cordis Heard, Monica Merryman

OFF-BROADWAY PRODUCTIONS FROM PAST SEASONS THAT CLOSED THIS SEASON

Title	Opened	Closed	Performances
The Club	10/14/76	5/21/78	667
Streamers	4/21/76	6/5/77	497
Ashes	2/9/77	7/3/77	167
On-the Lock-In	4/27/77	6/5/77	62
Agamemnon	5/18/77	6/19/77	61
Creditors/The Stronger	5/17/77	6/5/77	56
Dear Liar	4/28/77	6/12/77	53
Exiles	5/19/77	6/12/77	40

NATIONAL TOURING COMPANIES

(Failure to submit material necessitated several omissions)

ANNIE

Book by Thomas Meehan; Based on "Little Orphan Annie" comic strip; Music, Charles Strouse; Lyrics, Martin Charnin; Director, Mr. Charnin; Choreography, Peter Gennaro; Sets, David Mitchell; Costumes, Theoni V. Aldredge; Lighting, Judy Rasmuson; Musical Direction, Glen Clugston; Dance Arrangements, Peter Howard; Orchestrations, Philip J. Lang; Production Supervisor, Janet Beroza; Assistant Conductor, Steve Hinnenkamp; Wardrobe, Linda Lee; Production Assistants, Mark Miller, Kathy Meehan; General Management, Gatchell & Neufeld; Hairstylists, Charles LaFrance, Ed de Orienzo; Produced by Irwin Meyer, Stephen R. Friedman, Lewis Allen, Peter Crane, Alvin Nederlander Associates, JFK Center for the Performing Arts, Icarus Productions; Presented by Mike Nichols. Opened Thursday March 23, 1978 at O'Keefe Center, Toronto, Canada, and still touring May 31, 1978.

CAST

Annie	Kathy-Jo Kelly
Oliver Warbucks	Norwood Smith
Miss Hannigan	Jane Connell†1
Grace Farrell	Kathryn Boule
Rooster Hannigan	Gary Beach
FDR	Sam Stoneburner
Lily	Lisa Raggio
July	Dara Brown
Tessie	April Lerman
Pepper	Shelle Monahan
Duffy	Alyson Mord
Kate	Dana Tapper
Molly	Kristin Williams
Sandy	Himself
Bundles/Ickes	Gordon Stanley
Dog Catcher/Bert Healy/Hull	Michael Shaw
Dog Catcher/Jimmy Johnson/Guard	Edmond Dante
Lt. Ward/Justice Brandeis	Charles Cagle
Sophie/Cecile/Ronnie Boylan	Linda Rios
Drake	Tom Avera
Mrs. Pugh/Connie Boylan	Linda Lauter
Mrs. Greer/Page/Perkins	Jan Pessano†2
Annette/Bonnie Boylan	Penny Carroll
Fred McCracken/Howe	Michael Connolly
Alternates: Richard Flanders, Mimi Wallace	

MUSICAL NUMBERS: see Broadway Calendar, page 49.

Company Managers: John Corkill, Mark Andrews
Press: David Powers, Kevin Carroll O'Connor
Stage Managers: Martha Knight, Bethe Ward, B. J. Allen, Moose Peting

† Succeeded by: 1. Ruth Kobart, 2. Lynn Kearney

Martha Swope Photos

Lisa Raggio, Jane Connell, Gary Beach
Below: Norwood Smith, Kathy-Jo Kelly, Kathryn Boul

DRACULA

By Hamilton Deane and John L. Balderston; From Bram Stoker's novel "Dracula"; Director, Dennis Rosa; Scenery and Costumes, Edward Gorey; Scenery Supervision, Lynn Pecktal; Costumes Supervision, John David Ridge; Lighting, Roger Morgan; Wardrobe Supervisor, Byron Brice; Hairdresser, Frank Mellon; Assistant Director, Steven Deshler; Presented by Jujamcyn Theaters, Elizabeth Ireland McCann, John Wulp, Victor Lurie, Nelle Nugent, Max Weitzenhoffer; Opened Friday, May 19, 1978 at Mechanic Theatre in Baltimore, MD., and still touring May 31, 1978.

CAST

Lucy Seward	Margaret Whitton
Miss Wells	Victoria Page
Jonathan Harker	Nick Stannard
Dr. Seward	Dalton Dearborn
Abraham Van Helsing	David Hurst
R. M. Renfield	John Long
Butterworth	Fritz Sperberg
Count Dracula	Raul Julia†

STANDBYS AND UNDERSTUDIES: Jean LeClerc (Dracula), William Riker (Van Heising/Seward), Mary Dierson (Lucy/Miss Wells), Chaz Denny (Haker/Butterworth/Renfield), Fritz Sperberg (Harker)

A melodrama in 3 acts and 4 scenes. The action takes place in the 1920's in the library of Dr. Seward's sanatorium in Purley, England, in Lucy's boudoir, and in a vault.

Company Manager: James Mennen
Press: Solters & Roskin, Joshua Ellis, Milly Schoenbaum, Ellen Levene
Stage Managers: William Dodds, M. William Lettich, Chaz Denny, Mary Dierson

† Succeeded by Jean LeClerc. For Broadway production, see Broadway Calendar page 17.

Raul Julia   **Jean LeClerc**

BUBBLING BROWN SUGAR

Book, Loften Mitchell; Based on concept by Rosetta LeNoire; Director, Robert M. Cooper; Choreography-Musical Staging, Billy Wilson; Musical Direction-Arrangements, Danny Holgate; Sets, Clarke Dunham; Lighting, Barry Arnold; Costumes, Bernard Johnson; Projections, Lucie D. Grosvenor, Clarke Dunham; Choral Arrangements, Chapman Roberts; Additional Music, Danny Holgate, Emme Kemp, Lillian Lopez; Production Supervisor, I. Mitchell Miller; Production Coordinator, Sharon Brown; Presented by J. Lloyd Grant, Richard Bell, Robert M. Cooper, Ashton Springer in association with M.G.B. Associates; Opened June 22, 1976 at the Shubert Theatre in Chicago, Il., and closed at the National Theatre, Washington, D.C., on Oct. 9, 1977.

CAST

Skip	Ronald "Smokey" Stevens†1
Bill/Time Man/M.C.	Charles "Honi" Coles
Ray/Young Sage	Robert Melvin
Carolyn/Nightclub Singer	Marilyn Johnson†2
Norma	Yolanda Graves
Gene/Young Checkers	Marcus B. F. Brown
Helen	Vikki Baltimore
Laura	Nancy-Suzanne
Marsha/Young Irene	Ursuline Kairson†3
Newsboy/Son/Nightclub Singer	Keith Davis†4
Tony/Waiter/Dutch	Alan Zampese†5
Irene Paige	Mable Lee†6
John Sage/Dusty	Vernon Washington†7
Checkers/Rusty	Jay Flash Riley
Jim	J. Edward Adams
Ella	Terri Burrell
Judy/Dutch's Girl	Stephanie Kurz
Charlie/Count	Richard Casper
Gospel Lady	Lucille Futrell Harley
The Solitunes	Marcus B. F. Brown, Ronald Stevens, Keith Davis, Ursuline Kairson
Bumpy	Hugh Hurd

MUSICAL NUMBERS: "Harlem '70," "Bubbling Brown Sugar," "That's What Harlem Is to Me," "Bill Robinson Specialty," "Harlem Sweet Harlem," "Nobody," "Goin' Back in Time," "Some of These Days," "Moving Uptown," "Strolling," "I'm Gonna Tell God All My Troubles," "His Eye Is on the Sparrow," "Swing Low, Sweet Chariot," "Sweet Georgia Brown," "Honeysuckle Rose," "Stormy Monday Blues," "Rosetta," "Sophisticated Lady," "In Honeysuckle Time," "When Emaline Said She'd Be Mine," "Solitude," "C'mon Up to Jive Time," "Stompin' at the Savoy," "Take the 'A' Train," "Harlem Time," "Love Will Find a Way," "Dutch's Song," "Ain't Misbehavin'," "Pray for the Lights to Go Out," "I Got It Bad," "Harlem Makes Me Feel," "There'll Be Some Changes Made," "God Bless the Child," "It Don't Mean a Thing"

A musical revue in 2 acts and 9 scenes. The action takes place in Harlem at the present time, and between 1920 and 1940.

General Manager: Ashton Springer
Company Manager: Douglas Helgeson
Press: Max Eisen, Maurice Turet
Stage Managers: Jack Welles, Femi Sarah Heggie, Nancy-Suzanne, Jerry Cleveland

† Succeeded by: 1. Billy Newton-Davis, 2. Sandi Hewitt, 3. Vivian Reed for 12 weeks, 4. Myles G. Savage, 5. William Bremer, 6. Marilyn Johnson, 7. Charles "Honi" Coles

Jai Oscar St. John, Mable Lee, Richard Brown, Bobby Hill

BUBBLING BROWN SUGAR

Director, Ron Abbott; Musical Director, Jeff Laibson; Choreography restaged by Dyann Robinson; All other credits same as listed for preceding company; Presented by Tom Mallow in association with James Janek; Production Associates, Richard Martini, Jerry R. Moore; Wardrobe, Al Costa; Opened Tuesday, Aug. 23, 1977 in Uihlein Hall, Milwaukee, WI, and closed Apr. 22, 1978 at National Arts Centre, Ottawa, Canada.

CAST

Skip/Young Checkers/Solitune	Garry Q. Lewis
Ray/Young Sage/Solitune	Ralph Glenmore
Carolyn/Gospel Lady/Club Singer	Teri Lindsey
Norma	Veda Jackson
Gene/Gospel Lady's Son/Solitune	Bernard Marsh
Helen	Lynn Allen
Laura	Katherine Singleton
Marsha/Young Irene	Rhetta Hughes
Tony/Waiter	Greg Minahan
Irene Paige	Mable Lee
John Sage/Rusty	Richard Brown
Checkers/Dusty	Bobby Hill
Jim/Nightclub Singer	Glover Parham
Ella	Francine Claudia Moore
Time Man/M.C.	Jai Oscar St. John
Judy	Jan Birse
Charlie	Thomas Tofel
Dance Alternates: Jalia Murry, Ronn Elmore	

MUSICAL NUMBERS: see preceding listing. For original Broadway production, see THEATRE WORLD Vol. 33

General Manager: James Janek
Company Manager: Sheila R. Phillips
Press: Clarence Allsopp
Stage Managers: Robert S. McNally III, Rita McNally, Jalia Murry

CALIFORNIA SUITE

By Neil Simon; Director, Gene Saks; Restaged by Philip Cusack; Set, William Ritman; Costumes, Jane Greenwood; Lighting, Tharon Musser; Wardrobe Supervisor, Robert Killgoar; Hairstylist, Jennifer Berman; Assistant to Producers, Leslie Butler; Producers, Emanuel Azenberg, Robert Fryer; Opened Saturday, October 1, 1977 at the Playhouse in Wilmington, DE, and closed June 3, 1978 at the Shubert Theatre in Boston, MA.

CAST

Visitor from New York:
Hannah Warren .... Elizabeth Allen
William Warren .... Robert Reed†
Visitor from Philadelphia:
Marvin Michaels .... Warren Berlinger
Bunny .... Bea Swanson
Millie Michaels .... Patti Karr
Visitors from London:
Sidney Nichols .... Robert Reed†
Diana Nichols .... Elizabeth Allen
Visitors from Chicago:
Mort Hollender .... Warren Berlinger
Beth Hollender .... Patti Karr
Stu Franklyn .... Robert Reed†
Gert Franklyn .... Elizabeth Allen

UNDERSTUDIES: Mary Boucher (Hannah/Diana/Gert/Bunny), Martin Donegan (William/Sidney/Stu), Gary Gage (Marvin/Mort), Bea Swanson (Millie/Beth), Cathy B. Blaser (Bunny)

A comedy in two acts and four scenes. The action takes palce at the present time in a hotel suite in California.

General Manager: Jose Vega
Company Manager: Alan Wasser
Press: Bill Evans, Harry Davies
Stage Managers: Richard W. Evans, Jake Hamilton, Cathy B. Blaser

† Succeeded by Don Murray. For original Broadway production, see THEATRE WORLD, Vol. 33.

Martha Swope Photo

Patti Karr, Elizabeth Allen, Warren Berlinger, Robert Reed

CHICAGO

Book by Fred Ebb, Bob Fosse; Music, John Kander; Lyrics, Fred Ebb; Based on play "Chicago" by Maurine Dallas Watkins; Directed and Choreographed by Bob Fosse; Settings, Tony Walton; Costumes, Patricia Zipprodt; Lighting, Jules Fisher; Musical Director, Arthur Wagner; Orchestrations, Ralph Burns; Dance Music Arrangements, Peter Howard; Sound, Abe Jacob; Hair Styles, Romaine Green; Assistant to Mr. Fosse, Kathryn Doby; Associate General Manager, Frank Scardino; Wardrobe Supervisor, Ellen Anton; Assistant Choreographer, Tony Stevens; Produced in association with Martin Richards, Joseph Harris, Ira Bernstein; Presented by Robert Fryer and James Cresson; Opened Monday, Sept. 12, 1977 in the Colonial Theatre, Boston, MA., and still touring May 31, 1978.

CAST

Velma Kelly .... Carolyn Kirsch†1
Roxie Hart .... Penny Worth†2
Fred Casely .... Rick Emery
Sgt. Fogarty .... Geoffrey Webb
Amos Hart .... Rex Everhart†3
Liz .... Carla Farnsworth
Annie .... Susan Streater
June .... Kirsten Childs
Hunyak .... Susan Stroman
Mona .... Clare Leach
Matron .... Edye Byrde
Billy Flynn .... Jerry Orbach
Mary Sunshine .... M. O'Haughey
Go-to-Hell-Kitty .... Karen Tamburrelli
Harry .... Daniel Stewart
Aaron .... Jeremy Blanton†4
Baliff .... William H. Brown, Jr.
Court Clerk .... David Kottke
Martin Harrison .... J. Keith Ryan
Dance Alternates: Melanie Adam, Ron Schwinn

MUSICAL NUMBERS: "All That Jazz," "Funny Honey," "Cell Block Tango," "When You're Good to Mama," "Tap Dance," "All I Care About," "A Little Bit of Good," "We Both Reached for the Gun," "Roxie," "I Can't Do It Alone," "Chicago after Midnight," "My Own Best Friend," "I Know a Girl," "Me and My Baby," "Mister Cellophane," "When Velma Takes the Stand," "Razzle Dazzle," "Class," "Nowadays," "Keep It Hot," "R.S.V.P."

A "musical vaudeville" in two acts. The action takes place in the late 1920's in Chicago, Illinois.

General Managers: Joseph Harris, Ira Bernstein
Company Manager: Doug Helegson
Press: The Merlin Group, Cheryl Sue Dolby, Irene Gandy, Beatrice DaSilva
Stage Managers: Ed Aldridge, Craig Jacobs, James Lockhart

† Succeeded by: 1. Chita Rivera, 2. Gwen Verdon, 3. Haskell Gordon, 4. Jon Engstrom. For original New York production, see THEATRE WORLD, Vol. 32.

Carolyn Kirsch, Jerry Orbach, Penny Worth

A CHORUS LINE

Conceived, Directed and Choreographed by Michael Bennett; Book, James Kirkwood, Nicholas Dante; Music, Marvin Hamlisch; Lyrics, Edward Kleban; Set, Robin Wagner; Costumes, Theoni V. Aldredge; Lighting, Tharon Musser; Sound, Abe Jacob; Co-Choreographer, Bob Avian; Orchestrations, Bill Byers, Hershy Kay, Jonathan Tunick; Music Direction and Vocal Arrangements, Don Pippin; Musical Direction, Sherman Frank; Assistant to Choreographer, Baayork Lee; Associate Producer, Bernard Gersten; Wardrobe, Alyce Gilbert, Karen Lloyd; Hairstylist, Juan Rodriguez; Production Supervisor, Jason Steven Cohen; Assistant Conductor, Tony Geralis; Presented by the New York Shakespeare Festival (Joseph Papp, Producer) in association with Plum Productions; Opened Monday, May 3, 1976 at the Royal Alexandra Theatre, Toronto, Can., and still playing May 31, 1978. For original New York production, see THEATRE WORLD, Vol. 31.

CAST

Paul	Tommy Aguilar†1
Jarad	Michael Austin
Kristine	Christine Barker†2
Al	Steve Baumann†3
Vicki	Judy Burns†4
Tom	Ron Stafford†5
Maggie	Betty Lynd
Frank	Troy Garza†6
Val	Karen Jablons†7
Zach	Eivind Harum†8
Mike	Jeff Hyslop†9
Diana	Gina Paglia†10
Louis	Anthony Inneo
Greg	Mark Dovey†11
Bobby	Ron Kurowski†12
Connie	Jennifer Ann Lee†13
Lois	Wendy Mansfield†14
Judy	Murphy Cross†15
Richie	A. William Perkins†16
Barbara	Martie Hatem Ram†17
Larry	T. Michael Reed†18
Butch	Ken Rogers†19
Cassie	Pamela Sousa†20
Mark	Timothy Scott†21
Roy	Ron Simione†22
Sheila	Jane Summerhays†23
Bebe	Miriam Welch†24
Tricia	Nancy Wood†25
Don	Brandt Edwards†26
Rosemary	Gail Mae Ferguson
Claude	Gary Sullivan
Doug	Sam Viverito

MUSICAL NUMBERS: see Broadway Calendar, page 50.

General Managers: Emanuel Azenberg, Robert Kamlot
Company Managers: Maurice Schaded, Laurel Ann Wilson, Noel Gilmore
Press: Merle Debuskey, Horace Greeley McNab
Stage Managers: Jeff Hamlin, Frank Hartenstein, Kate M. Pollock, Scott Faris

† Succeeded by: 1. Guillermo Gonzalez, 2. P. J. Mann, 3. Frank Hooper, 4. Niki Harris, 5. Steve Belin, 6. Robert Warner, 7. Patti Colombo, 8. Buddy Vest, 9. C. J. McCaffrey, 10. Diane Fratantoni, 11. Larry Blum, 12. Ronald Stafford, 13. Cherylene Lee, 14. Bebe Neuwirth, 15. Shanna Reed, 16. Millard Hurley, 17. Michelle Stubbs, 18. John Fogarty, 19. Eric Riley, 20. Deborah Henry, 21. Scott Geralds, 22. Scott Faris, 23. Judy Burns, 24. Teresa Rossomando, 25. Janie Gleason, 26. Barry Thomas.

Scott Geralds, P. J. Mann, Barry Thomas
Martha Swope Photos

FDR

By Dore Schary; Director, Jeff Bleckner; Scenery and Lighting, H. R. Poindexter; Costumes, Noel Taylor; General Manager, David Hedges; Press, Seymour Krawitz; Presented by Don Gregory in association with Bill Loeb; Opened Monday, Sept. 12, 1977 at the Moore Theatre, Seattle, Wa., and closed Nov. 29, 1977 at the National Theatre, Washington, D.C.

CAST

Robert Vaughn
as
Franklin Delano Roosevelt

A one-character play in two parts, covering the Roosevelt years in public service.

Robert Vaughn as FDR

A CHORUS LINE

Musical Direction, Tom Hancock; Music Coordinator, Robert Thomas;Wardrobe Mistress, Mary Beth Regan; Associate Conductor, Nicholas Archer, Jr.; All other credits same as listed for preceding company of "A Chorus Line"; Opened Tuesday, May 11, 1975 at the Curran Theatre in San Francisco, CA., and still touring May 31, 1978. For original New York production, see THEATRE WORLD, Vol. 31.

CAST

Kristine	Cookie Vasquez
Val	Pamela Blair†1
Roy	Tim Cassidy†2
Mark	Jimmy Roddy†3
Maggie	Lisa Donaldson†4
Mike	Don Correia†5
Richie	Ronald Dennis†6
Judy	Patricia Garland†7
Greg	Andy Keyser
Don	Dennis Edenfield
Bebe	Nancy Lane†8
Connie	Lauren Kayahara†9
Diana	Chris Bocchino†10
Zach	Joe Bennett†11
Cassie	Pamela Peadon†12
Vicki	Mary Ann O'Reilly†13
Bobby	Michael Austin
Al	Don Percassi†14
Sheila	Charlene Ryan†15
Larry	Roy Smith†16
Butch	Sam Tampoya†17
Tom	Danny Taylor†18
Frank	Claude R. Tessier†19
Paul	Sammy Williams†20
Lois	Lee Wilson†21
Tricia	Linda Dangcil†22

MUSICAL NUMBERS: see Broadway Calendar, page 50.

General Manager: Emanuel Azenberg, Robert Kamlot
Company Manager: Lilli Afan
Press: Merle Debuskey, Margie Korshak
Stage Managers: Jeff Hamlin, Tom Porter, Martin Gold, Carlos Gorbea

† Succeeded by: 1. Lois Englund, 2. Noel Craig, 3. James Beaumont, 4. Christina Saffran, 5. William Mead, 6. Larry G. Bailey, 7. Victoria Tabaka, 8. Rise Clemmer, 9. Sachi Shimizu, 10. Chris Bocchino, 11. Anthony S. Teague, 12. Wanda Richert, 13. Denise Direnzo, 14. Jack Karcher, 15. Sally Benoit, 16. Keith Keen, 17. Dennis Birchall, 18. Michael Lane, 19. Jack Magradey, 20. Stephen Crenshaw, 21. Tina Paul, 22. Laura Klein

Larry Bailey and cast
Top: Chris Bocchino, Anthony Teague

FOR COLORED GIRLS WHO HAVE CONSIDERED SUICIDE WHEN THE RAINBOW IS ENUF

By Ntozake Shange; Arranged and Directed by Oz Scott; Set, Ming Cho Lee; Lighting, Jennifer Tipton; Costumes, Judy Dearing; Choreography, Paula Moss; Wardrobe Supervisor, Margaret Faison; Presented by Joseph Papp and Woodie King, Jr.; Production Supervisor, Jason Steven Cohen; Associate Producer, Bernard Gersten; A NY Shakespeare Festival Production in association with the Henry Street Settlement's New Federal Theater; Opened Aug. 10, 1977 at the Mark Taper Forum in Los Angeles, CA, and still touring May 31, 1978.

CAST

Lady in Orange	Barbara Alston
Lady in Pink	Beverly Anne
Lady in Red	Trazana Beverley†
Lady in Purple	Gloria Calomee
Lady in Green	Brenda J. Davis
Lady in Blue	Paula Larke
Lady in Yellow	Jonette O'Kelley

Understudies: Yvette Hawkins, LaTanya Richardson, Tawnya Pettiford

Performed without intermission.

General Managers: Emanuel Azenberg, Robert Kamlot
Press: Merle Debuskey, Owen Levy
Stage Managers: Robert Kellogg, Jacqueline Yancey

† Succeeded by LaTanya Richardson. For original NY production, see THEATRE WORLD, Vol. 33.

Martha Swope Photo

Jonette O'Kelley, Brenda Davis, Trazana Beverley, Paula Larke

GREASE

Book, Music and Lyrics, Jim Jacobs, Warren Casey; Director, Tom Moore; Musical Numbers and Dances Staged by Patricia Birch; Scenery, Douglas W. Schmidt; Costumes, Carrie F. Robbins; Associate Director, Michael Martorella; Assistant Choreographer, Kathi Moss; Musical Direction, Elizabeth Myers; Orchestrations, Michael Leonard; Vocal and Dance Arrangements, Louis St. Louis; General Management, Theatre Now, Inc.; Presented by Kenneth Waissman and Maxine Fox; Opened Oct. 10, 1976 at the Shubert in Boston, Ma., and still touring May 31, 1978. For original New York production, see THEATRE WORLD, Vol. 28.

CAST

Miss Lynch	Imogene Bliss
Patty Simcox	Ann-Ngaire Martin
Eugene Florczyk	Randy Powell
Jan	Patricia Douglas
Marty	Linda Lyons
Betty Rizzo	Nita Novy
Doody	Michael Riney
Roger	Dan Woodard
Kenickie	Kelly St. John
Sonny LaTierri	Terry Michos
Frenchy	Duffi
Sandy Dumbrowski	Gail Edwards
Danny Zuko	Peter Gallagher
Vince Fontaine	Stephen M. Groff
Johnny Casino/Teen Angel	Steve Yudson
Cha-Cha DiGregorio	Mary Garripoli

UNDERSTUDIES: Linda Nenno, Jacalyn Switzer, Robert Reynolds, John Everson
MUSICAL NUMBERS: See Broadway Calendar, page 53

MY FAIR LADY

Book and Lyrics, Alan Jay Lerner; Adapted from George Bernard Shaw's "Pygmalion"; Music, Frederick Loewe; Director, Jerry Adler; Choreography and Musical Numbers, Crandall Diehl; Scenery, Oliver Smith; Costumes, Cecil Beaton; Lighting, Ken Billington; Musical Director, Albert L. Fiorillo, Jr.; Hairstylist, Vincenzo Prestia; Production Associates, Richard Martini, Jerry R. Moore; Assistant Conductor, Philip Parnes; Wardrobe, James Jay; Production Assistant, David Kerley; Presented by Tom Mallow in association with James Janek; Opened Monday, October 10, 1977 at the American Theatre in St. Louis, Mo., and closed at Heinz Hall, Pittsburgh, Pa., May 28, 1978. For original Broadway production, see THEATRE WORLD, Vol. 12.

CAST

Buskers	Lisa Guignard, Dirk Lumbard, Robert Sullivan
Mrs. Eynsford-Hill	Enid Rodgers
Freddy Eynsford-Hill	Kevin Lane Dearinger
Eliza Doolittle	Anne Rogers
Colonel Pickering	Ronald Drake
Henry Higgins	Edward Mulhare
1st Cockney/Jamie/Footman	Ned Coulter
2nd Cockney/Servant/Ambassador	James Todkill
3rd Cockney/Servant/Footman/Flunkey	Rick McElhiney
4th Cockney/Bartender/Butler	Morgan MacKay
Harry/Lord Boxington/Zoltan Karpathy	Don Woodman
Alfred P. Doolittle	Thomas Bowman
Mrs. Pearce	Joyce Worsley
Mrs. Hopkins/Queen of Transylvania	Celia Tackaberry
Servants	Malita Barron, Julie Ann Fogt
Mrs. Higgins	Marie Paxton
Chauffeur/Constable	Scott Harris
Lady Boxington/Servant	Kristina Karlin
Flower Girl	Nancy Hess
Mrs. Higgin's Maid	Lynn Keeton

DANCERS: Andy Ferrell, Terry Gene, Lisa Guignard, Scott Harris, Nancy Hess, James Horvath, Lynn Keeton, Dirk Lumbard, Nancy Lynch, Peter Pederson, Linda Ravinsky, Robert Sullivan

MUSICAL NUMBERS: "Street Entertainers," "Why Can't the English?," "Wouldn't It Be Loverly?," "With a Little Bit of Luck," "I'm an Ordinary Man," "Just You Wait," "The Rain in Spain," "I Could Have Danced All Night," "Ascot Gavotte," "On the Street Where You Live," "Embassy Waltz," "You Did It," "Show Me," "Get Me to the Church on Time," "A Hymn to Him," "Without You," "I've Grown Accustomed to Her Face"

A musical in 2 acts and 18 scenes.

General Manager: James Janek
Company Manager: Robert C. Ossenfort
Press: F. Bev Kelley
Stage Managers: Jack Welles, Ric Barrett, Nancy Lynch

Anne Rogers, Edward Mulhare

Artistic Director-Producer, Philip Meister; General Manager, Deborah Teller; Tour Directors, Arthur Bicknell, Suzi Guernsey; Scenery and Lighting, Terry Bennett; Costumes, Sharon Hollinger; Company Manager, Kirk Wolfinger; Technical Director, Harvey Wilson; Stage Managers, Stephen Root, Alison Edwards, Jonathan Lutz; Opened Oct. 3, 1977 in Machia, ME, and closed May 13, 1978 in Amherst, MA.

COMPANY

Julian Bailey, Richard Bowne, Rodney Clark, Alison Edwards, Pamela Erb, Nancy Hammill, Jonathan Lutz, Richard Phillips, Stephen Root, Marc Weishaus, Harvey Wilson, Kirk Wolfinger

PRODUCTIONS

"As You Like It" by William Shakespeare; Director, Sue Lawless; Music, John Franceschina; "Othello" by William Shakespeare; Director, Philip Meister; "A Winter's Tale" by William Shakespeare; Director, Mario Siletti.

Below: Nancy Hamill, Richard Bowne in "Winter's Tale" Left: Nancy Hamill, Jonathan Lutz in "Othello" Top: Richard Bowne, Alison Edwards in "As You Like It"

PIPPIN

By Roger O. Hirson; Music and Lyrics, Stephen Schwartz; Directed and Choreographed by Bob Fosse; Scenery, Tony Walton; Costumes, Patricia Zipprodt; Lighting, Jules Fisher; Musical Direction, Roland Gagnon; Orchestrations, Ralph Burns; Dance Arrangements, John Berkman; Sound, Abe Jacob; Assistant to Choreographer, Louise Quick Bowen; Hairstylist, Ernest Adler; Wardrobe, A. T. Karniewich; Associate Conductor, Alyce Billington; General Managers, Joseph Harris, Ira Bernstein; Company Manager, Harold Kusell; Press, Fred Weterick; Stage Managers, John H. Lowe III, Bill Biskup, Julie Ostrow; Presented by Stuart Ostrow; Opened Monday, Sept. 7, 1977 in JFK Center Opera House, Washington, D.C., and still touring May 31, 1978. For original New York production, see THEATRE WORLD, Vol. 29.

CAST

Leading Player	Larry Riley
Pippin	Michael Rupert
Charles	Eric Berry
Lewis	Jerry Colker
Fastrada	Antonia Ellis†
Sword Bearer	Ken Urmston
The Head Field Marshall	David Pursley
Berthe	Thelma Carpenter
Beggar	Lee Mathis
Peasant	Clayton Strange
Noble	Andy Hostettler
Catherine	Alexandra Borrie
Theo	Shamus Barnes

STANDBYS AND UNDERSTUDIES: Lynn Archer (Berthe), Jo Jo Barnes (Theo), Clayton Strange (Leading Player), David Pursley (Charles), Dance Alternates: Gwen Hillier Lowe, Scott Fless

MUSICAL NUMBERS: "Magic to Do," "Corner of the Sky," "Welcome Home," "War Is a Science," "Glory," "Simple Joys," "No Time at All," "With You," "Spread a Little Sunshine," "Morning Glow," "On the Right Track," "Kind of Woman," "Extraordinary," "Love Song," Finale

A musical in eight scenes without intermission. The action takes place in 780 A.D. and thereabouts in the Holy Roman Empire and thereabouts.

† Succeeded by Carole Schweid

Larry Riley, Michael Rupert

Tony Russel, Kathryn Crosby

SAME TIME, NEXT YEAR

By Bernard Slade; Director, Warren Crane; Set, William Ritman; Costumes, Jane Greenwood; Lighting, Tharon Musser; Hairstylist, Steve Atha; Production Associates, Richard Martini, Jerry R. Moore; Wardrobe Supervisor, Thelma Davis; Production Assistant, David Kerley; General Manager, James Janek; Press, Max Eisen; Stage Managers, J. S. McKie, Jr., Richard Stack; Presented by Tom Mallow by arrangement with Morton Gottlieb; For original New York production, see THEATRE WORLD, Vol. 31. Opened Friday, January 13, 1978 in Greensboro, N.C., Auditorium, and closed April 22, 1978 in Theatre Maisenneuve, Montreal, Canada.

CAST

Doris .... Kathryn Crosby
George .... Tony Russel
Standbys: Rose Mary Taylor, Richard Stack

A comedy in two acts and six scenes. The action takes place in a guest cottage of a country inn in Northern California from 1951 to 1976.

Martha Swope Photo

See Broadway Calendar page 60.

SHENANDOAH

Book, James Lee Barrett, Peter Udell, Philip Rose; Based on screenplay of same title by Mr. Barrett; Music, Gary Geld; Lyrics, Peter Udell; Director, Philip Rose; Choreography, Robert Tucker; Scenery, C. Murawski; Lighting, Thomas Skelton; Costumes, Pearl Somner, Winn Morton; Orchestrations, Don Walker; Musical Direction, Richard Laughlin; Dance Arrangements, Russell Warner; Wardrobe Supervisor, Cathleen Gallagher; General Manager, Helen Richards; Company Manager, L. Liberatore; Stage Managers, Bert Wood, Brenda Gardner, Eileen Hawkins; Press, Merle Debuskey, Reuben Rabinovitch; Presented by Philip Rose, Gloria and Louis K. Sher; Opened Tuesday, Oct. 4, 1977 in Ariel Crown Theatre, Chicago, Il., and still touring May 31, 1977. For original New York production, see THEATRE WORLD, Vol. 31.

CAST

Charlie Anderson .... John Cullum†
Jacob .... Dean Russell
James .... Bill DeWitt
Nathan .... Robert Quigley
John .... Dan McGeachy
Jenny .... Suzy Brabeau
Henry .... J. J. Jepson
Robert (The Boy) .... Steve Grober
Anne .... Lola-Belle Smith
Gabriel .... Cal Boney
Reverend Byrd .... James Harwood
Sam .... Gordon Halliday
Sgt. Johnson .... Ed Sala
Lieutenant .... Kenneth Kantor
Tinkham .... Tim Wallace
Carol .... Ron Highley
Corporal .... Robert Johanson
Maurauder .... Jay Pierce
Engineer .... Leslie Feagan
Confederate Sniper .... Gary Barker

ENSEMBLE: Gary Barker, Freyda Thomas, Ron Highley, Leslie Feagan, Eileen Hawkins, Tim Wallace, Robert Johanson, Kenneth Kantor, Matt Gavin, Joel T. Myers, Jay Pierce, Ed Sala, Scott Bakula

MUSICAL NUMBERS: "Raise the Flag of Dixie," "I've Heard It All Before," "Pass the Cross to Me," "Why Am I Me," "Next to Lovin' I Like Fightin'," "Over the Hill," "The Pickers Are Comin'," "Meditation," "We Make a Beautiful Pair," "Violets and Silverbells," "Papa's Gonna Make It Alright"

A musical in two acts. The action takes place during the Civil War in the Shenandoah Valley of Virginia.

† Succeeded by John Raitt

Ed Sala, Robert Johanson, John Raitt
Above: Gordon Halliday, Suzy Brabeau   157

Kukla, Burr Tillstrom, Ollie
Left: Cyril Ritchard, Carol Swarbrick, David
Chaney, Bonnie Schon

SIDE BY SIDE BY SONDHEIM

Music and Lyrics by Stephen Sondheim; and Music by Leonard Bernstein, Mary Rodgers, Richard Rodgers, Jule Style; Director, Ned Sherrin; Musical Director, Paul Gemignani; Musical Staging, John Grigas; Scenery, Jay Moore; Costumes, Florence Klotz; Lighting, Ken Billington; Sound, Jack Mann; Wardrobe Supervisor, Kaye Nottbusch, Harry Hinkel; General Manager, Howard Haines; Stage Managers, John Grigas, Thomas M. Guerra; Press, Mary Bryant, Gertrude Bromberg; Presented by Harold Prince in association with Ruth Mitchell by arrangement with the InComes Company; Opened Sunday, Oct. 30, 1977 in the Drury Lane Theatre, Chicago, IL, and closed there Jan. 29, 1978. For original New York production, see THEATRE WORLD, Vol. 33.

CAST

Cyril Ritchard†
Carol Swarbrick
David Chaney
Bonnie Schon

MUSICAL NUMBERS: "Comedy Tonight," "Love Is in the Air," "If Momma Was Married," "You Must Meet My Wife," "The Little Things You Do Together," "Getting Married Today," "I Remember," "Can That Boy Foxtrot," "Company," "Another Hundred People," "Barcelona," "Marry Me a Little," "Sorry—Grateful," "I Never Do Anything Twice," "Bring on the Girls," "Ah, Paree!," "Buddy's Blues," "Broadway Baby," "You Could Drive a Person Crazy," "Everybody Says Don't," "Anyone Can Whistle," "Send in the Clowns," "Everybody Ought to Have a Maid," "A Boy Like That," "I Have a Love," "The Boy from . . .," "Pretty Lady," "You Gotta Have a Gimmick," "Losing My Mind," "Could I Leave You?," "I'm Still Here," "Side by Side by Sondheim"

A "musical entertainment" in two parts.

† Succeeded by Burr Tillstrom, Kukla and Ollie

SIDE BY SIDE BY SONDHEIM

Pianists, John Berkman, Terry Trotter; Scenery, Peter Docherty; Company Manager, John Caruso; Press, Mary Bryant, Richard Spittel, Dan Kephart, Philip Rinaldi; Stage Managers, John Grigas, Valentine Mayer. All other credits same as preceding listing. Opened Monday, March 6, 1978 at the Parker Playhouse in Ft. Lauderdale, FL, and still touring May 31, 1978.

CAST

Hermione Gingold
Larry Kert
Barbara Heuman
Millicent Martin

ALTERNATES: Elliott Reid for Miss Gingold, Gary Krawford for Mr. Kert, Marina MacNeal for Misses Martin and Heuman, Judy Balsam for pianists

MUSICAL NUMBERS: same as in preceding listing.

Martha Swope Photos

Barbara Heuman
Above: Millicent Martin

Larry Kert
Above: Hermione Gingold

SLY FOX

By Larry Gelbart; Based on Ben Jonson's play "Volpone"; Director, Arthur Penn; Sets and Lighting, George Jenkins; Costumes, Albert Wolsky; Wardrobe Supervisor, Josephine Zampredi; Hairdresser, Vincent Tucker; General Manager, Eugene V. Wolsk; Company Manager, James Awe; Stage Managers, Clint Jakeman, Kenneth Cox, Sanford Morris; Press, Merle Debuskey, Daniel Langan. Opened Wednesday, March 8, 1978 in the Fox Theatre, San Diego, CA, and closed at the Blackstone Theatre in Chicago, IL, May 27, 1978 because of Mr. Gleason's illness. For original New York production, see THEATRE WORLD, Vol. 33.

CAST

Simon Able	Cleavon Little
Sly's Servants	Jack Landron, Toshi Toda, Catherine Schreiber
Foxwell J. Sly	Jackie Gleason
Lawyer Craven	Edward Zang
Jethro Crouch	Irwin Corey
Abner Truckle	Bob Levine
Miss Fancy	Marie Wallace
Mrs. Truckle	Patty Dworkin
Crouch's Servant	Toshi Toda
Captain Crouch	Peter Johl
Chief of Police	David Tabor
Bailiff	Thomas Bade
Court Clerk	Sam Kressen
The Judge	Himself
Policemen	Kermit Brown, Thomas Bade, Sanford Morris

A comedy in two acts and seven scenes. The action takes place in San Francisco in the late 1800's.

Jackie Gleason, Cleavon Little

THE SOUND OF MUSIC

Book, Howard Lindsay and Russel Crouse; Music, Richard Rodgers; Lyrics, Oscar Hammerstein 2nd; Director, Forrest Carter; Choreography and Musical Numbers, Eivie McGehee; Musical Direction, Gordon Brown; Scenery, Peter Wolf; Lighting, David Gibson; Costumes, Arthur Boccia; Production Manager, Harold Goldfaden; Producer, Tom Hughes; Stage Managers, Al Grab, Paul Forste; Presented by James M. Nederlander, David Smerling, Julian Colby; Opened June 21, 1977 in Dallas, TX, and closed at the Arie Crown Theatre, Chicago, Il., Sept. 4, 1977. For original New York Production, see THEATRE WORLD, Vol. 16.

CAST

Maria Rainer	Shirley Jones
Sister Berthe	Phyllis Lyman
Sister Margaretta	Gail Higson
Mother Abbess	Karen Looze
Sister Sophia	Mary Kay Laughlin
Capt. Georg Von Trapp	H. M. Wynant
Franz	Jim Oyster
Frau Schmidt	Helen Noyes
Liesl	Claire Riley
Friedrich	Toby Parker
Louisa	Rachel Parker
Kurt	Andrew Forste
Brigitta	Sarah Jessica Parker
Marta	Piper Riley
Gretl	Megan Forste
Rolf Gruber	Guy Stroman
Elsa Schraeder	Sheila Smith
Ursula	Penny Peters McGuire
Max Detweiler	William LeMassena
Herr Zeller	Jon Vandertholen
Baron Elberfeld	Gary Daniel
Herr Ullrich	Bill Boss
Postulant	Connie Coit
Admiral von Schreiber	Paul Forste
Frau Ullrich	Sharon-Ann Hill
Baroness Elberfeld	Karen Nilsson
Frau Schweiger	Debra Suzanne Chapin

NEIGHBORS, NUNS, ETC: Debra Suzanne Chapin, Connie Coit, Gary Daniel, Agnes Guignard, Sharon-Ann Hill, Dianna Hughes, Mary Jo Lutticken, Andy McAvin, Penny Peters McGuire, Brad Moranz, Karen Nilsson, James Parker

MUSICAL NUMBERS: "Preludium," "The Sound of Music," "Maria," "My Favorite Things," "You Are 16," "The Lonely Goatherd," "How Can Love Survive?," "Do Re Mi," "Grand Waltz," "Landler," "So Long, Farewell," "Climb Every Mountain," "No Way to Stop It," "Ordinary Couple," "Processional"

A musical in 2 acts and 20 scenes.

Shirley Jones (C) Above: H. M. Wynant, Sheila Smith

Michael A. Del Medico as Gorky

"THIS ITALY OF YOURS" andante

Conceived, Written and Directed by Michael A. Del Medico; From the life and writings of Maxim Gorky; Production and Sound, P. Brandstein; Lighting, Joy Lilly; Production Staff, Nancy Ploeger, Diana De La Cuesta; General Manager, J. Bennett; Presented by Bari and Bennett Productions. Opened Monday, June 14, 1977 at Coolidge Theatre, Washington, D.C., and still touring May 31, 1978.

CAST
Michael A. Del Medico
as
Maxim Gorky

THE WIZ

Book, William F. Brown; Based on L. Frank Baum's "The Wonderful Wizard of Oz"; Music and Lyrics, Charlie Smalls; Direction and Costumes, Geoffrey Holder; Setting, Tom H. John; Lighting, Tharon Musser; Musical Direction, Larry Ball; Sound, Richard J. C. Miller; Choreography and Musical Numbers Staged by George Faison; Manager, Jose Vega; Wardrobe, Mario Brera; General Managers, Emanuel Azenberg, Eugene V. Wolsk; Company Manager, David W. Payne; Stage Managers, Kathleen A. Sullivan, Fred Seagraves, Jeanne Fornadel; Assistant to Managers, Kim Sellon, Nancy Nagel; Press, Merlin Group, Sandra Manley, Patt Dale; Presented by Ken Harper in association with 20th Century-Fox Film Corp.: Opened Wednesday, June 16, 1976 at the Ahmanson Theatre, Los Angeles, CA, and still touring May 31, 1978. For original New York production, see THEATRE WORLD, Vol. 31.

CAST

Aunt Em/Glinda	Roz Clark†1
Toto	Patches
Dorothy	Renee Harris
Uncle Henry	George Bell†2
Tornado	Regina Bell†3

Munchkins .... Sharon Brown, Charlotte Neveu, Keith Simmons, Patience Valentine, Tony Walker, Clent Bowers, Ilene Lewis, Alvin McDuffie, Deborah Sharpe

Addaperle	Vivian Bonnell

Yellow Brick Road .... Leon Jackson, Eran Smith, Dan Strayhorn, Lewis Whitlock, Bruce Taylor, Sean Walker

Scarecrow	Charles V. Harris†4

Crows .... Ruth Ashton, Jamilah Hunter, Cindy McGee, Henry Shaw, Graciela Simpson

Tinman	Ben Harney
Lion	Ken Prymus
Gatekeeper/Lord High Underling	George Bell†5
The Wiz	Kamal
Evillene	Carolyn Miller
Soldier Messenger	Tony Walker†6
Winged Monkey	Leon Jackson

EMERALD CITY CITIZENS: Ruth Karen Ashton, Carmen Benitez, Ron Blanco, Eddie Jordan, Ilene Lewis, Alvin McDuffie, Cindy McGee, Charlotte Neveu, Myles G. Savage, Henry Shaw, Braciela Simpson, Eran Smith, Bruce Taylor, Ron Taylor, Evelyn Thomas, Sean Walker, Lewis Whitlock

MUSICAL NUMBERS: see Broadway Calendar, page 59.

A musical in 2 acts and 16 scenes with a prologue.

† Succeeded by: 1. Peggie Blue, 2. Ron Taylor, 3. Evelyn Thomas, 4. Charles Valentino, 5. Clent Bowers, 6. Alvin McDuffie

Charles Valentino, Ken Prymus, Renee Harris, Ben Harney Above: Renee Harris, Vivian Bonnell

PRODUCTIONS THAT OPENED AND CLOSED
BEFORE SCHEDULED BROADWAY PREMIER

ABSENT FRIENDS

A comedy by Alan Ayckbourn; Director, Eric Thompson; Setting, Edward Burbridge; Costumes, Michele Suzanne Reisch; Lighting, Martin Aronstein; Press, Max Eisen; Presented by Claire Nichtern and Ashton Springer; Opened Monday, July 11, 1977 in Eisenhower Theatre/JFK Center, Washington, D.C., and closed Oct. 15, 1977 at Royal Alexandra Theatre, Toronto, Canada.

CAST

Colin .... Eli Wallach
Diana .... Anne Jackson
Paul .... Lee Richardson
Evelyn .... Dale Hodges
John .... Jacob Brooke
Marge .... Meg Wynn Owen

**Top Right: Eli Wallach, Anne Jackson,
Lee Richardson**

ALICE

Conceived, Written and Directed by Vinnette Carroll; From the works of Lewis Carroll; Music and Lyrics, Micki Grant; Choreography, Talley Beatty; Scenery, Douglas W. Schmidt; Costumes, Nancy Potts; Lighting, Jennifer Tipton; Incidental Music, Orchestrations, Vocal Arrangements, H. B. Barnum; Musical Director, Joyce Brown; Sound, Abe Jacob; Assistant Choreographer, Brenda L. Braxton; Wardrobe, Dean Jackson; Assistant Conductor, George Broderick; Assistant to Ms. Carroll, Gerard Campbell; Associate Producers, Luis Sanjurio, Shirley Hoffman; Production Assistants, Anthony Cookson, Stephen Graham; General Managers, Joseph Harris, Ira Bernstein; Stage Managers, Robert L. Borod, Alisa Jill Adler, Robert Charles, Kimako; Press, David Powers, Barbara Carroll; Presented by Mike Nicholas and Lewis Allen in association with Urban Arts Corps and Anita MacShane. Opened Wednesday, May 31, 1978 in the Forrest Theatre, Philadelphia, PA., and closed there June 11, 1978.

CAST

Charlie/Cook .... Charlene Harris
Caterpillar/Tweedledum/Cook/
  Fish/Horse .... Clinton Derricks-Carroll
Bartender/Mushroom/Cook .... Alberta Bradford
Gryph/Cook/Gryphon .... Thomas Pinnock
Waitress .... Marilyn Winbush
Carpenter/Tweedledee/Cook/Horse/Fish .... Cleavant Derricks
Chauffeur/Cook/Knight .... Douglas Houston
Duchess .... Jane White
Lily White/White Queen .... Alice Ghostley
Ted White/White King/White Knight .... Hamilton Camp
Prima/Cook .... Roumel Reaux
Secunda .... Clif De Raita
Tertia .... Christopher Deane
Regina/Black Queen .... Paula Kelly
Alice .... Debbie Allen
Eric/Cheshire Cat/Mock Turtle ..... Jeffrey Anderson-Gunter
Ronnie .... Ronald Dunham
Cheshire Cat's Girls .... Brenda Braxton, Linda James,
                         Juanita Grace Tyler, Kiki Shepard

ENSEMBLE: Adrian Bailey, Brenda Braxton, Roslyn Burrough, Nora M. Cole, Christopher Deane, Clif De Raita, Ronald Dunham, Ralph Farrington, Maggy Gorrill, Charlene Harris, Linda James, Dwayne Phelps, Roumel Reaux, Kiki Shepard, Juanita Grace Tyler, Marilynn Winbush, Charles Wynn, and Alternates: Ramon Colon, Debra Lyman

MUSICAL NUMBERS: "Disco," "Hall of Mirrors Ballet," "Father William," "Chess," "Workin' for the Man," "I am Real," "Children Are," "Everybody's Mad," "Alice," "Fun and Games," "It's Lonely," "Lobster Rock," "Consider"

A musical in 2 acts and 12 scenes with a prologue and epilogue. The action takes place at the present time in the Rabbit Hole, a discotheque.

Martha Swope Photos

**Cleavant Derricks, Debbie Allen, Clinton Derricks-Carroll
Above: Alice Ghostley, Debbie Allen, Paula Kelly**

BROADWAY

By Philip Dunning and George Abbott; Director, Robert Allan Ackerman; Settings, Karen Schulz; Costumes, Carrie F. Robbins; Lighting, Arden Fingerhut; Musical Supervisor, Jack Lee; Assistant to Director, Dennis Grimaldi; General Manager, Theatre Now, Inc. (William Court Cohen, Edward H. Davis, Norman E. Rothstein); Company Manager, Camille Ranson; Assistant to Producers, Tandy Cronyn; Hairdresser, Bert Anthony; Stage Managers, Joe Lorden, Jack Gianino; Presented by Roger Berlind, Steven Beckler, Thomas C. Smith; Press, Betty Lee Hunt, Maria Cristina Pucci, Jan W. Greenberg. Opened Tuesday, April 18, 1978 at the Wilbur Theatre, Boston, MA, and closed there May 14, 1978.

CAST

Nick Verdis	Joseph Leon
Pearl	Jill O'Hara
Roy Lane	William Atherton
Lil	Nancy Andrews
Mazie	Marion McCorry
Ruby	Jean DeBaer
Grace-Ann	Lesley Rogers
Katie	Laura Copland
Billie Moore	Teri Garr
Steve Crandall	Chris Sarandan
Dolph	Armin Shimerman
Porky	James Harder
Scar Edwards	Timothy Meyers
Joe	David J. Forsyth
Dan McCorn	Roy Poole
Benny	Robert D'Avi
Larry	Robert Sevra

UNDERSTUDIES: Laura Copland (Grace/Ruby/Pearl/Mazie), Lynn Charnay (Lil/Katie), Jack Gianino (Joe/Dolph/Larry/Benny), David J. Forsyth (Porky/Nick/Dan), Lesley Rogers (Billie), Robert Sevra (Roy/Steve/Scar)

A comedy in three acts. The action takes place in 1927 in the private party room of the Paradise Nightclub.

William Atherton, Teri Garr
(Elizabeth Wolynski Photo)

THE LAST MINSTREL SHOW

By Joe Taylor Ford; Director, Donald McKayle; Musical Direction, Howard Roberts; Set, Edward Burbridge; Costumes, Robert Mackintosh; Lighting, Ian Calderon; Orchestrations, Howard Roberts; Wigs and Make-up, Stanley James, Gene Sheppard; General Manager, Marilyn S. Miller; Associate Producer, Nadine Koval; Wardrobe, Judith Giles; Production Assistant, Victor Ouimet; Company Manager, Gintare Sileika; Stage Managers, Nate Barnett, Peter Lawrence, Frank Echols; Press, Betty Lee Hunt, Maria Cristina Pucci; Presented by Ken Marsolais in association with Martin Markinson, Donald Tick. Opened Tuesday, March 20, 1978 at the Wilbur Theatre, Boston, MA, and closed at the New Locust Theatre, Philadelphia, PA, April 30, 1978.

CAST

Forbes	Roger Alan Brown
Black Sally	Della Reese
J. J. Jones/Mr. Shine	Gregory Hines
George Cole/Mr. Tambo	Ned Wright
Uncle Tom Taylor/Mr. Salt	Eugene Jackson
Brother Bo Taylor/Mr. Pepper	Dick Vance
Sam Parks, Jr./Mr. Pompey	Jeffery V. Thompson
Preacher Simmons/Mr. Moses	Howard Roberts
Jimmie "Tuskegee" White/Mr. Rastus	Tucker Smallwood
Al Perletter/Mr. Interlocutor	Ralston Hill
Bert Pine/Mr. Bones	Clebert Ford
Patton Bridges	Rene Levant

STANDBYS: Sandra Phillips (Sally), Robert Gossett (Uncle Tom/Bert), John T. Grimes (Brother Bo/Preacher Simmons), Arvell Shaw (Sam), Clyde Williams (George), Robert Melvin (J.J.), Roger Alan Brown (Al/Jimmie), Frank Echols (Forbes), Tucker Smallwood (Patton)

MUSICAL NUMBERS: "A High Old Time in Dixie," "Wait Til the Sun Shines, Nelly," "Down Where the Watermelon Grows," "Shine, Shine, Shine," "At the Garbage Gentlemen's Ball," "T'Ain't No Sin," "Turkey in the Straw," "I'll Lend You Anything," "When the Bell in the Lighthouse Rings Ding, Dong," "Darktown Is Out Tonight," "Waitin' for the Robert E. Lee," "Oh, Dem Golden Slippers," "Good News," "Happy Days in Dixieland," "She's Getting More Like the White Folk Every Day," "I Don't Mind Walkin' in the Rain," "Pickaninny's Paradise," "Strut Miss Lizzie," "What He'd Done for Me," "Do Lord," "Gee, I'm Glad I'm from Dixie," "Dixie," "Can't You Hear Me Callin' Caroline," "Always Left Them Laughing"

A musical entertainment in 2 acts and 6 scenes. The action takes place backstage at the Variety Theatre, Cincinnati, Ohio, on the night of March 15, 1926.

Della Reese

NEFERTITI

Book and Lyrics, Christopher Gore; Music, David Spangler; Sets, Costumes, Visuals, Sam Kirkpatrick; Lighting, Gilbert V. Hemsley, Jr.; Director, Jack O'Brien; Choreography, Daniel Lewis; Musical Direction, John DeMain; Orchestrations, Robert Freedman; Dance Music Arrangements, Wally Harper; Conductor, Robert Billig; Assistant Producer, Virginia Hymes; General Managers, McCann & Nugent; Assistant to Director, Stephen Willems; Wardrobe, Stephanie Cheretun, Roger Girard; Assistant Conductor, Kevin Farrell; Company Managers, Mario De Maria, Victoria Heslin; Stage Managers, Alan Hall, Susie Cordon, Sal Provenza; Press, Ellen Levene, Linda Cioffoletti; Presented by Sherwin M. Goldman. Opened Monday, Sept. 20, 1977 at the Blackstone Theatre, Chicago, IL, and closed there Oct. 22, 1977.

CAST

Messenger from Egypt	Patrick Kinser-Lau
Penmut	Marilyn Cooper
Tushratta, King of Mitanni	Benjamin Rayson
Tadukhipa/Nefertiti	Andrea Marcovicci
Hap	Michael Nouri
Ipy, Grand Vizier and High Priest	Michael V. Smartt
Tiy, Great Wife of Egypt	Jane White
Akhnaton	Robert LuPone
General Ramose	Benjamin Rayson
Mitanni Scribe	G. Eugene Moose
Tutmose	Francisco LaGueruela
Sennet	Georgia Connor

CITIZENS: Georgia Connor, Ann Crumb, Florie Freshman, Sylvia Miranda, Anthony Balcena, Ramon Colon, Michael Corbett, Simeon Den, Patrick Kinser-Lau, Francisco LaGueruela, G. Eugene Moose, Ernest Pagnano, Sal Provenza, Lynda Karen Smith

MUSICAL NUMBERS: "The Diary of a Dying Princess," "Lama Su Apapi," "Penmut's Apology," "Everything Is Possible," "Breakfast at Thebes," "Father," "Pardon Me a Minute," "Beautiful Has Come," "Whatever Happened to Me?," "It Happens Very Softly," "Legions of the Night," "Light Will Shine," "Under the Sun," "The New World," "A Free Translation," "Someone Was Here," "Another Free Translation," "Dinner at Thebes," "Take Off the Sandal"

A musical in two acts.

Andrea Marcovicci, Robert LuPone, Marilyn Cooper
(Martha Swope Photo)

THE PRINCE OF GRAND STREET

By Bob Merrill; Director, Gene Saks; Choreography, Lee Theodore; Settings, David Mitchell; Costumes, Jane Greenwood; Lighting, Tom Skelton; Musical Direction and Vocal Arrangements, Colin Romoff; Orchestrations, Michael Gibson; Dance Arrangements, David Baker; General Manager, Oscar Olesen; Company Manager, James Walsh; Stage Managers, William Dodds, Wayne Carson, Vito Durante; Wardrobe, Warren Morrill, Ursula Jones; Assistant to Director, Toby Simpkins; Production Assistant, Bill Becker; Hairstylists, J. Masarone, Randy Coronato; Press, John Springer, Warren Knowlton, Suzanne Salter, Ann Todaro, Stephanie Buzzarte; Presented by Robert Whitehead and Roger L. Stevens, and the Shubert Organization. Opened Tuesday, March 7, 1978 at the Forrest Theatre, Philadelphia, PA, and closed April 15, 1978 at the Shubert Theatre in Boston, MA.

CAST

Itzak Goldfarb	Sam Leven
Nathan Rashumsky	Robert Preston
Jenny Abromowitz	Darlene Anders
Moishe Zweigman	Steven Gelfer
Yetta Feinstein	Bernice Massi
Martin Malovsky	Derek Wolshonak
Sam Teitelbaum/Sexton	Duane Bodin
Mrs. Schumacher	Annette C. Winter
Mrs. Schwartz	Molly Stark
Mr. Ginsburg/Foreman/Stephen Douglas	Alexander Orfaly
Mr. Gittleson/Stage Hand	Bob Carroll
Harry Metzger	David Margulies
Goldman	Alan Manson
Krantz	Sammy Smith
Leah	Neva Small
Julius Pritkin	Werner Klemperer
A Maid/Sarah	Susan Edwards
Stage Manager/Waiter	Walter Charles
Mark Twain	Addison Powell
Jim	Clyde Laurents
Maurice Markov	Richard Muenz
Young Mother	Nana
Yashka	Dean Badolato

MOURNERS: Dean Badolato, Duane Bodin, Bob Carroll, Walter Charles, Steven Gelfer, Clyde Laurents, Richard Muenz, Alexander Orfaly, Derek Wolshonak

CRIERS: Shellie Chancellor, Susan Edwards, Patricia Gadonnieux, Molly Stark, Annette C. Winter

WORKERS: Darlene Anders, Shellie Chancellor, Susan Edwards, Patricia Gadonnieux, Patti Mariano, Nana, Molly Star, Annette C. Winter

MUSICAL NUMBERS: "A Grand Street Tivoli Presentation," "Fifty Cents," "I'm a Girl with Too Much Heart," "I'm a Star," "Do I Make You Happy," "Stay with Me," "Sew a Button," "The Prince of Grand Street," "A Place in the World," "The Youngest Person I Know," "What Do I Do Now?"

A musical in 2 acts and 24 scenes. The action takes place in 1908 in and around the lower East Side of Manhattan.

Robert Preston, Neva Small
(Sy Friedman Photo)

Marc Jordan, D'Jamin Bartlett, David-James Carroll, Gene Barry

SPOTLIGHT

Book, Richard Seff; Based on story by Leonard Starr; Lyrics, Lyn Duddy; Music, Jerry Bresler; Director, David Black; Choreography, Tony Stevens; Settings, Robert Randolph; Costumes, Robert Mackintosh; Lighting, Roger Morgan; Musical Direction and Vocal Arrangements, Jack Lee; Orchestrations, Will Schaefer; Dance Arrangements, Wally Harper; General Manager, Eugene V. Wolsk; Company Manager, Steven Suskin; Stage Managers, Bob D. Bernard, Elise Warner, William McClary; Wardrobe, Lee Decker; Assistant to Director, Connie Kaplan; Production Assistant, Sheri Barron; Hairstylist, Jerry Maserone; Press, Seymour Krawitz, Louise Ment; Presented by Sheldon R. Lubliner. Opened Wednesday January 11, 1978 at the National Theatre, Washington, D.C., and closed there January 14, 1978.

CAST

Jack Beaumont	Gene Barry
Siggy Zimmer	Marc Jordan
Holly Beaumont	D'Jamin Bartlett
Chip Beaumont	David-James Carroll
Mr. Kleinsinger	William McClary
Carey	John Leslie Wolfe
Cosmo	Garon Douglass
Charlie/Waiter	James Braet
Myrna	Clare Culhane
Marie	Lenora Nemetz
Louisa May	Debbie Shapiro
Brawn	Gary Daniel
Mona	Cynthia Stewart
Contenders	Freda Soiffer, Michelle Stubbs, Eileen Casey
Lu Ellen	Terry Calloway
Janet/Night Woman	Michon Peacock
Passerby	Lloyd Sannes
Leaflet Man	Wayne Mattson
Young Man	Jeffrey Spielman
Young Woman	Michelle Stubbs
Louise Pembley	Polly Rowles

Standby: Carleton Carpenter

ENSEMBLE: Steven Anthony, James Braet, Terry Calloway, Eileen Casey, Clare Culhane, Gary Daniel, Garon Douglass, David Warren-Gibson, Barbara Hanks, Clay James, Wayne Mattson, Tim Millett, Marcia O'Brien, Michon Peacock, Loyd Sannes, Rochelle Seldin, Debbie Shapiro, Freda Soiffer, Jeffrey Spielman, Cynthia Stewart, Michelle Stubbs, John Leslie Wolfe

MUSICAL NUMBERS: "No Regrets," "What Am I Bio," "Spotlight," "You Need Someone," "Round and Round," "Tricks of the Trade," "Notice Me," "Everything," "Didn't You Used to Be Him?," "Such a Business," "Hole in the Wall," "The Stranger in the Glass," "You Are You," "Where Is Everybody?"

A musical in 2 acts and 13 scenes. The action takes place between 1955 and the present.

ANNUAL SHAKESPEARE FESTIVALS

ALABAMA SHAKESPEARE FESTIVAL
Anniston, Alabama
July 15–August 20, 1977

Artistic Director, Martin L. Platt; Managing Director, Anne F. Zimmerman-Ross; Associate Director, Bruce Hoard; Administrative Assistant, Glenda Knight; Sets and Lighting, Bob Moeller; Costumes, Lynne Emmert; Fencing Master, Normand L. Beauregard; Stage Managers, Arlene Ritz, Rebecca Wakefield; Company Manager, Margaret Jones; Production Assistants, Mary Ann O'Neal, Hank Snider, Blair Thomas; Original Music, Bruce Hoard

COMPANY

Allan Almeida, Charles Antalosky, Kathy Chandler, Marlene Egan, Robert Egan, Matthew Faison, William Forward, LaFain Freeman, Lorenzo Gunn, Bruce Hoard, Marilyn Jones, Jack Kyrieleison, David Licht, Lester Malizia, Judith Marx, Howard McMaster, Philip Pleasants, Robert Rieben, Elizabeth Schuette, Hank Snider, Ronn Tombaugh, Mark Varian, Clint Vriezelaar, Brian Whitney

REPERTOIRE

"Hamlet," "Rosencrantz and Guildenstern Are Dead" by Tom Stoppard, "Love's Labour's Lost," "The Imaginary Invalid" by Moliere adapted by Miles Malleson, "The Hollow Crown"

Martin L. Platt Photos

Charles Anatalosky, Philip Pleasants, Marlene Egan in "Hamlet" Left: Elizabeth Schuette, Matthew Faison in "Love's Labour's Lost"

CHAMPLAIN SHAKESPEARE FESTIVAL
Burlington, Vermont
July 6–August 27, 1977
Nineteenth Season

Producer-Director, Edward J. Feidner; Associate Producers, George B. Bryan, W. M. Schenk; Director, E. Keith Gaylord; Stage Managers, Andrew Mack, Brenda McMullan; Musical Director, James E. Kowal; Costumes, Polly Smith, Hinda Schreiber; Designers, Lisa M. Devlin, F. Patrick Orr; Technical Director, Daniel C. Boepple; Business Manager, Alice Cook; Press, Heidi Racht; Lighting, Steven Sysko, Duncan Stephens, Rick Whitmore; Props, Cathi Purington, Duncan Stephens

COMPANY

Ray Aranha, Jennifer Cover, Alan Altshuld, Dan Baumgarten, Kim Bent, Jonathan Bourne, Kent Cassella, Josh Conescu, Evelyne Germain, Hamilton Gillett, Deborah Gwinn, John Hutton, Michael Kluger, Jock MacDonald, Greg Patnaude, Jackie Patterson, Robert B. Putnam, Neave Rake, Chris Recchia, Sally Faye Reit, Jose Angel Santana, Muriel Stockdale, Craig A. Toth, Paul Ugalde

REPERTOIRE

"Two Gentlemen of Verona," "Macbeth," "Henry IV, Part I"

Craig A. Toth in "Henry IV Part I" Above: Jennifer Cover, Ray Aranha in "Macbeth"

COLORADO SHAKESPEARE FESTIVAL

Boulder, Colorado
July 22–August 18, 1977
Twentieth Year

Executive Director, Daniel S. P. Yang; Assistant Director, C. V. Bennett; Press, Beverly Shaw; Sound, Ed Spangler; Scenery, Dan Dryden; Costumes, Deborah M. Dryden, David A. Busse, Marla J. Jurglanis; Lighting, Paul Scharfenberger, Jim Doyle; Technical Director, Anthony Diemont; Stage Managers, Marci Auerbach, Greg Sullivan; Directors, Ronald E. Mitchell, J. H. Crouch, Edgar Reynolds

COMPANY

Bill Anthony, C. V. "Ben" Bennett, Andrew Burgreen, Shirley Carnahan, Richard Wells Chamberlain, George T. Crowley, Jr., Randolph Gale, Peter D. Giffin, Brad Gordon, Margo Gruber, William J. Johnson, Larry C. Lott, John Lymeropoulos, Jacklyn Maddux, Mark McQuown, Greg Michaels, David K. Miller, Joseph F. Muzikar, Mary Olson, Frederick Ponzlov, Rainard Rachele, Carl A. Rahal, Roderick L. Reinhart, Richard Rorke, Cathy Schaeffer, Randy Schaub, Margie Shaw, Anya Springer, Jim Stubbs, George Wall, Ricky Weiser, Denis Williams, Mark C. Zetterberg

PRODUCTIONS

"Much Ado about Nothing," "Richard II," "The Merchant of Venice"

Jerry Stowall Photos

**Right: George Wall, Carl A. Rahal in "Richard II"
Top: Joseph Muzikar, Jacklyn Maddux,
Larry C. Lott in "Much Ado about Nothing"**

**Jacklyn Maddux, Joseph Muzikar
in "Merchant of Venice"**

GLOBE OF THE GREAT SOUTHWEST

Odessa, Texas
June 17–August 21, 1977
Ninth Year

Producer-Director, Charles David McCally; Director, Durward Jacobs; Assistant Director, John Velz; Press, Wanda Snodgrass; Sets, Lighting, Technical Director, Ken Stacker; Costumes, Carolyn Jacobs, Hattie English, Mary Lynn Skinner; Sound, Vincent Neimann; Stage Managers, Eloise Bruce, Rhonda Clark, Patrick Rowan; Globe Founder, Marjorie Morris; Chairman Board of Governors, Dr. Dianne Peters

COMPANY

Kenneth Wayne Stacker, Janet Stanford, Rodney Clark, Jr., Patrick Rowan, Lissa LeGrand, James Bottom, Russ Odom, Eloise Bruce, Vincent Neimann, Rhonda Clark, John Amedro, Peter B. Nichols, John B. Cranford III, Billy Nelson, Robert J. Gibson, Sid A. Williams

PRODUCTIONS

"Measure for Measure," "Love's Labour's Lost," "She Stoops to Conquer" by Oliver Goldsmith

GREAT LAKES SHAKESPEARE FESTIVAL

Lakewood, Ohio
June 29–October 1, 1977

Artistic Director, Vincent Dowling; General Manager, William H. Witte; Press, Bill Rudman; Sets, John Ezell; Costumes, Michael Olich, Algesa O'Sickey; Lighting, Richard Coumbs; Musical Director, Stuart W. Raleigh; Technical Director, Richard Archer; Guest Directors, Daniel Sullivan, Roger Hendricks Simon

COMPANY

Norm Berman, John Q. Bruce, Bairbre Dowling, V. G. Dowling, Bernard Kates, Michael LaGue, Robert Lanchester, Dennis Lipscomb, George F. Maguire, MichaelJohn McGann, Holmes Osborne, Edith Owen, Clive Rosengren, Bruce Somerville, Sara Woods, Gusti

PRODUCTIONS

"Hamlet," "The Taming of the Shrew," "Peg o' My Heart" by J. Hartley Manners, "The Glass Menagerie" by Tennessee Williams, "The Importance of Being Oscar" by Michael MacLiammoir, *World Premier* of "In a Fine Frenzy" devised by Frederik N. Smith and conceived by Roger Hendricks Simon

Karabinus & Associates Photos

**Right Center: Sara Woods, Bernard Kates,
MichaelJohn McGann in "In a Fine Frenzy"
Top: Dennis Lipscomb,
Edith Owen in "Hamlet"**

**Sara Woods, Dennis Lipscomb
in "Taming of the Shrew"**

**John Q. Bruce, Bairbre Dowling
in "The Glass Menagerie"**

Robert Pickering, Alex Proctor, Ron Morhous
in "All's Well That Ends Well"

Cast of "King Henry VI Part I" Above: Ron Morhous,
Eugenia Wright in "Romeo and Juliet"

GLOBE PLAYHOUSE

Los Angeles, California
June 1, 1977–May 31, 1978

Executive Producer-Founder, R. Thad Taylor; Business Manager, Susan Marrone; Producer, The Shakespeare Society of America; Directors, Sydney Sims, Jean Blanchette, R. Lev Mailer, Gordon Smith, Molly Roden Ward, R. Thad Taylor, John Megna, Carl Reggiardo, Bill Campbell, J. D. Hall, Frank Geraci, Michael Fuller; Costumes, Joy Densmore, Doug Spesart, Sydney Sims, Jean Blanchette, Jacques Charvet, Andy Yelusch, Debbie Scott, Liz Delgado, Karen Kreider; Lights, George Gizienski, Gary Wissman, Michael J. Gossman, Robert Pickering, Betty Schneider, Lee Hausman; Stage Managers, Lou Clayton, Steven P. Munsie, Pamela Monroe, Marcus Beresford, Cavanaugh Yelling, Bonnie Ernst, Priscilla Guastavino, Lenore Daniels, Allen C. Barker

PRODUCTIONS AND CASTS

TITUS ANDRONICUS with William Frankfather, Dan Mahar, Tom C. Viers, Mark Koba, Bill Sykes, Colleen McMullen, John Carr, Marshall Gluskin, Nathan Loober, Derek Wooley, Channing Walker, Steven F. Munsie, Ralph Farquhar, Michael Siegal, Deena Booth, G. Oliver King, Karen Kreider, Michaela Conger, Michael Ross-Oddo, John Everson, Ted Frost, J. D. Hall, Dale Wann, Michael Speer, Bill Campbell, Sarah Boulton

ALL'S WELL THAT ENDS WELL with John Alderson, Harwood Benton, Sharon Borek, Suzanne Celeste Brown, Norma Chalfin, Geoffrey David, G. Oliver King, Dorene Ludwig, Mae Marmy, Ron Morhous, Steve F. Munsie, Robert Pickering, Alex Proctor, Richard W. Savin

MERRY WIVES OF WINDSOR with Martha Wissell, John Wyche, Jeffrey Coulas, Alan Johnson, Jeffrey Gerstein, Catherine Fiasca, Harry Pickup, Boyd Schlaefer, Kristine Kent, Celeste Barrett, Laird Thornton, Jennifer Cashoty, Adam Neumar

THE TAMING OF THE SHREW with Marc Billings, Eugene Brezany, Richard Cansino, Walter Cass, Angela Cheyne, Stephen D'Ambrose, Elizabeth Delgado, Leigh Kavanaugh, Joshua Lieberman, Wayne Marshall, Pierrino Mascarino, Jeffrey Moser, Joyce Nunley, Charles O'Connor, Fred Pinkard, Stephen E. Stuart, Dale Swann, Michael Tootikian, Terry Troutt, Larry Vigus II, Jeffrey Zimmerman

KING JOHN with Eugene Brezany, Janelle Buff, John Carr, Elizabeth Delgado, David Gatchell, Frank Gerachi, Eric Holms, Dick Johnson, Dudley Knight, John Light, Michael Lunsford, Cynthia Noel Macy, Steve Meigs, Ronald Morhous, Susan Peters, Robert Schiffler, Walter Scholz, Charles Sitler, Jr., Terry Troutt

TROILUS AND CRESSIDA with Ted Ball, Anita Barry, Marcus Beresford, Eugene Brezany, William Campbell, John Paul Davis, Elizabeth Delgado, Stephenie Dunnam, Horst Erhhardt, William Frankfather, Kenneth Gene, Frank Geraci, Tony Goodstone, Jim Habif, Danny Moreno, Heidi Mefford, Rich Meyer, Deborah Quinn, Robert Schiffler, Franklyn Seales, Charles Sitler, Jr., Calvin Ward, Bill Woodbury, Anita Barry

ROMEO AND JULIET with Haskell V. Anderson III, Robert Chandler, Carlyle Dukes, J. D. Hall, Ronald Morhous, Arnold Johnson, G. Oliver King, Stan Miller, Lynet Morrow, Michael Ross-Oddo, Frederick Schmidt, Larry Vigus II, Nigel Bullard, Paul Aron, Ben-Michael Lamb, Dan Rogers, Eugenia Wright, Cavanaugh Yelling

THE WINTER'S TALE with Haskell V. Anderson III, Neil Alan Barclay, Evan Cole, Oren Curtis, Kenneth Gene, Peter Ingolia, Olga James, Richard Klautsch, William Martel, Pamela Mundt, Noelle Nelson, Matt Siegel, Ralph Steadman, Helen Pugatch, Dick Rardin, Sarah Saltus, Maureen Jane Teefy, Edward Wilson, Cavanaugh Yelling, Craig Zehms

THE BOYS FROM SYRACUSE with Nigel Bullard, Eugene Brezany, Linda Deater, Mary Gavagan, Calvin Ward, Bill Campbell, Karen Kreidler, Gregory Kent Smith, Ben-Michael Lamb, Nancy Ries, Cynthia Noel Macy, Elizabeth Delgado, Joe Loevner, David Francis, Jean Blanchette

HENRY VI PART ONE with Paul Aron, Jeff Braun, Eugene Brezany, J. Keneth Campbell, James Reynolds, Stephen D'Ambrose, Kurt Dana, Todd Davis, Mark Fairchild, Evaughn Flaming, William Frankfather, Robert Gage, Karen Hensel, Daniel Mahar, Gregory Michaels, Karen Kreider, Robert Nadder, Marcus Smythe, Dale Swann, William Wright, Rob Zapple, Carl Walsh, Craig Wyckoff

TWO GENTLEMEN OF VERONA with Joe Barrett, Hal Bergem, Peter Brandon, Eugene Brezany, Elizabeth Delgado, Larry Eisenberg, Shannon Eubanks, Todd Davis, Leon Fermanian, Sharon Howard, Jose Rosario, David M. Scott, Sheryl Lee Ralph, Judy Knaiz, Lenore Daniels

OTHELLO with Haskell V. Anderson III, Sharon Anton, James E. Brodhead, Rushell C. Cheatham, Juanin Clay, Todd Davis, Christine Elie, Shannon Eubanks, Russ Fega, Jean Glaude, David Grant, J. D. Hall, Carl Scott Honaker, Steve Kimber, James Malbrough, Jon Mezz, Rafe Moore, Hykush Ohanessian, Pat Peach, Willie A. Thurman. Vance Valencia, Carl Walsh, Ivy White, Bob Wollman, Yahee

Robert Beseda, Paul Barry in "Cyrano de Bergerac"

NEW JERSEY SHAKESPEARE FESTIVAL

Madison, New Jersey
June 28–November 6, 1977
Thirteenth Year

Artistic Director, Paul Barry; Press, Ellen Barry; Stage Managers, James J. Thesing, Gary C. Porto; Lighting, Gary C. Porto; Costumes, Jeffrey L. Ullman, Dean H. Reiter; Sets, Don A. Coleman; Assistant Producer, Susan Socolowski; Administrative Assistants, Lillian Burwasser, Helen Marsh Rybka; Musical Director, Brian Lynner

COMPANY

Ellen Barry, Paul Barry, Robert Beseda, Nesbitt Blaisdell, Tom Brennan, Kale Brown, Roger Alan Brown, Jody Catlin, Richard Graham, Sue Lawless, Robin Leary, Brian Lynner, Virginia Mattis, Dana Mills, William Myers, Margery Shaw, Geddeth Smith, Ronald Steelman, Eric Tavaris, Curt Williams

Martin Amada, Joseph Bachalis, Kevin Paul Bain, Denise Bessette, Peter Bogyo, Leslie Brooks, Katherine Bruce, Marilyn Cervino, Anne Chapin, Lisa R. Churgin, Leslie-Marie Cocuzzo, Robert Mark Costello, George Crenshaw, James Cvitanich, Jerry Davis, Richard Dorfman, Thomas Ehas, Elisa Esposito, Kermit Frazier, Carla G. Froeberg, John Gilliom, Jan Granger, Michael Greenberger, Elyse Greenhut, William Hewitt, Bob Hull, Donna Jacobson, J. Douglas James, Larry Joshua, Philippa Keil, Sally Kessler, Adam Kraar, Carol Lang, Janice Lathen, Jason Lee, Alan Lipke, Sarah Loeffel, Andrea McCullough, Anne McIntosh, David McKennan, Guy Manna, Ilene Moskowitz, Aleta Moss, Susan F. Obrecht, Anne Marie Offer, Zoe Oka, Ellen M. Pavelka, Darci Picoult, Nancy Douglass Quinn, Joseph J. Quirinale, Jeffrey R. Sacks, Michael Sears, M. Howard Sheppard, Martin Sorsher, Joseph Lawrence Spiegel, Ellen Spier, James Swartz, Timothy Toney, Pamela Von Baumbaugh, David G. Von Salis, Barbara Wall, Jim Walker, David T. Wallace, Hillary Weisman, Karen Williams

PRODUCTIONS

"Much Ado about Nothing," "Titus Andronicus," "Cyrano de Bergerac" by Edmond Rostand, "An Enemy of the People" by Henrik Ibsen, "The Hot l Baltimore" by Lanford Wilson, "The Glass Menagerie" by Tennessee Williams

Left: Dana Mills, Geddeth Smith, Richard Graham in "Titus Andronicus"

**Kale Brown, Ellen Barry
in "The Glass Menagerie"**

**Jason Lee, Geddeth Smith, Robin Leary
in "Titus Andronicus"**

169

NEW YORK SHAKESPEARE FESTIVAL

Delacorte Theater/Central Park/NYC
July 6–August 28, 1977
Twenty-first Season

Producer, Joseph Papp; Associate Producer, Bernard Gersten; General Manager, Robert Kamlot; Press, Merle Debuskey, Bob Ullman, Richard Kornberg; Production Manager, Andrew Mihok; Technical Director, Darrell Ziegler; Wardrobe Supervisor, Joe Toland; Production Supervisor, Jason Steven Cohen

July 6–July 24, 1977

THREEPENNY OPERA

By Bertolt Brecht and Kurt Weill; New Translation by Ralph Manheim, John Willett; Director, Richard Foreman; Music Direction, Stanley Silverman; Scenery, Douglas W. Schmidt; Costumes, Theoni V. Aldredge; Lighting, Pat Collins; Sound, Roger Jay

CAST

Roy Brocksmith (Ballad Singer), Philip Bosco (Mack the Knife), Ellen Greene (Jenny), Jerome Dempsey (Peachum), Tony Azito (Samuel), Ed Zang (Filch), Gretel Cummings (Mrs. Peachum), Ralph Drischell (Matthew), Caroline Kava (Polly), William Duell (Jake), K. C. Wilson (Bob), Paul Ukena, Jr. (Ned), Robert Schlee (Jimmy), John Ridge (Walt), David Sabin (Tiger), Marc Jordan (Smith), Penelope Bodry (Lucy), Jack Eric Williams (Messenger), Beggars and Policemen: Pendleton Brown, Peter Iacangelo, George McGrath, Art Ostrin, Rick Petrucelli, Craig Rupp, Armin Shimerman, Jack Eric Williams, Ray Xito, Whores: Barbara Andres, Nancy Campbell, Alexandra Ivanoff, Lisa Kirchner, Mimi Turque

July 28–August 28, 1977

AGAMEMNON

By Aeschylus; Conceived by Andrei Serban, Elizabeth Swados, using fragments of the original Greek and Edith Hamilton's translation; Director, Andrei Serban; Music, Elizabeth Swados; Scenery, Douglas W. Schmidt; Costumes, Santo Loquasto; Lighting, Jennifer Tipton

CAST

Gloria Foster (Clytemnestra), Dianne Wiest (Cassandra), Jamil Zakkai (Agamemnon), Ron O'Neal (Aegisthus), Earle Hyman (Chorus Leader), SueLain Moy (Iphigenia), John De Vries (Watchman), William Parry (Herald), Chorus: Robin Bartlett, Richard Casselman, Bruce Cryer, Jon De Vries, Quitman Fludd III, Helena D. Garcia, Natalie Gray, Albert Harris, Rodney Hudson, Onni Johnson, Paul Kreppel, Paula Larke, Esther Levy, Tom Matsusaka, Valois Mickens, Joe Neal, Bill Parry, Paul Perri, Gerianne Raphael, Roger Lawson-Robinson, Eron Tabor, John Watson, Beverly Wideman

MOBILE THEATER

UNFINISHED WOMEN

By Aishah Rahman; Director, Bill Duke; Music, Jackie McLean; Lyrics, Aishah Rahman; Design, Linda Conaway; Costumes, Judy Dearing; Lighting, Shirley Prendergast; Musical Direction, Dona Summers

CAST

Kirk Kirksey (Charlie Chan), LaTanya Richardson (Wilma), Cheryl Tafathale Jones (Paulette), Socorro Santiago (Consuelo), Nikki Coleman (Mattie), Terria Joseph (Midge), Rosanna Carter (Head Nurse), Arthur Burghardt (Charles Parker), le Clanche du Rand (Pasha/Miss Wailing)

Fred Ohringer Photos

Top Right: Philip Bosco, Penelope Bodry in "Threepenny Opera"

Ron O'Neal, Gloria Foster
in "Agamemnon"

Cheryl Tafathale Jones, Socorro Santiago, Nikki Coleman, Latanya Richardson, Terria Joseph in "Unfinished Women"

OREGON SHAKESPEARE FESTIVAL

Ashland, Oregon
June 11–September 18, 1977
Forty-second Season

Founder, Angus L. Bowmer; President, Richard E. Bridenstine; Producing Director, Jerry Turner; General Manager, William W. Patton; Directors, Michael Addison, Elizabeth Huddle, Jane and William Glover, Pat Patton, Robert Loper, Jerry Turner; Designers, Richard L. Hay, Jeannie Davidson, Dirk Epperson, William Bloodgood, Robert Peterson; Production Coordinator, Pat Patton; Technical Director, R. Duncan Mackenzie; Stage Manager, Dennis Bigelow; Choreographer, Judith Kennedy; Fight Director, David L. Boushey; Sound, James Laseter; Wardrobe, Toni M. Lovaglia; Music Director, Mark Wardenburg; Press, Margaret Rubin

COMPANY

Denis Arndt, Larry R. Ballard, Jahnna Beecham, Catherine Butterfiled, Jack Wellington Cantwell, Mimi Carr, Ted D'Arms, Richard Denison, Joseph De Salvio, Patrick DeSantis, Cameron Dokey, David Eakle, James Edmondson, Richard Farrell, Jim Giancarlo, Keith Grant, Mary Hart, Terry Hays, Christine Healy, Ray Houle, Elizabeth Huddle, David Hudson, Alana Hunter, Jerry Jones, Dan Kremer, Kenned MacIver, David Marston, Susan Marston, Mary Molodovsky, Dan Moore, William Moreing, Barry Mulholland, Brian Mulholland, Allen Nause, Gayle Stuwe Neuman, Phil Neuman, Alexander Nibley, Thomas S. Oleniacz, William P. Ontiveros, Melody Page, Judd Parkin, Joann Johnson Patton, Kristin Patton, Shirley Patton, John Procaccino, Rex Rabold, Mack Ramsey, Richard Riley, Dale Thomas Rooklyn, Richard Rossi, Michael Santo, Clydine Scales, Thomas Arthur Scales, John Shepard, Jean Smart, David Smith, Robert Smith, Ronald Stanley Sopyla, Brian Thompson, Mary Turner, John Warren Tyson, Leslie Velton, Bruce Williams, Ronald Edmundson Woods, Michael Magruder, Jeff Ramscy, Peter White, Michael R. Hogan, Will Patton, Michael Leahy

PRODUCTIONS

"The Merchant of Venice," "King Henry VI Part III," "Antony and Cleopatra," "Measure for Measure," "The Rivals," "A Streetcar Named Desire," "A Moon for the Misbegotten"

Hank Kranzler Photos

Right: Ronald Edmundson Woods, Christine Healy, James Edmondson, Michael Santo in "Merchant of Venice" Above: Mimi Carr, Elizabeth Huddle, James Edmondson, Ted D'Arms in "Antony and Cleopatra" Top: Christine Healy, Dan Kremer in "Measure for Measure"

Michael Santo in "Henry VI Part III"

Denis Arndt, Jean Smart in "A Moon for the Misbegotten"

171

NATIONAL SHAKESPEARE FESTIVAL

Old Globe Theatre/San Diego, California
May 31–September 11, 1977
Twenty-eighth Season

Producing Director, Craig Noel; General Manager, Robert McGlade; Art Director, Peggy Kellner; Press, William B. Eaton; Technical Director, Terry Kempf; Stage Managers, Tom Corcoran, Anne Salazar; Costumes, Peggy Kellner, Robert Morgan; Lighting, John McLain; Composer, Conrad Susa; Dramaturge, Diana Maddox; Sound, Dan Dugan; Combats staged by Anthony DeLongis

COMPANY

Maureen Anderman, Ronnie B. Baker, Richard S. Fullerton, Nathan Haas, V. Craig Heidenreich, Byron Jennings, Richard Kneeland, Mark Lamos, John McMurtry, John H. Napierala, Mary-Joan Negro, Donovan Ward Scott, Norman Snow, Daniel J. Travanti, Geoffrey Wade, Geoffrey Beauchamp, Richard Allen Bradshaw, Dan Butler, Peter Davies, Leonardo Defilippis, Michael Newell, Dale Raoul, Douglas Sheeha, Deborah Taylor, Robert Thaler, R. Oliver Walker, Frank J. Adams, Katy Frank, Michael Hodges, Mark Kincaid, Maile Klein, Mark Koons, Matthew Redding, Keith Thompson, Michael Byers, C. Wayland Capwell, Aaron Fletcher, Edith Taylor Hunter, Bette Laws, Hugh Monahan, Lindy A. Nisbet, Mark Pinter, Chris Shaffer, Julie Sullivan

PRODUCTIONS

"Hamlet" directed by Jack O'Brien, "The Taming of the Shrew" directed by Laird Williamson, "Timon of Athens" directed by Eric Christmas, "Charley's Aunt" directed by Wayne Bryan
Bill Reid Photos

Lower Right: John McMurtry, Richard Kneeland in "Timon of Athens" Above: Maureen Anderman, Dan Travanti in "Taming of the Shrew" Top: Richard Kneeland, Maureen Anderman in "Hamlet"

Michael Byers in "Charley's Aunt"

SHAKESPEAREAN THEATER OF MAINE

Monmouth, Maine
June 28–September 4, 1977
Eighth Season

Artistic Director, Richard Sewell; General Manager, Glen Cooper; Press, Susan Beegel; Program Director, Lewis J. Alessio; Stage Managers, Jody Boese, John Tormey; Technical Director, Stephen R. Woody; Wardrobe, Linda Rice; Costumes, Florence L. Rutherford

COMPANY

David Bogan, Susanna Burns, Larry Cappiello, Al De Christo, Michele Delattre, John H. Fields, Gary Filsinger, Kim Gordon, Paul D. Haskell, Charmian Herd, Jenny Holan, Christopher Houston, Natalie Jensen, Michel Kinter, Peter Lind, Cecile Mann, Tom Markus, Bruce Martel, Ann Lynch Miles, Patricia Minot, Michael Morrison, Kate Pennington, Mary Pettingill, Michael Raymond, Deborah Shippee, Bill Silsby, James Siragusa, Tim Wheeler

PRODUCTIONS

"Don Juan in Hell" by George Bernard Shaw, "Twelfth Night," "Othello," "She Stoops to Conquer" by Oliver Goldsmith, "Measure for Measure," "Toad of Toad Hall" by Richard Sewell
No photos submitted.

PROFESSIONAL RESIDENT COMPANIES

(Failure to meet deadline necessitated several omissions)

ACT: A COMTEMPORARY THEATRE

Seattle, Washington
May 12, 1977–March 3, 1978
Thirteenth Season

Artistic Director, Gregory A. Falls; Musical Director, Stan Keen; General Manager, Andrew M. Witt; Technical Director/Lighting Design, Phil Schermer; Costumes, Sally Richardson; Scenery/-Props, Shelley Henze Schermer; Sound, Mac Perkins; Press, Louise Mortenson, Louise Campion Cummings; Company Manager, Jody Harris; Stage Managers, Eileen MacRae Murphy, Sandy Cruse; Production Assistants, Michael Weholt, Tina Lidnin; President, C. David Hughbanks

PRODUCTIONS AND CASTS

AS YOU LIKE IT by William Shakespeare: Mark Murphy, Dean Melang, Kurt Beattie, Richard Knisely, Paul Fleming, Kathleen Heaney, Marion Lines, Clayton Corzatte, Joseph Edward Meek, Glenn Mazen, Edward Baran, Richard Hawkins, Megan Dean, Jeffrey Prather, Jay Fernandez, John Hosking, John Aylward, Richard Hawkins, John Gilbert, Marie Mathay, Pernell McGuire, Mark Sather

TRAVESTIES by Tom Stoppard: Nicholas Hormann, Marion Lines, Glenn Mazen, Kathleen Heaney, Susan Ludlow, Sergei Tschernisch, Clayton Corzatte, John Aylward

LADYHOUSE BLUES by Kevin O'Morrison: Kathleen Heaney, Patricia Cosgrove, Constance Miller, Anne Gerety, Kathy Lichter

STREAMERS by David Rabe: Marcus Smythe, Steve Tomkins, Les Roberts, Justin Deas, Jay Fernandez, Ben Tone, Lee Corrigan, Merritt Olsen, James W. Monitor, Teotha Dennard, James W. Pearl

THE CLUB by Eve Merriam: Suzanne Walker, Katherine Benfer, Judith Moore, Karen McLaughlin, Carolyn Val-Schmidt, Mary Fain, Jean Bonard

ABSURD PERSON SINGULAR by Alan Ayckbourn: Donald Ewer, Barbara Berge, Robert Cornthwaite, Barbara Lester, Marion Lines, Saylor Cresswell

A CHRISTMAS CAROL adapted by Gregory A. Falls from Charles Dickens: John Gilbert, Jim Royce, John Michael Hosking, Richard Lee, Merritt Olsen, David Scott, Marie Mathay, Mark Sather, March Mattox, Richard Hawkins, James W. Monitor, Molly Pritchard, Robert John Zenk, Jean Smart, Brady Smith

THE ODYSSEY by Homer; Adapted by Gregory A. Falls and Kurt Beattie; Richard Lee, Marie Mathay, Merritt Olsen, John Hosking, Marcy Mattox, Robert Zenk, James W. Monitor, Richard Hawkins, Brenda Hubbard, David Colacci

Chris Bennion Photos

Right: Constance Miller, Kathleen Heaney, Kathy Lichter, Patricia Cosgrove, Anne Gerety in "Ladyhouse Blues" Above: Glenn Mazen, Nicholas Hormann in "Travesties" Top: Barbara Lester, Robert Cornthwaite in "Absurd Person Singular"

**Jim Royce, John Gilbert
in "A Christmas Carol"**

**Marcus Smythe, Les Roberts
in "Streamers"**

ACTORS THEATRE OF LOUISVILLE

Louisville, Kentucky
September 21, 1977–May 21, 1978
Tenth Season

Producing Director, Jon Jory; Administrative Director, Alexander Speer; Associate Director, Trish Pugh; Press, Ronette McNulty; Directors, Jon Jory, Elizabeth Ives, Charles Kerr, Daniel Stein, Michael Hankins, Ray Fry, Charles Maryan, Joe Morton, Patrick Tovatt; Choreographer, Margaret Castleman; Sets, Paul Owen, Richard Gould, David Hager, Michael Mottois, Richard Kent Wilcox; Costumes, Kurt Wilhelm; Lighting, Paul Owen, Jeff Hill, Ron Wallace, James Stevens, Michael Hottois, David Hager; Props, Cynthia Lee Beeman, Rebecca P. Ruff, Miles R. Vesich; Technical Director, Joseph Ragey; Costumiere, Mary Lou Owen; Stage Managers, Elizabeth Ives, Kimberly Francis Kearsley, Frazier Marsh, Bob Hornung, Bob Burrus

COMPANY

Jim Baker, Susan Berger, Leo Burmester, Bob Burrus, Jesse Caldwell, Margaret Castleman, Lynn Cohen, Barry Corbin, Peggy Cowles, Jeanne Cullen, Dawn Didawick, Denny Dillon, Harvey Evans, John H. Fields, Ray Fry, John Hancock, Ann Hodapp, Vinnie Holman, Lois Holmes, Robert Jackson, Victor Jory, Michael Kevin, Susan Kingsley, Marsha Korb, David Leary, Brian Lynner, Vaughn McBride, William McNulty, Gian Paul Morelli, Joe Morton, Adale O'Brien, Anne Pitoniak, Dennis Predovic, Dennis Sakamoto, Thurman Scott, James Secrest, David Shepherd, Howard Lee Sherman, Patrick Tovatt, Stephen van Benschoten, Dee Victor, Nan Wray

PRODUCTIONS

"Round and Round the Garden, "Living Together," "A Christmas Carol," "The Front Page," "Sizwe Bansi Is Dead," "The Mousetrap," "Lu Ann Hampton Laverty Oberlander," "Peg o' My Heart," "The Lion in Winter," *Premieres* of "Getting Out," "Does Anybody Here Do the Peabody?," "The Louisville Zoo," "An Independent Woman," "The Bridgehead," "Daddies," "Third and Oak," "How Do You Like Your Blue-Eyed Boy, Mr. Death?," "Andronicus" with music and lyrics by Jerry Blatt, "Criminal Dogs"

David S. Talbott Photos

**Left: Victor Jory, David Leary
in "Front Page" Top: Jim Baker,
Adale O'Brien in "Andronicus"**

**Michael Kevin, Brian Lynner, Thurman Scott,
William McNulty, Bob Burrus
in "The Bridgehead"**

**Lynn Cohen, Susan Kingsley
in "Getting Out"**

Mitchell Edmonds, Tanny McDonald
in "The Fourposter"

ALASKA REPERTORY THEATRE

Anchorage, Alaska
January 25–April 30, 1978
Second Season

Artistic Director, Robert J. Farley; Producing Director, Paul V. Brown; Production Manager, Gary D. Anderson; Designer, Jamie Greenleaf; Lighting, James Sale; Technical Director, Hugh Hall; Costumes, Carol Griffin; Business Manager, Mark Somers; Press, Jack Lloyd, Jane Bradbury; Stage Managers, Steven W. Login, Janet Ann Kruse; Chairman, Pamela Towill; Directors, Robert J. Farley, Clayton Corzatte, Dennis Brite

COMPANY

Betty Arnett, Mary Anne Dempsey, Mitchell Edmonds, Lou Favreax, Frank Geraci, Dana Hart, Geoffrey Hill, Margaret Hilton, Dana Ivey, Tanny McDonald, Deirdre Owens, Phillip Piro, Philip Pleasants, Marco St. John, J. J. Vincent, Tony Vita, Cynthia Wilson, Nicholas Cosco, Warren Elkins, John Mason, Steve McKean, Gina McMather, Susan Mendel, Scott Merrick, Jim Morrison, Tim Morrissey, Ernie Norris, Dave Roth, Don Ruddy, Luan Schooler

PRODUCTIONS

"Sherlock Holmes," "The Fourposter," "The Eccentricities of a Nightingale," "Diamond Studs"

Top Right: "Diamond Studs"
Below: Philip Pleasants, Lou Favreaux
in "Sherlock Holmes"

Dana Ivey, Marco St. John
in "Eccentricities of a Nightingale"   175

Bettye Fitzpatrick, Angela Wood, Pauline Flanagan,
Miriam Phillips, Bella Jarrett in "Echelon"

Michael Tylo, Robert Symonds, Bella Jarrett
in "The Shadow Box" Above: "Pay the Penalty"

Marilyn Lightstone, Cristine Rose, Maurice
Good, Dale Helward in "The Importance of
Being Earnest" Top Left: Dale Helward,
Pauline Flanagan in "Mary Stuart"

ALLEY THEATRE
Houston, Texas
October 15, 1977–May 28, 1978

Producing Director, Nina Vance; Managing Director, Iris Siff;
Business Manager, Bill Halbert; Press, Bob Feingold, Charles E.
Sanders; Administrative Director, Bettye Gardner; Producing Asso-
ciate, H. Wilkenfeld; Staff Director, Beth Sanford; Guest Directors,
Calina Volchyek, Leslie Yeo; Production-Company Manager, Bet-
tye Fitzpatrick; Stage Managers, George Anderson, Rutherford
Cravens, Trent Jenkins; Production Assistants, Paul Dupree, Janice
Heidke; Designers, Jonathan Duff, Matthew Grant, Michael J. Ce-
sario; Technical Director, William C. Lindstrom

PRODUCTIONS AND CASTS

MARY STUART by Friedrich Schiller; Adapted by Jean Stock
Goldstone, John Reich: Diana Barrington, Joyce Campion, Kenneth
Dight, Michael Guido, Eric House, Pauline Flanagan, Anthony
Manionis, Maurice Good, Bernard Frawley, Dale Helward, Claude
Bede, Randy Cheramie, Philip Davidson, Bobby L. Swain, Patrick
L. Byers, Vernon Grote

THE IMPORTANCE OF BEING EARNEST by Oscar Wilde:
Bernard Frawley, Dale Helward, Maurice Good, Pauline Flanagan,
Marilyn Lightstone, Joyce Campion, Cristine Rose, Richard Cur-
nock, David Wurst

ROOT OF THE MANDRAKE by Niccolo Machiavelli; Adapted
by Robert Symonds: Anthony Manionis, Philip Davidson, Robert
Symonds, Eric House, Dorothy Ann Haug, Dixie Taylor, Maurice
Good

ECHELON by Mikhail Roschin; Translated by Henry Heim; Inter-
national Premiere directed by Galina Volchek: Joel Stedman, Cris-
tine Rose, Bettye Fitzpatrick, Bella Jarrett, Lillian Evans, Pauline
Flanagan, Angela Wood, Donna O'Connor, Gale Childs, Lenore
Harris, Dale Helward, Bernard Frawley, Miriam Phillips, Robin
Bradley, Martin Rizley, Patti Slover, Chesley Santoro, Judy
Mueller, Gram Smith, Lealan Markham, Shawn Glanville, Dorothy
Price, Che Knight, Michael Guido, George Honea

THE SHADOW BOX by Michael Cristofer: David Wurst, Philip
Davidson, Gram Smith, Bettye Fitzpatrick, Robert Symonds, Michael Tylo, Bella Jarrett, Gale Childs, Miriam Philips

ABSURD PERSON SINGULAR by Alan Ayckbourn: Judy
Mueller, David Wurst, Robert Symonds, Lillian Evans, Cristine
Rose, Joel Parks

Alan B. Currie, Carl Davis Photos

ALLIANCE THEATRE COMPANY

Atlanta, Georgia
November 2, 1977–April 29, 1978

Artistic Director, Fred Chappell; Managing Director, Bernard Havard; Guest Directors, Martin L. Platt, Harry Rasky, Malcolm Black; Sets, William Schroder, Michael Stauffer, John Wulp, Philipp Jung, Michael Layton, Stephen Hendrickson; Lighting, Cassandra Henning, Carol Graebner, Michael Orris Watson, Guy H. Tuttle, Jane Reisman; Costumes, Michael Stauffer, Lynn Pecktal, Thom Coates; Production Manager, David W. Hughes; Stage Manager, Allen Wright; Press, Sandra Johnson

PRODUCTIONS AND CASTS

COLE: Russ Beasley, Sandra Dorsey, Lynn Fitzpatrick, Quitman Fludd III, Barbara Hancock, Vinni O'Neal, Bob Slater, John Sloman

A CHRISTMAS CAROL: Philip Pleasants, John W. Morrow, Jr., Robert C. Torri, Fergus G. Currie, Barbara Hancock, Melanie Webber, Rob Zapple, Mitchell Edmonds, Gib Manegold, Matthew Faison, Linda Wilson, Celine Rorke, Jennifer Cole, John Adcox, Malcolm Brush, Tim Rutland, Charles Antalosky, Mary Nell Santacroce, Bruce Hoard, George M. Brandt, Kitsy Battle, Susan Larkin, Sonny Goff, Morris Brown, Muriel Moore, Tim Webber, Thad Persons, Kelly Fine, Travis Fine, Lynn Fitzpatrick, Deborah LaVine

TIGER TAIL by Tennessee Williams (World Premiere, Jan. 19, 1978): Elizabeth Kemp, Thomas Toner, Lorrie Davis, Mary Nell Santacroce, Nick Mancuso, Charles Antalosky, Tyrone Kinlaw, Lorenzo Gunn, Sonny Keenum, Al Hamacher, Kenyatta Ferrell

THE DIARY OF ANNE FRANK: George Voskovec, Mary Nell Santacroce, Lynn Garretson, Burke Allison, Chondra Wolle, Harry Ellerbe, Al Hamacher, Christine Voskovec, Charles Antalosky, Lee Tombs

LU ANN HAMPTON LAVERTY OBERLANDER: Penny Fuller, Mary Nell Santacroce, Robert C. Torri, David Harscheid, Douglas R. Nielsen, Ben Jones, Theodore Martin, Charles Antalosky, Mercer Harris, Ron Culbreth, Susan Connors

THE TAMING OF THE SHREW: Tony Roberts, Diane D'Aquila, Gerard Parkes, Philip Pleasants, Susan Connors, David McCann, John Rose, Leo Leyden, Max Gulack, John Guerrasio, Skip Foster, Phillip Piro, Anne Haney, Edmund Lyndeck, John Olive, Dennis Haskins, Melanie Webber, Kitsy Battle, Jerry Hannah, Reid Pierce, Robert Holmes

Charles Rafshoon Photos

**Right: Elizabeth Kemp, Nick Mancuso
in "Tiger Tail" Top: Douglas R. Nielsen,
Penny Fuller in "Lu Ann Hampton
Laverty Oberlander"**

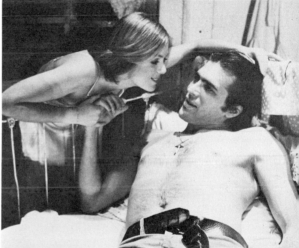

**George Voskovec, Lynn Garretson
in "The Diary of Anne Frank"**

**Tony Roberts
in "The Taming of the Shrew"**   177

AMERICAN CONSERVATORY THEATRE

San Francisco, California
October 15, 1977–June 10, 1978

General Director, William Ball; Executive Producer, James B. McKenzie; Executive Director, Edward Hastings; Conservatory Director, Allen Fletcher; Development Director, Edith Markson; Press, Cheryle Elliott; Guest Directors, Stephen Porter, Tom Moore; Scenery, Richard Seger, Ralph Funicello, Robert Blackman; Costumes, Robert Fletcher, Robert Morgan, Walter Watson, Cathy Edwards; Lighting, Richard Devin, Dirk Epperson, F. Mitchell Dana; Stage Managers, James L. Burke, Suzanne Fry

COMPANY

Wayne Alexander, Candace Barrett, Joseph Bird, Raye Birk, Libby Boone, Joy Carlin, Penelope Court, Peter Davies, Daniel Davis, Heidi Helen Davis, Barbara Dirickson, Peter Donat, Franchelle Stewart Dorn, Sabin Epstein, Kate Fitzmaurice, Melvin Buster Flood, Bennet Guillory, Lawrence Hecht, Elizabeth Huddle, David Hudson, Daniel Kern, Ruth Kobart, Gerald Lancaster, Anne Lawder, Deborah May, William McKereghan, Delores Y. Mitchell, Mark Murphey, Thomas Oglesby, Frank Ottiwell, William Paterson, Susan E. Pellegrino, Ray Reinhardt, Diane Salinger, Jay O. Sanders, Randall Smith, Robert Smith, Sydney Walker, Marrian Walters, J. Steven White, Bruce Williams, James R. Winker, Michael Winters

PRODUCTIONS

"Julius Caesar" by William Shakespeare, "The Master Builder" by Henrik Ibsen, "The Circle" by W. Somerset Maugham, "A Christmas Carol" by Charles Dickens, "All the Way Home" by Tad Mosel, "Hotel Paradiso" by Georges Feydeau and Maurice Desvallieres, "Absurd Person Singular" by Alan Ayckbourn, "The National Health" by Peter Nichols, "Travesties" by Tom Stoppard

William Ganslen Photos

Right: Jay O. Sanders in "Julius Caesar"

Peter Donat, Barbara Dirickson in "The Master Builder"

Michael Winters, Raye Birk, Elizabeth Huddle in "Hotel Paradiso"

William Paterson, Deborah May in "The Circle"

178

Charles Barney, Paul J. Curtis,
Arthur Yorinks in "Hurly-Burly"

AMERICAN MIME THEATRE
New York, N.Y.

Director, Paul J. Curtis; Administrator, Jean Barbour; Counsel, Joel S. Charleston

COMPANY

Jean Barbour
Charles Barney
Paul J. Curtis
Dale Fuller
Jean Gennis

Lynda Hodges
Deda Kavanagh
Andrew Levitt
Michael O'Brien
Arthur Yorinks

REPERTORY

"The Lovers," "The Scarecrow," "Dreams," "Hurly-Burly," "Evolution," "Sludge," "Six," "Abstraction"

David Eng Photos

AMERICAN THEATRE ARTS
Los Angeles, California
June 24, 1977–June 24, 1978

Artistic Director, Don Eitner; Production Director, Joseph Ruskin; Administrative Directors, Nancy Jeris, John Terry Bell; Conservatory Director, Carol Lawson Locatell; Art Director, James J. Agazzi; Costumes, Edguard Johnson; Lighting, Vance Sorell; Production Coordinator, Janice Christensen; Business Manager, William Thornton; Press, Kip Niven; Directors, Mike Robe, Joseph Ruskin, Rolly Fanton, Don Eitner, James J. Agazzi

PRODUCTIONS AND CASTS

SITTING by John Tobias: Dan Emerich, Bob Hollander, Nancy Jeris, Pat Ruskin, Ed Willkie

AFTER MAGRITTE by Tom Stoppard: Howard Adler, John Terry Bell, Betty Ferber, Lou Genevrino, Sara Shearer

IN GOOD KING CHARLES' GOLDEN DAYS by George Bernard Shaw: Craig Abernethy, John Terry Bell, Carla Borelli, Rob Clotworthy, Tanya George, Nancy Jeris, Carol Lawson Locatell, Nora Morgan, John Redman, Robert Sampson, Sara Shearer

THE INSTANT DOCTOR by Moliere, freely adapted: Craig Abernethy, Diana Armondo, Rob Barron, Dan Emerich, Bill Ferber, Mimi Hall, Len Lesser, Gwen Maynard, Alan Wedner

DEVOUR THE SNOW by Abe Polsky (World Premiere): Howard Adler, John Terry Bell, Hal Bokar, Judie Carroll, Rolly Fanton, Jeff Gallucci, Nora Morgan, Robert Sampson, Joseph Ruskin, Tony Venture, Ed Willkie

COLETTE by Elinor Jones: Gerald Anderson, John Terry Bell, Jack Broz, Earlene Davis, Gary Farr, Daniel Grace, Nancy Jeris, Carol Lawson Locatell, Sara Shearer

Betty Ferber. Ken Buckner Photos

Left Center: Carol Lawson Locatell, Daniel
Grace, Earlene Davis in "Colette" Right: Craig
Abernethy, Robert Sampson in "In Good King Charles . . ."

Hal Bokar, Joseph Ruskin, Robert Sampson
in "Devour the Snow"

ARENA STAGE
Washington, D.C.
October 7, 1977–June 11, 1978

Producing Director, Zelda Fichandler; Executive Director, Thomas C. Fichandler; Production Coordinator, George Spalding; Press, Thomas O'Connor; Directors, Patrick Adiarte, David Chambers, Liviu Ciulei, Susan Einhorn, Zelda Fichandler, Martin Fried, Richard Maltby, Jr., Marshall W. Mason, Steven Robman, Elizabeth Swados, Douglas C. Wager; Sets, John Lee Beatty, Sally Cunningham, Karl Eigsti, Ming Cho Lee, Santo Loquasto, Christopher Nowak, Tony Straiges, Patricia Woodbridge; Costumes, Kate Carmel, Rebecca Carroll, Laura Crow, Santo Loquasto, Sheila Roman, Stanley Simmons, Marjorie Slaiman; Lighting, Hugh Lester, William Mintzer, John J. Mulligan, Cheryl Thacker; Composers, Norman L. Berman, Robert Dennis, Mel Marvin, David Shire, Elizabeth Swados, Stanley Walden; Choreographers, B. H. Barry, Ethel Martin; Technical Director, Henry R. Gorfein; Stage Managers, Art Bundey, Julia Gillet, Dan Hild, John J. Mulligan, Mimi Jordan Sherin

COMPANY

Loni Ackerman, Jason Alexander, Cara Alfano, Christopher Allport, Peter Alzado, Stanley Anderson, Deborah Baltzell, Al Barkan, Christopher Bauer, Elizabeth Bauer, Richard Bauer, Doris Belack, Emily Benson, Janis Benson, Peter Benson, Joseph Bieber, Walter Bobbie, Dick Boccelli, Patricia Braunlich, David Brundage, Deborah Capponi, Mark Capponi, Russell Carr, Leslie Cass, Veronica Castang, Leonardo Cimino, Margery Cohen, Joel Colodner, Jarlath Conroy, Jeff Cooper, Ralph Cosham, Catherine Cox, James David Cromar, Lindsay Crouse, Liam Currier, Terrence Currier, Andrew Davis, Lydia deGreeve, Jossie DeGuzman, Paula Desmond, Tony Di Benedetto, Paul Edgar, Christine Estabrook, Karen Evans, Clarence Felder, Kevin Fisher, Robert Fisher, Kitty Fitzgibbon, Elizabeth Franz, Maricruz Fugon, Gale Garnett, John Gilliss, William C. Godsey, Carlos Juan Gonzalez, Robyn Goodman, Jeffrey Gordon, Rocky Greenberg, Almon Grimsted, Robin Groves, Ben Hammer, Mark Hammer, June Hansen, F. Thomas Hewitt, Sydney Hibbert, Derwyn Holder, George Clark Hosmer, Joanne Hrkach, Charles Hunter, Diane Kagan, Paul Kandel, Faizul Khan, Charles Lang, Daniel Lewin, Constance McCornick, Tom McDermott, Annie McGreevey, Christopher McHale, Sam McMurray, Edward Mercier, Jo Meyers, Timothy Meyers, Edward J. Moore, Gabor Morea, Joshua Mostel, Frank Muller, Robert Murch, Jim Nugent, Bill Nunnery, Terrence O'Hara, Estelle Omens, Joe Palmieri, Joanna Peled, David Perry, Marcia Phillips, Peter Phillips, Joyce Pinson, Don Plumley, C. C. H. Pounder, Andrew Prosky, Robert Prosky, Bill Randolph, David Sawyer, David Schechter, Scott Schofield, Rebecca Street, Eron Tabor, Kristoffer Tabori, Jay Tauber, David Teeple, David Toney, John Madden Towey, Jim Ward, Laura Waterbury, Nathan Wilansky, Halo Wines, John Wylie, Mark Zagaeski, and GUEST STARS: Eli Wallach, Anne Jackson

PRODUCTIONS

NIGHTCLUB CANTATA by Elizabeth Swados, THE NATIONAL HEALTH by Peter Nichols, STARTING HERE, STARTING NOW by Richard Maltby, Jr., David Shire, THE CAUCASIAN CHALK CIRCLE by Bertolt Brecht, COMEDIANS by Trevor Griffiths, A STREETCAR NAMED DESIRE by Tennessee Williams, HAMLET by William Shakespeare, GEMINI by Albert Innaurato, SEPARATIONS by Janet Neipris, DUCK HUNTING by Alexander Vampilov (English-language premiere), THE DESERT DWELLERS by Sidney Renthal, TRAPPERS by Anthony Giardina

Joe B. Mann Photos

Left Center: Edward J. Moore, Lindsay Crouse in "A Streetcar Named Desire" Above: Bill Nunnery, John Wylie, Veronica Castang, Halo Wines in "Caucasian Chalk Circle" Top: Mark Hammer, Stanley Anderson, Gale Garnett, John Madden Towey in "Duck Hunting"

Kristoffer Tabori, Richard Bauer in "Hamlet"

ASOLO STATE THEATER
Sarasota, Florida
June 1, 1977–May 31, 1978

Executive Director, Richard G. Fallon; Artistic Director, Robert Strane; Managing Director, Howard J. Millman; Assistant Artistic Director, Thomas Edward West; Press, Edith N. Anson; Sets, John Scheffler, Sandro La Ferla, Robert C. Barnes, Holmes Easley, David Emmons, Rick Pike; Costumes, Catherine King, Flozanne John; Lighting, Martin Petlock; Technical Director, Victor Meyrich; Stage Managers, Marian Wallace, Stephanie Moss

COMPANY

Susan Borneman, Deanna Dunagan, Kelly Fitzpatrick, David S. Howard, Trent Jones, William Leach, Bette Oliver, Mary Ed Porter, Walter Rhodes, Steven Ryan, Frederick Sperberg, Milt Tarver, Isa Thomas, Bradford Wallace, Robert Beseda, George Brengel, Hal Carter, Brit Erickson, Elizabeth Horowitz, Max Howard, Neal Kenyon, Bette Oliver, William Pitts, Robert Strane, Eberle Thomas, Stephen Van Benschoten

Fred Davis, Molly DePree, Bill Herman, Peter Ivanov, Beth Lincks, Steven J. Ranklin, Deborah Unger, John C. Wall, Kathleen Archer, Maryann Barulich, Howard A. Branch, Jr., Ritch Brinkley, Tom Case, Lou Ann Csaszar, John Green, Arthur Hanket, Angela L. Lloyd, Jean McDaniel, Kim Ivan Motter, Joseph Reed, Robert Walker, Kathleen Archer, Porter Anderson, Carolyn Blackinton, Raye Blakemore, Dov Fahrer, Marilyn Foote, Bruce Howe, Christine Joelson, Jeff King, Michael L. Locklair, Carolyn Ann Meeley, Mary Ann Mullen, Janet Nawrocki, Evan S. Parry, James St. Clair GUEST ARTISTS: John Ulmer, George Keathley, Paul Barry, John Franceschina, Normand Beauregard, Steven J. Rankin, Brian McFadden

PRODUCTIONS

"Waltz of the Toreadors," "Desire under the Elms," "Cyrano de Bergerac," "Saturday, Sunday, Monday," "The Royal Family," "Juno and the Paycock," "She Stoops to Conquer," "The School for Wives," "Travesties," "Richard III," *American Premiere* of "Cromwell" by David Storey, *World Premieres* of "My Love to Your Wife" by Neal Kenyon, Brian McFadden and John Franceschina, "A Troupe in a Trunk" by Jim Hoskins and John Franceschina

Gary Sweetman Photos

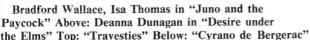

Bradford Wallace, Isa Thomas in "Juno and the Paycock" Above: Deanna Dunagan in "Desire under the Elms" Top: "Travesties" Below: "Cyrano de Bergerac"

Top: "Saturday, Sunday, Monday"
Below: "The Royal Family"

George Clark Hosmer, Peggity Price, Gwyllum
Evans, Cleo Holladay in "Relatively Speaking"

Mary Shelley, George Hosmer
in "Taming of the Shrew"

BARTER THEATRE
April 5–October 30, 1977
Forty-fifth Season

Artistic Director-Producer, Rex Partington; Business Manager, Pearl Hayter, Promotion Director, Ken Swiger; Development, Lucy Bushore; Director, Owen Phillips; Guest Directors, Ada Brown Mather, Byron Grant, John Beary, John Olon-Scrymgeour, Dorothy Marie; Scenery, Bennet Averyt, Parmelee Welles; Costumes, Sigrid Insull, Carr Garnett; Lighting, Grant Logan, Tony Partington; Technical Director, Grant Clifford Logan; Costumer, Martha Christian; Props, Lisa Greco; Stage Managers, Michael S. Mante;, Steven Woolf

COMPANY

Gwyllum Evans, Cleo Holladay, George Hosmer, Jane Ridley, Beth McDonald, John Morrow, Robert Rutland, Mary Shelley, Beverly Jensen
GUEST ARTISTS: Richard Babcock, Nel Cobb, Pete Edens, Stanley Flood, Rosalind Harris, David Harscheid, Lee Hines, Lisa Jacobson, Wayne Knight, Margaret Lunsford, Virginia Mattis, Peter More, Elizabeth Morgan, Peggity Price, Michelle Reilley, Con Roch, Alan Sharp, John Spencer, Susan Stevens, Beth Torgersen, Raymond McBride

PRODUCTIONS

"The Matchmaker" by Thornton Wilder, "The Taming of the Shrew" by William Shakespeare, "Relatively Speaking" by Alan Ayckbourn, "All My Sons" by Arthur Miller, "Hay Fever" by Noel Coward, "The Playboy of the Western World" by J. M. Synge, "Man with a Load of Mischief" by John Clifton, Ben Tarver, "The Mousetrap" by Agatha Christie, "Never Too Late" by Sumner Arthur Long, and *World Premiere* of "Bubba" by Sam Havens (August 31, 1977)

182

Left Center: Beverly Jensen
in "Bubba"

Jane Ridley, Gwyllum Evans in "Hay Fever" Above: Rex
Partington, Bruce McPherson, Virginia Mattis in "All My Sons"

CALIFORNIA ACTORS THEATRE

Los Gatos, California
October 6, 1977–May 21, 1978

Executive Producer, Sheldon Kleinman; General Manager, Francine Gordon; Artistic Director, Jame Dunn; Press, Richard Pontzious; Dramaturg, Dakin Matthews; Stage Managers, Joseph Broido, Frank Silvey; Sets, Ronald Krempetz; Costumes, Elaine Sausotte; Lighting, Eric Chasanoff; Props, Marguerite Robinson; Guest Directors, G. W. Bailey, Doug Johnson, Harvey Susser, Ed Hastings

COMPANY

Kurtwood Smith, Tom Ramirez, Martin Ferrero, Dakin Matthews, Carolyn Reed, Bonnie Gallup
GUEST ARTISTS: Zachary Berger, David Ogden Stiers, Harry Kersey

PRODUCTIONS

"Henry IV," "Henry V," "Scapino," "Steambath," "The Price," "You Can't Take It with You," *World Premiere* of "Save Grand Central," and *U. S. Premiere* of "Wild Oats"

John Naretto Photos

**Right: Kurtwood Smith, Zachary Berger
in "The Price" Top: Byron Jennings,
David Ogden Stiers in "Wild Oats"**

Leslie Harrell, Dakin Matthews in
"Save Grand Central"

Dakin Matthews as Falstaff
in "Henry IV"

Janet Sarno in "Night of the Iguana"
Below: Tana Hicken, Terry O'Quinn in "Ashes"

Paddy Croft, Robert Pastene in "The Rivals"
Below: Pat Karpen, Terry O'Quinn in
"The Runner Stumbles"

CENTER STAGE

Baltimore, Maryland
October 28, 1977–May 28, 1978

Artistic Director, Stan Wojewodski, Jr.; Managing Director, Peter W. Culman; Company Manager, Peter B. England; Business Manager, Mark Gallagher; Press, Linda Kinsey; Stage Manager, Ellen Raphael; Production Coordinator, William Yaggy; Technical Director, William Meyer; Costumer, Laura Castro; Sound, Kevin Carney; Designer, Charles Cosler; Directors, Robert A. Ackerman, Stan Wojewodski, Jr., Edward Berkeley, Marcia Rodd

PRODUCTIONS AND CASTS

THE GOODBYE PEOPLE by Herb Gardner with Marcia Rodd, Russell Horton, John Kellogg, Douglas Roberts, Stanley Weiman, Sammy Smith

THE RIVALS by Richard B. Sheridan with G. Brock Johnson, Doneil Szelag, Denise Koch, Lisa Goodman, Laura Esterman, Paddy Croft, Robert Pastene, Edmond Genest, Edward Cicciarelli, John Peilmeier, Paul C. Thomas, Daniel Thompson

THE RUNNER STUMBLES by Milan Stitt with G. Brock Johnson, Terry O'Quinn, Tana Hicken, Robert Pastene, Pat Karpen, Paddy Croft, Paul C. Thomas, Daniel Thompson

THE NIGHT OF THE IGUANA by Tennessee Williams with Jose Pacheco, Janet Sarno, Octavio Ciano, Paul Collins, Robert Wirtz, Joy Schoene, Bruce Godfrey, Lu Elrod, Daniel Szelag, Tana Hicken, Meg Wynn Owen, Sallyanne Tackus, Randall Duk Kim, Paul C. Thomas

ASHES by David Rudkin with Tana Hicken, Terry O'Quinn, Ellen Parks, George Taylor

BLITHE SPIRIT by Noel Coward with Cynthia Crumlish, Helen Carey, Munson Hicks, Bernard Frawley, Vivienne Shub, Paddy Croft, Pamela Lewis

Richard Anderson Photos

184   **Marcia Rodd, Russell Horton**
in "The Goodbye People"

CENTER THEATRE GROUP

AHMANSON THEATRE
Los Angeles, California
October 7, 1977–August 19, 1978

Managing Director, Robert Fryer; Manager, Charles Mooney; Assistant Manager, Barbara Stocks; Production Associate, Robert Linden; Production Coordinator, Michael Grossman; Production Administrator, Ralph Beaumont; Press, James H. Hansen, Ann Wareham; Technical Supervisor, H. R. Poindexter; Administrative Coordinator, Joyce Zaccaro

PRODUCTIONS AND CASTS

CHAPTER TWO by Neil Simon (*World Premiere* Oct. 7, 1977) for cast and credits, see Broadway Calendar, page 24

THE DEVIL'S DISCIPLE by George Bernard Shaw; Director, Frank Dunlop; Sets and Costumes, Carl Toms; Lighting, F. Mitchell Dana; Production Associate, Robert Linden; Stage Managers, Barbara-Mae Phillips, William O'Brien, Norman Abrams; Sound, William Young; Wardrobe Supervisor, Eddie Dodds; Music Coordinator, Bill Tynes. CAST: Rex Harrison, Margaret Hamilton, Luise Heath, Randy Pelish, Barnard Hughes, Carole Shelley, Fred Stuthman, Allan Lurie, Robert Cornthwaite, Betty Ramey, Peggy Rea, Chris Sarandon, John Orchard, Earl Boen, Benjamin Stewart, Norman Abrams, Timothy Askew, Tom Blank, Jason Buzas, Terry Collier, Ken Letner, George McDaniel, Dale Reynolds, Alexandra Stoddart, Peter Virgo, Jr., Jay Leslie, Keith Thompson, Bill Tynes, Gary Woodward

ABSURD PERSON SINGULAR by Alan Ayckbourn; Director, Stephen Porter; Sets, Edward Burbridge; Costumes, Noel Taylor; Production Supervisor/Lighting, Robert Randolph. CAST: Stockard Channing (Jane), Lawrence Pressman (Sidney), John McMartin (Ron), Eve Arden (Marion), Roberta Maxwell (Eva), Laurence Guittard (Geoffrey)

PAL JOEY '78 with Music by Richard Rodgers; Lyrics, Lorenz Hart; Book, John O'Hara; Adaptation by Jerome Chodorov, Mark Bramble; Choreography, Claudd Thompson; Scenery and Lighting, Robert Randolph; Costumes, Robert Fletcher; Musical Direction, John Myles; Orchestrations, Gil Askey; Musical Arrangements, D'Vaughn Pershing; Assistant Choreographer, Michele Simmons; Director, Michael Kidd; Stage Managers, Bill Holland, William S. O'Brien, Howard Chitjian. CAST: Lena Horne (Vera), Louisa Flaningam (Gladys), John LaMotta (Mike), Cleveland L. Pennington (Bartender), Myrna White (Stella), Ravah Daley (Agnes), Marjorie Barnes (Linda), Clifton Davis (Joey), Josephine Premice (Melba), Howard Chitjian (Waiter), Juleste Salve (Emilio), Simeon Den (Jacques), Roderick Spencer Sibert (Foreman), Norman Matlock (Ludlow), and Ensemble: Joel Blum, Le'Von Campbell, Stuart Carey, Reed Jones, Tim Millett, Stan Perryman, Anthony L. Seals, Jamilah Hunter, Lois Marie Hunter, Bonita Jackson, Christina Kumi Kimball, Julia Lema, Marilyn Mask, Sandi Orcutt, Myrna White, Melanie Winter, Michele Simmons, Mark Whitaker

Ken Veeder, Lydia Heston, Jay Thompson Photos

Right: Eve Arden, John McMartin, Roberta Maxwell, Stockard Channing Above: Eve Arden, Laurence Guittard, Roberta Maxwell, Lawrence Pressman in "Absurd Person Singular"

Rex Harrison, George McDaniel, Earl Boen, Jason Buzas in "The Devil's Disciple"

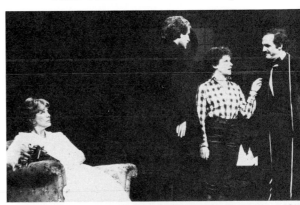

Josephine Premice, Lena Horne, Clifton Davis in "Pal Joey '78"

Clifton Davis, Lena Horne in "Pal Joey '78"

185

CENTER THEATRE GROUP
MARK TAPER FORUM

August 11, 1977–July 2, 1978
Eleventh Season

FOR COLORED GIRLS WHO HAVE CONSIDERED SUICIDE/WHEN THE RAINBOW IS ENUF by Ntozake Shange, with Jonelle Allen, Barbara Alston, Beverly Anne, Trazana Beverley, Candy Brown, Marilyn Coleman, Alfre Woodard

COMEDIANS by Trevor Griffiths, with Herbert Foster, Jim Dale, Philip Charles MacKenzie, Gerrit Graham, Avery Schreiber, John Devlin, Henry Jones, Scott Hylands, Sumant, Keene Curtis, Barry Dennen, Gordon Connell

GETTING OUT by Marsha Norman, with Janette Lane Bradbury, Susan Clark, Hugh Gillin, F. William Parker, John O'Connell, Bill Cobbs, Collin Wilcox, Sarah Cunningham, Griffin Dunne, James G. Richardson, Michael Fairman, Conchata Ferrell

BLACK ANGEL by Michael Cristofer (*World Premiere,* May 18, 1978); Director, Gordon Davidson; Set and Costumes, Sally Jacobs; Lighting, Tharon Musser. CAST: Joseph Maher (Martin), Tyne Daly (Simone), Neil Flanagan (Claude), Richard Dysart (Louis), David Spielberg (August), Vincent Duke Milana (1st Hooded Man), Bob Basso (2nd Hooded Man), Richard Riner (3rd Hooded Man/M.P.), Art LaFleur (Andy/M.P./Hooded Man), Jonathan Banks (Bob/M.P.)

A CHRISTMAS CAROL by Charles Dickens; Adapted by Doris Baizley; Director, John Dennis; Music, Susan Harvey. CAST: Tony Papenfuss, E. Lamont Johnson, Don McAlister, Nathan Cook, Alfre Woodard, Michael McNeilly, Frank Ford, Barry Moore, Doug Griffin, Dan Gerrity, Nancy Sheehy, Sab Shimono, Donna Fuller

MARK TAPER FORUM
NEW THEATRE FOR NOW

GETHSEMANE SPRINGS by Harvey Perr (*World Premiere,* Sept. 29, 1977); Director, John Sullivan. CAST: Andra Akers, Mathew Anden, John Anderson, Tyne Daly, Paul Hampton, Joanne Linville, Diana Scarwid, Charles Shull, James Sloyan, Gail Stickland, Joyce Van Patten

THE WINTER DANCERS by David Lan (*American Premiere,* Apr. 6, 1978); Director, Kenneth Brecher. CAST: John Kauffman, Constance Sawyer, Marcy Mattox, Sab Shimono, Yuki Shimoda, Haunani Minn, Ernest Harada, Ralph Brannen, Ken Ganado

ZOOT SUIT by Luis Valdez (*World Premiere,* Apr. 20, 1978); Director, Luis Valdez. CAST: Edward James Olmos, Arthur Hammer, Daniel Valdez, Abel Franco, Julio Medina, Lupe Ontiveros, Christine Avila, Pepe Serna, Rachel Levario, David E. Worden, Mike Gomez, Sheila Larken, Domingo Ambriz, Evelina Fernandez, Noah Keen, Vincent Duke Milana, Nelson D. Cuevas

Jay Thompson Photos

Right Center: Daniel Valdez in "Zoot Suit"
Above: John Kauffman, Marcy Mattox
in "The Winter Dancers" Top: Susan Clark,
Conchata Ferrell in "Getting Out"

Tyne Daly, Joseph Maher
in "Black Angel"

CENTER THEATRE GROUP
MARK TAPER FORUM
LABORATORY PRODUCTIONS
September 12, 1977–June 7, 1978

Director, John Sullivan; Manager, Susan E. Barton; Production Manager, Diane Keil; Stage Managers, Greg Dunn, Priscilla Guastavino, Karen Hendel, Bob Keil, Lynda A. Lavin, James T. McDermott

TRUE ROMANCES by Susan Yankowitz; Director, Judy Chaikin; Music, Elmer Bernstein; Lyrics, Miss Yankowitz; Designers, Terence Tam Soon, Michael M. Bergfeld; Musical Director, David Spear; Musical Numbers Staged by James Mitchell. CAST: Regina Baff, Joseph Burke, Alix Elias, Donna Fuller, Karen Hensel, John LaMotta, John Lansing, Ann McCurry, James Mitchell, Peter Riegert, Carol Schlanger, Tom Skerritt

MGMT by Jon Arlow; Director, Robert Calhoun; Designers, Erik Brenmark, Joyce Aysta, Thomas Ruzika. CAST: Barry Brown, Russell Johnson, Edwin Owens, James G. Richardson, Donegan Smith, Kent Smith, Herb Voland

SALOME by Kim Milford; Director, Gordon Hunt; Choreographer, Robert Talmage; Designers, Scott Johnson, Mary Malin, Dawn Chiang; Musical Director, Ron Stockert. CAST: Paul Ainsley, Marco Alpert, Doug Altman, Dennis Belfield, Beverly Bremers, Steve Bonino, Randy Brooks, Annette Charles, Dennis Cooley, James Dybas, Robert Fischer, Gail Heideman, Joe Kelly, Mickey McNeil, Kim Milford, Penelope Milford, Ron Stockert

TRIPTYCH by Oliver Hailey; Director, Michael Flanagan; Designers, Peter Clemons, Donna Casey, Karen M. Katz. CAST: Eileen Brennan, Jerry Hardin, Darryl Hickman, Bob Hogan, Heather MacRae

AT THE END OF LONG ISLAND by Richard Lees; Director, Asaad Kelada. CAST: Gretchen Corbett, Robert Hays, Louise Latham, Neva Patterson, John Randolph, Carol Rossen, William Schallert

BIG APPLE MESSENGER by Shannon Keith Kelley; Director, Jonathan Estrin. CAST: Sid Conrad, John Creamer, Bill Henry Douglass, Richard Erdman, Alan Feinstein, Jack Fletcher, Rick Hamilton, Ric Mancini, Rudy Ramos, Peter Riegert, Mike Robelo, Maurice Sneed, Dolph Sweet, Sal Viscuso

ORMER LOCKLEAR by Marc Norman; Director, Mr. Norman; Music, Tony Greco; Lyrics, Marc Norman; Choreographer, Sandra Duffy. CAST: Jeff Altman, Susan Krebs, Darrell Larson, Laura Owens

THE TAKING AWAY OF LITTLE WILLIE by Tom Griffin; Director, Wallace Chappell. CAST: Harry Basch, Robin Gammell, Cooper Neal, Sarah Rush, Shirley Slater, Timothy Wead, Nina Wilcox

IMPROVISATIONAL THEATRE
PROJECT

Director, John Dennis; Manager, Susan E. Barton; Stage Manager, Richard Serpe; Writer, Doris Baizley; Designers, Charles Berliner, Pamela Cooper; Composers, Harry Aguado, Susan Harvey; Choreographer, Carolyn Dyer. CAST: Nathan Cook, Donna Fuller, Noreen Hennessy, E. Lamont Johnson, Don McAlister, Michael McNeilly, Tony Papenfuss, Sab Shimono, Alfre Woodard

THE IMPACT COMPANY: Manager, David F. Walton; Stage Manager, August M. Amarino; Director, James Devney; Writers, Elizabeth Gray, Nicholas Kazan; Composers, Lenardo Dedman, Jeffrey Labes. CAST: Joan Brooker, Fran Ford, Dan Gerrity, Christopher Grant, Doug Griffin, Nancy Lane-Sheehy, Don McAlister, Stanford Miller, Barry Moore, Gwen Sampson

Richard Allen, Jay Thompson Photos

Right Center: Peter Riegert, Alan Feinstein, Dolph Sweet in "Big Apple Messenger" Above: Neva Patterson, John Randolph, William Schallert, Louise Latham in "At the End of Long Island" Top: Darryl Hickman, Eileen Brennan in "Triptych"

Nathan Cook, Noreen Hennessy, E. Lamont Johnson in "Concrete Dreams" **187**

Dan Hamilton in "The Royal Family"

CINCINNATI PLAYHOUSE IN THE PARK

Cincinnati, Ohio
October 11, 1977–June 11, 1978

Producing Director, Michael Murray; Managing Director, Robert W. Tolan; Directors, Michael Murray, R. G. Davis, Robert Brewer, John Going; Musical Director, Fred Goldrich; Sets, Neil Peter Jampolis, Karl Eigsti, John Lee Beatty, Joseph A. Varga; Costumes, Annie Peacock Warner, Jennifer von Mayrhauser, Caley Summers; Lighting, Neil Peter Jampolis, Marc B. Weiss, Jay Depenbrock; Press, Avis J. Yuni; Stage Managers, J. P. Valente, Ken Stauffer; Business Manager, R. C. Surber; Production Manager, William Kent Koefler

PRODUCTIONS AND CASTS

THE THREEPENNY OPERA: Hal Bennett, Grace Keagy, James Kisicki, Judith Lander, Gary McGurk, Pamela McLernon, Paul Merrill, Sally Mitchell, John Newton, Keith Prentice, William L. Schwarber, Luke Sickle, Adrian Sparks, Roy K. Stevens, David Upson, Linda Conway, Tony Davis, James P. Gubser, Rebecca Koborie, Mark O'Reilly, Anthony D. Stallsmith, Charlotte Maria Strayhorne, Jan van der Swaagh, Richard Wheeler

THE IMAGINARY INVALID: Sidney Armus, Daniel Sid Banzali, Michael Connolly, George Deloy, John Grassilli, Caroline Kava, Mary Ann Renz, Mimi Seton, Andrea Snow, Adrian Sparks

BENEFIT OF A DOUBT by Edward Clinton (*World Premiere,* Jan. 3, 1978): William Andrews, Elizabeth Council, Nancy Donohue, Tania Myren, Etain O'Malley, P. Jay Sidney

OF MICE AND MEN: Peter Bosche, Kent Broadhurst, Stephen Clarke, Lanny Flaherty, Susanne Marley, Robert Rutland, Luke Sickle, P. Jay Sidney, Robert Stocker, Eric Uhler

THE HOUSE OF BERNARDA ALBA: Claudine Catania, Diane Danzi, Viola Feldman, Sylvia Gassell, Vera Visconti Lockwood, Rochelle Parker, Marian Primont, Jana Robbins, Margaret Warncke, Toni Wein, Betty Alley, Elsie Ayer, Barbara Bratt, Carla Bussell, Julie Cunningham, Becky Duff, Dana Gilbert, Carol Henderson, Elizabeth Johnston, Jackie Kasten, Fredrica Lawlor, Suzanne Louiso, Lila Marcus, Jo Judson Martin, Maggie Nuelsen, Kimberly Osgood, Brette Parks, Christine Parks, Maureen Schaffner, Patricia Stucker, Juanita Van Styn, Amy Young, Laurie C. Young

THE ROYAL FAMILY: Barbara Caruso, Elizabeth Council, Ellen Fiske, Sam Gray, Birdie M. Hale, Dan Hamilton, James Kisicki, Marjorie Lovett, Samuel Maupin, Paul McMaster, John Newton, Moultrie Patten, William L. Schwarber, Christopher Wynkoop, Larry Boyd, Christine Parks, John Vissman

VANITIES: Robin Groves, Lynn Ritchie, Mercedes Ruehl

SIZWE BANSI IS DEAD: Larry Arrington-Bey, James Pickens, Jr.

WHAT'S A NICE COUNTRY LIKE YOU DOING IN A STATE LIKE THIS?: Jon Amos, Deb Girdler, Mary Haas, Timothy Hawkins, Freida Houck, Ann Pobereskin, Jim Slagle, Jim Semmelman

Sandy Underwood Photos

**Top Left: Nancy Donohue, Tania Myren
in "Benefit of a Doubt"
Left Center: Claudine Catania, Jana
Robbins in "House of Bernarda Alba"**

CLARENCE BROWN COMPANY
Knoxville, Tennessee
August 4, 1977–February 25, 1978

Director, Ralph G. Allen; General Manager, Julian Forrester; Advisers, Alvin Nielsen, Barry Gaines; Design, Robert Cothran; Production Manager, Margaret Wheeler; Press, Chris Grabenstein; Company Manager, Marsha Garfinkel; Stage Managers, Douglas Nigh, James Whisenand Long; Costumes, Marianne Custer; Directors, Wandalie Henshaw, Julian Forrester; Lighting, L. J. DeCuir, Barry Daniels; Incidental Music, Tim Duncan; Fight Choreography, Erik Fredricksen.

COMPANY

Jon Peter Benson, Richard Bowden, Douglas Brindley, Robert Browning, Robertson Carricart, Jay Doyle, Bernerd Engel, Richard Galuppi, Patrick Husted, Harris Laskawy, Charles Lutz, Harriet Nichols, Edward E. Shelnut, Mary-Elizabeth White, Evan Davis, Mary Saunders
GUEST ARTISTS: Mary Martin, Anthony Quayle, Philip Kerr

PRODUCTIONS

"Hamlet," "The Imaginary Invalid," "A Midsummer Night's Dream," and *U. S. Premiere* (Aug. 4, 1977) of "Do You Turn Somersaults?" by Aleksei Arbuzov with Mary Martin and Anthony Quayle.

Jonathan Daniel Photos

**Richard Galuppi in "The Imaginary Invalid"
Top: Anthony Quayle, Mary Martin
in "Do You Turn Somersaults?"**

COHOES MUSIC HALL
Cohoes, N.Y.
October 29, 1977–March 19, 1978

Executive Director, Louis J. Ambrosio; Business Manager, Kristine Koba; Press, Terri Garvey, Megan Seacord; Company Manager, Terilyn McGovern; Stage Manager, Barry J. W. Steinman; Technical Director, David Fletcher; Assistant Stage Manager, Suzanne Deak; Props, Paula Gouras; Lighting, Toni Golden; Costumes, Bob Wojewodski; Sets, Michael Anania

PRODUCTIONS AND CASTS

THE GLASS MENAGERIE: Maureen O'Sullivan, Elaine Hausman, Peter Webster, Robert Bacigalupi

VANITIES: Ellen Donkin, Donna Emmanuel, Elaine Hausman

MOON FOR THE MISBEGOTTEN: Gerald Richards, Robert Bacigalupi, Kaiulani Lee, Jon DeVries, Richard Harmel

THE UNEXPECTED GUEST: Robert Bacigalupi, Roger Baron, Yusef Bulos, Virginia Downing, Walter Hicklin, John Leighton, Thora Nelson, Ted Spian

PRIVATE LIVES: Christine Baranski, Richard Harmel, Elaine Hausman, Dale Hodges

Bob Mayette Photos

**Right Center: Maureen O'Sullivan
in "The Glass Menagerie"**

**Ellen Donkin, Elaine Hausman, Donna Emmanuel
in "Vanities"**

189

CLEVELAND PLAY HOUSE

Cleveland, Ohio
October 21, 1977–May 7, 1978

Director, Richard Oberlin; Associate Director, Larry Tarrant; Assistant Director, Robert Snook; Business Manager, Nelson Isekeit; Scenic Director, Richard Gould; Press, William Lempke, Paula Bond, Sherry Tarrant; Company Manager, Stanley R. Suchecki; Directors, Richard Halverson, Paul Lee, Evie McElroy, Richard Oberlin, Robert Snook, Larry Tarrant, Ray Walston, Jonathan Bolt, Terri White; Designers, Harriet Cone, Richard Gould, Eugene Hare, Barbara Leatherman, Estelle Painter, David Smith, Paul Rodgers; Stage Managers, Eugene Hare, Varney Knapp, Richard Oberlin; Technical Director, Russell Lowe

COMPANY

Kenneth Albers, Norman Berman, Sharon Bicknell, John Danielich, Ann Goldman, Jo Farwell, Jonathan Farwell, June Gibbons, Richard Halverson, Cheryl Kempe, Joe Lauck, Allen Leatherman, Paul Lee, Harper Jane McAdoo, Evie McElroy, Lizabeth Mackay, Todd Mandel, Richard Oberlin, James Richards, Carol Schultz, Robert Snook, Wayne S. Turney
GUEST ARTISTS: Mary Adams, Marge Adler, Mary Bradley, Kenneth Dolin, David O. Frazier, George Gould, Cookie Harlin, Providence Hollander, Dee Hoty, Douglas Jones, James Kisicki, Gay Marshall, Maeve McGuire, David Natale, Ellery Siegler, Erica Tarrant, Ray Walston, Terri White

PRODUCTIONS

THE LEARNED LADIES by Moliere, ROUND AND ROUND THE GARDEN by Alan Ayckbourn, THE PRAGUE SPRING by Lee Kalcheim, THE LITTLE FOXES by Lillian Hellman, KNOCK KNOCK by Jules Feiffer, THE CLUB by Eve Merriam, and *World Premieres* of GREAT EXPECTATIONS by Paul Lee adapted from Charles Dickens novel, and THE ROMANTICS by Maxim Gorki, translated and adapted by William Stancil

Herbert Ascherman, Jr. Photos

Right: Richard Halverson, Wayne S. Turney, Norm Berman in "Knock Knock" Above: "The Club" Top: Alma Maeve McGuire in "The Little Foxes"

Carol Schultz, Lizbeth Mackay, Kenneth Albers in "The Romantics"

Wayne S. Turney, James Richards, Paul Lee in "Great Expectations"

190

DALLAS THEATER CENTER
Dallas, Texas
October 1977–July 1978

Managing Director, Paul Baker; Associate Director, Mary Sue Jones; Stage Directors, Paul Baker, Judi Davis, Ken Latimer, Ryland Merkey, Albert Millaire; Sets, Yoichi Aoki, Virgil Beavers, Cheryl Denson, M. G. Johnston, Sallie Laurie, George Pettit, Peter Wolf; Costumes, Virgil Beavers, Cheryl Denson, John Henson, Rayanne Miller, Rodger Wilson; Lighting, Linda Blase, Robyn Flatt, John Henson, Allen Hibbard, Randy Moore, Sally Netzel; Stage Managers, Suzanne Chiles, Hanna Cusick, Andrew C. Gaupp, Mark Brenton Henager, Russell Henderson, Susan Sleeper; Press, Linda Blase, John Logan, Glenn Allen Smith, Lynn Trammell

COMPANY

Yoichi Aoki, Linda Blase, Judith Davis, Cheryl Denson, Keith Dixon, John Figlmiller, Robyn Flatt, Martha Robinson Goodman, Chris Hendrie, John Henson, Allen Hibbard, Mary Sue Jones, Kathleen Latimer, Ken Latimer, Sallie Laurie, John Logan, Rebecca Logan, Steven Mackenroth, Ryland Merkey, Norma Moore, Randy Moore, Louise Mosley, Sally Netzel, Patti O'Donnell, Mona Pursley, Bryant J. Reynolds, Synthia Rogers, Mary Rohde, Glenn Allen Smith, John R. Stevens, Randolph Tallman, Jacque Thomas, Lynn Trammell
GUEST ARTISTS: Mark Medoff, Albert Millaire

PRODUCTIONS

"Equus," "Absurd Person Singular," "The Imaginary Invalid," "Vanities," "Night of the Iguana," "Three Men on a Horse," and *World Premiere* of "Firekeeper" by Mark Medoff

Linda Blase Photos

Right Center: Mary Sue Jones, Warren Hammack in "Night of the Iguana" Above: Dick Trousdell, Rebecca Logan in "The Imaginary Invalid" Top: Mary Rohde, Steven Mackenroth in "Absurd Person Singular"

Tom Zinn, Robert Scevers in "Equus"

Preston Jones, John Figlmiller, Carlos Gonzalez in "Firekeeper" 191

COMPANY

Alan Abelew, Polita Barnes, Rogers Barnes, Deirdre Berthrong, Gar Campbell, Laurence Cohen, Stephen Downs, Sally Downs, Milton Earl Forrest, Myrna Gawryn, Susan Gelb, Daniel Grace, Donald Harris, Jane Harrison, Nora Heflin, Nancy Hickey, Mellissa Hubbert, Lance Larsen, Paul Linke, Marcina Motter, Andrew Parks, Louie Piday, Jerry Pojawa, Michael Prichard, Roxann Pyle, Russell Pyle, Dennis Redfield, Jack Rowe, Trish Soodik, Michael Stefani GUEST ARTISTS: Jill Basey, Vaughn Harris, Lisa James, Roy C. Kerry, Jerry Lee-Shu Loo, Jerome McAffee, Pat McGreal, Bruce McGuire, Rob Reed, Michael Sheehan, William T. Sutherland, Lisette Williams

PRODUCTIONS

"A Man's a Man" by Bertolt Brecht, and *World Premieres* of "Thighs" by Trish Soodik, "The Shooter's Bible" by Lance Larsen

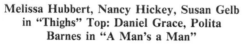

Melissa Hubbert, Nancy Hickey, Susan Gelb in "Thighs" Top: Daniel Grace, Polita Barnes in "A Man's a Man"

DETROIT REPERTORY THEATRE
Detroit, Michigan
November 3, 1977–June 18, 1978

Artistic Director-Producer, Bruce E. Millan; Audience Development Director, Robert Williams; General Manager, Marylynn Kacir; Costumiere, Marianna Hoad; Lighting, Dick Smith; Scenery, John Knox; Directors, Bruce E. Millan, Barbara Busby; Sound, Willie Hodge; Stage Manager, Robert Williams; Music Director, Kelly Smith

PRODUCTIONS AND CASTS

SUNDAY REVOLUTION by Metcalf Evans (*World Premiere,* Nov. 3, 1977): William Boswell, Robert Williams, Dee Andrus, Valarie Hawkins, John Hardy, Del Bondie, Valerie Paone

THE BLOOD KNOT by Athol Fugard with Robert Williams, Scott Dennis

LOST IN THE STARS by Maxwell Anderson and Kurt Weill, with Dee Andrus, Del Bondie, William Boswell, Annette Brodie, Perry Brown, Barbara Busby, Michael W. Campbell, Council Cargle, Sharon Castleberry, Albert B. Chisolm, Jr., Colleen Davis, John W. Hardy, Willie Hodge, Sullivan Horton, Jr., Jim Krul, Cheryl Lemans, Mac Lister, Marge Miller, Jesse Newton, Maggie Porter, Heidi Schneider, Robert Williams

Robert Williams, Scott Dennis in "Blood Knot" Right Center: Valarie Hawkins, Valerie Paone, William Boswell, Dee Andrus, Robert Williams in "Sunday Revolution"

Allan Carlsen, Michael Tolaydo in "Two Gentlemen
of Verona" Right Center: Gale Garnett, M. Jonathan
Steele in "Teeth 'n' Smiles" Top: Michael Tolaydo,
Margaret Whitton in "Hamlet"

FOLGER THEATRE GROUP

Washington, D.C.
October 12, 1977–July 16, 1978

Producer, Louis W. Scheeder; General Manager, Michael Shee-
han; Stage Managers, Pamela Horner, Laura Burroughs; Technical
Director, G. Kerry Comerford; Lighting, Hugh Lester, Elizabeth
Toth; Business Manager, Mary Ann deBarbieri; Press, Linda Leh-
man; Company Manager, Thomas Madden; Costumes, Bob Woje-
wodski, Dona Granata, Sheila McLamb, Susan Tsu, Karen M.
Hummel, Scenery, David Chapman, David Lloyd Gropman, Hugh
Lester; Music, Paul Schierhorn, William Penn; Directors, Louis W.
Scheeder, Jonathan Alper

PRODUCTIONS AND CASTS

TEETH 'N' SMILES by David Hare (*American Premiere*, Oct. 12,
1977); Music and Lyrics, Nick and Tony Bicat: Pamela Brook, Allan
Carlson, James Dean, Larry Dilg, Earle Edgerton, Gale Garnett,
Hubert Kelly, Peter Phillips, Paul Schierhorn, M. Jonathan Steele,
George Taylor

TWO GENTLEMEN OF VERONA by William Shakespeare:
Rosemary Brandenburg, Allan Carlsen, Richard Cochrane, Albert
Corbin, David Cromwell, James Dean, Franchelle Stewart Dorn,
Earle Edgerton, Carlos Juan Gonzalez, David Harscheid, John
Hertzler, Terry Hinz, Mikel Lambert, Shepard Sobel, Anne Stone,
Michael Tolaydo, Peter Vogt, Eric Zwemer

HAMLET by William Shakespeare: Chris Arnold, David Butler,
Allan Carlsen, Richard Cochrane, Albert Corbin, James Dean,
George Dunlap, Earle Edgerton, Kitty Fitzgibbon, David Har-
scheid, John Hertzler, Terry Hinz, Mike Lambert, Barry MacMil-
lan, Nick Matchwich, David McConeghey, John Neville-Andrews,
Jerry Paone, Shepard Sobel, Michael Tolaydo, Kate van Burek,
Peter Vogt, Margaret Whitton, Eric Zwemer

MACKEREL by Israel Horovitz (*World Premiere*. Apr. 12, 1978);
Director, Louis W. Scheeder: Brian Hartigan, Jo Henderson, Pat
Karpen, Elizabeth Kemp

RICHARD III by William Shakespeare: Elaine Bromka, Paul Col-
lins, Albert Corbin, Ralph Cosham, David Cromwell, James Dean,
George Dunlap, Earle Edgerton, John Elko, June Hansen, John
Healey, Jr., John Hertzler, Dale Hodges, Mikel Lambert, Robert
Lesko, David McConeghey, Norman Patrick Martin, John Neville-
Andrews, Chris Romilly, Alvin Lee Sanders, Shepard Sobel, Peter
Suddeth, Kate van Burek, Peter Vogt, Eric Zwemer

BLACK ELK SPEAKS by Christopher Sergel: Carl Alexander,
Henry "Kaimu" Bal, Richard Camargo, Clayton Corbin, Michael
Lamont, Jane Lind, Maria Antoinette Rogers

Photos by JEB

Brian Hartigan in "Mackerel"

James Whitmore as Will Rogers
Left: Max Morath in "The Ragtime Years"
Below: "All Night Strut"

FORD'S THEATRE SOCIETY

Washington, D.C.
December 16, 1977–July 20, 1978
Tenth Season

Executive Producer, Frankie Hewitt; Press, Alma Viator; General Manager, Maury Sutter; Assistant to Producer, Michael Howe; Technical Director, Tom Berra

PRODUCTIONS AND CASTS

THE ALL NIGHT STRUT! conceived and directed by Fran Charnas; Staging and Choreography, Arthur Faria; Musical Direction, William Roy; Set, Richard Ferrer; Costumes, Carol Oditz; Stage Manager, Sam Ellis. CAST: Michael Davis, Barbara Heuman, Marion Ramsey, Anthony White, Melanie Adam, Leslie Dockery, Luther Fontaine, Agnes Johnson, Bobby Longbottom, Jack Magradey, Liz Morris, Eric Riley, Christina Saffran, Jeff Spielman, Michelle Stubbs, Gary Sullivan

DIVERSIONS AND DELIGHTS: Vincent Price as Oscar Wilde (see Broadway Calendar, page 42)

JULES FEIFFER'S HOLD ME! with Sets by Kert Lundell, Costumes by Ruth Morley, Directed by Gene Borio. CAST: Maria Cellario, Rhoda Gemignani, William Lodge, Ray Stewart, Britt Swanson

THE RAGTIME YEARS: one-man show with Max Morath

THE AMERICAN DANCE MACHINE: *World Premiere* Feb. 4, 1978; Executive Director, Lee Theodore. CAST: Swen Swenson, Janet Eilber, Harold Cromer, Barry Preston, Nancy Chismar, Liza Gennaro, Amy Levine, Gina Martin, Marcia Oste, Debbi Bier Prouty, Christine von Scheidt, Larry Hyman, Joe Pugliese, Morgan Richardson, Joel Rosina, Kevin Ryan, Randy Skinner, Donald Young

WILL ROGERS' U.S.A.: a one-man show with James Whitmore as Will Rogers

THE ROBBER BRIDEGROOM by Alfred Uhry; Music, Robert Waldman; Director, Mary Porter Hall. CAST: Tom Wopat, Rhonda Coullet, Glynis Bell, Suzanne Costallos, Rosalind Harris, Trip Plymale, John Goodman, Ernie Sabella, David Sinkler, John Briggs, Aldyn McKean, David Lee Taylor, Margo Bruton, Dana Kyle, B. J. Hardin, Donalyn Petrucci, Tom Westerman

MOTHER COURAGE AND HER CHILDREN by Bertolt Brecht. Performed by The Acting Company (see Off Broadway Calendar page 98)

Richard Braaten Photos

Tom Wopat, Rhonda Coullet
in "The Robber Bridegroom"

GEORGE STREET PLAYHOUSE

New Brunswick, N.J.
October 7, 1977–June 4, 1978

Producing Director, Eric Krebs; Managing Director, John Herochik; Press, Tom Iovanne; Technical Director, Dan Stratman; Stage Managers, Lois J. Kier, Holly DeYoung; Designer, Dan Proett

COMPANY: Names not submitted

PRODUCTIONS

"The Rainmaker" by N. Richard Nash, directed by Eric Loeb; "Steambath" by Bruce Jay Freidman, directed by Peter Bennett; "Oh, New Brunswick! A Fully Clothed Revue"; "Man and Superman" by George Bernard Shaw, directed by Bob Hall; *World Premiere* of "Paris Was Yesterday" by Janet Flanner, adapted and directed by Paul Shyre, with Celeste Holm in a solo performance; "Serenading Louie" by Lanford Wilson, directed by Terry Schreiber; "Arsenic and Old Lace" by Joseph Kesselring, directed by Peter Bennett; "The Kids from Jersey"

Suzanne Karp Krebs Photos

Top Right: Mary Loane, Eric Loeb, Kathleen Claypool in "Arsenic and Old Lace" Below: Jaime Sanchez, Kerry Welch in "Steambath"

David Chandler, Cyril Mallett in "The Caretaker" Above: Linda Swenson, Lucy Holmes, Cindy Cooper in "Vanities"

GEVA

Rochester, N. Y.
October 12, 1977–April 9, 1978

Artistic Director, Gideon Y. Schein; Managing Director, Jessica L. Andrews; Business Manager, Timothy C. Norland; Press, Emily F. Leamon, John C. Marks, James Guido; Stage Manager, Timothy Toothman; Technical Director, Seth Price

COMPANY

Molly DePree, Christopher Fazel, Sharon James, Naomi Kay, Fredrick Nuernberg, Tony Pasqualini, S. Jay Rankin
GUEST ARTISTS: Nancy Rhodes, Karen R. Schulz, Richard Isackes, Woodie King, Jr., C. Richard Mills, Edna Watson

PRODUCTIONS

"The Front Page" by Ben Hecht and Charles MacArthur, "Death of a Salesman" by Arthur Miller, "The Farce of Scapin" by Moliere, "The Caretaker" by Harold Pinter, "A Raisin in the Sun" by Lorraine Hansberry, "Vanities" by Jack Heifner, "The Weak Spot" by George Kelly, "The Bald Soprano" by Eugene Ionesco, "The Russian Hut" by Larry Carr, "Box and Cox" by John Madison Morton, "A Pair of Lunatics" by W. R. Ralkes, "Star Quality" by William Morrison and Mark Long
Allen Friedman Photos

Philip Kerr, Benjamin Hendrickson
in "Otherwise Engaged" Left: W. H. Macey,
Lynn Cohen in "Battering Ram" Top: Barbara
Rush, Ruth Roman in "Night of the Iguana"

GOODMAN THEATRE

Chicago, Illinois
September 29, 1977–June 18, 1978
Fifty-second Season

Artistic Director, William Woodman; Managing Director, Janet Wade; General Manager, Roche Schulfer; Associate Artistic Director, Gregory Mosher; Press, Trisha Miller, Ann Fletcher, Joan Solomon; Production Manager, Philip Eickhoff; Stage Managers, Joseph Drummond, Christine Lawton; Costumes, James Edmund Brady, Michelle Demichelis, Julie Jackson, Virgil C. Johnson, Marsha Kowal, Barry Robison, Marjorie Slaiman; Sets, Maher Ahmad, Robert Christen, David Jenkins, Michael Merritt, David Mitchell, Joseph Nieminski, Helen Pond, Barry Robison, Herbert Senn; Business Manager, Barbara Janowitz

PRODUCTIONS AND CASTS

SAINT JOAN by George Bernard Shaw: Lynn Redgrave, Richard K. Allison, Eugene J. Anthony, Joseph Bova, George Brengel, Glenn Kovacevich, Leonard Kraft, Scott Larsson, Tony Lincoln, Robert Moberly, William Mowry, James Noble, Wyman Pendleton, Christopher Raynolds, Paul Shyre, David Whitaker

THE SEA GULL by Anton Chekhov (new version by Jean-Claude Itallie): Deborah Baltzell, Joseph Bell, Ruth Ford, Kinnaird Fox, Linda Kimbrough, Marge Kotlisky, William Mowry, Christopher Raynolds, Jack Roberts, Dennis Ryan, David Stettler, Jeremiah Sullivan, Robert Thompson

WORKING from Studs Terkel book, adapted by Stephen Schwartz (World Premiere): Steven Boockvor, Anne DeSalvo, Rex Everhart, Jay Footlik, Jo Henderson, David Patrick Kelly, Robin Lamont, Matt Landers, Bobo Lewis, Joe Mantegna, Joe Ponazecki, Jay Flash Riley, Brad Sullivan, Lynne Thigpen, Terri Treas

MUCH ADO ABOUT NOTHING by William Shakespeare: Eugene J. Anthony, Donald Brearley, Richard Clarke, Tom Doman, Laura Esterman, Patrick Hines, James Paul Ivey, Judity Ivey, Dennis Kennedy, Linda Kimbrough, Matthew Kimbrough, Tony Lincoln, William M. Mayfield, Katie McDonough, Timothy Oman, Christopher Raynolds, Raymon A. Rodriguez, Michael Sammer, Robert Scogin, Nicolas Surovy, Michael Tezla, Robert Thompson, John Walsh

THE NIGHT OF THE IGUANA by Tennessee Williams: Marcus Anast, Joseph Bell, Anne Edwards, Joyce Hazard, Art Kassul, David Mink, Alan Mixon, Ron Parody, Kathi O'Donnell, Michael Rieder, Ramon A. Rodriguez, Ruth Roman, Barbara Rush, Rebecca Taylor, Robert Thompson

OTHERWISE ENGAGED by Simon Gray: Barry Boys, James Greene, Sarah-Jane Gwillim, Benjamin Hendrickson, Philip Kerr, Marion Lines, Jack Roberts

Marge Kotlisky, William Mowry in "The Sea Gull"
Above: Lynn Redgrave in "St. Joan"

THE GUTHRIE THEATER

Minneapolis, Minnesota
June 6, 1977–February 25, 1978

Artistic Director, Michael Langham; Managing Director, Donald Schoenbaum; Associate Directors, Stephen Kanee, Ken Ruta; Production Manager, Jon Cranney; Lighting, Duane Schuler; Music Director-Conductor, Dick Whitbeck; Technical Directors, Terry Sateren, Bruce Margolis; Stage Managers, Robert Bye, Sharon Ewald, Michael S. Facius, Julie Haber, Bruce Margolis; Stage Managers, Robert Bye, Sharon Ewald, Michael S. Facius, Julie Haber, Mary Hunter, Paddy McEntee; Props, Michael Beery, Veda Hyde; Sound, Tom Bolstad; Wardrobe, Evelyn Bongard, Mary Jean Gauthier; Administrative Director, Donald Michaelis; Costumes, Jack Edwards, Lewis Brown, Jack Edwards, Annena Stubbs; Sets, Jack Barkla, John Conklin, John Ferguson, Ralph Funicello, Patrick Robertson; Directors, Michael Blakemore, Jon Cranney, Nick Havinga, Stephen Kanee, Michael Langham, Ken Ruta, Press, Cynthia Pierson

COMPANY

Don Amendolia, Peter Aylward, Fran Bennett, Robert Breuler, Barbara Bryne, Helen Burns, Cynthia Carle, Jeff Chandler, Oliver Cliff, Patricia Conolly, Sharon Ernster, Don R. Fallbeck, Patricia Fraser, Peter Michael Goetz, Mary Hara, James Hartman, James Hurdle, Roger Kozol, Matthew Kwiat, Karen Landry, Michael Laskin, Jack McLaughlin, James Noah, Holly Palance, Guy Paul, Fern Persons, Richard Russell Ramos, Barbara Reid, Ken Ruta, Frank S. Scott, Maura Shaffer, James Sweeney, Arnold Wilkerson

PRODUCTIONS

"She Stoops to Conquer," "A Moon for the Misbegotten," "La Ronde," "Catsplay," "The White Devil," "Design for Living," "A Christmas Carol," "Pantagleize"

SPECIAL EVENTS: Princess Grace in "Birds, Beasts and Flowers," and William Windom in "Thurber"

John Louis Anderson, Robert Ashley Wilson Photos

**Right Center: Oliver Cliff, Helen Burns
in "Catsplay" Above: Richard Russell Ramos,
Peter Michael Goetz, Sharon Ernster in "Moon for
the Misbegotten" Top: Jeff Chandler, Richard
Russell Ramos, Ken Ruta in "Design for Living"**

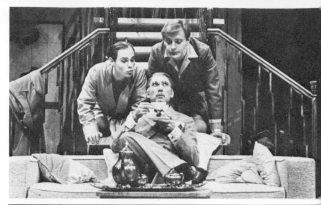

**Jeff Chandler, Helen Carey
in "La Ronde"**

**Richard Russell Ramos
in "Pantagleize"**

197

HARTFORD STAGE COMPANY

Hartford, Connecticut
October 14, 1977–June 18, 1978

Producing Director, Paul Weidner; Managing Director, William Stewart; Press, Dave Skal, Darlene Susco; Business Manager, Alan Toman; Technical Director, Randy Engels; Directors, Norman Ayrton, Edward Berkeley, Irene Lewis, Paul Weidner; Sets, John Conklin, James Guenther, Marjorie Kellogg, Hugh Landwehr; Costumes, Claire Ferraris, Linda Fisher, James Guenther, David Murin; Lighting, Beverly Emmons, Arden Fingerhut, Peter Hunt, Judy Rasmuson, Steve Woodring; Stage Managers, Fred Hoskins, Gary Lamagna

PRODUCTIONS AND CASTS

ALL THE WAY HOME by Tad Mosel: Joan Astley, Jack Alboukrek, Jacqueline Coslow, Wilhelmina Cox, Eric Foster, Alan Gifford, Brian Hartigan, Tana Hicken, Scott Lahman, David London, Ruth Maynard, Edwin J. McDonough, David O. Petersen, Daniel Shapiro, Anne Shropshire, Stephen Stout, Margaret Thomson, Robert Underwood, Teresa Wright

A FLEA IN HER EAR by Georges Feydeau: Jacqueline Coslow, Ted Graeber, Jeffrey Jones, Beth McDonald, Edwin J. McDonough, Richard Ooms, David O. Petersen, Jerry Reid, Theodore Sorel, Stephen Stout, Jill Tanner, Henry Thomas, Sigourney Weaver, Claudia Wilkens

PAST TENSE by Jack Zeman (*World Premiere*): Barbara Baxley, George Grizzard, Frank Rudnick, Robert Underwood

RAIN by John Colton and Clemence Randolph: Graham Beckel, Gertrude Blanks, Fred Burrell, Julia Curry, Jean DeBaer, Mark Dempsey, Paul Dion, Ted Graeber, I. M. Hobson, Ruby Holbrook, K. C. Kelly, Richard Mathews

HOLIDAY by Philip Barry: Linda Atkinson, George Bowe, Leah Chandler, Bob Dio, Joyce Fideor, Mark Fleischman, John Getz, Robin Haynes, Jill Larson, Ron Randell, Robbie Stevenson, Nicholas Wyman

THEY'D COME TO SEE CHARLIE by James Borrelli (*World Premiere*): Madison Arnold, Val Bisoglio, Peter Carew, Michael Dinelli, Joseph Mascolo, George Lee Miles, Gordon Oas-Heim, Tom Pedi, Peg Shirley, Ellis Williams

THE BLACK, THE BLUE AND THE GRAY by Irene Lewis and Edward Emmanuel: James Klawin, Tara Loewenstern, David McCarver, Thurman Scott, Francis X. Kuhn

THE OLD PLACE

Producing Director, Irene Lewis; Administrative Manager, Zeb Trachtenberg; Press, Marilyn Sponzo; Technical Directors, Jon King, Gayle Ruhlen; Directors, Mark Lamos, Irene Lewis; Sets, Hugh Landwehr; Costumes, Linda Fisher, Bob Wojewodski; Lighting, Spencer Mosse, Judy Rasmuson; Stage Manager, Dru Strange

EVE by Larry Fineberg (*American Premiere*); Director, Irene Lewis: John Carroll, Michael Galloway, Alexandra Johnson, Beverly May, Daniel Snyder, Joseph Sullivan

MACKEREL by Israel Horovitz; Director, Mark Lemos: Chris Ambrose, Jani Brenn, Cynthia Crumlish, Gerald Hiken, Janet Ward

Lanny Nagler Photos

George Grizzard, Barbara Baxley in "Past Tense" Top: Teresa Wright, David London in "All the Way Home"

Jeffrey Jones, Henry Thomas in "A Flea in Her Ear"

198

Joyce Fideor, Ron Randell, Linda Atkinson in "Holiday" Above: Joseph Mascolo, Michael Dinelli in "They'd Come to See Charlie"

Kate Mulgrew, Patrick Farrelly, Ron O'Neal
in "Othello" Right: David Snell, Giulia
Pagano in "Animal Kingdom" Below: Emily
Hacker, Karen Ludwig in "Miracle Worker"

Top Right: Peter Coffield, Swoosie Kurtz
in "The Middle Ages"

HARTMAN THEATRE COMPANY

Stamford, Connecticut
October 26, 1977–April 23, 1978
Third Season

Producing Directors, Margot and Del Tenney; Managing Director, Roger Meeker; Press, Deborah Weiner; General Manager, Jacqueline Frankel; Production Manager, J. D. Ferrara; Stage Manager, Joseph Kavanagh; Directors, Del Tenney, Tony Giordano, Melvin Bernhardt, Robert W. Smith, John Going, William E. Hunt; Designers, Roger Meeker, June Stearns, Richard Butler, J. D. Ferrara, Gerda Proctor, John Lee Beatty, Dennis Parichy, Zack Brown, Annette Beck, Linda Fisher, Jeffrey Schissler, Hugh Landwehr, Ruth A. Wells.

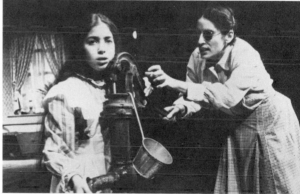

PRODUCTIONS AND CASTS

THE MOUSETRAP: Joanne Gibson, Stephen Temperley, Frederic Sperberg, Sally Chamberlin, John Wardwell, Margot Tenney, George Morfogen, Tom Mason

THE MIRACLE WORKER: Bob Horen, Patricia O'Connell, Patrick Farrelly, Emily Hacker, Trina Patterson, Casey Patterson, Sally Chamberlin, Frederic Sperberg, Karen Ludwig, Deloris Gaskins, Priscilla Cohen

THE MIDDLE AGES by A. R. Gurney, Jr. (*World Premiere*, Jan. 5, 1978); Director, Melvin Bernhardt; Peter Coffield, Patricia O'Connell, Swoosie Kurtz, Douglass Watson

OTHELLO: Ivar Brogger, David Canary, Carl Low, Ron O'Neal, John Blazo, Jr., Charles Berendt, Kate Mulgrew, Daniel P. Hannafin, Madelyn O'Neil, Paul Craggs, Margot Tenney, Stephanie Cotsirilos, Patrick Farrelly, Bob Horen, Mark Bell, Karl Blankenberg, Karen Fisher, J. J. Jefferson, Tom Kremer, Keith Luger, Lewis Popelowsky, William Sandwick

THE ANIMAL KINGDOM: Patrick Farrelly, Carl Low, Laurie Kennedy, Daniel P. Hannafin, David Snell, Ivar Brogger, Stephanie Cotsirilos, Giulia Pagano, Margot Tenney

JEROME KERN AT THE HARTMAN (*World Premiere*): David-James Carroll, Mercedes Ellington, Jeanne Lehman, James J. Mellon, Joyce Nolen, Michael Radigan, Jonathan Sprague, Sally Ann Swarm

Gerry Goodstein Photos

Jeanne Lehman, David-James Carroll
in "Jerome Kern at the Hartman" 199

**Benjamin Hendrickson, Margaret Phillips in
"The Sea Gull" Left: Beverly May, Jon DeVries in
"Birthday Party" Top: Gun-Marie Nilsson, Beth
Collins, Mercedes Ruehl in "Vanities"**

INDIANA REPERTORY THEATRE

Indianapolis, Indiana
October 21, 1977–April 9, 1978
Producing Director, Benjamin Mordecai; Artistic Director, Edward Stern; Business Manager, Stewart E. Slater; Press, Ed Cimbala; Production Manager, Chris Armen; Stage Managers, Joel Grynheim, James K. Tinsley; Technical Director, David L. Ramsey; Directors, William Guild, Thomas Gruenwald, Richard Harden, Charles Kerr, Edward Stern; Settings, Thomas Beall, Ursula Belden, John Doepp, Eric Head, Marjorie Kellogg, Van Phillips, David Potts; Costumes, Elizabeth Covey, Arnold S. Levine, Susan Tsu; Lights, Geoffrey T. Cunningham, Jeff Davis, John Doepp, Arden Fingerhut, Paul Gallo, Gersh, John Marriner, Lee Watson

PRODUCTIONS AND CASTS

THE PHILADELPHIA STORY by Philip Barry: James Beard, Wanda Bimson, Stephen C. Bradbury, Bruce Gray, Munson Hicks, Bernard Kates, Priscilla Lindsay, Beverly May, Thomas Stechschulte, Peter Thoemke

THE BIRTHDAY PARTY by Harold Pinter: Valery Daemke, Jon DeVries, Alfred Hinckley, Bernard Kates, Beverly May, Robert Stattel

THE COUNTRY GIRL by Clifford Odets: Ray Hill, Bernard Kates, John Lagioia, Charles Noel, Timothy Omen, Peter Thoemke, Christina Whitmore, Sara Woods

VANITIES by Jack Heifner: Beth Collins, Gun-Marie Nilsson, Mercedes Ruehl

THE SEA GULL by Anton Chekhov; Translated by Jean-Claude Van Itallie: Eunice Anderson, Wanda Bimson, Thomas Carson, Bruce Colville, David Gale, Gary Garth, Allison Giglio, Benjamin Hendrickson, Bernard Kates, Margaret Phillips, Peter Thoemke, Joseph Warren

HOW THE OTHER HALF LOVES by Alan Ayckbourn: Barbara Berge, John Bergstrom, Gary Garth, Allison Giglio, Bernard Kates, Sara Woods

TO KILL A MOCKINGBIRD (a narrative dramatization of Harper Lee's novel): Mark Buchan, Steve Cole, Gary L. Easterling, William Meisle, Alexandra O'Karma, Loren Reyher, Matthew Roberts, Peter Thoemke, Susan Yusen

Photos by Chilluffo

**William Meisle, Susan Yusen in "To Kill a
Mockingbird" Above: Allison Giglio
in "How the Other Half Loves"**

LONG WHARF THEATRE
New Haven, Connecticut
October 13, 1977–June 18, 1978
Thirteenth Season

Artistic Director, Arvin Brown; Executive Director, M. Edgar Rosenblum; Literary Manager, John Tillinger; Press, Rosalind Heinz; Directors, Arvin Brown, Davey Marlin-Jones, Kenneth Frankel, Edward Payson Call, Edward Gilbert, Patrick Adiarte; Sets, David Jenkins, John Conklin, Marjorie Kellogg, John Jensen, Mark Louis Negin, Steven Rubin, Joe Erdey; Costumes, Bill Walker, John Conklin, Linda Fisher; Lighting, Jamie Gallagher, Ronald Wallace, Joe Erdey; Stage Managers, Anne Keefe, James Harker, Jonathan Penzner, Franklin Keysar.

PRODUCTIONS AND CASTS

HOBSON'S CHOICE by Harold Brighouse: Richard Backus, Emery Battis, Frank Converse, Joyce Ebert, Mary Fogarty, Harry Groenier, Laurie Kennedy, Richard Mathews, Philip Polito, Ellin Ruskin, Susan Sharkey, William Swetland

THE LUNCH GIRLS by Leigh Curran (*World Premiere* Nov. 17, 1977): Carol Androsky, Octavio Ciano, Leigh Curran, Suzanne Lederer, Stephen D. Newman, Pamela Payton-Wright, Philip Polito, Susan Sharkey, Phyllis Somerville, Carol Williard

THE RECRUITING OFFICER by George Farquhar: Bob Ari, Emery Battis, Elaine Bromka, Helena Carroll, Clarence Felder, Harry Groenier, John Horton, Linda Hunt, Neil Hunt, Francesca James, Richard Mathews, Katherine McGrath, William Swetland, John Tillinger, Nicholas Woodeson, Max Wright

SPOKESONG by Stewart Parker (*American Premiere*, Feb. 2, 1978): John Horton, John Lithgow, Joseph Maher, Josef Sommer, Maria Tucci, Virginia Vestoff

S. S. GLENCAIRN by Eugene O'Neill: Victor Argo, Emery Battis, Beeson, Carroll, Nora Chester, David Clennon, Frederick Coffin, Lance Davis, le Clanche du Rand, Bob Harper, Owen Hollander, Peter Iacangelo, Richard Jamieson, Robert Lansing, Carol Jean Lewis, Marlena Lustik, Edwin J. McDonough, William Newman, C. C. H. Pounder, William Swetland

THE PHILADELPHIA STORY by Philip Barry: James Bigwood, Emery Battis, Alice Brereton, Blair Brown, Frank Converse, Barbara eda-Young, Jennie Harker, George Hearn, Skip Hinnant, Peter C. Johnson, Jan Miner, Douglas Stender, William Swetland

MACBETH by William Shakespeare: Emery Battis, Graham Beckel, Myra Carter, Charles Cioffi, Joyce Ebert, Julie Follansbee, Erik Fredricksen, Michael Govan, Ernest Graves, Kenneth Gray, Donna Haley, Richard Jamieson, Peter C. Johnson, Christopher Loomis, Cynthia Mason, Richard Mathews, Michael J. Miller, Dana Mills, William Newman, Steven Ryan, Michael Shannon, Mark Soper, Adrian Sparks, William Swetland, George Taylor

TWO BROTHERS by Conrad Bromberg (*World Premiere*, March 3, 1978): Joyce Ebert, Barbara eda-Young, Anna Levine, Beverly May, Tony Musante, James Noble, David Spielberg, John Tillinger, Patricia Triana

STARTING HERE, STARTING NOW with Lyrics by Richard Maltby, Jr., and Music by David Shire: Annie McGreevey, Eron Tabor, Laura Waterbury

William B. Carter, William L. Smith Photos

Right Center: John Lithgow, Virginia Vestoff in "Spokesong" Above: Suzanne Lederer, Stephen D. Newman in "The Lunch Girls" Top: Beeson Carroll, Robert Lansing in "S.S. Glencairn"

David Spielberg, Tony Musante in "Two Brothers"

201

LORETTO-HILTON REPERTORY THEATRE

St. Louis, Missouri
October 12, 1977–April 23, 1978

Producing Director, David Frank; Consulting Director, Davey Marlin-Jones; Associate Producer, Michael P. Pitek III; Assistant to Producers-Company Manager, Joyce Volker; Sets, Grady Larkins, Heidi Landesman, John Kavelin, John Conant; Costumes, John Carver Sullivan, Carr Garnett, Catherine Reich; Stage Managers, Glenn Dunn, Margaret Stuart-Ramsey, Jim R. Sprague; Technical Director-Production Coordinator, John Conant; Stage Directors, Davey Marlin-Jones, David Frank, Norman Gevanthor, Carl Schurr, Geoffrey Sherman; Lighting, Glenn Dunn, Peter E. Sargent, David Hitzert; Sound, Robert D. Wotawa; Press, Noeli Lytton

COMPANY

Brendan Burke, Peter Beiger, Alan Clarey, Jonathan Daly, Robert Darnell, Stephen Henderson, Keith Jochim, Joneal Joplin, Wil Love, J. Patrick Martin, Eric Singerman, Robert Spencer, Addie Walsh, Susan Malon Wall
GUEST ARTISTS: Patricia Ball, Clyde Burton, Joan Matthiessen, Jim R. Sprague, Mickey Hartnett, Patricia Kilgarriff, Dana Mills, Cara Duff-MacCormick, David Faulkner, Mary Fogarty, Linda Kampley, Kathleen Corny, Helen Hedman, Karen Looze, Michael McCarty, Karen McLaughlin, Marilyn Redfield, Steven Gilborn, Michael Thompson, Stephanie Lewis

PRODUCTIONS

"Macbeth," "Lu Ann Hampton Laverty Oberlander," "The Devil's Disciple," "The Runner Stumbles," "Canterbury Tales," "Ashes"

Michael Eastman Photos

Left: Mickey Hartnett in "Lu Ann Hampton Laverty Oberlander" Top: Cara Duff-MacCormick, Dana Mills in "The Devil's Disciple" Right Center: Cara Duff-MacCormick, David Faulkner in "The Runner Stumbles"

**Robert Darnell
as Macbeth**

**Robert Spencer, Kathleen Conry, Martha
Horstman in "Canterbury Tales"**

MANITOBA THEATRE CENTRE

Winnipeg, Canada
October 7, 1977–May 13, 1978

Artistic Director, Arif Hasnain; General Manager, Gregory Poggi; Press, Sarah Yates, Max Tapper; Production Manager, Dwight Griffin; Technical Director, Neil McLeod; Stage Directors, Timothy Bond, Alex Dmitriev, Edward Gilbert, Arif Hasnain, Irene Hogan, Stephen Katz, George Keathley, Kurt Reis, Gregory Tuck; Sets and Costumes, James Bakkom, Charles Dunlop, Michael Eagan, Debra Hanson, Mark Negin, Peter Wingate; Lighting, Donald Acaster, Joan Arhelger, Gilbert V. Hemsley, Edsel Hilchie, Neil McLeod, Monty Schneider, Bill Williams

PRODUCTIONS AND CASTS

THE LAST CHALICE by Joanna M. Glass (*World Premiere*): Frank Aldous, Robert S. Buck, Tom Celli, David Clement, John Gardiner, Patricia Hamilton, Adam Henderson, Irene Hogan, Roland Hewgill, Tim Whelan, Philippa King, George Sperdakos

HELLO AND GOODBYE by Athol Fugard: Peter Jobin, Toby Tarnow

KNOCK KNOCK by Jules Feiffer: Hy Anzell, Richard Blair, Harriet Hall, Bernie Passeltiner

OH COWARD by Noel Coward: David Brown, Paul Craig, Pat Galloway

SNOW WHITE AND THE SEVEN DWARFS by Clive Endersby: Pat Armstrong, Jay Brazeau, Paul Brown, Alexe Duncan, David Gillies, Jill Harris, Stan Lesk, Sam Moses, Candace O'Connor, Duncan Regehr, Patrusha Sarakula

THE CONTRACTOR by David Storey: Ian D. Clark, Tom Patrick Dineen, Terence Durrant, Alan Gifford, Dorothy D'Arcy Goldrick, Robert Haley, Louisa Martin, Margaret Martin, Tony Parr, Patrick Sinclair, Cedric Smith, Gordon Stokoe

THEATRE BEYOND WORDS: Paulette Hallich, Terry Judd, Larry Lefebvre, Harro Maskow, Robin Patterson

THE SEA HORSE by Edward J. Moore: Robert Haley, Kathleen Perkins

THE NIGHT OF THE IGUANA by Tennessee Williams: Anna Friedman, Alan Gifford, Patricia Hamilton, Arnie Hardt, Terry Harford, Araby Lockhart, John McEnery, Heather Summerhayes, Carol Teitel, Wanda Wilkinson

MEASURE FOR MEASURE by William Shakespeare: Bob Aarron, James Blendick, Jay Brazeau, Andy Carter, Dougal Clark, Brenda Curtis, Alexe Duncan, Peter Dvorsky, Alan Gifford, Lizz Graham, Adam Henderson, Mary Hitch, Kirk Inman, Nancy Kerr, Robin Marshall, Water Massey, Tom McBeath, Glen McCabe, John Peters, Booth Savage, Aaron Schwartz, Kerry Shale, Vandy Simpson, Neil Vipond

ASHES by David Rudkin: Leslie Carlson, Dorothy-Ann Haug, Wayne Robson, Dixie Seatle

THE ROYAL HUNT OF THE SUN by Peter Shaffer: Bob Aaron, Frank J. Adamson, Claude Bede, James Blendick, Peter Brockington, Remo Capone, William Dunlop, Alan Gifford, Janet-Laine Green, Adam Henderson, Richard Hilger, Kirk Inman, Peter Jobin, Colleen Letourneau, Dan MacDonald, Robin Marshall, Tom McBeath, John Peters, Claude Rae, Booth Savage, Robert Seale, Kerry Shale, Sean Sullivan, Tim Whelan

Daniel Teichman Photos

Right Center: John McEnery, Carol Teitel in "Night of the Iguana"

Brenda Curtis, Neil Vipond in "Measure for Measure" 203

MARRIOTT'S LINCOLNSHIRE THEATRE

Lincolnshire, Illinois
June 22, 1977–May 28, 1978

Producer, Richard S. Kordos; Press, John DeFrancisco, Gary Goodfriend; Stage Manager, Paul Ferris; Technical Director, Pat Nesladek; Costumes, Susan Clare; Props, Barbara Harris, Terry Jenkins; Technical Assistants, Lou Decrenscenzo, Donna Gavin, Laurie Manners, Rich Roeder, Tony Vaillancourt; Hairstylist, Bonnie Andrews; Directors, Dominic Missimi, Gene Patrick, Richard S. Kordos, Tony Mockus; Sets, Jeffrey Harris, George Pettit; Costumes Nancy Missimi, Pat Campano; Choreographer, Jim Bates

PRODUCTIONS AND CASTS

BLITHE SPIRIT by Noel Coward: Barbara Eden, Jo Morrison, Art Kassul, Roger Mueller, Susan Dafoe, Concetta Tomei, Jane MacIver

SCAPINO! by Frank Dunlop and Jim Dale from Moliere: Rita Moreno, Chris Anderson, Art Kassul, Steve Fletcher, Gary Prendergast, Kenneth Wilson-Blasor, Robert Strom, Angelina Reaux, Timothy Jenkins, Denise Blasor-Wilson, Michael Jon Sims, Tom Aulino, Norm Tobin

THE MUSIC MAN by Meredith Willson: Bobby Van, Susan Gordon-Clark, Anne Edwards, Bob Ackerman, Janet Lauer, Bruce Senesac, Gay Tonelli Woertz, Steven Vujovic, John Salewski, Laurence Russo, Barbara Moroz, Maurya Miller, Ed Krieger, Timothy Jenkins, George Gilbert, Mary Cobb, Susie Fenner, Patrick Hilsabeck, Nancy Ann Lewandowski, Suzanne Samorez, Scott Silver

6 RMS RIV VU by Bob Randall: Sheree North, Ron Parady, Barbara Kern, Roger Mueller, Patti Wilkus, Nathan Davis, Carole Lockwood, Robert Scogin

READY WHEN YOU ARE, C. B.! by Susan Slade: Susan Saint-James, James C. Hamilton, Marji Bank, Diane Ciesla, Concetta Tomei

TWIGS by George Furth: Cloris Leachman, Jack Callan, Tony Mockus, Charles Noel, Ward Ohrman, Frank Smith, George Womack, Weldon Bleiler

Joseph Jedd Photos

Right Center: Tony Mockus, Cloris Leachman, Charles Noel in "Twigs" Above: Concetta Tomei, Roger Mueller, Barbara Eden, Jane MacIver, Susan Dafoe in "Blithe Spirit" Top: Sheree North, Nathan Davis, Patti Wilkus, Ron Parady in "6 Rms Riv Vu"

Rita Moreno, Norm Tobin in "Scapino!"

Susan Gordon-Clark, Bobby Van in "The Music Man"

Tovah Feldshuh, Peggy Cass in "The Torch-Bearers" Right: James Noble, Karl Light, Carolyn Coates, Diana Crane in "Long Christmas Dinner" Top: Catherine Byers, David Selby, Stanja Lowe in "Toys in the Attic"

McCARTER THEATRE COMPANY

Princeton, N.J.
October 4, 1977–April 16, 1978

Producing Director, Michael Kahn; General Manager, Edward A. Martenson; Press, Michalann Hobson; Production Manager, Mark S. Krause; Directors, Nagle Jackson, Kenneth Frankel, Michael Kahn, Pat Hingle, William Woodman; Sets, Herbert Senn, Helen Pond, Christopher Nowak, Ed Wittstein, Raymond Recht, Howard Bay, Marjorie Kellogg; Costumes, Jane Greenwood, Bob Wojewodski, Virgil C. Johnson, David Graden, Jennifer von Mayrhauser; Lighting, Marc B. Weiss, Howard Bay, Richard Nelson, John McLain; Stage Managers, Audrey Frankowski, Suzanne Egan, Mark R. Paquette, Arthur Karp, Elizabeth Caldwell; Choreography, Elizabeth Keen, Michael Maurer

PRODUCTIONS AND CASTS

THREE BY THORNTON WILDER: Pamela Christian, Carolyn Coates, Diana Crane, Alice Drummond, Diane Franklin, Chris Hagen, Georgine Hall, Nicholas Kepros, Karl Light, James Noble, George Oliva, Joan Pape, Ricky Paul, Jobeth Williams

THE TORCH-BEARERS by George Kelly: Peggy Cass, Tovah Feldshuh, Farley Granger, Dina Merrill, Martha Greenhouse, Woody Eney, Betty Henritze, Lawrence Holofcener, J. Frank Lucas, Brad O'Hare, Claudette Sutherland, Ralph Williams

MUCH ADO ABOUT NOTHING by William Shakespeare: Eugene J. Anthony, Donald Brearley, Richard Clarke, Michael-Eliot Cooke, Roger DeKoven, Laura Esterman, Merwin Goldsmith, Michael Houlihan, Judith Ivey, Dennis Kennedy, Linda Kimbrough, Matthew Kimbrough, Tony Lincoln, Heather MacDonald, Kenneth Marshall, Timothy Oma, William Roerick, Marshall Shnider, Norman Snow, Nicolas Surovy, Gerald Walsh

THE CONFIRMATION by Howard Ashman (*Premiere*); Director, Kenneth Frankel: Herschel Bernardi, Marilyn Chris, Robert Tiesel, Minnie Gentry, Tara King, Alan Manson, Mara Mellin, Phillip Lindsay, Rosanna Carter

THE UTTER GLORY OF MORRISSEY HALL by Clark Gesner (*Premiere*); Director, Nagle Jackson: Patricia Falkenhain, Jane Rose, Daniel Arden, Gary Beach, Betsey Beard, Mary Carney, Marilyn Caskey, Lois Dawn Jeffory, Jeffrey Jones, Anne Kaye, Kate Kelly, Daniel Keyes, Alice Nagel, Cynthia Parva, Polly Pen, Jill P. Rose, Lauren Shub, Kathleen Swan, Diane Tarleton, Katherine Wolf

Cliff Moore Photos

Right Center: Herschel Bernardi, Marilyn Chris in "The Confirmation"

Catherine Wolf (R) in "The Utter Glory of Morrissey Hall"

205

Edgar Meyer, Stephen G. Arlen, Thom Bray
in "The Male Animal" Left: Marion Brasch,
Eric Tavaris, Mary Gallagher in "Table
Manners" Top: Jeffrey McLaughlin, Cheryl
Giannini, William LeMassena in "The Runner
Stumbles"

MEADOW BROOK THEATRE
Rochester, Michigan
September 19, 1977–May 21, 1978

Artistic and General Director, Terence Kilburn; Assistant to Director, Frank Bollinger; Directors, Terence Kilburn, Charles Nolte, John Ulmer, John Sharpe; Choreographer, John Sharpe; Sets, Peter Hicks, Don Beckman, Larry Reed, Lance Brockman, Douglas Wright; Costumes, Mary L. Bonnell, Christa Gievers; Lighting, Nancy Thompson, Fred Fonner, Larry Reed, Jean Montgomery; Stage Managers, Peter W. Hicks, Alice Galloway, Michael Shann, Douglas A. Wright; Wardrobe, Sue Ann Carbary; Props, Carolyn Hull

PRODUCTIONS AND CASTS

SHE STOOPS TO CONQUER: Jeanne Arnold, Dan C. Bar, Stephen Daley, Larry Gates, Patricia Reilly, Elizabeth Horowitz, Lynn Ann Leveridge, Richard Pilcher, Tom Spackman, Eric Tavaris, Eric Tull, Lori Altadonna, David Parker

PICNIC: Jeanne Arnold, Stephen Daley, Mary Benson, Jane Badler, Michel Cullen, Bella Jarrett, Melanie Resnick, Tom Spackman, Eric Tull, Patricia Reilly, Henrietta Kryskalla

TABLE MANNERS: Marion Brasch, Michel Cullen, Mary Gallagher, Peter McRobbie, Barbara Sohmers, Eric Tavaris

THE CORN IS GREEN: Michel Cullen, Peter McRobbie, Curtis Armstrong, Jeanne Arnold, Mary Benson, Leo Leyden, Marianne Muellerleile, Patricia Reilly, Michael Rothhaar, Tom Spackman, Steven Lutes, Rob Jones, Lori Altadonna, Leslie Bonnell, Pamela Bonnell, Wendy Bonnell

THE TEMPEST: Michel Cullen, Peter McRobbie, Curtis Armstrong, Mary Benson, Marianne Muellerleile, Michael Rothhaar, Tom Spackman, Thom Bray, Gilbert Cole, Louis Edmonds, Michael Hendricks, William LeMassena, Richard Hilger, Ginni Ness, G. Wood, Lori Altadonna, Jill Johnson, Steven Lutes, Rob Jones, Beth Taylor

THE RUNNER STUMBLES: Michel Cullen, Charlotte Bova, Cheryl Giannini, Jeffrey McLaughlin, Peter McRobbie, Marianne Muellerleile, William LeMassena, Patricia Reilly, Michael Rothhaar

THE MALE ANIMAL: Stephen G. Arlen, Thom Bray, William LeMassena, Louise Martin, Edgar Meyer, Priscilla Morrill, Patricia Reilly, Harold Roe, Tom Spackman, Marianne Muellerleile, Rachel Stephens, Margaret Christopher, Steven Lutes, Mary Pat Gleason, Michael Rothhaar

COLE: Marianne Challis, Connie Coit, Nancy Grahn, Henry J. Jordan, Michele Mullen, Frank Root, Richard Walker, Kevin Wilson

Dick Hunt Photos

**Tom Spackman, Jeanne Arnold
in "The Corn Is Green"**

Left Center: "Picnic"

MILWAUKEE REPERTORY THEATER

Milwaukee, Wisconsin
September 16, 1977–May 28, 1978

Artistic Director, John Dillon; Managing Director, Sara O'Connor; Business Manager, Peggy Rose; Press, Richard Bryant; Playwrights, Frank Cucci, Amlin Gray, Robert Ingham; Directors, Irene Lewis, Norman L. Berman, Sanford Robbins, Jewel Walker, Kenneth Frankel, Barry Boys, Sharon Ott; Sets, David Chapman, Fred Kolouch, R. H. Graham, Christopher M. Idoine, Valerie Kuehn, Grady Larkins, Elizabeth Mahrt, Joseph Tilford, Stuart Wurtzel; Lighting, Arden Fingerhut, R. H. Graham, Dennis McHugh, Spencer Mosse, Gregory Murphy, Joseph Tilford, Richard Winkler; Costumes, Rosemary Ingham, Marc Longlois, Barbara Murray, Carol Odita, Susan Tsu, Randy Barcelo, Elizabeth Covey; Fight Choreography, Michael Tezla; Conductors-Composers, Edmund Assaly, Mark van Hecke; Stage Managers, Rod Pilloud, Bennett Taber, Jim Riggs, Michael Tezla, E. A. Mathews

COMPANY

Eugene J. Anthony, Tom Blair, Barry Boys, Jacqueline Britton, Robert Burr, Faith Catlin, Vicki Childers, Peggy Cowles, Richard Cox, Regina David, Montgomery Davis, Rosemary De Angelis, Joyce Fideor, Ronald Frazier, Cara Gargano, Amlin Gray, Anthony Heald, Geraldine Kay, Dennis Kennedy, Lynn Mansbach, Susan Monts, John Mansfield, Durward McDonald, Daniel Mooney, Carol Morley, Jody Lee Olhava, James Pickering, Rose Pickering, Penelope Reed, Marta Rose, Ruth Schudson, Arlene Schulfer, Larry Shue, Gary Smiley, Bruce Somerville, Henry Strozier, Kristie Thatcher, Daniel Therriault, Michael Thompson, Sirin Devrim Trainer, A. C. Weary, Steven Williams

PRODUCTIONS

"Richard III," "Ah, Wilderness!," "Long Day's Journey into Night," "A Christmas Carol," "Custer," "Medal of Honor Rag," *American Premieres* of "Friends," "Just a Little Bit Less Than Normal," *World Premieres* of "The Portable Play," "High Time," "Namesake"

Mark Avery Photos

(Captions not submitted)

207

Barry Boys
in "The Morning Star"

MISSOURI REPERTORY THEATRE

Kansas City, Missouri
July 7, 1977–February 26, 1978

Producing Director, Patricia McIlrath; Press, David Stuart Hudson; Directors, Cyril Ritchard, James Assad, Harold Scott, John Reich, Francis J. Cullinan, Robert L. Smith; Sets, James Leonard Joy, John Ezell, Frederic James, Max Beatty, Baker S. Smith, Jack Montgomery; Costumes, Vincent Scassellati, Barbara Medlicott, Judith Dolan; Lighting, Joseph Appelt, Curt Ostermann, James Shehan, Michael Scott; Sound, Susan Selvey, Michael Schweppe, Douglas K. Faerber; Technical Director, Robert Scales; Stage Managers, Joseph DePauw, Joyce McBroom, James T. McDermott

COMPANY

James Armstrong, Walter Atamaniuk, Danie Barnett, Donna Lee Bolin, Barry Boys, Susie Bradley, Jackie Burroughs, Kevin Cloepfil, George Comiskey, William Cook, John Cothran, Ellen Crawford, Margaret Davis, Steve Doolittle, Barbara Edelman, Robert Elliott, June Finnell, Michael Genovese, Lorraine Gerrish, Buckner Gibbs, Nina Giliberto, Judy Goldman, Jolene Hainkel, Patton Hasegawa, Margaret Heffernan, Lisa Heffley, John Houston, Robin Humphrey, Harriet Levitt, Sally Longan, John Maddison, Laurie Maher, Vickie Marlatt, Steve Meyer, Kevin Mills, Mary Kay Moran, Eden Lee Murray, Rolla Nuckles, Lorca Peress, Madelyn Porter, Kathy Price, Juliet Randall, Jackie Riggs, Rita Rozran, Marci Sambol, Val Scassellati, Carl Schurr, Susan Selvey, David Stenstrom, Cheryl Strauss, Michael Tylo, Morton Walker, Von Washington, Alice White, Alfreda Williams, Kristin Williams, John Winfield

PRODUCTIONS

"The Misanthrope," "Old Times," "Mary Stuart," "The Hostage," "Purlie Victorious," "The Imaginary Invalid," "All My Sons," *World Premiere* of "The Morning Star"

Eden Lee Murray, Jackie Burroughs,
John Maddison, Steve Meyer in "The Hostage"

Mike Genovese, Richard C. Brown
in "The Imaginary Invalid"

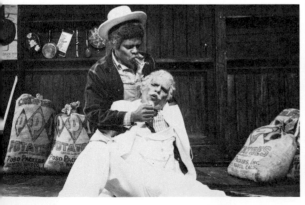

Von Washington, Robert Elliott
in "Purlie Victorious"

Juliet Randall, Barry Boys, Michael
Tylo, Robert Elliott in "The Misanthrope"

208

PAF PLAYHOUSE

Huntington Station, N.Y.
October 7, 1977–June 10, 1978

The Performing Arts Foundation of Long Island; Producer, Jay Broad, General Manager, Joel Warren, Business Manager, Michael Maso; Press, Richard Frankel, Susan Dember; Production Manager, Eugene Blythe; Technical Director, Steven Greer; Stage Managers, Jody Boese, David R. Schieve; Sets, David Chapman, Eldon Elder, Herbert Senn, Helen Pond, John Arnone, William Ivey Long, Marc B. Weiss; Costumes, David Toser, William Ivey Long, Laura Crow, Susan Hum Buck, Carol Oditz; Lighting, Richard Harden, Eldon Elder, Mitchell Dana, Marc B. Weiss, David F. Segal

PRODUCTIONS AND CASTS

EVENTS FROM THE LIFE OF TED SNYDER by Jay Broad; Director, Mr. Broad (*World Premiere*, Oct. 7, 1977): Robert Bella, Victoria Boothby, Clement Fowler, Pirie MacDonald, Stephen Stendera, Donald Casey, Pierre Epstein, Michael Hendricks, Gordon Oas-Heim, Judith Tillman

GIVE MY REGARDS TO BROADWAY by Dennis Turner (*World Premiere*, Nov. 18, 1977); Director, Anthony Stimac: Brian Brownlee, Jay Garner, David Christmas, Annie Kravat, Joseph Warren

DOWN AT THE OLD BULL AND BUSH by Dolores Sutton and Roderick Cook (*World Premiere*, Dec. 30, 1977); Director, Roderick Cook: Charlotte Fairchild, George Hall, Buck Hobbs, George S. Irving, Maria Karnilova, Patti Perkins, John Sloman

THE KILLING OF YABLONSKI by Richard Nelson (*World Premiere*, Feb. 10, 1978); Director, Peter Mark Shifter: Richard Bey, Deborah Mayo, Michael Miller, Elizabeth Parrish, Jon Polito, Jack Ramage, Joe Ragalbuto

HANCOCK'S LAST HALF HOUR by Heathcote Williams (*American Premiere*, Mar. 24, 1978); Director, Jay Broad: Jon Polito, James Cahill

JUNO'S SWANS by Elaine Kerr (*World Premiere*, May 5, 1978); Director, Michael Flanagan: Clement Fowler, Elaine Kerr, Tom Mason, Anna Shaler

Gerry Goodstein Photos

Jay Garner, Brian Brownlee, Annie Kravat in "Give My Regards to Broadway" Top: Elaine Kerr, Tom Mason in "Juno's Swans" Left: Jon Polito in "Hancock's Last Half Hour" Below: Elizabeth Parrish, Richard Bey, Jack Ramage, Deborah Mayo in "The Killing of Yablonski"

**James Cahill
in "The Gold Standard"**

Cameron Smith, Christopher Mynio
in "Pippin"

Geraldine Page
in "The Little Foxes"

PAPER MILL PLAYHOUSE

Millburn, N.J.
September 14, 1977–June 25, 1978

Executive Producer, Angelo Del Rossi; General Manager, Wade Miller; Press, Albertina Reilly, J. M. Gessner; Stage Managers, James Stefanile, Gregory Nicholas; Sets, Douglas W. Schmidt, Helen Pond, Herbert Senn, Clarke Dunham, Tony Walton; Costumes, Carrie F. Robbins, Anne Bass North, Vida Thomas, Bernard Johnson; Lighting, Helen Pond, Herbert Senn

PRODUCTIONS AND CASTS

GREASE by Jim Jacobs, Warren Casey; Director, Tom Moore: Imogene Bliss, Patricia Douglas, Duffi, Gail Edwards, Peter Gallagher, Mary Garripoli, Stephen M. Groff, Bernardo Hiller, Linda Lyons, Ann-Ngaire Martin, Nita Novy, Randy Powell, James Remar, Michael Riney, Dan Woodard, Steve Yudson

SHENANDOAH by James Lee Barrett, Peter Udell, Philip Rose, Gary Geld; Director, Philip Rose: Ed Ames, Christine Ebersole, Deborah Combs, Bill DeWitt, David Eric, Jay Bursky, Christopher Blount, Tim Waldrip, Robert Rosen, Steve Scott, Philip Casnoff, Peter Bosche, David Young, Timothy C. Wallace, John R. Briggs, Rex D. Hays, John Ganzer, Gene Masoner, Mark S. Zimmerman, Scott Bakula, Michael Calkins

FALLEN ANGELS by Noel Coward; Director, Philip Minor: Sandy Dennis, Jean Marsh, Gene Rupert, Robert Moberly, Stephen G. Arlen, Peggy Cosgrave

THE LITTLE FOXES by Lillian Hellman; Director, Philip Minor: Geraldine Page, Sandy Dennis, Rip Torn, Scott McKay, David Brooks, Amy Wright, Terry Layman, Douglas Stark, Beatrice Winde, Jim Mallette

BUBBLING BROWN SUGAR by Loften Mitchell; Director, Robert M. Cooper: Cab Calloway, Marilyn Johnson, Ursuline Kairson, David Bryant, Chip Garnett, Terry Burrell, Richard Casper, Ann Duquesnay, Mimi Moyer, Ronald "Smokey" Stevens, Lonnie McNeil, Lydia Abarca, Marcus B. F. Brown, Alton Lathrop, Edwetta Little, Rosemary Thompson, Linda Young, Ralph Bruneau, Leslie Dockery, Stanley Ramsey

PIPPIN by Roger O. Hirson, Stephen Schwartz; Director, Gene Foote: Northern J. Calloway, Cameron Smith, Joy Franz, Ted Thurston, Fay Sappington, Isabelle Farrell, Guy Allen, Sally Benoit, Terry Calloway, Kaylyn Dillehay, Laurent Giroux, Christopher Mynio, Deborah L. Phelan, Rick Schneider, Paul Solen, Karen Sutherland, Jeff Veazey

Terence Gili. Harold Brown Photos

Marilyn Johnson, Cab Calloway
in "Bubbling Brown Sugar"
Above: Ed Ames in "Shenandoah"

THE PHILADELPHIA COMPANY

Philadelphia, Pennsylvania
January 19–April 30, 1978

Artistic Director, Robert Hedley; Producing Director, Jean Harrison; Director, Dominic Garvey; Press, Karen Butler; Costumes, Gerry Woodard; Lighting, David Finck; Choreographer, Darrah Gustafson

PRODUCTIONS AND CASTS

THE TRANSFIGURATION OF BENNO BLIMPIE by Albert Innaurato: Brian Morgan, Carla Belver, Armando Matarazzo, Louis Lippa, Olivia Negron

THE FINAL CONCERT TOUR OF MICKEY COLOSSUS by Peter Mattaliano, Steve Jankowski: Jacqueline D. Boddie, Mary Lou DiFilippo, Liz Keller, Richard Lawson, Michael John Masiko, Rosemary McMenamin, Helen A. Morrison, Bella Weil

Top Right: Micheal J. Masiko in "The Final Concert Tour of Mickey Colossus and the Merchant of Death" *(J. C. Burke Photo)*

PHILADELPHIA DRAMA GUILD

Philadelphia, Pennsylvania
November 2, 1977–March 19, 1978

Artistic Director, Douglas Seale; Managing Director, James F. Freydberg; Chairman of the Board, Elkins Wetherill; Press, Kirby F. Smith; Artistic/Administrative Coordinator, Lillian Steinberg; Sets, John Kasarda; Costumes, Kristina Watson, David Murin; Lighting, Spencer Mosse; Production Manager, Patricia Christian; Directors, Michael Montel, Brian Murray, Richard Maltby, Jr.; Stage Managers, Jay Jacobson, Gloria Yetter; Production Assistant, Jona Huber; Technical Director, Allan Trumpler; Choreographer, Patrick Adiarte

PRODUCTIONS AND CASTS

THE SHOW-OFF by George Kelly: Joseph Costa, David Leary, Betty Leighton, Heather MacDonald, Michael Morin, William Newman, William Preston, Ellen Tovatt, Douglas Wing

TRAVESTIES by Tom Stoppard: Edward Atienza, Domini Blythe, Donald Ewer, David Rounds, Louise Troy, Valerie von Volz, Paxton Whitehead, Douglas Wing

SAINT JOAN by George Bernard Shaw: Domini Blythe, William Buell, Joseph Costa, Kenneth Dight, Judith Elder, Donald Ewer, Jack Gwillim, James E. Maxwell, Marilyn Meyrick, Richard Monette, Michael Morin, David Rounds, Geddeth Smith, Tony van Bridge, Douglas Wing

HOBSON'S CHOICE by Harold Brighouse: Domini Blythe, William Buell, Kenneth Dight, Donald Ewer, Betty Leighton, Heather MacDonald, David Rounds, Geddeth Smith, Ellen Tovatt, Louise Troy, Tony van Bridge, Douglas Wing

UNCLE VANYA by Anton Chekhov: William Buell, Donald Ewer, Jack Gwillim, Betty Leighton, Tarina Lewis, Robert Murch, David Rounds, Sherry Steiner, Louise Troy, Douglas Wing

STARTING HERE, STARTING NOW by Richard Maltby, Jr., David Shire: Loni Ackerman, Margery Cohen, George Lee Andrews, Harvey Evans

TONY VAN BRIDGE AS G.K.C.: the wit and wisdom of Gilbert Keith Chesterton, a solo performance

Peter Lester Photos

Right Center: Betty Leighton in "The Show-Off"

Louise Troy, David Rounds in "Hobson's Choice"

PITTSBURGH PLAYHOUSE
Pittsburgh, Pennsylvania
October 14, 1977–May 28, 1978

Executive Producer, Mark Lewis; Business Manager, Roderick Carter; Press, Jim Wilhelm, Marilyn McWilliams; Production Manager, Mary M. Turner; Technical Director, Alan Forino; Stage Managers, Joan B. Kendrall, Kimberly A. Blair, Renee Burkette; Designers, Boyd Ostroff, Robert Doepel, Joseph Kleban; Lighting, Jennifer Ford, Michael Ritchie; Costumes, Mary M. Turner, Shima Orans; Musical Director, Miriam Kelly; Choreographers, David Vinski, Ton Tassone; Directors, James Prescott, Don Wadsworth, Alexander Gray, Hugh Rose, Roderick Carter

COMPANY

Charles Altman, Maria A. Barney, Greg Besnak, Judy Bierman, David Butler, Patricia Cena, John Chmura, Claudia Cook, Carol Ebaugh, Jim Frederick, Leland Gantt, Patrice Haftman, John Hall, Charles Kloth, Gloria Macin, Michael McGovern, Doug Mertz, Ken Milchick, Jeff Paul, Sandy Reinert, Thomas Renne, Richard Ritzel, Pat Wade Robbins, Tim Rogers, Hugh Rose, Peggy Sanders, Michael Samreny, Marty Schiff, Elizabeth Thomas, Leonard B. Tolbert, Melanie Verliin, Wendy Walsh, D'Arcy Webb

PRODUCTIONS

"The Hot l Baltimore," "The Brave Little Tailor," "Playboy of the Western World," "A Christmas Carol," "The House of Blue Leaves," "Brecht on Brecht," "Arthur and the Sword of Camelot," "A Midsummer Night's Dream," "The Apple Tree," "Murder in the Cathedral," "The Frog Princess and the Witch"
Michael Friedlander Photos

**Top Left: Patrice Haftman, John Hall
in "A Midsummer Night's Dream"**

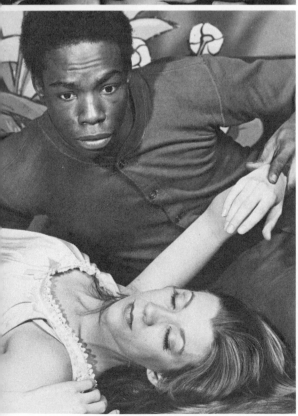

212 **Leland Gantt, Linda Johnson
in "The Apple Tree"**

**Doug Mertz, Michael McGovern
in "Arthur and the Sword of Camelot"**

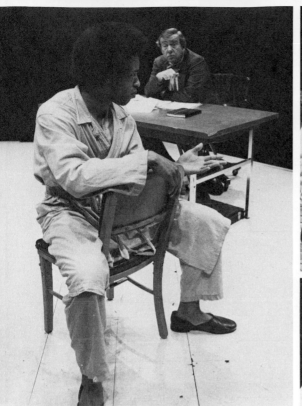

Damien Leake, Robert Nichols in "Medal of
Honor Rag" Right Center: Monica Merryman,
Elaine Kerr, Sharon Laughlin in "Father's
Day" Top: "You Never Can Tell"

PITTSBURGH PUBLIC THEATER

Pittsburgh, Pennsylvania
September 28, 1977–March 5, 1978
Third Season

General Director, Ben Shaktman; Administrative Manager, Mark
Rosenthal; Press, Christine Hurst, Joanne C. Malcolm; Production
Manager, George Allison Elmer; Stage Directors, Michael Flana-
gan, John Goin, Terry Schreiber, Ben Shaktman; Sets, Virginia
Dancy, Elmon Webb, Karl Eigsti, Henry Heymann; Costumes, Da-
vid Toser, Henry Heymann; Lighting, Bennet Averyt; Stage Man-
ager, Susana Meyer, David S. Rosenak; Props, David Lear;
Wardrobe, Martha Seely

PRODUCTION AND CASTS

FATHER'S DAY by Oliver Hailey: Ivar Brogger, Elaine Kerr,
Sharon Laughlin, Monica Merryman, Robert Murch, David Snell

YOU NEVER CAN TELL by George Bernard Shaw: Robert Black-
burn, Eva Brogger, Richard Dix, Avril Gentles, Kevin Hayes, I. M.
Hobson, Floyd King, Lodie Lynne McClintock, Joe McGrath, Gun-
Marie Nilsson, Erika Peterson, John Seidman

SLOW DANCE ON THE KILLING GROUND by William Hanley in repertory with MEDAL OF HONOR RAG by Tom Cole:
Jane Galloway, Damien Leake, Robert Nichols, Harry O'Toole

BALYASNIKOV by Aleksei Arbuzov (*World Premiere*, Dec. 21,
1977): John Abajian, Wanda Bimson, I. M. Hobson, William Rhys,
John Seidman, Joseph Wiseman

Jack Weinhold Photos

Joseph Wiseman
in "Balyasnikov"

PROFESSIONAL PERFORMING COMPANY

Chicago, Illinois

Producer, H. Adrian Rehner; Director, Jack Montgomery; Designer, Frank Bebey; Costumes, Leon Natker; Lighting, James Highland; Technicians, Bruce Taylor, Merle Hadgepath; Stage Manager, Sabrina Smith

COMPANY

Robert Jenkins, Oscar Grant, Larence Smith, Lenell Watson, Angela Mack, Phillip Pulliam, Dana Luellen, Maurice Adkins, David Block, Ato Williamson, Carey Cook, Orphus Black, Deborah Patterson, Sheila Hightower, Hallene Brooks, Sabrina Smith, George McCoy, Raynetta Green

PRODUCTIONS: "Here We Are," "Swapface," "Auditions"

Ray Hasch Photos

Professional Performing Company in "Swapface"

THE REPERTORY COMPANY

Philadelphia, Pennsylvania
September 29, 1977–June 10, 1978
Artistic Director, Joseph Aufiery; Administrative Director, Robin Dechert; Stage Directors, William Alderson, Joseph Aufiery, Danny Oreskes, Barry Sattels, Lorene White; Designers, Dennis Aufiery, Valjean Clark, Sue Dressler, Ben Sweetwood

COMPANY

John Bleasdale, Lin Kennedy, Sarah Jessica Labov, Margaret Lutz, Frank Lyons, Packy Lyons, Tom McManus, Marian Mazza, Tracey Moe, Danny Oreskes, Barry Sattels, Wally Schultz, Ben Sweetwood, Lorene White

PRODUCTIONS

"Our Town" by Thornton Wilder, "Luv" by Murray Schisgal, "The Glass Menagerie" by Tennessee Williams, "Rosencrantz and Guildenstern Are Dead" by Tom Stoppard, "A Flea in Her Ear" by Georges Feydeau, "Closing the Halls Where Once Fatima Stood" by Lanie Robertson (*World Premiere,* May 11, 1978), "The Typists" by Murray Schisgal, "The Tiger" by Murray Schisgal, "The Lover" by Harold Pinter, "Bedtime Story" by Sean O'Casey, "Bring in the Naked Girls" by Danny Oreskes (*World Premiere,* Apr. 12, 1978)

Jules Schick Photos

Marian Mazza, P. J. Lyons, Lin Kennedy in "A Flea in Her Ear"

Left Center: Reuben Tucker, Lin Kennedy in "Closing the Halls Where Once Fatima Stood"

ROBERT LEWIS ACTING COMPANY

New Rochelle, N.Y.
January 24 –June 25, 1978

Artistic Director, Robert Lewis; Associate Artistic Director, David Rotenberg; Administrative Director, Linda Strohmier; Designer, Beeb Salzer; General Manager, Barry Kramer; Technical Director, Richard Meyer; Stage Manager, John Fotia; Press, Bruce Cohen

PRODUCTIONS AND CASTS

THE CLUB CHAMPION'S WIDOW by John Ford Noonan (*World Premiere*, Jan. 24, 1978); Director, Robert Lewis: Maureen Stapleton, Lisa Sloan, John Braden, Berry Jenner

CALIGULA by Albert Camus, translated by Justin O'Brien: James Selby, Julius LaRosa, Chet Doherty, Glenn Z. Gress, Brian McEleney, Tony Howart, Peter Gallagher, Tom Dennis, Dan Desmond, Roger Grunwald, Paul Lawrence, Aida Berlyn, Cindy Rosmond, Stephen Dym, Timothy Doyle, Tom Mucciolo, John Griesemer, Jerry Kissel, Jim Boutilier, Elmore James

SUICIDE PROHIBITED IN THE SPRINGTIME by Alejandro Casona, translated by Adam D. Horvath (*American Premiere*, May 16, 1978); Director, David Rotenberg: Earle Hyman, Roger Grunwald, Lenka Peterson, Brian McEleney, Nancy Reardon, Annie Murray, Michael Lipton, Dan Desmond, Glenn Z. Gress, Brenda Lewis

Carol Lynn Rosegg Photos

**Right Center: Earle Hyman, Annie Murray, Michael Lipton in "Suicide Prohibited in Springtime"
Top: Maureen Stapleton in "The Club Champion's Widow"**

Brenda Lewis, Brian McEleney in "Suicide Prohibited in Springtime"

Aida Berlyn, Peter Gallagher in "Caligula"

ST. NICHOLAS THEATER COMPANY
Chicago, Illinois
September 1977–June 1978

Artistic Director, Steven Schachter; Managing Director, Peter Schneider; Business Manager, Bill Bifolck; Assistant to Artistic Director, Lois Hall; Production Coordinator, Catherine Goedert; Technical Directors, William Arnold, Edward Schuenemann; Design Coordinator, David Emmons; Musical Director, Alaric Jans; Press, Patricia Cox

COMPANY

Steve Anders, Mary Ann Brooks, Nick Faltas, Kim Nardelli, Barbara E. Robertson, Gail Silver, Denise Blasor-Wilson, Dory Ehrlich, Carole Helms, Marty Levy, Natalija Noulch, Michael Sassone, Jim Wise, Peter Weller

GUEST ARTISTS: Donal Donnelly, Geraldine Fitzgerald, Viveca Lindfors, Patti LuPone

PRODUCTIONS

"Ashes" by David Rudkin, "You Can't Take It with You" by Moss Hart and George S. Kaufman, "Uncommon Women and Others" by Wendy Wasserstein, "The Nuclear Family" by Mark Frost, "Spider" by Bobby Joyce Smith, "I'd Rather Be It" conceived and written by the women of the New York Ensemble, "The Slow Hours" by Bruce Burgun, "Marty" by Paddy Chayefsky, *World Premieres* of "The Woods" by David Mamet, and "Barnaby Sweet" by Glenn Allen Smith

James C. Clark Photos

Peter Weller, Patti LuPone in "The Woods"
Above: "Marty" Top: "The Nuclear Family"
Right Center: "Ashes"

THE SECOND CITY
Chicago, Illinois
June 1, 1977–May 31, 1978

Producer-Director, Bernard Sahlins; Associate Producer, Joyce Sloane; Director, Del Close

COMPANY

Will Porter
Nate Herman
Larry Coven
Don DePollo

James Belushi
Miriam Flynn
Maria Ricossa

PRODUCTION: "Sexual Perversity among the Buffalo"

Jay King Photo

Don DePollo, Maria Ricossa, Miriam Flynn, Will Porter in "Sexual Perversity among the Buffalo"

Zina Jasper, Judy Jurgaitis, Ronald Bishop
in "The Three Sisters" Top Right: David
Selby, Alley Mills, John Strasberg, Ellen
Endicott, Janet Ward in "Rib Cage" Below:
Richard Lupino, Douglas Stender, Jack
Marks, Carrie Nye, Robert Nichols in
"The Little Foxes"

STAGE WEST

West Springfield, Massachusetts
November 5, 1977–April 16, 1978

Artistic Director, Rae Allen; Managing Director, Stephen E.
Hays; Press, Ellen Kennedy; Directors, Larry Carpenter, Timothy
Near, Peter Mark Schifter; Stage Managers, Steven Woolf, Rachael
Lindhart, Michael S. Mantel; Technical Director, Jack Nardi; Sets,
Thomas Cariello, Laurence King, Jerry Rojo; Costumes, Christina
Weppner; Lighting, John Gisondi, Barley Harris, Barbara Ling

PRODUCTIONS AND CASTS

THE LITTLE FOXES by Lillian Hellman: Philip Curry, Jan Farrand, Richard Lupino, Jack Marks, Alley Mills, Robert Nicholas,
Carrie Nye, Sarallen, Douglas Stender

A CHRISTMAS CAROL by Charles Dickens, adapted by Rae
Allen and Timothy Near (*World Premiere*, Dec. 4, 1977): Kathleen
Bernard, Ronald Bishop, Scott C. Clement, Philip Curry, Anne
Cohen, Thomas Dillon, Jan Farrand, Amelia Hays, James Hil-
brandt, Judy Jurgaitis, Bev Lubin, Richard Lupino, Alley Mills,
Scott Myers, Kit Randal, Chris Romilly, Nancy Sellin, Jamie Shea,
Douglas Stender, Dale Westgaard, John Zamboni

LOOT by Joe Orton: Ronald Bishop, Gwyllum Evans, Chris
Romilly, Nancy Sellin, John Wallace Spencer, Douglas Stender

RIB CAGE by Larry Ketron (*World Premiere*, Jan. 7, 1978): Ellen
Endicott, James Hilbrandt, Alley Mills, David Selby, John Strasberg, Janet Ward

A BAGFUL OF STORIES by Peter Elbling and Timothy Near
(*World Premiere*, Jan. 9, 1978): Anne Cohen, Gregg Daniel, Thomas
Dillon, Josie Lawrence, Bev Lubin, Howard Schaffer

THE THREE SISTERS by Anton Chekhov: Ronald Bishop, Scott
C. Clement, Gwyllum Evans, Jeffrey Horowitz, Zina Jasper, Judy
Jurgaitis, Timothy Near, Chris Romilly, Nancy Sellin, John Wallace
Spencer, Douglas Stender, Sheryl Stoodley, George Touliatos, Maria
Vronskaya, Dale Westgaard

VANITIES by Jack Heifner: Anne Cohen, Timothy Near, Nancy
Sellin

Alan Epstein Photos

**Right Center: James Hilbrandt, Bev Lubin,
Judy Jurgaitis in "A Christmas Carol"**

**Timothy Near, Nancy Sellin,
Anne Cohen in "Vanities"**　　**217**

Robert Schuch, Susan Morgenstern
in "The Imaginary Invalid"

STAIRCASE THEATRE

Santa Cruz, California
June 10, 1977–June 10, 1978

Executive Producer, Karen Weinschenker; Artistic Director, Julia Steiny; Associate Producer, Greydon Morley; Production Coordinantor, Susan Edelman; Sets and Lighting, Lee Bauer, Lloyd Elliott Scott, Bruce Jordan, Larry Arsenault, Clyde Highbarger, Nancy Godfrey, Rustie; Costumes, Susan Ruttan, Lloyd Elliott Scott, Linda West-Groat, Carolyn Weible-Schmidt, Lori Muttersbach; Sound, Ron Holman; Technical Directors, Lee Bauer, Ron Holman, Bruce Jordan; Stage Managers, Beverly Adams Grant, David Hormel, Robin Knox, W. Terry Poland, Lori Muttersbach, Patricia Straub, Peter Ross

COMPANY

Larry Arsenault, Douglas Barry, Lee Bauer, Donna Blue, Shane Davis, Susan Edelman, Robert Gatto, Jim Gordon, Ellen Himelfarb, Bruce Jordan, Carol Karr, Mel Kinder, Susan Morgenstern, Greydon Morley, Lori Muttersbach, W. Terry Poland, Wendi Pope, Robyn Roberts, Susan Ruttan, Patricia Straub, Melita Ana Thorpe, Jay Crago Vaughn, Carolyn Weible-Schmidt, Karen Weinschenker, David West-Groat

PRODUCTIONS

"Jacques Brel Is Alive and Well and Living in Paris," "The Tavern," "The Two Disguised Gypsies," "A Little Night Music," "Rosencrantz and Guildenstern Are Dead," "Private Lives," "Company," "Misalliance," "The Imaginary Invalid," "The Hot l Baltimore," and *World Premiere* of "Misdemeanors" by John O'Brien

Alan Muttersbach Photos

218   **Jim Gordon, Karen Weinschenker**
in "Hot l Baltimore"

STUDIO ARENA THEATRE
Buffalo, N. Y.
September 30, 1977–April 29, 1978
Thirteenth SEason

Executive Producer, Neal Du Brock; General Manager, Stanley D. Silver; Associate to Producer, Michael T. Healy; Press, Blossom Cohan; Company Manager, Jane Abbott; Stage Managers, Don Walters, Robert C. Mingus; Technical Director, John T. Baun; Wardrobe, Diane R. Schaller, Mary-Camille Schwindler; Sound, Richard Menke; Production Assistant, William McMullen

PRODUCTIONS AND CASTS

SUNSET by Louis LaRusso II, Gary William Friedman, Will Holt (*World Premiere,* Sept. 30, 1977); Director, Tommy Tune: Alexis Smith, Buddy Vest, Bill Starr, Lisa Mordente, Ron Perlman, Yolanda Ray Raven, Cheryl Alexander, Christine Faith, Terry Rieser, Diva Gray

SEMMELWEISS by Howard Sackler (*World Premiere,* Nov. 4, 1977); Director, Edwin Sherin: Lewis J. Stadlen, Jack Bittner, Kathy Bates, Shepperd Strudwick, Leslie Barrett, Kim Hunter, Kent Broadhurst, Peter Blaxill, Chet Carlin, Mel Cobb, Kathleen Gray, K. McKenna, Elizabeth Parrish, Dennis Patella, Joel Stedman, Stephan Weyte

SAME TIME, NEXT YEAR by Bernard Slade: Rosemary Prinz, Richard Greene

THE CRUCIFER OF BLOOD by Paul Giovanni (*World Premiere,* Jan. 6, 1978); Directed by the author: Paxton Whitehead, Glenn Close, Timothy Landfield, Stephen Keep, Bill Herndon, Christopher Curry, Ian Trigger, Jacob Tuck Milligan, T. Ervin, Greg Houston

THE SHADOW BOX by Michael Cristofer: Suzanne Costallos, Joan Croydon, David Daniels, Eileen Letchworth, Pat McNamara, Gerald Richards, John Spencer, Rachel Taylor, Dan Kenefick

COWARD IN TWO KEYS by Noel Coward: Michael Allinson, Carolyn Coates, Gwyda DonHowe, James Mastrantonio

WHO'S AFRAID OF VIRGINIA WOOLF? by Edward Albee: Estelle Parsons, James Noble, Peter Burnell, Linda Kampley

Phototech Studio Photos

Right Center: Kathy Bates, Lewis J. Stadlen, Kim Hunter in "Semmelweiss" Above: Glenn Close, Timothy Landfield, Paxton Whitehead in "The Crucifer of Blood" Top: Peter Burnell, James Noble, Estelle Parsons in "Who's Afraid of Virginia Woolf?"

**Alexis Smith
in "Sunset"**

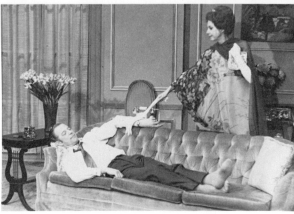

**Michael Allinson, Carolyn Coates
in "Coward in Two Keys"**

Darcy Pulliam, Nancy Reardon, Ellen Fiske
in "Tartuffe" Top: Dan Diggles, Ellen Fiske
in "The Plough and the Stars"

SYRACUSE STAGE

Syracuse, N. Y.
October 14, 1977–May 27, 1978

Producing Director, Arthur Storch; Managing Director, James Clark; Stage Directors, Peter Maloney, John Going, William Putch, Arthur Storch; Sets, Elmon Webb, Virginia Dancy, Eldon Elder, William Trotman, Neil Peter Jampolis, William Schroder; Costumes, James Berton Harris, William Schroder, Linda Fisher, Lowell Detweiler, Liz Bass, Nanzi Adzima; Lighting, James Stephens, Neil Peter Jampolis, Judy Rasmuson, Lee Watson; Stage Managers, David Semonin, Patricia Ann Speelman; Press, Susan Kindlund, Charlaine Martin

PRODUCTIONS AND CASTS

LOVE LETTERS ON BLUE PAPER by Arnold Wesker *(World Premiere)* with "The End of the Beginning" by Sean O'Casey: Richard Clarke, John Carpenter, Myra Carter, Jay Devlin

THE PLOUGH AND THE STARS by Sean O'Casey: Moultrie Patten, Robert Shrewsbury, Nancy Reardon, Gene O'Neill, Ellen Fiske, Dee Victor, Dan Diggles, Michael Houlihan, Lori Putnam, Tom Walsh, Darcy Pulliam, John Ahlin, Jonathan Putnam, Jack McClure

TARTUFFE by Moliere: Heidi D. L. Van De Carr, Darcy Pulliam, Lou Fusco, Ron George, Joyce Krempel, Nancy Reardon, Ellen Fiske, Gene O'Neill, Thomas Ruisinger, Moultrie Patten, Dan Diggles, Munson Hicks, Robert Shrewsbury, Michael Houlihan

THAT CHAMPIONSHIP SEASON by Jason Miller: Stephen C. Bradbury, David J. Forsyth, Thomas Connolly, Robert Fields, Edmund Lyndeck

CANDIDA by George Bernard Shaw: Robert Stattel, Beth Dixon, Michael Parish, Donald C. Moore, Penelope Allen, Daniel Zippi

VANITIES by Jack Heifner: Susanne Peters, Roxanne Hart, Rebecca Hollen

MUSICAL MIRAGE EXPRESS and JOURNEYS END IN LOVER'S MEETING by Gerardine Clark: Demetra Pittman, Trent Jones, Lydia Firestone, Kevin McClarnon, Kim Sullivan

Robert Lorenz Photos

Top: John Carpenter, Richard Clarke
220 **in "Love Letters on Blue Paper"**

Jay Devlin, John Carpenter in "The End of the Beginning"
Above: Roxanne Hart, Rebecca Hollen in "Vanities"

THEATRE BY THE SEA

Portsmouth, N. H.
September 27, 1977–June 4, 1978

Producing Director, Jon Kimbell; Business Manager, Kathleen Kimbell; Press, Sandi Bianco; Stage Directors, Miriam Fond, Russell Treyz, Alfred Gingold; Technical Director, Roger Rutledge; Sets, James E. Carroccio, John Shaffner, Leslie E. Rollins, Larry Fulton, Kathie Iannicelli; Costumes, Varel McComb, Kathie Iannicelli; Lighting, Dan Raymond, Ned Hallick; Wardrobe, Dolly Cripps; Props, Stephen Caldwell; Administration, Connie Barron, Jean Caldwell

PRODUCTIONS AND CASTS:

SLEUTH by Anthony Shaffer: Roby Brown, John K. Carroll

JUBALAY by Patrick Rose and Merv Campone (*World Premiere*); Director, Russell Treyz; Musical Director, John Clifton: Sydney Anderson, D. Michael Heath, Michael Maurice, Robert Molnar, Donna Pelc

MY THREE ANGELS by Sam and Bella Spewack: Tom Celli, Darcy Crandall, Nancy Walton Fenn, Frederic Major, David Penhale, Ginny Russell, James Ross Smith, Jeff Starbird, Keith Tarleton, Edward Trotta

THE SUNSHINE BOYS by Neil Simon: Sy Travers, Bill Farley, Tom Celli, Doris Yeager, Nancy Walton Fenn, Thomas Reardon, Dan Raymond

THE SHADOW BOX by Michael Cristofer: Frederic Major, Helen Auerbach, Robert Lowry, Holly Barron, Stephanie Voss, Nancy Walton Fenn, Jake Elwell, Thomas Reardon

THE GLASS MENAGERIE by Tennesse Williams: Benay Venuta, Alice Elliott, Chet Carlin, Robert Lowry

William L. Smith Photos

Right: Robert Molnar, Michael Maurice, Sydney Anderson, D. Michael Heath, Donna Pelc in "Jubalay" Top: Alice Elliott, Robert Lowry, Benay Venuta, Chet Carlin in "The Glass Menagerie"

THEATER CENTER

Philadelphia, Pennsylvania
October 5, 1977–June 17, 1978

Producing Director, Albert Benzwie; Press, Richard Stewart; Sets, Michael Koff; Costumes, Robin Frome; Stage Manager, Robert O'Neill

COMPANY

Lisa Emery, Eric Hutson, Christopher Whelan, David Robertson, Greg Maguire, Ron Long, Charles Musumeci, Paul Garabedian, Tim Moyer, Nan Lester

PRODUCTIONS

"The Blinds" by Richard Stewart (*World Premiere*, Oct. 5, 1977), "The Importance of Being Earnest" by Oscar Wilde, "Children of Our Mothers" by Barbara O'Toole (*World Premiere*, Nov. 30, 1977), "Tartuffe" by Moliere, "Herr Puntila and His Chauffeur Matti" by Bertolt Brecht, "Geographies of Northern Provinces" by Lanie Robertson (*World Premiere*, Mar. 22, 1978), "No Visitors Please" by Jack Engelhard (*World Premiere*, Apr. 26, 1978), "The Rendering" by Charles Brennan (*World Premiere*, Apr. 26, 1978), "House of Bedlam" by Kenneth Arnold

Richard Stewart Photo

Christopher Whelan, Greg Maguire, Lisa Emery, Tim Moyer in "The Blinds"

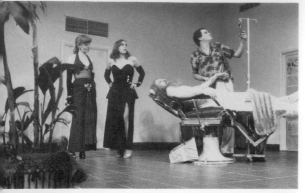

TRINITY SQUARE REPERTORY COMPANY

Providence, R. I.
October 11, 1977–May 21, 1978

Director, Adrian Hall; Administrator, G. David Black; Development Director, Marion Simon; General Manager, E. Timothy Langan; Press, Scotti DiDonato, Cynthia Boutin; Musical Director, Richard Cumming; Sets, Eugene Lee, Robert D. Soule; Lights, Eugene Lee, John F. Custer, Sean Keating; Costumes, James Berton Harris, Ann Morrell, Betsey Potter; Technical Director, David Ward; Props, Sandra Nathanson, Tom Waldon; Stage Managers, William Radka, Maureen F. Gibson, Dennis Blackledge, Beverly Andreozzi; Directors, Adrian Hall, Larry Arrick, George Martin, William Radka, Ann McBey Brebner

COMPANY

Kyle Baker, Robert Black, Ken Bradford, S. D. Brown, Bree Cavazos, William Damkoehler, Ann Gerety, Peter Gerety, Russell Gold, Tom Griffin, Richard Jenkins, Melanie Jones, David Kennett, Richard Kneeland, Joel Leffert, Howard London, George Martin, Derek Meader, Barbara Meek, Zakes Mokae, Nancy Nichols, Barbara Orson, Julie Pember, Ricardo Pitts-Wiley, Bonnie Sacks, Kevin Sessums, Margo Skinner, Norman Smith, Cynthia Strickland, Amy Van Nostrand, Daniel Von Bargen, Cynthia Wells

PRODUCTIONS

"Ethan Frome," "Rosmersholm," "A Christmas Carol," "Equus," "As You Like It," "The Show-Off," "Boesman and Lena," "Vanities," "American Buffalo," and *World Premiere* of "Seduced" by Sam Shepard

Robert Emerson, William L. Smith Photos

Left: Barbara Orson, William Damkoehler, Richard Kneeland, Peter Gerety, Julie Pember in "A Christmas Carol" Top: Cynthia Wells, Margo Skinner, George Martin, Richard Jenkins in "Seduced"

"Rosmersholm" Above: Richard Jenkins, Norman Smith, Peter Gerety in "American Buffalo"

Richard Kneeland, Kevin Sessums in "Equus"

"Cabaret"

VIRGINIA MUSEUM THEATRE
Richmond, Virginia
September 30, 1977–March 25, 1978

Managing Director-Producer, L. Bradford Boynton; General Manager, Loraine Slade; Production Manager, Doug Flinchum; Sets, Richard C. Hankins, Jeremy Conway; Costumes, Lana Fritz, Lori Adams, Martha Clermont; Lighting and Sound, Jim Bloch; Technical Directors, Thomas W. Hughes, David McCall; Music Director, Wilfred Allen Roper II; Stage Managers, Champe Leary, Nidal Mahayni, Press, Mike Hickey, Tom Stuart, Peggy Tregoning

PRODUCTIONS AND CASTS

VANITIES by Jack Heifner: Alice Elliott, Mary McTigue, Ellen Tobie

RICHARD III by William Shakespeare: Eunice Anderson, Charles Antalosky, Ronald Bisher, Mark Brandon, Larry Clark, Ken Costigan, Peter Cruger, Buck Dietz, Christopher Dunn, Herbert DuVal, Maury Erickson, Robert Foley, Una Harrison, Marion Johnson, Dana Kildron, Jack Kyrieleison, David MacEnulty, Howard McMaster, Joseph Martinez, William Meisle, Joseph Mullin, Dick Newdick, Scott Nicklin, Douglas Nielsen, Dennis Parrish, William E. Peterson, Philip Pleasants, John Reich, Nada Rowand, Louis Schaefer, Conor Shiel, Ronald Sopyla, Ellen Tobie, Mark Varian, Robert Walsh, Robin Wood

BERLIN TO BROADWAY WITH KURT WEILL: Betsy Blanks, Richard Casper, Mike Dantuono, Andrew Gale, Henrietta Valor

LET'S GET A DIVORCE by Victorien Sardou and Emile de Najac, translated by Brian Kelly (U.S. Premiere); Director, Tom Markus: James Beard, Maury Erickson, Rob Hall, Marie Goodman Hunter, Vance Jefferis, Shauna Kanter, Alexander Leidholdt, Tanny McDonald, Margery Murray, Kathy O'Callaghan, William E. Peterson, William Preston, Peter Silbert, Charmian Sorbello, Robert Walsh

MAN AND SUPERMAN by George Bernard Shaw: James Beard, Stephanie Braxton, Maury Erickson, Dan Hamilton, Shauna Kanter, Margery Murray, Kathy O'Callaghan, William Preston, Peter Silbert, Charmian Sorbello, Robert Walsh

CABARET by John Kander, Fred Ebb: Kay Cameron, Richard Casper, John Colbert, Bim Crane-Baker, Karen DiBianco, Keith Evans, Dale Furry, Alan Gilbert, Allan Gruet, Rob Hall, Jannet Horsley, John Hudson, Dave Jewett, Charmaine Jordon, Shauna Kanter, Bobby Longbottom, Steve Mabry, Bud Nease, Jan Neuberger, Scott Nicklin, Kathy O'Callaghan, William E. Peterson, William Preston, Rodney Reiner, Bill Roper, Rose Scudder, Jacqui Singleton, Cassie Stein, Pam Weller, Rebecca Woodley

"Richard III"

W. T. Martin, Judith Delgado in "A Chekhov Christmas"
(Keith Scott Morton Photo) **Left Center: Maggie Abeckerly,
Georgia Hester, Marjorie Fierst in "And Miss Reardon
Drinks a Little"** *(Geoffrey Gross Photo)* **Top: Tom Brennan,
Olympia Dukakis, in "One Flew Over the Cuckoo's Nest**
(Keith Scott Morton Photo)

THE WHOLE THEATRE COMPANY
Montclair, N.J.
October 18, 1977–June 3, 1978

Artistic Director, Olympia Dukakis; President, Arnold Mittelman; Business Manager, Sylvia Traeger; Press, Lucy Stille; Stage Directors, W. T. Martin, Arnold Mittelman, Bernard Hiatt, Louis Zorich, Olympia Dukakis; Sets, Paul Dorphley, Raymond C. Recht, Tony Negron; Costumes, Veronica Deisler, Sigrid Insull, Mary-Margaret Bergamini-Torias; Lighting, Marshall Spiller; Stage Managers, Julia Gillett, Ellen Zalk, Charles R. Traeger, Robert Stevenson; Technical Director, Joe Musco

COMPANY

Maggie Abeckerly, Jessica Allen, Remi Barclay, Jason Bosseay, Tom Brennan, Lyn Clifton, Judith Delgado, Paul Dorphley, Apollo Dukakis, Olympia Dukakis, Gerald Fierst, Marjorie Fierst, W. T. Martin, Arnold Mittelman, Glenna Peters, Stefan Peters, Ernie Schenk, Louis Zorich
GUEST ARTISTS: Jack Banning, John Basil Giletto, Ronald Willoughby, Jim Hillgartner, George Bohn, James Rebhorn, Judith L'Heureux, Georgia Hester, Carol Rosenfeld, Daniel Pollack

PRODUCTIONS

"Mother Courage," "A Chekhov Christmas," "Father's Day," "And Miss Reardon Drinks a Little," "One Flew Over the Cuckoo's Nest"

Glenna Peters, Apollo Dukakis
in "A Chekhov Christmas" *(Carl Selinger Photo)*

YALE REPERTORY THEATRE

New Haven, Connecticut
September 30, 1977–May 21, 1978

Director, Robert Brustein; Associate Directors, Andrei Serban, Walton Jones; Managing Director, Robert J. Orchard; Business Manager, Abigail P. Fearon; Press, Jan Geidt; Scenery, Michael Yeargan, Kate Edmunds, Jess Goldstein, Nancy Thun, Andrew Jackness; Costumes, Dunya Ramicova, Kate Edmunds, Jess Goldstein, Jeanne Button; Lighting, William B. Warfel, Thomas Skelton, William Connor, Robert Jared, James H. Gage, Tom Schraeder; Production Supervisor, John Robert Hood; Technical Directors, Bronislaw Sammler, George Lindsay, Jr.; Stage Managers, Frank S. Torok, James F. Ingalls.

PRODUCTIONS AND CASTS

THE GHOST SONATA by August Strindberg: Norma Brustein, Brenda Currin, Jeremy Geidt, Michael Gross, Shaine Marinson, Patrizia Norcia, Stephen Rowe, Douglas Simes, Priscilla Smith, Roy Steinberg, Mary Van Dyke, Max Wright

REUNION by David Mamet: Lindsay Crouse, Michael Higgins

TERRA NOVA by Ted Tally (*World Premiere*); Director, Travis Preston: Lindsay Crouse, Jeremy Geidt, Michael Gross, Michael Higgins, Arthur Hill, Stephen Rowe, Max Wright

SGANARELLE by Moliere: Mark Linn Baker, Norma Brustein, Peter Crombie, Joyce Fideor, Jeremy Geidt, David Marshall Grant, Michael Gross, Richard Crusin, Jonathan Marks, Elizabeth Norment, Patrizia Norcia, Marianne Owen, William Roberts, Eugene Troobnick, Frederic Warriner

MAN IS MAN by Bertolt Brecht: Mark Linn Baker, Jeremy Geidt, Joe Grifasi, Michael Gross, Richard Grusin, Patrizia Norcia, Estelle Parsons, John Seitz, John Shea

WINGS by Arthur Kopit (*World Premiere*); Director, John Madden: Constance Cummings, Ira Bernstein, Caris Corfman, Richard Grusin, Carol Ostrow, Marianne Owen, Geoffrey Pierson, Roy Steinberg

THE WILD DUCK by Henrik Ibsen: Blanche Baker, Norma Brustein, Jeremy Geidt, Michael Gross, Marianne Owen, Lee Richardson, William Roberts, Bruce Siddons, Douglas Simes, Shepperd Strudwick, Eugene Troobnick, Christopher Walken

THE 1940's RADIO HOUR by Walt Jones

GUEST ARTISTS: Mabou Mines' "The Be. Beaver Animation" by Lee Breuer, with JoAnne Akalaitis, Frederick Newmann, Ruth Maleczech, William Raymond, David Warrilow

Eugene Cook Photos

Right: Michael Higgins, Lindsay Crouse in "Reunion" Above: John Shea, Joe Grifasi, Estelle Parsons in "Man Is Man" Top: Max Wright, Jeremy Geidt, Michael Gross, Arthur Hill in "Terra Nova"

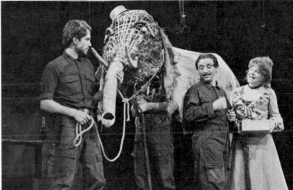

Shepperd Strudwick, Christopher Walken in "The Wild Duck"

Constance Cummings in "Wings"

PULITZER PRIZE PRODUCTIONS

1918–Why Marry?, 1919– No award, 1920–Beyond the Horizon, 1921–Miss Lulu Bett, 1922– Anna Christie, 1923–Icebound, 1924–Hell-Bent fer Heaven, 1925–They Knew What They Wanted, 1926–Craig's Wife, 1927–In Abraham's Bosom, 1928–Strange Interlude, 1929–Street Scene, 1930–The Green Pastures, 1931–Alison's House, 1932–Of Thee I Sing, 1933–Both Your Houses, 1934–Men in White, 1935–The Old Maid, 1936–Idiot's Delight, 1937–You Can't Take It with You, 1938–Our Town, 1939–Abe Lincoln in Illinois, 1940–The Time of Your Life, 1941– There Shall Be No Night, 1942–No award, 1943–The Skin of Our Teeth, 1944–No award, 1945– Harvey, 1946–State of the Union, 1947–No award, 1948–A Streetcar Named Desire, 1949–Death of a Salesman, 1950–South Pacific, 1951–No award, 1952–The Shrike, 1953–Picnic, 1954–The Teahouse of the August Moon, 1955–Cat on a Hot Tin Roof, 1956–The Diary of Anne Frank, 1957–Long Day's Journey into Night, 1958–Look Homeward, Angel, 1959–J. B., 1960–Fiorello!, 1961–All the Way Home, 1962–How to Succeed in Business without Really Trying, 1963–No award, 1964–No award, 1965–The Subject Was Roses, 1966–No award, 1967–A Delicate Balance, 1968–No award, 1969–The Great White Hope, 1970–No Place to Be Somebody, 1971–The Effect of Gamma Rays on Man-in-the-Moon Marigolds, 1972–No award, 1973–That Championship Season, 1974–No award, 1975–Seascape, 1976–A Chorus Line, 1977–The Shadow Box, 1978—The Gin Game

NEW YORK DRAMA CRITICS CIRCLE AWARDS

1936–Winterset, 1937–High Tor, 1938–Of Mice and Men, Shadow and Substance, 1939–The White Steed, 1940–The Time of Your Life, 1941–Watch on the Rhine, The Corn is Green, 1942– Blithe Spirit, 1943–The Patriots, 1944–Jacobowsky and the Colonel, 1945–The Glass Menagerie, 1946–Carousel, 1947–All My Sons, No Exit, Brigadoon, 1948–A Streetcar Named Desire, The Winslow Boy, 1949–Death of a Salesman, The Madwoman of Chaillot, South Pacific, 1950–The Member of the Wedding, The Cocktail Party, The Consul, 1951–Darkness at Noon, The Lady's Not for Burning, Guys and Dolls, 1952–I Am a Camera, Venus Observed, Pal Joey, 1953–Picnic, The Love of Four Colonels, Wonderful Town, 1954–Teahouse of the August Moon, Ondine, The Golden Apple, 1955–Cat on a Hot Tin Roof, Witness for the Prosecution, The Saint of Bleecker Street, 1956–The Diary of Anne Frank, Tiger at the Gates, My Fair Lady, 1957–Long Day's Journey into Night, The Waltz of the Toreadors, The Most Happy Fella, 1958–Look Homeward Angel, Look Back in Anger, The Music Man, 1959–A Raisin in the Sun, The Visit, La Plume de Ma Tante, 1960–Toys in the Attic, Five Finger Exercise, Fiorello!, 1961–All the Way Home, A Taste of Honey, Carnival, 1962–Night of the Iguana, A Man for All Seasons, How to Succeed in Business without Really Trying, 1963–Who's Afraid of Virginia Woolf?, 1964–Luther, Hello, Dolly!, 1965–The Subject Was Roses, Fiddler on the Roof, 1966–The Persecution and Assassination of Marat as Performed by the Inmates of the Asylum of Charenton under the Direction of the Marquis de Sade, Man of La Mancha, 1967–The Homecoming, Cabaret, 1968–Rosencrantz and Guildenstern Are Dead, Your Own Thing, 1969–The Great White Hope, 1776, 1970–The Effect of Gamma Rays on Man-in-the-Moon Marigolds, Borstal Boy, Company, 1971–Home, Follies, The House of Blue Leaves, 1972–That Championship Season, Two Gentlemen of Verona, 1973–The Hot l Baltimore, The Changing Room, A Little Night Music, 1974–The Contractor, Short Eyes, Candide, 1975–Equus, The Taking of Miss Janie, A Chorus Line, 1976–Travesties, Streamers, Pacific Overtures, 1977–Otherwise Engaged, American Buffalo, Annie, 1978— Da, Ain't Misbehavin'

AMERICAN THEATRE WING
ANTOINETTE PERRY (TONY) AWARD PRODUCTIONS

1948–Mister Roberts, 1949–Death of a Salesman, Kiss Me, Kate, 1950–The Cocktail Party, South Pacific, 1951–The Rose Tattoo, Guys and Dolls, 1952–The Fourposter, The King and I, 1953–The Crucible, Wonderful Town, 1954–The Teahouse of the August Moon, Kismet, 1955– The Desperate Hours, The Pajama Game, 1956–The Diary of Anne Frank, Damn Yankees, 1957–Long Day's Journey into Night, My Fair Lady, 1958–Sunrise at Campobello, The Music Man, 1959–J. B., Redhead, 1960–The Miracle Worker, Fiorello! tied with Sound of Music, 1961– Becket, Bye Bye Birdie, 1962–A Man for All Seasons, How to Succeed in Business without Really Trying, 1963–Who's Afraid of Virginia Woolf?, A Funny Thing Happened on the Way to the Forum, 1964–Luther, Hello, Dolly!, 1965–The Subject Was Roses, Fiddler on the Roof, 1966– The Persecution and Assassination of Marat as Performed by the Inmates of the Asylum of Charenton under the Direction of the Marquis de Sade, Man of La Mancha, 1967–The Homecoming, Cabaret, 1968–Rosencrantz and Guildenstern Are Dead, Hallelujah, Baby!, 1969–The Great White Hope, 1776, 1970–Borstal Boy, Applause, 1971–Sleuth, Company, 1972–Sticks and Bones, Two Gentlemen of Verona, 1973–That Championship Season, A Little Night Music, 1974–The River Niger, Raisin, 1975–Equus, The Wiz, 1976–Travesties, A Chorus Line, 1977– The Shadow Box, Annie, 1978— Da, Ain't Misbehavin', Dracula

1978 THEATRE WORLD AWARD WINNERS

VASILI BOGAZIANOS
of "P. S. Your Cat Is Dead"

NELL CARTER
of "Ain't Misbehavin' "

CARLIN GLYNN
of "The Best Little Whorehouse in Texas"

CHRISTOPHER GOUTMAN
of "The Promise"

WILLIAM HURT
of Circle Repertory Theatre

JUDY KAYE
of "On the 20th Century"

FLORENCE LACEY
of "Hello, Dolly!"

BO RUCKER
of "Native Son"

RICHARD SEER
of "Da"

ARMELIA McQUEEN
of "Ain't Misbehavin' "

GORDANA RASHOVICH
of "Fefu and Her Friends"

COLIN STINTON
of "The Water Engine"

229

THEATRE WORLD AWARDS PARTY, Thursday, May 25, 1978: Top: John Cullum, Anita Gillette, Monte Markham, Carol Channing, **Below:** Maureen Stapleton, Enid Markey, Nell Carter, Ken Page, Carol Channing, Florence Lacey, **Second Row from Bottom:** James Earl Jones, Judy Kaye, **Bottom:** Michael Moriarty, Carlin Glynn, Dustin Hoffman, Patricia Elliott

(Ron Reagan Photos)

Top: Ken Page, Gordana Rashovich, Melba Moore, Christopher Goutman, Below: Armelia McQueen, Dustin Hoffman, William Hurt, Vasili Bogazianos, Len Cariou, Second Row from Bottom: Bo Rucker, Irene Worth, Richard Seer, Bottom Row: Patricia Gillette, William Atherton, Jill O'Hara, Colin Stinton, Carol Lynley, Joseph Papp, Irene Worth

(*Ron Reagan Photos*)

| Sandy Dennis | Robert Redford | Julie Harris | Jon Voight | Marian Mercer |

PREVIOUS THEATRE WORLD AWARD WINNERS

1944–45: Betty Comden, Richard Davis, Richard Hart, Judy Holliday, Charles Lang, Bambi Linn, John Lund, Donald Murphy, Nancy Noland, Margaret Phillips, John Raitt

1945–46: Barbara Bel Geddes, Marlon Brando, Bill Callahan, Wendell Corey, Paul Douglas, Mary James, Burt Lancaster, Patricia Marshall, Beatrice Pearson

1946–47: Keith Andes, Marion Bell, Peter Cookson, Ann Crowley, Ellen Hanley, John Jordan, George Keane, Dorothea MacFarland, James Mitchell, Patricia Neal, David Wayne

1947–48: Valerie Bettis, Edward Bryce, Whitfield Connor, Mark Dawson, June Lockhart, Estelle Loring, Peggy Maley, Ralph Meeker, Meg Mundy, Douglass Watson, James Whitmore, Patrice Wymore

1948–49: Tod Andrews, Doe Avedon, Jean Carson, Carol Channing, Richard Derr, Julie Harris, Mary McCarty, Allyn Ann McLerie, Cameron Mitchell, Gene Nelson, Byron Palmer, Bob Scheerer

1949–50: Nancy Andrews, Phil Arthur, Barbara Brady, Lydia Clarke, Priscilla Gillette, Don Hanmer, Marcia Henderson, Charlton Heston, Rick Jason, Grace Kelly, Charles Nolte, Roger Price

1950–51: Barbara Ashley, Isabel Bigley, Martin Brooks, Richard Burton, James Daly, Cloris Leachman, Russell Nype, Jack Palance, William Smothers, Maureen Stapleton, Marcia Van Dyke, Eli Wallach

1951–52: Tony Bavaar, Patricia Benoit, Peter Conlow, Virginia de Luce, Ronny Graham, Audrey Hepburn, Diana Herbert, Conrad Janis, Dick Kallman, Charles Proctor, Eric Sinclair, Kim Stanley, Marian Winters, Helen Wood

1952–53: Edie Adams, Rosemary Harris, Eileen Heckart, Peter Kelley, John Kerr, Richard Kiley, Gloria Marlowe, Penelope Munday, Paul Newman, Sheree North, Geraldine Page, John Stewart, Ray Stricklyn, Gwen Verdon

1953–54: Orson Bean, Harry Belafonte, James Dean, Joan Diener, Ben Gazzara, Carol Haney, Jonathan Lucas, Kay Medford, Scott Merrill, Elizabeth Montgomery, Leo Penn, Eva Marie Saint

1954–55: Julie Andrews, Jacqueline Brookes, Shirl Conway, Barbara Cook, David Daniels, Mary Fickett, Page Johnson, Loretta Leversee, Jack Lord, Dennis Patrick, Anthony Perkins, Christopher Plummer

1955–56: Diane Cilento, Dick Davalos, Anthony Franciosa, Andy Griffith, Laurence Harvey, David Hedison, Earle Hyman, Susan Johnson, John Michael King, Jayne Mansfield, Sarah Marshall, Gaby Rodgers, Susan Strasberg, Fritz Weaver

1956–57: Peggy Cass, Sydney Chaplin, Sylvia Daneel, Bradford Dillman, Peter Donat, George Grizzard, Carol Lynley, Peter Palmer, Cliff Robertson, Pippa Scott, Inga Swenson

1957–58: Anne Bancroft, Warren Berlinger, Colleen Dewhurst, Richard Easton, Tim Everett, Eddie Hodges, Joan Hovis, Carol Lawrence, Jacqueline McKeever, Wynne Miller, Robert Morse, George C. Scott

1958–59: Lou Antonio, Ina Balin, Richard Cross, Tammy Grimes, Larry Hagman, Dolores Hart, Roger Mollien, France Nuyen, Susan Oliver, Ben Piazza, Paul Roebling, William Shatner, Pat Suzuki, Rip Torn

1959–60: Warren Beatty, Eileen Brennan, Carol Burnett, Patty Duke, Jane Fonda, Anita Gillette, Elisa Loti, Donald Madden, George Maharis, John McMartin, Lauri Peters, Dick Van Dyke

1960–61: Joyce Bulifant, Dennis Cooney, Sandy Dennis, Nancy Dussault, Robert Goulet, Joan Hackett, June Harding, Ron Husmann, James MacArthur, Bruce Yarnell

1961–62: Elizabeth Ashley, Keith Baxter, Peter Fonda, Don Galloway, Sean Garrison, Barbara Harris, James Earl Jones, Janet Margolin, Karen Morrow, Robert Redford, John Stride, Brenda Vaccaro

1962–63: Alan Arkin, Stuart Damon, Melinda Dillon, Robert Drivas, Bob Gentry, Dorothy Loudon, Brandon Maggart, Julienne Marie, Liza Minnelli, Estelle Parsons, Diana Sands, Swen Swenson

1963–64: Alan Alda, Gloria Bleezarde, Imelda De Martin, Claude Giraud, Ketty Lester, Barbara Loden, Lawrence Pressman, Gilbert Price, Philip Proctor, John Tracy, Jennifer West

1964–65: Carolyn Coates, Joyce Jillson, Linda Lavin, Luba Lisa, Michael O'Sullivan, Joanna Pettet, Beah Richards, Jaime Sanchez, Victor Spinetti, Nicolas Surovy, Robert Walker, Clarence Williams III

1965–66: Zoe Caldwell, David Carradine, John Cullum, John Davidson, Faye Dunaway, Gloria Foster, Robert Hooks, Jerry Lanning, Richard Mulligan, April Shawhan, Sandra Smith, Lesley Ann Warren

1966–67: Bonnie Bedelia, Richard Benjamin, Dustin Hoffman, Terry Kiser, Reva Rose, Robert Salvio, Sheila Smith, Connie Stevens, Pamela Tiffin, Leslie Uggams, Jon Voight, Christopher Walken

1967–68: David Birney, Pamela Burrell, Jordan Christopher, Jack Crowder (Thalmus Rasulala), Sandy Duncan, Julie Gregg, Stephen Joyce, Bernadette Peters, Alice Playten, Michael Rupert, Brenda Smiley, Russ Thacker

1968–69: Jane Alexander, David Cryer, Blythe Danner, Ed Evanko, Ken Howard, Lauren Jones, Ron Leibman, Marian Mercer, Jill O'Hara, Ron O'Neal, Al Pacino, Marlene Warfield

1969–70: Susan Browning, Donny Burks, Catherine Burns, Len Cariou, Bonnie Franklin, David Holliday, Katharine Houghton, Melba Moore, David Rounds, Lewis J. Stadlen, Kristoffer Tabori, Fredricka Weber

1970–71: Clifton Davis, Michael Douglas, Julie Garfield, Martha Henry, James Naughton, Tricia O'Neil, Kipp Osborne, Roger Rathburn, Ayn Ruymen, Jennifer Salt, Joan Van Ark, Walter Willison

1971–72: Jonelle Allen, Maureen Anderman, William Atherton, Richard Backus, Adrienne Barbeau, Cara Duff-MacCormick, Robert Foxworth, Elaine Joyce, Jess Richards, Ben Vereen, Beatrice Winde, James Woods

1972–73: D'Jamin Bartlett, Patricia Elliott, James Farentino, Brian Farrell, Victor Garber, Kelly Garrett, Mari Gorman, Laurence Guittard, Trish Hawkins, Monte Markham, John Rubinstein, Jennifer Warren, Alexander H. Cohen (Special Award)

1973–74: Mark Baker, Maureen Brennan, Ralph Carter, Thom Christopher, John Driver, Conchata Ferrell, Ernestine Jackson, Michael Moriarty, Joe Morton, Ann Reinking, Janie Sell, Mary Woronov, Sammy Cahn (Special Award)

1974–75: Peter Burnell, Zan Charisse, Lola Falana, Peter Firth, Dorian Harewood, Joel Higgins, Marcia McClain, Linda Miller, Marti Rolph, John Sheridan, Scott Stevensen, Donna Theodore, Equity Library Theatre (Special Award)

1975–76: Danny Aiello, Christine Andreas, Dixie Carter, Tovah Feldshuh, Chip Garnett, Richard Kelton, Vivian Reed, Charles Repole, Virginia Seidel, Daniel Seltzer, John V. Shea, Meryl Streep, A Chorus Line (Special Award)

1976–77: Trazana Beverley, Michael Cristofer, Joe Fields, Joanna Gleason, Cecilia Hart, John Heard, Gloria Hodes, Juliette Koka, Andrea McArdle, Ken Page, Jonathan Pryce, Chick Vennera

| Ted Agress | Jill Andre | Robert Ari | Christine Andreas | Anthony Austin |

BIOGRAPHIES OF THIS SEASON'S CAST

ABRAHAM, F. MURRAY Born Oct. 24, 1939 in Pittsburgh, Pa. Attended UTex. OB bow 1967 in "The Fantasticks," followed by "An Opening in the Trees," "Fourteenth Dictator," "Young Abe Lincoln," "Tonight in Living Color," "Adaptation," "Survival of St. Joan," "The Dog Ran Away," "Fables," "Richard III," "Little Murders," "Scuba Duba," "Where Has Tommy Flowers Gone?," "Miracle Play," "Blessing," "Sexual Perversity in Chicago," "Landscape of the Body," Bdwy in "The Man in the Glass Booth" (1968), "6 Rms Riv Vu," "Bad Habits," "The Ritz," "Legend."

ADDY, WESLEY. Born Aug. 4, 1913 in Omaha, NE. Attended UCLA. Bdwy debut 1935 in "Panic," followed by "How Beautiful with Shoes," "Hamlet," "Richard II," "Henry IV," "Summer Night," "Romeo and Juliet," "Twelfth Night," "Antigone," "Candida," "Another Part of the Forest," "Galileo," "Leading Lady," "The Traitor," "The Enchanted," "King Lear," "The Strong Are Lonely," "First Gentleman," "South Pacific," OB in "A Month in the Country," "Candida," "Ghosts," "John Brown's Body."

AGRESS, TED. Born Apr. 20, 1945 in Brooklyn, NY. Attended Adelphi U. Bdwy debut 1965 in "Hello, Dolly!" followed by "Dear World," "Look Me Up" (OB), "Shenandoah."

AIELLO, DANNY. Born June 20, 1935 in NYC. Debut 1975 in "Lamppost Reunion" for which he received a Theatre World Award, followed by "Wheelbarrow Closers," "Gemini."

ALANN, LLOYD. Born Aug. 15, 1952 in The Bronx, NY. Attended Lehman Col. Bdwy debut 1975 in "Grease."

ALDREDGE, TOM. Born Feb. 28, 1928 in Dayton, O. Attended Dayton U., Goodman Theatre. Bdwy bow 1959 in "The Nervous Set," followed by "UTBU," "Slapstick Tragedy," "Everything in the Garden," "Indians," "Engagement Baby," "How the Other Half Loves," "Sticks and Bones," "Where's Charley?," "Leaf People," "Rex," "Vieux Carre," "St. Joan," "Stages," OB in "The Tempest," "Between Two Thieves," "Henry V," "The Premise," "Love's Labour's Lost," "Troilus and Cressida," "Butter and Egg Man," "Ergo," "Boys in the Band," "Twelfth Night," "Colette," "Hamlet," "The Orphan," "King Lear," "Iceman Cometh."

ALEXANDER, C. K. Born May 4, 1920 in Cairo, Egypt. Graduate American U. Bdwy debut 1946 in "Hidden Horizon," followed by "The Happy Time," "Flight into Egypt," "Mr. Pickwick," "Can-Can," "Fanny," "The Matchmaker," "La Plume de Ma Tante," "Rhinoceros," "Carnival," "Tovarich," "Poor Bitos," "Ari," OB in "The Dragon," "Corruption in the Palace of Justice," "Justice Box," "Threepenny Opera," "The Cherry Orchard" (LC).

ALEXANDER, TERRY. Born Mar. 23, 1947 in Detroit, MI. Wayne State U. graduate. Bdwy debut 1971 in "No Place to be Somebody" OB in "Rashomon," "Glass Menagerie," "Breakout," "Naomi Court," "Streamers," "Julius Caesar."

ALICE, MARY. Born Dec. 3, 1941 in Indianola, MS. Debut OB 1967 in "Trials of Brother Jero," followed by "The Strong Breed," "Duplex," "Thoughts," "Miss Julie," "House Party," "Terraces," "Heaven and Hell's Agreement," "In the Deepest Part of Sleep," "Cockfight," Bdwy 1971 in "No Place to Be Somebody."

ALLEN, SCOTT. Born Aug. 29, 1948 in Morristown, NJ. Attended Union Col. Upsala Col., AMDA. Bdwy debut 1975 in "A Chorus Line."

ALLEN, SETH. Born July 13, 1941 in Brooklyn, NY. Attended Musical Theatre Acad. OB in "Viet Rock," "Futz," "Hair," "Candaules Commissioner," "Mary Stuart," "Narrow Road to the Deep North," "More Than You Deserve," "Split Lip," "The Misanthrope," Bdwy 1972 in "Jesus Christ Superstar."

ALLISON, PATTI. Born June 26, 1942 in St. Louis, MO. Graduate Webster Col., Ind. U. Broadway debut 1978 in "Angel."

ALLMON, CLINTON. Born June 13, 1941 in Monahans, TX. Graduate Okla. State U. Bdwy debut 1969 in "Indians," followed by "The Best Little Whorehouse in Texas," OB in "The Bluebird," "Khaki Blue," "One Sunday Afternoon."

ALMQUIST, GREGG. Born Dec. 1, 1948 in Minneapolis, MN. Graduate UMinn. Debut OB 1974 in "Richard III," followed by "A Night at the Black Pig," "Mother Courage," "King Lear."

ALPERN, MORRIS. Born Apr. 2, 1940 in Perth Amboy, NJ. Attended Monmouth Col., Miami U. OB in "Brecht on Brecht," "This Side of Paradise," "Harmony," "The Infantry," "Arthur."

ANANIA, JOHN. Born July 12, 1923 in Sicily. Attended HB Studio. Bdwy bow 1947 in "Sweethearts," followed by "Christine," "Little Me," "Cafe Crown," "Skyscraper," "Breakfast at Tiffany's," "Golden Rainbow," "The Penny Wars," "Applause," "Hello, Dolly!," OB in "What a Killing," "Fly Blackbird."

ANDALMAN, JEAN. Born May 5, 1951 in Chicago, IL. Graduate Sarah Lawrence Col. Bdwy debut 1972 OB in "The Bar That Never Closes," followed by "Thoughts," Bdwy 1976 in "Oh! Calcutta!"

ANDERMAN, MAUREEN. Born Oct. 26, 1946 in Detroit, MI. Graduate UMich. Bdwy debut 1970 in "Othello," followed by "Moonchildren" for which she received a Theatre World Award, "An Evening with Richard Nixon . . . ," "The Last of Mrs. Lincoln," "Seascape," "Who's Afraid of Virginia Woolf?," "A History of the American Film," OB in "Hamlet," "Elusive Angel," "Out of Our Father's House."

ANDERSSON, BIBI. Born Nov. 11, 1935 in Stockholm. SW. Attended Royal Dramatic Th. Sch. After success in Sweden on stage and film, made Bdwy debut 1973 in "Full Circle," followed by "The Night of the Tribades."

ANDRE, JILL. Born Feb. 16, 1935 in NYC. Attended CCNY, Columbia U. Debut OB 1952 in "Madwoman of Chaillot," followed by "Dark of the Moon," "Last Analysis," "Horseman Pass By," "From Here Inside My Head," "Kennedy's Children," "Stop the Parade," "Monkey, Monkey," "Battle of Angels," "Four Friends," "Augusta," "Wayside Motor Inn," Bdwy in "Sunrise at Campobello," "Great White Hope," "An Evening with Richard Nixon . . . ," "The Trip Back Down."

ANDREAS, CHRISTINE. Born Oct. 1, 1951 in Camden, NJ. Bdwy debut 1975 in "Angel Street," followed by "My Fair Lady," for which she received a Theatre World Award, OB in "Disgustingly Rich."

ANDREWS, GEORGE LEE. Born Oct. 13, 1942 in Milwaukee, WI. Debut OB 1970 in "Jacques Brel Is Alive . . . ," followed by "Starting Here Starting Now," Bdwy in "A Little Night Music" (1973), "On The 20th Century."

ANGELA, JUNE. Born Aug. 18, 1959 in NYC. Bdwy debut 1970 in "Lovely Ladies, Kind Gentlemen," followed by "The King and I" (1977).

ARDEN, DANIEL. Born Oct. 30, 1954 in Los Angeles, CA. Graduate NC School of Arts. Bdwy debut 1977 in "Equus."

ARI, BOB. Born July 1, 1949 in NYC. Graduate Carnegie-Mellon U. Debut OB in "Boys from Syracuse" (1976), followed by "Gay Divorce."

ARTHUR, PERRY. Born July 23, 1956 in Spirit Lake, IA. Attended Mansfield State Col., Drew U., AMDA. Bdwy debut 1977 in "Hair."

ATHERTON, WILLIAM. Born July 30, 1947 in Orange, Ct. Carnegie Tech graduate. Debut 1971 OB in "House of Blue Leaves," followed by "Basic Training of Pavlo Hummel," "Suggs" for which he received a Theatre World Award, "Rich and Famous," "The Passing Game," Bdwy 1972 in "The Sign in Sidney Brustein's Window."

ATKINS, EILEEN. Born June 16, 1934 in London, Eng. Attended Guildhall Sch. Bdwy debut 1966 in "The Killing of Sister George," followed by "The Promise," "Vivat! Vivat Regina!," "The Night of the Tribades."

ATTLES, JOSEPH. Born Apr. 7, 1903 in Charleston, SC. Attended Harlem Musical Conservatory. Bdwy bow in "Blackbirds of 1928," followed by "John Henry," "Porgy and Bess," "Kwamina," "Tambourines to Glory," "The Last of Mrs. Lincoln," "Bubbling Brown Sugar," OB in "Jerico-Jim Crow," "Cabin in the Sky," "Prodigal Son," "Day of Absence," "Cry of Players," "King Lear," "Duplex," "Do, Lord, Remember Me."

AUBERJONOIS, RENE. Born June 1, 1940 in NYC. Graduate Carnegie Inst. With LCRep in "A Cry of Players," "King Lear," and "Twelfth Night," Bdwy in "Fire," "Coco," "Tricks," "The Good Doctor," BAM Co. in "The New York Idea," "Three Sisters," "The Play's the Thing," "Julius Caesar."

AUSTIN, ANTHONY. Born June 6, 1966 in NYC. Debut OB 1974 in "Merry Wives of Windsor," followed by "Billy Irish," "Exiles."

AUSTIN, BETH. Born May 23, 1952 in Philadelphia, PA. Graduate Point Park Col., Pittsburgh Playhouse. Debut OB 1977 in "Wonderful Town" (ELT), Bdwy 1977 in "Sly Fox."

AYR, MICHAEL. Born Sept. 8, 1953 in Great Falls, MT. Graduate SMU. Debut 1976 OB in "Mrs. Murray's Farm," followed by "The Farm," "Ulysses in Traction," "Lulu," "Cabin 12."

Obba Babatunde   Christine Baranski   Charles Bari   Jayne Barnett   David Baumunk

AZITO, ANTONIO. Born July 18, 1948 in NYC. Attended Juilliard. Debut OB 1971 in "Red, White and Black," followed by "Players Project," "Secrets of the Citizens' Correction Committee," "Threepenny Opera." Bdwy 1977 in "Happy End."

BABATUNDE, OBBA. Born in Jamaica, NY. Attended Brooklyn Col. Debut OB 1970 in "The Secret Place," followed by "Guys and Dolls," "On Toby Time," "The Breakout," "Scottsbourough Boys," "Showdown Time," "Dream on Monkey Mt.," "Sheba," Bdwy 1978 in "Timbuktu."

BACIGALUPI, ROBERT. Born Oct. 21, 1949 in San Francisco, CA. Juilliard graduate. Debut 1975 in "The Robber Bridegroom," followed OB by "Edward II," "The Time of Your Life," "Mother Courage," "King Lear."

BAILEY, DENNIS. Born Apr. 12, 1953 in Grosse Pointe Woods, MI. UDetroit graduate. Debut 1977 OB in "House of Blue Leaves," Bdwy 1978 in "Gemini."

BAKER, LENNY. Born Jan. 17, 1945 in Boston, MA. Graduate Boston U. Debut OB 1969 in "Frank Gagliano's City Scene," followed by "The Year Boston Won the Pennant," "The Time of your Life," "Summertree," "Early Morning," "Survival of Joan," "Gallery," "Barbary Shore," "Merry Wives of Windsor," "Pericles," "Secret Service," "Boy Meets Girl," "Henry V," "Measure for Measure," Bdwy in "Freedom of the City" (1974), "I Love My Wife."

BALABAN, ROBERT. Born Aug. 16, 1945 in Chicago, IL. Attended Colgate, NYU. Debut 1967 OB in "You're a Good Man, Charlie Brown," followed by "Up Eden," "White House Murder Case," "Basic Training of Pavlo Hummel," "The Children," Bdwy in "Plaza Suite" (1968), "Some of My Best Friends."

BALSAM, MARTIN. Born Nov. 4, 1919 in NYC. Attended Actors Studio. Debut 1935 in "Pot Boiler" (OB), followed by "Ghost for Sale," "The Closing Door," "Sundown Beach," "Macbeth," "The Rose Tattoo," "Camino Real," "Middle of the Night," "The Porcelain Year," "You Know I Can't Hear You When the Water's Running," "Cold Storage."

BANCROFT, ANNE. Born Sept. 17, 1931 in NYC. Attended AADA. Bdwy debut 1958 in "Two for the Seesaw" for which she received a Theatre World Award, followed by "The Devils," "The Little Foxes" (1967), "A Cry of Players," "Golda."

BARANSKI, CHRISTINE. Born May 2, 1952 in Buffalo, NY. Graduate Juilliard Sch. Debut OB 1978 in "One Crack Out."

BARBOUR, THOMAS. Born July 25, 1921 in NYC. Princeton, Harvard graduate. Bdwy in "Portrait of a Queen," "Great White Hope," "Scratch," "The Lincoln Mask," OB in "Twelfth Night," "Admirable Bashville," "River Line," "The Lady's Not for Burning," "The Enchanted," "Antony and Cleopatra," "The Saintliness of Margery Kemp," "Dr. Willy Nilly," "Under the Sycamore Tree," "Epitaph for George Dillon," "Thracian Horse," "Old Glory," "Sjt. Musgrave's Dance," "Veil of Infamy," "Nestless Birds," "The Seagull," "Wayside Motor Inn," "Arthur."

BARI, CHARLES. Born July 15, 1954 in NYC. Attended Fredonia State UNY. Debut 1977 OB in "Carnival."

BARKER, MARGARET. Born Oct. 10, 1908 in Baltimore, MD. Attended Bryn Mawr. Bdwy debut 1928 in "The Age of Innocence," followed by, among others, "Barretts of Wimpole Street," "House of Connelly," "Men in White," "Gold Eagle Guy," "Leading Lady," "Member of the Wedding," "Autumn Garden," "See the Jaguar," "Ladies of the Corridor," "Master Builder," "Wayside Motor Inn" (OB).

BARNETT, JAYNE. Born Sept. 24, 1947 in Columbus, OH. Graduate Cincinnati Cons., Columbia U. Debut 1972 OB in "Dear Oscar," followed by "Washington Square," Bdwy in "Angel" (1978).

BARON, ROGER. Born NOv. 22, 1946 in Chicago, IL. Graduate Northwestern U. Bdwy debut 1976 in "The Heiress," followed by "The Crucible" (OB).

BARRETT, LAURINDA. Born in NYC in 1931. Attended Wellesley Col., RADA. OB in "The Misanthrope," "Palm Tree in a Rose Garden," "All Is Bright," Bdwy in "Too Late the Phalarope," "The Girls in 509," "The Milk Train Doesn't Stop Here Anymore," "UTBU," "I Never Sang for My Father," "Equus."

BARRIE, BARBARA. Born May 23, 1931 in Chicago, IL. Graduate UTex. Bdwy debut 1955 in "The Wooden Dish," followed by "Happily Never After," "Company," "Selling of the President," "Prisoner of Second Avenue," "California Suite," OB in "The Crucible," "Beaux Stratagem," "Taming of the Shrew," "Twelfth Night," "All's Well That Ends Well," "Horseman, Pass By," "Killdeer."

BARROWS, DIANA. Born Jan. 23, 1966 in NYC. Bdwy debut 1975 in "Cat on a Hot Tin Roof," followed by "Panama Hattie" (ELT), "Annie."

BARTON, DANIEL. Born Jan. 23, 1949 in Buffalo, NY. Attended Buffalo State, Albany State. Bdwy debut 1976 in "The Poison Tree," followed by "Timbuktu."

BARTLETT, D'JAMIN. Born May 21 in NYC. Attended AADA. Bdwy debut 1973 in "A Little Night Music" for which she received a Theatre World Award, OB in "The Glorious Age," "Boccacio," "2 by 5," "Lulu."

BATEMAN, BILL. Born Dec. 10 in Rock Island, IL. Graduate Augustana Co;. Debut 1974 OB in "Anything Goes," followed by Bdwy in "Hello, Dolly!" (1978).

BATES, KATHY. Born June 28, 1948 in Memphis, TN. Graduate Southern Methodist U. Debut OB 1976 in "Vanities."

BATTEN, TOM. Born in Oklahoma City. OK. Graduate USC. Bdwy debut 1961 in "How to Succeed in Business . . . ," followed by "Mame," "Gantry," "Mack and Mabel," "She Loves Me," "On the 20th Century."

BAUMANN, K. T. Born Aug. 13, 1946 in The Bronx, NY. Attended Neighborhood Playhouse. Bdwy debut 1967 in "The Prime of Miss Jean Brodie," followed by "Penny Wars," "Hello, Dolly!" (1978), OB in "Lemon Sky," "Effect of Gamma Rays . . . ," "Trelawny of 'The Wells'."

BAUMUNK, DAVID. Born Dec. 11 in Waynesboro, PA. Graduate George Washington U. Debut 1977 OB in "The Pirates of Penzance," followed by "Allegro."

BAYER, GARY. Born June 25, 1944 in Los Angeles, CA. Graduate UEvansville, NYU. Bdwy debut 1978 in "A History of the American Film."

BEACH, GARY. Born Oct. 10, 1947 in Alexandria, VA. Graduate NC Sch. of Arts. Bdwy bow 1971 in "1776," followed by "Something's Afoot," OB in "Smile, Smile, Smile," "What's a Nice Country like You . . . ," "Ionescapade," "By Strouse."

BECKHAM, BILLY. Born July 9, 1927 in Winnsboro, SC. Attended USC, Piscator's Workshop, New School. Debut 1948 OB in "All the King's Men," Bdwy in "Angel" (1978).

BEDFORD, PATRICK. Born May 30, 1932 in Dublin IR. Appeared with Dublin Gate Theatre before Bdwy bow 1966 in "Philadelphia Here I Come," followed by "The Mundy Scheme," "Small Craft Warnings" (OB), "Equus."

BELL, BRIAN. Born Apr. 18, 1945 in NYC. Graduate UDenver. Debut 1977 OB in "The Passion of Dracula."

BELL, JOAN. Born Feb. 1, 1935 in Bombay, Ind. Studied at Sylvia Bryant Stage Sch. Bdwy debut 1963 in "Something More," followed by "Applause," "Chicago."

BELLOMO, JOE. Born Apr. 12, 1938 in NYC. Attended Manhattan Sch. of Music. Bdwy bow 1960 in "New Girl in Town," followed by CC's "South Pacific" and "Guys and Dolls," OB in " Cindy," "Fantasticks."

BENNETT, MEG. Born Oct. 4, 1948 in Los Angeles, CA. Graduate Northwestern U. Bdwy OB 1971 in "Godspell," on Bdwy 1972 in "Grease."

BERETTA, JOANNE. Born Nov. 14 in San Francisco, CA. Attended San Francisco State Col. Debut 1976 OB in "The Club."

BEREZIN, TANYA. Born Mar. 25, 1941 in Philadelphia, Pa. Attended Boston U. Debut OB 1967 in "The Sandcastle," followed by "Three Sisters," "Great Nebula in Orion," "him," "Amazing Activity of Charlie Contrare," "Battle of Angels," "Mound Builders," "Serenading Louie," "My Life," "Brontosaurus."

BERNHARD, KAREN. Born Jan. 10, 1954 in NYC. Graduate Union Col. Debut 1978 OB in "The Offering," followed by "The Twilight Dinner."

BERRY, ERIC. Born Jan. 9, 1913 in London. Graduate RADA. NY debut 1954 in "The Boy Friend," followed by "Family Reunion," "The Power and the Glory," "Beaux Stratagem," "Broken Jug," "Pictures in the Hallway." "Peer Gynt," "Great God Brown," "Henry IV," "The White House," "White Devil," "Charley's Aunt," "The Homecoming" (OB), "Capt. Brassbound's Conversion," "Pippin."

BERTRAND, JACQUELINE. Born June 1, 1937 in Quebec City, Can. Attended Neighborhood Playhouse, LAMDA. Debut 1957 OB in "Madwoman of Chaillot," followed by "Geranium Hat," "Rhuy Blas," "Command Performance," "The Elizabethans," "Tovarich," "Dancing for the Kaiser," "Lulu."

BETSKO, KATHLEEN. Born May 6, 1939 in Coventry, Eng. Graduate UNH. Bdwy debut 1976 in "Equus," OB in "Ring Round the Moon," "A Slight Ache."

Susan Bigelow **Joseph Billone** **Verna Bloom** **Thomas Hewitt Brooks** **Candy Brown**

BEVERLEY, TRAZANA. Born Aug. 9, 1945 in Baltimore, MD. Graduate NYU. Debut 1969 OB in "Rules for Running Trains," followed by "Les Femmes Noires," "Geronamo," Bdwy in "My Sister, My Sister," "For Colored Girls Who Have Considered Suicide When the Rainbow Is Enuf" for which she received a Theatre World Award.

BIGELOW, SUSAN. Born Apr. 11, 1952 in Abington, PA. Attended UMd. Bdwy debut 1978 in "Working."

BILLONE, JOSEPH. Born Mar. 24, 1953 in Greenwich, CT. Graduate UCt., NYU. Debut 1978 OB in "Gay Divorce."

BINDIGER, EMILY. Born May 10, 1955 in Brooklyn, NY. Graduate HS Performing Arts. Debut 1973 OB in "Sisters of Mercy," Bdwy 1977 in "Shenandoah."

BIRNEY, REED. Born Sept. 11, 1954 in Alexandria, Va. Attended Boston U. Bdwy debut 1977 in "Gemini."

BISHOP, KELLY (formerly Carole). Born Feb. 28, 1944 in Colorado Springs, CO. Bdwy debut 1967 in "Golden Rainbow," followed by "Promises, Promises," "On The Town," "Rachel Lily Rosenbloom," "A Chorus Line."

BLACKTON, JACK. Born Mar. 16, 1938 in Colorado Springs, CO. OB in "The Fantasticks," "Put It in Writing," "Jacques Brel Is Alive . . . ," "Hark," "Kaboom," Bdwy in "Mame" (1966), "Side by Side by Sondheim."

BLAIR, PAMELA. Born Dec. 5, 1949 in Arlington, VT. Attended Ntl. Acad. of Ballet. Made Bdwy debut in 1972 in "Promises, Promises," followed by "Sugar," "Seesaw," "Of Mice and Men," "Wild and Wonderful," "A Chorus Line," OB in "Ballad of Boris K," "The Best Little Whorehouse in Texas."

BLAISDELL, NESBITT. Born Dec. 6, 1928 in NYC. Graduate Amherst, Columbia U. Debut 1978 OB in "Old Man Joseph and His Family," followed by "Moliere in Spite of Himself."

BLOOM, VERNA. Born Aug. 7 in Lynn, MA. Graduate Boston U. Bdwy debut 1967 in "Marat/Sade," followed OB by "Kool Aid," "The Cherry Orchard."

BLUM, MARK. Born May 14, 1950 in Newark, NJ. Graduate UPa., UMinn. Debut 1976 OB in "The Cherry Orchard."

BLUMENFELD, ROBERT. Born Feb. 26, 1943 in NYC. Graduated Rutgers, Columbia U. Bdwy debut 1970 in "Othello," OB in American Savoyards productions, "The Fall and Redemption of Man," "Tempest," "The Dybbuk," "Count Dracula."

BOBBIE, WALTER. Born Nov. 18, 1945 in Scranton, Pa. Graduate UScranton, Catholic U. Bdwy bow 1971 in "Frank Merriwell," followed by "Grass Harp," "Grease," "Drat!" (OB), "Tricks," "Going Up," "A History of the American Film."

BOEN, EARL. Born Aug. 8, 1941 in Pueblo, CO. Graduate Idaho State U. Debut 1978 OB in "The Devil's Disciple."

BOGAZIANOS, VASILI. Born Feb. 1, 1949 in NYC. Graduated San Francisco State Col. Debut 1978 OB in "P. S. Your Cat Is Dead" for which he received a Theatre World Award.

BONAFONS, KEN. Born Mar. 24, 1943 in New Orleans, LA. Graduate UNew Orleans. Bdwy debut 1977 in "Caesar and Cleopatra," followed OB in "Count Dracula."

BOND, RALEIGH. Born July 20, 1935 in Chicago, IL. Graduate Northwestern U. Debut 1961 OB in "Donogoo," followed by "Abe Lincoln in Illinois," "Evenings with Chekhov," "Red Roses for Me," "Taming of the Shrew," "Shortchanged Review," "Beaux Stratagem," Bdwy 1977 in "Sly Fox."

BOOCKVOR, STEVE. Born Nov. 18, 1942 in NYC. Attended Queens Col., Juilliard. Bdwy debut 1966 in "Anya," followed by "A Time for Singing," "Cabaret," "Mardi Gras," "Jimmy," "Billy," "The Rothchilds," "Follies," "Over Here," "The Lieutenant," "Musical Jubilee," "Annie," "Working."

BOOTH, ERIC. Born Oct. 18, 1950 in NYC. Graduate Emerson Col., Stanford U. Bdwy debut 1977 in "Caesar and Cleopatra," followed by "Golda," OB in "The Taming of the Shrew."

BORDO, ED. Born Mar. 3, 1931 in Cleveland, OH. Graduate Allegheny Col., LAMDA. Bdwy bow 1964 in "The Last Analysis," followed by "Inquest," "Zalmen or the Madness of God," "Annie," OB in "The Dragon," "Waiting for Godot," "Saved."

BORRELLI, JIM. Born Apr. 10, 1948 in Lawrence, MA. Graduate Boston Col. NY Debut OB 1971 in "Subject to Fits," followed by "Grease."

BOSCO, PHILIP. Born Sept. 26, 1930 in Jersey City, NJ. Graduate Catholic U. Credits: "Auntie Mame," "Rape of the Belt," "Ticket of Leave Man" (OB), "Donnybrook," "Man for All Seasons," "Mrs. Warren's Profession," with LCRep in "The Alchemist," "East Wind," "Galileo," "St. Joan," "Tiger at the Gate," "Cyrano," "King Lear," "A Great Career," "In the Matter of J. Robert Oppenheimer," "The Miser," "The Time of Your Life," "Camino Real," "Operation Sidewinder," "Amphitryon," "Enemy of the People," "Playboy of the Western World," "Good Woman of Setzuan," "Antigone," "Mary Stuart," "Narrow Road to the Deep North," "The Crucible," "Twelfth Night," "Enemies," "Plough and the Stars," "Merchant of Venice," and "A Streetcar Named Desire," "Henry V," "Threepenny Opera," "Streamers," "Stages," "St. Joan," "The Biko Inquest."

BOUTSIKARIS, DENNIS. Born Dec. 21, 1952 in Newark, NJ. Graduate Hampshire Col. Debut 1975 OB in "Another Language," followed by "Funeral March for a One-Man Band."

BOVA, JOSEPH. Born May 25, in Cleveland, OH. Graduate Northwestern U. Debut OB 1959 in "On the Town," followed by "Once Upon a Mattress," "House of Blue Leaves," "Comedy," "The Beauty Part," NYSF's "Taming of the Shrew," "Richard III," "Comedy of Errors," "Invitation to a Beheading," "Merry Wives of Windsor," "Henry V," "Streamers," Bdwy in "Rape of the Belt," "Irma La Douce," "Hot Spot," "The Chinese," "American Millionaire," "St. Joan."

BRACKEN, EDDIE. Born Feb. 7, 1920 in Astoria, NY. Bdwy bow 1931 in "The Man on Stilts," followed by "The Lady Refuses," "Life's Too Short," "Iron Men," "Brother Rat," "What a Life," "Too Many Girls," "Seven Year Itch," "Teahouse of the August Moon," "Shinbone Alley," "Beg, Borrow or Steal," "The Odd Couple," "You Know I Can't Hear You . . ." "Hello, Dolly!" (1978).

BRADLEY, HENRY. Born Nov. 23, 1931 in Albany, NY. Attended Am Th Wing, Black Theatre Workshop. Debut OB 1977 in "On the Lock-In."

BRANDEIS, RUTH. Born May 31, 1942 in NYC. Attended San Francisco State Col. OB in "Theatre of the Absurd," "Leave from Quintessence," "The Killers," "Nighthawk," "Against the Sun," "The Beard."

BREMSETH, LLOYD. Born July 27, 1948 in Minneapolis, MN. Attended UMinn. Debut 1968 in "Kiss Rock," followed by "Klara," "Sweet Shoppe Myriam," "Kiss Now," "Godspell."

BRENNAN, MIKE. Born Feb. 4, 1948 in NYC. Graduate Fordham U. Debut 1973 OB in "Arms and the Man," followed by "Gay Divorce."

BRIGHT, RICHARD. Born June 28, 1937 in Brooklyn, NY. OB in "The Balcony," "Does a Tiger Wear a Necktie?," "The Beard," "Survival of St. Joan," "Kool Aid," "Gogol," Bdwy 1977 in "The Basic Training of Pavlo Hummel."

BRISEBOIS, DANIELLE. Born June 28, 1969 in Brooklyn, NY. Bdwy debut 1977 in "Annie."

BROCKSMITH, ROY. Born Sept. 15, 1945 in Quincy, IL. Debut OB 1971 in "Whip Lady," followed by "The Workout," "Beggar's Opera," "Polly," "Threepenny Opera," Bdwy in "The Leaf People" (1975), "Stages," "Tartuffe."

BROOKES, JACQUELINE. Born July 24, 1930 in Montclair, NJ. Graduate UIowa, RADA. Bdwy debut 1955 in "Tiger at the Gates," followed by "Watercolor," "Abelard and Heloise," OB in "The Cretan Woman" for which she received a Theatre World Award, "The Clandestine Marriage," "Measure for Measure," "Duchess of Malfi," "Ivanov," "Six Characters in Search of an Author," "An Evening's Frost," "Come Slowly, Eden," "The Increased Difficulty of Concentration," "The Persians," "Sunday Dinner," "House of Blue Leaves," "A Meeting by the River," "Owners," "Hallelujah," "Dream of a Blacklisted Actor," "Knuckle," "Mama Sang the Blues."

BROOKS, JEFF. Born Apr. 7, 1950 in Vancouver, Can. Attended Portland State U. Debut 1976 OB in "Titanic," followed by "Fat Chances," Bdwy in "A History of the American Film" (1978).

BROOKS, JOEL. Born Dec. 17, 1949 in NYC. Graduated Hunter Col., UMin., AADA. Debut 1974 OB in "Auto Destruct," followed by "Fog and Mismanagement," "Museum."

BROOKS, THOMAS. Born June 13, 1949 in Bryn Mawr, PA. Graduate UPa. Debut 1978 OB in "Othello."

BROWN, CANDY A. Born Aug. 19 in San Rafael, CA. Attended MacAlester Col. Bdwy debut 1969 in "Hello, Dolly," followed by "Purlie," "Pippin," "Chicago."

| Kale Brown | Catherine Burns | Terence Burk | Gisela Caldwell | Philip Campanella |

BROWN, GWENDOLYN, (formerly Gwen Saska). Born Sept. 9, 1939 in Mishawaka, IN. Northwestern and Columbia graduate. Debut 1969 OB in "Geese," followed by "Macbeth," "In the Boom Boom Room," "Secret Service," "Boy Meets Girl," Bdwy 1977 in "The Trip Back Down," then "St. Joan."

BROWN, KALE. Born June 16, 1949 in San Rafael, CA. Attended U.S. International U., HB Studio. Debut 1978 OB in "Othello."

BROWN, KERMIT. Born Feb. 3, 1937 in Asheville, NC. Graduate Duke U. With APA in "War and Peace," "Judith," "Man and Superman," "The Show-Off," "Pantagleize," "The Cherry Orchard," OB in "The Millionairess," "Things," "Lulu," "Heartbreak House," "Glad Tidings."

BROWN, MIKE. Born Apr. 11, 1967 in Brooklyn, NY. Bdwy debut 1977 in "Golda."

BROWN, PENDLETON. Born Sept. 17, 1948 in Corry, PA. Attended HB Studio. Bdwy bow 1971 in "Soon," followed by "The Sign in Sidney Brustein's Window," "St. Joan."

BRUCE, KATHERINE. Born Dec. 25, 1941 in Cleveland, OH. Attended AADA. Debut 1967 OB in "The Rimers of Eldritch," followed by "Dinner at the Ambassador's," "The Adopted Moon."

BRUCE, SHELLEY. Born May 5, 1965 in Passaic, NJ. Debut OB 1973 in "The Children's Mass," Bdwy 1977 in "Annie."

BRUMMEL, DAVID. Born Nov. 1, 1942 in Brooklyn. Bdwy debut 1973 in "The Pajama Game," followed by "Music Is," OB in "Cole Porter," "Fantasticks."

BRYGGMAN, LARRY. Born Dec. 21, 1938 in Concord, CA. Attended CCSF, AmThWing. Debut 1962 OB in "A Pair of Pairs," followed by "Live like Pigs," "Stop, You're Killing Me," "Mod Donna," "Waiting for Godot," "Ballymurphy," "Marco Polo Sings a Solo," "Brownsville Raid," "Two Small Bodies," "Museum." Bdwy in "Ulysses in Nighttown," "Checking Out," "Basic Training of Pavlo Hummel."

BRYNNER, YUL. Born June 15, 1915 in Sakhalin Island, Japan. Bdwy debut 1946 in "Lute Song," followed by "The King and I," (also 1977 revival), "Home Sweet Homer."

BUCKLEY, BETTY. Born July 3, 1947 in Big Spring, TX. Graduate TCU. Bdwy debut 1969 in "1776," followed by "Pippin," OB in "Ballad of Johnny Pot," "What's a Nice Country Like You Doing in a State Like This?," "Circle of Sound."

BURGE, JAMES. Born Dec. 3, 1943 in Miami, FL. Graduate U Okla, Wayne State U. Bdwy bow 1970 in "Grin and Bare It," followed by "The Royal Family," OB in "Happy Hunter."

BURK, TERENCE. Born Aug. 11, 1947 in Lebanon, IL. Graduate S.IL.U. OB in "Religion," "The Future," "Sacred and Profane Love," Bdwy debut 1976 in "Equus."

BURKE, MICHAEL. Born Jan. 4, 1936 in Richmond, VA. Attended Randolph-Macon, Johns Hopkins U. Debut 1977 OB in "The Crucible."

BURKHARDT, GERRY. Born June 14, 1946 in Houston, TX. Attended Lon Morris Col. Bdwy debut 1968 in "Her First Roman," followed by "The Best Little Whorehouse in Texas."

BURNS, CATHERINE. Born Sept. 25, 1945 in NYC. Attended AADA. Bdwy debut 1968 in "The Prime of Miss Jean Brodie," OB in "Dream of a Blacklisted Actor," "Disintegration of James Cherry," "Operation Sidewinder," "Dear Janet Rosenberg, Dear Mr. Kooning" for which she received a Theatre World Award, "Two Small Bodies," "Voices."

BURSKY, JAY. Born Mar. 27, 1954 in Cleveland, OH. Graduated Indiana U. OB and Bdwy debut 1978 in "The Best Little Whorehouse in Texas."

BURTON, WARREN. Born Oct. 23, 1944 in Chicago, IL. Attended Wright Col. Bdwy bow in "Hair," followed by "A Patriot for Me," OB in "P.S. Your Cat Is Dead."

BUTTRAM, JAN. Born June 19, 1946 in Clarkesville, TX. Graduate NTexState. Debut 1974 OB in "Fashion," Bdwy 1978 in "The Best Little Whorehouse in Texas."

BYERS, CATHERINE. Born Oct. 7 in Sioux City, IA. Graduate UIowa, LAMDA, Bdwy debut 1971 in "The Philanthropist," followed by "Don't Call Back," "Equus," OB in "Petrified Forest," "All My Sons."

BYRDE, EDYE. Born Jan. 19, 1929 in NYC. Bdwy debut 1975 in "The Wiz."

CABLE, CHRISTOPHER. Born Mar. 18, 1930 in Alameda, CA. Graduate UCal. Debut 1965 OB in "Garden of Heavenly Faucets," followed by "The Drunkard," "Treasure Island," Bdwy in "Jesus Christ Superstar" (1977).

CALDWELL, GISELA. Born April 3 in Enid, OK. Graduate Geo. Washington U. Debut 1972 OB in "The Effect of Gamma Rays . . . ," followed by "Cappella," Bdwy in "Three Sisters" (1973), "Beggars Opera," "Measure for Measure."

CALKINS, MICHAEL. Born Apr. 27, 1948 in Chicago, IL. Graduate Webster Col. Debut 1973 OB in "Sisters of Mercy," followed by "Love! Love! Love!"

CALL, ANTHONY D. Born Aug. 31, 1940 in Los Angeles, CA. Attended UPa. Debut 1969 OB in "The David Show," Bdwy in "Crown Matrimonial," "The Trip Back Down."

CAMPANELLA, PHILIP. Born May 24, 1948 in Jersey City, NJ. Graduate St. Peter's Col., HB Studio. Debut 1970 OB in "Lady from Maxim's," followed by "Hamlet," "Tug of War," "Charles Abbott & Son," "She Stoops to Conquer," "Taming of the Shrew," "Misalliance," "The Play's the Thing," "The Caretaker," "Death of Lord Chatterly," "The Father," "Naked."

CANNING, JAMES J. Born July 2, 1946 in Chicago, IL. Graduate DePaul U. Bdwy debut 1972 in "Grease."

CARA, IRENE. Born Mar. 18, 1958 in NYC. Bdwy debut 1968 in "Maggie Flynn," followed by "The Me Nobody Knows," "Via Galactica," OB in "Lotta," "Ain't Misbehavin'"

CARIOU, LEN. Born Sept. 30, 1939 in Winnipeg, Can. Bdwy debut 1968 in "House of Atreus," followed by "Henry V" and "Applause" for which he received a Theatre World Award, "Night Watch," "A Little Night Music," "Cold Storage," OB in "A Sorrow Beyond Dreams."

CARLING, P. L. Born Mar. 31. Graduate Stanford U., UCLA. Debut 1955 OB in "The Chairs," followed by "In Good King Charles' Golden Days," "Magistrate," "Picture of Dorian Gray," "The Vise," "Lady from the Sea," "Booth Is Back in Town," "Ring Round the Moon," "Philadelphia, Here I Come," "Sorrows of Frederick," Bdwy in "The Devils" (1965), "Scratch," "Shenandoah."

CARLSEN, ALLAN. Born Feb. 7 in Chicago, IL. Attended UPa. Bdwy debut 1974 in "The Freedom of the City," OB in "The Morning after Optimism," "Iphigenia in Aulis," "Peg O' My Heart."

CARNEY, GRACE. Born Sept. 15, 1911 in Hartford, CT. Attended Columbia U, CCNY. Debut OB 1959 in "A Family Portrait," followed by "Billygoat Eddie," "Whitsuntide," Bdwy in "Donnybrook," "Eccentricities of a Nightingale," "Vieux Carre," "Angel."

CARNEY, MARY. Born Jan. 26, 1950 in Syracuse, NY. Graduate SONY Albany. Debut 1978 OB in "Othello."

CAROLI, VICTOR. Born May 11, 1942 in Lawrence, MA. Graduate IL. Wesleyan U. Debut 1977 OB in "The Crucible."

CARROLL, DAVID-JAMES. Born July 30, 1950 in Rockville Centre, NY. Graduate Dartmouth Col. Debut 1975 in "A Matter of Time," followed by "Joseph and the Amazing Technicolor Dreamboat," Bdwy "Rodgers and Hart" (1975), "Where's Charley?"

CARTER, NELL. Born Sept. 13 in Birmingham, AL. Bdwy debut 1971 in "Soon," followed by "Jesus Christ Superstar," "Dude," "Don't Bother Me, I Can't Cope," "Ain't Misbehavin'" for which she received a Theatre World Award, OB in "Iphigenia in Taurus," "Bury the Dead," "Fire in the Mindhouse," "The Dirtiest Show in Town."

CARTER, THELMA LOUISE. Born July 16 in Gary IN. Studied with Stella Adler. Debut 1975 OB in "Liberty Call," followed by "The Crucible."

CARVER, MARY. Born May 3, 1924 in Los Angeles, CA. Graduate USC. Debut 1950 OB in "Bury the Dead," followed by "Rhinoceros," "Life of Galileo," Bdwy in "Out West of 8th," "Low and Behold," "The Shadow Box."

CASHIN, TOM. Born Oct. 9, 1953 in Brooklyn, NY. Attended Hunter Col. Debut OB and Bdwy 1978 in "The Best Little Whorehouse in Texas."

CASSIDY, TIM. Born Mar. 22, 1952 in Alliance, OH. Attended UCincinnati. Bdwy debut 1974 in "Good News," followed by "A Chorus Line."

CASTANG, VERONICA. Born Apr. 22, 1938 in London, Eng. Attended Sorbonne. Bdwy debut 1966 in "How's the World Treating You?," followed by "The National Health," OB in "The Trigon," "Sjt. Musgrave's Dance," "Saved," "Water Hens," "Self-Accusation," "Kaspar," "Ionescapade," "Statements after and Arrest under the Immorality Act."

Eva Charney	**Paul Charles**	**Hye-Young Choi**	**Bryan Clark**	**Maris Clement**

CAVETT, DICK. Born Nov. 19, 1936 in Kearny, NE. Graduate of Yale U. Bdwy debut 1977 in "Otherwise Engaged."

CHAIKIN, SHAMI. Born Apr. 21, 1931 in NYC. Debut 1966 OB in "America Hurrah," followed by "Serpent," "Terminal," "Mutation Show," "Viet Rock," "Mystery Play," "Electra," "The Dybbuk."

CHAMBERS, MICHAEL. Born Apr. 13, 1940 in NYC. Graduate Goddard Col., Bristol Old Vic. Debut OB 1974 in "Mert and Phil," followed by "A Doll's House," Bdwy 1978 in "Sly Fox."

CHAMPION, GOWER. Born June 22, 1920 in Geneva, IL. Bdwy debut 1939 in "Streets of Paris," followed by "The Lady Comes Across," "Count Me In," "Tars and Spars," "Three for Tonight," "The Act."

CHANG, TISA. Born Apr. 5 in Chungking, CH. Attended CCNY. Bdwy debut 1970 in "Lovely Ladies, Kind Gentlemen," followed by "Brother" (OB), "Basic Training of Pavlo Hummel."

CHANNING, CAROL. Born Jan. 31, 1921 in Seattle, Wash. Attended Bennington Col. Bdwy debut 1941 in "No for an Answer," followed by "Let's Face It," "Proof Through the Night," "Lend an Ear" for which she received a Theatre World Award, "Gentlemen Prefer Blonds," "Wonderful Town," "The Vamp," "Show Girl," "Hello Dolly!" (also 1978 revival), "Four on a Garden," "Lorelei."

CHAPMAN, WILLIAM. Born Apr. 30, 1923 in Los Angeles, CA. Attended USCal. On Bdwy in "Candide," "Maria Golovin," "Greenwillow," "South Pacific" (CC 1961), "Shenandoah."

CHARLES, PAUL. Born July 29, 1947 in NYC. Attended Quintano Sch. Has appeared in "Best Foot Forward" (OB), "Kelly," "Royal Hunt of the Sun," "A Joyful Noise," "La Strada," "A Chorus Line."

CHARLES, WALTER. Born Apr. 4, 1945 in East Stroudsburg, PA. Graduate Boston U. Bdwy debut 1973 in "Grease," followed by "1600 Pennsylvania Avenue," "Knickerbocker Holiday."

CHARNEY, EVA. Born June 7 in Brooklyn, NY. Graduate Douglass Col., Boston U. Debut 1977 OB in "NYC Street Show," followed by "The Wanderers," "Caligula," Bdwy in "Hair" (1977).

CHIANESE, DOMINIC. Born Feb. 24, 1932 in NYC. Graduate Brooklyn Col. Debut 1952 OB with American Savoyards, followed by "Winterset," "Jacques Brel Is Alive . . . ," "Ballad for a Firing Squad," "City Scene," Bdwy in "Oliver!," "Scratch," "The Water Engine."

CHOI, HYE-YOUNG. Born Oct. 22, 1946 in Seoul, Korea. Graduate Manhattan Sch. of Music. Bdwy debut 1977 in "The King and I."

CHRISTIAN, ROBERT. Born Dec. 27, 1939 in Los Angeles. Attended UCLA. OB in "The Happening," "Hornblend," "Fortune and Men's Eyes," "Boys in the Band," "Behold! Cometh the Vanderkellans," "Mary Stuart," "Narrow Road to the Deep North," "Twelfth Night," "The Past Is the Past," "Going through Changes," "Black Sunlight," "Terraces," "Blood Knot," "Boesman and Lena," "Statements after an Arrest under the Immorality Act," Bdwy in "We Bombed in New Haven," "Does a Tiger Wear a Necktie?," "An Evening with Richard Nixon," "All God's Chillun."

CHRISTINA-JONES, LINDA. Born Mar. 19, 1947 in Tonawanda, NY. Graduate Wake Forest U. Debut 1977 OB in "The Bald Soprano."

CIBELLI, RENATO. Born Sept. 28, 1915 in The Bronx, NY. Attended RADA. Bdwy debut 1956 in "Happy Hunting," followed by "Milk and Honey," "Happiest Girl in the World," "Man of La Mancha" (original and 1977 revival).

CILENTO, WAYNE. Born Aug. 25, 1949, in The Bronx, NY. Graduate State U. Brockport. Bdwy in "Irene," "Rachel Lily Rosenbloom," "Seesaw," "A Chorus Line," "The Act," "Dancin'."

CISSEL, CHUCK. Born Oct. 3, 1948, in Tulsa, OK. Graduate UOkla. Bdwy debut 1971 in "Purlie," followed by "Lost in the Stars," "Via Galactica," "Don't Bother Me, I Can't Cope," "A Chorus Line."

CLANTON, RALPH. Born Sept. 11, 1914 in Fresno, CA. Attended Pasadena Playhouse. On Bdwy in "Victory Belles," "Macbeth," "Richard III," "Othello," "Lute Song," "Cyrano," "Antony and Cleopatra," "Design for a Stained Glass Window," "Taming of the Shrew," "Burning Glass," "Vivat! Vivat Regina!," "The Last of Mrs. Lincoln," OB in "Ceremony of Innocence," "Endecott and the Red Cross," "The Philanderer," BAM Co.'s "New York Idea," and "Three Sisters," "You Never Can Tell."

CLARK, BRYAN E. Born Apr. 5, 1929 in Louisville, KY. Graduate Fordham U. Bdwy debut 1978 in "A History of the American Film."

CLARK, CHERYL. Born Dec. 7, 1950 in Boston, MA. Attended Ind. U., NYU. Bdwy debut 1972 in "Pippin," followed by "Chicago," "A Chorus Line."

CLARK, JOSH. Born Aug. 16, 1955 in Bethesda, MD. Attended NC Sch. of Arts. Debut 1976 OB in "The Old Glory," followed by "Molly."

CLEMENT, CLARIS. Born July 11, 1950 in Philadelphia, PA. Graduate Rollins Col. Debut 1976 OB in "Noel and Cole," Bdwy 1978 in "On the 20th Century."

CLEMENTE, RENE. Born July 2, 1950 in El Paso, TX. Graduate West Tex. State U. Bdwy debut 1977 in "A Chorus Line."

CLOSE, GLENN. Born May 19, 1947 in Greenwich, CT. Graduate William & Mary Col. Bdwy debut 1974 with Phoenix Co. in "Love for Love," "Member of the Wedding," "Rules of the Game," followed by "Rex," OB in "The Crazy Locomotive," "Uncommon Women and Others."

COCA, IMOGENE. Born Nov. 18, 1908 in Philadelphia, PA. Bdwy debut 1925 in "When You Smile," followed by "Garrick Gaieties," "Flying Colors," "New Faces," "Fools Rush In," "Who's Who," "Folies Bergere," "Straw Hat Revue," "All in Fun," "Concert Varieties," "Janus," "Girls in 509," "On the 20th Century."

COE, JOHN. Born Oct. 19, 1925 in Hartford CT. Graduate Boston U. On Bdwy in "Passion of Josef D.," "Man in the Glass Booth," "La Strada," "Happy End," OB in "Marrying Maiden," "Thistle in My Bed," "John," "Wicked Cooks," "June Bug Graduates Tonight," "Drums in the Night," "America Hurrah," "Father Uxbridge Wants to Marry," "Nobody Hears a Broken Drum," "Dylan," "Screens," "The Kid."

COFFIELD, PETER. Born July 17, 1945 in Evanston, IL. Graduate Northwestern, UMich. With APA in "The Misanthrope," "Cock-a-Doodle Dandy" and "Hamlet," followed by "Abelard and Heloise," "Vivat! Vivat Regina!," "Merchant of Venice," "Tartuffe."

COFFIN, FREDERICK. Born Jan. 16, 1943 in Detroit, MI. Graduate UMich. Debut 1971 OB in "Basic Training of Pavlo Hummel," followed by "Much Ado about Nothing," "King Lear," "As You Like It," "Boom Boom Room," "Merry Wives of Windsor," "Secret Service," "Boy Meets Girl," "Hot Grog," Bdwy in "We Interrupt This Program" (1975).

COGGIN, BARBARA. Born Feb. 27 in Chattanooga, TN. Attended Peabody Col. Bdwy debut 1970 in "Lovely Ladies, Kind Gentlemen," followed by "Poor Murderer," OB in "The Drunkard," "One for the Money, etc.," "Judy: A Garland of Songs," "Rag Doll," "Museum."

COHEN, MARGERY. Born June 24, 1947 in Chicago, IL. Attended UWisc., UChicago. Bdwy debut 1968 in "Fiddler on the Roof," followed by "Jacques Brel Is Alive . . . ," OB in "Berlin to Broadway," "By Bernstein," "Starting Here Starting Now," "Unsung Cole."

COLE, KAY. Born Jan. 13, 1948 in Miami, Fl. Bdwy debut 1961 in "Bye Bye Birdie," followed by "Stop the World I Want to Get Off," "Roar of the Greasepaint . . . ," "Hair," "Jesus Christ Superstar," "Words and Music," "Chorus Line," OB in "The Cradle Will Rock," "Two if by Sea," "Rainbow," "White Nights," "Sgt. Pepper's Lonely Hearts Club Band."

COLLINS, STEPHEN. Born Oct. 1, 1947 in Des Moines, IO. Graduate Amherst Col. Bdwy debut 1972 in "Moonchildren," followed by "No Sex Please, We're British," "The Ritz," OB in "Twelfth Night," "More Than You Deserve," "Macbeth" (LC), "Last Days of British Honduras," BAM Co.'s "New York Idea," "Three Sisters," and "The Play's the Thing."

COLLINS, SUZANNE. Born in San Francisco, CA. Graduate USan Francisco. Debut 1975 OB in "Trelawny of the Wells," followed by "The Cherry Orchard."

COMBS, DAVID. Born June 10, 1949 in Reno, NV. Graduate UNev., Wayne State U. Bdwy debut 1975 in "Equus."

CONAWAY, JEFF. Born Oct. 5, 1950 in NYC. Attended NYU. Bdwy debut 1960 in "All the Way Home," followed by "Grease."

CONNER, BYRON. Born Dec. 5, 1953 in Gadsden, AL. Graduate Ithaca Col. Debut 1978 OB in "The Taming of the Shrew."

CONOLLY, PATRICIA. Born Aug. 29, 1933 in Tabora, E. Africa. Attended USydney. With APA in "You Can't Take It with You," "War and Peace," "School for Scandal," "Wild Duck," "Right You Are," "We Comrades Three," "Pantagleize," "Exit the King," "Cherry Orchard," "Misanthrope," "Cocktail Party" and "Cock-a-Doodle Dandy," followed by "A Streetcar Named Desire," "The Importance of Being Earnest."

Harriett Conrad   **Richard Cox**   **Peggy Cooper**   **Keene Curtis**   **Alma Cuervo**

CONRAD, HARRIETT. Born June 11, 1944 in NYC. Attended Queens Col., AADA, Neighborhood Playhouse. Debut 1972 on Bdwy in "Sugar," followed by "Man of La Mancha" (1977).

COOK, JILL. Born Feb. 25, 1954 in Plainfield, NJ. Bdwy debut 1971 in "On the Town," followed by "So Long, 174th Street," "Dancin'," OB in "Carnival."

COOLEY, DENNIS. Born May 11, 1948 in Huntington Park, CA. Attended Northwestern U. Bdwy debut 1970 in "Hair," followed by "Jesus Christ Superstar," "Creation of the World and Other Business," "Where's Charley?", "Shenandoah."

COONAN, SHEILA. Born June 28, 1922 in Montreal, Can. Attended McGill U. Appeared in "Red Roses for Me," "A Taste of Honey," "The Hostage," "The Great White Hope," OB in "Hogan's Goat," "Macbeth," "A Song for the First of May," "Happy Hunter."

COOPER, PEGGY. Born Mar. 31, 1931 in Huntington, WVa. Graduate Baldwin-Wallace Cons. Bdwy debut 1968 in "Zorba," followed by "La Strada," "The Rothschilds," "Goodtime Charley," "On the 20th Century."

COOPER, ROY. Born Jan. 22, 1930 in London, Eng. Bdwy debut 1968 in "The Prime of Miss Jean Brodie," followed by "Canterbury Tales," "St. Joan."

CORNTHWAITE, ROBERT. Born Apr. 18, 1917 in St. Helens, OR. Graduate USCal. Bdwy debut 1978 in "The Devil's Disciple."

COSTA, JOSEPH. Born June 8, 1946 in Ithaca, NY. Graduate Gettysburg Col., Yale U. Debut 1978 OB in "The Show-Off."

COSTER, NICOLAS. Born Dec. 3, 1934 in London. Attended Neighborhood Playhouse. Bdwy bow 1960 in "Becket," followed by "90 Day Mistress," "But Seriously," "Twigs," "Otherwise Engaged," OB in "Epitaph for George Dillon," "Shadow and Substance," "Thracian Horses," "O, Say Can You See," "Happy Birthday, Wanda June," "Naomi Court," "Old Glory."

COSTIGAN, KEN. Born Apr. 1, 1934 in NYC. Graduate Fordham U., Yale U. Debut 1960 OB in "Borak," followed by "King of the Dark Chamber," "The Hostage," "Next Time I'll Sing to You," "Curley McDimple," "The Runner Stumbles," "Peg o' My Heart," "The Show-Off," Bdwy 1962 in "Gideon."

COUNCIL, RICHARD. Born Oct. 1, 1947 in Tampa, FL. Graduate UFla. Debut OB 1973 in "Merchant of Venice," followed by "Ghost Dance," "Look We've Come Through," "Arms and the Man," "Isadora Duncan Sleeps with the Russian Navy," "Arthur," Bdwy 1975 in "The Royal Family."

COURTENAY, TOM. Born Feb. 25, 1937 in Hull, Eng. Graduate RADA. Made Bdwy debut 1977 in "Otherwise Engaged."

COWAN, EDIE. Born Apr. 14 in NYC. Graduate Butler U. Bdwy debut 1964 in "Funny Girl," followed by "Sherry," "Annie."

COX, RICHARD. Born May 6, 1948 in NYC. Yale graduate. Debut 1970 OB in "Saved," followed by "Fuga," "Moonchildren," "Three Sons," Bdwy in "The Sign in Sidney Brustein's Window" (1972).

CRABTREE, DON. Born Aug. 21, 1928 in Borger, TX. Attended Actors Studio. Bdwy bow 1959 in "Destry Rides Again," followed by "Happiest Girl in the World," "Family Affair," "Unsinkable Molly Brown," "Sophie," "110 in the Shade," "Golden Boy," "Pousse Cafe," "Mahagonny" (OB), "The Best Little Whorehouse in Texas."

CRAIG, DONALD. Born Aug. 14, 1941 in Abilene, TX. Graduate Hardin-Simmons Col., UTex. Debut 1975 OB in "Do I Hear a Waltz?" (ELT). Bdwy 1977 in "Annie."

CRAIG, JOEL. Born Apr. 26 in NYC. Attended Brandeis U. Bdwy debut 1961 in "Subways Are for Sleeping," followed by "Nowhere to Go but Up," "Hello, Dolly!," "Follies," "Cyrano," "Very Good Eddie," OB in "Out of This World," "Carnival."

CRISTOFER, MICHAEL. Born Jan. 22, 1945 in Trenton, NJ. Attended Catholic U. Made debut 1977 OB in "The Cherry Orchard" for which he received a Theatre World Award, followed by "Conjuring an Event."

CROFOOT, LEONARD JOHN. Born Sept. 20, 1948 in Utica, NY. Bdwy debut 1968 in "The Happy Time," followed by "Come Summer," "Gigi," OB in "Circus," "Joseph and the Amazing Technicolor Dreamcoat."

CROMWELL, DAVID. Born Feb. 16, 1946 in Cornwall, NY. Ithaca Col. graduate. Debut 1968 OB in "Up Eden," followed by "In the Boom Boom Room," Bdwy 1978 in "A History of the American Film."

CRONIN, JANE. Born Apr. 4, 1936 in Boston, MA. Attended Boston U. Bdwy debut 1965 in "Postmark Zero," OB in "Bald Soprano," "One Flew over the Cuckoo's Nest," "Hot l Baltimore," "The Gathering," "Catsplay."

CRONYN, HUME. Born July 18, 1911 in London, Can. Attended McGill U., AADA. Bdwy debut 1934 in "Hipper's Holiday," followed by "Boy Meets Girl," "High Tor," "Room Service," "There's Always a Breeze," "Escape This Night," "Off to Buffalo," "Three Sisters," "Weak Link," "Retreat to Pleasure," "Mr. Big," "Survivors," "Four-poster," "Madam, Will You Walk" (OB), "The Honcys," "A Day by the Sea," "Man in the Dog Suit," "Triple Play," "Big Fish, Little Fish," "Hamlet," "The Physicists," "A Delicate Balance," "Hadrian VII," "Promenade All," "Noel Coward in Two Keys," "Krapp's Last Tape," "Happy Days," "Act without Words," "The Gin Game."

CROWLEY, EDWARD. Born Sept. 5, 1926 in Lewiston, ME. Attended AADA. Bdwy debut 1958 in "Make a Million," followed by "Family Way," OB in "Admirable Bashville," "An Evening with GBS," "Once around the Block," "I Want You," "Lion in Love," "Telemachus Clay," "Hair," "How to Steal an Election," "In the Matter of J. Robert Oppenheimer," "An Evening for Merlin Finch," "Dylan," "Val, Christie and Others," "Danton's Death," "Arthur."

CROXTON, DARRYL. Born Apr. 5, 1946 in Baltimore, MD. Attended AADA. Appeared OB in "Volpone," "Murder in the Cathedral," "The Taking of Miss Janie," "Old Glory," "Divine Comedy," "Jack Gelber's New Play," Bdwy debut 1969 in "Indians," followed by "Sly Fox."

CUERVO, ALMA. Born Aug. 13, 1951 in Tampa FL. Graduate Tulane U., Yale U. Debut 1977 OB in "Uncommon Women and Others."

CULLUM, JOHN. Born Mar. 2, 1930 in Knoxville, TN. Graduate U. Tenn. Bdwy bow 1960 in "Camelot," followed by "Infidel Caesar," "The Rehearsal," "Hamlet," "On a Clear Day You Can See Forever" for which he received a Theatre World Award, "Man of LaMancha," "1776," "Vivat! Vivat Regina!," "Shenandoah," "Kings," "The Trip Back Down," "On the 20 Century," OB in "Three Hand Reel," "The Elizabethans," "Carousel," "In the Voodoo Parlor of Marie Leveau," "The King and I" (JB).

CUNLIFFE, JERRY. Born May 16, 1935 in Chicago, IL. Attended UChicago. Debut 1957 OB in "Anatol," followed by "Antigone," "Difficult Woman," "Tom Paine," "Futz," "Cherry Orchard," Bdwy in "Elizabeth I" (1972).

CURRY, CHRISTOPHER. Born Oct. 22, 1948, in Grand Rapids, MI. Graduated UMich. Debut 1974 OB in "When You Comin' Back, Red Ryder?" followed by "The Cherry Orchard," "Spelling Bee," "Ballymurphy," "Isadora Duncan Sleeps with the Russian Navy," "The Promise."

CURTIS, KEENE. Born Feb. 15, 1925 in Salt Lake City, UT. Graduate UUtah. Bdwy bow 1949 in "Shop at Sly Corner," with APA in "School for Scandal," "The Tavern," "Anatole," "Scapin," "Right You Are," "Importance of Being Earnest," "Twelfth Night," "King Lear," "Seagull," "Lower Depths," "Man and Superman," "Judith," "War and Peace," "You Can't Take It with You," "Pantagleize," "Cherry Orchard," "Misanthrope," "Cocktail Party," "Cock-a-Doodle Dandy" and "Hamlet," "A Patriot for Me," "The Rothschilds," "Night Watch," "Via Galactica," "Annie," OB in "Colette," "Ride across Lake Constance."

CWIKOWSKI, BILL. Born Aug. 4, 1945 in Newark, NJ. Graduate Monmouth and Smith Cols. Debut 1972 OB in "Charlie the Chicken," followed by "Summer Brave," "Desperate Hours," "Mandragola," "Two by John Ford Noonan," "Soft Touch," "Innocent Pleasures."

DAMON, CATHRYN. Born Sept. 11 in Seattle, WA. Bdwy debut 1954 in "By the Beautiful Sea," followed by "The Vamp," "Shinbone Alley," "A Family Affair," "Foxy," "Flora, The Red Menace," "UTBU," "Come Summer," "Criss-Crossing," "A Place for Polly," "Last of the Red Hot Lovers," OB in "Boys from Syracuse," "Secret Life of Walter Mitty," "Show Me Where The Good Times Are," "Effect of Gamma Rays on Man-in-the-Moon Marigolds," "Siamese Connections," "Prodigal," "Down by the River . . . ," "Sweet Bird of Youth," "The Cherry Orchard."

DANA, LEORA. Born Apr. 1, 1923 in NYC. Attended Barnard Col., RADA. Bdwy debut 1947 in "Madwoman of Chaillot," followed by "Happy Time," "Point of No Return," "Sabrina Fair," "Best Man," "Beekman Place," "The Last of Mrs. Lincoln," "The Women," "Mourning Pictures," OB in "In the Summer House," "Wilder's Triple Bill," "Collision Course," "Bird of Dawning Singeth All Night Long," "Increased Difficulty of Concentration," "Place without Mornings," "Rebel Women," "The Tennis Game."

DANIELE, GRACIELA. Born Dec. 8, 1939 in Buenos Aires. Bdwy debut 1964 in "What Makes Sammy Run?" followed by "Here's Where I Belong," "Promises, Promises," "Follies," "Chicago."

William Daprato   Leslie Denniston   Jack Davidson   Anne DeSalvo   Ronald Dennis

DAPRATO, WILLIAM J. Born Sept. 22, 1924 in The Bronx, NY. Attended Th. Sch. of Dramatic Arts. Debut 1963 OB in "The Burning," followed by "Holy Ghosts," "Awake and Sing," Bdwy in "Mike Downstairs," "Shenandoah."

DARKE, REBECCA. Born Dec. 6, 1935 in Brooklyn, NY. Credits: OB in "The Midnight Caller," "Who'll Save the Plowboy," "Undercover Man," "A Party for Divorce," "A Piece of Blue Sky," "Hey, Rube," Bdwy 1977 in "The Basic Training of Pavlo Hummel."

DAVID, CLIFFORD. Born June 30, 1932 in Toledo, OH. Attended Toledo U., Actors Studio. Bdwy bow 1960 in "Caligula," followed by "Wildcat," "Aspern Papers," "On a Clear Day You Can See Forever," "A Joyful Noise," "1776," OB in "Boys from Syracuse," "Camino Real," "Museum."

DAVIDSON, JACK. Born July 17, 1936 in Worcester, MA. Graduate Boston U. Debut 1968 OB in "Moon for the Misbegotten," followed by "Battle of Angels," "Midsummer Night's Dream," "Hot l Baltimore," "A Tribute to Lili Lamont," "Ulysses in Traction," "Lulu," "Hey, Rube." Bdwy in "Capt. Brassbound's Conversion" (1972), "Anna Christie."

DAVILA, DIANA. Born Nov. 5, 1947 in NYC. Bdwy debut 1967 in "Song of the Grasshopper," followed by "The Prime of Miss Jean Brodie," "Two Gentlemen of Verona," "Home Sweet Homer," "Stages," OB in "What the Butler Saw," "The Refrigerators," "People Are Living There," "Last Analysis," "The Seducers."

DAVYS, EDMUND. Born Jan. 21, 1947 in Nashua, NH. Graduate Oberlin Col. Debut 1978 OB in "Othello."

DAWSON, CURT. Born Dec. 5, 1941 in Kansas. RADA graduate. Debut 1968 OB in "Futz," followed by "Boys in the Band," "Not Now, Darling," "White Nights," "Enter a Free Man," "You Never Can Tell," Bdwy 1975 in "Absurd Person Singular."

DEAN, LAURA. Born May 27, 1963 in Smithtown, NY. Debut 1973 OB in "The Secret Life of Walter Mitty," followed by "A Village Romeo and Juliet," "Carousel," "Hey, Rube."

de BANZIE, LOIS. Born May 4 in Glasgow, Scot. Bdwy debut 1966 in "Elizabeth the Queen," followed by "Da," OB in "Little Murders," "Mary Stuart," "People Are Living There," "Ride Across Lake Constance," "The Divorce of Judy and Jane," "What the Butler Saw," "Man and Superman," "The Judas Applause."

DeFILIPPS, RICK. Born Apr. 16, 1950 in Binghamton, NY. Attended AMDA. Debut 1976 OB in "Panama Hattie" (ELT), followed by "Wonderful Town," "Beowulf."

DeFRANK, ROBERT. Born Nov. 29, 1945. Graduate Towson State, Essex Community Col. Debut 1977 OB in "The Crazy Locomotive," followed by "The Taming of the Shrew."

DE LAPPE, GEMZE. Born Feb. 28, 1925 in Portsmouth, VA. Attended Hunter Col. Credits in "Oklahoma!," "The King and I," "Paint Your Wagon," "Juno," "Brigadoon," OB in "Gorey Stories."

de LAVALLADE, CARMEN. Born Mar. 6, 1931 in New Orleans, LA. Bdwy debut 1954 in "House of Flowers," followed by "Josephine Baker and Company," OB in "Othello."

DEMPSEY, JEROME. Born Mar. 1, 1929 in St. Paul, MN. Toledo U graduate. Bdwy bow 1959 in "West Side Story," followed by "The Deputy," "Spofford," "Room Service," "Love Suicide at Schofield Barracks," "Dracula," OB in "Cry of Players," "Year Boston Won the Pennant," "The Crucible," "Justice Box," "Trelawny of the Wells," "The Old Glory," "Six Characters in Search of an Author," "Threepenny Opera."

DeMUNN, JEFFREY P. Born Apr. 25, 1947 in Buffalo, NY. Graduate Union Col. Debut 1975 OB in "Augusta," Bdwy 1976 in "Comedians," followed by "A Prayer for My Daughter."

DENGEL, JAKE. Born June 19, 1933 in Oshkosh, WI. Graduate Northwestern U. Debut OB in "The Fantasticks," followed by "Red Eye of Love," "Fortuna," "Abe Lincoln In Illinois," "Dr. Faustus," "An Evening with Garcia Lorca," "Shrinking Bride," APA's "Cock-a-Doodle Dandy" and "Hamlet," "Where Do We Go from Here?," "Woyzeck," "Endgame," "Measure for Measure," "Ulysses in Traction," Bdwy in "Royal Hunt of the Sun," "The Changing Room."

DENNIS, RONALD. Born Oct. 2, 1944 in Dayton, OH. Debut OB 1966 in "Show Boat," followed by "Of Thee I Sing," "Moon Walk," "Please Don't Cry," Bdwy in "A Chorus Line."

DENNIS, SANDY. Born Apr. 27, 1937 in Hastings, NE. Bdwy debut 1957 in "The Dark at the Top of the Stairs," followed by "Burning Bright" (OB), "Face of a Hero," "Complaisant Lover," "A Thousand Clowns" for which she received a Theatre World Award, "Any Wednesday," "Daphne in Cottage D," "How the Other Half Loves," "Let Me Hear You Smile," "Absurd Person Singular," "Same Time Next Year."

DENNISTON, LESLIE. Born May 19, 1950 in San Francisco, CA. Attended HB Studio. Bdwy debut 1976 in "Shenandoah."

DEROSKI, BONNIE. Born June 8, 1961 in Neptune, NJ. Debut 1977 OB in "Landscape of the Body."

DeSALVO, ANNE. Born Apr. 3 in Philadelphia, PA. OB in "Iphigenia in Aulis," "Lovers and Other Strangers," "The First Warning," "Warringham Roof," Bdwy 1977 in "Gemini."

DeSHIELDS, ANDRE. Born Jan. 12, 1946 in Baltimore, MD. Graduate U Wisc. Bdwy debut 1973 in "Warp," followed by "Rachel Lily Rosenbloom," "The Wiz," "Ain't Misbehavin'." OB in "2008½."

DEWHURST, COLLEEN. Born June 3, 1926 in Montreal, Can. Attended Downer Col., AADA. Bdwy debut 1952 in "Desire under the Elms," followed by "Tamburlaine the Great," "Country Wife," "Caligula," "All the Way Home," "Great Day in the Morning," "Ballad of the Sad Cafe," "More Stately Mansions," "All Over," "Mourning Becomes Electra," "Moon for the Misbegotten," "Who's Afraid of Virginia Woolf?," "An Almost Perfect Person," OB in "Taming of the Shrew," "The Eagle Has Two Heads," "Camille," "Macbeth," "Children of Darkness" for which she received a Theatre World Award, "Antony and Cleopatra" (CP), "Hello and Goodbye," "Good Woman of Setzuan" (LC), "Hamlet" (NYSF).

DIAMOND, BOB. Born May 10, 1941 in NYC. Studied at A.C.T. San Francisco. Debut 1971 OB in "One Flew over the Cuckoo's Nest," followed by "Les Femme Noire."

DILLEHAY, KAYLYN. Born Dec. 1, 1954 in Oklahoma City, OK. Attended Tex. Christian U., OkCityU. Debut 1976 OB in "Follies," followed by "Carnival," "Beowulf."

DILLON, MIA. Born July 9, 1955 in Colorado Springs, CO. Graduate Penn State U. Bdwy debut 1977 in "Equus," followed by "Da," OB in "The Crucible."

DINELLI, MICHAEL. Born Jan. 22, 1953 in Los Angeles, CA. Debut OB 1976 in "In the Boom Boom Room," Bdwy 1977 in "The Basic Training of Pavlo Hummel."

DISHY, BOB. Born in Brooklyn, NY. Graduate Syracuse U. Bdwy debut 1955 in "Damn Yankees," followed by "Can-Can" (CC'62), "Flora the Red Menace," "Something Different," "The Goodbye People," "A Way of Life," "The Creation of the World and Other Business," "American Millionaire," "Sly Fox," OB in "Chic," "When the Owl Screams," "Wrecking Ball," "By Jupiter," "Unknown Soldier and His Wife."

DITTMAN, DEAN. Born Sept. 12, 1932 in Frontenac, KS. Attended Kan. State Col., Sorbonne. Bdwy debut 1958 in "Most Happy Fella," followed by "Music Man," "Sunday Man," "On the 20th Century," OB in "The Cradle Will Rock."

DIXON, ED. Born Sept. 2, 1948 in Oklahoma. Attended OklaU. Bdwy in "Student Prince," "No, No, Nanette," "Knickerbocker Holiday," OB in "By Bernstein," "Wonderful Town," "Identity and Other Crises."

DIXON, MacINTYRE. Born Dec. 22, 1931 in Everett, MA. Emerson Col. graduate. OB in "Quare Fellow," "Plays for Bleecker Street," "Stewed Prunes," "Cat's Pajamas," "Three Sisters," "3 X 3," "Second City," "Mad Show," "Meow!," "Lotta," "Rubbers," "Conjuring an Event," Bdwy in "Xmas in Las Vegas," "Cop-Out," "Story Theatre," "Metamorphoses," "Twigs," "Over Here!"

DON, CARL. Born Dec. 15, 1916 in Vitebsk, Russia. Attended Western Reserve U. Bdwy debut 1954 in "Anastasia," followed by "Romanoff and Juliet," "Dear Me, the Sky Is Falling," "The Relapse," "The Tenth Man," "Zalmen," OB in "Richard III," "Twelfth Night," "Winterset," "Arms and the Man," "Between Two Thieves," "He Who Gets Slapped," "Jacobowsky and the Colonel," "Carnival."

| Pi Douglass | Adrienne Doucette | Richard Dow | Nina Dova | Craig Dudley |

DONHOWE, GWYDA. Born Oct. 20, 1933 in Oak Park, IL. Attended Drake U., Goodman Th. Bdwy debut 1957 in "Separate Tables," followed by "Half a Sixpence," "The Flip Side," "Paris Is Out," "Applause," with APA in "The Show-Off," "War and Peace," "Right You are," and "You Can't Take It with You," OB in "Philosophy in the Boudoir," "Rondelay," "How Far Is It to Babylon?"

DONLEY, ROBERT. Born in Cumberland Township, PA. Attended Waynesburg Col., Atlantic U. Debut 1947 on Bdwy in "Crime and Punishment," followed by "Andersonville Trial," "Something about a Soldier," "Unsinkable Molly Brown," "The Visit," "Twigs," "Anna Christie."

DONNELLY, DONAL. Born July 6, 1931 in Bradford, Eng. Bdwy debut 1966 in "Philadelphia, Here I Come!," followed by "A Day in the Death of Joe Egg," "Sleuth," OB in "My Astonishing Self."

DORRIN, JOHN. Born July 17, 1920 in Omaha, NE. Attended Los Angeles City Col. Bdwy debut 1944 in "Song of Norway," followed by "Silk Stockings," "Most Happy Fella," "Best Man," "My Fair Lady," "What Makes Sammy Run?," "Fade Out, Fade In," "Carousel," "Annie Get Your Gun," "Finian's Rainbow," "St. Joan," "I'm Solomon," "Oklahoma" (JB), "New Girl in Town" (ELT), "Gigi," "Show Boat" (JB), "Knickerbocker Holiday," "Finian's Rainbow" (JB).

DOUCETTE, ADRIENNE. Born Jan. 11, 1952 in Jersey City, NJ. Attended AMDA, AADA. Debut 1978 OB in "Allegro."

DOUGLASS, PI. Born in Sharon, CT. Attended Boston Conserv. Bdwy debut 1969 in "Fig Leaves Are Falling," followed by "Hello, Dolly!," "Georgy," "Purlie," "Ari," "Jesus Christ Superstar," "Selling of the President," "The Wiz," OB in "Of Thee I Sing."

DOVA, NINA. Born Jan. 15, 1926 in London, Eng. Attended Neighborhood Playhouse. Debut 1954 OB in "I Feel Wonderful," followed by "A Delicate Balance," "Naked," Bdwy in "Zorba," "The Rothschilds," "Saturday Sunday Monday."

DOW, RICHARD A. Born Aug. 30, 1941 in Cambridge, MA. Graduate UPa. Debut 1970 OB in "The Dirtiest Show in Town," followed by "Baba Goya," "Nourish the Beast," "Hothouse," "Action," "International Stud."

DREYFUSS, RICHARD. Born in Brooklyn, NY in 1948. Bdwy debut 1969 in "But Seriously," OB in "Line," "Julius Caesar."

DRISCHELL, RALPH. Born Nov. 26, 1927 in Baldwin, NY. Attended Carnegie Tech. OB in "Playboy of the Western World," "The Crucible," "The Balcony," "Time of Vengeance," "Barroom Monks," "Portrait of the Artist," "Abe Lincoln in Illinois," "The Caretaker," "A Slight Ache," "The Room," "The Year Boston Won the Pennant," "The Time of Your Life," "Camino Real," "Operation Sidewinder," "Beggar on Horseback," "Threepenny Opera," Bdwy in "Rhinoceros," "All in Good Time," "Rosencrantz and Guildenstern Are Dead," "The Visit," "Chemin de Fer," "Ah, Wilderness," "Stages."

DRUM, LEONARD. Born Feb. 21 in Pittsfield, MA. Graduate UNMex., Columbia. OB in "Kaleidoscope," "The Golden Six," "On the Town," "O Marry Me!," "The Giants' Dance," "Gay Divorce," Bdwy 1967 in "Marat/deSade."

DRUMMOND, ALICE. Born May 21, 1929 in Pawtucket, RI. Attended Pembroke Col. OB in "Royal Gambit," "Go Show Me a Dragon," "Sweet of You to Say So," "Gallows Humor," "American Dream," "Giants' Dance," "Carpenters," "Charles Abbot & Son," "God Says There Is No Peter Ott," "Enter a Free Man," "Memory of Two Mondays," "Secret Service," "Boy Meets Girl," "Savages," Bdwy debut 1963 in "Ballad of the Sad Cafe," followed by "Malcolm," "The Chinese," "Thieves," "Summer Brave," "Some of My Best Friends."

DUDLEY, CRAIG. Born Jan. 22, 1945 in Sheepshead Bay, NY. Graduate AADA, AmThWing. Debut 1970 OB in "Macbeth," followed by "Zou," "Othello."

DUELL, WILLIAM. Born Aug. 30, in Corinth, NY. Attended Ill. Wesleyan, Yale. OB in "Portrait of the Artist . . . ," "Barroom Monks," "Midsummer Night's Dream," "Henry IV," "Taming of the Shrew," "The Memorandum," "Threepenny Opera," Bdwy in "A Cook for Mr. General," "Ballad of the Sad Cafe," "Ilya, Darling," "1776," "Kings," "Stages."

DUKAKIS, OLYMPIA. Born in Lowell, MA. Debut 1960 OB in "The Breaking Wall," followed by "Nourish the Beast," "Curse of the Starving Class," Bdwy in "The Aspern Papers" (1962), "Abraham Cochrane," "Who's Who in Hell."

DUNNOCK, MILDRED. Born Jan 25 in Baltimore, MD. Graduate Goucher Col., Columbia U. Bdwy debut 1932 in "Life Begins," followed by "The Corn Is Green," "Richard III," "Only the Heart," "Foolish Notion," "Lute Song," "Another Part of the Forest," "The Hallams," "Death of a Salesman," "Pride's Crossing," "The Wild Duck," "In the Summer House," "Cat on a Hot Tin Roof," "Child of Fortune," "The Milk Train Doesn't Stop Here Anymore," "Traveller without Luggage," "Days in the Trees," "Tartuffe," OB in "The Trojan Women," "Phedre," "Willie Doesn't Live Here Anymore," "Colette," "A Place without Doors."

DUSSAULT, NANCY. Born June 30, 1936 in Pensacola, FL. Graduate Northwestern U. Debut 1958 OB in "Diversions," followed by "Street Scene," "Dr. Willy Nilly," "The Cradle Will Rock," "No for an Answer," "Whispers on the Wind," "Trelawny of 'The Wells'," "Detective Story," Bdwy in "Do Re Mi" (1960) for which she received a Theatre World Award, "Sound of Music," "Bajour," "Carousel," "Finian's Rainbow," "Side by Side by Sondheim."

EARLEY, CANDICE. Born Aug. 18, 1950 in Ft. Hood, TX. Attended Trinity U. Bdwy debut 1971 in "Hair," followed by "Jesus Christ Superstar," "Grease," "Civilization and Its Discontents" (OB).

EASTERBROOK, LESLIE. Born July 29, 1949 in Los Angeles, CA. Stephens Col. graduate. Bdwy debut 1976 in "California Suite."

EASTERBROOK, RANDALL. Born Jan. 15, 1951 in Peoria, IL. Graduate Northwestern U. Bdwy debut 1977 in "Hair."

EDE, GEORGE, Born Dec. 22, 1931 in San Francisco, CA. Bdwy debut 1969 in "A Flea in Her Ear," followed by "Three Sisters," "The Changing Room," "The Visit," "Chemin de Fer," "Holiday," "Love for Love," "Rules of the Game," "Member of the Wedding," "Lady from the Sea," "The Philanderer" (OB), "A Touch of the Poet."

EDMEAD, WENDY. Born July 6, 1956 in NYC. Graduate NYCU. Bdwy debut 1974 in "The Wiz."

EDMONDS, LOUIS. Born Sept. 24, 1923 in Baton Rouge, LA. Attended Carnegie Tech. OB in "Life in Louisiana," "Way of the World," "The Cherry Orchard," "Uncle Vanya," "Duchess of Malfi," "Ernest in Love," "The Rapists," "Amoureuse," Bdwy in "Candide," "Maybe Tuesday," "The Killer," "Passage to India," "Fire!," "Otherwise Engaged."

EDWARDS, BRANDT. Born Mar. 22, 1947 in Holly Springs, MS. Graduate UMiss. NY debut off and on Bdwy in "A Chorus Line."

EDWARDS, EDWARD. Born Mar. 26, 1950 in Dallas, TX. Attended UTx., SMU, Juilliard. Debut 1974 OB in "Who Here Has Seen the Color of the Wind," followed by "Moliere in Spite of Himself," "A Month in the Country," "Streamers."

EDWARDS, RONNIE CLAIRE. Born Feb. 9, 1933 in Oklahoma City, OK. Graduate UOk. Bdwy debut 1963 in "Paint Your Wagon," followed by "Trial of the Catonsville 9," "The Lincoln Mask," OB in "Patio/Porch."

EGAN, MICHAEL. Born Aug. 24, 1926 in Washington, PA. Graduate Buckness U. Bdwy debut 1956 in "The Great Sebastians," followed by "Luther," "A Cry of Players," "The Incomparable Max," "The Ritz," OB in "The Real Inspector Hound," "Drums in the Night," "Duck Variations," "American Buffalo," "Waiting for Godot."

ELIZONDO, HECTOR. Born Dec. 12, 1936 in NYC. Attended CCNY. Bdwy debut 1968 in "The Great White Hope," followed by "Prisoner of Second Avenue," "Sly Fox," OB in "Drums in the Night," "Steambath," "Dance of Death" (LC).

ELLERBE, HARRY. Born Jan. 13 in Columbia, SC. Graduate Georgia Tech. Bdwy debut 1931 in "Philip Goes Forth," followed by "Thoroughbred," "Strange Orchestra," "Ghosts," "Hedda Gabler," "Outward Bound," "Whiteoaks," "The Cocktail Party," "Oh, Mr. Meadowbrook," "The Desk Set," OB in "The Show-Off."

Antonia Ellis	David Eric	Laura Esterman	Laurie Faso	Louisa Flaningam

ELLIOTT, PATRICIA. Born July 21, 1942 in Gunnison, CO. Graduate U. Colo., London Academy. Debut with LCRep 1968 in "King Lear," and "A Cry of Players," followed OB in "Henry V," "The Persians," "A Doll's House," "Hedda Gabler," "In Case of Accident," "Water Hen," "Polly," "But Not for Me," "By Bernstein," "Prince of Homburg," Bdwy bow 1973 in "A Little Night Music" for which she received a Theatre World Award, followed by "The Shadow Box," "Tartuffe," "13 Rue de L'Amour."

ELLIS, ANTONIA. Born Apr. 30, 1944 in Newport, Isle of Wight. Bdwy debut 1975 in "Pippin."

ELMORE, STEVE. Born July 12, 1936 in Niangua, MO. Debut 1961 OB in "Madame Aphrodite," followed by "Golden Apple," "Enclave," Bdwy in "Camelot," "Jenny," "Fade In Fade Out," "Kelly," "Company," "Nash at 9," "Chicago."

ELVERMAN, BILL. Born Nov. 14, 1951 in Kenosha, WI. Graduate UWisc. Debut 1977 OB in "Museum."

ENO, TERRY. Born June 5, 1946 in Miami, FL. Attended Miami U., HB Studio. Bdwy debut in "Irene," followed by "Good News," OB in "Buy Bonds Buster," "Joseph and the Amazing Technicolor Dreamcoat."

ENSSLEN, DICK. Born Dec. 19, 1926 in Reading PA. Attended Musical Theatre Academy. Bdwy debut 1964 in "Anyone Can Whistle," followed by "Bajour," "Education of Hyman Kaplan," "Canterbury Tales," "Desert Song," "Annie."

EPPS, SHELDON. Born in Los Angeles, CA. Graduate Carnegie-Mellon U. Debut OB 1978 in "Julius Caesar."

EPSTEIN, PIERRE. Born July 27, 1930 in Toulouse, France. Graduate UParis, Columbia. Bdwy bow 1962 in "A Shot in the Dark," followed by "Enter Laughing," "Bajour," "Black Comedy," "Thieves," "Fun City," OB in "Incident at Vichy," "Threepenny Opera," "Too Much Johnson," "Second City," "People vs. Ranchman," "Promenade," "Cakes with Wine," "Little Black Sheep," "Comedy of Errors," "A Memory of Two Mondays," "They Knew What They Wanted," "Museum," "The Bright and Golden Land."

ERIC, DAVID. Born Feb. 28, 1949 in Boston, MA. Graduate Neighborhood Playhouse. Debut OB 1971 in "Ballad of Johnny Pot," followed by "Love Me, Love My Children," Bdwy in "Yentl" (1975), "Shenandoah."

ERWIN, BARBARA. Born June 30, 1937 in Boston, MA. Debut 1973 OB in "The Secret Life of Walter Mitty," followed by "Broadway," Bdwy 1977 in "Annie."

ESTERMAN, LAURA. Born Apr. 12, in NYC. Attended Radcliffe, LAMDA. Debut 1969 OB in "The Time of Your Life" (LCR), followed by "Pig Pen," "The Carpenters," "Ghosts," "Waltz of the Toreadors," "Macbeth" (LC), "The Seagull," "Rubbers," "Yanks 3, Detroit 0," "Golden Boy," "Out of Our Father's House," Bdwy 1974 "God's Favorite."

ESTEY, CAROL. Born Jan. 22, 1945 in Trenton, NJ. Bdwy debut 1967 in "Sherry," followed by "Ari," "Gantry," "A Mother's Kisses," "Dude," "Jesus Christ Superstar," "The Act," OB in "Love Me, Love My Children," "A Matter of Time."

EVANS, DILLON. Born Jan. 2, 1921 in London, Eng. Attended RADA. Bdwy debut 1950 in "The Lady's Not for Burning," followed by "School for Scandal," "Hamlet," "Ivanov," "Vivat! Vivat Regina!," "Jockey Club Stakes," "Dracula," OB in "Druid's Rest," "Rondelay," "Little Foxes."

EVANS, PETER. Born May 27, 1950 in Englewood, NJ. Graduate Yale, London Central School of Speech. Debut OB 1975 in "Life Class," followed by "Streamers," "A Life in the Theatre."

EVERHART, REX. Born June 13, 1920 in Watseka, IL. Graduate UMo., NYU Bdwy bow 1955 in "No Time for Sergeants," followed by "Tall Story," "Moonbirds," "Tenderloin," "Matter of Position," "Rainy Day in Newark," "Skyscraper," "How Now Dow Jones," "1776," "The Iceman Cometh," "Chicago," "Working."

FAGA, GARY. Born Nov. 23, 1953 in Brooklyn, NY. Attended Bklyn Col. Debut OB 1975 in "Hustlers," followed by "Dance with Me," Bdwy 1976 in "Equus."

FASO, LAURIE. Born Apr. 11, 1946 in Buffalo, NY. Graduate Denison U., Carnegie Tech. Debut OB 1974 in "Godspell," followed by "The Glorious Age," "Comedy of Errors" (CP), Bdwy 1976 in "Godspell."

FERGUSON, LOU. Born Aug. 8, 1944 in Trinidad, WI. Debut OB 1970 in "A Season in the Congo," followed by "Night World," "La Gente," "Shoe Shine Parlor," "The Defense," "Rum an' Coca Cola."

FERRER, JOSE. Born Jan. 8, 1912 in Santurce, PR. Princeton graduate. Bdwy debut 1935 in "A Slight Case of Murder," followed by "Spring Dance," "Brother Rat," "In Clover," "How to Get Tough about It," "Missouri Legend," "Mamba's Daughters," "Key Largo," "Charley's Aunt," "Vickie," "Let's Face It," "Othello," "Cyrano de Bergerac," "Volpone," "Angel Street," "Four One-Act Comedies," "The Alchemist," "The Long Voyage Home," "Insect Comedy," "Silver Whistle," "20th Century," "The Shrike," "Richard III," "Edwin Booth," "The Girl Who Came to Supper," "Man of La Mancha," OB in "A Life in the Theatre."

FIELDS, JOE. Born Jan. 23, 1935 in Uniontown, AL. Attended Karmu Theatre Sch. Debut 1969 OB in "Ceremonies in Dark Old Men," followed by "Of Mice and Men," "As You Like It," Bdwy in "Ain't Supposed to Die a Natural Death" (1971), "The Basic Training of Pavlo Hummel" for which he received a Theatre World Award.

FITCH, ROBERT. Born Apr. 29, 1934 in Santa Cruz, CA. Attended U. Santa Clara. Bdwy debut 1961 in "Tenderloin," followed by "Do Re Mi," "My Fair Lady" (CC), "Girl Who Came to Supper," "Flora the Red Menace," "Baker Street," "Sherry," "Mack and Mabel," "Henry, Sweet Henry," "Mame," "Promises, Promises," "Coco," "Lorelei," "Annie," OB in "Lend an Ear," "Half-Past Wednesday," "Anything Goes," "Crystal Heart," "Broadway Dandies," "One Cent Plain."

FITZGERALD, FERN. Born Jan. 7, 1947 in Valley Stream, NY. Bdwy debut 1976 in "Chicago," followed by "A Chorus Line."

FITZGERALD, GERALDINE. Born Nov. 24, 1914 in Dublin, Ire. Bdwy debut 1938 in "Heartbreak House," followed by "Sons and Soldiers," "Doctor's Dilemma," "King Lear," "Hide and Seek," "Ah, Wilderness," "The Shadow Box," "A Touch of the Poet," OB in "Cave Dwellers," "Pigeons," "Long Day's Journey into Night," "Everyman and Roach."

FLAGG, FANNIE. Born Sept. 21, 1944 in Birmingham, AL. Attended Pittsburgh Playhouse. Debut 1963 OB in "Just for Opening," followed by "Patio/-Porch."

FLANAGAN, WALTER. Born Oct. 4, 1928 in Ponta, TX. Graduate Houston U. On Bdwy in "Once for the Asking," "A Texas Trilogy," "A Touch of the Poet," OB in "Bedtime Story," "Coffee and Windows," "Opening of a Window," "The Moon Is Blue," "Laughwind," "The Dodo Bird."

FLANINGAM, LOUISA. Born May 5, 1945 in Chester, SC. Graduate UMd. Debut 1971 OB in "The Shrinking Bride," Bdwy 1976 in "The Magic Show."

FOGARTY, JACK. Born Oct. 23, 1923 in Liverpool, Eng. Attended Fordham and Columbia U. Debut 1952 OB in "No Exit," followed by "Hogan's Goat," "Sweeney Todd," "The Fantasticks."

FOOTE, GENE. Born Oct. 30, 1936 in Johnson City, TN. Attended ETSU. Bdwy debut 1961 in "Unsinkable Molly Brown," followed by "Bajour," "Sweet Charity," "Golden Rainbow," "Applause," "Pippin," "Chicago," "Celebration" (OB).

FORLOW, TED. Born Apr. 29, 1931 in Independence, MO. Attended Baker U. Bdwy debut 1957 in "New Girl in Town," followed by "Juno," "Destry Rides Again," "Subways Are for Sleeping," "Can-Can," "Wonderful Town" (CC), "A Funny Thing Happened on the Way to the Forum," "Milk and Honey," "Carnival" (CC), "Man of LaMancha" (original and 1977 revival), "A Night at the Black Pig" (OB).

FORSYTHE, HENDERSON. Born Sept. 11, 1917 in Macon, MO. Attended UIowa. OB in "The Iceman Cometh," "The Collection," "The Room," "A Slight Ache," "Happiness Cage," "Waiting for Godot," "In Case of Accident," "Not I" (LC), "An Evening with the Poet-Senator," "Museum," "How Far Is It to Babylon?," Bdwy in "The Cellar and the Well," "Miss Lonelyhearts," "Who's Afraid of Virginia Woolf?," "Malcolm," "Right Honourable Gentleman," "Delicate Balance," "Birthday Party," "Harvey," "Engagement Baby," "Freedom of the City," "Texas Trilogy," "The Best Little Whorehouse in Texas."

Elizabeth Franz   Arny Freeman   Florie Freshman   Colin Garrey Sue Anne Gershenson

FOSTER, FRANCES. Born June 11 in Yonkers, NY. Bdwy debut 1955 in "The Western Trees," followed by "Nobody Loves an Albatross," "Raisin in the Sun," "The River Niger," "First Breeze of Summer," OB in "Take a Giant Step," "Edge of the City," "Tammy and the Doctor," "The Crucible," "Happy Ending," "Day of Absence," "An Evening of One Acts," "Man Better Man," "Brotherhood," "Akokawe," "Rosalee Pritchett," "Sty of the Blind Pig," "Ballet Behind the Bridge," "Good Woman of Setzuan" (LC), "Behold! Cometh the Vanderkellans," "Orrin," "Boesman and Lena," "Do Lord Remember Me."

FOSTER, GLORIA. Born Nov. 15, 1936 in Chicago, IL. Attended IllStateU, Goodman Th. Debut 1963 OB in "In White America," followed by "Medea" for which she received a Theatre World Award, "Yerma," "A Hand Is on the Gate," "Black Visions," "The Cherry Orchard," "Agamemnon."

FRANKLIN, NANCY. Born in NYC. Debut 1959 OB in "Buffalo Skinner," followed by "Power of Darkness," "Oh, Dad, Poor Dad . . . ," "Theatre of Peretz," "Seven Days of Mourning," "Here Be Dragons," "Beach Children," "Safe Place," "Innocent Pleasures," Bdwy in "Never Live over a Pretzel Factory," "Happily Never After," "The White House."

FRANZ, ELIZABETH. Born June 18, 1941 in Akron, OH. Attended AADA. Debut OB 1965 in "In White America," followed by "One Night Stands of a Noisy Passenger," "The Real Inspector Hound," "Augusta," Bdwy in "Rosencrantz and Guildenstern Are Dead," "The Cherry Orchard."

FREEMAN, AL, JR. Born Mar. 21, 1934 in San Antonio, TX. Attended CCLA. Bdwy in "The Long Dream," "Tiger, Tiger Burning Bright," "Living Premise," "Blues for Mr. Charlie," "Dozens," "Look to the Lilies," OB in "Slave," "Dutchman," "Trumpets of the Lord," "Medea," "The Great MacDaddy," "One Crack Out."

FREEMAN, ANN. Born in Portsmouth, Eng. Bdwy debut 1967 in "Life with Father," followed by OB's "Present Laughter," "The Home," "The Crucible."

FREEMAN, ARNY. Born Aug. 28, 1908 in Chicago, IL. Bdwy bow 1949 in "A Streetcar Named Desire," followed by "The Great Sebastians," "Tall Story," "Hot Spot," "What Makes Sammy Run?," "Cactus Flower," "Minnie's Boys," "Much Ado about Nothing," "Sunshine Boys," "Working," OB in "Gay Divorce," "Dream Girl," "The Shrike," "Gun Play."

FREEMAN, MORGAN. Born June 1, 1937 in Memphis, TN. Attended LACC. Bdwy bow 1967 in "Hello, Dolly!," followed by "The Mighty Gents," OB in "Ostrich Feathers," "Niggerlovers," "Exhibition," "Black Visions," "Cockfight."

FRESHMAN, FLORIE. Born Nov. 30, 1954 in Brooklyn, NY. Graduate SUNY Purchase. Debut 1977 OB in "NYC Street Show," followed by "Allegro."

FREUND, JOSH. Born Oct. 1 1969 in NYC. Bdwy debut 1977 in "Golda."

GALE, DAVID. Born Oct. 2, 1936 in England. Debut 1958 OB in "Elizabeth the Queen," followed by "Othello," "White Devil," "Baal," "What Do They Know about Love Uptown?," "Joe Egg," "The Trial," "Dumbwaiter," "The Dodge Boys," "The Biko Inquest," Bdwy in "Of Mice and Men" (1974), "Sweet Bird of Youth."

GALIANO, JOSEPH. Born Mar. 26, 1944 in Beaumont, TX. Graduate SMU. Debut 1976 OB in "The Fantasticks."

GALLAGHER, HELEN. Born in 1926 in Brooklyn, NY. Bdwy debut 1947 in "Seven Lively Arts," followed by "Mr. Strauss Goes to Boston," "Billion Dollar Baby," "Brigadoon," "High Button Shoes," "Touch and Go," "Make a Wish," "Pal Joey," "Guys and Dolls," "Finian's Rainbow," "Oklahoma!," "Pajama Game," "Bus Stop," "Portofino," "Sweet Charity," "Mame," "Cry for Us All," "No, No, Nanette," OB in "Hothouse," "Tickles by Tucholsky," "The Misanthrope."

GALLERY, JAMES. Born in Auburn, NY. Graduate Lemoyne Col. Debut 1967 OB in "Arms and the Man," followed by "Shadow of a Gunman," "Where Do We Go from Here," "A Doll's House," "Hamlet," Bdwy in "Wilson in the Promise Land" (1970), "Sly Fox."

GALLOWAY, JANE. Born Feb. 27, 1950 in St. Louis, MO. Attended Webster Col. Debut 1976 OB in "Vanities," followed by "Domino Courts," "Comanche Cafe."

GALVIN, JAMES. Born Jan. 15, 1933 in NYC. Debut 1966 OB in "The Employment Agency," followed by "How to Succeed in Business . . . ," "Happy Hunter."

GARBER, VICTOR. Born Mar. 16, 1949 in London, Can. Debut 1973 OB in "Ghosts" for which he received a Theatre World Award, followed by "Joe's Opera," "Cracks," Bdwy in "Tartuffe," "Deathtrap."

GARDENIA, VINCENT. Born Jan. 7, 1923 in Naples, Italy. Debut 1955 OB in "In April Once," followed by "Man with the Golden Arm," "Volpone," "Brothers Karamazov," "Power of Darkness," "Machinal," "Gallows Humor," "Theatre of the Absurd," "The Lunatic View," "Little Murders," "Passing Through from Exotic Places," "The Carpenters," Bdwy in "The Visit" (1958), "Rashomon," "The Cold Wind and the Warm," "Only in America," "The Wall," "Daughter of Silence," "Seidman & Son," "Dr. Fish," "Prisoner of Second Avenue," "God's Favorite," "California Suite."

GARDNER, JEANNETTE. Born in Kinston, NC. Graduate Greensboro Col. Debut 1974 OB in "I'll Die if I Can't Live Forever," followed by "Carnival."

GARFIELD, DAVID. Born Feb. 6, 1941 in Brooklyn, NY. Graduate Columbia, Cornell U. OB in "Hang Down Your Head and Die," "Government Inspector," "Old Ones," "Family Business," Bdwy in "Fiddler on the Roof," "The Rothschilds."

GARFIELD, JULIE. Born Jan. 10, 1946 in Los Angeles, CA. Attended UWisc., Neighborhood Playhouse. Debut 1969 OB in "Honest-to-God Schnozzola," followed by "East Lynne," "The Sea," "Uncle Vanya" for which she received a Theatre World Award, Bdwy in "The Good Doctor," "Death of a Salesman," "The Merchant."

GARLAND, GEOFF. Born June 10, 1932 in Warrington, Eng. Debut 1961 OB in "The Hostage," followed by "Trelawny of 'The Wells'," "Timon of Athens," "Waiting for Godot," "Billy Liar," Bdwy in "Hamlet," "Imaginary Invalid," "A Touch of the Poet," "Tonight at 8:30," "Front Page," "Capt. Brassbound's Conversion," "Cyrano," "My Fat Friend," "Sly Fox."

GARRETT, BOB. Born Mar. 2, 1947 in NYC. Graduate Adelphi U. Debut OB 1971 in "Godspell," Bdwy in "Grease."

GARREY, COLIN. Born in Norwich, NY. Graduate AADA, RADA. Debut 1971 OB in "Ballad of Johnny Pot," followed by "As You Like It," "The Youth Hostel," Bdwy 1977 in "Miss Margarida's Way."

GARY, HAROLD. Born May 7, 1910 in NYC. Bdwy bow 1928 in "Diamond Lil," followed by "Crazy with the Heat," "A Flag Is Born," "Guys and Dolls," "Oklahoma!," "Arsenic and Old Lace," "Billion Dollar Baby," "Fiesta," "The World We Make," "Born Yesterday," "Will Success Spoil Rock Hunter?," "Let It Ride," "Counting House," "Arturo Ui," "A Thousand Clowns," "Enter Laughing," "Illya, Darling," "The Price," "The Sunshine Boys," "Pal Joey," OB in "Rosebloom," "Family Business."

GASSELL, SYLVIA. Born July 1, 1923 in NYC. Attended Hunter Col. Bdwy debut 1952 in "The Time of the Cuckoo," followed by "Sunday Breakfast," "Fair Game for Lovers," "Inquest," OB in "U.S.A.," "Romeo and Juliet," "Electra," "A Darker Flower," "Fragments," "Goa," "God Bless You, Harold Fineberg," "Philosophy in the Boudoir," "Stag Movie," "The Old Ones," "Where Memories are Magic."

GAYLORD, MARTHA. Born July 14, 1955 in Dallas, TX. Attended Yale U. Debut 1977 OB in "The Elusive Angel."

GEFFNER, DEBORAH. Born Aug. 26, 1952 in Pittsburgh, PA. Attended Juilliard, HB Studio. Debut 1975 OB in "Tenderloin," Bdwy in "Pal Joey," "A Chorus Line."

GELKE, BECKY. Born Feb. 17, 1953 in Ft. Knox, KY. Graduate Western Ky. U. Debut 1978 OB and Bdwy in "The Best Little Whorehouse in Texas."

GENNARO, MICHAEL. Born Sept. 20, 1950 in NYC. Graduate UNotre Dame, Neighborhood Playhouse. Debut 1975 OB in "The Three Musketeers," followed by "Godspell," "Julius Caesar."

GENTLES, AVRIL. Born Apr. 2, 1929 in Upper Montclair, NJ. Graduate UNC. Bdwy debut 1955 in "The Great Sebastians," followed by "Nude with Violin," "Present Laughter," "My Mother, My Father and Me," "Jimmy Shine," "Grin and Bare It," "Lysistrata," "Texas Trilogy," OB in "Dinny and the Witches," "The Wives," "Now Is the Time," "Man with a Load of Mischief," "Shay."

GERSHENSON, SUEANNE. Born Feb. 18, 1953 in Chicago, IL. Attended Indiana U. Debut 1976 OB in "Panama Hattie," followed by "Carnival."

| T. Galen Girvin | Rebecca Gilchrist | Paul Gleason | Joanna Gleason | Adam Grammis |

GIERASCH, STEFAN. Born Feb. 5, 1926 in NYC. On Bdwy in "Kiss and Tell," "Snafu," "Billion Dollar Baby," "Montserrat," "Night Music," "Hatful of Rain," "Compulsion," "Shadow of a Gunman," "War and Peace," "Of Mice and Men," "Tartuffe," OB in "7 Days of Mourning," "AC/DC," "Owners," "Nellie Toole & Co.," "The Iceman Cometh."

GILBERT, LOU. Born Aug. 1, 1909 in Sycamore, IL. Bdwy debut 1945 in "Common Ground," followed by "Beggars Are Coming to Town," "Truckline Cafe," "Dream Girl," "The Whole World Over," "Volpone," "Hope Is the Thing with Feathers," "Sundown Beach," "Detective Story," "Enemy of the People," "Anna Christie," "The Victim," "Whistler's Grandmother," "His and Hers," "Abie's Irish Rose," "Highway Robbery," "A Streetcar Named Desire," "Good as Gold," "Diary of Anne Frank," "The Egg," "In the Counting House," "Great White Hope," "Creation of the World and Other Business," "Much Ado about Nothing," OB in "A Month in the Country," "Big man," "Dynamite Tonight," "Good Woman of Zetuan," "Three Sisters," "The Tempest," "King Lear," "Baba Goya," "As You Like It," "Nourish the Beast," "The Old Ones," "Old Man Joseph and His Family."

GILBORN, STEVEN. Born in New Rochelle, NY. Graduate Swarthmore Col., Stanford U. Bdwy debut 1973 in "Creeps," followed by "The Basic Training of Pavlo Hummel," "Tartuffe," OB in "Rosmersholm," "Henry V," "Measure for Measure," "Ashes," "The Dybbuk," "Museum."

GILCHRIST, REBECCA. Born June 10, 1948 in Parkersburg, WV. Graduate WVa. U. Debut OB 1972 in "The Proposition," followed by "Hot Grog," Bdwy 1974 in "Grease."

GILFORD, JACK. Born July 25, 1907 in NYC. Bdwy debut 1940 in "Meet the People," followed by "They Should Have Stood in Bed," "Count Me In," "The Live Wire," "Alive and Kicking," "Once over Lightly," "Diary of Anne Frank," "Romanoff and Juliet," "The Tenth Man," "A Funny Thing Happened on the Way to the Forum," "Cabaret," "3 Men on a Horse," "No, No, Nanette," "The Sunshine Boys," "Sly Fox."

GILL, TERI. Born July 16, 1954 in Long Island City, NY. Graduate USIU. Bdwy debut 1976 in "Going Up," OB in "Allegro."

GILLETTE, ANITA. Born Aug. 16, 1938 in Baltimore, MD. Debut 1960 OB in "Russell Patterson's Sketchbook" for which she received a Theatre World Award, followed by Bdwy's "Carnival," "All American," "Mr. President," "Guys and Dolls" (CC), "Don't Drink the Water," "Cabaret," "Jimmy," "Rich and Famous" (OB), "Chapter Two."

GINGOLD, HERMIONE. Born Dec. 9, 1897 in London, Eng. Bdwy debut 1953 in "John Murray Anderson's Almanac," followed by "Sleeping Prince," "First Impressions," "From A to Z," "Milk and Honey," "Oh, Dad, Poor Dad, Mama's Hung You . . . ," "A Little Night Music," "Side by Side by Sondheim."

GIRVIN, T. GALEN. Born Apr. 7, 1948 in Coatesville, PA. Graduate West minster Col. Debut 1974 OB in "Pop!," followed by "Boys from Syracuse" (ELT), "Disgustingly Rich."

GLEASON, JOANNA. Born June 2, 1950 in Toronto, Can. Graduate UCLA. Bdwy debut 1977 in "I Love My Wife" for which she received a Theatre World Award.

GLEASON, PAUL. Born May 4, 1941 in Miami, FL. Graduate Fla. State U. Debut 1973 OB in "One Flew over the Cuckoo's Nest," followed by "Economic Necessity," "Niagara Falls," "Alfred the Great."

GLOVER, JOHN. Born Aug. 7, 1944 in Kingston, NY. Attended Towson State Col. Debut 1969 OB in "A Scent of Flowers," followed by "Government Inspector," "Rebel Women," "Treats," Bdwy in "The Selling of the President," "Great God Brown," "Don Juan," "The Visit," "Chemin de Fer," "Holiday," "The Importance of Being Earnest."

GLYNN, CARLIN. Born Feb. 19, 1940 in Cleveland, OH. Attended Sophie Newcomb Col., Actors Studio. Debut 1959 OB in "Waltz of the Toreadors," Bdwy debut 1978 in "The Best Little Whorehouse in Texas" for which she received a Theatre World Award.

GODREAU, MIGUEL. Born Oct. 17, 1946 in Puerto Rico. Appeared with Alvin Ailey Dance Co., Harkness Ballet, Bdwy in "Dear World," "Timbuktu."

GOLEMBO, ALICE. Born Jan. 18, 1949 in Baltimore, MD. Graduate NC Sch. of Arts, Goodman Theatre. Bdwy debut 1977 in "Golda."

GOODMAN, ROBYN. Born Aug. 24, 1947 in NYC. Graduate Brandeis U. Debut 1973 OB in "When You Comin' Back, Red Ryder?," followed by "Richard III," "Museum."

GORMAN, CLIFF. Born Oct. 13, 1936 in NYC. Attended UCLA. OB in "Hogan's Goat," "Boys in the Band," "Ergo," Bdwy in "Lenny," "Chapter Two."

GOUTMAN, CHRISTOPHER. Born Dec. 19, 1952 in Bryn Mawr, PA. Graduate Haverford Col., Carnegie-Mellon U. Debut 1978 OB in "The Promise" for which he received a Theatre World Award.

GRAFF, ILENE. Born Feb. 28 in NYC. Graduate Ithaca Col. Bdwy debut 1968 in "Promises, Promises," followed by "Grease," "I Love My Wife."

GRAHAM, DONNA. Born Sept. 28, 1964 in Philadelphia, PA. Bdwy debut 1977 in "Annie."

GRAMMIS, ADAM. Born Dec. 8, 1947 in Allentown, PA. Graduate Kutztown State Col. Bdwy debut 1971 in "Wild and Wonderful," followed by "Shirley MacLaine Show," "A Chorus Line," OB in "Dance Continuum," "Joseph and the Amazing Technicolor Dreamcoat."

GRANT, BYRON. Born June 14, 1936 in Columbus, GA. Graduate Huntingdon Col., Southern Ill. U., AMDA. Debut 1978 OB in "Gay Divorce."

GRAVES, ERNEST. Born May 5, 1919 in Chicago, IL. Attended Goodman Theatre. Bdwy bow 1941 in "Macbeth," followed by "The Russian People," "Cyrano de Bergerac," "Eastward in Eden," "Venus Is," "Ceremony of Innocence" (OB), "Poor Murderer," "Golda."

GREENE, ELLEN. Born Feb. 22 in NYC. Attended Ryder Col. Debut 1973 in "Rachel Lily Rosenbloom," followed OB by "In the Boom Boom Room," "Threepenny Opera."

GREENE, JAMES. Born Dec. 1, 1926 in Lawrence, MA. Graduate Emerson Col. OB in "The Iceman Cometh," "American Gothic," "The King and the Duke," "The Hostage," "Plays for Bleecker Street," "Moon in the Yellow River," "Misalliance," "Government Inspector," "Baba Goya," LCRep 2 years, "You Can't Take It with You," "School for Scandal," "Wild Duck," "Right You Are," "The Show-Off," "Pantagleize," "Festival of Short Plays," "Nourish the Beast," "One Crack Out," Bdwy in "Romeo and Juliet," "Girl on the Via Flaminia," "Compulsion," "Inherit the Wind," "Shadow of a Gunman," "Andersonville Trial," "Night Life," "School for Wives," "Ring Round the Bathtub," "Great God Brown," "Don Juan."

GREENE, REUBEN. Born Nov. 24, 1938 in Philadelphia, PA. With APA in "War and Peace," "You Can't Take It with You," and "Pantagleize," OB in "Jerico-Jim Crow," "Happy Ending," "Boys in the Band," "Twilight Dinner."

GREENE, RICHARD. Born Jan. 8, 1946 in Miami, FL. Graduate Fla. Atlantic U. Debut 1971 with LCRep in "Macbeth," followed OB by "Play Strindberg," "Mary Stuart," "Narrow Road to the Deep North," "Twelfth Night," and "The Crucible," "Family Business," Bdwy 1977 in "Romeo and Juliet."

GRIFFITH, KRISTIN. Born Sept. 7, 1953 in Odessa, TX. Juilliard graduate. Bdwy debut 1976 in "A Texas Trilogy." OB in "Rib Cage."

GRIGLAK, JEFFREY. Born June 14, 1951 in Pittsburgh, Pa. Graduate Carnegie-Mellon U. Debut 1978 OB in "The Taming of the Shrew" (ELT).

GRIMES, TAMMY. Born Jan. 30, 1934 in Lynn, MA. Attended Stephens Col., Neighborhood Playhouse. Debut 1956 OB in "The Littlest Revue," followed by "Clerambard," "Molly," Bdwy in "Look after Lulu" (1959) for which she received a Theatre World Award, "The Unsinkable Molly Brown," "Rattle of a Simple Man," "High Spirits," "The Only Game in Town," "Private Lives," "Musical Jubilee," "California Suite," "Tartuffe."

GRIZZARD, GEORGE. Born Apr. 1, 1928 in Roanoke Rapids, VA. Graduate UNC. Bdwy bow 1954 in "All Summer Long," followed by "The Desperate Hours," "Happiest Millionaire" for which he received a Theatre World Award, "Disenchanted," "Big Fish, Little Fish," with APA 1961-62, "Who's Afraid of Virginia Woolf?," "Glass Menagerie," "You Know I Can't Hear You . . .," "Noel Coward's Sweet Potato," "Gingham Dog," "Inquest," "Country Girl," "Creation of the World and Other Business," "Crown Matrimonial," "The Royal Family," "California Suite."

GROVER, STANLEY. Born Mar. 28, 1926 in Woodstock, IL. Attended UMo. Appeared in "Seventeen," "Wish You Were Here," "Time Remember'd," "Candide," "13 Daughters," "Mr. President," CC's "South Pacific," "Finian's Rainbow" and "The King and I," "Company," "Desert Song," "Don't Call Back," OB in "Lyle," "Finian's Rainbow."

Jonathan Hadary   Sarah-Jane Gwillim   Tobias Haller   Barbara Hanks   Rex Hays

GUIDALL, GEORGE. Born June 7, 1938 in Plainfield, NJ. Attended UBuffalo, AADA. Bdwy debut 1969 in "Wrong Way Light Bulb," followed by "Cold Storage," OB in "Counsellor-at-Law."

GULACK, MAX. Born May 19, 1928 in NYC. Graduate CCNY, Columbia U. Debut OB 1952 in "Bonds of Interest," followed by "Warrior's Husband," "Worm in the Horseradish," "Marcus in the High Grass," "Country Scandal," "Song for the First of May," "Threepenny Opera."

GUNTON, BOB. Born Nov. 15, 1945 in Santa Monica, CA. Attended UCal. Debut 1974 OB in "Who Am I?," followed by "The Kid," "Desperate Hours," Bdwy in "Happy End," (1977), "Working."

GWILLIM, SARAH-JANE. Born March 4 in Plymouth, Eng. Attended London Central Sch. of Speech. Debut 1977 OB in "You Never Can Tell," Bdwy in "St. Joan" (1977).

GWYNNE, FRED. Born July 10, 1926 in NYC. Harvard Graduate. Bdwy debut 1952 in "Mrs. McThing," followed by "Love's Labour's Lost," "Frogs of Spring," "Irma La Douce," "Here's Love," "The Lincoln Mask," "More Than You Deserve" (OB), "Cat on a Hot Tin Roof," "A Texas Trilogy," "Angel."

HADARY, JONATHAN. Born Oct. 11, 1948 in Chicago, IL. Attended Tufts U. Debut 1974 OB in "White Nights," followed by "El Grande de Coca-Cola," "Songs from Pins and Needles," "Gemini" (also Bdwy 1977).

HAFNER, JULIE J. Born June 4, 1952 in Dover, OH. Graduate Kent State U. Debut 1976 OB in "The Club."

HAGERTY, MICHAEL. Born Sept. 2, 1951 in Cincinnati, OH. Graduate Carnegie-Mellon U. Debut 1975 OB in "Dubliners," followed by "Disgustingly Rich."

HAIGH, KENNETH. Born Mar. 25, 1930 in Yorkshire, Eng. Attended Central School. Bdwy debut 1957 in "Look Back in Anger," followed by "Caligula," "Endecott and the Red Cross" (OB), "California Suite."

HALL, DAVIS. Born Apr. 10, 1946 in Atlanta, GA. Graduate Northwestern U. Bdwy debut 1973 in "Butley," OB in "The Promise."

HALL, GRAYSON. Born in Philadelphia, PA. Attended Temple U., Cornell U. Debut 1953 OB in "Man and Superman," followed by "La Ronde," "Six Characters in Search of an Author," "The Balcony," "The Buskers," "The Love Nest," "Shout from the Rooftops," "The Last Analysis," "Friends and Relations," "The Screens," "Secret of the Citizens Correction Committee," "The Sea," "What Every Woman Knows," "Jack Gelber's New Play," "Happy End," "Rib Cage," Bdwy in "Subways Are for Sleeping," "Those That Play the Clowns," "The Leaf People," "Happy End."

HALLER, TOBIAS. Born Sept. 30, 1951 in Baltimore, MD. Graduate Towson State U. Debut 1971 OB in "Now There's Just the Three of Us," followed by "The Screens," "Gorey Stories," Bdwy in "The Last of Mrs. Lincoln" (1972).

HALLEY, BEN, JR. Born Aug. 6, 1951 in Harlen, NY. Graduate CCNY, Yale. Bdwy debut 1978 in "A History of the American Film."

HALLIDAY, GORDON. Born Apr. 2, 1952 in Providence, RI. Attended RI Col., AADA, Bdwy debut 1975 in "Shenandoah."

HAMILTON, MARGARET. Born Dec. 9, 1902 in Cleveland, OH. Attended Cleveland Playhouse. Bdwy debut 1932 in "Another Language," followed by "Dark Tower," "Farmer Takes a Wife," "Outrageous Fortune," "The Men We Marry," "Fancy Meeting You Again," "Annie Get Your Gun" (CC), "Goldilocks," "UTBU," LC's "Show Boat" and "Oklahoma!," "Come Summer," "Our Town," BAM Co.'s "New York Idea," and "Three Sisters," "The Devil's Disciple."

HAMILTON, ROGER. Born in San Diego, CA., May 2, 1928. Attended San Diego Col., RADA. OB in "Merchant of Venice," "Hamlet," "Live Like Pigs," "Hotel Passionato," "Sjt. Musgrave's Dance," Bdwy in "Someone Waiting," "Separate Tables," "Little Moon of Alban," "Luther," "The Deputy," "Rosencrantz and Guildenstern Are Dead," "The Rothschilds," "Pippin."

HAMMER, BEN. Born Dec. 8, 1925 in Brooklyn, NY. Graduate Bklyn Col. Bdwy bow 1955 in "The Great Sebastians," followed by "Diary of Anne Frank," "Tenth Man," "Mother Courage," "The Deputy," "Royal Hunt of the Sun," "Golda," OB in "The Crucible," "Murderous Angels."

HANKS, BARBARA. Born Sept. 1, 1951 in Salt Lake City, UT. Graduate UUtah. Debut 1978 OB in "Gay Divorce."

HANLEY, KATIE. Born Jan. 17, 1949 in Evanston, IL. Attended Carnegie-Mellon U. Debut 1971 OB in "Godspell," followed by "Grease."

HAREWOOD, DORIAN. Born Aug. 6, 1951 in Dayton, OH. Attended U Cincinnati. Bdwy debut 1972 in "Two Gentlemen of Verona," followed by "Over Here," "Don't Call Back" for which he received a Theatre World Award, "Streamers," "The Mighty Gents."

HARGER, GARY. Born Aug. 19, 1951 in New Haven, CT. Ithaca Col. graduate. Bdwy debut 1975 in "Shenandoah."

HARPER, JAMES. Born Oct. 8, 1948 in Bell, CA. Attended Marin Col., Juilliard. Debut 1973 OB in "King Lear," followed by "Robber Bridegroom," "The Time of Your Life," "Mother Courage," "Edward II."

HARRIS, ALBERT. Born Feb. 16, 1945 in Philadelphia, PA. Attended Temple U. Debut 1967 OB in "The Poker Session," followed by "Promenade," "Agamemnon," "Company."

HARRIS, BAXTER. Born Nov. 18, 1940 in Columbus, KS. Attended U Kan. Debut 1967 OB in "America Hurrah," followed by "The Reckoning," "Wicked Women Revue," "More Than You Deserve," "Pericles," "him," "Battle of Angels," "Down by the River . . . ," Bdwy in "A Texas Trilogy" (1976), "Dracula."

HARRIS, PAMELA. Born Jan. 2, 1953 in Chicago, IL. Graduate Goodman Theatre, UMich. Debut 1977 OB in "The Crucible."

HARRISON, KEN. Born Oct. 26, 1947 in Santa Barbara, CA. Studied at American Conservatory Theatre. Bdwy debut 1977 in "Anna Christie."

HARTMAN, ELEK. Born Apr. 26, 1922 in Canton, OH. Graduate Carnegie Tech. OB in "Where People Gather," "Goa," Bdwy in "We Bombed in New Haven" (1968), "Angel."

HAWKINS, TRISH. Born Oct. 30, 1945 in Hartford, CT. Attended Radcliffe, Neighborhood Playhouse. Debut OB 1970 in "Oh! Calcutta!" followed by "Iphigenia," "The Hot l Baltimore" for which she received a Theatre World Award, "him," "Come Back, Little Sheba," "Battle of Angels," "Mound Builders," "The Farm," "Ulysses in Traction," "Lulu," Bdwy 1977 in "Some of My Best Friends."

HAYNES, TIGER. Born Dec. 13, 1907 in St. Croix, VI. Bdwy bow 1956 in "New Faces," followed by "Finian's Rainbow," "Fade Out—Fade In," "The Pajama Game," "The Wiz."

HAYS, REX DAVID. Born June 17, 1946 in Hollywood, CA. Graduate San Jose State U., Brandeis U. Bdwy debut 1975 in "Dance with Me," followed by "Angel."

HEARD, CORDIS. Born July 27, 1944 in Washington, DC. Graduate Chatham Col. Bdwy debut 1973 in "Warp," OB in "Vanities."

HEARD, JOHN. Born Mar. 7, 1946 in Washington, DC. Graduate Clark U. Debut 1974 OB in "The Wager," followed by "Macbeth," "Hamlet," "Fishing," "G. R. Point" for which he received a Theatre World Award, "Creditors," "The Promise," Bdwy in "Warp" (1973).

HEARN, GEORGE. Born June 18, 1934 in St. Louis, MO. Graduate Southwestern Col. OB in "Macbeth," "Antony and Cleopatra," "As You Like It," "Richard III," "Merry Wives of Windsor," "Midsummer Night's Dream," "Hamlet," "Horseman, Pass By," Bdwy in "A Time for Singing," "The Changing Room," "An Almost Perfect Person."

HEATH, LUISE. Born Apr. 18, 1951 in Brooklyn, NY. Attended Howard U., Juilliard. Debut 1970 OB in "The Black Quartet," followed by "The Last Sweet Days of Isaac," "Ragtime Blues," NEC productions, "The Devil's Disciple." Bdwy in "Via Galactica," "1600 Pennsylvania Ave.," "River Niger."

HEATH, SIGRID. Born Jan. 29, 1947 in St. Lucia, BWI. Attended UNC. Debut 1976 OB in "Lovesong," followed by "Identity and Other Crises."

HEDAYA, DAN. Born in Brooklyn, NY. Graduate Tufts Col. Debut 1974 OB in "Last Days of British Honduras," followed by "Conjuring an Event," "Museum," Bdwy in "The Basic Training of Pavlo Hummel" (1977).

HEFFERNAN, JOHN. Born May 30, 1934 in NYC. Attended CCNY, Columbia, Boston U. OB in "The Judge," "Julius Caesar," "Great God Brown," "Lysistrata," "Peer Gynt," "Henry IV," "Taming of the Shrew," "She Stoops to Conquer," "The Plough and the Stars," "Octoroon," "Hamlet," "Androcles and the Lion," "A Man's a Man," "Winter's Tale," "Arms and the Man," "St. Joan" (LCR), "Peer Gynt" (CP), "Memorandum," "Invitation to a Beheading," "Shadow of a Gunman," "The Sea," Bdwy in "Luther," "Tiny Alice," "Postmark Zero," "Woman Is My Idea," "Morning, Noon and Night," "Purlie," "Bad Habits," "Lady from the Sea," "Knock Knock," "Sly Fox."

Reily Hendrickson   **Michael Hirsch**   **Cynthia Herman**   **Nicholas Hormann**   **Celeste Holm**

HEMSLEY, WINSTON DeWITT. Born May 21, 1947 in Brooklyn, NY. Bdwy debut 1965 in "Golden Boy," followed by "A Joyful Noise," "Hallelujah, Baby," "Hello, Dolly!," "Rockabye Hamlet," "A Chorus Line," OB in "Buy Bonds Buster."

HENDRICKSON, REILY. Born Apr. 30, 1930 in Chicago, IL. Graduate AADA. Debut 1962 OB in "The Country Girl," followed by "Exiles," "The Seagull," "Blithe Spirit," "The Hostage," "Ring Round the Moon," "Hotel Paradiso," "The Happy Hunter."

HENNING, DOUG. Born May 3, 1947 in Winnipeg, Can. Graduate McMaster U. Bdwy debut 1974 in "The Magic Show."

HENRITZE, BETTE. Born May 3 in Betsy Layne, KY. Graduate UTenn. OB in "Lion in Love," "Abe Lincoln in Illinois," "Othello," "Baal," "Long Christmas Dinner," "Queens of France," "Rimers of Eldritch," "Displaced Person," "Acquisition," "Crime of Passion," "Happiness Cage," "Henry VI," "Richard III," "Older People," "Lotta," "Catsplay," Bdwy in "Jenny Kissed Me" (1948), "Pictures in the Hallway," "Giants, Sons of Giants," "Ballad of the Sad Cafe," "The White House," "Dr. Cook's Garden," "Here's Where I Belong," "Much Ado about Nothing," "Over Here," "Angel Street."

HERMAN, CYNTHIA. Born July 23, 1947 in Peoria, IL. Juilliard graduate. Bdwy debut 1974 in "Three Sisters," followed by "Beggar's Opera," "Measure for Measure," "Scapin," OB in "Uncommon Women and Others."

HEWETT, CHRISTOPHER. Born Apr. 5 in England, attended Beaumont Col. Bdwy debut 1956 in "My Fair Lady," followed by "First Impressions," "Unsinkable Molly Brown," "Kean," "The Affair," "Hadrian VII," "Music Is," OB in "Tobias and the Angel," "Trelawny of the Wells," "Finian's Rainbow." (JB)

HIGGINS, JOEL. Born Sept. 28, 1943 in Bloomington, IL. Graduate Mich State U. Bdwy debut 1975 in "Shenandoah" for which he received a Theatre World Award, followed by "Music Is," "Angel," OB in "Camp Meeting."

HIGGINS, MICHAEL. Born Jan. 20, 1926 in Bklyn. Attended Theatre Wing. Bdwy bow 1946 in "Antigone," followed by "Our Lan'," "Romeo and Juliet," "The Crucible," "The Lark," "Equus," OB in "White Devil," "Carefree Tree," "Easter," "The Queen and the Rebels," "Sally, George and Martha," "L'Ete," "Uncle Vanya," "The Iceman Cometh," "Molly."

HIKEN, GERALD. Born May 23, 1927 in Milwaukee, WI. Attended UWis. OB in "Cherry Orchard," "Seagull," "Good Woman of Setzuan," "The Misanthrope," "The Iceman Cometh," "The New Theatre," Bdwy in "Lovers," "Cave Dwellers," "Nervous Set," "Fighting Cock," "49th Cousin," "Gideon," "Foxy," "Three Sisters," "Golda."

HINES, PATRICK. Born Mar. 17, 1930 in Burkesville, TX. Graduate Tex. U. Debut OB in "Duchess of Malfi," followed by "Lysistrata," "Peer Gynt," "Henry IV," "Richard III," "Hot Grog," Bdwy in "Great God Brown," "Passage to India," "The Devils," "Cyrano," "The Iceman Cometh," "A Texas Trilogy," "Caesar and Cleopatra."

HIRSCH, JUDD. Born Mar. 15, 1935 in NYC. Attended AADA. Bdwy debut 1966 in "Barefoot in the Park," followed by "Chapter Two," OB in "On the Necessity of Being Polygamous," "Scuba Duba," "Mystery Play," "Hot l Baltimore," "Prodigal," "Knock Knock."

HIRSCH, MICHAEL. Born Jan. 1, 1947 in Brooklyn, NY. Graduate Ithaca Col. Debut 1978 OB in "Company."

HLIBOK, BRUCE. Born July 31, 1960 in NYC. Debut OB and Bdwy 1978 in "Runaways."

HODES, GLORIA. Born Aug. 20 in Norwich, CT. Operatic training before Bdwy debut 1969 in "Gantry," followed by OB's "The Club" for which she received a Theatre World Award.

HOFFMANN, JACK. Born Mar. 6, 1950 in Indianapolis, IN. Graduate Denison U. Debut 1974 OB in "Anna K," followed by "Dear Oscar," "Waiting for Godot," "Boys from Syracuse," "Carnival."

HOGAN, JONATHAN. Born June 13, 1951 in Chicago, IL. Graduate Goodman Theatre. Debut OB 1972 in "The Hot l Baltimore," followed by "Mound Builders," "Harry Outside," "Cabin 12," "5th of July," Bdwy in "Comedians" (1976), "Otherwise Engaged."

HOIT, MICHAEL. Born Oct. 18, 1949 in Chicago, IL. Graduate UIll. Debut 1975 OB in "Godspell," followed by "Words," "Joseph and the Amazing Technicolor Dreamcoat," Bdwy in "Godspell" (1977), "Hair" (1977).

HOLLAND, ANTHONY. Born Oct. 17, 1933 in Brooklyn, NY. Graduate UChicago. OB in "Venice Preserved," "Second City," "Victim of Duty," "New Tenant," "Dynamite Tonight," "Quare Fellow," "White House Murder Case," "Waiting for Godot," "Tales of the Hasidim," Bdwy in "My Mother, My Father and Me," "We Bombed in New Haven," "Dreyfus in Rehearsal," "Leaf People."

HOLLIDAY, KENE. Born June 25, 1949 in NYC. Graduate UMd. Debut 1976 OB in "Streamers."

HOLM, CELESTE. Born Apr. 29, 1919 in NYC. Attended UCLA, UChicago. Bdwy debut 1938 in "Glorianna," followed by "The Time of Your Life," "Another Sun," "Return of the Vagabond," "8 O'Clock Tuesday," "My Fair Ladies," "Papa Is All," "All the Comforts of Home," "Damask Cheek," "Oklahoma!," "Bloomer Girl," "She Stoops to Conquer," "Affairs of State," "Anna Christie," "The King and I," "His and Hers," "Interlock," "Third Best Sport," "Invitation to a March," "Mame," "Candida," "Habeas Corpus," OB in "A Month in the Country," "John Brown's Body."

HOLMES, PRUDENCE WRIGHT. Born in Boston, MA. Attended Carnegie Tech. Debut 1971 OB in "Godspell," followed by "Polly," "The Crazy Locomotive," Bdwy 1977 in "Happy End."

HORMANN, NICHOLAS. Born Dec. 22, 1944 in Honolulu, HI. Graduate Oberlin, Yale. Bdwy debut 1973 in "The Visit," followed by "Chemin de Fer," "Holiday," "Love for Love," "Rules of the Game," "Member of the Wedding," "St. Joan," OB in "Ice Age," "Marco Polo."

HORNE, CHERYL. Born Nov. 15 in Stamford, CT. Graduate SMU. Debut 1975 OB in "The Fantasticks."

HORTON, RUSSELL. Born Nov. 11, 1941 in Los Angeles, CA. Graduate UCLA. Debut 1966 OB in "Displaced Person," followed by "How's the World Treating You?," LC's "Galileo," "Antigone," "What Did We Do Wrong?," "The Last Resort," "Scribes," "City Sugar."

HOSBEIN, JAMES. Born Sept. 24, 1946 in Benton Harbor, MI. Graduate UMich. Debut 1972 OB in "Dear Oscar," followed by "Darrel and Carol and Kenny and Jenny," Bdwy 1977 in "Annie."

HOTY, TONY. Born Sept. 29, 1949 in Lakewood, OH. Attended Ithaca Col., WVaU. Debut 1974 OB in "Godspell" (also Bdwy 1976), followed by "Joseph and the Amazing Technicolor Dreamcoat."

HOWARD, JOE. Born Nov. 24, 1948 in Yonkers, NY. Graduate Hamilton Col. Bdwy debut 1976 in "So Long, 174th Street," followed by "Shenandoah."

HUDGINS, MARILYN. Born June 24 in Washington, DC. Graduate SBV Col., URedlands. Bdwy debut 1978 in "Hello, Dolly!"

HUDGINS, WAYNE. Born June 19, 1950 in Amarillo, TX. Graduate UWash. Bdwy debut 1976 in "Shenandoah."

HUGHES, BARNARD. Born July 16, 1915 in Bedford Hills, N.Y. Attended Manhattan Col. OB in "Rosmersholm," "A Doll's House," "Hogan's Goat," "Line," "Older People," "Hamlet" "Merry Wives of Windsor," "Pericles," BAM Co.'s "Three Sisters," Bdwy in "The Ivy Green," "Dinosaur Wharf," "Teahouse of the August Moon" (CC), "A Majority of One," "Advise and Consent," "The Advocate," "Hamlet," "I Was Dancing," "Generation," "How Now, Dow Jones?," "Wrong Way Light Bulb," "Sheep On The Runway," "Abelard and Heloise," "Much Ado About Nothing," "Uncle Vanya," "The Good Doctor," "All Over Town," "Da."

HULCE, THOMAS. Born Dec. 6, 1953 in Plymouth, MI. Graduate NC Sch. of Arts. Bdwy debut 1975 in "Equus," followed OB in "A Memory of Two Mondays," "Julius Caesar."

HUMPHREY, CAVADA. Born June 17 in Atlantic, City, NJ. Graduate Smith Col. Debut 1943 OB in "A Man's House," followed by "Moon in Capricorn," "Girl of the Golden West," "Dear Liar," "Life Is a Dream," "Madame de Sade," "Henry's Daughter," Bdwy in "House in Paris," "Song of Bernadette," "As the Girls Go," "Time Remembered," "The Devil's Disciple," "Richard III," "Othello," "Henry IV," "You Can't Take It with You," "Candida."

HUNT, LINDA. Born Apr. 2, 1945 in Morristown, NJ. Attended Goodman Theatre. Debut 1975 OB in "Down by the River Where the Waterlilies . . . ," followed by "The Tennis Game," Bdwy in "Ah, Wilderness."

HURT, WILLIAM. Born Mar. 20, 1950 in Washington, DC. Graduate Tufts U., Juilliard. Debut 1976 OB in "Henry V," followed by "My Life," "Ulysses in Traction," "Lulu," "5th of July." He received a 1978 Theatre World Award for his performances with Circle Repertory Theatre.

| Marcia Hyde | Elmore James | Memrie Innerarity | Page Johnson | Nancy Kammer |

HYDE, MARCIA. Born Dec. 9, 1948 in Oklahoma City, OK. Graduate Colo. Women's Col., UDenver. Debut 1976 OB in "Heartbreak House," followed by "The Balcony," "Bingo," "Tartuffe," "Old Man Joseph and His Family," "Moliere in spite of Himself."

HYMAN, EARLE. Born Oct. 11, 1926 in Rocky Mount, NC. Attended New School, Theatre Wing. Bdwy debut 1943 in "Run, Little Chillun," followed by "Anna Lucasta," "Climate of Eden," "Merchant of Venice," "Othello," "Julius Caesar," "The Tempest," "No Time for Sergeants," "Mr. Johnson" for which he received a Theatre World Award, "St. Joan," "Hamlet," "Waiting for Godot," "Duchess of Malfi," "Les Blancs," OB in "The White Rose and the Red," "Worlds of Shakespeare," "Jonah," "Life and Times of J. Walter Smintheus," "Orrin," "Cherry Orchard," "House Party," "Carnival Dreams," "Agamemnon," "Othello."

INNERARITY, MEMRIE. Born Feb. 11, 1945 in Columbus, MS. Attended USMiss. Debut 1976 OB in "The Club."

JABLONS, KAREN. Born July 19, 1951 in Trenton, NJ. Juilliard graduate. Debut 1969 OB in "The Student Prince," followed by "Sound of Music," "Funny Girl," "Boys from Syracuse," Bdwy in "Ari," "Two Gentlemen of Verona," "Lorelei," "Where's Charley?," "A Chorus Line."

JACOBI, LOU. Born Dec. 28, 1913 in Toronto, Can. Bdwy bow 1955 in "Diary of Anne Frank," followed by "The Tenth Man," "Come Blow Your Horn," "Fade Out-Fade In," "Don't Drink the Water," "A Way of Life," "Norman, Is That You?," "Unlikely Heroes," "The Sunshine Boys," "Cheaters."

JAMES, CLIFTON. Born May 29, 1921 in Spokane, WA. Attended Ore. U., Actors Studio. Has appeared in "The Time of Your Life" (CC), "The Cave Dwellers," "Great Day in the Morning," "Andorra," "And Things That Go Bump in the Night," "The Coop" (OB), "Trial of Lee Harvey Oswald," "The Shadow Box."

JAMES, ELMORE. Born May 3, 1954 in NYC. Graduate SUNY/Purchase. Debut 1970 OB in "Moon on a Rainbow Shawl," "The Ups and Downs of Theopholus Maitland," "Carnival."

JAMES, FRANCESCA. Born Jan. 23 in Montebello, CA. Attended Carnegie-Mellon U. Bdwy debut 1971 in "The Rothschilds," OB in "The Father," "Life of Galileo."

JAMES, JESSICA. Born Oct. 31, 1933 in Los Angeles, CA. Attended USC. Bdwy debut 1970 in "Company," followed by "Gemini," OB in "Nourish the Beast," "Hothouse," "Loss of Innocence," "Rebirth Celebration of the Human Race," "Silver Bee," "Gemini."

JANS, ALARIC. Born Jan. 27, 1949 in St. Louis. MO. Attended Harvard U. OB and Bdwy debut 1978 in "The Water Engine."

JANSEN, JIM. Born July 27, 1945 in Salt Lake City, UT. Graduate U Utah. NYU. Debut OB 1973 in "Moonchildren," followed by "Marco Polo Sings a Solo," "Chez Nous," Bdwy 1974 in "All Over Town."

JENKINS, CAROL MAYO. Born Nov. 24, in Knoxville, TN. Attended Vanderbilt U., UTn., London Central Sch. of Speech. Bdwy debut 1969 in "The Three Sisters," followed by "There's One in Every Marriage," "Kings," OB in "Zinnia."

JOHNSON, ROBERT. Born Apr. 17, 1951 in Wilmington, DE. Graduate Ithaca Col. Bdwy debut 1977 in "Shenandoah."

JOHNSON, KURT. Born Oct. 5, 1952 in Pasadena, CA. Attended LACC, Occidental Col. Debut 1976 OB in "Follies," followed by "Walking Papers," "A Touch of Marble," Bdwy in "Rockaby Hamlet," "A Chorus Line."

JOHNSON, MEL, JR. Born Apr. 16, 1949 in NYC. Graduate Hofstra U. Debut 1972 OB in "Hamlet," followed by "Love! Love! Love," Bdwy 1978 in "On the 20th Century."

JOHNSON, PAGE. Born Aug. 25, 1930 in Welch, WV. Graduate Ithaca Col. Bdwy bow 1951 in "Romeo and Juliet," followed by "Electra," "Oedipus," "Camino Real," "In April Once" for which he received a Theatre World Award, "Red Roses for Me," "The Lovers," "Equus," OB in "The Enchanted," "Guitar," "4 in 1," "Journey of the Fifth Horse," APA's "School for Scandal," "The Tavern" and "The Seagull," "Odd Couple," "Boys In The Band," "Medea."

JOHNSTON, JUSTINE. Born June 13 in Evanston, IL. Debut 1959 OB in "Little Mary Sunshine," followed by "The Time of Your Life" (CC), "The Dubliners," Bdwy in "Pajama Game," "Milk and Honey," "Follies," "Irene," "Molly," "Angel," BAM Co.'s "New York Idea."

JONES, EDDIE. Born in Washington, PA. Debut 1960 OB in "Dead End," followed by "Curse of the Starving Class," Bdwy 1974 in "That Championship Season."

JONES, JAMES EARL. Born Jan. 17, 1931 in Arkabutla, MI. Graduate Mich U. OB in "The Pretender," "The Blacks," "Clandestine on the Morning Line," "The Apple," "A Midsummer Night's Dream," "Moon on a Rainbow Shawl" for which he received a Theatre World Award. "PS 193," "Last Minstrel," "Love Nest," "Bloodknot," "Othello," "Baal," "Danton's Death" (LC). "Boesman and Lena," "Hamlet" (NYSF) "Cherry Orchard," Bdwy in "The Egghead," "Sunrise at Campobello," "The Cool World," "A Hand Is on the Gate," "Great White Hope," "Les Blancs," "King Lear," "The Iceman Cometh," "Of Mice and Men," "Paul Robeson."

JORDAN, ALAN. Born Mar. 21, 1943 in Toronto, Can. Graduate Neighborhood Playhouse. Debut 1974 OB in "The Proposition," followed by "Battle of Angels," "Exiles."

JOSLYN, BETSY. Born Apr. 19, 1954 in Staten Island, NY. Graduate Wagner Col. Debut 1976 OB in "The Fantasticks."

JOURDAN, LOUIS. Born June 18, 1921 in Marseilles, France. Bdwy debut 1954 in "The Immoralist," followed by "Tonight in Samarkand," "13 Rue de L'Amour."

JUDE, PATRICK. Born Feb. 25, 1951 in Jersey City, NJ. Bdwy debut 1972 in "Jesus Christ Superstar," followed by 1977 revival.

JULIA, RAUL. Born Mar. 9, 1940 in San Juan, PR. Graduate UPR. OB in "Macbeth," "Titus Andronicus" (CP), "Theatre in the Streets," "Life Is a Dream," "Blood Wedding," "Ox Cart," "No Exit," "Memorandum," "Frank Gagliano's City Scene," "Your Own Thing," "Persians," "Castro Complex," "Pinkville," "Hamlet," "King Lear," "As You Like It," "Emperor of Late Night Radio," "Threepenny Opera," "The Cherry Orchard," Bdwy bow 1968 in "The Cuban Thing," followed by "Indians," "Two Gentlemen of Verona," "Via Galactica," "Where's Charley?"

JUNG, CALVIN. Born Feb. 17, 1945 in NYC. Graduate Hillsdale Col. Debut 1972 OB in "Chickencoop Chinaman," followed by "Dawn Song," "Year of the Dragon," "A Memory of Two Mondays," "They Knew What They Wanted," "Museum," Bdwy 1976 in "Sly Fox."

KAGEN, DAVID. Born Sept. 27, 1948 in Somers Point, NJ. Graduate Carnegie Tech. Debut 1978 OB in "Family Business."

KAHN, MADELINE. Born Sept. 29, 1942 in Boston, MA. Graduate Hofstra U. Bdwy debut in "New Faces of 1968," followed by "Two by Two," "She Loves Me," "On the 20th Century," OB in "Promenade," "Boom Boom Room," "Marco Polo Sings a Solo."

KAIRSON, URSULINE. Born March 28 in Chicago, IL. Attended Wilson Jr. Col. Bdwy debut 1970 in "Hair," followed by "Purlie," "Bubbling Brown Sugar," OB in "The Rhinegold."

KAMMER, NANCY. Born Mar. 27, 1953 in Valdosta, GA. Attended NYU. Appeared with dance companies before debut OB 1977 in "Carnival."

KAMP, DIANE. Born Aug. 7, 1948 in Oskaloosa, IA. Graduate Calvin Col., UMich. Debut 1978 OB with Acting Co. in "The Other Half," "King Lear," and "Mother Courage."

KANAR, ZWI. Born July 17, 1931 in Skalbmierz, Poland. Studied with Decroux and Marceau. Debut 1978 OB in solo mime show.

KANSAS, JERI. Born Mar. 10, 1955 in Jersey City, NJ. Debut 1978 OB in "Gay Divorce."

KARR, PATTI. Born July 10 in St. Paul, MN. Attended TCU. Bdwy debut 1953 in "Maggie," followed by "Carnival in Flanders," "Pipe Dream," "Bells Are Ringing," "New Girl in Town," "Body Beautiful," "Bye Bye Birdie," "New Faces of 1962," "Come on Strong," "Look to the Lilies," "Different Times," "Lysistrata," "Seesaw," "Irene," "Pippin," OB in "A Month of Sundays," "Up Eden."

KASZNAR, KURT. Born Aug. 12, 1913 in Vienna, Aust. Bdwy debut 1936 in "Eternal Road," followed by "The Army Play by Play," "Joy to the World," "Make Way for Lucia," "Montserrat," "Happy Time," "Waiting for Godot," "Seventh Heaven," "Look after Lulu," "Sound of Music," "Barefoot in the Park," OB in "Six Characters in Search of an Author," "The Play's the Thing."

KAVA, CAROLINE. Born in Chicago, IL. Attended Neighborhood Playhouse. Debut 1975 OB in "Gorky," followed by "Threepenny Opera," Bdwy 1978 in "Stages."

| K. C. Kelly | Laura Kenyon | Richard Kevlin-Bell | Alexandra Korey | Michael Kolba |

KAVANAUGH, RICHARD. Born in 1943 in NYC. Bdwy debut 1977 in "Dracula."

KAYE, JUDY. Born Oct. 11, 1948 in Phoenix, AZ. Attended UCLA, Ariz. State U. Bdwy debut 1977 in "Grease," followed by "On the 20th Century" for which she received a Theatre World Award.

KEEP, STEPHEN. Born Aug. 24, 1947 in Camden, SC. Attended Columbia, Yale. Bdwy debut 1972 in "Paul Sills Story Theatre" and "Metamorphosis," followed by "Shadow Box," OB in "Clarence," "The Cherry Orchard," "Esther."

KELL, MICHAEL. Born Jan. 18, 1944 in Jersey City, NJ. Attended HB Studio. Debut 1972 OB in "One Flew over the Cuckoo's Nest," followed by "Boom Boom Room," "Golden Boy," "Streamers."

KELLY, K. C. Born Nov. 12, 1952 in Baraboo, WI. Attended UWisc. Debut 1976 OB in "The Chicken Ranch," followed by Bdwy in "Romeo and Juliet" (1977), "The Best Little Whorehouse in Texas."

KENIN, ALEXA. Born Feb. 16, 1962 in NYC. Debut 1977 OB in "Landscape of the Body," followed by "Elusive Angel."

KENNEDY, MIMI. Born Sept 25, 1948 in Rochester, NY. Graduate Smith College. Bdwy debut 1975 in "Grease," OB in "Hot Grog."

KENYON, LAURA. Born Nov. 23, 1948 in Chicago, IL. Attended USCal. Debut 1970 OB in "Peace," followed by "Carnival," Bdwy in "Man of La Mancha" (1971), "On the Town."

KERMOYAN, MICHAEL. Born Nov. 29, 1925 in Fresno, CA. Attended Stanford U., USC. Bdwy bow 1954 in "The Girl in Pink Tights," followed by "Whoop-Up," "Happy Town," "Camelot," "Happiest Girl in the World," "Fly Blackbird," "Ross," "Tovarich," "Anya," "The Guide," "Desert Song," "The King and I," OB in "Carousel," "Sandhog," "Angels of Anadarko."

KERNAN, DAVID. Born June 23, 1939 in London, Eng. Bdwy debut 1977 in "Side by Side by Sondheim."

KERT, LARRY. Born Dec. 5, 1934 in Los Angeles, CA. Attended LACC Bdwy bow 1953 in "John Murray Anderson's Almanac," followed by "Ziegfeld Follies," "Mr. Wonderful," "Walk Tall," "Look, Ma, I'm Dancin'," "Tickets Please," "West Side Story," "A Family Affair," "Breakfast at Tiffany's," "Cabaret," "La Strada," "Company," "Two Gentlemen of Verona," "Music! Music!," "Musical Jubilee," "Side by Side by Sondheim."

KEVLIN-BELL, RICHARD. Born Jan. 28, 1945 in Brooklyn, NY. Graduate St. John's U., Bklyn Col. Debut 1969 OB in "Get Thee to Canterbury," followed by "Macbeth," "Company."

KEYES, DANIEL. Born Mar. 6, 1914 in Concord, MA. Attended Harvard. Bdwy debut 1954 in "The Remarkable Mr. Pennypacker," followed by "Bus Stop," "Only in America," "Christine," "First Love," "Take Her, She's Mine," "Baker Street," "Dinner at 8," "I Never Sang for My Father," "Wrong Way Light Bulb," "A Place for Polly," "Scratch," "Rainbow Jones," "Angel," OB in "Our Town," "Epitaph for George Dillon," "Plays for Bleecker St.," "Hooray! It's a Glorious Day!," "Six Characters in Search of an Author," "Sjt. Musgrave's Dance," "Arms and the Man," "Mourning Becomes Electra," "Salty Dog Saga," "Hot l Baltimore."

KEZER, GLENN. Born Apr. 2, 1923 in Okemah, OK. Graduate UOkla. Bdwy in "My Fair Lady," "Camelot," "Fade Out—Fade In," "Half a Sixpence," "Little Murders," "Trial of Lee Harvey Oswald," "The Other Man," OB in "Walk in Darkness," "Brigadoon" (CC), "Oh, Say Can You See L.A.," "Firebugs," "The David Show," "Promenade," "Threepenny Opera."

KILEY, RICHARD. Born Mar. 31, 1922 in Chicago, IL. Attended Loyola U. Bdwy debut 1953 in "Misalliance" for which he received a Theatre World Award, followed by "Kismet," "Sing Me No Lullaby," "Time Limit!," "Redhead," "Advise and Consent," "No Strings," "Here's Love," "I Had a Ball," "Man of La Mancha" (also LC and 1977 revival), "Her First Roman," "The Incomparable Max," "Voices," "Absurd Person Singular," "The Heiress," "Knickerbocker Holiday."

KILLMER, NANCY. Born Dec. 16, 1936 in Homewood, IL. Graduate Northwestern U. Bdwy debut 1969 in "Coco," followed by "Goodtime Charley," "So Long, 174th Street," OB in "Exiles."

KILTY, JEROME. Born June 24, 1922 in Pala Indian Reservation, CA. Attended Guildhall Sch., London. Bdwy debut 1950 in "The Relapse," followed by "Love's Labour's Lost" (CC), "Misalliance," "A Pin to See the Peepshow," "Frogs of Spring," "Quadrille," "Othello," "Henry IV," OB in "Dear Liar."

KIMBROUGH, CHARLES. Born May 23, 1936 in St. Paul, MN. Graduate Ind. U., Yale. Bdwy bow 1969 in "Cop-Out," followed by "Company," "Love for Love," "Rules of the Game," "Candide," "Mr. Happiness," "Same Time, Next Year," OB in "All in Love," "Struts and Frets," "Troilus and Cressida," "Secret Service," "Boy Meets Girl."

KIMMINS, KENNETH. Born Sept. 4, 1941 in Brooklyn, NY. Graduate Catholic U. Debut 1966 OB in "The Fantasticks," followed by "Adaptation," "All My Sons," Bdwy in "Fig Leaves Are Falling," "Gingerbread Lady," "Company," "Status Quo Vadis," "Magic Show."

KINGSLEY, PETER. Born Aug. 14, 1945 in Mexico City, Mex. Graduate Hamilton Col., LAMDA. Debut 1974 OB in "The Beauty Part," followed by "Purification," "Moliere in spite of Himself," "Old Man Joseph and His Family."

KIRSCH, CAROLYN. Born May 24, 1942 in Shreveport, LA. Bdwy debut 1963 in "How to Succeed . . .," followed by "Folies Bergere," "La Grosse Valise," "Skyscraper," "Breakfast at Tiffany's," "Sweet Charity," "Hallelujah, Baby!," "Dear World," "Promises, Promises," "Coco," "Ulysses in Nighttown," "A Chorus Line," OB in "Silk Stockings."

KITT, EARTHA. Born Jan. 26, 1928 in North, SC. Appeared with Katherine Dunham and in clubs before Bdwy debut in "New Faces of 1952," followed by "Mrs. Patterson," "Shinbone Alley," "Timbuktu."

KLAVUN, WALTER. Born May 8, 1906 in NYC. Yale graduate. Bdwy debut 1928 in "Say When," followed by "No More Ladies," "Arms for Venus," "Annie Get Your Gun," "Twelfth Night," "Dream Girl," "Auntie Mame," "Say, Darling," "Desert Incident," "How to Succeed in Business . . .," "What Makes Sammy Run," "Twigs," OB in "Mornings at 7," "Dandy Dick," "The Dubliners," "Ballad of the Sad Cafe."

KLIBAN, KEN. Born July 26, 1943 in Norwalk, CT. Graduate UMiami, NYU. Bdwy debut 1967 in "War and Peace," followed by OB in "Puppy Dog Tails," "Istanboul," "Persians," "him," "Elizabeth the Queen," "Judith," "Man and Superman," "Boom Boom Room," "Ulysses in Traction," "Lulu."

KLINE, KEVIN. Born Oct. 24, 1947 in St. Louis, MO. Graduate Ind. U., Juilliard. Debut 1970 OB in "Wars of Roses," followed by "School for Scandal," "Lower Depths," "The Hostage," "Women Beware Women," "Robber Bridegroom," "Edward II," "The Time of Your Life," "Beware the Jubjub Bird," "Dance on a Country Grave." Bdwy in "Three Sisters," "Measure for Measure," "Beggar's Opera," "Scapin," "On the 20th Century."

KLUNIS, TOM. Bdwy debut 1961 in "Gideon," followed by "The Devils," "Henry V," "Romeo and Juliet," "St. Joan," OB in "The Immoralist," "Hamlet," "Arms and the Man," "Potting Shed," "Measure for Measure," "Romeo and Juliet," "The Balcony," "Our Town," "Man Who Never Died," "God Is My Ram," "Rise, Marlowe," "Iphigenia in Aulis," "Still Life."

KNIGHT, SHIRLEY. Born July 5 in Goessel, KS. Attended Phillips U., Wichita U. Bdwy debut 1964 in "The Three Sisters," followed by "We Have Always Lived in a Castle," "The Watering Place," "Kennedy's Children," OB in "Journey to the Day," "Rooms," "Happy End," "Landscape of the Body."

KNIGHT, TED. Born in 1924 in Terryville, CT. Attended American Theatre Wing. Bdwy debut 1977 in "Some of My Best Friends."

KNIGHT, WILLIAM. Born Dec. 6, 1934 in Los Angeles, CA. Graduate CCLA. Bdwy debut 1970 in "Oh! Calcutta!," followed by "An Evening with Richard Nixon . . .," OB in "The Minister's Black Veil," "Santa Anita '42," "Elusive Angel."

KNUDSON, KURT. Born Sept. 7, 1936 in Fargo, ND. Attended NDState U., Hamline U, UMiami. Debut 1976 OB in "The Cherry Orchard."

KOLBA, MICHAEL. Born Oct. 1, 1947 in Moorhead, MN. Graduate Moorhead U., UHawaii. Debut 1976 OB in "The Cherry Orchard," followed by "Measure for Measure."

KOREY, ALEXANDRA. Born May 14 in Brooklyn, NY. Graduate Columbia U. Debut 1976 OB in "Fiorello!" (ELT), Bdwy in "Hello, Dolly!" (1978).

KRAMER, JOEL. Born July 1, 1943 in The Bronx, NY. Graduate Queens Col., UMich. Debut 1963 OB in "St. Joan of the Stockyards," followed by "Playboy of the Western World," "Measure for Measure," "Man Who Corrupted Hadleyburg," "Call Me Madam," "Castaways," "Esther."

| Philip Krause | Berit Lagerwall | Stephen Lang | Urylee Leonardos | Michael Leslie |

KRAUS, PHILIP. Born May 10, 1949 in Springville, NY. Carnegie Tech graduate. Bdwy debut 1973 in "Shelter," followed by "Equus," OB in "Julius Caesar."

KREININ, REBECCA. Born May 4, 1955 in Pittsburgh, PA. Graduate Pittsburgh Playhouse. Debut 1978 OB in "Moliere in spite of Himself."

KRUGER, DANIEL D. Born May 30, 1942 in Genesco, IL. Attended Ill. State U. Debut 1972 OB in "Secret Life of Walter Mitty," followed by "Call Me Madam," "Allegro."

KUHLMAN, RON. Born Mar. 6, 1948 in Cleveland, OH. Graduate Ohio U. Debut 1972 OB in "A Maid's Tragedy," followed by "A Chorus Line" (Bdwy 1975).

KURTZ, MARCIA JEAN. Born in The Bronx, NY. Juilliard graduate. Debut 1966 OB in "Jonah," followed by "America Hurrah," "Red Cross," "Muzeeka," "The Effect of Gamma Rays . . . ," "The Year Boston Won the Pennant," "The Mirror," "The Orphan," "Action," "The Dybbuk," Bdwy in "The Chinese and Dr. Fish," "Thieves."

KURTZ, SWOOSIE. Born Sept. 6, in Omaha, NE. Attended USCal., LAMDA. Debut 1968 OB in "The Firebugs," followed by "The Effect of Gamma Rays . . . ," "Enter a Free Man," "Children," "Museum," "Uncommon Women and Others," Bdwy in "Ah, Wilderness" (1975), "Tartuffe," "A History of the American Film."

KUSS, RICHARD. Born July 17, 1927 in Astoria, NY. Attended Ithaca Col. Debut 1951 OB in "Mother Said No," followed by "A Maid's Tragedy," Bdwy in "J.B.," "Wait until Dark," "Solitaire/Double Solitaire," "Golda."

LACEY, FLORENCE. Born July 22, 1948 in McKeesport, PA. Graduate Pittsburgh Playhouse. Bdwy debut 1978 in "Hello, Dolly!" for which she received a Theatre World Award.

LADD, MARGARET. Born Nov. 8, 1942 in Providence, RI. Graduate Bard Col. OB in "The Knack," "Free, Free, Free," "The Experiment," "Museum," "Passing Game," Bdwy in "The Great Indoors," "Sheep on the Runway."

LAGERFELT, CAROLYN. Born Sept. 23 in Paris. Graduate AADA. Bdwy debut 1971 in "The Philanthropist," followed by "4 on a Garden," "Jockey Club Stakes," "The Constant Wife," "Look Back in Anger" (OB), "Otherwise Engaged."

LAGERWALL, BERIT. Born May 8, 1945 in Sweden. Debut 1977 OB in "A Servant of Two Masters," followed by "Old Man Joseph and His Family," "Moliere in spite of Himself."

LAMONT, ROBIN. Born June 2, 1950 in Boston, MA. Attended Carnegie-Mellon U. Debut 1971 OB in "Godspell," followed by "Thoughts," Bdwy in "Godspell" (1976), "Working."

LAMOS, MARK. Born March 10, 1946 in Chicago, IL. Attended Northwestern U. Bdwy debut 1972 in "The Love Suicide at Schofield Barracks," followed by "The Creation of the World and Other Business," "Cyrano," OB in "City Sugar."

LANCASTER, LUCIE. Born Oct. 15, 1907 in Chicago, IL. Bdwy debut 1947 in "Heads or Tails," followed by "Mr. Pickwick," "The Girl Who Came to Supper," "Bajour," "How Now, Dow Jones," "Little Boxes" (OB), "70 Girls 70," "Pippin."

LANDERS, MATT. Born Oct. 21, 1952 in Mohawk Valley, NY. Attended Boston Cons. Debut OB 1974 in "Godspell," followed by Bdwy in "Grease" (1975), "Working."

LANE, NANCY. Born June 16, 1951 in Passaic, NJ. Attended Va. Commonwealth U., AADA. Debut 1975 OB and Bdwy in "A Chorus Line."

LANG, STEPHEN. Born July 11, 1952 in NYC. Graduate Swarthmore Col. Debut 1975 OB in "Hamlet," followed by "Henry V," Bdwy in "St. Joan" (1977).

LANGELLA, FRANK. Born Jan. 1, 1940 in Bayonne, NJ. Graduate Syracuse U. Debut 1963 OB in "The Immoralist," followed by "The Old Glory," "Good Day," "White Devil," "Yerma," "Iphigenia in Aulis," "A Cry of Players," "Prince of Homburg," Bdwy in "Seascape," "Dracula."

LANSBURY, ANGELA. Born Oct. 16, 1925 in London, Eng. Bdwy debut 1957 in "Hotel Paradiso," followed by "A Taste of Honey," "Anyone Can Whistle," "Mame," "Dear World," "Gypsy," "The King and I" (1978).

LANSING, JOHN. Born Oct. 16, 1949 in Baldwin, NY. Attended Hofstra Col. Bdwy debut 1972 in "The Sign in Sidney Brustein's Window," followed by "Grease."

LATHRAM, ELIZABETH. Born Apr. 23, 1947 in Washington, DC. Graduate UOre. Debut 1971 OB in "Godspell," followed by "Moonchildren," "Children of Adam," Bdwy 1976 in "Godspell."

LEAGUE, JANET. Born Oct. 13 in Chicago, IL. Attended Goodman Theatre. Debut 1969 OB in "To Be Young, Gifted and Black," followed by "Tiger at the Gates," "The Screens," "Mrs. Snow," "Please Don't Cry and Say No," Bdwy in "First Breeze of Summer," (1975) "For Colored Girls Who Have Considered Suicide . . ."

LEDERER, SUZANNE. Born Sept. 29, 1948 in Great Neck, NY. Graduate Hofstra U. Bdwy debut 1974 in "The National Health," followed by "Days in the Trees," OB in "Treats."

LEE, KAIULANI. Born Feb. 28, 1950 in Princeton, NJ. Attended American U. Bdwy debut 1975 in "Kennedy's Children," OB in "Ballad of the Sad Cafe," "Museum," "Safe House."

LEEDS, MICHAEL. Born Nov. 14, 1951 in NYC. Graduate Ithaca Col. Bdwy debut 1976 in "Pal Joey," followed by "The Act."

LeMASSENA, WILLIAM. Born May 23, 1916 in Glen Ridge, NJ. Attended NYU. Bdwy bow 1940 in "Taming of the Shrew," followed by "There Shall Be No Night," "The Pirate," "Hamlet," "Call Me Mister," "Inside U.S.A.," "I Know, My Love," "Dream Girl," "Nina," "Ondine," "Fallen Angels," "Redhead," "Conquering Hero," "Beauty Part," "Come Summer," "Grin and Bare It," "All over Town," "A Texas Trilogy," OB in "The Coop," "Brigadoon," "Life with Father," "F. Jasmine Addams," "The Dodge Boys."

LEON, JOSEPH. Born June 8, 1923 in NYC. Attended NYU, UCLA. Bdwy debut 1950 in "Bell, Book and Candle," followed by "Seven Year Itch," "Pipe Dream," "Fair Game," "Gazebo," "Julia, Jake and Uncle Joe," "Beauty Part," "Merry Widow," "Henry, Sweet Henry," "Jimmy Shine," "All over Town," "California Suite," "The Merchant," OB in "Come Share My House," "Dark Corners," "Interrogation of Havanna," "Are You Now or Have You Ever Been."

LEONARDOS, URYLEE. Born May 14, in Charleston, SC. Attended Manhattan Sch. of Music. Bdwy debut 1943 in "Carmen Jones," followed by "Shangri-La," "Bells Are Ringing," "Wildcat," "Sophie," "Milk and Honey," "110 in the Shade," "Bajour," "Ilya, Darling," "Dear World," "Desert Song," "1600 Pennsylvania Ave.," OB in "Billy Noname," "Fixed."

LESLIE, MICHAEL. Born Mar. 31, 1952 in Neptune, NJ. Graduate Rutgers, Cornell U. Bdwy debut 1977 in "Hair."

LETNER, KEN. Born Oct. 25, 1932 in Nevada City, CA. Graduate U. San Francisco. Debut 1975 OB in "Our Father," followed by "The Devil's Disciple," "Julius Caesar."

LEVERIDGE, LYNN ANN. Born Mar. 16, 1948 in NYC. Attended Hofstra U. Debut 1970 OB In "Saved," followed by "Beggar's Opera," "The Contractor," "Black Tuesday."

LEVINE, ANNA. Born Sept. 18, 1955 in NYC. Attended Actors Studio. Debut 1975 OB in "Kid Champion," followed by "Uncommon Women and Others," "City Sugar."

LEVINE, ROBERT. Born Sept. 4, 1931 in Brooklyn, NY. Graduate Syracuse U. Debut 1960 OB in "Opening of a Window," followed by "Enemy of the People," "The Miser," "King Lear," "A Cry of Players," "Suggs," "Good Woman of Setzuan," "The Time of Your Life," "Bananas," "In the Matter of J. Robert Oppenheimer," "The Last Resort," Bdwy in "Golda."

LINDIG, JILLIAN. Born Mar. 19, 1944 in Johnson City, TX. Debut 1969 OB in "Brownstone Urge," followed by "AC/DC," Bdwy in "Equus."

LINDSEY, GENE. Born Oct. 26, 1936 in Beaumont, TX. Graduate Baylor U, Southwestern U. OB in "By Jupiter," "Gogo Loves You," "Bernstein's Theatre Songs," "The Deer Park," "Troubles in Tahiti," "Columbus," "Ramblings," "Unsung Cole," Bdwy in "My Daughter, Your Son," "Cactus Flower."

LITHGOW, JOHN. Born in Rochester, NY. Graduate Harvard U. Bdwy debut 1973 in "The Changing Room," followed by "My Fat Friend," "Comedians," "Anna Christie," OB in "Hamlet," "Trelawny of the Wells," "A Memory of Two Mondays," "Secret Service," "Boy Meets Girl."

248

| Elisa London | David Little | Barbara Luna | Greg Macosko | Rebecka Malka |

LITTLE, DAVID. Born Mar. 21, 1937 in Wadesboro, NC. Graduate Wm. & Mary Col., Catholic U. Debut 1967 OB in "MacBird," followed by "Iphigenia in Aulis," "Antony and Cleopatra," "Antigone," "An Enemy of the People," "Three Sons," Bdwy in "Thieves," "Zalmen, or the Madness of God."

LIVINGSTON, RUTH. Born March 25 in New Haven, CT. Graduate UMich., AmThWing. Debut OB 1976 in "The Rimers of Eldritch," followed by "Play Me, Zoltan," Bdwy in "Romeo and Juliet" (1977)."

LLOYD, CHRISTOPHER. Born Oct. 22, 1938 in Stamford, CT. Attended Neighborhood Playhouse. Bdwy debut 1969 in "Red, White and Maddox," followed by "Happy End," OB in "Kaspar," "Total Eclipse," "Macbeth," "The Seagull," "In the Boom Boom Room," "Happy End."

LOEB, ERIC. Born Apr. 26, 1943 in Berkeley, CA. Graduate UWis. Bdwy debut 1975 in "Sweet Bird of Youth," followed by "The Water Engine."

LOEWENSTERN, TARA. Born Nov. 11, 1951 in Los Angeles, CA. Attended SMU, UTx, RADA. Debut 1977 OB in "The Crucible."

LOKEY, BEN. Born Dec. 15, 1944 in Birmingham, AL. Graduate West Tx. State, UUtah. Bdwy debut 1977 in "A Chorus Line."

LOMBARD, MICHAEL. Born Aug. 8, 1934 in Brooklyn, NY. Graduate Bklyn Col., Boston U. OB in "King Lear," "Merchant of Venice," "Cages," "Pinter Plays," "LaTurista," "Elizabeth the Queen," "Room Service," "Mert and Phil," Bdwy in "Poor Bitos," "The Devils," "Gingerbread Lady," "Bad Habits," "Otherwise Engaged."

LONDON, ELISA. Born June 30 in Oakland, CA. Graduate Yale U. Debut 1977 OB in "The Crucible."

LOUDON, DOROTHY. Born Sept. 17, 1933 in Boston, MA. Attended Emerson Col., Syracuse U. Debut 1961 OB in "World of Jules Feiffer," Bdwy 1963 in "Nowhere to Go but Up" for which she received a Theatre World Award, followed by "Noel Coward's Sweet Potato," "Fig Leaves Are Falling," "Three Men on a Horse," "The Women," "Annie."

LOUISE, MARY. Born July 10, in Baltimore, MD. Attended American Theatre Wing. Debut 1962 OB in "Fly Blackbird," followed by "Unsung Cole," Bdwy in "Funny Girl."

LOVE, EDWARD. Born June 29, 1952 in Toledo, OH. Graduate Ohio U, NYU. Debut 1972 OB in "Ti-Jean and His Brothers," Bdwy 1975 in "Raisin," followed by "A Chorus Line," "Dancin'."

LUCAS, J. FRANK. Born in Houston, TX. Graduate TCU. Debut 1943 OB in "A Man's House," followed by "Coriolanus," "Edward II," "Long Gallery," "Trip to Bountiful," "Orpheus Descending," "Guitar," "Marcus in the High Grass," "Chocolates," "To Bury a Cousin," "One World at a Time," Bdwy in "Bad Habits," "The Best Little Whorehouse in Texas."

LUCKINBILL, LAURENCE. Born Nov. 21, 1938 in Ft. Smith, AR. Graduate UArk., Catholic U. Bdwy debut in "A Man for All Seasons," followed by "Beekman Place," "Poor Tonight," "Fantasticks," "Tartuffe," "Boys in the Band," "Horseman, Pass By," "Memory Bank," "What the Butler Saw," "A Meeting by the River," "Alpha Beta," "A Prayer for My Daughter," "Life of Galileo."

LUDWIG, KAREN. Born Oct. 9, 1942 in San Francisco, CA. Bdwy debut 1964 in "The Deputy," followed by "The Devils," OB in "Trojan Women," "Red Cross," "Muzeeka," "Huui, Huui," "Our Late Night," "The Seagull," "Museum."

LUGENBEAL, CAROL. Born July 14, 1952 in Detroit, MI. Graduate U.S. International U. Bdwy debut 1974 in "Where's Charley?," followed by "On the 20th Century."

LUNA, BARBARA. Born Mar. 2 in NYC. Bdwy debut 1951 in "The King and I," followed by "West Side Story" (LC), "A Chorus Line."

LuPONE, PATTI. Born Apr. 21, 1949 in Northport, NY. Juilliard graduate. Debut 1972 OB in "School for Scandal," followed by "Women Beware Women," "Next Time I'll Sing to You," "Beggar's Opera," "Scapin," "Robber Bridegroom," "Edward II," "The Time of Your Life," Bdwy in "The Water Engine," "Working."

LuPONE, ROBERT. Born July 29, 1946 in Brooklyn, NY. Juilliard graduate. Bdwy debut 1970 in "Minnie's Boys," followed by "Jesus Christ Superstar," "The Rothschilds," "The Magic Show," "A Chorus Line," "St. Joan," OB in "Charlie Was Here and Now He's Gone."

LYDIARD, ROBERT. Born Apr. 28, 1944 in Glen Ridge, NJ. Graduate Fla. Atlantic U. Debut 1968 OB in "Your'e a Good Man, Charlie Brown," followed by "Johnny Johnson," "Dear Oscar," "Oh, Lady! Lady!," Bdwy 1978 in "Hello, Dolly!"

LYMAN, DEBRA. Born July 17, in Philadelphia, PA. Graduate Phila. Col. Debut 1967 OB in "By Jupiter," Bdwy in "Sugar" (1972), "My Fair Lady," "Chicago."

LYMAN, DOROTHY. Born Apr. 18, 1947 in Minneapolis, MN. Attended Sarah Lawrence Col. Debut OB in "America Hurrah," followed by "Pequod," "American Hamburger League," "Action," "Fefu and Her Friends."

LYNCH, RICHARD. Born Feb. 12, 1940 in Brooklyn, NY. Attended Actors Studio. Bdwy debut 1965 in "The Devils," followed by "Lady from the Sea," "Basic Training of Pavlo Hummel," OB in "Live Like Pigs," "One Night Stands of a Noisy Passenger," "Things That Almost Happen," "12 Angry Men," "The Orphan," "Action."

MacDONALD, PIRIE. Born Mar. 24, 1932 in NYC. Graduate Harvard U. Debut 1957 OB in "Under Milk Wood," followed by "Zoo Story," "Innocent Pleasure," Bdwy in "Shadow and Substance," "Golden Fleecing," "Big Fish, Little Fish," "Death of a Salesman," "But Not for Me."

MacDONALD, SUSAN. Born Sept. 4, 1953 in Westport, CT. Attended HB Studio. Debut 1977 OB in "The Passing Game."

MACOSKO, GREG. Born Mar. 4, 1947 in Berea, OH. Graduate Albion Col. Debut 1971 OB in "The Screens," followed by "Little Mahagonny," "Riverwind," "Rabinowitz Gambit."

MADDEN, SHARON. Born July 8, 1947 in St. Louis, MO. Debut 1975 OB in "Battle of Angels," followed by "The Hot l Baltimore," "Who Killed Richard Cory?," "Mrs. Murray's Farm," "The Passing of Corky Brewster," "Brontosaurus," "Ulysses in Traction," "Lulu."

MAGEE, JACK. Born May 12, 1950 in Fort Lee, NJ. Graduate UDayton. Debut 1978 OB in "Life of Galileo."

MAGEE, KAREN. Born June 2, 1949 in Cleveland, OH. Graduate Ohio U. Debut 1974 OB in "Pop," followed by "A Funny Thing Happened on the Way . . .," "Anyone Can Whistle," "Babes in Arms," "Carnival."

MAGGIORE, CHARLES. Born Mar. 19, 1936 in Valley Stream, NY. Attended Bates Col., Adelphi U., Neighborhood Playhouse. Bdwy debut 1967 in "Spofford," followed by "Sly Fox," OB in "Six Characters in Search of an Author," "Rivals," "The Iceman Cometh," "Othello," "The Elizabethans," "Three Musketeers."

MAIN, LAURIE. Born Nov. 29, 1922 in Melbourne, Aust. After career in Eng., made Bdwy debut 1959 in "First Impressions," followed by "Jolly's Progress," "Camelot," "Lord Pengo," "13 Rue de L'Amour."

MALIS, CLAIRE. Born Feb. 17, in Gary, IN. Graduate UInd., AADA. Debut 1969 OB in "The Man with the Flower in His Mouth," followed by "Berkeley Square," "My Life," "P.S. Your Cat Is Dead."

MALKA, REBECKA. Born Apr. 4, 1952 in Khartoum, Sudan. Attended Adelphi, Cornell U. Debut 1976 OB in "Boys from Syracuse," Bdwy in "The Merchant" (1977).

MANTEGNA, JOE. Born Nov. 13, 1947 in Chicago, IL. Attended Goodman Th. Sch. Bdwy debut 1978 in "Working."

MARCIONA, ANTHONY. Born Sept. 27, 1961 in The Bronx, NY. Debut 1965 OB in "Survival of St. Joan," followed by "Chickencoop Chinaman," "Good Citizen," "Landscape of the Body," Bdwy in "Zorba" (1967), "Georgy," "Gypsy" (1974).

MARINAN, TERENCE. Born Dec. 11, 1949 in Duluth, MN. Attended UMinn., RADA. Debut 1978 OB in "The Show-Off."

MARKHAM, MONTE. Born June 21, 1935 in Manatee, FL. Graduate UGa. Bdwy debut 1973 in "Irene" for which he received a Theatre World Award, followed by "Same Time, Next Year" (1978).

MARLOWE, LYNN. Born Oct. 13, 1952 in Springfield, IL. Graduate UIll. Debut 1975 OB in "Do I Hear a Waltz?," followed by "The Boys from Syracuse," "Gay Divorce."

Samuel Maupin   Kathleen McKiernan   Francis McDonald   Becky McSpadden   Bernie McInerney

MARRIOTT, TED. Born Dec. 21, 1949 in San Bernardino, CA. Attended ULas Vegas, Cal. State U. Debut 1977 OB in "Carnival."

MARTIN, MARY. Born Dec. 1, 1913 in Weatherford, TX. Attended Ward-Belmont Col. Bdwy debut 1938 in "Leave It to Me," followed by "One Touch of Venus," "Lute Song," "Annie Get Your Gun," "South Pacific," "Kind Sir," "Peter Pan," "The Skin of Our Teeth," "The Sound of Music," "Jennie," "Hello, Dolly!," "I Do! I Do!," "Do You Turn Somersaults?"

MARTIN, MILLICENT. Born June 8, 1934 in Romford, Eng. Attended Italia Conti Sch. Bdwy debut 1954 in "The Boy Friend," followed by "Side by Side by Sondheim."

MARTIN, VIRGINIA. Born Dec. 2, 1932 in Chattanooga, TN. Attended Theatre Wing. Appeared in "South Pacific," "Pajama Game," "Ankles Aweigh," "New Faces of 1956," "How to Succeed in Business . . . ," "Little Me," OB in "Buy Bonds Buster," "Joseph and the Amazing Technicolor Dreamcoat."

MARTINEZ, TONY. Born Jan. 27, 1920 in Santurce, PR. Attended UPR. Bdwy debut 1967 in "Man of La Mancha," and in revival.

MASIELL, JOE. Born Oct. 27, 1939 in Brooklyn, NY. Attended HB Studio. Debut 1964 in "Cindy," followed by "Jacques Brel Is Alive and . . . ," "Sensations," "Leaves of Grass," "How to Get Rid of It," "A Matter of Time," "Tickles by Tucholsky," "Not at the Palace," Bdwy in "Dear World," "Different Times," "Jacques Brel Is . . ."

MASON, CRAIG. Born July 1, 1950 in Rochester, MN. Graduate Yale U. Debut 1978 OB in "Allegro."

MASONER, GENE. Born Jan. 22, in Kansas City, KS. Attended UKan., HB Studio. Debut OB 1969 in "Your Own Thing," followed by "White Devil," "Cherry," "3 Drag Queens from Datona," Bdwy in "Shenandoah" (1975), "Angel."

MASTERS, ANDREA. Born Nov. 16, 1949 in Chicago, IL. Attended Mills Col., Columbia U. Debut 1975 OB in "The Long Valley," Bdwy in "The Basic Training of Pavlo Hummel" (1977).

MASTERS, BEN. Born May 6, 1947 in Corvallis, OR. Graduate UOre. Debut 1970 OB in "Boys in the Band," followed by "What the Butler Saw," "The Cherry Orchard," Bdwy in "Capt. Brassbound's Conversion."

MATALON, ZACK. Born in Jamaica, WI. Attended London U. Bdwy bow 1960 in "Irma La Douce," followed by "Look: We've Come Through," "Golda."

MATHEWS, WALTER. Born Oct. 10, 1926 in NYC. Graduate NYU, Ohio U. Bdwy debut 1951 in "St. Joan," followed by "The Long Dream," "King Lear," "Mr. Roberts," "Equus."

MATTHEWS, ANDERSON. Born Oct. 21, 1950 in Springfield, OH. Carnegie-Mellon U. Graduate. Bdwy debut 1975 in "The Robber Bridegroom," followed by OB in "Edward II," "The Time of Your Life," "Mother Courage," "King Lear."

MAUPIN, SAMUEL. Born Dec. 27, 1947 in Portsmouth, VA. Graduate Va. Commonwealth U. Debut 1977 OB in "The Passion of Dracula."

MAXWELL, ROBERTA. Born in Canada. Debut 1968 OB in "Two Gentlemen of Verona," followed by "A Whistle in the Dark," "Slag," "The Plough and the Stars," "Merchant of Venice," "Ashes," Bdwy in "The Prime of Miss Jean Brodie" (1968), "Henry V," "House of Atreus," "The Resistible Rise of Arturo Ui," "Othello," "Hay Fever," "There's One in Every Marriage," "Equus," "The Merchant."

MAY, BEVERLY. Born Aug. 11, 1927 in East Wellington, BD, Can. Graduate Yale U. Debut 1976 OB in "Female Transport," Bdwy 1977 in "Equus."

MAYER, CHARLES. Born Apr. 4, 1904 in Germany. Attended State Th. Sch. Debut OB 1944 in "Korbin," followed by "Beavercoat," "Marriage Proposal," "Jacknife," "Boubouroche," "Golden Boy," "The Lawyer," "Flight into Egypt," "Ice Age," "Chez Nous," "Catsplay," Bdwy in "A Bell for Adano," "Red Mill," "Now I Lay Me Down to Sleep," "Springtime Folly," "Thieves," "Fiddler on the Roof" (1976).

McALLISTER, SHAWN. Born Jan. 22, 1944 in San Antonio, TX. Attended Palm Beach Jr. Col. Debut 1974 OB in "Meegan's Game," followed by "Aaron Burr," "The Crucible," "The Book of Lambert," "The Patriots," "Battle of Brooklyn," "Native Son."

McARDLE, ANDREA. Born Nov. 5, 1963 in Philadelphia, PA. Bdwy debut 1977 in "Annie" for which she received a Theatre World Award.

McCALLUM, DAVID. Born Sept. 19, 1933 in Scotland. Attended Chapman Col. Bdwy debut 1968 in "The Flip Side," followed by "California Suite."

McCARTY, MARY. Born in 1923 in Kansas. Bdwy debut 1948 in "Sleepy Hollow" for which she received a Theatre World Award, followed by "Small Wonder," "Miss Liberty," "Bless You All," "A Rainy Day in Newark," "Follies," "Chicago," "Anna Christie."

McCLAIN, MARCIA. Born Sept. 30, 1949 in San Antonio, TX. Trinity U. graduate. Debut 1972 OB in "Rainbow," followed by "A Bistro Car on the CNR," Bdwy 1974 in "Where's Charley?" for which she received a Theatre World Award.

McCOY, BASIA. Born Dec. 15, 1916 in Plains, PA. Graduate Carnegie-Mellon U. Debut 1948 OB in "The Fifth Horseman," followed by "Mary Stuart," "The Crucible."

McDONALD, FRANCIS. Born Dec. 14, 1939 in Raleigh, NC. Graduate UNC, UGa. Debut 1975 OB in "The Doctor and the Devils," followed by "The Crucible," "Book of Lambert," "Native Son."

McFARLAND, ROBERT. Born May 7, 1931 in Omaha, NE. Graduate UMich, Columbia U. Debut 1978 OB in "The Taming of the Shrew."

McGILL, EVERETT. Born Oct. 21, 1945 in Miami Beach, FL. Graduate UMo., RADA. Debut OB 1971 in "Brothers," followed by "The Father," "Enemies," Bdwy in "Equus" (1974), "A Texas Trilogy," "The Merchant."

McGREEVEY, ANNIE. Born in Brooklyn, NY. Graduate AADA. Bdwy debut 1971 in "Company," followed by "The Magic Show," OB in "Booth Is Back in Town."

McGREGOR-STEWART, KATE. Born Oct. 4, 1944 in Buffalo, NY. Graduate Beaver Col., Yale U. Bdwy debut 1975 in "Travesties" followed by "A History of the American Film," OB in "Titanic."

McINERNEY, BERNIE. Born Dec. 4, 1936 in Wilmington, DE. Graduate UDel., Catholic U. Bdwy debut 1972 in "That Championship Season," followed by OB in "Life of Galileo."

McINTYRE, MARILYN. Born May 23, 1949 in Erie, PA. Graduate Penn State U., NC Sch. of Arts. Debut 1977 OB in "The Perfect Mollusc," followed by "Measure for Measure," "The Promise."

McKIERNAN, KATHLEEN. Born in NYC. Graduate Mt. St. Vincent, Catholic U. Debut 1973 OB in "Last Chance Saloon," followed by "The Crucible," "Native Son."

McMARTIN, JOHN. Born in Warsaw, IN. Attended Columbia U. Debut 1959 OB in "Little Mary Sunshine" for which he received a Theatre World Award, followed by "Too Much Johnson," "The Misanthrope," Bdwy in "The Conquering Hero," "Blood, Sweat and Stanley Poole," "Children from Their Games," "A Rainy Day in Newark," "Sweet Charity," "Follies," "Great God Brown," "Don Juan," "The Visit," "Chemin de Fer," "Love for Love," "Rules of the Game."

McMILLAN, KENNETH. Born July 2, 1934 in Brooklyn. Bdwy debut 1970 in "Borstal Boy" followed by "American Buffalo," OB in "Red Eye of Love," "King of the Whole Damn World," "Little Mary Sunshine," "Babes in the Wood," "Moonchildren," "Merry Wives of Windsor," "Where Do We Go from Here?," "Kid Champion," "Streamers."

McQUEEN, ARMELIA. Born Jan. 6, 1952 in North Carolina. Attended HB Studio, Bklyn. Consv. Bdwy debut 1978 in "Ain't Misbehavin'" for which she received a Theatre World Award.

McSPADDEN, BECKY. Born Dec. 14, 1949 in Norfolk, VA. Graduate UNeb. Bdwy debut 1974 in "Candide," followed by OB in "Company."

MEDFORD, KAY. Born Sept. 14, 1920 in NYC. Bdwy debut 1951 in "Paint Your Wagon," followed by "Two's Company," "John Murray Anderson's Almanac," "Lullaby" for which she received a Theatre World Award, "Black-Eyed Susan," "Almost Crazy," "Wake Up, Darling," "Mr. Wonderful," "A Hole in the Head," CC's "Carousel" and "Pal Joey," "A Handful of Fire," "Bye Bye Birdie," "In the Counting House," "The Heroine," "Funny Girl," "Don't Drink the Water," OB in "Where Memories Are Magic."

MEISTER, FREDERIKKE. Born Aug. 18, 1951 in San Francisco, CA. Graduate NYU. Debut 1978 OB in "Museum."

| Cynthia Meryl | Alan Mixon | Anne Miyamoto | Brooks Morton | Stephanie Musnick |

MERCADO, HECTOR. Born in NYC in 1949. Graduate H. S. Performing Arts. Attended Harkness Ballet Sch., HB Studio. Bdwy debut 1960 in "West Side Story," followed by "Man of LaMancha" (and 1977 revival), "Mass," "Dr. Jazz," "1600 Pennsylvania Ave.," "Your Arms Too Short to Box with God."

MERRYMAN, MONICA. Born June 2, 1950 in Sao Paulo, Brazil. Graduate EMichU. Debut 1975 OB in "East Lynne," followed by "A Night at the Black Pig," "Vanities."

MERSON, SUSAN. Born Apr. 25, 1950 in Detroit, MI. Graduate Boston U. Bdwy debut 1974 in "Saturday Sunday Monday," followed by OB "Vanities."

MERYL, CYNTHIA. Born Sept. 25, 1950 in NYC. Graduate Ind.U. Bdwy debut 1976 in "My Fair Lady," OB in "Before Sundown," "The Canticle," "The Pirate," "Dames at Sea," "Gay Divorce."

METCALF, MARK. Born Mar. 11 in Findlay, OH. Attended UMich. Debut OB 1973 in "Creeps," followed by "The Tempest" (LC), "Beach Children," "Hamlet," "Patrick Henry Lake Liquors," "Streamers."

MILES, ROSS. Born in Poughkeepsie, NY. Bdwy debut 1962 in "Little Me," followed by "Baker Street," "Pickwick," "Darling of the Day," "Mame," "Jumpers," "Goodtime Charley," "Chicago," "Dancin'."

MILGRIM, LYNN. Born Mar. 17, 1944 in Philadelphia, PA. Graduate Swarthmore Col., Harvard U. Debut 1969 OB in "Frank Gagliano's City Scene," followed by "Crimes of Passion," "Macbeth," "Charley's Aunt," "The Real Inspector Hound," "Rib Cage," "Museum," Bdwy 1977 in "Otherwise Engaged."

MILLER, BETTY. Born Mar. 27, 1925 in Boston, MA. Attended UCLA. OB in "Summer and Smoke," "Cradle Song," "La Ronde," "Plays for Bleecker St.," "Desire under the Elms," "The Balcony," "The Power and the Glory," "Beaux Stratagem," "Gandhi," "Girl on the Via Flaminia," "Hamlet," APA's "You Can't Take It with You," "Right You Are," "The Wild Duck" and "The Cherry Orchard," Bdwy in "A Touch of the Poet" (1977).

MILLIGAN, JACOB. Born Mar. 25, 1949 in Kansas City, MO. Graduate UKC. Bdwy debut 1976 in "Equus," OB in "Beowulf."

MILLIGAN, JOHN. Born in Vancouver, Can. Attended Bristol Old Vic School. Credits include "The Matchmaker," "The First Gentleman," "Love and Libel," "Look Back in Anger," "Hilary," "The Devils," OB in "Esther."

MILLS, STEPHANIE. Born in 1959 in Brooklyn, NY. Bdwy debut 1975 in "The Wiz."

MINAMI, ROGER. Born June 16, 1945 in Honolulu, HI. Attended Long Beach State Col. Bdwy debut 1977 in "The Act."

MINNELLI, LIZA. Born Mar. 12, 1946 in Los Angeles, CA. Attended UParis, HB Studio. Debut 1963 OB in "Best Foot Forward" for which she received a Theatre World Award, Bdwy in "Flora, the Red Menace," "Liza," "Chicago," "The Act."

MISTRETTA, SAL. Born Jan. 9, 1945 in Brooklyn, NY. Ithaca Col. graduate. Bdwy debut 1976 in "Something's Afoot," followed by "On the 20th Century."

MITCHELL, CAMERON. Born Nov. 4, 1918 in Dallastown, PA. Attended Franklin-Marshall Col. Debut 1938 OB in "At a Certain Hour," followed by "Peace and Plenty," Bdwy in "Jeremiah," "Death of a Salesman" for which he received a Theatre World Award, "Southern Exposure," "Les Blancs," "November People."

MIXON, ALAN. Born Mar. 15, 1933 in Miami, FL. Attended UMiami. Bdwy bow 1962 in "Something about a Soldier," followed by "Sign in Sidney Brustein's Window," "The Devils," "The Unknown Soldier and His Wife," "Love Suicide at Schofield Barracks," "Equus," OB in "Suddenly Last Summer," "Desire under the Elms," "Trojan Women," "Alchemist," "Child Buyer," "Mr. and Mrs. Lyman," "A Whitman Portrait," "Iphigenia in Aulis," "Small Craft Warnings," "Mourning Becomes Electra," "The Runner Stumbles," "Old Glory," "The Gathering," "Ballad of the Sad Cafe."

MIYAMOTO, ANNE. Born in Honolulu, HI. Graduate UHaw., NYU. Debut 1962 OB in "Yanks Are Coming," Bdwy 1977 in "Basic Training of Pavlo Hummel."

MOLINE, PATRICIA. Born Sept. 30, 1950 in Liverpool, Eng. Graduate Wichita State U. Bdwy debut 1973 in "The Pajama Game," OB in "Gay Divorce."

MONFERDINI, CAROLE. Born in Eagle Lake, TX. Graduate North Tex. State U. Debut 1973 OB in "The Foursome," followed by "The Club."

MOOR, BILL. Born July 13, 1931 in Toledo, OH. Attended Northwestern U., Dennison U. Bdwy debut 1964 in "Blues for Mr. Charlie," followed by "Great God Brown," "Don Juan," "The Visit," "Chemin de Fer," "Holiday," "P.S. Your Cat Is Dead," "Night of the Tribades," "The Water Engine," OB in "Dandy Dick," "Love Nest," "Days and Nights of Beebee Fenstermaker," "The Collection," "The Owl Answers," "Long Christmas Dinner," "Fortune and Men's Eyes," "King Lear," "Cry of Players," "Boys in the Band," "Alive and Well in Argentina," "Rosmersholm," "The Biko Inquest."

MOORE, CHARLOTTE. Born July 7, 1939 in Herrin, IL. Attended Smith Col., Washington U. Bdwy debut 1972 in "The Great God Brown," followed by "Don Juan," "The Visit," "Chemin de Fer," "Holiday," "Love for Love," "Member of the Wedding," OB in "Out of Our Father's House."

MOORE, JONATHAN. Born Mar. 24, 1923 in New Orleans, LA. Attended Piscator's Sch. Debut OB 1961 in "After the Angels," followed by "Berkeley Square," "Checking Out," "The Biko Inquest," Bdwy in "Dylan," "1776."

MOORE, MAUREEN. Born Aug. 12, 1951 in Wallingford, CT. Bdwy debut 1974 in "Gypsy," OB in "Unsung Cole," "By Strouse."

MOORE, MELBA. Born Oct. 29, 1945 in NYC. Graduate Montclair State Col. Bdwy debut 1968 in "Hair," followed by "Purlie" for which she received a Theatre World Award, "Timbuktu."

MORENZIE, LEON. Born in Trinidad, WI. Graduate Sir George William U. Debut 1972 OB in "Ti-Jean and His Brothers," followed by "The Cherry Orchard," "Cockeyed Tiger," "Twilight Dinner," "Rum and Coca Cola," Bdwy in "The Leaf People."

MORIARTY, MICHAEL. Born Apr. 5, 1941 in Detroit, MI. Graduate Dartmouth LAMDA. Debut OB 1963 in "Antony and Cleopatra," followed by "Peanut Butter and Jelly," "Long Day's Journey into Night," "Henry V," "Alfred the Great," "Our Father's Failing," Bdwy in "Trial of the Catonsville 9," "Find Your Way Home" for which he received a Theater World Award, "Richard III" (LC).

MORRISEY, BOB. Born Aug. 15, 1946 in Somerville, MA. Attended UWis. Debut 1974 OB in "Ionescapade," followed by "Company."

MORTON, BROOKS. Born Oct. 3, 1932 in KY. Attended Northwestern U. Debut 1962 OB in "Riverwind," followed by "Sunday Dinner," CC's "West Side Story," "Say, Darling," Bdwy in "Marathon '33," "Beyond the Fringe," "Three Sisters," "Ivanov," "Prime of Miss Jean Brodie," "Her First Roman," "Penny Wars," "Company," "Bad Habits," "Sly Fox."

MOSTEL, JOSHUA. Born Dec. 21, 1946 in NYC. Graduate Brandeis U. Debut 1971 OB in "The Proposition," followed by "More Than You Deserve," "The Misanthrope," Bdwy in "Unlikely Heroes," "American Millionaire," "A Texas Trilogy."

MULREAN, LINDA. Born Nov. 17, 1950 in Boston, MA. Graduate Manhattanville Col. Debut 1973 OB in "The Karl Marx Play," followed by "Fashion," "Antigone," "The Specialist."

MURPHY, ROSEMARY. Born Jan. 13, 1927 in Munich, Ger. Attended Neighborhood Playhouse, Actors Studio. Bdwy debut 1950 in "Tower beyond Tragedy," followed by "Look Homeward, Angel," "Period of Adjustment," "Any Wednesday," "Delicate Balance," "Weekend," "Death of Bessie Smith," "Butterflies Are Free," "Ladies at the Alamo," "Cheaters."

MURRAY, BRIAN. Born Oct. 9, 1939 in Johannesburg, SA. Debut 1964 OB in "The Knack," followed by "King Lear," "Ashes," Bdwy in "All in Good Time," "Rosencrantz and Guildenstern Are Dead," "Sleuth," "Da."

MURRAY, DON. Born July 31, 1929 in Hollywood, CA. Attended AADA. Debut 1948 in "The Insect Comedy" (CC), followed by "The Rose Tattoo," "The Skin of Our Teeth" (1955), "The Hot Corner," "The Norman Conquests," "Same Time Next Year."

MURRAY, PEG. Born in Denver, CO. Attended Western Reserve U. OB in "Children of Darkness," followed by "A Midsummer Night's Dream," "Oh, Dad, Poor Dad . . . ," "Small Craft Warnings," "Enclave," "Landscape of the Body," Bdwy in "The Great Sebastians" (1956), "Gypsy," "Blood, Sweat and Stanley Poole," "She Loves Me," "Anyone Can Whistle," "The Subject Was Roses," "Something More," "Cabaret," "Fiddler on the Roof," "Royal Family."

MUSNICK, STEPHANIE. Born Apr. 12, 1950 in Philadelphia, PA. Graduate Villanova U. Bdwy debut 1977 in "Gemini."

Mary Ann Niles   **Bill Noone**   **Elizabeth Owens**   **Don Nute**   **Giulia Pagano**

NATHAN, VIVIAN. Born Oct. 26, 1921 in NYC. Bdwy debut 1948 in "Sundown Beach," followed by "Montserrat," "Rose Tattoo," "Camino Real," "Anastasia," "Lovers," "Semi-Detached," "The Investigation," "The Watering Place," "Golda," OB in "Bullfight," "Long Day's Journey into Night."

NAUGHTON, JAMES. Born Dec. 6, 1945 in Middletown, CT. Graduate Brown, Yale U. Debut 1971 OB in "Long Day's Journey into Night" for which he received a Theatre World Award, followed by "I Love My Wife" (Bdwy 1977).

NEGRO, MARY-JOAN. Born Nov. 9, 1948 in Brooklyn, NY. Debut 1972 OB in "The Hostage," followed by "Lower Depths," "Women Beware Women," "Ladyhouse Blues," "The Promise," Bdwy in "Three Sisters," "Measure for Measure," "Beggar's Opera."

NEILSON, RICHARD. Born Nov. 30, 1924 in London, Eng. Debut 1959 OB in "Heloise," followed by "O Say Can You See," "Tea Party," Bdwy in "Pickwick" (1964), "Wise Child," "My Fair Lady," "Equus."

NELSON, BARRY. Born in 1920 in Oakland, CA. Bdwy debut 1943 in "Winged Victory," followed by "Light Up the Sky," "The Moon Is Blue," "Wake Up, Darling," "Rat Race," "Mary, Mary," "Nobody Loves an Albatross," "Cactus Flower," "Everything in the Garden," "Only Game in Town," "Fig Leaves Are Falling," "Engagement Baby," "Seascape," "Norman Conquests," "The Act."

NELSON, GAIL. Born March 29 in Durham, NC. Oberlin Col. graduate. Bdwy Debut 1968 in "Hello, Dolly!," followed by "Applause," "Music! Music!" OB in "Six," "By Strouse."

NELSON, MARK. Born Sept. 26, 1955 in Hackensack, NJ. Graduate Princeton U. Debut 1977 OB in "The Dybbuk."

NEUCHATEAU, CORINNE. Born July 20, 1952 in Staten Island, NY. Attended Barnard Col. Bdwy debut 1977 in "Golda."

NEWELL, JAMES S. Born Nov. 20, 1940 in Chicago, IL. Graduate Xavier U., St. Louis U., Wayne State U. Debut 1976 OB in "The Fantasticks," followed by "Allegro."

NICHOLS, JOSEPHINE. Born Nov. 11, 1913 in Lawrenceville, IL. Graduate UOkla., Columbia U. Debut 1960 OB in "The Prodigal," followed by "Roots," "The Golden Six," "The Adding Machine," "The Storm," "Uncommon Women and Others," Bdwy in "On an Open Roof," "The Skin of Our Teeth."

NILES, MARY ANN. Born May 2, 1933 in NYC. Attended Miss Finchley's Ballet Acad. Bdwy debut in "Girl from Nantucket," followed by "Dance Me a Song," "Call Me Mister," "Make Mine Manhattan," "La Plume de Ma Tante," "Carnival," "Flora the Red Menace," "Sweet Charity," "George M!," "No, No, Nanette," "Irene," OB in "The Boys from Syracuse." CC's "Wonderful Town" and "Carnival."

NIMOY, LEONARD. Born Mar. 26, 1931 in Boston, MA. Graduate Boston Col., Antioch Col., Pasadena Playhouse. Bdwy debut 1973 in "Full Circle," followed by "Equus" (1977).

NOONE, BILL E. Born May 1, 1944 in Montgomery, WVa. Graduate SMU. Debut OB 1973 in "Medea," followed by "Moliere in spite of Himself."

NORTH, ALAN. Born Dec. 23, 1927 in NYC. Attended Columbia U. Bdwy bow 1955 in "Plain and Fancy," followed by "South Pacific," "Summer of the 17th Doll," "Requiem for a Nun," "Never Live over a Pretzel Factory," "Dylan," "Spofford," "Finian's Rainbow" (JB).

NUTE, DON. Born Mar. 13, in Connellsville, Pa. Attended Denver U. Debut OB 1965 in "The Trojan Women," followed by "Boys in the Band," "Mad Theatre for Madmen," "The Eleventh Dynasty," "About Time," "The Urban Crisis," "Christmas Rappings," "The Life of a Man," "A Look at the Fifties."

O'BRIEN, SYLVIA. Born May 4, 1924 in Dublin, Ire. Debut OB 1961 in "O Marry Me," followed by "Red Roses for Me," "Every Other Evil," "3 by O'Casey," "Essence of Woman," "Dear Oscar," Bdwy in "Passion of Josef D," "Right Honourable Gentleman," "Loves of Cass McGuire," "Hadrian VII," "Conduct Unbecoming," "My Fair Lady," "Da."

O'DELL, K. LYPE. Born Feb. 2, 1939 in Claremore, OK. Graduate Los Angeles State Col. Debut 1972 OB in "Sunset," followed by "Our Father," "Ice Age," "Prince of Homburg," "Passion of Dracula."

OEHLER, GRETCHEN. Born in Chicago, IL. Attended Goodman Theatre Sch. Debut 1971 OB in "The Homecoming," Bdwy 1977 in "Dracula."

O'HARA, JILL. Born Aug. 23, 1947 in Warren, PA. Attended Edinburgh State Teachers Col. Bdwy debut 1968 in "George M!," followed by "Promises, Promises" for which she received a Theatre World Award, OB in "Hang Down Your Head and Die," "Hair," "Master Builder," "Alfred the Great," "Wayside Motor Inn."

O'HARA, PAIGE. Born May 10, 1956 in Ft. Lauderdale, FL. Debut 1975 OB in "The Gift of the Magi," followed by "Company."

O'KEEFE, PAUL C. Born Apr. 27, 1951 in Boston, MA. Graduate Columbia U. Bdwy debut 1958 in "The Music Man," followed by "Sail Away," "Oliver," "A Texas Trilogy," "Passing Game" (OB).

OMENS, ESTELLE. Oct. 11, 1928 in Chicago, IL. Graduate UIowa. OB in "Summer and Smoke," "The Grass Harp," "Legend of Lovers," "Plays for Bleecker St.," "Pullman Car Hiawatha," "Brownstone Urge," "Gandhi," "Shadow of a Gunman," "Bright and Golden Land," Bdwy in "The Watering Place."

O'NEAL, RON. Born Sept. 1, 1937 in Utica, NY. Attended Ohio State U. Debut 1968 OB in "American Pastoral," followed by "No Place to Be Somebody" for which he received a Theatre World Award," Dream on Monkey Mountain," "Agamemnon," Bdwy in "All over Town."

ORBACH, JERRY. Born Oct. 20, 1935 in NYC. Attended Northwestern U. Bdwy debut 1961 in "Carnival," followed by "Guys and Dolls," "Carousel," "Annie Get Your Gun," "The Natural Look," "Promises, Promises," "6 Rms Riv Vu," "Chicago," OB in "Threepenny Opera," "The Fantasticks," "The Cradle Will Rock," "Scuba Duba."

O'SHEA, MILO. Born June 2, 1926 in Dublin, Ire. Bdwy debut 1968 in "Staircase," followed by "Dear World," "Mrs. Warren's Profession" (LC), "Comedians," "A Touch of the Poet," "Waiting for Godot" (OB).

OSUNA, JESS. Born May 28, 1933 in Oakland, CA. OB in "Blood Wedding," "Come Share My House," "This Side of Paradise," "Bugs and Veronica," "Monopoly," "The Infantry," "Hamp," "The Biko Inquest," Bdwy in "The Goodbye People."

OWENS, ELIZABETH. Born Feb. 26, 1938 in NYC. Attended New School, Neighborhood Playhouse. Debut 1955 OB in "Dr. Faustus Lights the Lights," followed by "Chit Chat on a Rat," "The Miser," "The Father," "Importance of Being Earnest," "Candida," "Trumpets and Drums," "Oedipus," "Macbeth," "Uncle Vanya," "Misalliance," "Master Builder," "American Gothics," "The Play's the Thing," "The Rivals," "Death Story," "The Rehearsal," "Dance on a Country Grave," "Othello," Bdwy in "The Lovers," "Not Now Darling," "The Play's the Thing."

PACINO, AL. Born Apr. 25, 1940 in NYC. Attended Actors Studio. Bdwy bow 1969 in "Does a Tiger Wear a Necktie?" for which he received a Theatre World Award, followed by "The Basic Training of Pavlo Hummel," OB in "Why Is a Crooked Letter?," "Peace Creeps," "The Indian Wants the Bronx," "Local Stigmatic," "Camino Real" (LC).

PAGANO, GIULIA. Born July 8, 1948 in NYC. Attended AADA. Debut 1977 OB in "The Passion of Dracula."

PAGE, GERALDINE. Born Nov. 22, 1924 in Kirksville, MO. Attended Goodman Theatre. OB in "7 Mirrors," "Summer and Smoke," "Macbeth," "Look Away," "The Stronger." Bdwy debut 1953 in "Midsummer," for which she received a Theatre World Award, followed by "The Immoralist," "The Rainmaker," "Innkeepers," "Separate Tables," "Sweet Bird of Youth," "Strange Interlude," "Three Sisters," "P.S. I Love You," "The Great Indoors," "White Lies," "Black Comedy," "The Little Foxes," "Angela," "Absurd Person Singular."

PAGE, KEN. Born Jan. 20, 1954 in St. Louis, MO. Attended Fontbonne Col. Bdwy debut 1976 in "Guys and Dolls" for which he received a Theatre World Award, followed by "The Wiz," "Ain't Misbehavin."

PALMER, BETSY. Born Nov. 1, 1929 in East Chicago, IN. Graduate DePaul U., Actors Studio. Bdwy debut 1955 in "The Grand Prize," followed by "Affair of Honor," "Roar Like a Dove," "South Pacific" (CC), "Cactus Flower," "Eccentricities of a Nightingale," "Same Time, Next Year."

PALMER, LELAND. Born June 16, 1945 in Port Washington, NY. Bdwy debut 1966 in "Joyful Noise," followed by "Applause," "Pippin," OB in "Your Own Thing."

| William Parry | Ellen Parker | William Paulson | Frances Peter | John Pielmeier |

PANKIN, STUART. Born Apr. 8, 1946 in Philadelphia, PA. Graduate Dickinson Col., Columbia U. Debut OB 1968 in "Wars of the Roses," followed by "Richard III," "Timon of Athens," "Cymbeline," "Mary Stuart," "Narrow Road to the Deep North," "Twelfth Night," "The Crucible," "Wings," "A Glorious Age," "Joseph and the Amazing Technicolor Dreamcoat," BAM's "Three Sisters."

PAOLUCCI, ROBERT. Born in Quincy, MA. Graduate Fordham U. Debut 1974 OB in "Inherit the Wind," followed by "The Taming of the Shrew."

PAPE, JOAN. Born Jan. 23, in Detroit MI. Graduate Purdue U. Debut 1972 OB in "Suggs," followed by "Bloomers," "Museum," Bdwy in "The Secret Affairs of Mildred Wild," "Cat on a Hot Tin Roof," "A History of the American Film."

PARKER, ELLEN. Born Sept. 30, 1949 in Paris, Fr. Graduate Bard Col. Debut 1971 OB in "James Joyce Liquid Memorial Theatre," followed by "Uncommon Women and Others," Bdwy 1977 in "Equus."

PARKS, KATHERINE. Born May 11, 1946 in Louisville, KY. Graduate Stephens Col. UMo. Debut 1978 OB in "Old Man Joseph and His Family," followed by "Moliere in spite of Himself."

PARRY, WILLIAM. Born Oct. 7, 1947 in Steubenville, OH. Graduate Mt. Union Col. Bdwy debut 1971 in "Jesus Christ Superstar," followed by "Rockabye Hamlet," "The Leaf People," OB in "Sgt. Pepper's Lonely Hearts Club Band," "The Conjuror," "Noah," "The Misanthrope," "Joseph and the Amazing Technicolor Dreamcoat," "Agamemnon."

PARSONS, ESTELLE. Born Nov. 20, 1927 in Lynn, MA, Attended Boston U., Actors Studio. OB in "Threepenny Opera," "Automobile Graveyard," "Mrs. Dally Has a Lover" for which she received a Theatre World Award, "In the Summer House," "Monopoly," "Peer Gynt," "Mahagonny," "Silent Partner," "Barbary Shore," "Oh Glorious Tintinnabulation," with LCR in "East Wind," "Galileo," "People Are Living There," and "Mert and Phil," Bdwy in "Happy Hunting," "Whoop-Up!," "Beg, Borrow or Steal," "Ready When You Are, C. B.," "Malcolm," "Seven Descents of Myrtle," "A Way of Life," "And Miss Reardon Drinks a Little," "Norman Conquests," "Ladies at the Alamo," "Miss Margarida's Way."

PAULSON, WILLIAM. Born Mar. 17, 1954 in NYC. Attended Hunter Col., Neighborhood Playhouse. Bdwy debut 1976 in "Night of the Iguana," OB in "The Crucible."

PEARL, IRWIN. Born Oct. 14, 1945 in Brooklyn, NY. Graduate Hofstra U. Bdwy bow 1970 in "Minnie's Boys," followed by "Fiddler on the Roof" (1976), OB in "Big Hotel," "Ergo," "Invitation to a Beheading," "Babes in Arms," "The Taming of the Shrew."

PENDLETON, AUSTIN. Born Mar. 27, 1940 in Warren, OH. Attended Yale U. Appeared with LC Rep. Co. 1962–63, and in "Oh, Dad, Poor Dad . . .," "Fiddler on the Roof," "Hail Scrawdyke," "The Little Foxes," "An American Millionaire," "The Runner Stumbles," OB in "The Last Sweet Days of Isaac," BAM Co.'s "Three Sisters," "The Play's the Thing," "Julius Caesar," and "Waiting for Godot."

PENDLETON, WYMAN. Born Apr. 18, 1916 in Providence, RI. Graduate Brown U. Bdwy in "Tiny Alice," "Malcolm," "Quotations from Chairman Mao Tse-Tung," "Happy Days," "Henry V," "Othello," "There's One in Every Marriage," "Cat on a Hot Tin Roof," OB in "Gallows Humor," "American Dream," "Zoo Story," "Corruption in the Palace of Justice," "Giant's Dance," "Child Buyer," "Happy Days," "Butter and Egg Man," "Othello."

PENN, EDWARD. Born in Washington, DC. Studied at HB studio. Debut 1965 OB in "The Queen and the Rebels," followed by "My Wife and I," "Invitation to a March," "Of Thee I Sing," "Fantasticks," "Greenwillow," "One for the Money," "Dear Oscar," "Speed Gets the Poppys," "Man with a Load of Mischief," "Company," Bdwy bow 1975 in "Shenandoah."

PERCASSI, DON. Born Jan. 11 in Amsterdam, NY. Bdwy debut 1964 in "High Spirits," followed by "Walking Happy," "Coco," "Sugar," "Molly," "Mack and Mabel," "A Chorus Line."

PESATURO, GEORGE. Born July 29, 1949 in Winthrop, MA. Graduate Manhattan Col. Bdwy debut 1976 in "A Chorus Line."

PETER, FRANCES. Born June 27 in Chicago, IL. Attended Goodman Theatre Sch. AmThWing. Debut 1949 OB in "Lady from the Sea," followed by "Misbegotten Angels," "Delightful Season," "Sold to the Movies," "Sorry, Wrong Number," "Count Dracula."

PETRICOFF, ELAINE. Born in Cincinnati, OH. Graduate Syracuse U. Bdwy debut 1971 in "The Me Nobody Knows," OB in "Hark!," "Ride the Winds," "Cole Porter," Bdwy debut 1973 in "Grease."

PETTY, ROSS. Born Aug. 29, 1946 in Winnipeg, Can. Graduate UManitoba. Debut 1975 OB in "Happy Time," followed by "Maggie Flynn," "Carnival."

PHELPS, ELEANOR. Born in Baltimore, MD. Vassar graduate. Bdwy debut 1928 in "Merchant of Venice," followed by "Richard II," "Criminal Code," "Trick for Trick," "Seen But Not Heard," "Flight to the West," "Queen Bee," "We the People," "Six Characters in Search of an Author," "Mr. Big," "Naughty-Naught," "The Disenchanted," "Picnic," "My Fair Lady" (1956 & 76), "40 Carats," "Crown Matrimonial," "Royal Family," OB in "Garden District," "Color of Darkness," "Catsplay."

PHILLIPS, MARY BRACKEN. Born Aug. 15, 1946 in Kansas City, MO. Attended Kansas U. Debut 1969 OB in "Perfect Party," followed by "Look Where I'm At," "Hot Grog," Bdwy in "1776," "Different Times," "Hurry Harry."

PHILLIPS, PETER. Born Dec. 7, 1949 in Darby, PA. Graduate Dartmouth Col., RADA. Debut 1976 OB in "Henry V," followed by "The Cherry Orchard," "Total Eclipse," "Catsplay," Bdwy in "Equus" (1977)

PICARDO, ROBERT. Born Oct. 27, 1953 in Philadelphia, PA. Graduate Yale U. Debut 1975 OB in "Sexual Perversity in Chicago," followed by "Visions of Kerouac," "The Primary English Class," "Gemini" (also Bdwy '77).

PICKLES, CHRISTINA. Born Feb. 17, 1938 in Eng. Attended RADA. Bdwy in APA's "School for Scandal," "War and Peace," "The Wild Duck," "Pantagleize," "You Can't Take It with You," "The Seagull" and "The Misanthrope," "Inadmissible Evidence," "Who's Who in Hell," "Sherlock Holmes," OB in "Chez Nous."

PIELMEIER, JOHN. Born Feb. 23, 1949 in Altoona, PA. Graduate Catholic U., Penn State. Debut 1978 OB in "Count Dracula."

PILCHER, RICHARD. Born Apr. 12, 1946 in St. Louis, MO. Graduate UMo. Bdwy debut 1978 in "13 Rue de L'Amour."

PINCUS, WARREN. Born Apr. 13, 1938 in Brooklyn, NY. Attended CCNY. OB in "Miss Nefertiti Regrets," "Circus," "Magician," "Boxcars," "Demented World," "Give My Regards," "Electronic Nigger," "Last Pad," "Waiting for Godot," "In the Time of Harry Harrass," "Yoshe Kolb," Bdwy in "Zalmen, or the Madness of God," "Gemini."

PINHASIK, HOWARD. Born June 5, 1953 in Chicago, IL. Graduate Ohio U. Debut 1978 OB in "Allegro."

POLE, FRANCES. Born June 12, 1907 in St. Paul, MN. Debut 1958 OB in "'Tis Pity She's a Whore," followed by "Mornings at 7," "Ice Age," Arsenic and Old Lace," "The Adopted Moon."

POLENZ, ROBERT. Born June 9, 1953 in Trenton, NJ. Graduate Muskingam Col. Bdwy debut 1974 in "Over Here," followed by "Candide," OB in "Apple Pie," "Children of Adam."

POLIS, JOEL. Born Oct. 3, 1951 in Philadelphia, PA. Graduate USC, Yale. Debut 1976 OB in "Marco Polo," followed by "Family Business."

POMERANTZ, JEFFREY DAVID. Born July 2, 1945 in NYC. Attended Northwestern U., RADA. Bdwy debut (as Jeffrey David-Owen) 1975 in "The Leaf People," followed by "The Ritz," "Equus," OB in "John Gabriel Borkman," "Museum."

PONAZECKI, JOE. Born Jan. 7, 1934 in Rochester, NY. Attended Rochester U., Columbia. Bdwy bow 1959 in "Much Ado about Nothing," followed by "Send Me No Flowers," "Call on Kuprin," "Take Her, She's Mine," "Fiddler on the Roof," "Xmas in Las Vegas," "3 Bags Full," "Love in E-Flat," "90 Day Mistress," "Harvey," "Trial of the Catonsville 9," "Country Girl," "Freedom of the City," "Summer Brave," "Music Is," OB in "The Dragon," "Muzeeka," "Witness," "All Is Bright," "The Dog Ran Away," "Dream of a Blacklisted Actor," "Innocent Pleasures."

POTTER, CAROL. Born May 21, 1948 in NYC. Graduate Radcliffe Col. Debut 1974 OB in "The Last Days of British Honduras," followed by "Gemini" (1977 OB & Bdwy).

POWERS, NEVA RAE. Born in Oakland City, IN. Graduate Cincinnati Cons. Debut 1974 OB in "The Boy Friend," followed by "Love! Love! Love!"

| William Preston | Kitty Rea | Lee Roy Reams | Roxanne Reese | Robert Rhys |

PRESTON, ROBERT. Born June 8, 1918 in Newton Highlands, MA. Attended Pasadena Playhouse. Bdwy debut 1951 in "20th Century," followed by "The Male Animal," "Men of Distinction," "His and Hers," "The Magic and the Loss," "Tender Trap," "Janus," "Hidden River," "Music Man," "Too True to Be Good," "Nobody Loves an Albatross," "Ben Franklin in Paris," "The Lion in Winter," "I Do! I Do!," "Mack and Mabel," "Sly Fox."

PRESTON, WILLIAM. Born Aug. 26, 1921 in Columbia, PA. Graduate Penn. State U. Debut OB 1972 in "We Bombed in New Haven," followed by "Hedda Gabler," "Whisper into My Good Ear," "A Nestless Bird," "Friends of Mine," "Iphigenia in Aulis," "Midsummer," "The Fantasticks."

PRICE, GILBERT. Born Sept. 10, 1942 in NYC. Attended AmThWing. OB in "Kicks & Co.," "Fly Blackbird," "Jerico-Jim Crow" for which he received a Theatre World Award, "Promenade," "Slow Dance on the Killing Ground," "Six," "Melodrama Play," Bdwy in "Roar of the Greasepaint ..." (1965), "Lost in the Stars," "The Night That Made America Famous," "!600 Pennsylvania Ave.," "Timbuktu."

PRICE, VINCENT. Born May 27, 1911 in St. Louis, MO. Attended Yale, ULondon. Bdwy bow 1935 in "Victoria Regina," followed by "Shoemaker's Holiday," "Heartbreak House," "The Lady Has a Heart," "Outward Bound," "Angel Street," "Richard III," "Black-Eyed Susan," "Darling of the Day," "Diversions and Delights."

PROFANATO, GENE. Born Dec. 9, 1964 in NYC. Bdwy debut 1970 in "Lovely Ladies, Kind Gentlemen," followed by "The King and I" (1977).

PUMA, MARIE. Born in Brooklyn, NY. Graduate CUNY. Debut 1969 OB in "Romeo and Jeannette," followed by "Purification," "Naked."

PURSLEY, DAVID. Born July 13, 1938 in Lewisburg, PA. Graduate Harvard, Baylor U. Debut 1969 OB in "Peace," followed by "The Faggott," "Wings," "Three Musketeers," "Happy End" (1977 Bdwy).

QUARRY, RICHARD. Born Aug. 9, 1944 in Akron, OH. Graduate U. Akron, NYU. Bdwy bow 1970 in "Georgy," followed by "Oh! Calcutta!," "Grease."

QUAYLE, ANTHONY. Born Sept. 7, 1913 in Ainsdale, Eng. Attended RADA. Bdwy debut 1936 in "Country Wife," followed by "Tambourlaine the Great," "Firstborn," "Galileo," "Halfway up the Tree," "Sleuth," "Do You Turn Somersaults?"

RABB, ELLIS. Born June 20, 1930 in Memphis, TN. Attended Carnegie Tech., Yale. Debut OB 1956 in "Midsummer Night's Dream," followed by "Misanthrope," "Mary Stuart," "The Tavern," "Twelfth Night," "The Importance of Being Earnest," "King Lear," "Man and Superman," "Life in the Theatre," Bdwy in "Look after Lulu," "Jolly's Progress," "Right You Are ...," "Scapin," "Impromtu at Versailles," "Lower Depths," "School for Scandal," "Pantagleize," "Cock-a-Doodle Dandy," "Hamlet," "The Royal Family." Founder and director of APA.

RACHELLE, BERNIE. Born Oct. 7, 1939 in NYC. Graduate Yeshiva U., Hunter Col. OB in "Winterset," "Golden Boy," "Street Scene," "World of Sholom Aleichem," "Diary of Anne Frank," "Electra," "Nighthawks," "House Party," "Dancing in NY."

RADIGAN, MICHAEL. Born May 2, 1949 in Springfield, IL. Graduate Springfield Col., Goodman Theatre. Debut 1974 in "Music! Music!" (CC), OB in "Broadway Dandies," "Beowulf."

RAGNO, JOSEPH. Born Mar. 11, 1936 in Brooklyn, NY. Attended Allegheny Col. Debut 1960 OB in "Worm on the Horseradish," followed by "Elizabeth the Queen," "A Country Scandal," "The Shrike," "Cymbeline," "Love Me, Love My Children," "Interrogation of Havana," "The Birds," "Armenians," "Feedlot," Bdwy in "Indians," "The Iceman Cometh."

RAMSAY, REMAK. Born Feb. 2, 1937 in Baltimore, MD. Graduate Princeton U. Debut 1964 OB in "Hang Down Your Head and Die," followed by "The Real Inspector Hound," "Landscape of the Body," Bdwy in "Half a Sixpence," "Sheep on the Runway," "Lovely Ladies, Kind Gentlemen," "On the Town," "Jumpers," "Private Lives," "Dirty Linen."

RAMSEL, GENA. Born Feb. 10, 1950 in El Reno, OK. Graduate SMU. Bdwy debut 1974 in "Lorelei," OB in "Joe Masiell Not at the Palace."

RAMSEY, JOHN. Born Jan. 23, 1940 in Scranton, PA. Graduate Brown U., Yale. Debut 1964 in "Sunset," followed by Bdwy in "House of Atreus," "Find Your Way Home," "Sly Fox."

RASCHE, DAVID. Born Aug. 7, 1944 in St. Louis, MO. Graduate Elmhurst Col., UChicago. Debut 1976 OB in "John," followed by "Snow White," "Isadora Duncan Sleeps with the Russian Navy," Bdwy in "Shadow Box" (1977).

RASHOVICH, GORDANA. Born Sept. 18 in Chicago, IL. Graduate Roosevelt U., RADA. Debut 1977 OB in "Fefu and Her Friends" for which she received a Theatre World Award.

RATHBURN, ROGER. Born Nov. 11, 1940 in Perrysburg, OH. Attended Ohio State U., Neighborhood Playhouse. Bdwy debut 1971 in "No, No, Nanette" for which he received a Theatre World Award, OB in "Children of Adam."

RAWLINS, LESTER. Born Sept. 24, 1924 in Farrell, PA. Attended Carnegie Tech. Bdwy in "Othello," "King Lear," "The Lovers," "A Man for All Seasons," "Herzl," "Romeo and Juliet," "Da," OB in "Endgame," "Quare Fellow," "Camino Real," "Hedda Gabler," "Old Glory," "Child Buyer," "Winterset," "In the Bar of a Tokyo Hotel," "The Reckoning," "Nightride."

RAY, LESLIE ANN. Born May 27, 1946 in NYC. Graduate Hofstra U, AADA. Debut 1969 OB in "Trumpets and Drums," followed by "Godspell," "Anna K.," "Hamlet," "Bonus Army," Bdwy in "Angel" (1978).

RAYSON, BENJAMIN. Born in NYC. Bdwy debut 1953 in "Can-Can," followed by "Silk Stockings," "Bells Are Ringing," "A Little Night Music," "Happy End."

REA, KITTY. Born Jan. 13, 1952 in Bethesda, MD. Graduate San Francisco State U. Debut OB 1974 and Bdwy 1976 in "Godspell."

REAMS, LEE ROY. Born Aug. 23, 1942 in Covington, KY. Graduate U. Cinn. Cons. Bdwy debut 1966 in "Sweet Charity," followed by "Oklahoma!" (LC). "Applause," "Lorelei," "Show Boat" (JB), "Hello, Dolly!" (1978).

REDGRAVE, LYNN. Born in London Mar. 8, 1943. Attended Central Schl. of Speech. Bdwy debut 1967 in "Black Comedy," followed by "My Fat Friend," "Mrs. Warren's Profession" (LC), "Knock Knock," "St. Joan."

REED, ALAINA. Born Nov. 10, 1946 in Springfield, OH. Attended Kent State U. Bdwy debut in "Hair" (original and 1977), OB in "Sgt. Pepper's Lonely Hearts Club Band."

REED, GAVIN. Born June 3, 1935 in Liverpool, Eng. Attended RADA. Debut 1974 OB in "The Taming of the Shrew," followed by "French without Tears," Bdwy in "Scapino" (1974), "Some of My Best Friends."

REED, PAMELA. Born Apr. 2, 1949 in Tacoma, WA. Graduate UWash. Bdwy debut 1978 in "The November People," OB in "The Curse of the Starving Class."

REEHLING, JOYCE. Born Mar. 5, 1949 in Baltimore, MD. Graduate NC Sch. of Arts. Debut 1976 OB in "Hot 1 Baltimore," followed by "Who Killed Richard Cory?," "Lulu," "5th of July."

REESE, ROXANNE. Born June 6, 1952 in Washington, DC. Graduate Howard U. Debut 1974 OB in "Freedom Train," followed by "Feeling Good," "No Place to Be Somebody," Bdwy 1976 in "For Colored Girls Who Have Considered Suicide ..."

REINKING, ANN. Born Nov. 10, 1949 in Seattle, WA. Attended Joffrey Sch., HB Studio. Bdwy debut 1969 in "Cabaret," followed by "Coco," "Pippin," "Over Here" for which she received a Theatre World Award, "Goodtime Charley," "A Chorus Line," "Chicago," "Dancin'."

RENENSLAND, HOWARD. Born Apr. 4, 1948 in Leavenworth, KS. Graduate Washburn U., Trinity U. Debut 1977 O B in "Nest of Vipers," followed by "Happy Hunter."

REPOLE, CHARLES. Born May 24 in Brooklyn, NY. Graduate Hofstra U. Bdwy debut 1975 in "Very Good Eddie" for which he received a Theatre World Award, followed by "Finian's Rainbow" (JB).

RHYS, ROBERT C. Born Jan. 23, 1951 in Lexington, MA. Attended Ntl. Th. Inst. Bdwy debut 1972 in "Jumpers," followed by "The Rocky Horror Show," OB in "YMCA," "Joseph and the Amazing Technicolor Dreamcoat."

RICE, SARAH. Born Mar. 5, 1955 in Okinawa. Attended Ariz State U. Debut 1974 OB in "The Fantasticks."

RICHARDS, ARLEIGH. Born Nov. 28, 1949 in Gary, IN. Graduate Swarthmore Col., Neighborhood Playhouse. Debut 1977 OB in "The Crucible," followed by "Fefu and Her Friends."

Ruth Rivera   **Jess Richards**   **Mariellen Rokosny**   **Gil Rogers**   **Janine Ruane**

RICHARDS, JESS. Born Jan. 23, 1943 in Seattle, WA. Attended U. Wash. Bdwy debut 1966 in "Walking Happy," followed by "South Pacific." (LC), "Blood Red Roses," "Two by Two," "On the Town," for which he received a Theatre World Award, "Mack and Mabel," OB in "One for the Money," "Lovesong," "A Musical Evening with Josh Logan."

RIDGE, JOHN. Born May 13, 1924 in Brooklyn, NY. Attended LIU, NYU, Pratt Inst. Debut OB 1969 in "TheTriumph of Robert Emmet," Bdwy 1972 in "Mourning Becomes Electra," followed by "Threepenny Opera" (LC).

RIFICI, JOE. Born Nov. 25, 1952 in NYC. Graduate Wagner Col. Bdwy debut 1975 in "Grease."

RINALDI, JOY. Born in Yonkers, NY. Graduate Stephens Col., AADA. Debut OB 1969 in "Satisfaction Guaranteed," Bdwy 1973 in "Grease."

RINEHART, ELAINE. Born Aug. 16, 1952 in San Antonio, TX. Graduate NC Sch. of Arts. Debut 1975 OB in "Tenderloin," Bdwy in "The Best Little Whorehouse in Texas."

RIVELLINO, STEVEN. Born May 22, 1952 in NYC. Graduate Pace U. Debut 1975 OB in "Boy Meets Boy," followed by "Carnival" (ELT).

RIVERA, CHITA. Born Jan. 23, 1933 in Washington, DC. Attended Am. Sch. of Ballet. Bdwy debut 1950 in "Guys and Dolls," followed by "Call Me Madam," "Can-Can," "Shoestring Revue" (OB), "Seventh Heaven," "Mr. Wonderful," "West Side Story," "Bye Bye Birdie," "Bajour," "Chicago."

RIVERA, RUTH. Born Aug. 5, 1946 in Santurce, PR. Attended Brooklyn Col. Bdwy debut 1977 in "Cold Storage."

ROBARDS, JASON. Born July 26, 1922 in Chicago, IL. Attended AADA. Bdwy debut 1947 with D'Oyly Carte, followed by "Stalag 17," "The Chase," "Long Day's Journey into Night," for which he received a Theatre World Award, "The Disenchanted," "Toys in the Attic," "Big Fish Little Fish," "A Thousand Clowns," "Hughie," "The Devils," "We Bombed in New Haven," "The Country Girl," "Moon for the Misbegotten," "A Touch of the Poet," OB in "American Gothic," "The Iceman Cometh," "After the Fall," "But for Whom Charlie," "Long Day's Journey into Night."

ROBBINS, REX. Born in Pierre, SD. Bdwy debut 1964 in "One Flew Over the Cuckoo's Nest," followed by Scratch," "The Changing Room," "Gypsy," "Comedians," "An Almost Perfect Person," OB in "Servant of Two Masters," "The Alchemist," "Arms and the Man," "Boys in the Band," "A Memory of Two Mondays," "They Knew What They Wanted," "Secret Service," "Boy Meets Girl," BAM Co.'s "Three Sisters," "The Play's the Thing" and "Julius Caesar."

ROBERTS, DORIS. Born Nov. 4, 1930 in St. Louis, MO. Attended Actors Studio, Neighborhood Playhouse. Bdwy debut 1956 in "The Desk Set," followed by "Have I Got a Girl for You," "Malcolm," "Marathon '33," "Under the Weather," "The Office," "The Natural Look," "Last of the Red Hot Lovers," "Secret Affairs of Mildred Wall," "Cheaters," "Bad Habits," "Ladies at the Alamo," OB in "Death of Bessie Smith," "American Dream," "Color of Darkness," "Don't Call Me by My Rightful Name," "Christy," "Boy in the Straight-Back Chair," "A Matter of Position," "Natural Affection," "The Time of Your Life."

ROBERTSON, WILLIAM. Born Oct. 9, 1908 in Portsmouth, VA. Graduate Pomona Col. Bdwy debut 1936 in "Tapestry in Grey," followed by "Cup of Trembling," "Liliom," "Our Town," "Caesar and Cleopatra," OB in "Uncle Harry," "Shining Hour," "Aspern Papers," "Madame Is Served," "Tragedian in spite of Himself," "Kibosh," "Sun-Up," "The Last Pad," "Hamlet," "Girls Most Likely to Succeed," "The Petrified Forest," "The Minister's Black Veil," "Santa Anita," "Babylon," "Midsummer Night's Dream," "A Touch of the Poet," "The Zykovs," "Rimers of Eldrich," "The Crucible," "Lulu."

RODERICK, WILLIAM. Born Dec. 17, 1912 in NYC. Bdwy bow 1935 in "Romeo and Juliet," followed by "St. Joan," "Hamlet," "Our Town," "Importance of Being Earnest," "The Land is Bright," "Autumn Hill," "This Is the Army," "Magnificent Yankee," "Tonight at 8:30," "The Heiress," "Medea," "Macbeth," "Burning Glass," "Right Honourable Gentleman," "Marat/de Sade," "Homecoming," "We Bombed in New Haven," "Elizabeth the Queen" (CC), "Waltz of the Toreadors," "Night of the Iguana," "The Merchant," OB in "Madam, Will You Walk," "Cherry Orchard," "Come Slowly, Eden," "A Passage to E. M. Forster," "Trials of Oz."

ROGERS, GIL. Born Feb. 4, 1934 in Lexington, KY. Attended Harvard. OB in "The Ivory Branch," "Vanity of Nothing," "Warrior's Husband," "Hell Bent fer Heaven," "Gods of Lightning," "Pictures in the Hallway," "Rose," "Memory Bank," "A Recent Killing," "Birth," "Come Back, Little Sheba," "Life of Galileo," Bdwy in "The Great White Hope," "The Best Little Whorehouse in Texas."

ROKOSNY, MARIELLEN. Born June 20, 1955 in Elizabeth, NJ. Graduate Ithaca Col. Debut 1978 OB in "Lulu."

ROOP, RENO. Born Dec. 19 in Narva, Estonia. Graduate Goodman Theatre. Debut 1965 OB in "Medea, followed by "Hamlet," "Timon of Athens," "How Far Is It to Babylon?," Bdwy in "Emperor Henry IV," "Freedom of the City."

ROSE, GEORGE. Born Feb. 19, 1920 in Bicester, Eng. Bdwy debut with Old Vic 1946 in "Henry IV," followed by "Much Ado about Nothing," "A Man for All Seasons," "Hamlet," "Royal Hunt of the Sun," "Walking Happy," "Loot," "My Fair Lady," (CC '68), "Canterbury Tales," "Coco," "Wise Child," "Sleuth," "My Fat Friend," "My Fair Lady," "She Loves Me," BAM's "The Play's the Thing," "The Devil's Disciple," and "Julius Caesar."

ROSE, JOHN. Born Aug. 24, 1939 in Ottawa, KS. Attended City Col. San Francisco, USC. Bdwy debut 1976 in "The Night of the Iguana," followed by "St. Joan."

ROSEN, ABIGAIL. Born Sept. 18, 1946 in Basle, Switz. Bard Col. graduate. OB in "The Living Premise," "International Playgirls," "Home Movies," "Cinderella," "Beclch," "A Small Disturbance," Bdwy in "Where's Daddy?," "Sign in Sidney Brustein's Window."

ROSEN, ROBERT. Born Apr. 24, 1954 in NYC. Attended Indiana U., HB Studio. Bdwy debut 1975 in "Shenandoah."

ROSENBAUM, DAVID. Born in NYC. Debut OB 1968 in "American Hurrah," followed by "The Cavedwellers," "Evenings with Chekhov, "Out of the Death Cart," "After Miriam," "The Indian Wants the Bronx," "Allergy," "Family Business," Bdwy in "Oh! Calcutta!" (1972).

ROSS, JUSTIN. Born Dec. 15, 1954 in Brooklyn, NY. Debut 1974 OB in "More Than You Deserve," Bdwy 1975 in "Pippin," followed by "A Chorus Line."

ROSSOMME, RICHARD. Born Apr. 5, 1936 in Los Angeles, CA. Graduate San Jose State Col., Pasadena Playhouse. Debut 1975 OB in "Tenderloin," followed by "Allegro."

ROWLES, POLLY. Born Jan. 10, 1914 in Philadelphia, PA. Attended Carnegie Tech. Bdwy debut 1938 in "Julius Caesar," followed by "Richard III," "Golden State," "Small Hours," "Gertie," "Time Out for Ginger," "Wooden Dish," "Goodbye Again," "Auntie Mame," "Look after Lulu," "A Mighty Man Is He," "No Strings," "Best Laid Plans," "Killing of Sister George," "40 Carats," "The Women," OB in "Older People," "Mrs. Warren's Profession," "The Show-Off."

ROY, RENEE. Born Jan. 2, 1935 in Buffalo, NY. Attended Hartford Col. Bdwy debut 1954 in "Ankles Aweigh," followed by "Nature's Way," "By Jupiter," "Zelda," OB in "Company."

RUANE, JANINE. Born Dec. 17, 1963 in Philadelphia, PA. Bdwy debut 1977 in "Annie."

RUCKER, BO. Born Aug. 17, 1948 in Tampa, FL. Studied with Stella Adler, Lee Strasburg. Debut 1978 OB in "Native Son" for which he received a Theatre World Award.

RUDD, PAUL. Born May 15, 1940 in Boston, MA. OB in "Henry IV," followed by "King Lear," "A Cry of Players," "Midsummer Night's Dream," "An Evening With Merlin Finch," "In the Matter of J. Robert Oppenheimer," "Elagabalus," "Streamers" (LC), "Henry V" (CP), "Boys in the Band," "Da," "The Show-Off," Bdwy in "The Changing Room," "The National Health," "The Glass Menagerie," "Ah, Wilderness!," "Romeo and Juliet."

RUISINGER, THOMAS. Born May 13, 1930 in Omaha, NE. Graduate SMU, Neighborhood Playhouse. Bdwy debut 1959 in "Warm Peninsula," followed by "The Captain and the Kings," "A Shot in the Dark," "Frank Merriwell," "The Importance of Being Earnest," OB in "The Balcony," "Thracian Horses," "Under Milk Wood," "Six Characters in Search of an Author," "Papers."

| Richard Ryder | Janet Sarno | Sam Schacht | Lois Saunders | Michael Scott |

RULE, CHARLES. Born Aug. 4, 1928 in Springfield, MO. Bdwy bow 1951 in "Courtin' Time," followed by "Happy Hunting," "Oh, Captain!," "Conquering Hero," "Donnybrook," "Bye, Bye Birdie," "Fiddler on the Roof," "Henry, Sweet Henry," "Maggie Flynn," "1776," "Cry for Us All," "Gypsy," "Goodtime Charley," "On the 20th Century."

RUPERT, MICHAEL. Born Oct. 23, 1951 in Denver, CO. Attended Pasadena Playhouse. Bdwy debut 1968 in "The Happy Time" for which he received a Theatre World Award, followed by "Pippin."

RUSKIN, JEANNE. Born Nov. 6 in Saginaw, MI. Graduate NYU. Bdwy debut 1975 in "Equus."

RUSSAK, GERARD. Born Sept. 11, 1927 in Paterson, NJ. Attended NY Col of Music. Bdwy bow 1967 in "Marat/deSade," followed by "Zorba," "Knickerbocker Holiday," OB in "The Fantasticks," "Lulu."

RUSSELL, CRAIG. Born Jan. 10, 1948 in Toronto, Can. Debut 1977 OB in "A Man and His Women."

RUSSELL, DAVID. Born Aug. 9, 1949 in Allenwood, PA. Ithaca Col. graduate. Bdwy debut 1975 in "Shenandoah."

RUVOLO, DANNY. Born May 22, 1956 in East Rockaway, NY. Attended HB Studio. Bdwy debut 1974 in "Ulysses in Nighttown," followed by "A Chorus Line."

RYAN, CHARLENE. Born in NYC. Bdwy debut 1964 in "Never Live over a Pretzel Factory," followed by "Sweet Charity," "Fig Leaves Are Falling," "Coco," "A Funny Thing Happened on the Way to the Forum," "Chicago."

RYDER, RICHARD. Born Aug. 20, 1942 in Rochester, N Y. Attended Colgate U., Pratt Inst. Bdwy debut 1972 in "Oh! Calcutta!," followed by "Via Galactica," OB in "Rain," "Oh, Pshaw!," "The Dog beneath the Skin," "Polly," "Lovers," "Green Pond."

SABELLICO, RICHARD. Born June 29, 1951 in NYC. Attended C. W. Post Col. Bdwy debut 1974 in "Gypsy," OB in "Gay Divorce."

SABIN, DAVID. Born Apr. 24, 1937 in Washington, DC. Graduate Catholic U. Debut 1965 OB in "The Fantasticks," followed by "Now Is the Time for All Good Men," "Threepenny Opera" (LC), "You Never Can Tell," Bdwy in "The Yearling," "Slapstick Tragedy," "Jimmy Shine," "Gantry," "Ambassador," "Celebration," "Music Is," "The Water Engine."

SACHS, ANN. Born Jan. 23, 1948 in Boston, MA. Carnegie Tech graduate. Bdwy debut 1970 in "Wilson in the Promise Land," followed by "Dracula," OB in "Tug of War," "Sweetshoppe Miriam," "Festival of American Plays."

SALIS, NANCY. Born Aug. 14, 1952 in Christopher, IL. Graduate UIll. Debut 1976 OB in "Follies," followed by "Joe Masiell Not at the Palace."

SAND, PAUL. Born Mar. 5, 1935 in Santa Monica, CA. Attended UCLA. Bdwy bow 1961 in "From the Second City," followed by "Story Theatre," "Metamorphosis," OB in "Journey to the Day," "Wet Paint," "Hotel Passionato," "Mad Show," "Tales of the Hasidim."

SARANDON, CHRIS. Born July 24, 1942 in Beckley, WVa. Graduate UWVa., Catholic U. Bdwy debut 1970 in "The Rothschilds," followed by "Two Gentlemen of Verona," OB in "Marco Polo Sings a Solo," "The Devil's Disciple."

SARNO, JANET. Born Nov. 18, 1933 in Bridgeport, CT. Graduate SCTC, Yale U. Bdwy debut 1963 in "Dylan," followed by "Equus," OB in "6 Characters in Search of an Author," "Who's Happy Now," "Closing Green," "Fisher," "Survival of St. Joan," "The Orphan."

SAUNDERS, LOIS ANN. Born May 14, 1939 in Toledo, OH. Attended Centenary Col., HB Studio. Debut 1964 OB in "Great Scott!," followed by "Man with a Load of Mischief," "Follies," "The Crucible."

SCALZO, JOSEPH. Born Feb. 13, 1949 in Danbury, CT. Graduate Hartwick, Col. Debut 1974 OB in "The Window," Bdwy 1977 in "Caesar and Cleopatra," followed by "Some of My Best Friends."

SCARDINO, DON. Born in Feb. 1949 in NYC. Attended CCNY. On Bdwy in "Loves of Cass McGuire," "Johnny No-Trump," "My Daughter, Your Son," "Godspell," "Angel," OB in "Shout from the Rooftops," "Rimers of Eldrich," "The Unknown Soldier and His Wife," "Godspell," "Moonchildren," "Kid Champion," "Comedy of Errors," "Secret Service," "Boy Meets Girl," "Scribes."

SCHACT, SAM. Born Apr. 19, 1936 in The Bronx, NY. Graduate CCNY. OB in "Fortune and Men's Eyes," "Cannibals," "I Met a Man," "The Increased Difficulty of Concentration" (LCR), "One Night Stands of a Noisy Passenger," "Owners," "Jack Gelber's New Play," Bdwy in "The Magic Show," "Golda."

SCHAEFER, CRAIG. Born Aug. 24, 1953 in San Gabriel, CA. Attended UCLA. Debut 1975 OB in "Tenderloin," followed by "Joseph and the Amazing Technicolor Dreamcoat."

SCHENKKAN, ROBERT. Born Mar. 19, 1953. Graduate Cornell U., UTex. Debut 1978 OB in "The Taming of the Shrew."

SCHILLING, WILLIAM. Born Aug. 30, 1939 in Philadelphia, Pa. AADA graduate. Debut 1975 OB in "An Evening with John L. Lewis," followed by "The Wobblies," "Native Son."

SCHLEE, ROBERT. Born June 13, 1938 in Williamsport, PA. Lycoming Col. graduate. Debut 1972 OB in "Dr. Selavy's Magic Theatre," followed by "Hotel for Criminals," "Threepenny Opera."

SCHNABEL, STEFAN. Born Feb. 2, 1912 in Berlin, Ger. Attended UBonn, Old Vic. Bdwy bow 1937 in "Julius Caesar," followed by "Shoemaker's Holiday," "Glamour Preferred," "Land of Fame," "Cherry Orchard," "Around the World in 80 Days," "Now I Lay Me Down to Sleep," "Idiot's Delight," "Love of Four Colonels," "Plain and Fancy," "Small War on Murray Hill," "A Very Rich Woman," "A Patriot for Me," OB in "Tango," "In the Matter of J. Robert Oppenheimer," "Older People," "Enemies," "Little Black Sheep," "Rosmersholm," "Passion of Dracula."

SCHRAMM, DAVID. Born Aug. 14, 1946 in Louisville, KY. Attended Western Ky. U., Juilliard. Debut 1972 OB in "School for Scandal," followed by "Lower Depths," "Women Beware Women," "Mother Courage," "King Lear," "Duck Variations," Bdwy in "Three Sisters," "Next Time I'll Sing to You," "Edward II," "Measure for Measure," "The Robber Bridegroom."

SCHULL, REBECCA. Born Feb. 22 in NYC. Graduate NYU. Bdwy debut 1976 in "Herzl," followed by "Golda," OB in "Mother's Day," "Fefu and Her Friends."

SCHWEID, CAROLE. Born Oct. 5, 1946 in Newark, NJ. Graduate Boston U., Juilliard. Bdwy debut 1970 in "Minnie's Boys," followed by "A Chorus Line," OB in "Love Me, Love My Children," "How To Succeed in Business . . .," "Silk Stockings" (ELT), "Children of Adam."

SCOTT, GEORGE C. Born Oct. 18, 1927 in Wise, Va. OB in "Richard II" for which he received a Theatre World Award, followed by "As You Like It," "Children of Darkness," "Desire under the Elms," Bdwy in "Comes a Day," "Andersonville Trial," "The Wall," "General Seeger," "Little Foxes," "Plaza Suite," "Uncle Vanya," "Death of a Salesman," "Sly Fox."

SCOTT, MICHAEL. Born Jan. 24, 1954 in Santa Monica, CA. Attended Cal. State U. Debut 1978 OB and Bdwy in "The Best Little Whorehouse in Texas."

SEAMON, EDWARD. Born Apr. 15, 1937 in San Diego, CA. Attended San Diego State Col. Debut 1971 OB in "The Life and Times of J. Walter Smintheous," followed by "The Contractor," "The Family," "Fishing," "Feedlot," "Cabin 12," Bdwy in "The Trip Back Down."

SEER, RICHARD. Born Oct. 13, 1949 in Anchorage, AK. Graduate Cal. State U. Debut 1972 OB in "Hey Day," followed by "Joseph and the Amazing Technicolor Dreamcoat," Bdwy in "Da" for which he received a 1978 Theatre World Award.

SELDES, MARIAN. Born Aug. 23, 1928 in NYC. Attended Neighborhood Playhouse. Bdwy debut 1947 in "Medea," followed by "Crime and Punishment," "That Lady," "Tower Beyond Tragedy," "Ondine," "On High Ground," "Come of Age," "Chalk Garden," "The Milk Train Doesn't Stop Here Anymore," "The Wall," "A Gift of Time," "A Delicate Balance," "Before You Go," "Father's Day," "Equus," "The Merchant," "Deathtrap," OB in "Different," "Ginger Man," "Mercy Street," "Candle in the Wind," "Isadora Duncan Sleeps with the Russian Navy."

SELL, JANIE. Born Oct. 1, 1941 in Detroit, MI. Attended UDetroit. Debut 1966 OB in "Mixed Doubles," followed by "Dark Horses," "Dames at Sea," "By Bernstein," Bdwy in "George M!," "Irene," "Over Here" for which she received a Theatre World Award, "Pal Joey," "Happy End."

SERRECCHIA, MICHAEL. Born Mar. 26, 1951 in Brooklyn, NY. Attended Brockport State U. Teachers Col. Bdwy debut 1972 in "The Selling of the President," followed by "Heathen!," "Seesaw," "A Chorus Line," OB in "Lady Audley's Secret."

| Joan Shangold | Denny Shearer | Susan Sharkey | Armin Shimerman | Laurie Dawn Skinner |

SETRAKIAN, ED. Born Oct. 1, 1928 in Jenkintown, WVa. Graduate Concord Col., NYU. Debut 1966 OB in "Drums in the Night," followed by "Othello," "Coriolanus," "Macbeth," "Hamlet," "Baal," "Old Glory," "Futz," "Hey Rube," Bdwy in "Days in the Trees," "St. Joan," "The Best Little Whorehouse in Texas."

SHAKAR, MARTIN. Born Jan. 1, 1940 in Detroit, MI. Attended Wayne State U. Bdwy bow 1969 in "Our Town," OB in "Lorenzaccio," "Macbeth," "The Infantry," "Americana Pastoral," "No Place to Be Somebody," "World of Mrs. Solomon," "And Whose Little Boy Are You?," "Investigation of Havana," "Night Watch," "Owners," "Actors," "Richard III," "Transfiguration of Benno Blimpie," "Jack Gelber's New Play," "The Biko Inquest."

SHANGOLD, JOAN. Born in Albany, NY. Debut 1977 OB in "The Crucible."

SHARKEY, SUSAN. Born Dec. 12 in NYC. Graduate UAriz. Debut 1968 OB in "Guns of Carrar," followed by "Cuba Si," "Playboy of the Western World," "Good Woman of Setzuan," "Enemy of the People," "People Are Living There," "Narrow Road to the Deep North," "Enemies," "The Plough and the Stars," "The Sea," "The Sykovs," "Catsplay."

SHAWHAN, APRIL. Born Apr. 10, 1940 in Chicago, IL. Debut OB 1964 in "Jo," followed by "Hamlet," "Oklahoma!" (LC), "Mod Donna," Bdwy in "Race of Hairy Men," "3 Bags Full" for which she received a Theatre World Award, "Dinner at 8," "Cop-Out," "Much Ado about Nothing," "Over Here," "Rex," "A History of the American Film."

SHAWN, DICK. Born Dec. 1 in Buffalo, NY. Attended UMiami. Bdwy debut 1948 in "For Heaven's Sake, Mother," followed by "A Funny Thing Happened on the Way . . .," "The Egg," "Peterpat," "Fade Out-Fade In," "I'm Solomon," "Musical Jubilee," OB in "Rebirth Celebration of the Human Race," "The Second Greatest Entertainer in the Whole Wide World."

SHEA, JOHN V. Born Apr. 14 in North Conway, NH. Graduate Bates Col., Yale. Debut OB 1974 in "Yentl, the Yeshiva Boy," followed by "Gorky," "Battering Ram," "Safe House," Bdwy in "Yentl" (1975) for which he received a Theatre World Award, "Romeo and Juliet."

SHEARER, DENNY. Born July 30, 1941 in Canton, OH. Attended HB Studio. Debut 1968 OB in "Up Eden," Bdwy 1977 in "Bubbling Brown Sugar."

SHEARIN, JOHN D. Born Sept. 27, 1944 in Charlotte, NC. Graduate Wm. and Mary Col., Penn StateU. Debut 1976 OB in "Love and Intrigue," followed by "P.S. Your Cat Is Dead."

SHELLEY, CAROLE. Born Aug. 16, 1939 in London, Eng. Bdwy debut 1965 in "The Odd Couple," followed by "The Astrakhan Coat," "Loot," "Noel Coward's Sweet Potato," "Hay Fever," "Absurd Person Singular," "The Norman Conquests," OB in "Little Murders," "The Devil's Disciple," "The Play's the Thing."

SHELTON, REID. Born Oct. 7, 1924 in Salem, OR. Graduate U. Mich. Bdwy bow 1952 in "Wish You Were Here," followed by "Wonderful Town," "By the Beautiful Sea," "Saint of Bleecker Street," "My Fair Lady," "Oh! What a Lovely War!," "Carousel" (CC), "Canterbury Tales," "Rothschilds," "1600 Pennsylvania Avenue," "Annie," OB in "Phedre," "Butterfly Dream," "Man with a Load of Mischief," "Beggars Opera," "The Contractor," "Cast Aways."

SHELTON, SLOANE. Born Mar. 17, 1934 in Asheville, NC. Attended Berea Col., RADA. Bdwy debut 1967 in "Imaginary Invalid," followed by "Touch of the Poet," "Tonight at 8:30," "I Never Sang for My Father," "Sticks and Bones," "The Runner Stumbles," "Shadow Box," OB in "Androcles and the Lion," "The Maids," "Basic Training of Pavlo Hummel," "Play and Other Plays," "Julius Caesar."

SHIMERMAN, ARMIN. Born Nov. 5, 1949 in Lakewood, NJ. Graduate UCLA. Debut 1976 in "Threepenny Opera" (LC), followed by "Silk Stockings" (ELT), Bdwy 1977 in "St. Joan."

SHUMAN, JOHN. Born Aug. 10 in Boston, MA. Debut 1975 OB in "The Hot 1 Baltimore," followed by "Moonchildren," Bdwy in "13 Rue de L'Amour" (1978).

SHYRE, PAUL. Born Mar. 8, 1926 in NYC. Attended UFla., AADA. Debut 1956 OB in "Pictures in a Hallway," followed by "Purple Dust," "Cock-a-Doodle Dandy," "U.S.A.," Bdwy in "I Knock at the Door," "Absurd Person Singular," "St. Joan."

SILVER, SHELDON. Born Nov. 30 in Philadelphia, PA. Graduate Temple U., Ill. State U. Debut 1976 OB in "Fiorello!," followed by "Allegro."

SIMMONDS, STANLEY. Born July 13 in Brooklyn, NY. Attended Roosevelt Col. Bdwy debut 1927 in "My Maryland," followed by "Castles in the Air," "Simple Simon," "If the Shoe Fits," "Brigadoon," "Call Me Madam," "Silk Stockings," "Li'l Abner," "Fiorello," "Let It Ride," "I Can Get It for You Wholesale," "How to Succeed in Business . . .," "Pickwick," "Kelly," "Half a Sixpence," "How Now, Dow Jones," "Maggie Flynn," "Jimmy," "Mack and Mabel," "On the 20th Century."

SIMS, MARLEY. Born Feb. 23, 1948 in NYC. Graduate Hofstra U. Debut OB 1971 in "The Me Nobody Knows," followed by "Godspell." (OB and Bdwy).

SKINNER, LAURIE DAWN. Born June 23, 1952 in Ft. Campbell, KY. Debut 1975 OB in "The Three Sisters," followed by "Panama Hattie," "Brigadoon," Bdwy 1977 in "The Act."

SLACK, BEN. Born July 23, 1937 in Baltimore, MD. Graduate Catholic U. Debut 1971 OB in "Oedipus at Colonus," followed by "Interrogation of Havana," "Rain," "Thunder Rock," "Trelawny of the Wells," "Heartbreak House," "The Dodge Boys," Bdwy 1976 in "Legend."

SLOMAN, JOHN. Born June 23, 1954 in Rochester, NY. Graduate SUNY/-Geneseo. Debut 1977 OB in "Unsung Cole."

SMITH, EBBE ROE. Born June 25, 1949 in San Diego, CA. Graduate San Francisco State U. Debut 1978 OB in "Curse of the Starving Class."

SMITH, LOIS. Born Nov. 3, 1930 in Topeka, KS. Attended UWash. Bdwy debut 1952 in "Time Out for Ginger," followed by "The Young and Beautiful," "Wisteria Trees," "Glass Menagerie," "Orpheus Descending," "Stages," OB in "Sunday Dinner," "Present Tense," "The Iceman Cometh," "Harry Outside."

SMITH, RUFUS. Born July 11, 1917 in Smithfield, VA. Attended UVa. Bdwy bow 1938 in "Knickerbocker Holiday," followed by "Queen of Spades," "Park Avenue," "Street Scene," "Allegro," "Mr. Roberts," "Paint Your Wagon," "Pipe Dream," "Goldilocks," "Fiorello," "A Gift of Time," "Come on Strong," "The Advocate," "3 Bags Full," "Annie Get Your Gun," "Halfway Up the Tree," "The Education of Hyman Kaplan," "On the 20th Century."

SNOW, NORMAN. Born Mar. 29, 1950 in Little Rock, AR. Juilliard graduate. Debut 1972 OB in "School for Scandal," followed by "Lower Depths," "Hostage," "Timon of Athens," "Cymbeline," "U.S.A.," "Women Beware Women," "One Crack Out," Bdwy in "Three Sisters," "Measure for Measure," "Beggar's Opera," "Next Time I'll Sing to You."

SNYDER, DREW. Born Sept. 25, 1946 in Buffalo, NY. Graduate Carnegie Tech. Bdwy debut with APA in "Pantagleize," followed by "Cocktail Party," "Cock-a-doodle Dandy," and "Hamlet," NYSF's "Henry VI," "Richard III," and "Sticks and Bones," "The Cretan Bull," "Quail Southwest," "Wayside Motor Inn."

SNYDER, NANCY E. Born Dec. 2, 1949 in Kankakee, IL. Graduate Webster Col., Neighborhood Playhouse, Bdwy debut 1976 in "Knock, Knock," OB in "The Farm," "My Life," "Lulu," "Cabin 12," "5th of July," "My Cup Ranneth Over."

SOCKWELL, SALLY. Born June 14 in Little Rock, AR. Debut 1976 OB in "Vanities."

SOBOLOFF, ARNOLD. Born Nov. 11, 1930 in NYC. Attended Cooper Union. OB in "Threepenny Opera," "Career," "Brothers Karamazov," "Vincent," "Bananas," "Papp," "Camino Real," "Are You Now or Have You Ever Been?," "Music! Music!," "The Sea," Bdwy in "Mandingo," "The Egg," "Beauty Part," "One Flew over the Cuckoo's Nest," "Anyone Can Whistle," "Bravo Giovanni," "Sweet Charity," "Mike Downstairs," "Cyrano," "The Act."

SPIEGEL, BARBARA. Born Mar. 12 in NYC. Debut 1969 in LCRep in "Camino Real," "Operation Sidewinder" and "Beggar on Horseback," followed OB by "Feast for Flies," "Museum."

SQUIBB, JUNE. Born Nov. 6 in Vandalia, IL. Attended Cleveland Play House, HB Studio. Debut 1956 OB in "Sable Brush," followed by "Boy Friend," "Lend an Ear," "Another Language," "Castaways," "Funeral March for a One-Man Band," "Gorey Stories," Bdwy in "Gypsy" (1960), "The Happy Time."

SQUIRE, KATHERINE. Born Mar. 9, 1903 in Defiance, OH. Attended Ohio Wesleyan, Cleveland Playhouse. Bdwy debut 1932 in "Black Tower," followed by "Goodbye Again," "High Tor," "Hipper's Holiday," "What a Life," "Liberty Jones," "The Family," "Chicken Every Sunday," "Goodbye, My Fancy," "Sin of Pat Muldoon," "Shadow of a Gunman," "Traveling Lady," OB in "Roots," "This Here Nice Place," "Boy on a Straight-Back Chair," "Catsplay."

| Gordon Stanley | Helen Stenborg | Wesley Stevens | Susan Tabor | Robin Swados |

STANLEY, GORDON. Born Dec. 20, 1951 in Boston, MA. Graduate Brown U., Temple U. Debut 1977 OB in "Lyrical and Satirical," followed by "Allegro."

STENBORG, HELEN. Born Jan. 24, 1925 in Minneapolis, MN. Attended Hunter Col. OB in "A Doll's House," "A Month in the Country," "Say Nothing," "Rosmersholm," "Rimers of Eldrich," "Trial of the Catonsville 9," "Hot l Baltimore," "Pericles," "A Doll's House," "Elephant in the House," "A Tribute to Lili Lamont," "Museum," "5th of July," Bdwy in "Sheep on the Runway."

STEPHENSON, ALBERT. Born Aug. 23, 1947 in Miami, FL. Attended Boston Consv. Bdwy debut 1973 in "Irene," followed by "Debbie Reynolds Show," "The Act."

STERLING, JAN. Born Apr. 3, 1923 in NYC. Attended Fay Compton Sch. Bdwy debut 1938 in "Bachelor Born," followed by "When We Are Married," "Grey Farm," "This Rock," "Rugged Path," "Dunnigan's Daughter," "This Too Shall Pass," "Present Laughter," "Two Blind Mice," "Small War on Murray Hill," "Perfect Setup," "Front Page," "November People," OB in "Friday Night," "Come Back, Little Sheba."

STERNE, RICHARD. Born Feb. 26, 1942 in Philadelphia, PA. Graduate Northwestern U. Bdwy bow 1964 in "Hamlet," followed by "Crown Matrimonial," OB in "Beyond Desire," "Naked."

STERNHAGEN, FRANCES. Born Jan. 13, 1932 in Washington, DC. Vassar Graduate. OB in "Admirable Bashful," "Thieves' Carnival," "Country Wife," "Ulysses in Nighttown," "Saintliness of Margery Kemp," "The Room," "A Slight Ache," "Displaced Person," "Playboy of the Western World" (LC). Bdwy in "Great Day in the Morning," "Right Honourable Gentleman," with APA in "Cocktail Party," and "Cock-a-doodle Dandy," "The Sign in Sidney Brustein's Window," "Enemies" (LC), "The Good Doctor," "Equus," "Angel."

STEVENS, WESLEY. Born Apr. 6, 1948 in Evansville, IN. Graduate UVa., Ohio State U. Debut 1978 OB in "Othello."

STEVENSON, MARGOT. Born Feb. 8, 1918 in NYC. Brearley School graduate. Bdwy debut 1932 in "Firebird," followed by "Evensong," "A Party," "Barretts of Wimpole Street," "Symphony," "Truly Valiant," "Call It a Day," "Stage Door," "You Can't Take It With You," "Golden Wings," "Little Women" (CC), "Rugged Path," "Leading Lady," "The Young and Beautiful," "The Apple Cart," "Triple Play," "Lord Pengo," "Hostile Witness," "The Royal Family," OB in "Autumn Ladies and Their Lovers' Lovers," "Quail Southwest," "Mama Sang the Blues."

STEWART, JEAN-PIERRE. Born May 4, 1946 in NYC. Graduate CCNY. OB in "Henry IV," "King Lear," "Cry of Players," "In the Matter of J. Robert Oppenheimer," "The Miser," "Long Day's Journey into Night," "American Night Cry," "The Old Ones" "Dancing for the Kaiser," "Primary English Class," "Mama Sang the Blues," "Museum."

STINTON, COLIN. Born Mar. 10, 1947 in Kansas City, MO. Attended Northern Ill. U. Debut 1978 OB and Bdwy in "The Water Engine" for which he received a Theatre World Award.

STOVALL, COUNT. Born Jan. 15, 1946 in Los Angeles, CA. Graduate UCal. Debut 1973 OB in "He's Got a Jones," followed by "In White America," "Rashomon," "Sidnee Poet Heroical," "A Photo."

STREEP, MERYL. Born Sept. 22 in Summit, NJ. Graduate Vassar, Yale. Debut 1975 OB in "Trelawny of the Wells," followed by "27 Wagons Full of Cotton" for which she received a Theatre World Award, "A Memory of Two Mondays," "Secret Service," "Henry V," "Measure for Measure" (CP), "The Cherry Orchard," (LC), Bdwy in "Happy End" (1977).

STRONG, MICHAEL. Born Feb. 8, 1923 in NYC. Graduate Brooklyn Col., Neighborhood Playhouse. Bdwy debut 1941 in "Spring Again," followed by "Russian People," "Counter-Attack," "Eve of St. Mark," "Men to the Sea," "Whole World Over," "Detective Story," "Anastasia," "Firstborn," "Gypsy," "A Far Country," "Rhinoceros," "Emperor's Clothes," "Enemy of the People," LCRep's "After the Fall," "Incident at Vichy," "But for Whom Charlie," and "Marco Millions," OB in "A Month in the Country," "Dance of Death," "The Sponsor."

STUART, IAN. Born May 25, 1940 in London, Eng. Attended St. Ignatius Col. Debut 1972 OB in "Misalliance," followed by "Count Dracula," Bdwy 1977 in "Caesar and Cleopatra."

STUTHMAN, FRED. Born June 27, 1919 in Long Beach, CA. Attended UCal. Debut 1970 OB in "Hamlet," followed by "Uncle Vanya," "Charles Abbot & Son," "She Stoops to Conquer," "Master Builder," "Taming of the Shrew," "Misalliance," "Merchant of Venice," "Conditions of Agreement," "The Play's the Thing," "Ghosts," "The Father," "Hot l Baltimore," "Cherry Orchard," "The Devil's Disciple," Bdwy in "Sherlock Holmes" (1975).

SUDDETH, J. ALLEN. Born Aug. 3, 1952 in Vienna, Aust. Graduate Ohio U. Debut 1978 OB in "Moliere in spite of Himself."

SULLIVAN, BRAD. Born Nov. 18, 1931 in Chicago, IL. Graduate UMaine, AmThWing. Debut 1961 OB in "Red Roses for Me," followed by "South Pacific" (LC), "Hot-house," Bdwy in "Basic Training of Pavlo Hummel," (1977), "Working."

SULLIVAN, IAN. Born Apr. 1, 1933 in NYC. Attended Boston U. Bdwy debut 1970 in "Man of La Mancha" (also 1977 revival), followed by "Vivat! Vivat Regina!," "My Fair Lady" (1976), "Home Sweet Homer."

SUROVY, NICOLAS. Born June 30, 1944 in Los Angeles, CA. Attended Northwestern U., Neighborhood Playhouse. Debut 1964 OB in "Helen" for which he received a Theatre World Award, followed by "Sisters of Mercy," Bdwy 1977 in "The Merchant."

SUTHERLAND, STEVEN. Born May 18 in London, Eng. Attended Bristol Old Vic School. Bdwy debut 1977 in "Otherwise Engaged."

SUTORIUS, JAMES. Born Dec. 14, 1944 in Euclid, OH. Graduate Ill. Wesleyan, AMDA. Bdwy debut 1970 in "The Cherry Orchard," followed by "The Changing Room," "The November People," OB in "Servant of Two Masters," "Hamlet," "Sexual Perversity in Chicago."

SWADOS, ROBIN. Born May 10, 1953 in NYC. Graduate UMass. Debut 1977 OB in "Hello and Goodbye," followed by "The Would-Be Fiance."

SWANSEN, LARRY. Born Nov. 10, 1930 in Roosevelt, OK. Graduate OKU. Bdwy debut 1966 in "Those That Play the Clowns," followed by "Great White Hope," "The King and I," OB in "Dr. Faustus Lights the Lights," "Thistle in My Bed," "A Darker Flower," "Vincent," "MacBird," "Unknown Soldier and His Wife," "Sound of Music," "Conditioning of Charlie One," "Ice Age," "Prince of Homburg."

SWARBRICK, CAROL. Born Mar. 20, 1948 in Inglewood, CA. Graduate UCLA, NYU. Debut 1971 OB in "Drat!," followed by "The Glorious Age," Bdwy 1978 in "Side by Side by Sondheim."

SWIFT, ALLEN. Born Jan. 16, 1924 in NYC. Debut 1961 OB in "Portrait of the Artist," followed by "Month of Sundays," "Where Memories Are Magic," Bdwy in "Student Gypsy" (1963), "Checking Out."

SWITKES, WILLY. Born Nov. 12, 1929 in New Haven, CT. Graduate Catholic U. Debut 1960 OB in "A Country Scandal," followed by "The Firebugs," "Conerico Was Here to Stay," Bdwy 1976 in "Sly Fox."

SYERS, MARK. Born Oct. 25, 1952 in Trenton, NJ. Graduate Emerson Col. Bdwy debut 1976 in "Pacific Overtures" followed by "Jesus Christ Superstar" (1977).

SYMINGTON, DONALD. Born Aug. 30, 1925 in Baltimore MD. Bdwy debut 1947 in "Galileo," followed by "Mourning Pictures," CC's "Caesar and Cleopatra," "Dream Girl" and "Lute Song," "A Girl Can Tell," OB in "Suddenly Last Summer," "Lady Windermere's Fan," "Rate of Exchange," "Shrinking Bride," "Murderous Angels," "An Evening with the Poet Senator," "The Tennis Game."

TABOR, SUSAN. Born May 28, 1939 in Detroit, MI. Skidmore, NYU graduate. Debut 1962 OB in "Electra," followed by "What Every Woman Knows," Bdwy in "Inadmissible Evidence" (1965), "California Suite."

TAMBOR, JEFFREY. Born July 8, 1944 in San Francisco, CA. Attended SF State Col., Wayne State U. Debut 1976 OB in "Measure for Measure," Bdwy 1976 in "Sly Fox."

TANDY, JESSICA. Born June 7, 1909 in London, Eng. Attended Greet Acad. Bdwy debut 1930 in "The Matriarch," followed by "Last Enemy," "Time and the Conways," "White Steed," "Geneva," "Jupiter Laughs," "Anne of England," "Yesterday's Magic," "A Streetcar Named Desire," "Hilda Crane," "Fourposter," "The Honey's," "A Day by the Sea," "Man in the Dog Suit," "Triple Play," "Five Finger Exercise," "The Physicists," "A Delicate Balance," "Home," "All Over," LCRep's "Camino Real," "Not I" and "Happy Days," "Noel Coward in Two Keys," "The Gin Game."

Diane Tarleton   **Ian Trigger**   **Judith Townsend**   **Edmond Varrato**   **Trish Van Devere**

TARBUCK, BARBARA. Born Jan. 15, 1942 in Detroit, MI. Graduate UMich., LAMDA. Debut 1970 in LC's "Landscape" and "Silence," followed by "Amphitryon," "The Birthday Party," "The Crucible," "The Carpenters," "Great American Refrigerator," "An Evening with Sylvia Plath," "Biography for a Woman," "Hothouse," "The Water Engine."

TARLETON, DIANE. Born in Baltimore, MD. Graduate UMd. Bdwy debut 1965 in "Anya," followed by "A Joyful Noise," "Elmer Gantry," "Yentl," OB in "A Time for the Gentle People," "Spoon River Anthology," "International Stud."

TAYLOR, CLARICE. Born Sept. 20, in Buckingham County, VA. Attended New Theater School. Debut 1943 OB in "Striver's Row," followed by "Major Barbara," "Family Portrait," "Trouble in Mind," "The Egg and I," "A Medal for Willie," "Nat Turner," "Simple Speaks His Mind," "Gold Through the Trees," "The Owl Answers," "Song of the Lusitanian Bogey," "Summer of the 17th Doll," "Kongi's Harvest," "Daddy Goodness," "God Is a (Guess What?)," "An Evening of One Acts," "5 on the Black Hand Side," "A Man Better Man," "Day of Absence," "Brotherhood," "Akokawe," "Rosalee Pritchett," "Sty of the Blind Pig," "Duplex" (LC), "Wedding Band," Bdwy 1975 in "The Wiz."

THOME, DAVID. Born July 24, 1951 in Salt Lake City, UT. Bdwy debut 1971 in "No, No, Nanette," followed by "Different Times," "Good News," "Rodgers and Hart," "A Chorus Line."

THORNE, RAYMOND. Born Nov. 27, 1934 in Lackawanna, NY. Graduate UConn. Debut 1966 OB in "Man with a Load of Mischief," followed by "Rose," "Dames at Sea," "Love Course," "Blue Boys," Bdwy 1977 in "Annie."

TILLINGER, JOHN. Born June 28, 1938 in Tabriz, Iran. Attended URome. Bdwy debut 1966 in "How's the World Treating You?," followed by "Halfway up the Tree," "The Changing Room," OB in "Tea Party," "Pequod," "A Scent of Flowers," "Crimes of Passion," "Claw," "Ashes," "Chez Nous."

TILLSTROM, BURR. Born Oct. 13, 1917 in Chicago, IL. Attended UChicago. Bdwy debut 1978 in "Side by Side by Sondheim."

TIPPIT, WAYNE. Born Dec. 19, 1932 in Lubbock, TX. Graduate UIowa. Bdwy bow 1959 in "Tall Story," followed by "Only in America," "Gantry," OB in "Dr. Faustus," "Under the Sycamore Tree," "Misalliance," "The Alchemist," "MacBird," "Trainor, Dean, Liepolt & Co.," "Young Master Dante," "Boys in the Band," "Wayside Motor Inn."

TOLAN, KATHLEEN. Born Aug. 10, 1950 in Milwaukee, WI. Attended NYU, HB Studio. Debut 1974 OB in "Hothouse," followed by "More Than You Deserve," "Wicked Women Revue," "Museum."

TORN, RIP. Born Feb. 6, 1931 in Temple, TX. Graduate UTx. Bdwy bow 1956 in "Cat on a Hot Tin Roof," followed by "Sweet Bird of Youth," for which he received a Theatre World Award, "Daughter of Silence," "Strange Interlude," "Blues for Mr. Charlie," "Country Girl" (CC), "Glass Menagerie," OB in "Chaparral," "The Cuban Thing," "The Kitchen," "Deer Park," "Dream of a Blacklisted Actor," "Dance of Death," "Macbeth," "Barbary Shore," "Creditors."

TORRES, ANDY. Born Aug. 10, 1945 in Ponce, PR. Attended AMDA. Bdwy debut 1969 in "Indians," followed by "Purlie," "Don't Bother Me, I Can't Cope," "The Wiz," "Guys and Dolls," OB in "Billy Noname."

TOVATT, ELLEN. Born in NYC. Attended Antioch Col., LAMDA. Debut 1962 OB in "Taming of the Shrew," followed by "The Show-Off," Bdwy in "The Great God Brown," "The Visit," "Chemin de Fer," "Holiday," "Love for Love," "Rules of the Game," "Herzl."

TOWERS, CONSTANCE. Born May 20, 1933 in Whitefish, MT. Attended Juilliard, AADA. Bdwy debut 1965 in "Anya," followed by "Show Boat" (LC), "Carousel" (CC), "Sound of Music" (CC'67, JB '70 & '71), "Engagement Baby," "The King and I" (CC'68, JB '72, Bdwy '77).

TOWNSEND, JUDITH. Born Nov. 16, 1951 in Chesapeake, VA. Graduate E. Carolina U., Fla. State U. Debut 1978 OB in "The Taming of the Shrew."

TRIGGER, IAN. Born Sept. 30, 1942 in Eng. Graduate RADA. NY debut 1973 OB in "The Taming of the Shrew," followed by "Scapino," "True History of Squire Jonathan," Bdwy in "Scapino," "Habeas Corpus," "13 Rue de L'Amour."

TROOBNICK, GENE. Born Aug. 23, 1926 in Boston, MA. Attended Ithaca Col., Columbia U. Bdwy bow 1960 in "Second City," followed by "The Odd Couple," "Before You Go," "The Time of Your Life," OB in "Dynamite Tonight," "A Gun Play," "Tales of the Hasidim."

TUMARIN, BORIS. Born Apr. 4, 1910 in Riga, Latvia. Attended Berlin Arts Acad., Actors Workshop. Debut 1941 OB in "The Emperor's New Clothes," followed by "Winter Soldiers," "The Family," "A Chekhov Carnival," "Paths of Glory," "The Victors," "Three Sisters," "Merchant of Venice," "Whisper into My Good Ear," "Firebugs," "A Month in the Country," "Giant's Dance," "Caucasian Chalk Circle," "The Tenth Man" (CC), "The Head of Hair," Bdwy in "The Prescott Proposals," "Anastasia," "The Innkeepers," "The Devil's Advocate," "Garden of Sweets," "Venus at Large," "Traveller without Luggage," "Man in the Glass Booth," "The Merchant."

UNGER, JUDY. Born Aug. 22, 1970 in NYC. Bdwy debut 1977 in "Golda."

URMSTON, KENNETH. Born Aug. 6, 1929 in Cincinnati, OH. Attended Xavier U. Bdwy debut 1950 in "Make A Wish," followed by "Top Banana," "Guys and Dolls," "John Murray Anderson's Almanac," "Can-Can," "Silk Stockings," "Oh Captain!," "Bells Are Ringing," "Redhead," "Madison Avenue," "Tenderloin," "We Take the Town," "Lovely Ladies, Kind Gentlemen," "Follies," "Pippin."

VALE, MICHAEL. Born June 28, 1922 in Brooklyn, NY. Attended New Sch. Bdwy debut 1961 in "The Egg," followed by "Cafe Crown," "Last Analysis," "Impossible Years," "Saturday, Sunday, Monday," "Unexpected Guests," "California Suite," OB in "Autograph Hound," "Moths," "Now There's the Three of Us," "Tall and Rex," "Kaddish," "42 Seconds from Broadway," "Sunset."

VALENTINE, JAMES. Born Feb. 18, 1933 in Rockford, IL. Attended ULondon, Central Sch. of Drama. Bdwy debut 1958 in "Cloud 7," followed by "Epitaph for George Dillon," "Duel of Angels," "Ross," "Caesar and Cleopatra," "The Importance of Being Earnest."

VALOR, HENRIETTA. Born Apr. 28 in New Cumberland, PA. Northwestern U. graduate. Bdwy debut 1965 in "Half a Sixpence," followed by "Applause," "Jacques Brel Is Alive and Well . . . ," OB in "Fashion," "Jacques Brel . . . ," "A Bistro Car on the CNR."

VAN DEVERE, TRISH. Born Mar. 9, 1947 in Englewood, NJ. Graduate Ohio Wesleyan U. Debut 1967 OB in "Kicking Down the Castle," Bdwy 1975 in "All God's Chillun Got Wings," followed by "Sly Fox."

VAN NORDEN, PETER. Born Dec. 16, 1950 in NYC. Graduate Colgate U., Neighborhood Playhouse. Debut 1975 OB in "Hamlet," followed by "Henry V," "Measure for Measure," "A Country Scandal," "Hound of the Baskervilles," "Tartuffe," "Antigone," "Bingo," "Taming of the Shrew," "The Balcony," Bdwy 1977 in "Romeo and Juliet," "St. Joan."

VANNUYS, ED. Born Dec. 28, 1930 in Lebanon, IN. Attended Ind.U. Debut 1969 OB in "No Place to Be Somebody," followed by "Conflict of Interest," "The Taming of the Shrew," Bdwy in "Black Terror."

VAN SCOTT, GLORY. Born in Chicago, IL. Graduate Goddard Col., Antioch-Union. Debut 1962 OB in "Fly Blackbird," followed by "Billy Noname," "Don't Bother Me, I Can't Cope," "Love! Love! Love!," Bdwy in "Great White Hope," "Kwamina," "Show Boat," "Porgy and Bess."

VARRATO, EDMOND. Born Nov. 25, 1919 in Blairsville, PA. Attended State U., AmThWing. Bdwy debut 1948 in "Ballet Ballads," followed by "La Plume de Ma Tante," "Something More," "Pickwick," "Marat/deSade," "St. Joan," "Mike Downstairs," "Man of La Mancha."

VENNEMA, JOHN C. Born Aug. 24, 1948 in Houston, TX. Graduate Princeton U., LAMDA. Bdwy debut 1976 in "The Royal Family." OB in "Statements after . . . ," "The Biko Inquest."

VERDON, GWEN. Born Jan. 13, 1926 in Culver City, CA. Bdwy debut 1950 in "Alive and Kicking," followed by "Can-Can" for which she received a Theatre World Award, "Damn Yankees," "New Girl in Town," "Redhead," "Sweet Charity," "Children, Children," "Chicago."

VESTOFF, VIRGINIA. Born Dec. 9, 1940 in NYC. Bdwy debut 1960 in "From A to Z," followed by "Irma La Douce," "Baker Street," "1776," "Via Galactica," "Nash at 9," "Boccaccio," OB in "The Boy Friend," "Crystal Heart," "Fall Out," "New Cole Porter Revue," "Man with a Load of Mischief," "Love and Let Love," "Short-Changed Review," "The Misanthrope."

Martin Vidnovic   Holly Villaire   David Vogel   Terri White   Peter White

VIDNOVIC, MARTIN. Born Jan. 4, 1948 in Falls Church, VA. Attended Cincinnati Consv. of Music. Debut 1972 OB in "The Fantasticks," followed by Bdwy in "Home Sweet Homer" (1976), "The King and I" (1977).

VILEEN, ELLIOTT. Born Dec. 14, 1950 in Pittsburgh, PA. Graduate RI Sch. of Design, Temple U. Debut 1977 OB in "The Passion of Dracula."

VILLAIRE, HOLLY. Born Apr. 11, 1944 in Yonkers, NY. Graduate UDetroit, UMich. Debut 1971 OB in "Arms and the Man," followed by "Purity," "Eyes of Chalk," "Anna-Luse," "Village Wooing," "The Fall and Redemption of Man," BAM Co.'s "New York Idea," "Three Sisters," and "Julius Caesar," Bdwy in "Scapino" (1974), "Habeas Corpus."

VINOVICH, STEVE. Born Jan. 22, 1945 in Peoria, IL. Graduate UIll., UCLA, Juilliard. Debut 1974 OB in "The Robber Bridegroom," followed by "King John," "Father Uxbridge Wants to Marry," Bdwy in "Robber Bridegroom" (1976), "The Magic Show."

VITA, MICHAEL. Born in 1941 in NYC. Studied at HB Studio. Bdwy debut 1967 in "Sweet Charity," followed by "Golden Rainbow," "Promises, Promises," "Chicago," OB in "Sensations," "That's Entertainment."

VITELLA, SEL. Born July 7, 1934 in Boston, MA. Graduate San Francisco Inst. of Music. Debut 1975 OB in "The Merchant of Venice," followed by "Gorey Stories," Bdwy in "Something's Afoot" (1976).

VOGEL, DAVID. Born Oct. 19, 1922 in Canton, OH. Attended UPa. Bdwy debut 1948 in "Ballet Ballads," followed by "Gentlemen Prefer Blondes," "Make a Wish," "The Desert Song," OB in "How to Get Rid of It," "The Fantasticks."

VON SCHERLER, SASHA. Born Dec. 12, in NYC. Bdwy debut 1959 in "Look after Lulu," followed by "Rape of the Belt," "The Good Soup," "Great God Brown," "First Love," "Alfie," "Harold," "Bad Habits," OB in "Admirable Bashville," "The Comedian," "Conversation Piece," "Good King Charles' Golden Days," "Under Milk Wood," "Plays for Bleecker Street," "Ludlow Fair," "Twelfth Night," "Sondra," "Cyrano de Bergerac," "Crimes of Passion," "Henry VI," "Trelawny of the Wells," "Screens," "Soon Jack November," "Pericles," "Kid Champion," "Henry V," "Comanche Cafe," "Museum."

VON SYDOW, MAX. Born July 10, 1929 in Lund, Swed. Attended Stockholm Royal Acting Acad. Bdwy debut 1977 in "The Night of the Tribades."

VOSKOVEC, GEORGE. Born June 19, 1905 in Sazava, Czech. Graduate Dijon U. Bdwy debut 1945 in "The Tempest," followed by "Love of 4 Colonels," "His and Hers," "The Seagull," "Festival," "Uncle Vanya," "A Call on Kuprin," "Tenth Man," "Big Fish, Little Fish," "Do You Know the Milky Way?," "Hamlet," "Cabaret," "Penny Wars," "All Over," OB in "The Alchemist," "East Wind," "Galileo," "Oh Say Can You See L. A.?," "Room Service," "Brecht on Brecht," "All Is Bright," "The Cherry Orchard," "Agamemnon."

WALKER, CHET. Born June 1, 1954 in Stuttgart, AR. Bdwy debut 1972 in "On the Town," followed by "Ambassador," "Pajama Game," "Lorelei," "Pippin."

WALKER, KATHRYN. Born in Jan. in Philadelphia, PA. Graduate Wells Col., Harvard, LAMDA. Debut 1971 OB in "Slag," followed by "Alpha Beta," "Kid Champion," "Rebel Women," Bdwy in "The Good Doctor" (1973) "Mourning Pictures," "A Touch of the Poet."

WALKER, RANDOLPH. Born Feb. 8, 1929 in London, Eng. Rollins Col. graduate. Debut 1975 OB in "Don Juan in Hell," followed by "The Heretic," "Chalk Garden," "Royal Family," "Lion in Winter," Bdwy 1977 in "The King and I."

WALLACE, LEE. Born July 15, 1930 in NYC. Attended NYU. Debut OB 1966 in "Journey of the Fifth Horse," followed by "Saturday Night," "An Evening with Garcia Lorca," "Macbeth," "Booth Is Back In Town," "Awake and Sing," "Shepherd of Avenue B," "Basic Training of Pavlo Hummel," "Curtains." Bdwy in "Secret Affairs of Mildred Wild," "Molly," "Zalmen, or the Madness of God," "Some of My Best Friends."

WALTHER, GRETCHEN. Born Mar. 8, 1938 in NYC. Attended Northwestern U., HB Studio. Bdwy debut 1962 in "Something about a Soldier," OB in "Innocent Pleasures."

WARD, CHARLES. Born Oct. 24, 1952 in Los Angeles, CA. Soloist with American Ballet Theatre before 1978 Bdwy debut in "Dancin'."

WARD, DOUGLAS TURNER. Born May 5, 1930 in Burnside, LA. Attended UMich. Bdwy bow 1959 in "A Raisin in the Sun," followed by "One Flew over the Cuckoo's Nest," "Last Breeze of Summer," OB in "The Iceman Cometh," "The Blacks," "Pullman Car Hiawatha," "Bloodknot," "Happy Ending," "Day of Absence," "Kongi's Harvest," "Ceremonies in Dark Old Men," "The Harangues," "The Reckoning," "Frederick Douglass through His Own Words," "River Niger." "The Brownsville Raid," "The Offering."

WARREN, JOSEPH. Born June 5, 1916 in Boston, MA. Graduate Denver U. Bdwy debut 1951 in "Barefoot in Athens," followed by "One Bright Day," "Love of Four Colonels," "Hidden River," "The Advocate," "Philadelphia, Here I Come," "Borstal Boy," "The Lincoln Mask," OB in "Brecht on Brecht," "Jonah," "Little Black Sheep," "Black Tuesday," "The Show-Off."

WATERSTON, SAM. Born Nov. 15, 1940 in Cambridge, MA. Graduate Yale. Bdwy bow 1963 in "Oh, Dad, Poor Dad . . .," followed by "First One Asleep Whistle," "Halfway up the Tree," "Indians," "Hay Fever," "Much Ado About Nothing," OB in "As You Like it," "Thistle in My Bed," "The Knack," "Fitz," "Biscuit," "La Turista," "Posterity For Sale," "Ergo," "Muzeeka," "Red Cross," "Henry IV," "Spitting Image," "I Met a Man," "Brass Butterfly," "Trial of the Catonsville 9," "Cymbeline," "Hamlet," "A Meeting by the River," "The Tempest," "A Doll's House," "Measure for Measure," "Chez Nous," "Waiting for Godot."

WEAVER, FRITZ. Born Jan. 19, 1926 in Pittsburgh, PA. Graduate UChicago. Bdwy debut 1955 in "Chalk Garden," for which he received a Theatre World Award, followed by "Protective Custody," "Miss Lonely-hearts," "All American," "Lorenzo," "The White House," "Baker Street," "Child's Play," "Absurd Person Singular," OB in "The Way of the World," "White Devil," "Doctor's Dilemma," "Family Reunion," "The Power and the Glory," "Great God Brown," "Peer Gynt," "Henry IV," "My Fair Lady" (CC), "Lincoln," "The Biko Inquest."

WEBB, ROBB. Born Jan. 29, 1939 in Whitesburg, KY. Attended Ohio State U. Debut 1976 OB in "Who Killed Richard Cory?," Bdwy 1977 in "Sly Fox."

WEDGEWORTH, ANN. Born Jan. 21 in Abilene, TX. Attended UTex. Bdwy debut 1958 in "Make A Million," Followed by "Blues for Mr. Charlie," "Last Analysis," "Thieves," "Chapter Two," OB in "Chapparal," "The Crucible," "Days and Nights of Beebee Fenstermaker," "Ludlow Fair," "Line."

WEEKS, JAMES RAY. Born Mar. 21, 1942 in Seattle, WA. Graduate UOre., AADA. Debut 1972 in LCRep's "Enemies," "Merchant of Venice" and "A Streetcar Named Desire," followed by OB's "49 West 87th," "Feedlot," Bdwy in "My Fat Friend," "We Interrupt This Program."

WELDON, CHARLES. Born June 1, 1940 in Wetumka, OK. Bdwy debut 1969 in "Big Time Buck White," followed by "River Niger," OB in "Ride a Black Horse," "Long Time Coming and a Long Time Gone," "Jamimma," "In the Deepest Part of Sleep," "Brownsville Raid," "Great MacDaddy," "The Offering."

WENDSCHUH, RONALD. Born Apr. 19, 1939 in Minnesota. Graduate Luther Col., UMin. Debut 1977 OB in "The Crucible."

WESTON, JACK. Born in 1924 in Cleveland, OH. Attended Cleveland Playhouse, AmThWing. Bdwy debut 1950 in "Season in the Sun," followed by "South Pacific," "Bells Are Ringing," "California Suite," "The Ritz," "Cheaters."

WHITE, ALICE. Born Jan. 6, 1945 in Washington, DC. Oberlin Col. graduate. Debut 1977 OB in "The Passion of Dracula."

WHITE, PENNEY. Born Oct. 28 in Pensacola, FL. Graduate Northwestern U. Bdwy debut 1971 in "Metamorphoses," OB in "Second City," "Some Other Time" (LC), "Inside My Head," "Telemachus Clay," "Bag of Flies," "Museum."

WHITE, PETER. Born Oct. 10, 1937 in NYC. Graduate Northwestern U., Yale. Debut 1968 OB in "Boys in the Band," followed by "John Brown's Body," "Life of Galileo," Bdwy in "P.S. Your Cat Is Dead" (1976).

WHITE, TERRI. Born Jan. 24, 1953 in Palo Alto, CA. Attended USIU. Debut OB 1976 in "The Club."

WHITENER, WILLIAM. Born Aug. 17, 1951 in Seattle, WA. With Joffrey Ballet before Bdwy debut 1978 in "Dancin'."

WHITMORE, JAMES. Born Oct. 1, 1922 in White Plains, NY. Attended Yale U. Bdwy debut 1947 in "Command Decision," followed by "A Case of Libel," "Inquest," "Will Rogers, U.S.A.," "Bully."

Charles LaVont Williams **Hattie Winston** **Kai Wulff** **Gretchen Wyler** **Richard Zavaglia**

WIDDOES, KATHLEEN. Born Mar. 21, 1939 in Wilmington, DE. Attended Paris' Theatre des Nations. Bdwy debut 1958 in "The Firstborn," followed by "World of Suzie Wong," "Much Ado about Nothing," "The Importance of Being Earnest," OB in "Three Sisters," "The Maids," "You Can't Take It with You," "To Clothe the Naked," "World War 2 1/2," "Beggar's Opera," "As You Like It," "A Midsummer Night's Dream."

WIENEKE, M. LYNNE. Born Sept. 5, 1951 in Saginaw, MI. Graduate UMich. Debut 1978 OB in "Allegro."

WILCOX, RALPH. Born Jan. 30, 1951 in Milwaukee, WI. Attended UWisc. Debut 1971 OB in "Dirtiest Show In Town," followed by "Broadway," "Miracle Play," Bdwy in "Ain't Supposed to Die a Natural Death," "The Wiz."

WILKINSON, KATE. Born Oct. 25 in San Francisco, CA. Attended San Jose State Col. Bdwy debut 1967 in "Little Murders," followed by "Johnny No-Trump," "Watercolor," "Postcards," "Ring Round the Bathtub," "The Last of Mrs. Lincoln," OB in "La Madre," "Earnest in Love," "Story of Mary Surratt," "Bring Me a Warm Body," "Child Buyer," "Rimers of Eldritch," "A Doll's House," "Hedda Gabler," "Real Inspector Hound," "The Contractor," "When the Old Man Died."

WILLARD, DEL. Born May 8, 1935 in Rutland, VT. Debut OB 1963 in "The Brig," followed by "A Recent Killing," "Come Back, Little Sheba," "A View from the Bridge."

WILLIAMS, CHARLES LAVONT. Born Sept. 10, 1956 in Chicago, IL. Attended Kennedy-King Col. Bdwy debut 1977 in "Hair."

WILLIAMS, SAMMY. Born Nov. 13, 1948 in Trenton, NJ. Bdwy debut 1969 in "The Happy Time," followed by "Applause," "Seesaw," "A Chorus Line."

WILSON, ELIZABETH. Born Apr. 4, 1925 in Grand Rapids, MI. Attended Neighborhood Playhouse. Bdwy debut 1953 in "Picnic," followed by "Desk Set," "Tunnel of Love," "Big Fish, Little Fish," "Sheep on the Runway," "Sticks and Bones," "Secret Affairs of Mildred Wild," "The Importance of Being Earnest," OB in "Plaza 9," "Eh?," "Little Murders," "Good Woman of Setzuan," "Uncle Vanya," "Threepenny Opera."

WILSON, K. C. Born Aug. 10, 1945 in Miami, FL. Attended AADA. Debut 1973 OB in "Little Mahagonny," followed by "The Tempest," "Richard III," "Macbeth," "Threepenny Opera," "The Passion of Dracula."

WILSON, MARY LOUISE. Born Nov. 12, 1936 in New Haven, CT. Graduate Northwestern U. OB in "Our Town," "Upstairs at the Downstairs," "Three-penny Opera," "A Great Career," "Whispers on the Wind," "Beggar's Opera," Bdwy in "Hot Spot," "Flora, the Red Menace," "Criss-Crossing," "Promises, Promises," "The Women," "Gypsy," "The Royal Family," "The Importance of Being Earnest."

WINGATE, MARTHA. Born July 28, 1953 in Boston, MA. Attended Western Was. State Col., UWash. Bdwy debut 1977 in "Hair."

WINSTON, HATTIE. Born Mar. 3, 1945 in Greenville, MS. Attended Howard U. OB in "Prodigal Son," "Day of Absence," "Pins and Needles," "Weary Blues," "Man Better Man," "Billy Noname," "Sambo," "The Great Mac-Daddy," "A Photo," Bdwy in "The Me Nobody Knows," "Two Gentlemen of Verona."

WINSTON, LEE. Born Mar. 14, 1941 in Great Bend, KS. Graduate UKan. Debut 1966 OB in "The Drunkard," followed by "Show Boat" (LC), "Little Mahagonny," "Good Soldier Schweik," Bdwy 1976 in "1600 Pennsylvania Avenue," "The Adopted Moon."

WINTER, MELANIE. Born Feb. 12, 1958 in Burbank, CA. Debut 1977 OB in "Wonderful Town."

WINTERS, MARIAN. Born Apr. 19, 1924 in NYC. Attended Brooklyn Col. Debut 1949 OB in "King John," followed by "Dream Girl" (CC), "Hippolytus," "Sing Me No Lullaby," "The Cherry Orchard," Bdwy in "I Am a Camera" for which she received a Theatre World Award, "The Dark Is Light Enough," "Auntie Mame," "Tall Story," "The 49th Cousin," "Nobody Loves an Albatross," "Mating Dance," "Deathtrap."

WINTERS, SHELLEY. Born Aug. 18, 1922 in East St. Louis, IL. Attended Drama Workshop, Actors Studio. Bdwy debut 1941 in "The Night before Christmas," followed by "Meet the People," "Rosalinda," "Oklahoma!," "A Hatful of Rain," "Girls of Summer," "Night of the Iguana," "Under the Weather," "Minnie's Boys," "The Effect of Gamma Rays on Man-in-the-Moon Marigolds" (1978), OB in "Cages."

WONG, JANET. Born Aug. 30, 1951 in Berkeley, CA. Attended UCal. Bdwy debut 1977 in "A Chorus Line."

WOOD, G. Born Dec. 31, 1919 in Forrest City, AR. Graduate Carnegie Tech, NYU. Bdwy bow 1953 in "Cyrano de Bergerac," followed by "Richard III," "Shangri-La," "The Crucible," "The Seagull," "Imaginary Invalid," "A Touch of the Poet," "Tonight at 8:30," "Henry V," "Who's Who in Hell," "The Importance of Being Earnest," OB in "La Ronde," "Cradle Song," "The Lesson," "Thor with Angels," "A Box of Watercolors," "Tobias and the Angels," "The Potting Shed."

WOOD, JOHN. Born in 1931 in Derbyshire, Eng. Attended Oxford U. Bdwy debut 1967 in "Rosencrantz and Guildenstern Are Dead," followed by "Sherlock Holmes," "Travesties," "Tartuffe," "Deathtrap."

WOODWARD, CHARLAINE. Born Dec. 29 in Albany, NY. Graduate Goodman Sch. of Drama., SUNY. Debut 1975 OB in "Don't Bother Me, I Can't Cope," Bdwy in "Hair" (1977), "Ain't Misbehavin'."

WOODS, RICHARD. Born May 9, 1921 in Buffalo, NY. Graduate Ithaca Col. Bdwy in "Beg, Borrow or Steal," "Capt. Brassbound's Conversion," "Sail Away," "Coco," "Last of Mrs. Lincoln," "Gigi," "Sherlock Holmes," "Murder among Friends," "The Royal Family," "Deathtrap," OB in "The Crucible," "Summer and Smoke," "American Gothic," "Four-in-One," "My Heart's in the Highlands," "Eastward in Eden," "The Long Gallery," "The Year Boston Won the Pennant," "In the Matter of J. Robert Oppenheimer" (LC), with APA in "You Can't Take It with You," "War and Peace," "School for Scandal," "Right You Are," "The Wild Duck," "Pantagleize," "Exit the King," "The Cherry Orchard," "Cock-a-doodle Dandy," and "Hamlet."

WORTH, IRENE. Born June 23, 1916 in Nebraska. Graduate UCLA. Bdwy debut 1943 in "The Two Mrs. Carrolls," followed by "The Cocktail Party," "Mary Stuart," "Toys in the Attic," "King Lear," "Tiny Alice," "Sweet Bird of Youth," "The Cherry Orchard" (LC).

WORTH, PENNY. Born Mar. 2, 1950 in London, Eng. Attended Sorbonne, Paris. Bdwy debut 1970 in "Coco," followed by "Irene," "Annie."

WRIGHT, BOB. Born in 1911 in Columbia, MO. Attended UMo. Bdwy bow 1948 in "Make Mine Manhattan," followed by "Kiss Me, Kate," "Hit the Trail," "South Pacific" (CC), "Tall Story," "Merry Widow" (LC), "Sound of Music" (CC), "Man of La Mancha."

WRIGHT, MARY CATHERINE. Born Mar. 19, 1948 in San Francisco, CA. Attended CCSF, SF State Col. Bdwy debut 1970 in "Othello," followed by "A History of the American Film," OB in "East Lynn," "Mimi Lights the Candle," "Marvin's Gardens," "The Tempest," "Doctor in Spite of Himself," "Love's Labors Lost."

WRIGHT, WILLIAM. Born Jan. 21, 1943 in Los Angeles, CA. Graduate UUtah, Bristol Old Vic. Debut 1973 OB in "Merchant of Venice" (LC), "The Way of the World," Bdwy 1976 in "Equus."

WULFF, KAI. Born Dec. 18, 1950 in Hamburg, Ger. Bdwy debut 1976 in "Equus."

WYLER, GRETCHEN. Born Feb. 16, 1932 in Oklahoma City, OK. Bdwy debut 1950 in "Where's Charley?," followed by "Guys and Dolls," "Silk Stockings," "Damn Yankees," "Rumple," "Bye Bye Birdie," "Sly Fox."

ZABELSKI, LUCIEN. Born Aug. 5, 1949 in Torrington, CT. Graduate UCt., RADA. Debut 1972 OB in "Hope Is the Thing with Feathers," followed by "Under Milk Wood," "Naked."

ZAKKAI, JAMIL. Born in Bagdad. Graduate Hofstra U. Debut 1960 OB in "The Connection," followed by "The Dybbuk," "In the Jungle of Cities," "Tonight We Improvise," "Agamemnon."

ZAKS, JERRY. Born Sept. 7, 1946 in Germany. Graduate Dartmouth, Smith Col. Bdwy debut 1973 in "Grease," OB in "Death Story," "Dream of a Blacklisted Actor," "Kid Champion," "Golden Boy," "Marco Polo," "One Crack Out."

ZALKIND, DEBRA. Born Mar. 30, 1953 in NYC. Graduate Juilliard. Appeared with several dance companies before Bdwy debut 1978 in "The Best Little Whorehouse in Texas."

ZANG, EDWARD. Born Aug. 19, 1934 in NYC. Graduate Boston U. OB in "Good Soldier Schweik," "St. Joan," "Boys in the Band," "The Reliquary of Mr. And Mrs. Potterfield," "Last Analysis," "As You Like It," "More than You Deserve," "Polly," "Threepenny Opera," BAM Co.'s "New York Idea," "The Misanthrope."

ZAVAGLIA, RICHARD. Born Mar. 25, 1937 in Newark, NJ. Attended HB Studio, AADA. OB in "Skaters," "As You Like It," "Life of Galileo."

Barbara Ashley (1950)

Geraldine Brooks (1975)

Ilka Chase (1960)

HORTENSE ALDEN, 76, Texas-born actress, died Apr. 2, 1978 in Tucson, AZ. She made her Broadway debut at 15, subsequent;y appearing in such productions as "Liliom," "It's a Boy!," "As You Like It," "The Locked Door," "Firebrand," "Arabesque," "Ghosts," "A Month in the Country," "Lysistrata," "Grand Hotel," "Thunder on the Left," "But Not for Love," "Arms of Venus," "Here Come the Clowns," "Ned McCobb's Daughter," "Garden District," and 1968 off Broadway in "The Late, Late Show." She was divorced from novelist James T. Farrell. A son survives.

BARBARA ASHLEY, age unreported, Brooklyn-born actress and singer, died Mar. 1, 1978. Born Geraldine Barbieri, she had appeared in "The Canteen Show," "Ballet Ballads," "The Liar," and in 1950 "Out of This World" for which she received a Theatre World Award. No reported survivors.

JEAN BARRERE, 59, NY-born stage manager and former actor, died in his sleep Aug. 29, 1977 in his home in Croton-on-Hudson, NY. His career began as an actor in 1936 in "Brother Rat," and he was subsequently involved with over 35 productions, including "Too Many Heroes," "Pajama Game," "Life with Father," "South Pacific," "The Loud Red Patrick," "Sunrise at Campobello," "Copper and Brass," "The Highest Tree," "Unsinkable Molly Brown," "Fanny," "Devil's Advocate," "Something about a Soldier," "Venus at Large," "Tovarich," "Rugantino," "Hamlet," "Comedy in Music," "Do I Hear a Waltz?," and "The Devils." Surviving are his widow, two sons and a daughter.

GEORGE BATSON, 61, playwright, died July 25, 1977 in NYC. His first comedy, "Treat Her Gently," opened on Bdwy in 1941. Other plays include "Time on Your Hands," "Punch and Julia," "Ramshackle Inn," "Magnolia Alley," "A Date with April," and "House on the Rocks." He was also active as a producer in England. No reported survivors.

JACOB BEN-AMI, 86, Russian-born actor, director, and founder of the Jewish Art Theatre, died July 22, 1977 in NYC. He achieved acclaim on both the Yiddish and English-speaking stages in such plays as "Green Fields," "The Mute," "Naomi," "Samson and Delilah," "Idle Inn," "Johannes Kreisler," "The Failures," "Man and the Masses," "Diplomacy," "Welded," Eva LeGallienne's Civic Repertory Theatre productions, "Evensong," "Day of Judgement," "The Tenth Man," "The Dybbuk," "Walking to Waldheim" and "In My Father's Court." He is survived by a son, and a niece, actress Jennifer Warren.

ABNER BIBERMAN, 69, Philadelphia-born stage and screen actor, and film and tv director, died June 20, 1977 at his home in San Diego, CA. He went to Hollywood after working in NY with the Group Theatre, and appearing in such productions as "Sailors of Cattaro," "Panic," "Waiting for Lefty," "Till the Day I Die," "Winterset," "Siege," and "Roosty." He had roles in over 100 films. His widow and three sons survive.

DON BLACKMAN, 65, Broadway and Hollywood actor, died Sept. 11, 1977 of a heart attack in his San Fernando, CA home. Prior to his acting career he was a lightweight boxing champion. He had appeared in such plays as "Emperor Jones," "Othello," "The Iceman Cometh," "John Henry" and "Golden Boy." Two sisters survive.

ALEX BRADFORD, 51, Alabama-born gospel singer, composer and minister, died in his sleep Feb. 15, 1978 in NYC after suffering a stroke. He collaborated on several gospel plays, including "Your Arm's Too Short to Box with God." For his performance in "Don't Bother Me, I Can't Cope," he received an Obie Award. He also appeared in "Black Nativity." Surviving are his widow and two daughters.

GERALDINE BROOKS, 52, NY-born actress, died June 19, 1977 of cancer in Riverhead, NY. After her Bdwy debut in 1944 in "Follow the Girls," she appeared in "Winter's Tale," "Time of the Cuckoo," "Brightower," "Fiddler on the Roof," and off Broadway's "Jules Feiffer's Hold Me!" in 1977. She had also appeared in numerous tv shows and in films. She is survived by her husband, writer Budd Schulberg, her mother and a sister.

CAMERON BURKE, 25, actor and dancer, was killed May 30, 1978 by a hit-and-run driver while riding his bicycle in Babylon, L.I., NY. From his home in Portland, Maine, he came to NY to study dancing, subsequently appearing with several companies. At his death, he was appearing off Broadway in the musical "The Best Little Whorehouse in Texas." His parents surv;ve.

RICHARD CARLSON, 65, Minnesota-born stage, film and tv actor, died Nov, 25, 1977 after a cerebral hemorrhage in Sherman Oaks, CA. Before moving to Hollywood, he performed in "Now You've Done It," "Ghost of Yankee Doodle," "Whiteoaks" and "Stars in Your Eyes." He appeared in over 40 films, but was probably best known for his tv series "I Led Three Lives." Surviving are his widow and two sons.

JOHN CAZALE, 42, Boston-born stage and screen actor, died March 12, 1978 of cancer in NYC. He had appeared Off Broadway in "The Indian Wants the Bronx" and "Line" for which he received Obies, and in "The Resistible Rise of Arturo Ui," "The Local Stigmatic," and several NY Shakespeare Festival productions, including "Measure for Measure." His mother, a sister and brother survive.

ILKA CHASE, 72, NY-born stage and film actress, radio and tv personality, playwright, and novelist, died Feb. 15, 1978 of internal hemorrhaging in Mexico City. Her Bdwy career began in 1924 in "The Red Falcon," followed by "Shall We Join the Ladies?," "Antonia," "Embers," "Happy Husband," "Animal Kingdom," "Forsaking All Others," "Days without End," "Wife Insurance," "While Parents Sleep," "Small Miracle," "Revenge with Music," "On to Fortune," "Co-Respondent Unknown," "The Women," "Keep Off the Grass," "Beverly Hills," "In Bed We Cry" which she wrote. She had roles in 21 films. Her third husband, Dr. Norton S. Brown. survives.

GENE COFFIN, 72, costume designer for stage, films and tv, died Oct. 18, 1977 in NYC. Among his many stage credits are "Dear Charles," "Someone Waiting," "Affair of Honor," "Jolly's Progress," "The 49th Cousin," "Arsenic and Old Lace," and "Sailor's Delight." His widow and son survive.

ROBIN CRAVEN, (nee Robin Harry Cohen in London), 71, stage and tv actor, died May 15, 1978 of a stroke and heart failure in NYC. After his Bdwy debut in 1939 in "Dear Octopus," he appeared in "Hand in Glove," "Present Laughter," "The Corn Is Green," "The King and I," "Witness for the Prosecution," "My Fair Lady," "Passage to India," and "Foxy." His widow survives.

CARTER DE HAVEN, 90, stage and screen actor, died July 20, 1977 in Hollywood, CA. His career on Bdwy began as a child and stardom came at an early age. After marrying actress Flora Parker, they became a team in musicals and vaudeville. Among his many credits are "Miss Dolly Dollars," "Queen of the Moulin Rouge," "The Girl in the Taxi," "All Aboard," and "His Little Widows." He appeared in many two-reel comedies and full-length films before retiring in the early 1930's to write, direct and produce. Surviving are two sons, and a daughter, actress Gloria De Haven.

DERRICK DE MARNEY, 71, actor, producer and director, died Feb. 18, 1978 in his native London. His Bdwy appearances included "The Matriarch," "The Last Enemy," "The Tudor Wench," "Young Mr. Disraeli" and "The Importance of Wearing Clothes." His deceased brother Terence was also a noted actor. No reported survivors.

NAT DORFMAN, 82, veteran Broadway press agent, and playwright, died July 3, 1977 of a heart attack in NYC. He had represented more than 300 productions before becoming public information director of the NYC Opera, from which job he had just retired. He wrote sketches for "The International Revue," "Lew Leslie's Blackbirds" and "Rhapsody in Black," and such plays as "Take My Tip" and "Errant Lady." He is survived by a son and daughter.

FRED F. FINKLEHOFFE, 67, film and stage producer, playwright, screenwriter and director, died Oct. 5, 1977 at his home in Springtown, PA. His career began as co-author of the hit "Brother Rat" that took him to Hollywood for several years. His later Bdwy credits as a producer include "The Heiress," "The Traitor," "Affairs of State," "Ankles Aweigh," "Show Time," and "Laugh Time." His second wife and a daughter survive.

WILL GEER, 76, Indiana-born character actor on stage, films and tv, died Apr. 22, 1978 of a respiratory ailment in Los Angeles, CA. After performing in touring companies, he made his Bdwy debut in 1928 in "The Merry Wives of Windsor," subsequently appearing in over 50 productions, including "Let Freedom Ring," "Bury the Dead," "Of Mice and Men," "The Cradle Will Rock," "Tobacco Road," "Flamingo Road," "On Whitman Avenue," "Alice Adams," "Coriolanus," "Wisteria Trees," "The Vamp," "Hamlet," "As You Like It," "110 in the Shade" and "Horseman, Pass By." He was best known for his six years as the grandfather in the tv series "The Waltons." He was divorced from actress Herta Ware. Surviving are a son and two daughters, including actress Ellen Geer.

LEO GENN, 72, British actor on stage and film, died Jan. 26, 1978 in his native London. He left a law practice to become an actor. His Bdwy debut was in 1938 in "The Flashing Stream," and he subsequently appeared in "Another Part of the Forest," "Small War on Murray Hill," "The Hidden River," "The Devil's Advocate," "Fair Game for Lovers," and "The Only Game in Town." His widow survives.

KATHRYN GIVNEY, 81, Wisconsin-born stage and film actress, died Mar. 16, 1978 in her home in Hollywood, CA. After her NY debut in "Ballyhoo" in 1927, she appeared in "Nightstick," "The Behavior of Mrs. Crane," "Lost Horizons," "If This Be Treason," "Fulton of Oak Falls," "Life with Father," "The Royal Family," "Wallflower," "Good Night, Ladies," and "This, Too, Shall Pass" among others. After 1946 she moved to Hollywood and was prominent in numerous films. No reported survivors.

CHARLOTTE GREENWOOD, 87, Philadelphia-born comedienne, noted for her long legs, high kicks and gangly mannerisms on stage, film, and in vaudeville, died Jan. 18, 1978 in her home in Los Angeles, CA. After her Bdwy debut in 1905 in "The White Cat," she performed in "The Passing Show of 1912," "Betty Pepper," "So Long, Letty," "Linger Longer, Letty," "Music Box Revue," "Ritz Revue," "LeMaire's Affairs," "Post Road," "I Remember Mama" (on tour), and "Out of This World." In 1930 she made the film of "So Long, Letty," and subsequently was featured or starred in many movies. She was married twice, but left no known survivors.

JEAN HAGEN, 54, stage, screen, radio and tv actress, died Aug. 29, 1977 of throat cancer in Woodland Hills, CA. After a career in radio, she made her Bdwy debut in 1946 in "Swan Song," followed by "Another Part of the Forest," "Ghosts," "Born Yesterday," and "The Traitor." Her film career began in 1949. She was probably best known as Danny Thomas' wife in the tv series "Make Room for Daddy." No reported survivors.

HILDEGARDE HALLIDAY, 75, NJ-born actress, died of cancer Oct. 10, 1977 in NYC. After her Bdwy debut in 1923 in "The Failures," she appeared in "Garrick Gaieties," "The Chief Thing," "New Faces of 1934," "Crazy with the Heat," "Walk into My Parlor," "Odds on Mrs. Oakley," and "My Romance." In recent years she had been teaching. Two cousins survive.

BILL HINNANT, 42, stage, tv and film actor, drowned Feb. 17, 1978 while vacationing in the Dominican Republic. He made his Bdwy debut in 1955 in "No Time for Sergeants," and subsequently appeared in "All Kinds of Giants," "Put It in Writing," "You're a Good Man, Charlie Brown" in which he played Snoopy, "American Hamburger League," "God Bless Coney," "Here's Love," "Frank Merriwell" and "Hurry Harry." Surviving are his mother, a sister, and brother, actor Skip Hinnant.

HARRIET HOCTOR, 74, prominent dancer and choreographer in the 1930's and 1940's, died June 9, 1977 in Arlington, VA. She began her career in vaudeville and made her Bdwy debut in 1920 in "Sally," and was subsequently featured in "Topsy and Eva," "A La Carte," "The Three Musketeers," "Show Girl," "Simple Simon," "Vanities," "Hold Your Horses" and "Ziegfeld Follies." She performed regularly in vaudeville at the Palace and other key showcases in NY and London. In later years she operated a school of ballet in Boston. Several nieces and nephews survive.

Will Geer (1970)

Leo Genn (1966)

Bill Hinnant (1965)

Oscar Homolka (1965)

Alfred Lunt (1954)

Paul McGrath (1968)

EDWARD HOLMES, 66, Canadian-born stage, film and tv actor, died July 12, 1977 in NYC. His Bdwy credits include "Richard III," "Measure for Measure," "Taming of the Shrew," "Merchant of Venice," "Henry VIII," "Gideon," "Dinner at 8" and "Freedom of the City." Surviving are a son and three grandchildren.

OSCAR HOMOLKA, 79, Vienna-born versatile actor on stage, film and tv, died Jan. 28, 1978 of pneumonia in Sussex, Eng., where he had lived for the last 12 years. His Broadway credits include "The Emperor Jones," "Bonaparte," "Trial of Mary Dugan," "Karl and Anna," "Power and Glory," "Innocent Voyage," "I Remember Mama," "The Last Dance," "Bravo!," "The Master Builder" and "Rashomon." He had appeared in over 100 films. His fifth wife, actress Joan Tetzel, died Oct. 31, 1977. Two sons survive.

ARNOLD HORWITT, 59, writer and lyricist, died Oct. 20, 1977 of cancer in Santa Monica, CA. He wrote sketches and/or lyrics for "Make Mine Manhattan," "Girls against the Boys," "Call Me Mister," "Two's Company," "Are You with It?" "Inside U.S.A.," and "Plain and Fancy." He is survived by his widow, two daughters and a son.

JACOB JACOBS, 86, a prominent figure in the Yiddish theatre, died Oct. 14, 1977 in Brooklyn. At the age of 13 he came to the U.S. from Czechoslavakia. He was an actor, producer, lyricist, playwright and director, and established several Yiddish theatres. His most popular song was "Bei Mir Bist du Schoen." He acted in such productions as "Soul of a Woman," "Motke from Slobodke," "Women of New York," "Farblondjete Honeymoon," "A Cowboy in Israel," "Hello Charlie," "Oh What a Wedding!" and "The President's Daughter." Surviving are his actress daughter, Thelma Mintz, and two grandchildren.

SAUL LEVITT, 66, playwright and author, died Sept. 30, 1977 of a heart attack in his native NYC. He was best known for his play "The Andersonville Trial," and "The Trial of the Catonsville Nine" which he co-authored. His one-character play "Lincoln" was produced off Broadway last year. Surviving are his widow and a son.

ALBERT LEWIS, 93, Polish-born producer, director, writer for stage, screen and tv, and former actor, died Apr. 6, 1978 in Beverly Hills, CA. Among the productions with which he was associated are "Rain," "The Nervous Wreck," "The Jazz Singer," "The Donovan Affair," "The Spider," "Mirrors," "Cabin in the Sky," "My Fair Ladies," "Banjo Eyes," "Chicago," "Icebound," "Uncle Willie" and "Three Wishes for Jamie." He is survived by two sons, Burton and Arthur who is also a producer.

KATHLEEN LOCKHART, 84, retired stage, radio and film actress, died Feb. 17, 1978 in Los Angeles, CA. Before moving to Hollywood she appeared in "The Bunk of 1926," "Three Faces East," "Irene," "The Talking Parrot," "Bitter Sweet," "Suspect," "The Children's Hour," "Little Father of the Wilderness," "The Way of the World" and "Happily Ever After." She was the widow of actor Gene Lockhart, and mother of actress June Lockhart who survives.

GUY LOMBARDO, 75, popular band leader and theatrical producer, died Nov. 5, 1977 after open heart surgery in Houston, TX. Death was attributed to respiratory, kidney and heart failure. For more than half a century Mr. Lombardo and His Royal Canadians played "the sweetest music this side of heaven" for New Year's Eve celebrations. In 1955 he began producing summer musical extravaganzas at Jones Beach Theatre on Long Island. His productions include "Arabian Nights," "Show Boat," "Song of Norway," "Hit the Deck," "Paradise Island," "Around the World in 80 Days," "Mardi Gras!," "South Pacific," "The Sound of Music," "Fiddler on the Roof" and "Finian's Rainbow." Born in Canada, he and his band came to the U.S. in 1924. His widow and two brothers survive.

ALFRED LUNT, 84, one of America's most celebrated actors, died Aug. 3, 1977 of cancer in Chicago, IL. With his wife, Lynn Fontanne, they became the world's most distinguished acting couple until their retirement in 1960. He was born in Milwaukee, WI, and began his career in stock. In 1917 he made his NY debut in "Romance and Arabella," and met Miss Fontanne in 1919 in "A Young Man's Fancy;" they were married in 1922. Other credits include "Clarence," "Banco," "Sweet Nell of Old Drury," "The Guardsman," "Arms and the Man," "Goat Song," "At Mrs. Beam's," "Juarez and Maximilian," "Ned McCobb's Daughter," "Brothers Karamozov," "The Second Man," "The Doctor's Dilemma," "Marco Millions," "Volpone," "Caprice," "Elizabeth the Queen," "Reunion in Vienna," "Design for Living," "Taming of the Shrew," "Point Valaine," "Idiot's Delight," "Amphitryon '38," "There Shall Be No Night," "The Pirate," "O Mistress Mine," "I Know My Love," "Quadrille," "The Great Sebastians," and their last performances were in "The Visit." They retired to their home in Genosee Depot, WI. Miss Fontanne survives.

MICHEAL MacLIAMMOIR, 78, Irish actor, playwright, designer and poet, died Mar. 6, 1978 at his home in Dublin. He was a co-founder of the Dublin Gate Theatre. He had appeared on Bdwy in "John Bull's Other Island," "The Old Lady Says No," "Where Stars Walk," "I Must Be Talking to My Friends," and "The Importance of Being Oscar." He had appeared in films and over 300 plays. No reported survivors.

PAUL McGRATH, 74, Chicago-born stage, radio, film and tv actor, died Apr. 13, 1978 in his sleep during a visit to London. His career began in 1924 and his credits include "Made in America," "The Good Fairy," "Here Today," "Ode to Liberty," "Room Service," "Mrs. Moonlight," "Susan and God," "Lady in the Dark," "In Bed We Cry," "Common Ground," "The Big Knife," "The Small Hours," "Command Decision," "Candida," "A Girl Can Tell," "The Gang's All Here," "Bicycle Ride to Nevada" and "Brightower." He was the host on radio's "Inner Sanctum" series, and in several tv serials, such as "Love of Life" and "The Guiding Light." Surviving is his widow, former actress Anne Sargent.

MAGGIE McNAMARA, 48, stage and film actress, died Feb. 18, 1978 in her native NYC from an overdose of pills. She had appeared in "The King of Friday's Men" and "Step on a Crack." She was in the Chicago company of "The Moon Is Blue" and repeated her role in the film. Her marriage to David Swit ended in divorce. Two sisters and a brother survive.

DANNY MEEHAN, 47, actor, dancer, singer and composer, died Mar. 29, 1978 of cancer in NYC. His Bdwy bow in 1958 in "Whoop-Up" was followed by "Do Re Mi," "Funny Girl," "Ulysses in Nighttown," "Poison Tree," and Off-Broadway in "Smiling the Boy Fell Dead," "Thracian Horses," "O, Oysters," "New Cole Porter Revue." Surviving are his widow and daughter.

ZERO MOSTEL, 62, (Brooklyn-born Samuel Joel Mostel), actor on stage, tv and film, and artist, died Sept. 8, 1977 of a cardiac arrest in Philadelphia, PA. He was performing in a pre-Broadway production of "The Merchant." His career began as a comic in nightclubs and on radio. "Keep 'Em Laughing" in 1942 marked his Broadway debut, followed by "Top Notchers," "Concert Varieties," "Beggar's Holiday," "Flight into Egypt," "A Stone for Danny Fisher," "Once Over Lightly," "Good Woman of Setzuan," "Good as Gold," "Rhinoceros," "A Funny Thing Happened on the Way to the Forum" and "Fiddler on the Roof." He received "Tonys" for the last three mentioned, and revived "Fiddler" in 1976. He is survived by his widow, former dancer Kathryn Harkin, and two sons, Tobias and actor Josh Mostel.

PHYLLIS NEILSON-TERRY, 84, London-born actress, died Sept. 25, 1977 in her country home outside London. She is a niece of the great Victorian actress, Ellen Terry, and a cousin of Sir John Gielgud. After achieving stardom at an early age in England, she came to the U.S. in 1914 in "Twelfth Night," and subsequently in "The Adventure of Lady Ursula," "Trilby," "The Great Pursuit" and "Separate Tables." Her second husband, actor Heron Carvic, survives.

GEORGE OPPENHEIMER, 77, NY-born drama critic, playwright, and writer for stage and screen, died Aug. 14, 1977. For the last 20 years he had worked for the Long Island newspaper, Newsday, as a columnist and critic. His plays include "The Manhatters," "Here Today," "Another Love," "Dance Me a Song" and "A Mighty Man Is He." He collaborated on several films for Samuel Goldwyn and MGM. He also wrote the pilot and 29 episodes of the popular tv series "Topper." A brother survives.

OLGA PETROVA, 93, stage and film actress, and playwright, died Nov. 30, 1977 in Clearwater, FL. As Muriel Harding, she began her career as a chorus girl in her native England. After coming to the U.S. she achieved success in vaudeville and in such plays as "The Quaker Girl," "Panthea," "The White Peacock" and "Hurricane" both of which she wrote, and "What Do We Know." Her autobiography "Butter with My Bread" was published in 1942. She was divorced from her first husband, and her second, actor Lewis Willoughby, pre-deceased her by several years.

H. R. POINDEXTER, 41, set and light designer for stage, tv and dance, died Sept. 24, 1977 of a heart attack in Los Angeles, CA. In 1971 he received a "Tony" for "Paul Sills' Story Theatre." His other credits include "My Sweet Charlie," "Clarence Darrow," "Belle of Amherst," "The Constant Wife," "Music Is," "Abelard and Heloise," "Night of the Iguana," "A Funny Thing Happened on the Way to the Forum," and this season's "Diversions and Delights" and "Paul Robeson." He had been technical supervisor for the Mark Taper Forum and the Ahmanson Theatre in Los Angeles. Surviving are his mother and two sons.

H. C. POTTER, 73, Broadway and Hollywood director, died Aug. 31, 1977 in NYC. Among his play credits are "Button, Button," "Doctor X," "Experience Unnecessary," "Double Door," "Wednesday's Child," "Post Road," "Kind Lady," "A Bell for Adano," "Anne of the Thousand Days," "Point of No Return" and "Sabrina Fair." His widow and three sons survive.

SIR TERENCE RATTIGAN, 66, one of England's most prolific and successful playwrights, died Nov. 30, 1977 of bone cancer in his home in Bermuda. While in his 20's he wrote "French without Tears" which had one of the longest runs in British theatre history. Since 1936 there was rarely a season without one of his plays. His last, "Cause Celebre," opened in London in July 1977. He was last represented on Broadway in 1974 by "In Praise of Love" co-starring Julie Harris and Rex Harrison. Other NY productions of his plays are "First Episode," "After the Dance," "Grey Farm," "Flare Path," "While the Sun Shines," "O Mistress Mine," "The Winslow Boy," "Harlequinade," "The Browning Version," "Who Is Sylvia?," "The Deep Blue Sea," "The Sleeping Prince," "Separate Tables," "Variations on a Theme," "Ross," and "The Girl Who Came to Supper." He also wrote many film scripts. No reported survivors.

ALAN REED, (nee Teddy Bergman), 69, NY-born stage, radio, film and tv actor, died June 14, 1977 in West Los Angeles, CA. His career began in 1927 with the Provincetown Theatre in Greenwich Village, NY. Among his Bdwy credits are "Merry Wives of Windsor," "Love's Old Sweet Song," "Hope for a Harvest" and "The Pirate." He was the voice of Fred on tv's "The Flintstones," and on radio was Daddy to Fanny Brice's Baby Snooks. After moving to Los Angeles in 1943, he appeared in over 50 films. His widow and three sons survive.

DANIEL REED, 86, retired actor, director and producer, died Feb. 9, 1978 in Montrose, NY. After his Broadway debut in 1912 in "Oliver Twist," he appeared in, among others, "The Unknown Warrior," "Hope Is the Thing with Feathers," "The Vigil," "Love Me Long," "My Heart's in the Highlands," "Spoon River Anthology," "Come Back, Little Sheba," "Borned in Texas," "Mary Rose," "Barefoot in Athens," "Time of the Cuckoo," "Carousel," "Shadow of a Gunman" and "Man and Superman." Surviving are his widow, publicist Isadora Bennett, and daughter, folk singer Susan Reed.

CYRIL RITCHARD, 79, Australian-born actor, singer, and director, died Dec. 18, 1977 of a cardiac arrest in Chicago, IL, where he was performing in "Side by Side by Sondheim." He collapsed on stage Nov. 25, and remained in a coma until his death. After making his theatrical debut at 19 in Australia, he went to England and with his wife, the late Madge Elliott, became the stars of several musicals. His NY debut was in "Puzzles of 1925," subsequently appearing in "Love for Love," "Make Way for Lucia," "The Relapse," "Peter Pan," "Visit to a Small Planet," "The Pleasure of His Company," "Happiest Girl in the World," "Romulus," "Too True to Be Good," "Irregular Verb to Love," "Roar of the Greasepaint," "Sugar" and "Musical Jubilee." A foster son, a brother and sister survive.

HERMAN SHAPIRO, 80, former actor and stage manager, died Mar. 28, 1978 of a heart condition in Cranford, NJ. After training to be a lawyer, he began his 38-year Broadway career in 1930 as an actor in "Once in a Lifetime." He appeared in other productions before becoming a stage manager for such productions as "The Heiress," "The Shrike," "A Streetcar Named Desire," "Mr. Roberts," "Carousel," "West Side Story," "My Fair Lady," and "Annie Get Your Gun." He worked for many years at NY City Center. He is survived by his widow, a son and a daughter.

Zero Mostel (1967)

H. R. Poindexter (1977)

Cyril Ritchard (1965)

Regina Wallace (1958)

Ethel Waters (1949)

Peggy Wood (1960)

SYDNEY SMITH, 68, retired stage, radio and film actor, and teacher, died Mar. 4, 1978 in Seattle, WA. Among his Broadway credits are "Taps," "Present Arms," "Allure," "Richard II," "Hamlet," "Henry IV," "R.U.R.," "Harriet," "Curious Savage," "Horse Eats Hat," and "Edwin Booth." Before his retirement, he taught in the U. of Northern Illinois in DeKalb. Surviving are his widow, a son and a daughter.

LAURA STUART, 39, stage and tv actress, died Dec. 26, 1977 of cancer in NYC. She had appeared Off Broadway in "Electra," "The Trojan Women" and "Women at the Tomb," and on Broadway in "Fiddler on the Roof" (for over 500 performances), "Private Lives" and "The Norman Conquests." She had been a regular on the tv series "Another World." She is survived by her mother and two sisters.

MYRTLE TANNEHILL, 91, actress, and third generation of a theatrical family, died in July 1977 in her home in Yorktown Heights, NY. After her stage debut in the early 1900's, her many credits include "Dear Brutus," "Get-Rick-Quick Wallingford," "Broadway Jones," "Bonehead," "The Broken Wing," "Dream Maker," "Dodsworth," "Philadelphia Story" and "Pygmalion." Two sisters survive.

WILLIAM TANNEN, 65, stage and film character actor, died Dec. 2, 1977 in Woodland Hills, CA. He had acted on Broadway in, among others, "Garrick Gaieties of 1930," "School for Scandal," "Keeping Expenses Down," "Lucrece," "Evensong," "The Return of Hannibal." He leaves his widow.

JOAN TETZEL, 56, stage, radio and film actress, died Oct. 31, 1977 at her home in Sussex, Eng. Born in NYC, she began her Broadway career at 16 in "Dramatic School," subsequently appearing in "Lorelei," "Liliom," "Happy Days," "The Damask Cheek," "Harriet," "Peepshow," "Pretty Little Parlor," "I Remember Mama," "Strange Bedfellows," "Red Gloves," "The Winner," "The Masterbuilder," "U.S.A.," "One Flew over the Cuckoo's Nest" and "How the Other Half Loves." She was married to Oscar Homolka who died in January 1978. Her mother and three brothers survive.

FRANK THOMPSON, 56, Oklahoma-born costume designer for stage, films, opera and ballet, died June 4, 1977 in Los Angeles, CA. He created costumes for such Broadway productions as "The Linden Tree," "Rape of Lucretia," "Late Love," "Nude with Violin," "Tenth Man," "Viva Madison Avenue," "Pal Joey," "Harold," "Photo Finish," "Guys and Dolls," "Kismet," "The Zulu and the Zayda," NY City Center productions, "A Place for Polly," "The Gingerbread Lady" and "The Country Girl." Surviving are a sister and brother.

AUSTIN TREVOR, (nee Schilsky), 80, Irish-born stage and screen character actor, died Jan. 22, 1978 in London. His career began in 1915 on Broadway in "Hamlet," which led to contracts with the Stratford Festival and Old Vic in London. Other Broadway roles were in "Escape," "The Patriot," "Roulette," "Call It a Day," "Once Is Enough" and "Don't Listen, Ladies." No reported survivors.

REGINA WALLACE, 86, stage, film and tv actress for 50 years, died Feb. 13, 1978 after a stroke in Englewood, NJ. After her 1913 debut in "Good Little Devil," her credits include "Pagans," "Nobody's Money," "The Breaking Point," "The Show-Off," "Divorce a la Carte," "Housewarming," "First Lady," "Antony and Cleopatra," "Run Sheep Run," "The Male Animal" (original and revival), "Counsellor-at-law," "Yes, My Darling Daughter," and "My Fair Lady" which she played for six years. No reported survivors.

ETHEL WATERS, 80, world-renowned singer and actress, died Sept. 1, 1977 of kidney and heart failure in Chatsworth, CA. Her career began at 17 as a singer in vaudeville in Philadelphia. Her records made her an international favorite, and she made her Broadway debut in 1927 in "Africana," followed by "Lew Leslie's Blackbirds of 1930," "Rhapsody in Black," "As Thousands Cheer," "At Home Abroad," "Mamba's Daughters," "Cabin in the Sky," "Blue Holiday," "An Evening with Ethel Waters," and her best-known role was in "The Member of the Wedding" which she repeated in the film version and received an Academy Award nomination. She was married and divorced twice. There were no immediate survivors.

ADA MAE WEEKS, also known as Ada May, 80, popular musical comedy star in the 1920's, died Apr. 25, 1978 in her NYC home. The Brooklyn-born actress appeared in several "Ziegfeld Follies," was a headliner at the Palace, and on Broadway in "Jim Jam Jems," "The O'Brien Girl," "Listen, Lester," "Lollipop" and "Rio Rita." She later appeared in Charlie Chaplin's "Monsieur Verdoux." She is survived by her husband, Mario Castegnaro, and a sister.

RUDOLF WEISS, 77, Vienna-born actor, died Apr. 6, 1978 after a stroke in NYC. After fleeing the Nazi invasion of Austria where he had been a successful actor, he made his Broadway debut in 1940 in "Two on an Island," and subsequently appeared in "Flight to the West," "The Potting Shed," "The Tenth Man," and off-Bdwy in "The Iceman Cometh," "Naked," "Stalag 17," "Kiss Mama," "The Deadly Game," "The Play's the Thing," and his last in 1971 "Whose Little Boy Are You?" Surviving are his widow and a niece, Eva Weith Slane.

JOHN F. WHARTON, 83, lawyer, writer, and one of the founders of the Playwrights Producing Company, died Nov. 24, 1977 of complications from emphysema. Among his many theatrical clients was Cole Porter and he became the co-executor of his estate and sole trustee of his Musical and Literary Property Trusts. The Playwrights Company presented many distinguished productions by its members Maxwell Anderson, Robert Sherwood, Elmer Rice, S. N. Behrman and Sidney Howard, but it was dissolved in 1960 after 69 plays. Mr. Wharton was also instrumental in establishing the reduced-price ticket booth on Times Square. He is survived by his second wife, former actress Mary Mason, a daughter and a step-daughter.

PEGGY WOOD, Brooklyn-born versatile actress of stage screen and tv, died Mar. 18, 1978 of a cerebral hemorrhage in Stamford, CT. After her debut in 1910 in "Naughty Marietta," she appeared in 70 Broadway productions, including "Maytime" (her first starring role), "Buddies," "Marjolaine," "Clinging Vine," "Candida," "Trelawney of 'The Wells'," "Merchant of Venice," "Bitter Sweet," "Old Acquaintance," "Blithe Spirit," "Getting Married," "Charley's Aunt" and "The Girls in 509." She was also starred in several London productions. She was probably best known for the mother in the tv series "I Remember Mama" (1949–1957). From 1959 to 1966 she served as president of ANTA. She was nominated for an Academy Award for her performance in the film "The Sound of Music." After the death of her first husband, poet-novelist-playwright John Van Alstyn Weaver, she married William A. Walling who died in 1973. A son, David Weaver, survives.

269